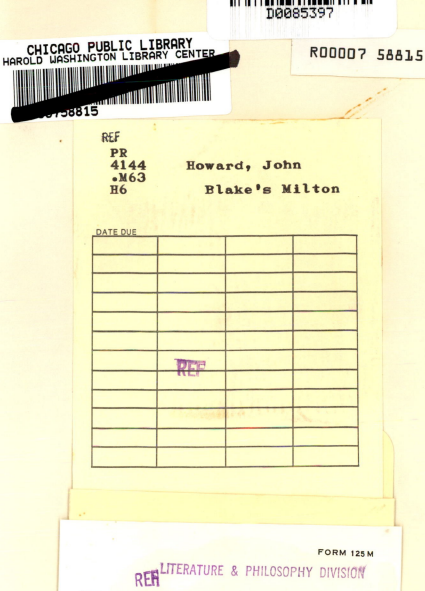

Blake's *Milton*

Blake's *Milton*

A Study in the Selfhood

John Howard

Rutherford ● *Madison* ● *Teaneck*
Fairleigh Dickinson University Press
London: Associated University Presses

Associated University Presses, Inc.
Cranbury, New Jersey 08512

Associated University Presses
108 New Bond Street
London W1Y OQX, England

Ref
PR
4144
,M63
,H6
Cop. 1

Library of Congress Cataloging in Publication Data
Howard, John, 1934–
    Blake's Milton: a study in the selfhood.
    Bibliography: p.
    Includes index.
    1. Blake, William, 1757–1827. Milton. 2. Blake,
William, 1757–1827—Philosophy. I. Title.
PR4144.M63H6   821'.7   75-10140
ISBN 0-8386-1756-5

PRINTED IN THE UNITED STATES OF AMERICA

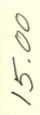

For
Rob, Lisa, and Laura

Contents

Acknowledgments

I wish to thank the students in my courses who have contributed much to my understanding of Blake. I wish also to thank Professor Gayle Smith for his thorough reading of my manuscript and his encouragement; Professors Morris Freedman, George Panichas, Neil Isaacs, and John Kinnaird for their helpful advice and encouragement. Special thanks to Charles Rutherford who obtained for me the invaluable services of Sally Fields, Linda Mitchell, Linda Robinson, Sharon Landolt, and Sue Cody, to whom I am grateful for kindness as well as expert help in preparing my manuscript. I am grateful also for the conscientious editing of Mrs. Mathilde E. Finch. My thanks to Roberta Howard, my wife, for encouragement, and for her help in proofreading and indexing. Finally, my thanks to the many scholars and critics, both mentioned and unmentioned in this book, who have made my reading of Blake easier and more delightful.

I wish to thank the following publishers for having given me permission to quote from published works:
Columbia University Press for permission to quote from *The Works of John Milton*. Edited by F. A. Patterson *et al.*
Doubleday & Company Inc., and Professor David Erdman for permission to quote from *The Poetry and Prose of William Blake*.

Huguenot-Thomas Paine Historical Association of New
Rochelle, N.Y., for permission to quote from *The Life
and Works of Thomas Paine*. Edited by William M. Van
der Weyde.

Thomas Nelson & Sons Limited for permission to quote
from *The Works of George Berkeley,* Bishop of Cloyne.
Edited by A. A. Luce and T. E. Jessop.

Oxford University Press for permission to quote from *The
Complete Writings of William Blake* edited by Geoffrey
Keynes. © Oxford University Press 1966. Reprinted by
permission of the publisher.

Introduction: Sublime Allegory

I. FALL AND REDEMPTION

By January 1803, William Blake had still not gained recognition as a poet of religious or revolutionary themes. He had not achieved acceptance as a painter, and his designs were a source of trouble to him. His *Four Zoas,* an attempt at a vast visionary poem, remained unengraved, incomplete, and perhaps incoherent. Even his engraving, as satisfactory as it could be, had not won him reputation enough to withstand the growing financial difficulties of the late 1790s. His life at Felpham, his new career as a miniature painter, and his adventures in engraving and publishing the insipid ballads of William Hayley had become a degradation below humiliation. He was now reduced to writing vain boasts to his brother about his future career as a publisher, boasts so empty that Blake himself must have felt painfully their hollow promise. Yet, from this ruin of personal pride and ever-changing worldly ambition, his phoenixlike energies lifted him above the ashes of despair to write and engrave two final epic works, whose imaginative range and literary skill far out-matched his early productions. In the first of these epics, *Milton,* Blake did what he had not done before in his poetry. He himself became part of the vision, both an actor and a

11

spectator who provided a local habitation for the vision in the "reality" that we recognize as this earth. Also added to this embodiment of the disembodied was a new dimension of vastness, a transcendant view of totality that at once out-soared all his previous flights and illuminated the world of the poetry he had left behind him. And it is from Blake's inclusion of himself in the poem that this new view of a larger reality stems, for his personal involvement forces us to see how his poetry reflects psychological meanings. We must recognize that Blake's visionary world is one of the reality of the psyche.

This personal involvement in a long narrative poem was not an unusual phenomenon in the romantic period. Looking back to what may have been Milton's sublimations of his own personal frustrations in *Paradise Lost* and *Samson Agonistes,* as well as the open inclusion of his personal voice in *Paradise Lost,* the romantic poets found precedent for such an approach. Keat's personal ambitions for, and doubts about, poesy find expression in *Endymion* and *Lamia,* while in *The Fall of Hyperion,* his picture of his own dreamlike experience of death and rebirth before the altar of Moneta casts a revealing symbolic meaning over the episodes of the Hyperion story and further intensifies the relationship between his life and his poetic narrative. Shelley's persona in *The Triumph of Life* duplicates this process, and we see how in *Adonais* his presence, more than a mere conventional pastoral device, is a way of showing how truly he laments his own outcast lot. This process is perhaps pushed to its limits in the "egotistical sublime" of *The Prelude,* when Wordsworth himself becomes the central figure of his epic of poetic and spiritual growth. But it is more than self-inclusion that defines the personal involvement of these poets, for a particular type of psychological process seems to be at the heart of all these poems. The defeat of worldly hope, the despair arising from ambition's failure, or the tortured and passionate failure of love, had led each poet to a crisis of personality that evoked a rebirth, a new creativity born of an inner awareness of power and dedication. Wordsworth, suffering from the decay of hopes of the French Revolution, Shelley from the death of hope for any earthly reform, and Keats from the loss of hope for worldly success, had responded with a new burst of energy that turned their poetry into psychic exploration. In a sense they had all experienced the process of psychic fall and redemption, whose cosmic archetype is the story of *Paradise Lost*.

It is with Blake's view of the process in *Milton* that we are concerned here. Blake's vision of the fall and redemption offers a way of talking about the individual's "spiritual" makeup, a way of mapping out the architecture and landscape of the personality. Blake describes how the personality permits its own instincts of fear to imprison its creativity in delusion, an imprisonment that lasts until its creativity reasserts itself in a defiant act of self-annihilation. This imprisonment and subsequent freedom are embodied in his vision of the fall and redemption in *Milton*.[1] For Blake, man's redemption can come only from his true self, his immortal spirit, which is the human center of creativity, the bounteous, generous cornucopia of productivity within the soul. The imprisoning instincts he called the selfhood, which is a false covering over the immortal spirit. Blake saw the selfhood as survival-oriented, manifesting itself as a hold-fast defense mechanism toward exterior reality as well as repressive enchainments of the creativity within. But Blake's view of the selfhood encompassed even more. Because he believed that the exterior world is an emanation of the immortal, creative part of personality, his concept of the selfhood also encompassed all the defensive structures of society and man's history.

The psychological language necessary to express the conflict between these two forces of personality had not yet been created, and only in the imaginative analogies of poetry could a successful vehicle be found. But the age certainly had need for such language. Without it, the writer could only project his undelineated feelings onto exterior phenomena, and describe those phenomena in a way that reflected his but semi-conscious feelings. The romantics' exaggeration of the wondrous boy Chatterton, the supposed young genius crushed by an oppressive literary establishment, was a projection of the repression of the inner self felt by many. Shelley's lament for youthful genius crushed by the conservative and murderous critics was certainly a projection of his own feelings about the restrictive establishment. And the conservative attitude of previous years had been immortalized by Boswell's projection into the character of Samuel Johnson the parentally dictatorial narrowness that would permit Kit Smart freedom only because he was harmless, or that despised Wilkes the morning star of liberty and of libertinism, or that had scolded the secretive rake Boswell himself. Though Blake had no ready-made language to reveal how these objective symbols were reflections of interior states of mind, he had certainly become aware of the phenomenon, and his task was to put together a language and poetic structure that could express what he saw. He called it *sublime allegory*.

II.   SUBLIME ALLEGORY

Behind *Milton* is the cosmological conception that the eternal forces exist in a realm other than that of time or space, though repeatedly manifesting themselves in time and space in accidental, varying, but essentially the same forms. These eternal forces are by no means obvious to men, even though they are the causes of the events of time and space. Their obscurity results from their being dimmed by the individual's belief that what is reported by the senses alone is real. In fact, the individual can perceive those forces only if he actively controls his perception, giving to the object world the spiritual perception which, unaided, the object world cannot give.

Here a problem in language arises, a problem curiously similar to Milton's own problem of expressing the eternal.

Words convey images, and images by nature are results of
sense experience. How can an image of this world convey a
meaning that transcends its own limited scope? Blake's solution is to force the words to convey a view of the world
that contradicts the spatial-temporal world to which we are
accustomed. For example, Blake pictures Rahab, the biblical harlot, as "standing on Carmel" (19.28),[2] an understandable relationship to us since we know from the book of
Joshua that Rahab belongs in Canaan. But she is addressing
Milton, whose earthly time and place put him out of all
possible "real" connection with Rahab. Moreover, Tirzah,
one of the biblical daughters of Zelophehad, standing with
Rahab, is said to be natural religion! The customary
categories of the phenomenological world are not ignored;
they are vehemently violated, as the eighteenth-century
concept of natural religion is transported back thousands of
years to be equated with an obscure biblical personage.
This is Blake's way of putting into language a concept of
reality essentially different from the concept that had
formed the assumptions of language. Events of time and
space are subservient to the laws of time and space in those
accepted assumptions, while for Blake temporal and spatial
events directly manifest transcendent forces not even per-
ceivable by the senses, much less expressible by a language not freed from its sensual bonds.

Blake's tool for conveying his concept was the symbol.
For our purposes, a symbol is an image or identity that
stands for a reality greater than any single, temporal manifestation of that reality in the phenomenal world. Although
this reality is spiritual, it is known in the phenomenal world
by its manifestation. The seeing through this manifestation
to the reality is the poet's talent if he demonstrates what
Blake calls *vision*. Vision is the comprehension of spiritual
reality. The poet's expression of spiritual reality through a
coherent, though perhaps obscure and paradoxical set of
symbols, is myth.

Blake's symbols are eclectically derived, though his principal source is the Bible. But a number of his most important symbols seem original. For instance Los, the character symbolizing the imagination, has possible archetypes in Apollo, Christ, Prometheus, Plato's Demiurge, and many other forms representing a creative intellect, but he is essentially Blake's own creation. Even the symbols with discoverable sources are colored by Blake's idiosyncratic interpretations. The Satan of *Milton,* for instance, has the self-aggrandizing characteristics of the Satan of *Paradise Lost,* but he is also the Satan of Revelation with his delusive, worldly power. But more than these, he is the principle of self-righteousness within each individual that Blake could have uncovered only in his personal experience.[3] Here we detect one of Blake's characteristic uses of the symbol. Blake's symbolism of the cosmos was a way of revealing the human psyche as he saw it. In fact, what we perceive as an analogy between the individual and the all-inclusive divinity was for Blake an equation. On the one hand, the divinity *is* collective man, while on the other hand, as collective man evolves in spiritual patterns, so does the individual. Inevitably, Blake's cosmos contains the elements of total human history as well as ontogeny. Thus the Satan of Revelation and the Satan of *Paradise Lost* are spiritual identities that were manifested to John of Patmos and to John Milton, but they also stand for a principle working within the individual psyche. What is described as working and existing in an objective cosmos, works and exists within each man's mind. Furthermore, Blake's psychology has an ethical tinge, for the elements of the cosmos are divided into moral categories tending to good or evil. As an example, a key moral value that emerges in Blake's *Milton* is transcendent mercy, while justice, the traditional Christian balance of mercy, is a descendant and ultimately ephemeral value. This ethical valuation appears in psychological ways when we see the principles of freedom, forgiveness, and love dramatized by the symbolic characters of the poem. Though Blake's ethical valuation may disturb us if we see it as a code for interaction between men, his valuation makes sense to us as a psychological principle working within the mind. Blake's insistence on reliance on freedom, forgiveness, and love means that man must free his impulses, feel no guilt, attempt to restrict no feeling, and respond affectionately to his own true nature. In short, Blake's moral teaching strikes its most profound note when heard as a voice to the psyche. The harmony of mind that Blake would have man hear and feel and sing, is from himself to himself.

This symbolic double reference to the inner world of the mind and the outer cosmos is not the only complexity we have to deal with. The discernible outlines of his symbols at times change. The symbols themselves may coalesce, becoming part of an aggregate that itself has its own name. Thus, the Shadowy Female, symbol for delusion, seems to be an aggregation of female symbols, two of which are Rahab and Tirzah, who themselves stand for holiness and natural religion. Moreover, the same spiritual force may appear under different symbolic names, according to the momentarily appropriate manifestation. Thus Satan may be Urizen struggling with one aspect of Milton, or the covering cherub threatening Europe, or the red dragon of Revelation. Further, and perhaps most frustratingly, an individual symbol may suddenly be divided into a number of subcategories that represent an aspect of that symbol but are not that symbol's complete identity. Unfortunately for the reader who may begin to murmur, Milton himself at one point is divided into four categories. But with patience to prevent that murmur, the reader can see that Blake has meaning as well as art in this maneuvering.

Blake's own phrase for this symbolic language was *sublime allegory*. In a letter to Thomas Butts (July 1803), Blake informs his friend that he had recorded his three previous years in a "memento" to future generations "by a Sublime Allegory, which is now perfectly completed into a Grand Poem." He defines the term as "allegory address'd to the

Intellectual powers, while it is altogether hidden from the Corporeal Understanding.''[4] By corporeal Blake means bodily, that which experiences materially, that empirical reason which Coleridge put on the lower level of mental powers as understanding. The intellectual power for Blake is the power that permits perception to transcend the limits of experience; it is the imagination. Blake's statement, therefore, is not a statement of purposeful obscurantism but one that recognizes that many men may not permit their "intellectual powers" to take precedence over their "corporeal understanding" in seeing his meaning. They remain in a limited time-and-space world.

Blake's conception of sublime allegory derives from the notions of allegory articulated by several contemporaries: Fuseli, William Hayley, Thomas Taylor, and Anselm Bayley, as Joseph Wittreich has recently explained. For Blake the writing of a sublime allegory was part of the conception of epic poetry. Wittreich points out that Hayley and Fuseli believed that allegory ''must transcend topical reference and merge with a grand mythology that serves simultaneously as the new epic machinery and as the poem's unifying structure.''[5] This means that the allegory, though containing topical reference, must be using that reference to direct the reader's mind to the transcendental truth beyond the topical manifestation. Blake is following this path when Satan begins to transcend any one particular manifestation of evil and becomes a symbolic aggregate of many specific manifestations. Yet there are undoubted traces of topical events evident in the poem. Blake's own personal life is involved, overtly as Blake becomes an actor in the poem, and covertly as the characters perform actions that suggest Blake's relationship to his patron Hayley, his struggle with the soldier Scolfield, and his trial for sedition. Moreover, portions of the poem seem to make reference to events and persons of the recent past, pointing a critical finger at John Hunt for his attacks on aspects of Methodism. In fact, it seems as though Blake's moral stance forces his sublime allegory into moral satire. Hence Blake sounds at times like a Hebrew prophet pointing out the evil that will lead to destruction.[6]

Wittreich makes another point about the tradition of epic that illuminates this contrary stance of *Milton*. Before *Paradise Lost,* an epic was written as if the poet and audience agreed about the ethical values behind the poem.[7] But, "from Milton's point of view, and from Blake's, the poet . . . is a generator of values rather than a confirmer of those that already exist."[8] The epic poet's generation of value spoken of by Wittreich requires that Blake enter into mental warfare with those contemporary values which Blake saw as evil. In many ways in his works, Blake is on the attack.[9] But in *Milton* that attack was in the tradition not only of epic, but of the prophet as well. Martin Price has suggested similarities between the prophetic satire of Blake and the Augustan traditions of satire. Distinguished from them primarily by a shift away from moral judgment as a standard,[10] Blake's resemblance is in his awareness of the depth to which "attitudes are rooted in systems of belief" which, in a mad world, pervert sanity. Blake's effort was to "give unmistakable form to error and thus rob it of vague and mysterious authority."[11] It is the prophet who "must commit himself to vision that strips away illusion."[12] Florence Sandler has shown how *Milton* is in the tradition of Revelation, a tradition of unveiling evil. She points out also the paradoxical situation wherein the objects of Blake's attack, the Deists, were also in the tradition of unveiling the evils of religion. Blake, like the deists, was critical of much of Christianity, particularly in its reliance on fear and in the alliance of "priest and monarch."[13] Unlike the deists, he did not wish to exchange "priestly mystery for reason."[14]

The object of Blake's attack in *Milton* is suggested by the names of those whom he sees as manifestations of evil: Bacon, Newton, Locke, Hume, Gibbon, Bolingbroke, Voltaire, and Rousseau. These represent the rational, scientific, and in some cases, skeptical energies of the seventeenth and eighteenth centuries. Blake saw the results of this rationalism in materialism and in the deceit of political opportunists, which were replacing the shopworn deceits of priestcraft. For Blake, the rationalists, no matter how they might differ from orthodox Christianity, were essentially agents of the same force that lay behind orthodoxy: the selfhood. Blake found the scientific interest of Bacon, Locke's empiricism, Newton's mathematical laws, Gibbon's sneering skepticism, Bolingbroke's, Voltaire's, and Rousseau's natural religion to be delusions, spawned by the selfhood and used by the selfhood to control man in society. These delusions served the selfhood's purpose—to control the essential deity in man, the imagination, which itself is the main threat to the selfhood.

Thus Blake is involved in a double effort: to remove the covering of delusion surrounding human life and to illuminate the true source of human life and creativity. His method seems to be one of opposition. He proceeds by naming the evil, the process of naming evil itself a method of satiric reduction.[15] He also uses mockery. He had the habit of picking up key words from his antagonists, and using them, almost as ironic allusions, in a manner that reversed the basic point of his antagonist's original argument.[16] This is Blake's mental warfare. Perhaps he is following Thomas Taylor, who at the end of his translation of Plotinus's *Concerning the Beautiful,* calls out: "Rise then, my friends, and the victory will be ours. The foe is indeed numerous, but, at the same time feeble; and the weapons of truth, in the hands of vigorous union, descend with irresistible force, and are fatal wherever they fall."[17] Taylor's foe is materialism. Blake too calls out in the preface to *Milton:* "Rouse up, O Young man of the new age! set your forheads against the ignorant Hirelings! For we have Hirelings in the Camp, the Court & the University; who would if they could, for ever depress Mental & prolong Corporeal War."

To a great extent it is the mental war that makes the poem important to us. Certainly *Milton* pleases; it contains some ideas that fascinate us. But there is more here than pleasure. It is the faith that Blake shows, not the religious faith

per se, but the immense courage to assert his disbelief in
some of the main dogmas of his time, the faith that allows
him to undergo the labor of inventing and engraving a complex literary work, that must stand on its refusal to comply
with some of the most accepted philosophical principles of
his day. The other benefits of *Milton* are real enough. The
beliefs are fascinating and speak of ways of perception that
we ourselves can find useful; and Blake's intellectual construction is a great mental pleasure to unfold in its intricate
and subtle meanings. But its greatest value is in its display
of that same kind of faith which he found in Whitfield and
Wesley. What greater miracle than "Men who devote their
lifes whole comfort to intire scorn & injury & death"
(23.1–2)? And this is not the same as that martyrdom which
seeks death. Blake's faith seeks to enlighten others about
life and about the easily accepted, perhaps mistaken, overly
self-assured dogmas of culture and the restrictive, repressive, defensive elements of the mind that imprison man's
creativity, keeping him from truth and happy light. His
spirit is not simply that of the Satanic rebel, optimistic
revolutionary, or Old Testament prophet. It is the spirit of
persistent and open rejection of the cant, the dogmas, the
worn-out myths that men too easily accept as justification
for exploitation, injustice, war, and despair. Though no
rationalist, Blake is the epitome of the Enlightenment's
pursuit of truth. There is really no adequate name for Blake.
Debunker, skeptic, philosopher are names that do not describe him. In one sense he is the member of the loyal
opposition, but his loyalty is to truth, not to a worldly establishment. In another sense, he is close to Voltaire (though
Blake would not appreciate the comparison).

Thus Blake had moved beyond any language of the
eighteenth century to express the unity in the human
psyche of cosmic, historic, topical, and personal existence.
To follow the track of Blake's courageous flight, we must
map out the landscape in which he journeyed to the true
promised land.

Blake's *Milton*

1

The Spiritual World

I. MATERIALISTS AND SPIRITUALISTS

Upon examining the cosmic framework within which the action of *Milton* occurs, one finds Blake's characteristic two-edged sword carving out the lineaments of the spiritual world and revealing the current delusion of materialism used by the selfhood to control mankind. With the burin of prophetic vision Blake exposes Bacon, Newton, and Locke as representatives of this delusion.[1] Bacon, Newton, and Locke share the assumptions that matter has an independent existence, and that, like a machine, it is governed by mechanical causation that is discoverable and knowable. Bacon's inductive method, which assumes that matter is independent and understandable, aims at the dissection of nature into its parts "as did the school of Democritus."[2] Blake must have sensed something sinister in Bacon's preference for "the school of Leucippus and Democritus."[3] Not only is Bacon's favoring of these materialistic philosophers a key to his own philosophy's easy conjoining with the

25

philosophy of atomism in the *Novum Organon,* but, in his essay "of atheisme," he attempts to make the point that the philosophy of Democritus and Epicurus is not at odds with religion. But Blake saw the Baconian science as another manifestation of that earthly delusion which manifested itself in Bacon's materialistic forebears and pointed to its further manifestation in Newton. Bacon's attempts to find the forms of nature were no other than attempts to find a cause-and-effect relationship in matter[4] that would make the natural world self-sufficient under a few simple laws. The rules of reasoning in this attempt are set out in Book III of Newton's *Mathematical Principles of Natural Philosophy.* These rules include the rules of natural cause and effect, and the rule of precedence of the inductive method, based on observations of phenomena, over hypotheses not based on phenomena.[5] It is the observation of phenomena as a source of truth that implies the reality of matter. The latest manifestation of delusion, Locke's empiricism, asserts, in Locke's distinction between primary and secondary ideas, the assumption of the independent existence of matter. Primary ideas exist in matter itself. Locke writes: "The particular bulk, number, figure, and motion of the parts of fire, or snow, are really in them,—whether any one's senses perceive them or not and therefore they may be called real qualities, because they really exist in those bodies."[6] In all three philosophers, matter has the real, independent existence upon which knowledge is based.

The delusion of Bacon, Newton, and Locke is also manifest in the thought of Hartley and Priestley. Hartley, the follower of Locke, traces thought to the mechanical workings of the vibratiuncles in the brain, as though thought were governed by a mechanical cause-and-effect relationship.[7] Priestly, though attempting to rid Christianity of various corruptions such as the belief in the duality of matter and spirit, gives the most obvious support to the high valuation of matter:

It has been the opinion of many philosophers, and among others of Mr. Locke, that, for any thing that we know to the contrary, a capacity of thinking might be given to matter. Dr. Hartley, however, notwithstanding his hypothesis would be much helped by it, seems to think otherwise. He also supposes that there is an intermediate *elementary body* between the mind and the gross body; which may exist, and be the instrument of giving pleasure or pain to the sentient principle, after death. But I own I see no reason why his scheme should be burdened with such an incumbrance as this.

I am rather inclined to think that, though the subject is beyond our comprehension at present, man does not consist of two principles so essentially different from one another as *matter* and *spirit,* which are always described as having not one common property, by means of which they can affect or act upon each other; the one occupying space, and the other not only not occupying the least imaginable portion of space, but incapable of bearing relation to it; insomuch that, properly speaking, my mind is no more *in my body* than it is in the moon. I rather think that the whole man is of some *uniform composition,* and that the property of *perception,* as well as the other powers that are termed mental, is the result (whether necessary or not) of such an organical structure as that of the brain. Consequently, that the whole man becomes extinct at death, and that we have no hope of surviving the grave but what is derived from the scheme of revelation.[8]

In Priestley the ultimate implication is made. Man, both mind and body, is matter, and the extinction of his body is the extinction of his mind. Here, hope for eternal life is removed to faith, while reason reports only of death. The farther this hope is removed from man, the closer comes the sinister and gripping fear that there is no spiritual existence at all, and ultimately that death is the final eclipse of the individual. In such a philosophic world view, man's fear drives him to any servility to avoid death, making him an easy prey to the survival-determined selfhood.

But the century's materialism had not gone without its opponents, both direct and oblique. In his *Essay on Spirit*, Robert Clayton saw nature as a result of direct spiritual causation,[9] and Abraham Tucker, in *The Light of Nature*, imagined a kind of cosmic assembly line of pure spirits working on gravity and other laws of nature.[10] But a more direct opponent, Thomas Taylor, launched more than one attack against materialism. To pursue matter "through its infinite divisions and wander in its dark labyrinths is the employment of the philosophy in vogue," wrote Taylor in his introduction to Plotinus's *Concerning the Beautiful*.[11] "All modern sects are in a state of barbarous ignorance: for Materialism, and its attendant Sensuality, have darkened the eyes of the *many,* with the mists of error."[12] Matter is for Taylor a "nonentity."[13] But the most philosophic attack on materialism came from Berkeley, who insisted that "the very notion of what is called matter or *corporeal substance,* involves a contradiction in it."[14] There are conclusive proofs "against the existence of material substance."[15] Berkeley's attack on material substance was part of an attack on the Lockean notion that ideas are derived from the senses reacting to the material world. For Berkeley no ideas exist anywhere but in the perceiving mind. "Their *esse* is *percepi,* nor is it possible they should have existence out of the mind of thinking things which perceive them."[16] It is spirit that perceives.[17] "The cause of ideas is an incorporeal active substance or spirit."[18]

But Berkeley took pains not to deny the existence of a world exterior to the mind of the individual. His attack essentially was directed against the notion "of absolute or external existence of unperceiving substances,"[19] but since he could not disbelieve in the existence of exterior reality, he postulated a divine mind that at all times perceives the infinite universe. This perception is an archetype in the divine mind. The individual's perception of the forms of the archetype is ectypal.[20] Thus things do exist, but not as material objects independent of mind. Matter cannot account for causation.[21] The "substratum" of matter is an unnecessary and delusory invention.[22]

Blake's visionary cosmos is the symbolic embodiment of the anti-materialist principle that matter cannot have its own independent system of cause and effect. Matter is brought into motion by spiritual cause. When Blake writes "every Natural Effect has a Spiritual Cause" (26.44), he is on the side of Berkeley, but with a visionary's allegiance.

II. TIME AND SPACE

Blake countered the concepts of materialism by his picture of the cosmos as a spiritually animated, nonmechanistic, visionary creation that functions in accordance with the purposes of eternity.[23] His picture is heavily detailed and sometimes confusing, but its basic patterns remain clear. It directly denies the temporal and spatial concepts of the universe of Newton's astronomy, for in Blake's universe space is a symbolic creation of the mind, figuring forth in the objectification of the exterior world the inner rooms and framework of the psyche. And in this universe, time is a sequential cover, a separation from eternity that will disappear.[24]

Blake conceives of time as the sequence of events extending from the fall of man from eternity into the physical creation, which has the absolute limit of six thousand years,[25] to his eventual return to eternity.[26] He embodied this concept in the myth of the fall of Albion, "when Albion was slain upon his Mountains" (3.1). The mythic Albion, on a cosmic level, represents all of the life of eternity that is fallen into the physical world. To bring that life back to eternity is the purpose of creation. Throughout *Milton* Albion sleeps on his couch; and though Blake dramatizes Albion's rousing himself at the end of the poem, Albion relapses, his relapse suggesting that man refuses to return to eternity because he refuses to relinquish the delusions of the selfhood. Blake's many references to sleeping, couches, and waking suggest that temporal existence is merely a brief episode of sleep in the eternal world. But this sleep has been changed to death by Satan (29.32–33), that is, the delusion that the material world has independent, real existence turns the "sleep" of this life into a potential everlasting death.[27] On a psychological level this condition of Albion represents a psychic malfunction of the mind caused by the selfhood's domination of the whole personality.

Blake's sequencing of time runs as follows: Albion's fall into a deathlike sleep preceded the initial episode of the poem, the shaping of Urizen by Los, which is Los's characteristic attempt to stop the degenerative process begun in the fall. Blake describes the seven passing ages of Los's formation of Urizen (3.6–27), which are to be taken as events prior to the formation of the world of time and space. When the formation of Urizen was complete, Los viewed his semi-successful attempt with terror (3.28), recognizing his own defensive posture in the inadequacy of his achievement. This recognition led to the separation of Enitharmon and Los's Spectre from Los's bosom and back (3.29–36). Among these three, the process of creation was then taken up as a serious pursuit. They built the looms of generation and Golgonooza (3.38–39), which symbolize the spiritual machinery that brings about material formation and process. In essence Los's pursuit constitutes the spiritual causation that leads to all natural effect. Blake then tells how Los's power was subdivided among all his children, from Orc to Satan, all of whom have been given form: "First Orc was Born then the Shadowy Female; then All Los's Family/ At last Enitharmon brought forth Satan Refusing Form, in vain" (3.40–41).

Satan's formation coincides with the beginning of man as it is recorded in the Bible, for in *Milton* Satan and Adam occur at the same interval in the temporal sequence: "The Divine hand found the Two Limits: first of Opacity, then of Contraction/ Opacity was named Satan, Contraction was named Adam" (13.20–21).[28] The limit is a limit to the fall from eternity, a kind of absolute end of degeneration beyond which mankind cannot go.[29] This merciful act occurred during the six thousand years of time, following the sending of two guards to the world to time. These two, Lucifer and Molech, had themselves fallen, and the degenerative process would have gone on had it not been limited. The formation of Adam preceded the descent of Elohim, Shaddai, Pahad, and Jehovah, whom Blake sees as guards also subject to corruption. Jehovah, the perfection of "hypocritic holiness" (13.25), without corrupting Jesus, formed a false body (a church) around him, which perverted his teachings (13.22–26).

Milton's descent to Blake marks the nearing of the end of the six thousand years of time. Los himself announces this end: "Fellow Labourers! The Great Vintage & Harvest is now upon Earth" (25.17). The harvest and vintage stand for the spiritual life that will proceed after the end of time, also symbolized in the awakening of Albion (25.23). In psychological terms, the end of temporal existence is really an end to the delusion that independent matter constitutes reality. The consummation of the creation, leading to the awakening of Albion (25.61–2), occurs when man acquires spiritual vision. Each individual may experience this vision during his lifetime and all of mankind will experience it at the last judgment. At any time, an individual may transcend his narrow sensual view and acquire spiritual vision, thus causing the world of time and space to be consumed for that individual. When all men accomplish this change, then Albion, who represents sleeping, collective man, will truly awake, not simply rouse himself and relapse, as he does at the end of the poem (39.32–52).

The spread of time thus can be a psychic spectrum as well as cosmic. Blake's description of infinity as a vortexlike projection from the individual which changes with time but includes all the individual's experience within it or behind it (15. 21–35), suggests that time is an illusion of sequence caused by the selfhood. Moreover, Blake's mundane shell is, in part, a psychological time-space continuum where place, or events of place, are essentially past time. Late in the poem the twenty-seven heavens of the mundane shell are given in temporal sequence from Adam to Luther, suggesting a sequential ordering of the past in space, the oldest in time being the most distant in space, the youngest the closest (37.35–43). That "All these are seen in Milton's Shadow" (37.44) suggests that the history of cosmic man can be contained within the confines of a single individual. This past time in the mind is the individual's memory, yet it can aid the delusion of independent material existence, since men may think, with Locke, that nothing enters the mind except from the exterior world of phenomena. But past time has its real existence only within the mind, for personal consciousness is the human imagination itself, which has no beginning or end, merely different manifestations. The individual personality has "destin'd lineaments permanent for ever & ever" (22.25), and "can never Die" (32.24). Death as the eclipse of identity, and time as the inevitable sequence of events for the personality, are delusions. Time is, in essence, a visionary construction, a mercy to the fallen soul. When one delves below the smallest particle of time, he is in touch with eternity and has in his possession the sum of time, of "Six Thousand Years" (28.63).

Space is a series of symbolic constructs that deny the normal spatial relationships that one dwelling in a spatial world customarily accepts. For Blake, space, like time, is essentially "visionary" (29.20). The Newtonian notion of space, limiting "existence" to external, sensuous objects, neglects the unsensed existence of eternity. For Blake, events in the exterior world are really manifestations of spiritual, interior causes. Their existence is not only not limited by an exterior spatial world, but their existence itself is caused by an internal vision of man. The laws, therefore, of spatial relationship, so important in a Newtonian universe of "Length Bredth Highth" (4.27), are illusions in

Blake's universe of mental space.[30] Rather, the spatial relationships in *Milton* are indicators of spiritual relationships.
Thus the opposing points of the compass, the inner and
outer view of man, above and below, within and without,
represent not spatial, but psychological opposites. An
example of this symbolism can be seen in the relationship
between inner and outer, and within and without. In the
statement "travellers to Eternity pass *outward* to Satan's
seat,/ But travellers to Eternity pass *inward* to Golgonooza" (17.29–30; italics mine) the directions reflect not
spatial paths but flows of psychic energy. *Within* the mind is
eternal vision. That vision lies *within* the nerves of the eye
that is spiritually open, "and *in this hallowed center* holds
the heavens of bright eternity" (28.38; italics mine) while
"Spectrous cunning" (28.41) waits *without*. "*Within* the
Center [of the Flower] Eternity expands" (31.48; italics
mine) When the fallen vision assumes reality to exist only in
the exterior world, it is turning *outward* to Satan's seat, that
is, it is being deluded by the selfhood that spatial existence
alone is real. To turn *inward* to the imagination is to put the
visionary existence on a higher plane of reality and thus to
become spiritual. To attempt to deduce knowledge about
God from the *outward* natural world is to deduce knowledge only of Satan. The empirical philosophy of five senses
is traveling *outward;* traveling *inward* is the philosophy of
the visionary.

III. EDEN, BEULAH, ULRO

Recognizing that portions of space symbolize psychological reality, we can examine the places known as Eden,
Beulah, and Ulro to see their meaning.[31] Blake's universe,
the supreme, timeless part of it, is called eternity or Eden.
It contains God, the spiritual life, and is God. It can expand
to become a single entity or contract and divide into mul-
titudes. In eternity the individual identity exists as a part of
the whole, at the same time retaining the capability of indi-

viduality. Psychologically, expanded eternity is that selfless harmony with others which allows one to identify with a group. Eternity is known also as the Divine Body of Jesus as well as the Human Imagination. The connection of eternity with the imagination implies that the essence of human life is spiritual existence; it also implies that the individual's imagination is the spiritual essence of the individual, while his body, senses, and reason are merely enclosures of the spirit, keeping it from contact with eternity.

The life of eternity seems characterized by strenuous, excessive, unwearying mental strife. So exceedingly active is eternity that the "female" portion of eternity is unable to withstand it and fades away. Therefore a temporal region of rest and sleep is provided, called Beulah. It is not eternity, but not exactly time either. Beulah is a sleep of eternity that *may* lead into a fall, but not inevitably. The active portions of eternity turn to Beulah for rest and for correction of error. There they have an "emanation" to repose in before they return to eternity.

The masculine nature of eternity is intended to suggest the selflessness that underlies Blake's whole ethical point of view. Eternity is a place where there is nothing for the comfort of the self. From each individual a constant outpouring of creative energy flows in a selfless stream of activity. Though *Milton* gives us brief pictures of the eternal tables, and of a bard before a divine assembly, suggesting a calm, Lucretian existence, the brief hints of the earlier *Book of Urizen*—where eternity seems conceived as a place of joy mixed with pain, of constant death of the self in creation, and metaphorically of "unquenchable burnings" (*BU* 4.13)—help us to see what Blake means by "the great Wars of Eternity in fury of Poetic Inspiration,/ To build the Universe stupendous: Mental forms Creating" (30.19–20). This is life "too exceeding unbounded" (30.22), a terrible joy that consumes the "weak & weary" (31.1). It is a life of selfless creative activity.[32] The presence of terror and pain in eternity is inevitable, because the individual is without his defenses. It is the desire to avoid the inevitable pain of selflessness that leads the weak and weary to a land of rest and, potentially at least, to the selfhood. Yet, despite its terrors, eternity is not deadly. The wars of eternity are changed to fixity and finality only when the fall into the world of Ulro occurs. They are then turned from a state of flux to "a frozen bulk subject to decay and death" (34.54). In eternity what are manifested in the physical world as war and hunting are the fluxile "fountains of the River of Life" (35.2). This fall from the freedom of eternity results from the selfhood's reaching for fixity because it believes fixity to give unthreatening permanence and stability. But what exists in defenseless freedom then becomes enclosed in a fortress, which is really a prison.

The world of eternity, where mental forms are continuously being created, thus stands also for creativity.[33] In eternity form and shape are created. Eternity is selfless in that it refuses to concern itself with survival, always turning the attention to the shaping of creation. Eternity exists when man builds the universe, that is, creates mental form (30.19–20). The psychological truth of this idea becomes clear when one reflects on his own experience. Anyone who has painted, written, composed, built, constructed a work of art, architecture, or artifact subsequently becomes aware of the timelessness of the act. What seemed to be experienced as a few minutes may actually have taken hours. Man experiences creativity as timelessness or eternity. Eternity is thus a symbolic place representing a combination of the individual creative urges of the imagination with the nonself-centered impulses.

Around eternity, and between eternity and this world, is the realm of Beulah. It is a realm of dream, of contrariety, where contrariety is truth. It is a pleasant rest. It is a land of sexual delusion. It is the realm of the daughters who inspire. Beulah is certainly suggested by the Beulah in *Pilgrim's Progress,* which is a land adjacent to the celestial city (Blake's eternity) where weary pilgrims (Blake's mental warriors in eternity) may rest and be refreshed. Here is renewed the contract between bride and bridegroom (Blake's male and emanation; contrarieties). It is beyond the valley of the shadow of death (not in the lower world of time and space). From Blake's Beulah an individual may fall away from eternal life just as the soul, crossing the river from Bunyan's Beulah, may itself yet be lost. Thus Blake's Beulah's pleasant connotations must be balanced against the fact that Beulah is the place from which souls are drawn down into spiritual death, to generation. It is an intermediary between eternity and the world as it appears to us. The sleepers of Beulah may be lured down "the River Storge (which is Arnon) into the Dead Sea" (34.30); that is, the sleeping individual may be lured into a great delusion. Just as the Arnon flows into the Dead Sea, souls descend to embodiment in flesh. Parental appetite (Storge) wishes to lure the souls into the worlds of the flesh. But just as the flowing Arnon and souls fall into the Dead Sea and into flesh, so does the unwary and over-relaxed soul fall into delusion.

It is the tinge of the selfhood inherent in Beulah that leads potentially to the delusion of this world. A place "where no dispute can come" (30.3), a place of shade and sleep (30.2), a place protected like an infant cradled in its mother's arms (30.11–12), a place of "mild & pleasant Rest" (30.14) is created essentially for those who cannot withstand absolute selflessness. It is a bounded, nonexcessive place, representing the need for protection. It was founded originally to give a place of rest to those who might "consume" (30.27). This kind and merciful motive for its foundation, however, does not cancel the ambivalence of Beulah, for in its own extremes Beulah can become the world of Ulro. This "lovely Shadow" (30.2) is a "Temporal Habitation" (30.29), the first step of the descent to the delusion of time and space. It is the first time-structuring act of the mind anxious to avoid feelings of insecurity. It is a shadow into which the eternals go, a dovelike covering (31.3), a child in its mother's arms. In essence it is the first bit of protective covering from selflessness that can become the incrustation of the selfhood. No creativity is said to exist in Beulah, though it may be a place of inspiration. The daughters of Beulah may inspire a poet's song (2.1), but they are not themselves the creators. As a land of rest and inspiration Beulah may function as a place of dreams where the weary may rest and restore their creative energies. But if it becomes a permanent haven, then the individual has begun the fall into Ulro.

Beulah as a place thus symbolizes that mental state of noncreativity wherein the weary mind seeks refreshment; the strife of creativity is relaxed so that the paradoxical, the contrary, the apparently illogical is not disputed. In its relaxed ambience the pursuit of creation is dropped for the refreshment of pleasure. This mental state, though there is no exact word for it, is a state between creative struggle and delusory stasis. It is between eternity and Ulro.

The symbol *Ulro* represents delusion in many forms but, particularly in *Milton,* the delusion that the material universe had independent and exclusive reality. This empirical delusion appears in Blake's occasional equations of spatial existence with Ulro. As space, Ulro is mentioned when Los sees the world without Bowlahoola and Allamanda as a visionless polypus that would tremble "thro all the Ulro space" (24.39). This equation is also suggested by the "watchers of Ulro" (20.50), who behold the spatial world, and by the fact that the spatially visible wild Thyme is "Los' messenger . . . in Ulro dark" (35.54-55). But more frequently Ulro means not space but the delusion of the mind that equates space with total reality. As delusion, Ulro is mentioned when Satan falls into a "World of deeper Ulro" (9.34), when "the shades of Death & Ulro" (14.12) appear in Milton's visage, or when Milton's wives and daughters must remain in the "dark Ulro till the Judgemnt" (17.5). Its destructive qualities appear when Blake thinks of it as a nether region of Beulah (21.6–7; 22.46; 27.45; 37.16). It is a result of the delusive Tirzah at the end of Book I:

"The Three Heavens of Ulro, where Tirzah & her Sister/ Weave the black Woof of Death" (29.55–56). Here the three heavens, usually associated with Beulah in the poem, are associated with Ulro and given over to Tirzah's perverting influence. Tirzah's weaving carries the meaning of materialization, and death here represents the delusion that the physical world has independent reality. Thus Ulro in *Milton* becomes a symbol for the same delusion of materialism as that attacked by Berkeley.

The connection between the senses as agents of delusion and Ulro as a state of delusion is suggested when Satan grows "Opake against the Divine Vision" (9.31) and falls into "a World of deeper Ulro" (9.34), opacity being later referred to as a possible condition for the eye (28.34) and ear (29.35–37). It is Hartley, following Newton, who calls the nerve fibers of the brain pellucid, because "Opacity of any Body . . . [is] an argument that its Pores are so large and irregular, as to disturb and interupt the vibration of the Aether."[34] Blake has ironically substituted opacity for the pellucid quality of the nerves assigned to them by Hartley. Associated with Satan, opacity stands for the limited Lockean view of reality that grows in thought divided from vision.[35] This deceptive potentiality of the senses is suggested in the symbol the *False Tongue* (2.10), which appears in: "Ulro, Seat of Satan,/ Which is the False Tongue beneath Beulah: it is the Sense of Touch" (27.45–46). The false tongue symbolizes the sense that *may* delude one into believing that what it detects is alone real. The delusive false tongue is also the part of materialism which has changed the belief in Christ's mercy to a belief in retribution.

Tell also of the False Tongue! vegetated
Beneath your land of shadows: of its sacrifices. and
Its offerings; even till Jesus, the image of the Invisible God
Because its prey; a curse, an offering. and an atonement,
For Death Eternal in the heavens of Albion, & before the Gates

Of Jerusalem his Emanation, in the heavens beneath
Beulah.
(2.10–15)

Thus Ulro, along with its associated symbols, is the spatial
equivalent of the particular delusion of the selfhood that the
material universe has independent reality, a delusion that
leads eventually to a belief in retribution. It is the work of
the rational philosophy of Bacon, Newton, and Locke.

IV. SPACE AS MENTAL FORM

There are several other spatial relationships in *Milton*,
but these do not fit neatly into the structure of Eternity-
Beulah-Ulro. However, as psychological states of mind
they make abundant sense. Blake had Swedenborg as an
example in using spatial relationships to symbolize mental
states. Swedenborg insisted that space belongs only to the
natural world and that heaven is indeterminate and unmeasurable. For Swedenborg it is a gross absurdity to apply
the idea of space to heavenly things.[36] The progression
through space in the spiritual world represents a change of
the mental interior: "Motions, progressions, and changes of
place, in the other [spiritual] life are changes of the state of
the interior of life [i.e., the states of psychic being] and
nevertheless it really appears to spirits and angels as if they
actually existed."[37] This is also Blake's meaning in his spatial concepts. They are spiritual relationships, and the indeterminate and unmeasurable spatial relations between these
symbolic states is of no consequence in determining their
meaning.[38]

The diagram of the cosmic world on plate thirty-three of
Milton, though not containing all of Blake's spatial symbols
(e.g., Beulah), is itself a picture of the various psychic elements. The flames surrounding the four globes are the
flames of eternity. As such they represent creativity and
selflessness. The globes of the fallen Urizen, Urthona,

Tharmas, and Luvah constitute chaos (34.32). Chaos traditionally holds the primal matter of all creation, but in
Blake's view these globes are the dire ruin that constitute a
spatial world (34.39). Traditionally, chaos exists before creation. But for Blake, these globes are ruins after a fall. Thus
Blake's chaos is really a fallen mental perception resulting
from the delusion of the independent existence of matter.
Since the independent existence of primal matter is not an
acceptable idea for Blake, that matter is not only a chaos,
but a ruin, without form or order. Psychologically, Blake is
denying that our sensations of a natural world have the
power to shape thought. Within the chaos, however, is the
mundane shell or, as Blake calls it here, the "Egg form'd
World of Los" (34.33). It is proper here to imagine chaos as
the external world and the mundane shell as part of the
internal mind of man. The mundane shell is a twenty-
sevenfold creation, but it is an interior, not exterior creation. It is a "Concave Earth" (17.21), a "shadow of all
things upon our Vegetative Earth/ Englarg'd into dimension
& deform'd into indefinite space" (17.22–23). The mundane shell is the world of memory within the vegetated
man.[39] When projected into space, that is, when it is assumed to have independent existence, it is deformed. Then
it is seen as the outer sphere of a limited spatial world,
much like the eighth sphere in the Ptolemaic universe,
which contains the fixed stars (37.47–55). As a shadow it is
human memory. The "shadow" is described in the culmination of the poem when Blake describes the twenty-seven
churches associated with "Milton's Shadow" (37.44). Conceived solely as objective events in historical sequence,
these churches are delusion. Though they exist in the memory, they can become delusions when they are assumed to
have had independent existence. They are delusory coverings of the true vision when so perverted, though they all
have sprung from an impulse of the creative imagination.

In Blake's diagram the mundane shell encloses a strange
design appearing as tongues of flame, but if viewed upside

down, one can see the flames as tentaclelike projections. This is the polypus "of living fibres down . . . [in] the Sea of Time & Space" (34.25). This polypus, without the shaping function of Los, would constitute the fallen world. It would be a "Fibrous Vegetation/ A Polypus of soft affections without Thought or Vision" (24.37–38). In essence it would represent sensation without thought. It may appear to be the flame of thought, but it is only an inverted delusion. The polypus is said to be the abode of the five females (here representing the five senses) whose amorous songs lure souls into the flesh (34.27–30). As a symbol of affection, pleasure, or appetite, the polypus is a place of sensation. It seems perplexing at first that the "Heads of the Great Polypus" are also "Cities of the Levites" (38.1–3), but when one recollects that the Levites are the priestly caste of the Hebrews and that sensation, empirical philosophy, natural religion, deism, and druidism were also associated with the "churches" as attempts to deny spirituality, then one begins to accept Blake's unusual double meaning for polypus. It represents the sensory apparatus on the individual level and the delusory apparatus on the cosmic level of meaning. That Blake equates it with Ulro (34.24) makes its delusory nature clear.

Blake's design shows the names of Satan and Adam within the mundane shell, signifying that the mundane shell contains the stated limits of the fall: opacity and contraction. Man can go no farther from eternity, and at this limit Los begins his creative work that leads to a return to eternity. Sensation and memory are in the mundane shell, but the truly saving process is imaginative creativity: to create, or to give form, is the function of Los.

V. LOS'S WORLD

From the time of the fall of Urizen to the present of Milton's descent, form-giving is Los's central function, but form-giving has a large scope of meaning. It is the entire process of birth, growth, and fruition. In terms of Blake's myth of the fall, form-giving is an attempt to give a solid form to that which would endlessly disorganize in its fall from eternity. That form, moreover, is the step back toward eternity. In that form what has fallen is, like a seed, being dropped into the world for growth into spiritual existence. The world of growth is a world of process carried on by Los's sons. The words of St. Paul (used by Blake in "To Tirzah" in *Songs of Experience*) "it is raised a spiritual body," derive from St. Paul's implied comparison between soul and seed. This is the function of Los: to give the form that the spiritual seed will take in the process of moving toward the great harvest, the last vintage, or spiritual vegetation of the soul. The whole process should also be taken as a symbol of mental activity. The work of Los is to give images to ideas, to create forms of thought. Here Blake is giving the imagination a central place in his psychological picture of man. Sensation is a dangerous polypus. Memory can be a construct of delusion. But imagination is the magnificent work of Los.[40]

Unfortunately, the form-giving of Los becomes an elaborate allegory that drifts back and forth across the basic ground of the psychological analogue between space and mind as it develops its theme: "every Natural Effect has a Spiritual Cause, and Not/ A Natural" (26.44–45). Blake's world of Los becomes a fanciful extension of the thesis that Los is the spiritual cause of all natural effects. This mythic explanation of natural phenomena accounts for events in ways other than scientific, and its details are so elaborated as to render the picture paradoxical at times. Blake, however, in elaborating the thesis in such detail is only extending an idea that has occurred before in the eighteenth century. Swedenborg's spiritual world constitutes the groundwork for Blake's thesis, but Blake proceeds exhaustively to give substance to such suggestions as those of Robert Clayton: "All Nature, therefore, seems to be animated, or alive; and this whole World to be replete with

Spirits formed with different Kinds and Degrees of abilities, according to the various Ends and Uses, for which they were designed by their Creator''[41]; or the more elaborate ideas of Abraham Tucker, whose *mundane soul* is in part the spiritual cause of natural events. For Tucker the mundane soul is the spatial repository for spirits after they have left their vehicular state. Like an ocean, it is everywhere. Spirits exist in this ocean as individuals, yet there is a telecommunication between them that makes awareness universal. Moreover, each spirit has its own function, in which it finds great satisfaction, as an effective cause in the material world.[42] Blake's ornate, mythical world of Los is similar in that the individual spirits associated with Los are seen as the spiritual causes of natural events.

The complications of the thesis of spiritual causation appear generally in such oblique and unclear statements as this: that the four arts—poetry, painting, music, and architecture, which is science—in eternity are the four faces of man; but in time and space only science exists, and its function is to make manifest the other three arts (27.55–62). Blake's statement here, unpoetic and jumbled beyond complete explication, rests on the thesis that eternity (spirituality) is manifested in time and space (nature). Yet Blake's successful elaborations of spiritual causation overbalance his failures. The thesis lies behind the grand comparison of the black storm and the face of Los:

Like the black storm, coming out of Chaos, beyond the stars:
It issues thro the dark & intricate caves of the Mundane Shell
Passing the planetary visions, & the well adorned Firmament
The Sun rolls into Chaos & the stars into the Desarts;
And then the storms become visible, audible & terrible,
Covering the light of day, & rolling down upon the mountains,
Deluge all the country round. Such is a vision of Los;

When Rintrah & Palamabron spoke; and such his stormy
    face
Appeared, as does the face of heaven, when covered with
    thick storms
Pitying and loving tho in frowns of terrible perturbation.
                  (23.21–30)

The natural world of storm, stars, sun, light, mountains,
and country are the sensational phenomena corresponding
to the spiritual event of Los's frown, and in this brilliant
passage the phenomenal and spiritual are so interconnected
that the thesis is exemplified as well as stated. The same
thesis lies behind the two magnificent pictures of nature in
the lamentations of Beulah. The nightingale, lark, and choir
of birds; the thyme and all the spring flowers are visions of
the lamentation of Beulah insofar as the spiritual event can
be seen as a sensational phenomenon (31.28–64). The constellations in their grand course through the sky, the calm
ocean, the gorgeously clothed fly, and the wind-swept trees
on mountains are visions of eternity if seen with the imagination (25.66–26.10). "But we see only as it were the hem
of their garments/ When with our vegetative eyes we view
these wond'rous Visions" (26.11–12).[43] The spiritual cause
can be seen only after we realize that our imprisoning sensation perceives only a mere portion, and that portion a
small one, of the totality of existence, which is mainly
spiritual and always spiritually caused.

Time and space are spiritually caused. The sons of Los
build up time: like a castle expanding from the couch of
sleep to the towers and outworks, time is expanded by
building blocks of moments into ages.[44] Space, like the
moment of time, is built from the smallest structure, the
globule of blood. The world we inhabit is thus a series of
visionary creations of the sons of Los. But the senses themselves without imagination cannot report the essential
spirituality of that vision. They give only a partial report.
The notions of material science, based on the extension of

the senses by the telescope and microscope,[45] cannot give that vision, and it is therefore a delusion to think that the limited capability of mere sensation can give an all-inclusive view even of the spatial world (29.15–18).

Blake's elaboration of spiritual causation also illustrates creativity's function as guardian against the destructive urges. The sons of Los are spiritual causes, both good and bad. After Los's separation from Enitharmon, he begot a series of sons, all of whom work on the building of Golgonooza (3.39–42). Orc, Palamabron, Rintrah, Antamon, and Ozoth are workers helping Los to give form to chaos. Yet Los's fallen sons and daughters, Satan, Tirzah, Rahab, and others, are trying to destroy Los's forms. In this struggle Los and his unfallen sons act the role of guardians, and their role is associated with the role of the prophet. As the prophet in the Old Testament is the guardian of the truth of Israel against the evil practice of the Israelites, so Los is the guardian against evil. Furthermore, his function of guardian is associated with the guardianship of the seven eyes of God.[46] The seven eyes (Lucifer, Molech, Elohim, Shaddai, Pahad, Jehovah, and Jesus; Milton himself is the eighth) are sequentially sent to guard the world of time and space, presumably from destruction (13.12–25). Blake does not clearly explain why they become fallen, but their connection to Los makes it clear that their mission is to guard against destruction. The seven eyes are connected to Los in their common source, Revelation. When Blake says that Los is the "Fourth Zoa, that stood around the Throne Divine" (24.76), he is referring to the vision of the throne of God in Revelations 4, where the divine throne is surrounded by twenty-four elders, and "four beasts" (Rev. 4:6), or *zoa* in Greek. The fourth beast, an eagle, which in Swedenborgian correspondence represents prophecy, is an appropriate symbol for Los, the "Spirit of Prophecy" (24.71). But in Revelation the throne divine is also fronted by the "seven Spirits of God" (4:5), who are seen in chapter 5 of Revelation as the seven eyes of the Lamb of God.

These are Blake's "Seven Eyes of God [who] continually/ Guard round . . . the Generations of Tirzah/ Because of Satan" (24.6–7). They share the duty of Los who, as the "Fourth Zoa . . . [is] also set/ The Watchman of Eternity" (24.8–9). Though fallen, as the seven eyes are fallen, Los prevents the destruction of any event of time and space (22.15–25) through his prophetic or imaginative function. "They vanish not from me & mine, we guard them first & last" (22.23). Los bends his force against the east to prevent destruction (26.18–20), and he gives safe conduct to "the Spirits to be vegetated" (29.47). As a prophet he walks "up and down" (22.18) in the six thousand years of time, preserving the eternal lineaments of all the generations of men (22.18–25). They are preserved in Los's halls, where the mercy of time as a preserver against chaotic destruction allows all Los's fallen sons, who are sons of the spirit of prophecy, to work against eternal destruction (24.68–76). Los, as time, is a guard against the eternally destructive urges, and is merciful in the same sense that Enitharmon's decisions to give space to Satan is a kind decision (13.16). Psychologically, the guardian-prophet embodies the imaginative creativity that, through its insistence on giving form to the formless, keeps in check the selfhood's destructiveness, which is manifested externally in a class of men who are destroyers. Historically, Los's guardianship manifests itself as faith in the preservative power of vision and imagination against reason, science, and Lockean epistemology. Religiously, it causes a reliance on the inspired but personally interpreted word of the Bible, as opposed both to the rationalism of deism and to the dogma of orthodoxy.

Los's guardianship, however, has its dark side. One remembers that the seven eyes of God are in some degree fallen, and Los himself is a fallen zoa. His attempts to recreate Urizen have been only partially successful and his effort leaves him terrified and weeping. As a preserver from chaos he succeeds, but as a restorer to eternity he is doomed to failure. His work, the mundane shell, has this double aspect. It is a form that preserves from chaos, but it is also a hardened shell that restricts. The eternal vision is given shape in the material world to prevent the chaotic dissolution of man, but the manifested vision becomes "frozen to unexpansive deadly destroying terror" (35.1). In the world of time and space, the perfection of eternity does not exist and the material product of creativity inevitably will be imperfect. Los's fallibility is part of the reason for Palamabron's and Rintrah's distrust (22.27–28). Los himself, after Satan slays Thullough, alters his world with rage (9.12–18). He also mistakenly resists Milton's journey at first (17.35–36).

The larger meaning of this potential fallibility of the creative side of the mind suggests a discrimination to be made between intention and achievement. Creativity is thought of as producing something new. But there is always an analogue in the past for every new venture; nothing comes to flower without its roots. Newness is only the slightly different manifestation of an eternal archetype, a manifestation that can never equal the archetype in perfection. Yet, though inevitably incomplete and imperfect in achievement, creativity's imperfection does not hurt its saving power; in fact, it can be viewed as a cause of that power. Because of its imperfection in achievement, creativity can never cease. After all, eternity, for Blake, is a life of ceaseless creativity. Perfect creation is never promised, and the dark aspects of Los are warning that the products of creativity are not its final goal.

Moreover, and perhaps paradoxically, the past cannot become a conscious determinant in man's creativity. To permit such would be to exchange creativity for imitation. Imitation of nature is the preservation of chaos. One must give form not to the material world, but to the eternal vision that resides in the imagination. The product will be flawed because form-giving in the material world cannot be perfect. But unless the imagination's visions are given form,

the world remains a chaos. Here the psychological implications are clear. The fall into chaos, the necessity of form to
stop the fall, and the necessity of a process to return what is
fallen to eternity are most appropriate as symbolic treatment for an idea in consciousness. If the idea is not given
form, it will fall away from consciousness and be lost, never
to be in the eternity of another's mind. The idea, like the
spirit and like the seed, must be given form to ensure the
"glorious spiritual/ Vegetation" (25.60–61).

   Blake uses varying symbols for the processes of spiritual
embodiment. The process of Los's form-giving is described
in the symbols of building and producing: "The Passions &
Desires descend upon the hungry winds . . . / The Sons of
Los clothe them & feed & provide houses & fields"
(26.28–30). The passions and desires, the souls, the spirits,
are unembodied creatures seeking forms provided by the
sons of Los. At times Blake refers to the souls as spectres
choosing their forms (26.38; 28.10–43), but he reverts to
calling them "Spirits to be Vegetated" (29.47).[47] The use of
spectre here merely as a synonym for spirit is not entirely
inconsistent with the spectre's meaning as rational power
(40.34). The spectre is the rational power of man seeking
form just as desires and passions seek form. These mental
functions are being vegetated just as spirits are, and the
shape they take, human form or otherwise, is a matter of
choice. The sleeper is another symbol for the spirit to be
vegetated (26.29). This symbol is derived from the part of
Blake's myth that sees the spirit as a sleeper of Beulah
falling away from eternal vision. The sleeper then must
have a form so that he can begin the process of return. Still
another symbol for the process is that of the gateway. The
souls descend and ascend to and from the body by a north
and south gate (26.12–17). Though not consistent in itself
(at first all souls descend through both gates; later they are
said to ascend through the north gate) the conception is
based on the myth of the gates from Porphyry's *Concerning
the Cave of the Nymphs*. In Porphyry the northern gate is

"the gate through which souls descend,"[48] while the southern gates "are . . . avenues . . . of souls ascending to the Gods."[49] Blake seems to have reversed the two gate's directions, but the essential meaning remains. The gates are the entrance ways of the spirits to be vegetated. The process of being vegetated may, however, suggest limitation. Although the spirit is said to be given inner form, like a garden (26.31–32), (i.e., given an inner spiritual shape), or given sexual texture (4.4) (i.e., put into the body as either male or female), it is really enclosed in the five senses (5.19–26) (i.e., limited from eternal vision). Blake's strangest symbolic formulation of the embodiment process is in the use of the term *vehicle*. Twice Blake uses Abraham Tucker's strange conception of the vehicular state. Tucker had fantasized about the vehicular body as a very tiny, elastic, material husk that contains the spiritual essence. The vehicle, as he called it, can travel from one state, or life, to another after death. It travels through several existences before it dissolves, permitting the soul to rejoin the sea of spirit. It implants on the soul the character derived from its past experience. Picking up Tucker's notion, Blake uses it to suggest the transformation of identity. In *Milton,* Lazarus is the "Vehicular Body of Albion the Redeem'd" (24.27), and Los is a "Vehicular Terror" (17.31). Los is the vehicular, or present state of the transformed Urthona, even as Lazarus is a state of the transformed Albion. In all of these symbols, Blake is depicting the spiritual essence receiving material form so that essence, or soul, may avoid chaos and return to eternity.

The process of creation Los has performed in part, but part has been performed by his sons. As a direct agent Los has given form to the fallen Urizen (3.6–27) and still creates the sun each morning (29.41), but the processes of creativity are spread among a minutely articulated hierarchy of spirits. Los is father and ruler of these spirits. Some are in opposition to him, such as Satan. Some have fallen into vegetation in past time and are no longer part of Los's processes: "Twelve Sons successive fled away in that thousand years of sorrow" (23.62). Among Los's remaining sons are Rintrah, Palamabron, Sotha, Theotormon, Orc, Bromion, Ozoth, and Antamon, who are each manifested in Los's processes in different ways. Rintrah and Palamabron, scantly depicted as governors "over Day & Night" (29.27), are also the operators of the plow and harrow in the symbol of spiritual growth and vegetation (4.1–2). Sotha and Theotormon have direct involvement in giving material form to the spirit,[50] when they induce the unwilling spirits, or spectres, to choose a material form.[51] Like Rintrah and Palamabron, they are agents effecting a transformation (28.21–28).

Orc, however, insofar as he constitutes the nervous system of each human, is not so much an efficient as a material cause of the embodiment in form. As the means of sensation in material form, he is associated with the polypus. His identity is also slightly confused when he is said to be a manifestation of Satan, who is a manifestation of Urizen, and simultaneously to be a manifestation of Luvah. But this confused set of identifications is merely an attempt to suggest that the vision of man (Luvah as an eternal) usurped by his reason (Satan) degenerates to become mere sensation (Orc) (29.28–39). Orc is imprisoned in the nerves, which are falsely assumed to be the only connecting links between the senses and the seat of awareness: "Orc incessant howls burning in fires of Eternal Youth" (29.29); Orc's freedom symbolizes the removal of the delusion that passive sensation constitutes awareness. Orc is also the pleasure principle. The fire of eternal youth is the pleasurable sensation of the nerves, which is good in itself, but deadly when considered the only pleasure. The danger of being imprisoned in the materialistic delusion is expressed in the vague statement that "sleep [i.e., being born into this world] was transformed/ To Death" (29.32–3) in the "optic vegetative Nerve" (29.32) and in the equally vague statement about the "Nerves of the Nostrils" and opacity (29.35–39). The sons of Ozoth work within the eye, in a still different fashion. They do not create the eye, which is a material manifestation of Orc, but they create the vision of the eye. They give various delights in two ways. To those who possess artificial riches (i.e., the wealthy) they give scorn, hardening the optic nerve and thereby shutting out natural beauty, so that the eye becomes "opake" like a black pebble. But to the poor they give internal vision, which allows them to see internally even as a diamond is clear within. This internal vision enables them to behold eternity (28.37–38).

The symbolism associated with Orc and Ozoth is not always perspicuous, but in Blake's best depictions of Los's spiritual agents, he makes the agent take on several layers of meaning. Antamon exemplifies this success:

> And sometimes two Spectres like lamps quivering
> And often malignant they combat (heart-breaking sorrowful
> & piteous)
> Antamon takes them into his beautiful flexible hands,
> As the Sower takes the seed, or as the Artist his clay
> Or fine wax, to mould artful a model for golden ornaments.
> The soft hands of Antamon draw the indelible line;
> Form immortal with golden pen; such as the Spectre admir-
> ing
> Puts on the sweet form; then smiles Antamon bright thro his
> windows
> The Daughters of beauty look up from their Loom & pre-
> pare.
> The integument soft for its clothing with joy & delight.
> (28.11–20)

Here Antamon is the spiritual agent as a painter, a sculptor, and a sower. His skill is such that the beautiful form he creates entices the spectre or spirit to take the form. On another level he is a true sower of seeds, for like a phallus producing semen, he permits the spirit to take embodiment in the human seed. The looms of the daughters of beauty, which are wombs, provide the bodily integument that is a clothing or garment of the spirit. Thus the artistic creative process and the biological procreative process are manifestations of the same spiritual cause. Blake derived this concept from the interpretation of generation found in Porphyry's *Concerning the Cave of the Nymphs.*[52] In Porphyry's view the humid soul is "insnared by corporeal love"[53] and descends "into generation and the tenacious vestment of the body,"[54] where the nymphs weave on the bodily bones the purple garment of flesh. Like Porphyry's nymphs, Blake's daughters of beauty weave the body for the enticed soul, but Blake has changed the emphasis of Porphyry by making the beauty of the form rather than corporeal love the enticement, and by adding Antamon as the spiritual and artistic agent. Blake has kept the paradigm of Porphyry's myth, but used it in his own meaning, making the process a universal creative process on both biological and artistic levels.

The work of creation is notably the work of both male and female. Enitharmon, like Los's sons, has her place. She is the creator of space and of the body. The space created for Satan is an act of mercy (13.12–13), and Enitharmon herself, like Orc, constitutes space: "By mortals . . . Enitharmon is nam'd Space" (24.68). As such she is the emanated ground for the creative activity to work. With her daughters, she constitutes the female procreativity that gives flesh to bare form (29.51–53).

The instruments used for the processes described in the world of Los are interconnected. Los's forge, with its associated chains, anvil, furnace, hammer, bellows, and iron ladles, has a double function: to furnish the instruments necessary for the harvest (6.8–13) and to give shape to the spectres (26.38). The harvest is the spiritual harvest that is being grown from the labors of Rintrah and Palamabron, whose plow and harrow are its preparatory forerunners. Los's winepress is associated with his harvest as well as Satan's mills. Satan's mills are the places where the husks of the harvest are ground away. Thus, Satan, the destroyer, yet has a function in the process of spiritual growth, though he does not comprehend it. The forge-harvest series of metaphors represents the process of spiritual birth and maturation. The same kind of meaning exists in the picture of Enitharmon's looms, which are called the looms of Cathedron. From the material point of view, Cathedron's looms are the womb where the garment of flesh is woven. From a spiritual point of view, the loom of Cathedron is a couch where the sleeper reposes until his awakening ($\kappa\alpha\theta\epsilon\delta\rho o\nu$ means throne and can be a place of idle sitting or reclining, i.e., a couch). Thus the death couch of eternity is a loom where spirits are woven flesh for the world of time and space. However, the weaving symbol, along with the mills of Satan, and the concept of space, is also a potential source of evil wherein the selfhood works. In fact, the garment woven on the looms is a hood or covering that must eventually be put off. The body must die; the selfhood must be put off.

Just as the symbolic instruments function in the process of spiritual birth and maturation, so do the locations of Los's world, but because of the multiplicity of meaning Blake puts on some locations, they sometimes seem rather obscure symbols. The world of Los is distinct from either eternity, the Ulro vision, or Beulah; for as Blake makes Milton's identity divide, he shows Milton's redeemed portion traveling in the mundane shell, which is the egg-formed world of Los; while Milton's eternal human portion resides in eternity, his elect portion becomes the rock Sinai as part of the Ulro delusion, and his shadow portion remains visible to Blake. Los's mundane shell holds the various locations of Los's world, such as Bowlahoola, Allamanda, Udan Adan, and Entuthon Benython. Bowlahoola on one level is the place where the soul enters the material form, choosing the form it desires.[55] Los's forge is in Bowlahoola (24.51). Allamanda is the cultivated land, the place where souls are matured appropriately.[56] Away from these are the lake of Udan Adan,[57] which is a destructive area belonging to Satan's camp (αδυνατειν means to be unable), Satan's mills, and Entuthon Benython (εντυθεν means thenceforth, βενθοσ means the depths of the sea),[58] which suggests the nonentity of matter.[59] From Blake's spiritual viewpoint, matter is the nonentity that must be given a unique name. The locations of these places in relation to Eternity, Beulah, and Ulro are not detailed, but it is necessary only to see them as places associated with Los and his functions to see that as places they are symbols for spiritual ideas that take shape in many forms. Bowlahoola is also law and the human stomach (24.48, 67). As spiritual idea, it is the principle of form manifested in human relationships as law and in the human digestive system as stomach. Allamanda is the principle of cultivation that in human relationships is commerce (27.42), in human economy the growing wheat field. Golgonooza is the principle of conception in the human body as the skull, in human history as a new Golgotha where a birth of the new conception of self-annihilation will occur.[60]

Perhaps Blake's symbolic universe would not be too confusing if all these place-symbols remained in this unfamiliar context. But Blake also attempts to relate the symbolic places with the familiar surroundings of England and the Holy Land of the Bible. This represents Blake's attempt to integrate the spiritual and cosmic world with the phenomenal existence of common experience. The implication is that great action of cosmic significance can and does occur in the homely places of everyday life. Moreover, the place names of England become parallels to places in the Holy Land. Tyburn is Calvary, Lambeth is Jerusalem. The banks of Cam are Rephaim's vale. Yet not all the places are equivalent. However, Carmel, Ephraim, the deserts of Midian, and the other biblical places, take on a familiar atmosphere because of the general admixture. The first effect is a shock to our normal sense of time and place, but the ultimate effect is a recognition that spiritual action is repeated at different temporal intervals with the same import, the same problem, the same goal. The sacrifice of Calvary, with its implications of oppression from worldly men, is now the sacrifice at Tyburn.

The English place names are involved in further complexities through Blake's tendency to see analogy between geographic entities and the human body. Thus the material form of the British Isles is seen as the giant Albion, asleep. Parts of his body are locations in the British Isles, Tyburn, for instance, being the resting place of his left foot. The myth of Albion's fall is seen as the formation of the material form of the British Isles. The myth of the sleep of Albion and his awakening represents the awakening of the people of England from that sleep. Thus the analogy of body to geography tends to lose its distinct boundary and Albion becomes a symbol for the spiritual condition of the people of England. But the rockiness and hardness of the material entity is indeed an appropriate symbol for what Blake saw as the spiritual condition of his fellow men.

These, then, are the main elements of Blake's mythic world. The spiritual and psychological condition—Eternity, Beulah, and Ulro; Los and Enitharmon and their progeny; and the complex mixture of various places in biblical and English geography and times—are all indicative of the anti-materialistic, essentially spiritual and imaginative belief that drove Blake to mental warfare against those he considered agents of the selfhood. Los's creation of form can be seen as the creation of form for fallen spirits. But this myth is also a way of saying that the imagination gives shape to perception.[61] The world of Los symbolizes mental process.[62] Embodiment represents a putting off of the less definite and becoming more definite. This is the process of evolving thought.

2

Fall into Selfhood

I. INTELLECTUAL BACKGROUND OF THE SELFHOOD

In exploring the psyche in *Milton*, Blake was not in *terra incognita*. Though his poetic vehicle blazed a new trail that brought him farther into many unfamiliar recesses, he set out from roads that others had opened. In fact, he linked up two high roads of thought about the pysche before carrying his exploration farther than any of his predesessors. The philosophic highroad that examined the motivation of man generally found in man two basic drives, one altruistic or benevolent, the other self-interested. Generally, the philosophers saw man either as driven by one of these motives or as reconciling both within himself. Essentially they were concerned with the motivation of the individual's response to the social group, and thus were concerned with the mapping of the psyche. But the road of the spiritualist traveled over the question of man's relationship with God, revealing in the individual two basic drives, one the love of God, the other self-interest. The spiritualist approach found man's love of God in opposition to worldliness, and thus created an equation of self-interest with worldliness. Blake formed a link between the philosophic and spiritualist concepts by developing a view of the self that makes it both a set of interior psychological principles and a set of exterior forces manifest in the world of men.

The philosophers meandered around the problem of the self-involvement of man, talking about it in several terms: self-love, self-interest, self, or self-preservation. It is self-preservation that is the basic motive that Blake uncovers as the root of the selfhood from which stem all the evil thorns and vines that prick and bind the essential man. Relatively few writers felt comfortable with the egocentric conclusion that self, or self-preservation, or self-love, was the primary motive of moral action. But those who did were in accord with Holbach, who stated the position most clearly:

> Newton calls it *inert force*. The moralists have called it *self-love*, which is only a tendency to preserve himself—the desire of happiness—the love of his well-being—of pleasure—the promptitude of seizing all that appears favourable to his existence and a marked aversion to all that menaces or disturbs him . . . . This *self*-gravitation is, then, a necessary disposition in man, and in all beings, which by a diverse means tends to preserve them in the existence that they have received so long as nothing deranges the order of their machine or its primitive tendency.[1]

Holbach's equation of self-love with self-preservation implies, of course, preservation in the corporeal world. This concept lies behind Mary Wollstonecraft's remark: "Self-preservation is, literally speaking, the first law of nature; and that care necessary to support and guard the body is the first step to unfold the mind, and inspire a manly spirit of independence."[2]

The view of man as a creature driven primarily by a desire for self-preservation had many opponents. Ann Radcliffe, in *The Romance of the Forest*, attacked the notion when she put the concept into the specious reasoning of the murderous Marquis de Montalt, who is trying to persuade another to commit murder: "Self preservation is the great law of nature; when a reptile hurts us, or an animal of prey threatens us, we think no further but endeavour to annihilate it. When my life, or what may be essential to my life, requires the sacrifice of another, or if even some passion, wholly unconquerable, requires it, I should be a madman to hesitate."[3] This parody of Wollstonecraft, emphasizing the complete and narrow egoism of self-love and its readiness to destroy others to preserve the self from even an imagined danger or for purely malicious reasons, is a parody similar to Blake's Satanic parody of the self. But Ann Radcliffe here, in attacking that philosophy, which Godwin saw, later in his life, as the "grovelling principle, born in France,"[4] had behind her other writers who distrusted self-love.

Adam Smith discriminated between self-love and other principles of human action and denied that self-love has any significance in making moral judgments. In *The Theory of Moral Sentiments* he wrote:

> According to Mr. Hobbes . . . man is driven to take refuge in society . . . because without the assistance of others he is incapable of subsisting with ease or safety. Society, upon this account, becomes necessary to him, and whatever tends to its support and welfare, he considers as having a remote tendency to his own interest . . . . When those authors [Hobbes and others] . . . deduce from self-love the interest which we take in the welfare of society, and the esteem upon that account which we bestow upon virtue, they do not mean, that . . . our sentiments are influenced by any benefit we receive from the one, or any detriment we suffer from the other . . . [it is our sympathy that does so]. Sympathy, however, cannot, in any sense, be regarded as a selfish principle.[5]

Hume, like Smith, denies that self-love is the motivating

force in any virtuous act. To destroy the idea that self-love is a cause of moral action, he states in his *Principles of Morals* the view of those who believe in self-love: "That whatever affections one may feel, or imagine he feels for others, no passion is, or can be, disinterested; that the most generous friendship, however sincere, is a modification of self-love; and that, even unknown to ourselves, we seek only our own gratification."[6] But Hume furnishes instances that are "marks of a general benevolence in human nature, where no *real* interest binds us to the object . . . if we consider rightly of the matter, we shall find that the hypothesis which allows of a disinterested benevolence, distinct from self-love . . . is more conformable to the analogy of nature than . . . this latter principle [i.e., self love]."[7]

Yet others, rather than insist on a separation between self-love and a disinterested principle of motivation, tried to harmonize self-love and benevolence. In his *Essays on Human Knowledge,* Bolingbroke wrote: "That true Self Love and social are the same . . . I have always thought most undeniably evident; or that the author of nature has so constituted the human system, that they coincide in it. . . . "[8] David Hartley conceived of self-interest as one of the motivating causes of human action, but whether it be gross self-interest, refined self-interest, or rational self-interest, self-interest does not contradict the principles of benevolence, piety, moral sense, and the love of God; ultimately it is eclipsed in them.[9] The harmony of self-interest and benevolence conceived by Bolingbroke and Hartley is akin to that of Rousseau. Though Rousseau had spent some time in the circle of Holbach, he did not fully subscribe to the Holbachian principle. In *A Dissertation on the Origin and Foundation of the Inequality of Mankind,* he wrote: "There is another principle [compassion] which has escaped Hobbes; which, having been bestowed on mankind, to moderate, on certain occasions, the impetuosity of egoism, or before its birth, the desire of self-preservation, tempers the ardour with which he preserves his own welfare, by an innate repugnance at seeing a fellow creature suffer."[10] Rousseau distinguished between degrees of self-interest, calling the desire for self-preservation "self respect" and the desire for aggrandizement "egoism." The principle of egoism would not exist in a state of nature. Thus Rousseau's distinction leaves him able to accept the principle of self-preservation.

I do not wish to imply that Blake was responding directly to any of these writers, only that the principle of self-interest was an important consideration for the eighteenth century, especially the notion of self-preservation. Blake's basic stance against the selfhood conforms in principle with the stance that self-interest, self-love, self-preservation, or selfishness, has no part in moral action. He would have agreed with Hume and Smith in their antagonism to self-love, though he would have denied the ultimate value of any concern for moral virtue. He would not have agreed with Holbach. It is likely that he would have felt suspicious of Hartley, Bolingbroke, and Rousseau.

Rather than seeing self primarily in its relation to other men, Swedenborg and Boehme viewed self in its relation to God. Both saw self as the principle separating man from unity with divinity.[11] Swedenborg's influence on Blake has been long established. He seems to accord well with Blake on the question of self-love. In a *Treatise Concerning Heaven and Hell* Swedenborg wrote:

> Self-love is that principle in any one that leads him to seek his own good only, and that of others no further than it may be subservient thereto; nay such a one is a mercenary in the whole of his zeal and regards for his religion, his country, or any human society.[12]

The opposite of self-love is love of God. Swedenborg explained:

> The odiousness of Self-love will manifestly appear by comparison with its opposite, or that Love which is celes-

tial, consisting in the love of uses for the sake of usefulness, and the Love of good for the sake of goodness,
whether a man exercise himself therein in behalf of religion, his country, or fellow citizens, studying and labouring to promote their interest and welfare with all the
sincerity of a cordial affection, and takes pleasure in the
work, without any view to consequences respecting Self.
This is to love God with all our heart, and our neighbour
as ourselves; and as we do this from the Love which is
from God, so in doing it we glorify him, who is the giver of
every good and perfect gift. But how different is the man of
Self, who, being the idol of his own vanity, considers
others as his slaves, and only estimates them by the
service and worship they pay him; little knowing, that so
far as he departs from the disinterested Principle of
celestial Love, so far is he distant from the kingdom of
Heaven.[13]

Here, though Swedenborg was concerned with the question
of morals, as were the eighteenth-century philosophers, he
was more concerned with the separation between man and
God caused by self-love.

The principle is even clearer in Boehme, whose conception of the cosmos is akin to Blake's. Boehme's concept is
that the life of this physical existence is not the essential life,
but merely a manifestation of one aspect of God, and that the
mistake of wanting to maintain physical existence,that is,
not to die, is the mistake of the selfhood. Boehme seemed to
conceive of the individual in the physical world as a projection in the material world of the divine essence, a single
manifestation of God which, by the individual's own will,
returns to God. To continue to will to be manifested in the
physical world is spoken of as eternal dying, or as being
foolishly unaware of one's true nature:

Now all Men are proceeded out of this only Man
[Boehme's God here], he is the Stem or Body, the other
are all his branches, and receive Power from their Stem,

and bring forth Fruit upon one; and each Twig enjoys the Tree's *Ens*; What Folly [and Madness] is it then, that the Twig wills to be an own [selfish] Tree; and grows up of itself as a strange Plant, as if its Fellow-twig did not stand also in its Stem?[14]

Boehme dropped the tree metaphor but repeated the same idea:

If the human Will (which is departed out of the Unity of Eternity, and entered into a self-Fulness, viz. into a selfish Lust and Desire) does again break itself off from Self-hood, and enter into the Mortfication of Self-will, and introduces its Desire again only into the first Mother, the first Mother [by which Boehme means an aspect of God] does again choose it to be its Child and makes it again one with the only Will of Eternity. But that (Will or Person) which continues in Self-hood, he continues in the eternal Dying.[15]

It should be noted that the selfhood as described by Boehme is precisely that desire for self-preservation praised by Holbach and Wollstonecraft and respected by Rousseau. Blake's logical extension of Boehme's concept is that the act of self-annihilation consists of a willingness to forgo survival in a world of time and space, for such survival is meaningless at best and, at worst, an evil opposing man's divine urge to transcend the limits of this life, either by death or in creative vision.

Thus in both Swedenborg and Boehme the self is that which divides man from God. But the general distrust of the self was shared by Swedenborg, Boehme, Smith, and Hume, to different degrees and with different emphases, to be sure. And this distrust stands opposed to the high valuation given to self-preservation whose spokesmen, descending from Hobbes, can be found in Holbach and Wollstonecraft, with the implicit alliance of Hartley, Bolinbroke, and Rousseau.

II. MECHANISM OF THE SELFHOOD

Blake's concept of the selfhood in *Milton* is best imagined as a defensive covering that both imprisons the immortal spirit and defends against threats from without the personality. Though only part of the whole man, the selfhood suffers the delusion that it is all important, that it is the essence of the man, thereby elevating its function of self-preservation in the physical world above the functions of the truly more important element of personality, the creative and loving spirit. From this central delusion proliferate all the mechanisms of personality that contaminate human thought and activity. These delusion-caused mechanisms act in two directions: inwards, to suffocate any altruistic or selflessly creative thought that would endanger the delusion of the elevated status of self-preservation; and outwards, to control the threats from the exterior world of men. Yet, although delusion breeds these mechanisms, its failure to control completely the imagined interior or exterior threats to its status leads inevitably to a final solution: it must destroy the threat. In the selfhood's mechanisms of interior control we recognize familiar mental processes such as repression or projection, but in the mechanisms for exterior control Blake suggests more sinister processes. The selfhood, itself deluded, works on the deluded selfhoods of other men to control them, relying on the mechanisms of authority, mystification, and imputation of guilt, all forms of threat to self-preservation that keep one man from harming another. It is a logical extension of its defensive posture that the selfhood should seek inevitably to grasp the power of social institutions in order to protect its own interest, and one expects therefore to see in this world those with the strongest, most deluded selfhoods struggling fiercely and successfully to gain control over such mind-controlling institutions as the church or state. Thus the individual's selfhood extends its branches out of the individual into the collective body of man, and by a kind of analogy between individual and society, the authority and control of the state become a selfhood striving to preserve the status quo.

Sporadically in his earlier poems Blake had suggested much of the phenomenon of the selfhood's mechanisms, which became the central focus of *Milton*. Processes such as threatening authority, the preaching of chastity, mystification, and imputation of guilt, which had previously appeared separately, Blake now joined together as tentacles stemming from the single selfhood. One of Blake's most characteristic pictures had been that of an authority figure who uses delusive counter-threats of punishment to control any imagined threats to its position. For instance, in *America,* when Orc enacts his revolutionary defiance of the authority of religion and morality, Albion's angel sends forth a fear-inspired but futile cry: "Sound! sound! my loud war-trumpets, & alarm my Thirteen Angels" (9.1) (though his cry evokes from Boston, one of the thirteen, the heroic defiance: "No more I follow, no more obediance pay"). Albion's angel relies here on his threatening posture to enforce his will. And in *The Song of Los* the kings of Asia, threatened by the "thought creating fires of Orc" suddenly realize that their ability to cause famine, pestilence, and poverty, has lost its power to delude man (6.9–7.7). Thus, threatening authority is not always a successful means of control. But when threats of corporeal retribution, such as Albion's angel uses, fail to delude, the threat of eternal retribution is always at hand. To propose eternal death is to attack the most cherished fears of the slavish selfhood, which will avoid all "sin" in order to avoid eternal death. The hypertensive, parrotlike speech of the angel who is warning Blake of his danger in *The Marriage of Heaven and Hell* dramatizes the extremity of this delusion: "O pitiable foolish young man! O horrible! O dreadful state! consider the hot burning dungeon thou art preparing for thyself to all eternity, to which thou art going in such a career" (*MHH* 17). But the delusion of the angel's prospect is revealed as Blake's view of hell changes in the following episode, a change that illustrates how the angel has imposed a delusion on Blake, and suggests that a delusion has been imposed on him. The threat of eternal punishment to his self-preservation has led him to a slavish and nervous delusion. Ultimately the slave will wish to be in absolute control and to threaten others with punishment, as does the angel of *The Marriage.* For the slave always desires to enter the class of slave drivers, and to throw down the slave driver into slavery in a cycle of fear-inspired struggle for control. In the appearance of the terrible revolutionary fires of Orc in the vineyards of France (*Europe* 15.2), Blake had depicted the start of the overthrow, but he certainly became aware of the dangers of success, for his picture of another revolutionary, Fuzon, reveals the final course of the cycle. Fuzon revolts from Urizen's rule (*Book of Urizen* 28.8–9), recognizing his delusion (*Book of Ahania* 2.10–14), but he also sends his symbolic "Globe of wrath" (*B.A.* 2.16) against Urizen, whom it appears to destroy. Fuzon then shows that his overthrow of Urizen is merely a replacement of one authority figure by another:

> Fuzon, his tygers unloosing
> Thought Urizen slain by his wrath.
> I am God said he, eldest of things!
> (*B.A.* 3.36–38)

Blake stated his view of the ceaseless struggle for control most succinctly in "The Grey Monk":

> The hand of Vengeance found the Bed
> To which the Purple Tyrant fled
> The iron hand crush'd the Tyrant's head
> And became a Tyrant in his stead.
> (11. 31–35)

The delusion of power lies beneath Fuzon's assumption of godhead, a delusion that implies that there are either tyrants or slaves, and that there is an eternal cycle of revolution locking the man in from true freedom.

Blake depicted a related delusory means of mental control in the preaching of chastity. He saw the drive for self-preservation in man's tendency to make moral sanctions against sexuality. For in sexual relationships the individual may wish to give love as well as to receive pleasure. Lust uses others for its own pleasure, but love eclipses self in giving pleasure. He suggested these two attitudes in "the Clod and the Pebble." If one seeks not to please self, "Nor for itself has any care/ But for another gives its ease," one has a heaven. But the fearful, anxious selfhood cannot permit self-surrender, and will "bind another to its delight" to create a hell. Secretly desiring pleasure, the defensive selfhood yet condemns sexuality as sin:

> Dire shriek'd his invisible Lust
> Deep groan'd Urizen! stretching his awful hand
> Ahania (so named his parted soul)
> He siez'd on his mountains of Jealousy.
> He groand anguishd & callled her Sin.
> (*Book of Ahania* 2.30–35)

It is the frustration of the drive for sexual pleasure that can become a means for control. The man full of sexual desire, held from easy fulfillment by the preaching of chastity, is at the command of the woman who grants fulfillment. The sexual urge of the male can make him a slave to the promising, alluring, but ungiving and hence dominating female:

> But Los saw the Female & pitied
> He embrac'd her, she wept, she refus'd
> In perverse and cruel delight
> She fled from his arms, yet he followed.
> (*Book of Urizen* 19.10–13)

Instead of becoming a selfless haven for man, the female uses him to promote her own power. "Forbid all Joy, & from her childhood shall the little female/ Spread nets in every secret path" (*Europe* 6.8–9). She will enjoy her power:

The joy of woman is the Death of her most best beloved
Who dies for Love of her
In torments of fierce jealousy & pangs of adoration.
        (*Four Zoas*, night 2; p. 34, ll. 63–65)

Thus the teaching of chastity becomes a delusive and sinister technique for domination.

Blake's word for the technique of delusion was mystery. Mystery consists of half truths, hypocrisy, and all forms of mystification that delude man and thereby reduce their potential for threatening. The "mind-forg'd manacles" ("London" 1.8) are controls that take shape in the tree of mystery, whose "fruit of Deceit" ("The Human Abstract" 1.17) produces poverty, unhappiness, cruelty, religious anxiety, sorrow, and humility, all forms of debilitation that remove the power to revolt. Perhaps one of the subtlest forms of mystery is the half truth, which consists in removing particulars from a total context, leaving only vague general principles. This technique Blake brilliantly exemplified in the response of Bromion to Theotormon in *Visions of the Daughters of Albion*. In anguish over Oothoon's supposed unchastity, and unable to comprehend Oothoon's eloquent statement of undefiled love and her belief in a spiritual world, Theotormon considers the existence of a world where thoughts go, and seems about to break through to a spiritual perception not based on the empirical world. But to subvert that chance, Bromion, breaking into the poem, offers the subtleties of science as the way to perceive another world. He offers the microscope to find "places yet unvisited by the voyager, and . . . worlds/ Over another kind of seas, and in atmospheres unknown" (*V.D.A.* 4.17–18). But the world he offers is merely a world discoverable by the extension of the senses, not truly another kind of world. Blake thus has depicted the replacing of spiritual discovery with scientific exploration, which was the latest technique of mystery that also had worked when "Rintrah gave Abstract Philosophy to Brama" (*Song of Los* 3.11) or when "Palamabron gave an abstract law" to Trismegistus, Pythagoras, Socrates, and Plato (*Song of Los* 3.18–19). But doubt is also part of mystery, for, at his fall, in *The Four Zoas,* Urizen, the prince of light, who had represented faith, "is chang'd to Doubt" (night 2; p. 27, 1.15). Mystery can be the work of the priest or the deist, and can aid any form of tyranny in its maintenance of control:

> The Priest sat by and heard the child.
> In trembling zeal he siez'd his hair:
> He led him by his little coat:
> And all admir'd the Priestly care.
>
> And standing on the altar high,
> Lo what a fiend is here! said he:
> One who sets reason up for judge
> Of our most holy Mystery.
> ("A Little Boy Lost" 11. 9–16)

Blake had shown how mental control begins with the creation of a sense of guilt, which is a refinement of the anxiety to preserve the self. Assimilated in early childhood, the teachings of parents, teachers, nurses, and other authority figures constitute the notions of guilt.

> To her father white
> Came the maiden bright:
> But his loving look,
> Like the holy book,
> All her tender limbs with terror shook.
> ("A Little Girl Lost" 11.25–29)

But guilt works on the individual even when the authority figure is absent, and in extreme forms it behaves "like a gestapo headquarters within the personality, mercilessly tracking down dangerous or potentially dangerous ideas and every remote relative of those ideas, accusing, threatening, tormenting in an interminable inquisition to establish guilt for trivial offenses or crimes committed in dreams.''[16]

Why wilt thou Examine every little fibre of my soul
Spreading them out before the Sun like Stalks of flax to dry
The infant joy is beautiful but its anatomy
Horrible Ghast & Deadly nought shalt thou find in it
But Death Despair & Everlasting brooding Melancholy

Thou wilt go mad with horror if thou dost Examine thus
Every moment of my secret hours Yea I know
That I have sinnd & that my Emanations are become
    harlots
I am already distracted at their deeds & if I look
Upon them more Despair will bring self murder on my soul
O Enion thou art thyself a root growing in hell
Tho thus heavenly beautiful to draw me to destruction.
        (*Four Zoas,* night 1; p. 4, 11. 28–37)

The sense of guilt, torturing from within, but inherited from childhood's assimilation of exterior teaching, is a form of slavery to exterior authority. In *Europe,* the youth of Albion are said to behold Albion's Angel, an agent of the restrictor Urizen. "Their parents brought them forth, & aged ignorance preaches canting/ On a vast rock, perceivd by those senses that are clos'd from thought" (*Europe,* 12.7–8). Until the twentieth century no one could have stated more clearly the process by which the parental injunctions, the oughts and shoulds, the fear-inspiring rules of the conscience, are instilled into the mind. Thought occurs in the imagination, but the conscience is an unseen set of rules absorbed from the world perceived by the senses, controlling man when he knows it not.

Blake had shown other sinister means by which the selfhood works on the inner spirit. The delusions of the selfhood itself are always present. Ideas that sooth the fears of the individual selfhood allow the complacent selfhood a delusive ease. It is easy to accept the physical world as the sum of all existence when one is well fed, and clothed, and housed, and in bodily contentment (*Four Zoas,* night 2; p. 35, 1. 16–p. 36, 1.13). But the deluded selfhood cannot tolerate the suggestion that unsettling reminders of other joys or other dangers should be heard. In *Europe,* where one may read the sons of Urizen as a single voice of the narrowly selfish soul, one finds

> Sieze all the spirits of life and bind
> Their warbling joys to our loud strings
> Bind all the nourishing sweets of earth
> To give us bliss, that we may drink the sparkling wine of
>   Los
> And let us laugh at war,
> Despising toil and care,
> Because the days and nights of joy, in lucky hours renew.
>   (*Europe* 4.3–9)

Deluded, the selfhood attacks the man's inner promptings as if they were themselves delusions, repressing all inconvenient thoughts. Ironically, it is Blake's picture of the repression of anger in "The Poison Tree" that is characteristic of the fully developed selfhood. Yet anger is in a way a non-self-oriented emotion, since the immediate and unpremeditated expression of anger usually leaves the individual without a second defense. In practice the expression of anger can "clear the air" and thereby permit a more complete relationship of love. But the selfhood cannot trust such defenseless expression and it therefore represses anger, only to have it go underground and spring up in deceitful and malicious ways. The apple on the poison tree that slays the speaker's enemy is the fruit of the selfhood's repression.

But if the selfless promptings cannot be repressed, they must be removed. For instance, the selfhood-dominated individual, feeling a potentially love-filled and consequently self-destroying desire, will project and objectify that desire on another, castigating that other for the desire he himself feels, calling it sin. Blake depicted this projection symbolically in terms of separation of male and female. In *The Book of Ahania,* chapter one, Fuzon's "sounding beam" (2.27) strikes the restrictive and moralistic Urizen in his "cold loins" (2.29), causing the separation of Urizen and Ahania, whom Urizen then names sin, though in secret he kisses and weeps over her. The symbolic inference is that Urizen's selfhood-dominated conscience cannot admit into consciousness the realization of his own lust, suggested symbolically by Fuzon's loin-dividing beam, and he therefore projects his guilt onto the object of his secret lust, Ahania, bestowing on her the frightening responsibliity for sin that his selfhood cannot bear. Thus the removal is accomplished by projection. But, in the end, projection will not help. To obey the promptings of the selfhood is ultimately schizophrenic, for the selfhood will inevitably wish to reject the immortal, selfless, creative impulse that is the individual's true identity. The guilt-ridden, fear-inspired drive for survival, which is the selfhood, would entirely repress or project that true identity. The unchallenged selfhood would lead man to a catatonic crouch of the mind, depicted pictorially by Blake in his pictures of Urizen in *The Book of Urizen,* where the aged and bearded Urizen is bent to the embryo-like postures that characterize some manifestation of schizophrenia. Symbolizing the complete rejection of the mind's creativity, Urizen's fall from eternity leads quickly to his urge to hide under "a roof vast, petrific around . . . like a womb" (5.28–29). Urizen remains in a "dreamless night" (7.7) and becomes a world of "Forgetfulness, dumbness, necessity/ In chains of the mind locked up" (10.24–5).

Of course, the extremes of both interior and exterior control may have afforded the troubled selfhood no relief. The selfhood must therefore proceed to the final solution: destruction. In its insane desire for self-preservation the selfhood will remove all threats; it will destroy all other forms to preserve its own physical existence. Indeed, Blake made this clear when the unheeded threats of Albion's Angel in *America* are followed by his destructive plagues (14.4–5). But among other threatening forms are the beautiful creations of the immortal spirit (the imagination); and the danger in them is that beauty and creativity (one's own or another's) demand for a time that selfhood be forgotten. The shaping spirit turns on the dross of matter to create form, but the selfhood cannot cease its introspection, its egoism, to permit the outward flow of energy. This is the meaning of Urizen's separation from eternity in *The Book of Urizen*. Urizen's desire for self-preservation will not permit him to endure the fluctuations, the unquenchable burning of a creative eternity, and he seeks for a "solid without fluctuation" (4.11) for an escape from the constant death of the self. His self-involved state, symbolized in his "Self-clos'd, all repelling" (3.3) condition, even in eternity, leads ultimately to a "petrific abominable chaos" (3.26). Thus the selfhood turns on the immortal spirit, and since the spirit cannot be destroyed, the selfhood rejects it completely, turning away like a vampire from the light, bending itself ever inwardly until it is frozen in the fixed and deadly forms of matter. From the fear of its own inadequacy, the selfhood follows the path of destruction as far as it will lead; ironically, that fear, which is inherent in the drive for survival, in extreme form, leads to the destruction of complete life.

Thus Blake had already suggested the selfhood's mechanisms for exterior control: delusive teachings of authority, chastity, mystery, and guilt; and for interior control: repression and projection of inner promptings of otherness. Ultimately the selfhood attempts destruction of all that cannot be controlled.

III.   THE ARCHETYPE OF THE FALL

The processes of control of the exterior world and the individual's own mind, which I have described as the protective mechanism of the selfhood, are the focal points of *Milton*. Distinguishable in the poem are two large patterns dealing with the selfhood, one showing the descent into its aberrations, the other the means to escape them. These two patterns constitute roughly the divisions of the work between the Bard's Song and Milton's journey.[17] The pattern of descent into the selfhood begins with delusion, then leads to attempts to control the exterior world, next results in the repression or rejection of any unwanted personal impulses, and finally culminates in destruction.

The full spectrum of the pattern emerges in the drama of the fall of Satan. Delusion is the key to Satan's fall, and it becomes more exaggerated and dangerous as he progresses in his plunge. The first indication of Satan's deluded state occurs when Los warns Satan that it is not wise to hide his anger: "If you account it Wisdom when you are angry to be silent, and/ Not to shew it: I do not account that Wisdom but Folly" (4.6–7). That this warning might properly have been made to Palamabron, who failed to make a complete complaint of Satan's abuses at his first meeting with Los (7.29–30), does not lessen the suggestion that Satan is undergoing one of the first steps in the pattern. Satan wishes to usurp Palamabron's function of driving the harrow (4.16), but Palamabron's refusal has bred anger in him. The delusion that has brought about Satan's desire is later explained by Leutha, but for the moment his desire serves as an indication of his incipient fall. His delusion shows itself clearly after he has in fact usurped Palamabron's function. Palamabron suggests the depths of his delusion: "You know Satans mildness and his self-imposition, Seeming a brother, being a Tyrant, even thinking himself a brother/ while he is murdering the just" (7.21–23). Satan weeps and accuses Palamabron "of crimes/ Himself had wrought" (7.34–35). Almost convinced by Satan's "blandishments," Los is unable to make judgment between Palamabron and Satan. "What could Los do? How could he judge, when Satans self, believ'd/ That he had not oppres'd the horses of the Harrow, nor the servants" (7.39–40). Satan exculpates himself "for himself believ'd/ That he had not oppres'd not injur'd the refractory servants" (8.2–3). Satan is convinced of Palamabron's "turpitude" (8.7). Such delusion is obvious in daily life as the refusal of an individual to understand his own motives. This inability usually means that the individual has his own self-interest at stake and is avoiding the self-awareness that threatens his weak self-image. Here Satan's delusion simply keeps him from recognizing his desire to dominate Palamabron, whose higher function serves as a threat to Satan's concept of himself. For the harrow, the plow, the instruments of harvest are instruments of creative activity.[18] Blake calls the harrow a scheme of human conduct invisible and incomprehensible to mortals who think Satan's mills everything (4.12–13). However, Satan's mills are destructive (4.17), though we certainly recognize their useful function. Assigned to destruction, and perhaps not understanding his function, Satan's threatened selfhood secretly seeks to usurp Palamabron's station. This kind of delusion is the result of an extreme form of the selfhood, which perceives the higher status of others as a threat to itself. It is latent paranoia. That the successful completion of his usurpation would not satisfy Satan is suggested when Blake describes the action as Satan's "primitive tyrannical attempts on Los" (7.5), primitive here implying the first as well as undeveloped attempts. Being part of the creative force in Los's function, Palamabron is only the first victim of the selfhood, whose primitive attempts will evolve into a comprehensive and sinister program of delusion, control, and destruction.[19]

The danger of Satan's attempts is seen quickly, for after Los has refused retribution and declared a day of mourning in which the plow is driven over all nature in an attempt to eliminate from the psyche the scars of the past (a mistaken and unsuccessful one, for this attempt is only a form of repression), Satan becomes embroiled with the other sons of Los: Rintrah, Theotormon, Bromion, Michael, and Thullough, as well as Palamabron. It is Thullough, "the friend of Satan" (8.33), who faintly reproves him; in his rage Satan browbeats Michael and slays his friend Thullough (8.39). Satan's self-delusion has led inexorably to destruction. The final solution of the threatened selfhood has turned on its closest mark, the friend who mildly points out errors.

The mental war against delusion begins when it becomes obvious to Palamabron that Satan's guilt should no longer be concealed. He summons a great assembly, and his words are a prayer for protection as well as a caution learned from Satan's slaying of his own friend. "O God, protect me from my friends, that they have not power over me/ Thou hast given me power to protect myself from my bitterest enemies" (9.5–6). Satan, however, has gained no self-knowledge. In deeper delusion, he reaches for further means of control and assigns to himself authority, as well as the doctrine of moral retribution in its form of punishment for sin:

For Satan flaming with Rintrahs fury hidden beneath his
    own mildness
Accus'd Palamabron before the Assembly of ingratitude! of
    malice;
He created Seven deadly Sins drawing out his infernal
    scroll,
Of Moral laws and cruel punishments upon the clouds of
    Jehovah
To pervert the Divine voice in its entrance to the earth
With thunder of war & trumpets sound, with armies of dis-
    ease
Punishments & deaths mustered & number'd; Saying I am
    God alone
There is no other! let all obey my principles of moral indi-
    viduality
I have brought them from the uppermost innermost reces-
    ses
Of my Eternal Mind, transgressors I will rend off for ever,
As now I rend this accused Family from my covering.
                    (9.19–29)

The defensiveness of Satan's posture is evident. His counteraccusations, his threats of retribution, his assumption of an authoritative position, his threat to turn away transgressors, are defense mechanisms of a threatened selfhood whose insane overcompensation leads to even greater delusion and restriction of the personality.

Further degeneration follows as Satan becomes opaque before the assembly (9.31). He is hidden in "a world of deeper ulro" (9.34). In essence he is separated from the other members of Los's assembly, a separation demanded by the anxious selfhood. This separation puts Satan into his space, which is known among other titles as Canaan (10.4–5). Canaan, according to Swedenborg, represents the worship of externals without internals.[20] Blake, following Swedenborg, uses the word for the generation into which Urizen was drawn to become Satan (10.1–2). It is the delusion of space, which creates the illusion of infinite distance, though in reality it is limited by the narrow perception of the senses. Canaan thus represents mistaken vision, mistaken worship; it is a symbol of delusion and destruction, the ultimate end of selfhood. And as the twelve tribes of Israel divided when they invaded Canaan, the act of separation continues as Satan "triumphant divided the Nations" (10.21). Thus the act of separation of Satan from the eternals recalls Urizen's similar separation, and it symbolizes that rejection of the creative side of personality (Los's world) which the selfhood sees as a threat. Separation as a symbolic act thus becomes a characteristic of Satan's world, and we see it working not only on Satan but also on all those under the control of the selfhood. But mere separation is again no final solution to the selfhood's fears. The selfhood must destroy. Satan in Canaan is a "mighty Fiend Against the Divine Humanity mustring to war" (10.11). He sets his "face against Jerusalem to destroy the Eon of Albion" (11.1).[21] Psychologically the deluded, repressive, destructive self turns away from the openness and freedom of brotherhood, becomes self-involved, limiting its focus to its own interests, and separates itself from whatever threatens those interests. Then it extends its tentacles into the exterior world to hold fast. It produces controlling institutions that mirror itself in the whole body politic of man. This state is summed up in the following passage, where the mills are equivalent to organized religion; the moony space, the limited world known as the physical cosmos; Albion's temples, the most ancient forms of worship; Satan's Druid sons, priests or deists; and the synagogues, churches:

And the Mills of Satan were separated into a moony Space
Among the rocks of Albions Temples, and Satans Druid sons
Offer the Human Victims throughout all the Earth, and Albions
Dread Tomb immortal on his Rock, overshadowed the whole Earth;
Where Satan making to himself Laws from his own identity.
Compell'd others to serve him in moral gratitude & submission
Being call'd God: setting himself above all that is called God.
And all the Spectres of the Dead calling themselves Sons of God
In his Synagogues worship Satan under the Unutterable Name.

(11.6–14)

Here the selfhood has established delusive controls in the symbolic act of proclaiming itself God, in establishing "Druid sons," in existing under the unutterable name, and in using laws of moral gratitude and submission. Thus the orthodoxy of religion stems from the selfhood.

The separation of Satan involves yet another kind of separation, that between wrath and pity. The danger of separated wrath is hinted when Los warns Rintrah and Palamabron that they should have patience: "O Sons we live not by wrath, by mercy alone, we live!" (23.34). By giving in to wrath, which leads to "Martyrdoms & Wars" (23.49), twelve sons separated from Los (23.62). But Satan's situation is more complicated. Early in the Palamabron-Satan quarrel, Los warns against "pity false" (7.42). He knows that "pity divides the soul/ And man, unmans" (8.19–20). In the contention between Satan, Bromion, Theotormon, Palamabron, Rintrah, Thullough, and Michael, Bromion and Theotormon "contended on the side of Satan/ Pitying his youth and beauty" (8.30–31). Satan is thus associated with pity, although in the solemn assembly he is consumed with wrath (9.11–12). This ambiguity is resolved when Rintrah rears up barriers between Satan and Palamabron (9.43–45) that result in "Satan not having the Science of Wrath, but only of Pity" (9.46). "Wrath is left to wrath & pity to pity" (9.47).[22] It is important to discern exactly what Blake means by pity. It is not mercy or commiseration. It is only a part of an attitude, and by itself it is a state, an element of the selfhood. To have pity for suffering and not to have wrath against the cause of suffering, whether the cause is another man, or ultimately a God, is, essentially, to accept the state of suffering as an inevitable condition. A reformer or a revolutionary cannot act without the implication that he feels wrath against the cause of suffering as well as pity for the sufferer; but a bishop who preaches unmurmuring acceptance of an unfair earthly lot, a governmental apologist who always strives to reinforce the status quo, these are capable of feeling only pity, for their response to suffering allows no suggestion of change or hint that anything is wrong. They have no wrath. Satan's pity is the kind that weeps for suffering but refuses to alleviate it. It is, in fact, the pity felt by the keeper of the status quo, who pities the suffering that he himself inflicts to protect himself. And pity deludes those pitied into accepting their state. Paradoxically, the pity does not preclude destruction, because the rigid adherence to the status quo implied in the pity means that Satan will stop at nothing to maintain control. Thus, in his pity, he is still a mighty fiend mustering to war, which is wrath separated from pity. The separation of wrath and pity thus exemplifies the selfhood's work.

Leutha's explanation of Satan's usurpation of Palamabron's harrow emphasizes delusion as the original cause of Satan's fall, but it still illustrates the pattern of delusion, control, separation, and destruction.[23] Satan's actions stem from a "feminine delusion of false pride self-deceiv'd" (11.26). Though this delusion is said to account for Satan's assuming "wrath in the day of mourning" (11.25), it is clear that the delusion occurred before the slaying of Thullough. Leutha is that feminine delusion (personified now as well as dramatized) who had influenced Satan to usurp Palamabron's function. Leutha's motive was desire for Palamabron, yet since she was denied satisfaction by the envy of Elynittria, she worked by indirection. Her effect on Satan is stupefaction of "the masculine perceptions . . . hence rose his [Satan's]/ Delusory love to Palamabron" (12.5–7). Only Satan's "feminine" perceptions were awake (12.6). This division of sexes is a division of mental power similar to the division of pity and wrath. It is delusion resulting from repression, a condition Blake associates with the domination of the selfhood.

Once in possession of the horses of Palamabron, Satan is challenged. When the resting horses are disturbed by Leutha at noon, Satan compels the gnomes, the servants of the harrow, to curb the horses (12.15–17). The result is separation, for the harrow "cast thick flames & orb'd us round in concave fires/ A Hell of our own making" (12.21–22).[24] Separation leads again to destruction. Satan drives the harrow among the constellations to "devour Albion and Jerusalem the emanation of Albion/ Driving the Harrow in Pity's path" (12.27–28). Further separation occurs in Leutha's formation of the serpent, which is really the restriction of material form. Satan, in serpent form, uses irritating speech as he strives to control the gnomes (12.29–34). And even further separation follows when Satan takes the prophetic wine meant for Palamabron:

Wild with prophetic fury his former life became like a
    dream

Cloth'd in the Serpents folds, in selfish holiness demanding
  purity
Being most impure, self-condemn'd to eternal tears, he
  drove
Me from his inmost Brain & the doors clos'd with thunders
  sound.

(12.45–48)

Leutha's final view of Satan is as a "sick one" (13.4),
"Who calls the individual Law, Holy: and despises the
Saviour/ Glorying to involve Albions Body in fires of eternal War" (13.5–6). Thus the pattern continues to be revealed as Satan always moves toward forms of destruction.[25] Tumbling down the psychic track of delusion, separation, and destruction, Satan plummets into the egocen-
tricity of the selfhood.

Based upon the analogy between the history of cosmic
man and of an individual's life, the fall of Satan symbolizes
the fall of any individual into the selfhood. Blake's view of
cosmic history represents the fall as the beginning of a constant descent into materialism and enslavement, a fall that
was limited only by divine mercy. In *Milton* there are several references to other falls, and in these references Blake
reinforces the idea that the cosmic fall of Satan is a
paradigm of the fall of any individual. This notion comple-
ments Blake's view of the last judgment expressed in his
"Vision of the Last Judgement." As there was an original
fall for all men, so there is an individual fall for each man,
just as there will be a Last Judgment for all men as there is a
last judgment for each man.[26] One must realize that Blake is
not interested in the temporal sequence of history. Rather,
he shows the multiplicity of falls symbolizing the psychic
nature of the fall.

Indeed, suggestions that Satan's fall in the Bard's Song is
the beginning of cosmic history occur when Palamabron
calls a solemn assembly after Satan's slaying of Thullough.
When the assembly's judgment fell on Rintrah, Los cursed
heaven, rent nations; "He displacd continents, the oceans

fled before his face/ He alter'd the poles of the world, east, west & north & south" (9.16–17). As Burnet's *Sacred Theory of the Earth* pointed out, the slanting poles of the earth and the disorganized geological arrangements of earth's topography resulted from the fall of Adam. But Satan's destination after the fall is the spatial universe as we know it. "And Satan vibrated in the immensity of the Space! Limited/ To those without but Infinite to those within" (10.8–9). This reversal of time sequence, wherein Satan's fall instead of Adam's produces the slanting poles of earth, results from Blake's evaluation of the physical world as a delusion. Blake's picture of the delusion of the physical world, stemming from Satan's fall, symbolizes the individual's selfhood-caused delusion that the physical world is all in all. This space is the infinite Newtonian universe, which is clearly a delusion suffered by those limited to sensory knowledge. His space is given the traditional time limit for creation. The eternals "gave a Time to the Space,/ Even Six Thousand years" (13.16–17). Moreover, at his fall Satan assumes the shape of the serpent, being "cloth'd in Serpents folds" (12.46). As Raine has suggested, the serpent is a traditional symbol of materialism.[27]

These hints, however, are not meant to suggest that the picture of Satan's fall is the beginning of cosmic history. Falls have clearly occurred prior to Satan's. To insure that one does not mistake Satan's fall as that beginning, Blake inserts several other references to falls in the work. The most obvious is the description of Los's limiting Urizen's degeneration at the beginning of the Bard's Song. Since Satan is one of Los's progeny after the fall (which produced Enitharmon, the mother of Satan), then clearly Satan's fall is not the first. Urizen's fall occurred when "Albion was slain upon his Mountains/ And in his Tent, thro envy of Living Form" (3.1–2). This fall seems also related to Luvah's usurpation in eternity of "the World of Urizen to the South" (19.19). At this event, the four zoas, who are derived from the four creatures of Revelation (4: 6–9) and who sit around the divine throne, "fell towards the Center sinking downward in dire Ruin" (34.39). This fall creates the cosmos in which Satan's fall later occurs, and it is drawn by Blake for the reader to see on plate thirty-three. When Los announces the coming of the last vintage, he gives an order to the fall of Albion and Satan. The workers of the vintage are to gather all men from the beginning, "Since Men began to be Wove into Nations by Rahab & Tirzah/ Since Albions Death & Satans Cutting-off from our awful Feilds" (25.29–30). These three events are not intended to be taken as three simultaneous events, listed in parallel, but three discrete events at different times. Blake is concerned with the analogy of the different falls to point out the paradigm of the individual fall. The analogy of the fall into degeneration is implied in another episode in *Milton* when Blake mentions

> Lambeth's Vale
> Where Jerusalems foundations began; where they were laid
> in ruins
> Where they were laid in ruins from every Nation & Oak
> Groves rooted.
> (6.14–16)

This fall may refer to the foundation of the New Jerusalem Church, which Blake saw as corrupted by the priestcraft that overtook it in the early 1790s. The priestcraft is the oak grove planted by the druid. Lambeth had been the place where the early Swedenborgian society met on Sunday evenings at the home of Jacob Duché, who was the minister of the "Lambeth Asylum for Female Orphans."[28] Or it may stand for the residence of a Bishop, who is really a druid of the State Church's oak groves. Here then, an event that is suggestive of the fall (Jerusalem laid in ruins) is not connected to the other allusions to the fall, a fact that supports the contention that the fall is a background analogy for Satan's fall, which itself is a fall that can occur in any man.[29]

There are yet other falls in the poem. Los fears that Palamabron and Rintrah, because of their intransigent resistance to Milton, may be "generated" as his other twelve sons (twelve tribes of Israel) (plates 23 & 24). Even the seven eyes of God, who are supposed to guard the fallen world, have themselves suffered a fall. Lucifer fell from pride, Molech from impatience, Elohim from weariness, Shaddai from anger, Pahad from terror, and finally Jehovah from hypocritical holiness, which enveloped Christ and punished him as a transgressor (13.16–27). The fallen state of the seven eyes of God constitutes the "Seven Angels [who] bear my [Satan's] Name" (38.55), whom Satan claims as his own in the final section of the poem. At this point in *Milton* Satan is the symbol of the selfhood, who has brought dire change in the spatial forms of the seven eyes of God. The danger of the fall into selfhood encompasses all. In fact, the individual's fall into selfhood can be symbolized by any part of the creation and the fallen creation itself.

All of these falls contain to some degree the pattern of degeneration stemming from the mechanisms of the selfhood. The first fall, that of Urizen, suggests delusion as a cause, though it entails separation and restriction. Urizen had envied the "Living Form" of Albion and the "sports of Wisdom in the Human Imagination/ Which is the Divine Body of the Lord Jesus" (3.2–4). Mental delusion in the form of envy led directly to Urizen's isolation in darkness with a chained mind (3.6). This fall is explicable in terms of the selfhood's receiving threats in the form of perceiving beauty and life outside of the self. Since that beauty could not be controlled, Urizen's attempts were to isolate himself from it in an exterior world. Doubtless Los's attempt to set limits to Urizen's degeneration succeeds, but Urizen is far from regeneration, and the result is one that causes Los to fear that he himself had undergone such a change. Again the threat to the self has disastrous effect. Los, who "became what he beheld" (3.29),[30] undergoes the symbolic act of separation into spectre and emanation. The globe of blood that comes from him becomes Enitharmon, and the blue fluid becomes the spectre (3.29–37). Blake does not elaborate further on the cause of this separation, but it clearly results from the threat to his own selfhood. Los's fallen state is suggested in the fact that his ensuing labors have mixed values. His creation of Golgonooza is an attempt to create a way to regenerate the selfhood, and the "Looms of Generation" (3.38) are means of limiting the fall into selfhood, though the perverting influence of Tirzah in the process of weaving flesh and the threat of Satan's morality (29.47–54) represent a continuing force to cause the fall into selfhood.

IV. TOPICAL THEMES IN THE BARD'S SONG

References to actual events like the decay of the Swedenborgian society teasingly suggest the possibility that there is a consistent topical allegory in *Milton*. But the poem is not topical allegory. It shows an archetype: an "image of a class"[31] of experience, as Blake calls it in his *Descriptive Catalogue*. Just as Chaucer's pilgrims are the images of an immortal "substance" manifesting its eternal identity in time (with varying accidentals that go with each age, though the eternal identity is repeatedly manifested without essential change),[32] so the characters of the Bard's Song are eternal archetypes performing an archetypal action. This archetype is repeated throughout different ages of time, with varying accidentals. As an archetype, it forms a pattern to which many possible events conform: Milton's experience with Cromwell,[33] Cowper's experience with John Newton,[34] Pitt's experience with England, or Blake's experience with Hayley. These possibilities, the last two of which I shall discuss, are not topical allegories, for the multiple possibilities deny the essence of topical allegory, which is limited to a single historical manifestation.[35] These possibilities should be seen as manifestations of the archetype because the sublime allegory is a way of making

known the spiritual, and consequently timeless and repeated cause of natural events. Existing in a realm removed
from the laws of time and space, spiritual causes are manifested repeatedly in the events of time and space, and
therefore separate events of time and space may be manifestations of the same thing.

Blake's life at Felpham may fit into the Satan-Palamabron
story in more than one way. Traditionally, Satan is William
Hayley, Blake's patron and employer. Satan's characteristics of officious interference and his usurpation of Palamabron's tools are identified with Hayley's officious concern
for Blake and his inducement to Blake to do miniature
painting.[36] But this traditional explanation severs the poem
into discrete sections—the Bard's Song justifying Blake's
very personal dispute with Hayley, and the remaining section dealing with Milton and Blake—without clear connection between the two. However, it is possible to pay Blake
the compliment of suggesting that he had enough insight
into himself to see that the dramatization of Satan's actions
described his own actions as well as Hayley's.[37] To begin
with, Blake's reference to the plow and harrow in his letter
to Butts (Sept. 23, 1800), and Butts's answer urging Blake
to take up the plow, meaning the work offered him at present, can be viewed as Blake's coveting the work offered by
Hayley.[38] Satan's usurpation of Palamabron's tools may be
Blake's falling into the miniature work suggested by
Hayley. The mills left by Satan may be the mill of Blake's
engraving drudgery left behind in London. Satan's
delusion—blaming Palamabron—may derive from Blake's
complaints about Hayley as evidenced in his letter to Butts
(Jan. 10, 1802).[39] It would be an honest and magnanimous
insight if Blake were to intend his statement about Satan's
thinking himself wronged and mildly cursing Palamabron to
refer to his own distrust of Hayley.

Blake's remark in the letter to Butts (25 April, 1803)
about corporeal friends being spiritual enemies brings out
Blake's concern about hypocritical friendship:

And now My Dear Sir Congratulate me on my return to London with the Full approbation of Mr Hayley & with Promise—But Alas!

Now I may say to you what perhaps I should not dare to say to any one else. That I can alone carry on my visionary studies in London unannoyed & that I may converse with my friends in Eternity. See Visions, Dream Dreams, & prophecy & speak Parables unobserv'd & at liberty from the Doubts of other Mortals, perhaps Doubts proceeding from Kindness. but Douts are always pernicious Especially when we Doubt our Friends Christ is very decided on this Point. "He who is Not With Me is Against Me" There is no Medium or Middle state & if a Man is the Enemy of my Spiritual Life while he pretends to be the Friend of my Corporeal. he is a Real Enemy—but the Man may be the friend of my Spiritual Life while he seems the Enemy of my Corporeal but Not Vice Versa.[40]

When similar sentiments appear in the Bard's Song, though they may be said to refer to Satan's false friendship to Palamabron, in context they are ambiguous, referring possibly to Palamabron as well as Satan. Palamabron too stands accused of "officious brotherhood." Besides, even in Blake's letter, the statement is meant as a general principle applied to Blake and Hayley, a general principle that, in the poem, has an unclear reference. It is even possible that the corrective issued by Los to Palamabron may be such a warning as the warning issued to Hayley by Lady Hesketh about his anxious care about Blake.[41]

Satan's slaying of Thullough and subsequent trial parallel Blake's ejection of Scolfield from his garden and Blake's subsequent trial. Scolfield, a soldier, had been ejected by Blake from Blake's garden, and subsequently accused Blake of seditious words. He was supported by another soldier, Cock, a witness to the events, in his allegation.[42] Scolfield and Cock seem to fit the paradigm of Thullough and Michael. In the subsequent trial Blake was exculpated, just as Satan escaped judgment at his trial before the solemn assembly. Satan's departure from the company of the eternals coincides with Blake's departure for London. Satan is said to remove to, among other places, Babylon, which, in a letter of Hayley's once refers to London.[43]

The association of Blake with Satan would make the ensuing identification of Blake with Milton in the struggle against Satan much more appropriate than anything that could be gained from seeing Hayley as Satan. In either hypothetical reading, Satan as Hayley or as Blake, it is clear that the essence of the narrative is not topical allegory. Entirely too much remains unexplained. The narrative undoubtedly has elements of Blake's personal life, but it is a narrative that aims to discover dramatically and symbolically the psychological mechanisms of the fall into the selfhood. We must view it in this way to see how the thematic structure of the poem is built up. The selfhood was not Hayley's alone, and the dramatic picture at the end of *Milton* of Blake emerging with a new vision, suggests that he had seen the selfhood in William Blake. Indeed, it is a cynical irony to view Blake as quietly sitting in judgment on Hayley, making him into a Satan, and condemning him behind a covert allegory, in a mean and unforgiving way that suggests the very selfhood Blake takes to task.

Just as the parallels to Blake's life do not constitute topical allegory, so the political parallels do not either. But some passages in the Bard's Song suggest the cause of political evil. In the picture of the fall of Satan, Blake frequently views the mechanism of destruction as war, suggesting the possibility that the selfhood was working in the bloody wars sweeping over Europe. From the beginning, *Milton* points to the "class of Men whose whole delight is in Destroying . . . who would if they could, for ever depress Mental & prolong Corporeal War" (I. Preface). There is evidence that Blake was thinking of the politicians behind the horrors of war between 1793 and 1802. Although he wrote Flaxman (October 19, 1801)[44] of his rejoicing at the prospect of peace, in a letter to Butts (September 1801)[45] he recalls Pitt, the prosecutor of the war, who had constantly to drain money from English pockets, as prescribing "distress for a medicinal potion." Blake's commentaries on Bacon and Watson, made just prior to his arrival at Felpham, suggest his distrust of politicians: "The prince of darkness is a Gentleman & not a man he is a Lord Chancellor."[46]

A review of the popular characterization of Willian Pitt will underscore the way in which Blake could transform the topical into sublime allegory. Pitt had long been associated with the war, and, for Blake, the wordly realities of men like Pitt, Fox, and Burke were the present historical manifestations of the struggles of the selfhood. The themes in the Bard's Song of usurpation (a form of control), restriction, and destruction fit the popular character of Pitt.[47] According to the contemporary historian Robert Bissett, the viewpoints of Burke, Fox, and Pitt in 1792 represented three distinct attitudes toward the war with France. Burke was for it to restore monarchy; Fox against it because it would make France a military democracy; Pitt for it to protect England from revolution. In the popular mind these three attitudes became: "On the one side party zeal represented Mssrs. Burke and Pitt, and their respective adherents the abettors of tyranny; on the other, Mr. Fox, and his adherents as the abettors of jacobinism and democracy."[48] Pitt's popular character was not improved when he allowed the taxes for the war to fall heavily on the middle class (of which Blake was a part).[49] Pitt had the support of the moneyed class, but after the sedition bills of 1794–95, he lost the support of the middle and lower classes. Besides financial oppression, Pitt could be accused also of political repression. Pitt's attempt to control the radical drives in England appear clearly in 1794. His fear of the corresponding and constitutional societies, when it was discovered that plans for a national convention were being made, led him to infer that conspiracy was afoot. He wished to enact a temporary suspension of the *habeas corpus* act. He proposed a bill "empowering his majesty to secure and detain all persons suspected of designs against his crown and government."[50] Although in parliamentary debate Fox objected that there was no conspiracy since all was public knowledge, the bill was enacted. In 1795 after the King was assaulted by cries of "bread" and "peace," Pitt attempted to broaden the acts considered as sedition in order to have stronger control of the populace. "The law of treason was at once extended, and Pitt carried a 'sedition' bill."[51] Pitt's character as political repressor could not help him with the literati of the day. "The minister was not deemed favourable to writers as a class. . . . The laws in question, and other acts, tended to restrain the market for literary commodities. . . ."[52] Though Pitt's popularity with the literary world decreased, his political power increased. By 1797 Gillray could caricature his dominance over Parliament by showing him as a "giant-Factotum amusing himself."[53] Opposition in Parliament to Pitt's war effort was virtually nonexistent, though as the war bore wearily on, financial problems and military setbacks made some trouble for Pitt. Yet, in 1797 he imposed additional taxes, and made stirring appeals to the spirit of the nation. In 1798 the *habeas corpus* was again suspended, and further bills were passed repressing secret societies. The war was taking a heavy toll, though Pitt manfully persisted.[54] He was indeed prescribing distress to England, from lake's point of view.

Pitt's reputation with those of Blake's mind also suffered from another suspicion: that he was a usurper. This notion had begun early. In 1788 caricatures sponsored by the opposition implied that Pitt was usurping the royal position during the king's illness. "In some form or other the thesis that Pitt was arrogating to himself the powers of the Crown by a Regency Bill imposing restrictions on the Regent's powers (although he was known to be preparing to return to the bar when the Bill came into force) appears in all the Foxite prints."[55] From 1791 opposition prints view Pitt as "an arrogant upstart, usurping the powers of the crown, or

presuming on Royal Favor.''[56] Gillray's print showing Pitt
as a giant fungus is a fine example.[57] It is precisely in the
characterization of Pitt as usurper and warmonger that
Blake creates Satan.

Besides the general similarity between the popular
characterization of Pitt and Blake's Satan, there are other
similarities between the political events of the time and the
Bard's Song that suggest that Blake saw the manifestation
of the selfhood in the "real" world. Satan's curb of the
horses suggests Pitt's attempts in the early days of the war
to check resistance at home. Satan "compell'd the Gnomes
to curb the horses" (12.17). This left "the horses of the
Harrow . . . maddend with tormenting fury" (7.18). In 1793
Pitt had supported repressive measures against "traitorous
correspondence," had supported the suspension of *habeas
corpus*, had refused to back parliamentary reform (though
before the war he had supported it), and in 1795 had supported a sedition bill.[58] The repression sweeping England
was even to fall in 1798 on Blake's former "employer,"
Joseph Johnson.[59]

Pitt's fears of revolt in the lower classes were not un-
founded. There were meetings of the corresponding and
constitutional societies, led by Daniel Adams and Thomas
Hardy, organizers of the working classes. "In the course of
their preparations [for a national assembly] they had called
several meetings; especially one at Chalk Farm near
Hampstead. There several intemperate speeches were
made; and when festivity intermingled with politics, very
inflamatory toasts were proposed, and the meeting was undoubtedly seditious."[60] Like Pitt, Satan too has his difficulties with the workers of the mills. After Palamabron's
influence, Satan found his mills all confusion:

The servants of the Mills drunken with wine and dancing
    wild
With shouts and Palamabrons songs, rending the forests
    green

With ecchoing confusion, tho the Sun was risen on high.
                    (8.5–10)

Another episode in Pitt's political life seems apt. Satan's mills are kept in order by devices of mental control, but when Satan's friend Thullough reproves him, he resorts to destruction. Pitt had borne the presence of Thurlow in his cabinet uncomfortably for several years, but in 1792, when Thurlow opposed the libel bill supported by Pitt, Pitt had the king remove him from the chancellorship.[61] In general, the usurpation theme, with Satan's yearning for Palamabron's station, his attempts to control the genii, gnomes, and horses, his delusion about his own motives, his claim to be "God alone" (9.25) with all the moral power of retribution, and his final state, "a mighty Fiend against the Divine Humanity mustring to War" (10.11), is a sublime characterization of Pitt, whom Blake could see as one manifestation of the selfhood.

The notion that the Bard's Song illustrates the archetypal motivation behind England's political struggles and war is appropriate to the larger structure of *Milton*. Milton hears the Bard's Song some one hundred years after his earthly death and, though not exact, the lapse of time suggests the possibility that the events of the Bard's Song have a phenomenal manifestation well after Milton's death. Assuming the stretch of time, we can see reason why Milton turns against himself, accusing himself of being Satan. John Milton's reliance on war to establish a government, illustrated in his letter to General Monk, suggests the warmongering of the Bard's Song that was destroying England. William Pitt, the prime minister, and his lower counterpart, John Milton, the Latin secretary of the commonwealth, have both been the manifestations of the selfhood. Milton must return to rid the world of the remnants of that selfhood, and it is in Lambeth of the 1790s that Blake sees him return.

3

The Blossoming
of the Selfhood

I. EMPIRICISM AND NATURAL RELIGION

Blake's fully developed narrative seems bewildering at first, but the psychological pattern of the fallen selfhood gives unity to many of the poem's apparently unconnected elements. It is the interior processes of the selfhood that are developed through Satan's campaign into full-fledged cultural phenomena such as Lockean epistemology, natural religion, state religion, restrictive morality, and war. In other words, the interior selfhood develops into the exterior selfhood. Yet Blake frequently represents this phenomenon in symbols that convey meaning on both levels. For instance, the symbolic polypus stands both for the selfhood's limiting of perception to the bodily nerves of an individual and for the doctrine of empiricism in the body politic. The inference of these double symbols is that the interior delusion of the selfhood develops into exterior phenomena that tend to perpetuate the selfhood's delusion.

92

Blake tends to present his symbols in twisted heaps, but we may separate them to get a clear view. How the self-hood generates the cultural phenomena of empiricism and natural religion will concern us first. We shall see how delusion, like a vegetating tree, branches out into the symbol of Druidism, which in turn grows into doubt, reason, mathematics, a Newtonian universe, and finally the philosophy of empiricism.[1] Delusion's many-tentacled quality is conveyed when Blake symbolizes empiricism as the polypus. The delusion of empiricism is also closely associated with Tirzah, who represents natural religion. The stems of the selfhood bloom as different cultural phenomena and stretch through time from the earliest days to the present.

We may begin with the picture of Satan at the end of the poem since virtually all the symbols of the selfhood culminate in it. Many details of his appearance suggest his delusive and destructive character. Satan is said to be "gorgeous and beautiful" (38.12), and the term gorgeous connotes the superficial and tawdry quality of his beauty, for it is a beauty of delusion. The delusion of Satan in the Palamabron-Satan quarrel is still the delusion of this mock God standing before Blake:

Satan heard! Coming in a cloud, with trumpets & Flaming fire,
Saying I am God the judge of all, the living & the dead
Fall therefore down & worship me. submit thy supreme
Dictate, to my eternal Will & to my dictate bow
I hold the Balances of Right & Just & mine the Sword
Seven Angels bear my Name & in those Seven I appear
But I alone am God & I alone in Heaven & Earth
Of all that live dare utter this, others tremble & bow
Till All Things become One Great Satan, in Holiness
Oppos'd to Mercy, and the Divine Delusion Jesus be no more.

(38.50–39.2)

To maintain control of the exterior world, Satan has assumed the appearance of the God of justice, morality, and punishment who holds the "Balances of Right & Just & mine the Sword." He has corrupted the seven eyes of God, whose dark aspect now becomes part of the pompous delusion of mystery's show. And ironically, Jesus, the true God, is said to be a delusion by the delusion.

Satan is then described as a perverse imitation of the Godhead:

Loud Satan thunderd, loud & dark upon mild Felphams
   Shore
Coming in a Cloud with Trumpets & with Fiery Flame
An awful Form eastward from midst of a bright Paved-work
Of precious stones by Cherubim surrounded: so permitted
(Lest he should fall apart in his Eternal Death) to imitate
The Eternal Great Humanity Divine surrounded by
His Cherubim & Seraphim in ever happy Eternity
Beneath sat Chaos: Sin on his right hand Death on his left
And Ancient Night spread over all the heavn his Mantle of
   Laws
He trembled with exceeding great trembling & astonish-
   ment.

(39.22–31)

Here Blake shows how the delusion worshiped by the orthodox is really Satan's imitation of God. Chaos, sin, death, and law signify the destructive and moralistic nature of state religion, which intends to terrify and enslave. Blake has described a picture of the delusion that is the external God of this world, and of the delusion that is our internal selfhood.[2]

Details of this entire final presentation of Satan are related to the symbols of the corrupted seven eyes and Druidism, which are tied together in Blake's discovery of the real delusion. When Satan says: "Seven Angels bear my Name & in those Seven I appear" (38.55), we discover that Satan imitates God by imitating the picture from Revelation of the throne divine surrounded by the seven eyes of God. Earlier in the poem, the seven eyes had been connected with the Druids. As Milton converses with the seven, they inform him that

> We were Angels of the Divine Presence & were Druids in
>   Annandale
> Compelld to combine into Form by Satan, the Spectre of
>   Albion
> Who made himself a God . . . .
>   (32.11–13)

The seven are the Druids, the first priests. Satan's systematic transformation of himself into a God depends on a priestly caste, and Blake has introduced Satan's agency of Druidism as the earliest form of priestcraft. Early in the poem Blake had displayed a corrupting force, for not only did the "stony Druid Temples overspread the island white" (6.20) but they spread over the whole earth, leaving "Oak Groves rooted" (6.16) where once "Jerusalem's foundations began . . . [which were thence] laid in ruins" (6.15). In these "high-rear'd Druid temples/ Which reach the stars of heaven & stretch from pole to pole" (9.14–15), the ritual of Satan took the form of sacrifice: "Satan's Druid sons/ Offer the Human Victims throughout all the Earth" (11.7–8). The Druid rocks were already present when Los shaped Urizen. Here Blake connects the moralistic, sacrificial nature of Druidism with rationalism. Urizen is reconstructed "among indefinite Druid rocks & snows of doubt & reasoning" (3.8). The doubt and reason of Druidism characterize the rationalism which has lost the creative imagination that alone believes. Visionless, the Druid had created a God from the natural world, just as the eighteenth century had created a delusory God in its natural religion.[3] But the accretion of meanings in the symbol of Druidism goes well beyond this outline of the selfhood's connection. Blake further associated mathematics with Druidism; for the cor-

rupted form of the seven eyes, forced into becoming the
selfhood's tools for destructive moralism, and restrictive
control, are also forced into mathematical delusion:

Those combin'd by Satan's Tyranny [i.e. now Druids], first
in the blood of War
And Sacrifice & next in the Chains of imprisonment, are
Shapless Rocks
Retaining only Satan's Mathmatic Holiness, Length,
Bredth, & Highth.
(32.16–18)

To mark the opposition between the selfhood's Druidical,
rational mathematical delusion and the deeper, true humanity, Blake contrasts "Druidical Mathematical Proportion of
Length, Bredth, Highth" (4.27) with "Naked Beauty"
(4.28), and has Satan's "Mathmatic Proportion" fall before
"Living Proportion" (5.44) "among the rocks of the
Druids" (5.42).

The mathematical, rational delusion of the Druid reaches
into the present of Blake's day, and Blake connected this
sort of reason with the delusive concept of a Newtonian
universe. To see this connection, however, we must see
how the cultural phenomena of Blake's day represents that
connection. In the work of Thomas Paine, Blake found the
ultimate results of Druid rationalism. In *The Age of Reason*
Paine had set forth his notion of Deism, with several remarks that must have piqued Blake's interest. For Paine
only reason can reveal anything about God, and the way to
use reason is to examine the created world of God—the
physical world. "That which is now called natural
philosophy, embracing the whole circle of science, of which
astronomy occupies the chief place, is the study of the
works of God, and the power and wisdom of God in His
works, and is the true theology."[4] Like a well-conditioned
Baconian, Paine clearly relies on causation in the natural
universe to establish any statement about God. He writes:

"everything we behold carries in itself the internal evidence that it did not make itself . . . and it is the conviction arising from this evidence that carries us on, as it were, by necessity to the belief of a first cause eternally existing, of a nature totally different to any material existence we know of, and by the power of which all things exist; and this first cause man calls God."[5] Though this conclusion seems acceptable, Blake must have been interested in the way Paine translated this causation into the metaphors of mechanics and mathematics. The universe has "vast machinery."[6] Its "structure is an ever existing exhibition of every principle upon which every part of mathematical science is founded. The offspring of this science is mechanics; for mechanics is no other than the principles of science applied practically."[7] Significantly, from mechanics Paine slips into the terminology of a mill: "The man who proportions the several parts of a mill uses the same scientific principles as if he had the power of constructing a universe; but as he cannot give to matter that invisible agency by which all the component parts of the immense machine of the universe have influence upon each other and act in motional unison together, without any apparent contact, and to which man has given the name of attraction, gravitation and repulsion, he supplied the place of that agency by the humble imitation of wheels and cogs."[8] Moreover, Paine's universe is boundless. He is fascinated by the "immensity," the "vast distance" of space.[9] His deduction about God from this universe is that "the creation we behold is the real and ever existing Word of God, in which we cannot be deceived. It proclaims His power, it demonstrates His wisdom, it manifests His goodness and beneficence."[10] In Paine, then, Blake could find the Druidic universe of mathematics. The mathematical proportion of the Druid, and its snowy reasoning, is Blake's symbol for the "mathematical science" whose principles underlie the "vast machinery" of the Deistic, Newtonian universe. In *Milton* Blake picks up Paine's simile of the mill to represent Satan's workhouse.[11]

Satan, first of all, is said to be the "Miller of Eternity"
(3.42). Though his mills have a function in Los's world,
they are just the kind of universal mill Paine describes: they
are "Starry Mills" (4.2). To mortals such as Paine who see
only as delusive rationalism dictates, Satan's "Mills seem
every thing" (4.12). The mills are involved in the eternal
work of death (4.17). They are the astronomical "Wheels of
Heaven" (4.10), much like Paine's orrery, which mechanically grind along in the material creation. The ironic position of Satan is revealed when we learn that Satan is "Newton's Pantocrator" (4.11), the all-ruler of creation. But the
mills, as astronomical laws, are nothing other than inhu-
man, "Druidical Mathmatical Proportion of Length Bredth
Highth" (4.27), which is easily mocked by the beauty of
human form (4.27–28).

Satan's eternal mills become the astronomical universe
when Satan separates himself from eternity. His separation
is his creation in his own bosom of a "vast unfathomable
abyss" (9.35), which he enters: "His Spectre raging furious
descended into its Space" (9.52), and his mills are separated from eternity (11.6). Thus Satan's space is an interior
delusion that is the Newtonian Universe. Blake complicates
this symbol when he associates the fall into this space with
birth, or, in Porphyry's terms, the descent of the soul into
matter.

The nature of a female Space is this: it shrinks the Organs
of Life till they become Finite & Itself seems Infinite
And Satan vibrated in the immensity of the Space! Limited
To those without but Infinite to those within.
                              (10.6–9)

In these symbolic terms Blake is saying that a delusion
causes the view that the spatial, created universe is infinite,
a delusion that represents a falling away from the vision of
eternity. Space is the "Aereal Void" (35.52), the "Chaotic
Voids" (37.47), the "Newtonian" void (37.46) of modern

astronomy. But in the end Blake will always insist that "the Satanic Space is Delusion" (36.20). It is a "Void Outside of Existence, which if enter'd into/ Becomes a Womb" (41.37–42.1). Here the reason for Blake's connection of the birth motif with the Newtonian delusion becomes apparent. Birth is an entrance to a world where the five senses narrow perception, limiting the entrance of knowledge to those inlets supposed by Lockean empiricism to be the only inlets of knowledge. The delusion of space, like a womb, encloses the spiritual perceptions so that the imagination's limitless vision is constricted, peering only through the five senses. The enclosed spirit has but a "little narrow orb closed up & dark" (5.21) for an eye, pitifully weak tongue and nostrils, and a shell for an ear, shutting out the melody of eternity and hearing only discord (5.19–37). These senses are constrictors of true vision. They are the result of the mortals' "Sexual texture" (4.4), by which Blake means the physical manifestation resulting from sexual generation, that is, birth in the physical body. Paine's astronomical view of theology is thus connected to Lockean empiricism—a delusion that underlies the deceit of natural religion.

Thus the Druids' mathematics, the mills, the void, and the senses of the physical body stem from rationalistic delusion. The Druids' naturalistic world view is no other than that of natural religion, which creates a God from the false delusion of the Newtonian universe. The Druid, Satan's mills, and space are associated as symbols of the exterior manifestation of the selfhood's delusion. The delusion of the Druid is that of the "idiot Reasoner [who] laughs at the Man of Imagination/ And from laughter proceeds to murder by undervaluing calumny" (32.6–7). The Druid and Deist are aligned against the man whose spiritual vision transcends the spatial world of death and the selfhood.

The rationalism of the eighteenth century that underlies natural religion is attacked repeatedly by Blake in his acerbic remarks on the process of questioning and reasoning.

The "idiot reasoner" (32.6) is the "idiot Questioner" whose purpose is the destruction of spiritual wisdom:

The idiot Questioner who is always questioning
But never capable of answering; who sits with a sly grin
Silent plotting when to question, like a thief in a cave;
Who publishes doubt & calls it knowledge; whose Science
   is Despair,
Whose pretence to knowledge is Envy, whose whole Sci-
   ence is
To destroy the wisdom of ages to gratify ravenous Envy;
That rages round him like a Wolf day & night without rest
He smiles with condescention; he talks of Benevolence &
   Virtue
And those who act with Benevolence & Virtue, they mur-
   der time on time.
               (41.12–20)

The last two lines of this quotation suggest still another facet of the selfhood that Blake associated with natural religion. The hypocritical moralism of many rationalistic philosophers led not to their extolled benevolence, but to further control. Blake's remark about the talk of benevolence may relate to the whole body of eighteenth-century moral philosophers, including Hutcheson and Adam Smith, but his mention of Bolingbroke and Hume (40.12) as part of the religion of nature suggests that he is aiming particularly at their hypocritical praise of benevolence. For Bolingbroke the "great and fundamental principle of this law [law of human nature] [is] universal benevolence."[12] Hume, extolling benevolence, but seeing its ultimate value in its utility (i.e., survival value), writes: "it seems undeniable that nothing can bestow more merit on any human creature than the sentiment of benevolence in an eminent degree; and that a part, at least, of its merit arises from its tendency to promote the interest of our species, and bestow happiness on human society."[13] Blake's general disapproval of these philosophers must have found an exception in what would be his own approval of benevolence, but from his point of view all the talk of benevolence could not obscure the visionless rationalism that killed the imagination. Indeed, we may see in Hume's skepticism why Blake could characterize Hume as a questioner "who is always questioning/ But never capable of answering" (41.12–13), though the word *idiot* is the antithesis of any quality properly attributable to Hume.[14]

The "idiot questioner" is one aspect of rationalism. Another is that of the "Reasoning Spectre" (39.10) of Albion, who must be reclaimed before Albion can awake.[15] On the cosmic level, reason is a soporific, a deadly sleep of the cosmic soul that keeps mankind from true vision and true faith. The "Reasoning Spectre" has produced the eighteenth century's "Rational Demonstration" (41.3) in opposition to faith in the savior. On the individual level Blake sees the basic power of reason merely as a part of the material form: "The Negation is the Spectre; the Reasoning Power in Man" (40.34).[16] The spectre in this respect represents the physical aspect of any man, which wishes to maintain its existence at all costs. The reasoning power then becomes its mechanism for doing so, and its principal method is to object to, to question, to negate that spiritual perception which makes physical existence a mere part, and not an essential part, of mankind. We can see how, on both levels, the reason is negative. It is that defensive posture of the psyche which abstracts all feeling, intuition, or emotion from any consideration, and attempts to solve anxiety-producing problems with objectivity and coolness. While this mental process constitutes much intellectual thought, its tendency to abstract intellectual content from feeling can go so far as to refuse to consider feeling as significant. Consequently, the focus of this process is frequently too limited to enable man to find a satisfactory answer to the question he is asking. The repressed feeling is not expressed, though the isolated intelligence carries a consistent and coherent set of relationships within its nar-

row confines. This less-than-complete awareness of the
deeper and more human aspects of man is no other than the
sleep of Albion, whose product is both eighteenth-century
rationalism and the defense mechanism of the individual's
selfhood.

When Blake writes that the spectre forces the seven eyes
to combine into form, he is saying that the body of the
eighteenth century's rationalistic teaching, including
natural religion, stems from the defense mechanism of the
isolated intellect. In this sense the Druidism of earlier times
is akin to eighteenth-century rationalism. Both are results
of that "False Tongue! vegetated/ Beneath your [Daughters
of Beulah] land of shadows" (2.10–11) which is the delusion of the selfhood's rationalism. This rationalism resulted
in, among other things, Lockean empiricism, which is the
phenomenon that Blake points out in the symbol of the
polypus.[17] Used in its meaning both as a cuttle fish and a
polyp-like tumor, the polypus's symbolism has two levels
of meaning: that of a cuttle fish that floats in the sea of time
and space; and that of a tumor, which is a morbid interior
growth. These two levels point to the dual symbolism of the
polypus: on one level it represents the nerves of any individual; on another it represents cosmic matter, which is,
after all, no other than the stuff of the fallen cosmic man,
Albion. On either level the polypus represents Blake's reduction to absurdity of Lockean empiricism as it is expressed in Hartley's physiology. Hartley's tracing of thought to
the vibratiuncles within the fibers of the brain is suggested
when Blake links the polypus with the nervous system:

Orc incessant howls burning in fires of Eternal Youth
Within the vegetated mortal Nerves; for every Man born is
    joined
Within into One mighty Polypus, and this Polypus is Orc.
        (29.29–31)

The polypus as nerve would be the source of all sensation

and ultimately of all perception and thought according to the Lockean-Hartleyan idea that the only gateway of knowledge is through the senses. But Blake explicitly denies this function of the polypus:

> were it not for Bowlahoola & Allamanda
> No Human Form but only a Fibrous Vegetation
> A Polypus of soft affections without Thought or Vision
> Must tremble in the Heavens & Earths thro all the Ulro
>   space.
>   (24.36–39)

The nerves themselves do not carry thought or vision in Blake's anti-empirical view of spiritual causation.

On the cosmic level the symbolic meaning of polypus expands to become the nervous fibers of matter. When Ololon first sees the Ulro, she sees:

>   a vast Polypus
> Of living fibres down into the Sea of Time & Space growing
> A self-devouring monstrous Human Death Twenty-seven
>   fold
> Within it sit Five Females & the nameless Shadowy Mother
> Spinning it from their bowels with songs of amorous delight
> And melting cadences that lure the Sleepers of Beulah
>   down
> The River Storge (which is Arnon) into the Dead Sea:
> Around this Polypus Los continual builds the Mundane
>   Shell.
>   (34.24–31)

The evil associations of the monstrous "self-devouring" tumor and the cuttlefish aspect of the polypus in the "Sea of Time and Space" coincide in this use of the symbol. Furthermore, its association with the six females is the association of the delusion that material formation constitutes the totality of existence. And its association with the twenty-sevenfold human death links the polypus and the churches.

This linking marks the identification of the "Forty-eight Starry Regions . . . [as] Cities of the Levites/ The Heads of the Great Polypus" (38.1–2). The Levites were the priestly tribe of Israel, and their headship of the polypus here connects the organized church and Lockean empiricism. This strange connection stands, nevertheless, for Blake's vision of the selfhood's delusions. The fear inspired by the materialism implicit in empiricism is, for Blake, much like the fear inspired by organized religion:

Thy purpose & the purpose of thy Priests & of thy Churches
Is to impress on men the fear of death; to teach
Trembling & fear, terror, constriction; abject selfishness.
                        (38.36–38)

Behind the empirical philosophy is the unstated inference that spirit is unreal and that matter and its vibrations cause thought, thereby making the death of the body the end of thought and hence of personal identity. Behind the moralistic threats of an organized church is the inference of eternal punishment. Both fear-inspiring notions are delusions, causing and caused by the selfhood's drive to perpetuate its material existence. In a cyclic feeding of fear on fear, the selfhood creates from its own self-centeredness a fear of death that accentuates its self-centeredness. The delusion that material existence constitutes all is the turning point of this cycle, and Blake thus symbolizes the delusions arising from it in the form of a polypus, a cancer.

But Blake tied rationalism, empiricism, and religion into other symbols too. He saw the rationalism underlying natural religion degenerating into nature worship. Bolingbroke envisaged natural religion as the original religion from which all other "allegorical religions" had descended. Conceiving of these allegorical religions as mysterious, and following Pope, Bolingbroke had remarked that "where mystery begins, religion ends."[18] For Bolingbroke, natural philosophy is the tree trunk of all knowledge, and all organized religions are corruptions. Thus he conceived of natural religion as the historically primary religion. Mathew Tindall had the same concept when he suggested that the Gospel was a "republication" of natural religion.[19] But to Tindall the essence of natural religion was in the rational faculty of man and what it could deduce from its surroundings. "By Natural Religion I understand the Belief of the Existence of a God, and the Sense and Practice of those Duties, which result from the Knowledge, we, by our Reason, have of him, and his Perfections; and of ourselves, and our own Imperfections and of the Relation we stand in to him, and to our Fellow-Creatures; so that the Religion of Nature takes in every Thing that is founded on the Reason and Nature of Things."[20] Still other natural religionists see the primacy of natural religion as a matter of rational deduction from nature. Hartley, for instance, proposes the definition of natural religion in three ways: (1) the learning of love and reverence to God from the light of nature and a consideration of God's works; (2) regulation of action dictated by the moral sense; (3) rational self-interest,[21] all three being essentially the same. Hartley and Tindall both maintain that there is a harmony and supplementation between natural and revealed religion, but Paine has the ultimate statement in that he denies the value of revealed religion. For Paine the only word of God is his creation. To conjecture of the worker by the work, however, is not Blake's idea of the way to come to knowledge of God. The reason is a fallible instrument, and man can as easily deduce a Setebos (as Browning's Caliban does) as a benevolent deity. In reaction to this system of thinking, Blake goes so far as to arraign nature herself, in the symbol of Tirzah, as a delusory force.

Tirzah is one of the central symbols of natural religion in *Milton*. Her activity in the poem, however, is not that of a rational philosopher, but of a perverted generative principle, not unlike the tumor aspect of the polypus. She is the cause of division in all the materializations that occur. Her associated symbols are the loom and spindle (but these are

not the same as Enitharmon's, whose mild influence is far
different from Tirzah's), and since she is associated with
the generation of the material world, she becomes a symbol
for Blake of the religion of the material world. The essence
of that religion is the delusion that the material world constitutes the whole of reality. Thus her material formations
are at least in part delusory.[22]

The physical body itself is to Blake an ambivalent object.
In his myth of the fall of the cosmic man, Albion, it represents a limit to a process of individual degeneration begun
in eternity and not completely restored until the individual
escapes the body. But when the body is considered the
totality of existence, then the perverse delusion of Tirzah
has come about. Her perversion works in a subtle fashion.
Material form itself is the gift of the daughters of Enitharmon to weak souls seeking a material form that will stop
their deteriorating evanescence. The intention of Enitharmon's daughters is thus a kind one, but "Rahab & Tirzah
pervert/ Their mild influences" (29.53–54). Tirzah (Rahab
will be considered soon), the daughter of Rahab and a de-
scendent of Leutha (13.41), is responsible for the perversion of the three gates into Beulah's heavens. These three
heavens, in head, heart, and loins, can lead into Beulah, a
higher view of reality than the narrow empirical view that
convinces one that the physical body is everything. But
Tirzah "ties the knot of nervous fibres into a white brain!/
She ties the knot of bloody veins, into a red hot
heart! . . . She ties the knot of milky seed into two lovely
Heavens/ Two yet but one: each in the other sweet
reflected" (19.55-20.1). In essence, Tirzah has convinced
man that his reality consists of the sexual garments. For
Blake the sexual garment is the physical result of sexuality,
the corporealization of form. From this conception, we can
see how the sexual delusions through which Milton journeys (2.3) are the material shapes of this world. They are
derivations of the Beulah, the female energy of eternity.
They may be delusive, but they "delight the wanderer and

repose/ His burning thirst & freezing hunger" (2.4–5). They are spoken of as the three heavens of Beulah, head, heart, and loins, which are gates in each individual daughter of Albion. These gates are guarded, but they yield "intoxicating delight" (5.10) to those who can transcend the delusion of Tirzah. Perhaps it is simplest here to see that Blake's myth merely represents the ambivalence of earthly beauty according to the way it is perceived. As a sum of all, it fails. As a part of the whole, it is a mercy. Thus, the gates into paradise available through the influence of the daughters of Beulah are turned into a corporeal form recognized as the sole existence by the materialist.

Blake amplifies the symbol of Tirzah as the vegetative power that conceals the true spirit of man under the guise of a *nation*, Blake's suggestive word that has at least two implications. It suggests the nationalism that results in war. It suggests also that the nationalistic distinction between men, who in eternity are all one, is a force that must be broken to return to eternity. *Nation* is cognate with *natus* (birth), and with *nature*. In both cases, it is the divisive corporealization of identity. This dividing and separating process is a work of Tirzah. Los sees Tirzah as destructive because she has seduced away twelve of his sons, who have been woven into nations by her delusions (23.61–24.16). Becoming a nation is to be born into a new state, but that state is really one of a smaller, more defensive consciousness. Blake implies that the Israelites, who separated into twelve tribes after the invasion of Canaan, had really lost a higher identity. Their selfhoods would not allow the social urge to unite them in a larger group, and they had started the long pattern of narrowing of identity. Fear of too great a tax on the resources of love, because there are too many to love, leads the selfhood to reduce the number to be loved until, finally, it rejects all but its sole self. The process of becoming a nation is thus a shrinking process, motivated by fear. Tirzah's delusion is a spur to the selfhood's fear of the social bond because it makes survival in this existence more important than it could be if a spiritual existence were conceived. Fear for self is greater than love for others when the individual conceives of this life as his only one. Tirzah's delusion is the cause of the defensiveness of the nations,[23] which is dramatized in the lamentations arising from the threat implied in Ololon's journey:

And all Nations wept in affliction Family by Family
Germany wept towards France & Italy: England wept &
　　trembled
Towards America: India rose up from his golden bed:
As one awakened in the night: they saw the Lord coming
In the Clouds of Ololon with Power & Great Glory!
　　　　　　　　(31.12–16)

The modern nations lamenting here are the spiritual descendants of that delusory force which reappears in the end of the poem with Satan:

And all beneath the Nations innumerable of Ulro
Appeard, the Seven Kingdoms of Canaan & Five Baalim
Of Philistea, into Twelve divided, called after the Names
Of Israel:
　　　　　　　　(40.23–26)

They are the twelve sons of Los who fell into generation when they invaded Canaan, which is Satan's space:

　　　　　　it fell down and
Became Canaan: closing Los from Eternity in Albions
　　Cliffs
A mighty Fiend against the Divine Humanity mustring to
　　War.
　　　　　　　　(10.9–11)

Thus the nations of Tirzah are the nations of war.

Tirzah's delusion is that the physical world of nature is all. No doubt Rousseau's reliance on nature ("O nature! O my mother! I am here under thy guardianship alone")[24] is the reason why Tirzah is said to have "created Rousseau" (22.41) when the old churches failed to delude men. This delusion lies behind Blake's equation of Tirzah with natural religion. He writes:

Therefore bright Tirzah triumphs: putting on all beauty.
And all perfection, in her cruel sports among the Victims,
Come bring with thee Jerusalem with songs on the Grecian
  Lyre
In Natural Religion! in experiements on Men,
Let her be Offered up to Holiness! Tirzah numbers her;
She numbers with her fingers every fibre ere it grow;
Where is the Lamb of God? where is the promise of his
  coming?
Her shadowy Sisters form the bones, even the bones of
  Horeb:
Around the marrow! and the orbed scull around the brain!
His Images are born for War! for Sacrifice to Tirzah!
To Natural Religion! to Tirzah the Daughter of Rahab the
  Holy!
                    (19.44–54)

Tirzah is here associated with materialization (enclosure by bones and skull), which is materialization of the spiritual attempts of man (the images of the lamb of God), and a perversion of them to destructive purposes (war). Thus natural religion to Blake is the delusion that sees only the material form of spiritual truths.[25] The delusion of the natural principle, represented by Tirzah, is represented in the cultural phenomena of Blake's day by the history of Hartley's doctrine of the association of ideas. In his own fantastical language, Hartley, on a hint from Newton, explains how the nerves of the body may send signals to the brain by means of vibrations. But he stops short of seeing his mechanistic explanation as the end of the process. In fact he insists on a spiritual existence for consciousness, thus reinforcing a kind of duality of belief that is part of the

Cartesian split between body and spirit. But Joseph Priestly, as we have seen in his edition of Hartley, could not
admit the duality. He writes:

> I am rather inclined to think that, though the subject is
> beyond our comprehension at present, man does not con-
> sist of two principles so essentially different from one
> another as *matter* and *spirit*, which are always described
> as having not one common property, by means of which
> they can affect or act upon each other; the one occupying
> space, and the other not only not occupying the least
> imaginable portion of space, but incapable of bearing rela-
> tion to it; insomuch that, properly speaking, my mind is no
> more *in my body* than it is in the moon. I rather think that
> the whole man is of some *uniform composition*, and that
> the property of *perception*, as well as the other powers
> that are termed *mental*, is the result (whether necessary or
> not) of such an organical structure as that of the brain.
> Consequently, that the whole man becomes extinct at
> death, and that we have no hope of surviving the grave but
> what is derived from the scheme of revelation.[26]

Blake would here find an example of the perverting
influence of Tirzah. It is Tirzah who teaches Priestly that
matter alone gives man a complete explanation (Priestley's
acceptance of revelation being not different from Blake's
but Blake not accepting the principle of materialism). The
success of the delusion is, in Blake's myth, the success of a
female power, since materialization is a result of the separation of sexes and hence the existence of the female.

In a sense Tirzah's delusion is a usurpation of sorts. It is
for this reason that Blake selected the name *Tirzah*. She is
one of the daughters of Zelophehad, who insisted that
Moses give them the property that their sonless father
would have had, and Moses caused "the inheritance of
their father to pass unto them" (Numbers 27.7). These
daughters are named Mahlah, Noah, Hoglah, Milcah, and
Tirzah (Numbers 27.1) and they are five of the six wives
and daughters of Milton.[27] Blake implies by this allusion

that he does not agree with the Lord that the Daughters of Zelophehad spoke rightly. In fact, this use of the name implies the same sort of usurpation that Leutha has undertaken. Tirzah and her sisters are symbols for delusion that is aggressive and demanding. "The stamping feet of Zelophehad's Daughters are covered with Human gore/ Upon the treddles of the Loom" (29.58–59). The looms of Tirzah's delusion are cruel.[28] Natural religion, with its rationalistic doubt, its empirical, visionless materialism, is a cruel delusion separating man from the true God and leading him inevitably to the wars of self-defensiveness.

II. STATE RELIGION AND WAR

We must return now to the final picture of Satan at Felpham to pursue a slightly different exterior manifestation of the selfhood. Blake's picture of the selfhood's manifestation connects Satan's delusion with Urizen, the covering cherub, the hermaphrodite, the twenty-seven churches, the shadowy female, the chain of jealousy, and Rahab. All symbolize state religion in some way. Satan's statement: "I alone am God" (38.56), which recalls the delusion of Satan in the Palamabron-Satan section, the delusion of Urizen in the *Book of Urizen*, where he assumes the role of the lawgiving God (4.24–40), and the delusion of Fuzon in the *Book of Ahania* (3.36–39), is Blake's characteristic statement symbolizing self-deification. Blake also associated it with priestcraft. We learn in *Milton* that Satan is Urizen drawn down into generation, and the character of Urizen is that of the "primeval priest" from the *Book of Urizen* (2.1). It is Urizen's priestcraft with which Milton struggles on the Arnon as Urizen attempts to baptize Milton:

Urizen stoop'd down
And took up water from the river Jordan: pouring on
To Milton's brain the icy fluid from his broad cold palm.
(19.7–9)

Urizen freezes Milton's feet in "Marble beds" (19.2) of the cathedral floor, marble paid for by the painful labor of the poor man. Urizen here is still the primeval priest, and Los's equation of Urizen and Satan is Blake's way of symbolizing the exterior manifestation of the selfhood in state religion.

The connection between Satan's statement and state religion is reinforced by its allusion to the speech imputed to the Prince of Tyre in the Book of Ezekiel.[29] (This biblical allusion is background for several elements in *Milton*: the lamentation device, the covering cherub, the reference to Tyre, and the delusion of Satan.) Satan's delusion of Godhead is like that of the Prince of Tyre, who "hast said I am a God, I sit in the seat of God" (Ezek. 28.2). The prince's delusion stems from his pride and the worldly glory of Tyre and its riches in the realm of commerce (Ezek. 27), though for this pride Tyre will be cast down (Ezek. 28.10, 19). The delusion of Godhead, coupled with worldly wealth, power, and dominion, represents the alliance between religion and government that Blake called "State Religion." Furthermore, Blake's connection of Satan with the delusion suggests that state religion is satanic.

Blake further develops the symbolism of state religion in his reference to the covering cherub. Ezekiel has said of Tyre: "Thou art the anointed cherub that covereth" (28.14), and from the beginning of *Milton*, Blake incorporated and expanded the covering cherub as a symbol of delusion. Satan's fall begins the references to the covering cherub. Satan descends "on the seven mountains of Rome/ In the whole place of the Covering Cherub, Rome, Babylon, Tyre" (9.50–51). This descent has followed Satan's first statement that he is God. The covering cherub appears next as a satanic aspect of the descended Milton: "The Cherub on Sinai Glow'd" (20.23–24), recalling Ezekiel's statement that the covering cherub "wast upon the holy mountain of God" (Ezek. 28.14). But Blake has reversed the values in this allusion. The Sinai of Blake is a place where the restrictions of the Ten Commandments were introduced to afford the theocracy of Moses the power over the Israelites. In this evaluation of the decalogue, Blake, who can read black in the Bible where others read white, is following the critical asperity of Paine and Voltaire against the acts of Moses. But the covering cherub acts throughout cosmic time, and it is reflected in the contemporary world for Blake, who has Palamabron warn Los that "the Covering Cherub advances from the East" (23.10). Palamabron has mistaken the journeying Milton for the covering cherub (23.14), though indeed Milton's historical association with the Puritan oligarchy of Cromwell provides some basis for seeing one aspect of Milton as that of state religion. But Milton's failure was only one manifestation of the covering cherub who had reappeared in Blake's day.

Blake could have found a herald of church-state establishment in the man he referred to as Hand (23.15), John Hunt. Hunt's hysterical fears that Methodism would destroy the established church, whose priests are "the only men competent to search into the truth of what they teach" (*The Examiner* [May 7, 1808], p. 301), would have been an appropriate object of attack for Blake. Hunt, whose *Examiner* attacked Blake directly in August 1808, had earlier written: "The mild spirit of Christianity, and the Church of England Establishment which cherishes it, are in danger. The intolerant disciples of merciless Calvin, the gloomy Methodists, are swarming through the land . . . . The welfare of the country therefore demands some check to this growing evil. . ." (*The Examiner*, [Jan. 12, 1808], p. 369). And in a transparently specious attempt to win his argument for establishment, he wrote later: "Most of the Church's corruptions arise from its connexion with the state, with the great and the rich, in short, with the world. Will the Godly be less corruptible when they are abroad in the same temptation?" (*The Examiner*, [Dec. 25, 1808], p. 826). Blake undoubtedly noticed that Hunt was *not* proposing a change in the corrupting combination of church and state, only sounding a warning to keep a segment of men out of it.

But Blake had completed the main body of *Milton* before 1808, and he undoubtedly had other manifestations of the alliance of church and state in mind. In 1804 Blake had no further to look than Bishop Watson to find a current example of state religion. The Bishop, though he had early been a relatively liberal Whig, by 1798 was supporting Pitt in the prosecution of the war. His *Address to the People of Great Britian* displays a hysterical chauvinism and simplistic anxiety about keeping the status quo. In a time of growing poverty, Watson could scoff at the possibility of losing the war, insisting that "men and money are the sinews of war"[30] and that the English need only give more. He defended Pitt's ten percent tax increase thus: "Instead of calling for a tenth of a man's income, I wish the minister had called for a tenth or for such other portion of every man's *whole property* [italics mine] as would have enabled him not merely to make a temporary provision for the war, but to have paid off, in a few years, the whole or the greatest part of the national debt."[31] "Patriotism" can go no further. The reason for Watson's wish soon emerges in his use of religion to support the state. The atheists, who of course support France and are attempting to undermine the religion of the English in order to overthrow the government, are endeavouring to propagate these tenets.[32] Watson makes the dominion of the government a function of religious control of the populace: "No government can long subsist, if the bulk of the people have no reverence for a supreme being, no fear of perjury; no apprehension of futurity, no check from conscience. . . . "[33] Watson admits that the doctrine of rewards and punishments in a future life is a tool for political control: "they [who wish to overthrow the government] will first attempt to persuade you that there is nothing after death, no heaven for the good, no hell for the wicked, that there is no God, or none who regards your actions . . . [then] they will think you properly prepared to perpetrate every crime which . . . [they deem appropriate to their purposes]."[34] Never has the usefulness of religious fear to the state been so blatantly stated! When a bishop can exhort men to war, stand for higher taxes, and praise state control, then Blake certainly has reason to see church as a tool for power. Moreover, the orthodox Watson does not shun an alliance with Deism to maintain the status quo. He states that there are "many deists in this country who are sensible of the advantages of regular government, and who would be as unwilling as the most orthodox believers in the kingdom, that our own should be overturned."[35] Here Blake could see the sinister alliance of natural religion and state religion, given voice by a bishop in favor of maintaining the government that was bleeding England of its men and money. Blake symbolizes the constricting alliance of state religion with the rationalist philosopher when the covering cherub is equated with the "Spectre of Albion" (24.28). The covering cherub who "advances from East" (23.10) had advanced at least as far as the Bishop of Llandaff's diocess, even if the bishop did not go there himself.

But state religion has existed in the past history of Christianity:

I saw the Covering Cherub
Divide Four-fold into Four Churches when Lazarus arose
Paul, Constantine, Charlemaine, Luther.
(24.30–32)

Though Paul formed no state religion, and Luther himself formed no state religion (though the doctrine of *cujus regio ejus religio* soon followed), Constantine and Charlemagne were political, not religious authorities. Blake's insertion of political authority in this catalogue indicates the covering cherub's nature. State religion is a matter of authority over people.

The full complexity of state religion emerges in the final section of *Milton*. Milton's shadow, condensing into a visible form, is said to be the covering cherub (37.5–9). This vision contains Rahab and Satan, who are the forming agents of the twelve false Gods (37.20–34), and the twenty-seven churches (37.35–43). The twenty-seven churches are various forms of hermaphroditism: "Giants mighty Hermaphroditic" (37.37), "a Male within a female hid" (37.40), and "Male-Females" (37.42). The hermaphroditic forms constitute the combination of "a Dragon red & hidden harlot" (37.43). Blake had used the hermaphroditic beast and whore previously in his annotations to Watson's *Apology for the Bible*, where he had written "The Beast & Whore rule without control."[36] Blake's symbols here for state religion are derived from Revelation. The beast and dragon both represent Satan. The "great red dragon" appears first, "having seven heads and ten horns, and seven crowns upon his heads" (Rev. 12:13). He is equated with the Devil: "And the great dragon was cast out, that old serpent, called the Devil, and Satan" (Rev. 12:9). In the ensuing vision the dragon appears as a beast: "And I stood upon the sand of the sea, and saw a beast rise up out of the sea, having seven heads and ten horns, and upon his horns ten crowns, and upon his heads the name of blasphemy" (Rev. 13:1). The similarity in headdress is the indicator of identity. The beast-dragon is worshiped (Rev. 13:4). The headdress then reappears on the beast, accompanied by the "woman [who] was arrayed in purple and scarlet color" (Rev. 17:4). Her name is "Mystery, Babylon the Great, the Mother of Harlots and Abominations of the Earth" (Rev. 17:5). The woman "sits upon a scarlet-colored beast, full of names of blasphemy, having seven heads and ten horns" (Rev. 17:3). The headdress of the beast marks the significant connection of the whore and beast. Blake has taken the two symbols from Revelation, which itself attacks corruption in the church, and shows them to be permanent forces of corruption working from the time of Adam to the time of Bishop Watson. The whore and dragon are the hermaphroditic twenty-seven churches.

The covering cherub, a hermaphroditic monstrosity, is the delusory notion of holiness covering over the selfhood's urges to power, symbolized in the beast and the whore.

The hermaphrodite is not an androgynous identity. It is two separate principles, male and female, struggling for domination.[37] Each has its own selfhood, and each has its own turn to dominate. The hermaphrodite, as connected with the church and Milton, is introduced early in the poem, when Milton's shadow is said to be hermaphroditic and twenty-sevenfold (14.36–40).[38] This represents John Milton's mistaken alliance with the Cromwellian dictatorship. Milton's alliance is merely another manifestation of that hermaphrodite which has twenty-seven manifestations, all the churches from Adam to the present being the result of its work. The number twenty-seven becomes a sign for the power urge of this force. At times Blake refers to "twenty-seven Heavens" (35.65), with the "Twenty-seven Churches" (35.63). These heavens are the "Heavens of Ulro" (34.49), which are said to be "Twenty-seven fold" (34.26). They are the "Heavens builded on Cruelty" (32.3), "the Twenty-seven Heavens & their Churches" (37.35). It is from Swedenborg that Blake derives the equation of heaven and church. Swedenborg had equated heaven and churches in his cyclic concept of church history,[39] the formation of new heavens corresponding to the periodic formation of new churches upon earth.[40] Blake changed Swedenborg's conception by increasing the number of churches from four to twenty-seven, and by showing their corruption under the hermaphrodite when the churches became synagogues of Satan (11.14). Blake's language for the corrupt church, however, is derived from Revelation, where John of Patmos uses the phrases "synagogue of Satan" (Rev. 2:9) and "Satan's seat" (Rev. 2:13), referring to an evil that has crept into the churches of Pergamos and Smyrna. Blake, seeing the permanent work of the hermaphrodite, sees "Satan's seat" (20.39; 27.1–2) blocking the way to Golgonooza, the true spiritual vision. Satan's synagogues are webs to be removed (38.42), and just as Swedenborg saw the totality of heaven as a grand man,[41] Blake shows the totality of the corrupted church in a monstrous human effigy, "the wicker man of Scandinavia" (37.11).

The connection between the hermaphrodite and the covering cherub also lies behind the struggle between the Shadowy Female and Orc. As the hermaphrodite is one sex dominating the other, the Shadowy Female is dominating the male Orc.[42] She does so by weaving what she calls the human form, but since she is essentially only part of total humanity, she is actually weaving a delusive covering for the purpose of domination. And in the garment, Blake's symbolism expands across a broad spectrum of meaning, illuminating the phenomenological result of the spiritual cause. Into the fabric the Shadowy Female weaves "sighs & heart broken lamentations/ The misery of unhappy Families . . . . dire sufferings poverty pain & woe . . . the sick Father & his starving Family . . . the Prisoner in his stone Dungeon & the Slave at the Mill . . . Kings . . . Councellors & Mighty Men/ The Famine . . . Pestilence . . . War . . . Holiness . . . anxiety & care & desperation & death/ and repentance for sin & sorrow & punishment & fear" (18.6–24). These evils, the poor man's oppression under the powerful who wield all the weapons of the state to oppress the poor, are the phenomenal result of the hermaphroditic church. These evils are woven into the garment that is the covering of the covering cherub, which Blake probably considers to be the priestly garment of Aaron,[43] gorgeously woven and embroidered with jewels (Exod. 28). Blake is implying in his picture of the garment that the priest-tyrant is oppressing humanity to maintain its power. Orc himself lets us know the garment's association with state religion when he tells the Shadowy Female to take a female, not the human form "& not thy Covering Cherub" (18.37).

The delusive control of the female, manifest exteriorly in

hermaphroditic state religion, is also part of the interior mind of the individual, and manifests itself in the domination of jealousy. The struggle for dominance between the sexes symbolized in the hermaphrodite (and implied in the usurpation of the male role by Zelophehad's daughters) is amplified in the symbol of the chain of jealousy. Jealousy is an interior manifestation of the selfhood, which Blake in *Milton* depicts as an excessive quality of the female selfhood. Of the many ways in which jealousy may affect people, in *Milton* it works as a female will to prevent the male not only from loving another but also from deriving satisfaction from the jealous female herself. The female denies all sexual gratification to the male, usually by personal denial and by the use of the term *whore* to cast the idea of sin on intercourse with another. This double-bind produces in the male a state of nongratification that turns him into a slave. This slavery could not be obtained by simply driving off the other women, for sexual gratification would ensure only male fidelity. This indeed is the key, for male fidelity is not the female's object. The male must be in the position of slavery, of begging servitude, for the selfhood-dominated female, with her insidious jealousy, thirsts for absolute control. Thus the chain of jealousy is a device ultimately of the selfhood.

Jealousy is first mentioned immediately after Satan's fall. Los notes its presence: "whence is this Jealousy running along the mountains" (10.14). Jealousy has infected Elynitria and Ocalythron, who, in turn, infect the sun and moon with it. Later the Shadowy Female, who is holding Orc in the chain of jealousy, beholds Oothoon and Leutha hovering over Orc's couch. "Jealous her darkness grew:/ Howlings filled all the desolate places in accusations of Sin" (18.42–43). Orc's desire for Oothoon and Leutha is frustrated, and it is even suggested that they are implicated in Orc's torture: "Orc in vain/ Stretch'd out his hands of fire & wooed: they triumph in his pain" (18.44–45). The chain of jealousy is pointed out to Milton by Tirzah and Rahab:

"behold the fires of youth/ Bound with the Chain of Jealousy" (19.37–38). The purpose of Milton's journey is to "set free/ Orc from his Chain of Jealousy" (20.60–61), thus indicating that the removal of jealousy is involved with the ultimate purpose of self-annihilation. Later Rintrah and Palamabron, mistaking Milton's purpose, fear that he comes to establish yet another church. And the association between the hermaphroditic control behind the churches and jealousy is marked by their seeing the danger of this new formation in the daughters of Los weaving "a new Religion from new Jealousy of Theotormon" (22.38). Perhaps it is with the chain of jealousy that Rintrah and Palamabron wish to chain Blake-Milton: "Let us descend & bring him chained/ To bowlahoola" (23.17–18). Further on, the Divine Voice, speaking to the Shadowy Female, points to her jealousy as the cause of evil, and in particular shows the kind of jealousy that denies sexual gratification:

Then thou wast lovely, mild & gentle. now thou art terrible
In jealousy & unlovely in my sight, because thou hast cruelly
Cut off my loves in fury till I have no Love left for thee
Thy love depends on him thou lovest & on his dear loves
Depend thy pleasures which thou hast cut off by jealousy
Therefore I shew my Jealousy & set before you Death.
                    (33.5–10)

The Divine Voice is suggesting that jealousy is one of the prime motives for the present evil and that it consists in denial of all loves. It warns that jealousy spreads to the male also and can result only in the female's loss of all meaning, in "Death." Ironically, the selfhood's desire for control by means of jealousy leads nowhere.[44]

The speech of the Divine Voice also throws light on the story of the fall, for it is in Leutha's desire for Palamabron that Satan's original delusion began. Indeed, her jealousy is not stated, but the resultant jealousy of Elynitria and Ocalythron suggests it. Moreover, the association of jealousy with the symbol of the hermaphrodite is made stronger. For what else but a hermaphrodite is Satan with Leutha dwelling "in Satan's brain" (12.6)? Indeed, the unchaining of Orc is tantamount to unloosing Satan in the mistaken view of Palamabron and Rintrah (22.33). The unchaining from jealousy, however, is a beneficial act. All in all, jealousy, as Blake perceived, was a means of control, and consequently the weapon of the selfhood. In the cultural phenomenon that results from this form of the selfhood, the hermaphrodite takes the form of state religion. On the familiar and personal level it becomes sexual morality, a means of control.

The hermaphroditic urge is connected to still other symbols of the exterior phenomena of the selfhood. The "Mystery, Babylon the Great, the Mother of Harlots and Abominations of the Earth" (Rev. 17:5) that John of Patmos sees upon the beast is Blake's "Mystery the Virgin Harlot Mother of War/ Babylon the Great, the Abomination of Desolation" (22.48–49).[45] Babylon appears several times in *Milton*. She is "Mortal Virtue the cruel Virgin Babylon" (5.27). She is part of the covering cherub, along with Rome and Tyre (9.51). She is beheld in the spectre of Satan (38.23–28), and is said to bind Jerusalem. Her warfare against Jerusalem is mentioned by Palamabron, who sees her purpose "To destroy Jerusalem as a Harlot" (22.47), but the Divine Voice prophesies that Babylon will "bring Jerusalem in thine [Babylon's] arms in the night watches; and/ No longer turning her a wandering Harlot in the streets" (33.21–22). Finally she is equated with another biblical character, Rahab, in the climax of the poem, when the gathering of evil ties many of the symbolic threads together:

> Rahab Babylon appeard
> Eastward upon the Paved work across Europe & Asia
> Glorious as the midday Sun in Satans bosom glowing
> A Female hidden in a Male, Religion hidden in War

Named Moral Virtue; cruel two-fold Monster shining bright
A Dragon red & Hidden Harlot which John in Patmos saw.
                          (40.17–22)

Rahab has been an actress throughout the poem. She is the
daughter of Leutha, mother of Tirzah (13.41), and the first
of Milton's wives (17.11).[46] With Tirzah she attempts to lure
Milton across the Jordan (19.27–20.6), where she is given
the character of "Rahab the Holy" (19.54), to whom
Jerusalem is to be offered up (19.46–48)—a hint of her identity as Babylon. Her purpose in creating Voltaire (22.41)
ultimately is "to destroy Jerusalem" (22.47). The aggregate
of all existence that cannot be redeemed is "Satan/ and
Rahab" (31.18–19), the two being seen in the covering
cherub of the final vision (37.7–8), where they constitute "a
Dragon red & hidden Harlot (37.43). The final equation of
Rahab and Babylon then lets us know that the hermaphroditic dragon-and-harlot consists of Satan and Babylon-
Rahab.[47]
      The equation of Rahab and Babylon is an interesting equa-
tion of biblical characters derived from Joshua and Revelation in a meaningful way that throws light on Blake's concept of history. In Joshua Rahab is a harlot of Jericho who
conspires with the spies of Joshua in return for a pledge of
safety when the Israelites take Jericho (Josh. 2). When indeed he had conquered, Joshua kept the word of his spies,
sparing Rahab and her family and possessions. "And
Joshua saved Rahab the harlot alive, and her father's
household, and all that she had; and she dwelleth in Israel
even unto this day (Josh. 6:25; italics mine). Blake read the
anachronistic statement about the duration of Rahab's
dwelling in Israel as a hint of the sinister symbolic meaning
of Rahab's alliance with Israel.[48] Blake saw Rahab as an
indication of the selfhood's servitude for the sake of survival and her corrupting influence once she had entered the
nation of Israel. This was an early form of hermaphroditic
control, similar to Leutha's hiding in Satan's bosom. Rahab

is the daughter of Leutha indeed. That she dwells in Israel "even unto this day" was a token for Blake that Rahab represents a spiritual force manifested throughout history. She reappears as Babylon in Revelation, where her method of corruption is hinted. Earthly wealth has been her weapon (Rev. 18:12–13), the "sorceries" (Rev. 18:23) by which men were deceived. John of Patmos foresees her fall, and in her place "the holy city, new Jerusalem, coming down from God out of heaven." (Rev. 21:2). Blake's depiction of the struggle of Rahab-Babylon against Jerusalem is, for Blake, a re-vision in the modern world of the same evil seen by John of Patmos; for Blake, Rahab-Babylon was a permanent evil that worked its corruption particularly on religion. Her two qualities that seem to be his focus of interest are the delusion of holiness and virtue. In her holy aspect (20.54) Rahab-Babylon is the delusion of mystery, the obfuscation of detail used by the priest to maintain control, mystery (22.48) and holiness being synonymous. But this delusion is a hypocrisy, a lie to gain control, and Blake underlines that lie in his ironic twists around the notion of virginity and harlotry combined. Joshua's Rahab was a harlot and John of Patmos's Babylon was a harlot, but the present manifestation that Blake sees is a virgin harlot. Rahab-Babylon is a delusion who teaches the value of chastity in order to control men, but she is the same prostitute who has sold herself to Joshua or to any modern politician. She is religion prostituting herself to the state. She preaches moral virtue so that the state may control the people. She is moral virtue, the cruel virgin. Blake could have heard her voice in John Hunt's insinuation that Methodism favored licentiousness (*The Examiner* [Aug. 28, 1808], p. 556), Hunt's attack on spiritual feeling, which he claimed to be nothing other than sensuality disguised (*The Examiner,* [Aug. 14, 1808]), and even Hunt's distaste for the Song of Solomon and his consequent rejection of the allegory of the marriage of Christ and the Church (*The Examiner* [Aug. 28, 1808], p. 556). But John Hunt was only one manifestation of restrictive religious prudery. It is for the teaching of "self-righteousness" (22.42) that "Rahab creates Voltaire" (22.40).

But Rahab-Babylon is more than state religion. She is religion hidden in war.[49] As such she is an extension of moral righteousness, for war is no other than the extension of the morality of a society. Justice within a nation's boundaries requires moral virtue, and the extension of justice beyond its boundaries requires war. Shifting the analogy from the body politic to the individual, we see that survival of selfhood requires the prudent virtues that control the inner impulses of man as well as his social actions. Both justice and prudence are, for Blake, extensions of the selfhood, and the moral teachings that constitute their weapons are symbolized in the virgin harlot, the deceiver who has sold herself to the state or the selfhood. Rahab-Babylon is both within a man as a domineering, restrictive superego and within collective man as state religion.

The root of state religion is power, the power over men's minds that religious teaching affords. The priest, the direct exerciser of that power, is of importance to the political authority of any society. In the attempt to survive, every political organization will seize every means possible for organizing and controlling the people of a society—particularly the religious interest. The priest thus becomes allied to the state because the state needs the priest's power. The priest becomes a tool, a puppet. The real religious urges of man are left to wander away, and since their appearance would expose the true purpose of the corrupt priesthood, true religion is blasphemed as an imposter, a delusion, or fraud. Blake's view of priesthood is surprisingly like that of the Deists, with whom he so vehemently disagrees in other respects.[50] Bolingbroke saw the deterioration of natural religion in the corruptions stemming from priesthood: "The great principle that maintained all the corruptions of natural religion was that of priestcraft."[51] Furthermore, all religions are subject to the corruption by priesthood: "In short, the whole scheme of religion was applied then, as it is in many countries, Christian and others, still, to the advantage of those who had conduct of it."[52] The universality of corruption of priests, and consequently the alliance of state and church for the sake of power, is, almost a century later, Paine's theme in *The Age of Reason*: "All national institutions of churches, whether Jewish, Christian, or Turkish, appear to me no other than human inventions, set up to terrify and enslave mankind, and monopolize power and profit."[53] Thus the universality of corruption did not exempt the Christian church, which, in fact, is one of the worst: "Of all the systems of religion that ever were invented, there is none more derogatory to the Almighty, more unedifying to man, more repugnant to reason, and more contradictory in itself, than this thing called Christianity. . . . As an engine of power, it serves the purpose of despotism; and as a means of wealth, the avarice of priests; but so far as respects the good of man in general, it leads to nothing here or hereafter."[54] Though Blake could disagree with Paine's deistic rationalism, he certainly shared his distrust of priestcraft. And when Watson, attacking Paine, called for renewed war efforts against the French, particularly on the grounds of religion, Blake found Rahab-Babylon the whore allied with the beast, the hermaphroditic covering cherub. The deists pointed abstractly to the problem, but Blake saw it in prophetic symbols.[55]

Blake uses these symbols of state religion to demonstrate how the defensive impulses of the selfhood lead from moralism to war. The connection between the priest's power, political power, and war lies in the selfhood's connection between delusion, control, and destruction. The method of control is the morality preached by the priest, drummed into the individual in order to control the instincts toward freedom, both political and spiritual. Within the individual the superego and the defense mechanisms of the ego, partially embracing some of the teachings and partially reacting against the threatening urges of the unconscious drives for expression of the libidinous, the destructive, and the anti-social instincts, struggle to control these urges, which, if given full expression, would endanger the survival of the individual. The selfhood thus accepts moral teachings insofar as compliance with morality helps avoid threats of punishment for immoral action. Thus morality is a survival mechanism that is an extension of the selfhood, a mechanism that becomes a tool for political control. Fear of punishment for immoral action works on an individual to keep the social order. But between the various political bodies, actions considered immoral lead to attempts by one political body to punish another political body. This attempt is war. The state religion of the political body comes to the aid of the political authority in both external and internal morality, giving its sanction to legal punishment by adding the threats of spiritual punishment through laws of supposedly divine origin, and giving its sanction to external punishment by supporting a holy war. Survival of an individual in the material form is the motive being exploited, and for the individual, such as Blake, who believed that spiritual existence was real, the slavish submission to the control of authority that uses punishment or war to enforce its will is a slavery to the selfhood. In *Milton*, then, the selfhood's symbols are involved in preaching war and morality. And the symbols even suggest that present-day England is involved in this aspect of the selfhood.

Blake makes it clear that moral law is a result of the selfhood.[56] In the Palamabron-Satan section of the poem, Satan is shown creating the moral law: "He created Seven Deadly Sins drawing out his infernal scroll,/ Of Moral laws and cruel punishments upon the clouds of Jehovah" (9.21–22). The hint that the moral law is Jehovah's marks the selfhood as the true author of the decalogue, which has been formulated in order to control others: "Satan making to himself Laws from his own identity/ Compell'd others to serve him in moral gratitude & submission/ Being Call'd

God" (11.10–12). When Blake has Satan call "the Individual Law, Holy" (13.5), he means that the selfhood-
engendered moral law, which has taken the form of the
decalogue, has become part of the teaching of holiness. The
effect of this delusion is pointed out when the unformed and
uninformed souls call out to Los for righteousness and
punishment, which is the moral attitude Blake ascribes to
the delusion of morality:

And loud the Souls howl round the Porches of Golgonooza
Crying O God deliver us to the Heavens or to the Earths,
That we may preach righteousness & punish the sinner with
   death.

(25.12–14)

The association of decalogue and state religion is reinforced
by the references to Sinai and Horeb, the two biblical locations where the decalogue is said to have been given to
Moses (Exod. 20 and Deut. 5.2).[57] As Milton descends, he
finds his body to be "The Rock Sinai" (17.14); he perceives
the "Cruelties of Ulro . . . [which he writes down] In iron
tablets" (17.9–10), and he journeys "among the Rocks of
Horeb" (17.28). The influence of Horeb reaches to the vale
of Surrey (29.57). These references to the source of moral
law are thus spread throughout human history, in Milton's
day and in Blake's. The work of Sinai and Horeb is the
creation of the cruel morality that has been the tool of state
religion.

And morality is further associated, through state religion,
with war. Blake saw state religion in the theocracy of Israel,
Moses as political leader and Aaron as high priest controlling the Israelites by the supposed word of God. Paine had
forcefully belabored the thesis that Moses was a destructive
warmonger, using religion to reinforce his political ambition. Though Blake could disagree with Paine's deism, his
remarks in his annotations to Watson's *Apology for the
Bible* show that he shared Paine's disgust with the warmon-

gering of Moses. Paine had seen the Israelites' conquest of Canaan as a theocratic warmonger's invasion of the most immoral character. Blake remarked on the bishop's defense of the invasion: "the destruction of the Caananites by Joshua was the unnatural design of wicked men. To Extirpate a nation by means of another nation is as wicked as to destroy an individual by means of another individual which God considers (in the Bible) as Murder & commands it shall not be done."[58] Blake was again reading black in the Bible where the bishop read white. The invasion of Canaan becomes a symbol in *Milton* for the promise of control that leads to war. Satan's space becomes Canaan (10.9–10), and Rahab and Tirzah invite Milton to reinvade Canaan, saying "Let us bind thee in the bonds of War & be thou King/ Of Canaan and reign in Hazor" (20.5–6). The promise of war has stretched from Moses to Milton to Blake's day, and it is with the moral law of Moses that war is associated.

The moral law, moreover, requires a continuous series of atonements for crime. Early in the poem Blake points out the cruelty of this system, for the continued existence of those he calls the elect is entirely dependent on the moral law: "For the Elect cannot be Redeemed, but Created continually/ By Offering & Atonement in the Cruelties of Moral Law" (5.11–12). Jesus' atonement is required, not by the true God, but by the "False Tongue" (2.10), and "Ideas themselves (which are/ The Divine Members) may be slain in offerings for sins" (35.5–6). Thus the process of human morality has been elevated to divine punishment, and when Satan appears finally at Felpham, he appears with the traditional emblems of justice: "I hold the Balances of Right & Just & mine the Sword" (38.54). The principle of punishment lies behind justice in the world of man as it lies behind the notion of divine justice. Blake had told Crabb Robinson that he deplored the notion of the atonement and he makes it clear in his annotations to Watson that "all Penal Laws court Transgression & therefore are cruelty & Murder."[59]

Blake's view of morality is also antithetical to that of the deists. Almost all deists had seen the essence of natural religion in morality. Bolingbroke saw God's creatures determined by Him to seek happiness, which can be found only in morality.[60] John Toland hints that the essence of Christianity lies in its reasonableness, which is the faculty allowing man to choose and then to "deserve rewards & punishments."[61] By the end of the century the essence of Christianity for many is its morality. Priestley thought that the mission of Christ was to give proof of retribution so that man would be virtuous.[62] Paine, like many other deists, agrees that morality was the path to heaven for the deist; but for Blake it was the road to war.

Blake makes a connection between divinely sanctioned morality and war quite explicit. The image of Satan's fall into the selfhood, wherein he creates the moral law, is associated "With thunder of war & trumpets sound, with armies of disease/ Punishments & deaths muster'd & number'd" (9.24–25). Satan becomes "A mighty Fiend against the Divine Humanity mustring to War" (10.11), and he glories "to involve Albions Body in fires of eternal War" (13.6). Indeed, war is the ultimate result of the selfhood, for when delusion fails to control the individual's interior urges, or those of the body politic, or the threats of external bodies politic, then the selfhood must destroy those urges and threats. Blake has made it clear that Satan's essential character is that of the destroyer. He appears throughout history in many forms, but always "there is a Class of Men whose whole delight is in Destroying" (I. Preface). They would forever "depress Mental & prolong Corporeal War" (I. Preface). (Here we become aware of Blake's distinction between types of war so that we can see that Blake's "mental fight" is of higher character than the war of the destroyer.) These destroyers, "like the silly Greek & Latin slaves of the Sword" (I. Preface), are worshipers of the "detestable Gods of Priam; in pomp/ Of warlike selfhood" (14.15–16). Satan's tyranny leads "first in the blood of War/ And Sacrifice" (32.16–17).

The association of religion with the impulse to destroy, manifest in Watson's support of war, is given symbolic embodiment in the hermaphroditic pictures of Rahab-Babylon and Satan. In attempting to allure Milton, Rahab sounds like a destroyer. Speaking of Christ's images, men, she calls: "His images are born for War" (19.53). She appears in her complete hermaphroditic form as "A Female hidden in a Male, Religion hidden in War/ Namd Moral Virtue" (40.20–21). She is a "cruel two-fold Monster shining bright/ A dragon red & hidden harlot" (40.22–23). Thus, religiously sanctioned moral virtue is the harlot Rahab-Babylon, who lies behind the destructive impulse to war symbolized by the dragon Satan. If the whore of state religion appeared as Bishop Watson, the dragon half of the hermaphrodite was Pitt.

As I have pointed out, Pitt was thought the cause of England's ills by many of the liberal persuasion. Fuseli blamed Pitt for England's ills. Gilbert Wakefield saw Pitt as a "demon of destruction."[63] Blake had written "Bacon & Newton would prescribe ways of making the world heavier to me & Pitt would prescribe distress for a medicinal potion."[64] In the early 1790s Pitt and Burke seemed the executors of war, and Pitt's advocacy of the sedition and gagging bills, as well as his method of taxation, generally reinforced the liberal conception. As the war with France went on into the latter half of the decade, peace seemed more and more remote. With Nelson's victory at Trafalgar, the hope for peace with France, called forth by the peace negotiations of 1796–97, died. It must have seemed as if the eternal burden of war was the English lot when in 1800 Parliament rejected the French offer of peace. And though Pitt resigned in February 1801, war efforts continued. Finally the Peace of Amiens, signed in March 1802, gave a temporary relief to the war. But by July 1803, with the renewal of French and English war efforts, Pitt returned to Parliament to speak strongly for the effort that would be needed.[65] Throughout the decade preceding the writing of *Milton*, Blake must have seen Pitt as the embodiment of a mighty fiend mustering to war. With the church behind him, Pitt was the present manifestation of the dragon form of the hermaphrodite.

If Pitt is indeed represented by Satan, Satan's watch fiends are the vigilante groups that sprang up in England. One must be secretive to evade them (23.39–40). The spirits to be generated by Los must be given special guidance lest "Satan's Watch-Fiends touch them" (29.50). And there is the creative moment in which man can have a renovating vision, this moment being beyond the discovery of Satan's watch fiends (35.42–45). The watch fiends are, on the individual level, the defenses that control human thought,[66] but on the level of the body politic they are "the despicable instruments that are easily to be found in all great cities, as spies that were to attend the conventicles of sedition and to become members of the societies [constitutional and corresponding] in order to betray the secrets with which they might be interested."[67] In every country there are the vigilantes whose misdirected patriotism leads to the suppression of free speech. They are Satan's watch fiends.

But one of the worst results, supposed by Blake to stem from the political status quo, was the impoverished condition of England. Blake refers to this condition in his picture of the shadowy female's garment (18.5–25) most forcefully, but it is hinted at in the gnomes being forced to work (12.16–18), as are the genii of the mills (8.16); in the black slaves (21.21), in the sorrows of slavery (24.61), and most poignantly in Blake's vision of Satan's bosom:

I also stood in Satans bosom & beheld its desolations!
A ruind Man: a ruind building of God not made with hands;
Its plains of burning sand, its mountains of marble terrible:
Its pits & declivities flowing with molten ore & fountains
Of pitch & nitre: its ruind palaces & cities & mighty works;
Its furnaces of affliction in which his Angels & Emanations
Labour with blackend visages among its stupendous ruins
Arches & pyramids & porches colonades & domes.
(38.15–22)

Here the spiritual world becomes apparent in the laboring angel with blackened visage, who is really the English workman who supports the luxury and sickly grandeur of the powerful. Blake is referring to the economic slavery wherein the income of the workers is not in proportion to the cost of living. During the last years of the century England was in dire straits. "The distress produced by increasing pressure of population on means of subsistence, and by great displacements and revolutions of industry, was aggravated by a terrible period of commercial crises and depression, a succession of extremely bad harvests and a great French war. The price of the necessaries of life rose out of all proportion to the rate of wages and fluctuated with a violence that was extremely disastrous to the labouring poor."[68] Nearly a seventh part of the population was on relief by 1803.[69] Though the parliament and the king may have been aware of the problem, they were helpless against it. Blake saw that the problem required more drastic measures, and it is Los who "listens to the Cry of the Poor Man" (42.34). The prophetic imagination alone can bring a cure to the ills caused by the selfhood. For that reason Blake quotes at the beginning of the poem the words of Moses: "Would to God that all the Lord's people were Prophets" (I. Preface). Moses speaks these words of Eldad and Midad who had gone to the people to prophesy while the other twenty-eight elders had gone to the tabernacle. The thirty elders had been called together after Moses had complained to God of his burden. For the Israelites had complained bitterly of lack of meat. The problem of hunger lies behind Blake's poor man and the misery of the Israelites, whom Moses was leading to conquer the promised land just as Pitt was leading England.

The full development of the selfhood, then, extends to a large number of symbols in Milton, encompassing the interior psychodynamics of the selfhood as well as its cultural manifestations.[70] Natural religion, state religion, and war are seen as manifestations of the selfhood working throughout history.

III. STATE RELIGION AND NATURAL RELIGION

At the finale of *Milton* Ololon discovers that her self-hood's "Feminine portions" (40.10), Tirzah and Rahab, had led to:

> this Newtonian Phantasm,
> This Voltaire & Rousseau, this Hume & Gibbon & Boling-
> broke
> This Natural Religion, this impossible absurdity.
> (40.11–13)

Blake apparently meant to imply that these writers, to us so apparently different, were all generated in the delusion of Tirzah; therefore we should explore briefly how he may have connected the strange assortment of eighteenth-century writers. I believe that the connection of Bolin-broke, Voltaire, and Rousseau resides in the doctrine of future reward and punishment, a doctrine shared by both state and natural religion, which constitutes a mechanism for political control used by the state. The connection of Hume and Gibbon, however, is probably because of their skepticism, which I shall discuss in the next chapter.

Blake saw authority in the preceding century in the orthodox churches which, to his mind, had been part of the means of establishing political power over men through control of their minds. The control was built upon the preaching of a doctrine of eternal rewards and punishments for moral action. Although natural religion had begun to erode the power of orthodoxy, it also fell prey to the old deceits and showed signs of becoming allied with the seat of political power. As Blake states the process: "Seeing the churches at their Period in Terror & despair/ Rahab created Voltaire, Tirzah created Rousseau" (22.40–41). Natural religion was thus merely a substitute for orthodoxy. Both, therefore, could be forms of state religion. To combat this tendency Blake attacked the weapon of both orthodoxy and natural religion: the belief that man's moral action earned for him eternal rewards and punishments. His view of this tendency need not be seen as historically accurate, but it is possible to find examples that demonstrate his conception.

Blake's attitude toward the doctrine of rewards and punishments seems to follow Boehme's. For Boehme, sin is a characteristic of the selfhood. All men are elected to heaven, but they are at liberty to choose between the selfhood and the divinity. To choose the selfhood is not to be judged, punished, or damned, but to act freely. God does not use the carrot and stick method. In fact, heaven and hell are states of mind resulting from the choice. Satan chose hell: "hell is given to the devil for his house and habitation, because he introduced his life's form into the anger of God."[71] Man likewise: "Now the free will may reach to which [heaven or hell] it pleases; both gates stand open to him."[72]

It is the freedom of choice that would make Boehme palatable to Blake, just as the lack of freedom, deduced from Swedenborg's general principles, made Blake attack Swedenborg's *Divine Providence*. Though Swedenborg insisted that there is no such thing as predestination,[73] Blake, reacting to Swedenborg's notion that placement of an individual in heaven or hell is both foreseen and provided,[74] marked up his copy of *Divine Providence*, with sneering jibes such as "cursed folly," or "more abominable than Calvin," or "Lies and Priestcraft."[75] Swedenborg's vision was thus perverted by the same doctrine of eternal damnation that had affected orthodoxy. Rahab and Tirzah "perverted Swedenborg's Visions" (22.46).

Nor did the moral philosophers provide Blake with anything so palatable as Boehme's making heaven or hell a matter of free will. For it is possible to conceive of the doctrine of reward and punishment as providing no more real free will than that doctrine of predestination which Blake ascribed to Swedenborg, because the fear of punishment leaves no real choice. What choice is there when the quivering soul must face an angry, unforgiving God? The moral philosophers, such as Adam Smith, ignore this question when they write, as Smith does here: "those important rules of morality are the commands and laws of the Deity, who will finally reward the obedient and punish the transgressors of their duty."[76] The characterization of God as stern judge emerges with more force in one of Smith's uncharacteristic apostrophes:

> How unnatural, how impiously ungrateful, not to reverence the precepts that were prescribed to him by the infinite goodness of his Creator, even though no punishment was to follow their violation. The sense of propriety too is here well supported by the strongest motives of self-interest. The idea that, however we may escape the observation of man, or be placed above the reach of human punishment, yet we are always acting under the eye, and exposed to the punishment of God, the great avenger of injustice, is a motive capable of restraining the most headstrong passions, with those at least who, by constant reflection, have rendered it familiar to them.[77]

Though Blake does not mention Adam Smith, nowhere are the doctrine and the implied characterization of God put more clearly. This characterization belongs to both natural and state religion.

There is a subtlety in natural religion's treatment of the question of eternal rewards and punishments. David Hartley, arguing from both natural religion and revealed religion, foresees punishment for man, but ultimately, since God is benevolent, all mankind will be in a happy state after death.[78] Bolingbroke, describing natural religion and seeing the will of God revealed in his works, felt that among the universal characteristics of natural religion, which include rules of moral life, laws to maintain society, and reverence for a supreme being, was the notion of reward for virtue and punishment for vice.[79] Moreover, Bolingbroke suggests that established religion is necessary.[80] Yet he goes out of his way to reject the notion of God as a vengeful creator.[81]

Even Thomas Paine in the recent *The Age of Reason* had spoken of morality without vengefulness: "Deism, then, teaches us without the possibility of being deceived, all that is necessary or proper to be known. The creation is the Bible of the Deist. . . . The probabilities that we may be called to account hereafter will, to a reflecting mind, have the influence of belief . . . it is the fool only, and not the philosopher, or even the prudent man, that would live as if there were no God."[82] The hints of reward and punishment of these believers in Natural Religion do not necessarily imply the vision of a stern judge, but they display a tendency to hint at punishment.

What Blake would see as the French counterpart of natural religion in Voltaire and Rousseau undoubtedly troubled him, not only for its moral emphasis but also because of its easy acceptance of the unity of church and state. The coupling of rational Voltaire and romantic Rousseau was not unusual in England at this time, especially by the Joseph Johnson circle, probably because the theism and anti-fanaticism of Voltaire seemed mirrored in the profession of faith of the savoyard vicar in Rousseau's *Emile*. Indeed, there is much in this section of *Emile* that would have charmed Blake: the distrust of abstract ideas;[83] a belief in man's free will;[84] a distrust of reason as the sole guide to virtue;[85] a distrust of pure self-interest.[86] But Blake would have objected strenuously to Rousseau's emphasis on virtue and his tentative acceptance of eternal punishment: "O righteous and merciful Being! Whatever be thy decrees, I acknowledge their rectitude; if thou punishest the wicked, my weak reason is dumb before thy justice."[87] But Rousseau also believes in state religion. Though the savoyard vicar himself is a believer in natural religion, he carries out the duties of a priest with good will. In his description of natural religion, he finds the natural duty of man to worship God "in spirit and truth."[88] "With regard to exterior forms, if, for the sake of peace and good order, their uniformity be expedient, it is merely an affair of government."[89] The demand for uniformity rings an anxious note. Who demands uniformity? Whose order requires it? The answer to these questions is supplied in Rousseau's long footnote to the vicar's statement. He writes: "Modern governments are undoubtedly indebted to Christianity for their most solid authority, and the rarity of revolutions; it has even rendered them less sanguinary."[90] Blake could see in Rousseau's statement a willingness to accept the state's use of religion to consolidate power and authority. The Rousseau who changed his faith twice, according to geographic location, justifies the change in his *Confessions*: "it was the exclusive right of the sovereign power in every country to fix the mode of worship, and these unintelligible opinions; and that consequently it was the duty of a citizens to admit the one and conform to the other in the manner prescribed by the law."[91] Rousseau, the natural religionist, is thus quite willing to accept the alliance between church and state that forces man to adhere to an intellectual authority he may privately disavow. How close this is to the Test Act and established religion is obvious.

This slanted view of Rousseau has little resemblance to the real Rousseau who existed in rich human diversity, but it probably reflects the reasons for Blake's distrust. Blake was certainly aware of Rousseau's emphasis on virtue. In *Jerusalem*, chapter 3, he attacked Rousseau for his unforgiving nature as revealed in *The Confessions*. He points out that Rousseau did not find his cherished natural virtue and morality in his friends, by which Blake implies that morality is meaningless in friendship. Moreover, the notion that Rousseau would not forgive his friends for their failures is evidence for Blake that the doctrine of virtue leads not to brotherhood but to the isolation of the self-righteous. Rousseau certainly emphasized virtue. He felt that the virtue of man, the love of good and hatred of evil, is natural to man.[92] Man's conscience is his guide.[93] It is Rousseau's belief in virtue that ultimately leads him to accept the doctrine of rewards and punishments and all with which that doctrine is

associated. For Rousseau sees God as just,[94] and the unstated, though implied, inference that God does punish and
reward in the afterlife puts Rousseau in the camp of natural
religion. His belief in state religion, coupled with his acceptance of the doctrine of reward and punishment, therefore is
the probable reason that Blake associates him with the evils
of Tirzah.

Blake's view of Voltaire was undoubtedly much the
same. For Voltaire the basic principle of natural religion
was the morality common to the human race.[95] His statement of the belief of the theist in the *Philosophical Dictionary* is concise: "The theist is a man firmly convinced of the
existence of a supreme being as good as it is powerful,
which has created all the extended, vegetating, feeling, and
reflecting beings, which perpetuates their species, which
punishes crimes without cruelty and rewards virtuous action with kindness."[96] The stern god implied by Adam
Smith may not be present, but the doctrine of reward and
punishment remains constant. Voltaire disliked the violence and viciousness of fanatical Christianity, and his aversion to a cruel God is in line with that dislike. This same
aversion emerges in the *Philosophical Dictionary* in the
section on "Religion," question number eight.[97] Here Voltaire discriminates between a state and a theological religion, the state religion having priests (*imams,* he calls them),
churches (mosques), religious days, and established rites.
The priests have respect but no power. They teach morals
and are servants of the state. "A state religion can never
cause any turmoil." In his long war against the fanaticism
of the Catholic Church it is parodoxical that Voltaire was
willing to receive communion in his attempt to avoid the
retaliation of the Church. Thus both Rousseau and Voltaire,
reacting to conditions in France, can be seen as favoring an
alliance of church and state. Both also taught the doctrine
of morality and a system of rewards and punishments. It is
for this reason that Blake focuses on them as manifestations
of Rahab and Tirzah, the symbols of religious domination.

Though far different from Rousseau's and Voltaire's teachings, English orthodoxy shared the doctrine of future reward and punishment, and of established religion. William Paley, whose *Evidences of Christianity* (1794) became a "compulsory subject to all candidates for admission to Cambridge University,"[98] could presume in that work that the Creator intended "for these, his rational and accountable agents, a second state of existence, in which their situation will be regulated by their behaviour in the first state;"[99] in the second state they will receive "reward and punishment" according to their "comparative merit and demerit."[100] In his earlier *Moral and Political Philosophy* (1785), also "one of the lecture books for the students of the University of Cambridge,"[101] he summarizes his defense of the ecclesiastical establishment thus: "The knowledge and profession of Christianity cannot be upholden without a clergy: a clergy cannot be supported without a legal provision, a legal provision for the clergy cannot be constituted without the preference of one sect of Christians to the rest."[102] He does concede that any test for orthodoxy should be simple, and that the imposition of taxes to support the clergy should be done with "liberality and justice."[103] He would, of course, not proscribe toleration of dissenters—so long as they remained within the boundaries of political order. He would have: "a comprehensive national religion, guarded by a few articles of peace and conformity, together with a legal provision for the clergy of that religion; and with a *complete* toleration of all dissenters from the established church, without any other limitation or exception, than what arises from the conjunction of dangerous political dispositions with certain religious tenets."[104] Here then the Archdeacon Paley, whose orthodox tests fed the minds of Cambridge students at the end of the century, was in sympathy with Voltaire and Rousseau, who, as Blake saw them, were the latter-day saviors of state religion.

But the evil of state religion was not born with Paley in

England. Gibbon's ironic comment, "the various modes of worship which prevailed in the Roman world were all considered by the people as equally true; by the philosophers as equally false; and by the magistrates as equally useful,"[105] suggests an attitude that saw religion's only use in social control, an attitude reflected in the history of the Church of England. It had become a political tool. Bishops were appointed and sat in the House of Lords for political reasons.[106] Warburton could insist on the maintenance of the Test and Corporation Acts as "necessary safeguards for the welfare of the Established Church as the institution responsible for the religious and moral well-being of the national life."[107] (It was Warburton who also believed that man could not be moral without the doctrine of reward and punishment.)[108] Bishop Horsley had found it necessary to point out that clergymen were "more than mere hired servants of the State of laity."[109] Perhaps the alliance of church and state for many was a harmless assurance of national morality. But during the war with France another aspect of the alliance emerged: patriotic religion. In his *Reflections on the Revolution in France*, Burke could still grind away on the theme: "The majority of the people in England, far from thinking a national Establishment unlawful, hardly think it lawful to be without one."[110] This is the Burke who calls for war against France. Pitt, Blake's warmonger, had also stood against the abolition of the Test Act.[111] But the most enthusiastic of all war supporters was Bishop Watson, who called for increased taxes, more men, and more determination in the effort against an atheistic France: "Under whatever circumstances the war was begun, it is now become just . . . its continuance is now become necessary: for what necessity can be greater than that which arises from the enemy having threatened us with destruction as a nation."[112] Indeed, the English Church had become politically useful, and, when a bishop sounds so bloodthirsty, one begins to wonder about Rousseau's assertion that Christianity had rendered wars less sanguinary.

Thus it is the preaching of morality, the alliance of church and state (or state religion), and the backing of war that Blake sees in the cultural phenomena generated by the selfhood, with natural religion ready to take up the task when orthodoxy fails. He sees the power structure of the English establishment as a political means for control, with consequent exploitation, poverty, and the failure of true religion. The religious war against France is being waged with the blood of the enslaved, who cannot even afford bread.

4
Regeneration

I. DISCOVERY OF THE SELFHOOD

Escape from the selfhood, symbolized in several ways in *Milton*, results from a change of the mental balance of the mind. Escape occurs when man leaves the labyrinth of rational thinking for intuitive and imaginative realms of thought on the Daedalian wings of creativity. The rational thinking to be left behind is the sacrificial process of isolating mental concepts from their unconsciously generated, emotional, intuitive, and imaginative impulses. The wings of thought must be lifted by emotion to escape from rationality's labyrinthine ways. Its flight must be imaginative in that it must generate a view of life from within the mind, not solely from the reports of the senses,[1] and it must be intuitive insofar as it must allow the breathings from the unconscious, from the afflatus below any control, to direct the flight of consciousness. In this way the terrible wall between the sensation-oriented, survival-motivated parts of the mind and the outgoing altruistic impulses that focus only on others can be surmounted and the non-self-

142

centered part can begin to soar into the light. This flight will free the whole psyche, leaving behind the tyranny of the selfhood.

Such airy thinking is not fitted to the survival-motivated reality around us. It is imprudent, for instance, to rely on an imaginative concept of brotherhood of man to provide one's family with food. Yet, to become so prudent as to think *only* of providing one's family with food is to sink from some of the most valuable senses of belonging; indeed, paradoxically, it is almost to lose the necessary support of the herd altogether. But how does man regain this lost harmony of the psyche? Blake's answer, though never put in such twentieth-century terms, is very similar to what we call symbolic play. This concept is not one of sublimation of man's sexual urge, but one that sees the instinct to play as a necessary and innate part of human growth. Blake would think of this impulse as creativity. To balance the excess of narrowly focused prudence, one must create, and in creating bring to balance those seldom exercised, but ultimately essential, feelings of brotherhood that keep the mind healthy. Creativity knits together the fibers of consciousness and unconsciousness, of self and other, thus strengthening the whole psyche for any eventuality. Creativity tends to expand the borders of identity to include all of existence.

And in so expanding the realm of awareness, creativity opens the way to truth. The truth revealed by the creative play of the mind gives to the phenomena of existence a new perspective that includes the *total* reality of phenomena—a reality with subject and object knit together, with the natural an expression of the spiritual, with the temporal an expression of the timeless. Furthermore, when man drops the narrowness of isolated rationality, the resulting change in his mental activity will lead to changes in his behavior. As his non-self-centered urges begin to expand the domain of the self to include all, then the selfhood's rigid holds and its excessively prudent attitude toward others, that attitude which lies behind all government, law, and extremes of justice, will begin to relax. Anxiety about personal security or esteem (which is an extension of security) will be reduced, and the grip that represses and divides the whole man will be eased. The ultimate cause of anxiety, fear of death, will decrease, and, as a consequence, the fear of the causes of death, which included one's fellow man, will subside, allowing the prudent behavior patterns of morality to loosen their stern control. A freeing from internal anxiety will thus lead to a freeing of external rigidity. Moreover, when all men free themselves from the fear-induced control that the selfhood has over the other parts of the psyche, which are the instruments that the tyrant uses to control man in the aggregate, the tyrant is powerless. Thus the individual must concentrate on opening himself up to the promptings of the unconscious through creativity. For Blake these concepts, here presented in abstract terms, appear as symbolic statement and as poetic doctrine that carry the concepts without putting them in such doctrinaire formulation. He embodies these concepts in that symbolic language which itself is a result of the healthy creative play of the mind.[2]

A portion of this symbolic presentation deals with the removal of delusion, which, on the individual level, is the removal of the psychological barriers against creative thinking. It finds its doctrinal expression in Blake's holding up of faith, imagination, inspiration, and prophecy, and is given symbolic embodiment in images of removal of coverings, awakening, mental war, and creative art.

In Milton's peroration at the climax of the poem, wherein he describes the virtues he wishes to substitute for the evils of the selfhood, Milton mentions "Faith in the Saviour" (4.3) as the counterpoise to rational demonstration. The value of faith is also emphasized when Palamabron describes the work of Whitfield and Wesley as they strove against the delusions wrought by Tirzah and Rahab:

But then I rais'd up Whitefield, Palamabron raisd up
 Westley,
And these are the cries of the Churches before the two
 Witnesses'
Faith in God the dear Saviour who took on the likeness of
 men:
Becoming obedient to death, even the death of the Cross
The Witnesses lie dead in the Street of the Great City
No Faith is in all the Earth: the Book of God is trodden
 under Foot:
He sent his two Servants Whitefield & Westley: were they
 Prophets
Or were they Idiots or Madmen? shew us Miracles!
Can you have greater Miracles than these? Men who devote
Their lifes whole comfort to intire scorn & injury & death.
                        (22.55–23.2)

The cries of the churches, delayed in this passage until after
the picture of the two witnesses, Whitfield and Wesley, are
the faithless demands to be shown miracles, given toward
the end of the passage. Blake's inference is that Whitfield
and Wesley are themselves miracles because of their dedication. The churches' demand for miracles as justification
for faith ironically testifies that there is no faith in "all the
Earth."

The churches' cry for miracles reflects the controversy
over miracles in the eighteenth century.[3] Blake's antagonism to Gibbon and Hume arose in part because of
their attitudes toward miracles, which were similar to the
skeptical attitude dramatized in the church's rejection of
Whitfield and Wesley. Blake found in Gibbon's *Decline and
Fall of the Roman Empire* a picture of state religion in the
alliance between politics and religion as Christianity
emerged under Constantine. Though Blake might not have
quarreled with some parts of Gibbon's view, Gibbon's
ironic tone reveals an attitude very different from anything
Blake could have felt. Gibbon's explanation for Christiani-

ty's growth and eventual enfranchisement was given, not in tones of veneration, but in ironic language that accounted for Christianity's success on natural, rational principles. Miracles were not needed to account for its success. The growth of Christianity resulted from the most natural of motives, but, in Gibbon's phrasing, ones hardly noble. As Gibbon's explanations unfold, the connotations of venerable concepts gradually change, until the reader finds Jewish zeal becoming "inflexible perseverance."[4] Belief in immortality becomes a "doctrine . . . removed beyond the senses and the experience of mankind . . . to amuse the leisure of the philosophic mind."[5] Christian morality becomes an "indolent or even criminal disregard to the public welfare."[6] Christian unity becomes the "progress of ecclesiastical authority."[7] His most telling irony falls on the miracles ascribed to the early church. He speaks only of the ascription, or the claims, of miraculous events, never suggesting that the claims could be valid. With a grand sneer he writes of: "the occasional prodigies, which might sometime be effected by the immediate interposition of the Deity when he suspended the laws of Nature for the service of religion . . . ,"[8] a statement followed by an epic catalogue of miracles which, given in a lump, makes the concept of miracles seem preposterous. One cannot escape Gibbon's skeptical attitude when he then explains how belief in miracles continued into modern times: "Credulity performed the office of faith, fanaticism was permitted to assume the language of inspiration, and the effects of accident or contrivance were ascribed to supernatural powers."[9] And Gibbon's rationalist sneer was matched by Hume's deadly logic. In his *Essay on Miracles* Hume observed that the intellectual finds the proof of God in order and design, but the vulgar and ignorant in departure from order and design.[10] Hume's philosophical and Gibbon's historical skepticism represent the doubt that Blake found easily answered in the exemplars Whitfield and Wesley.

But Palamabron's reference to Whitfield and Wesley also constitutes an allusion to Revelation, which ties Blake's concept of faith to that of prophecy.[11] In Revelation 11, God raises two witnesses during the 1,260-day reign of the Gentiles who tread the holy city under foot. The two witnesses "shall prophesy" (Rev. 11:3), presumably to keep the faith during a time of tyranny. Eventually they will be killed by the "Beast . . . and their bodies shall lie in the street of the great city" (Rev. 11:8). Blake's allusion marks Whitfield and Wesley as prophets during a time of spiritual corruption. They have been raised by Rintrah and Palamabron, who were themselves the "Two Witnesses" that rose during the corruption of the great beast Satan (9.8). Thus Blake implies that as the beast appears throughout history, so will appear a witness against the beast. There will always be that prophetic spirit of faith which will challenge tyranny.[12]

The prophetic spirit, latent in every man, requires the working of the imagination. For Blake the imagination is the permanent identity of each individual that is never to be destroyed. He insists that "the Imagination is not a State: it is the Human Existence itself" (32.32). It is the creative, inspired focus of consciousness on a reality greater than the mere natural world, and its business is the conceptualization of form. The "Human Imaginations [are] Worlds of Eternity in which we shall live forever" (I. Preface). The connection between the individual's imagination and creativity is suggested in the connection between the Divine-Human Imagination and the "sports of Wisdom" and "Divine Vision" that inhere in the Imagination (3.2–3). These sports consist of the eternal work of creation of form, "To build the Universe stupendous: Mental forms Creating" (30.20). When this function is perverted, then the individual dwells in Ulro, a "nether region of the Imagination" (21.6). The generative function of the creative imagination is suggested further in the concept of the "Poetic Genius/

Who is the eternal all-protecting Divine Humanity" (14.1–2). The poetic genius is the prophetic spirit, but here Blake is following the lead of Paine, who writes:

> In the former part of "The Age of Reason," I have said that the word prophet was the Bible word for poet, and that the flights and metaphors of Jewish poets have been foolishly erected into what are now called prophecies. I am sufficiently justified in this opinion, not only because the books called prophecies are written in poetical-language, but because there is no word in the Bible, except it be the word prophet, that describes what we mean by a poet.[13]

Although Blake dropped Paine's derogatory tone, his notion of poetry as prophecy is the same as Paine's. To Blake, moreover, poetry and prophecy are a divine manifestation, for the divine humanity is the creative imagination. Furthermore, the imagination's sensitivity to unconscious dictates provides what Blake called inspiration. Divinity inspires the man from within, that is, from the unconscious. The bard sings his song "According to the inspiration of the Poetic Genius" (14.1). Memory, which is a consciousness of past temporal events, is opposed to inspiration, which, by contrast, is an expression from the unconscious. This concept appears in Milton's finding himself with the daughter of memory and not with the daughter of inspiration (14.29). And in his peroration Milton asserts that he had come "To cast off the rotten rags of Memory by Inspiration" (41.4).

Inspiration produces in the individual the creativity that is prophecy, which lifts man's vision above the staleness and rigidity of the mental constructs produced by excessive rationality and, through the creative play of the mind, leads man to new truth. This new truth reveals phenomena from an eternal, infinite, universal view rather than from a temporal, limited, self-centered one.[14] It is the seeing of truth that is the function of prophecy. Prophecy must see into the present, the true nature of things now. And the switch from rationality to prophetic vision is dramatized by the visions of Jesus at the beginning and end of the poem. Covered with the mists of rationality, the true nature of Jesus can be only dimly discerned: "The Lamb of God is seen thro "mists & Shadows" (14.25) at the beginning of Milton's journey; but through prophetic vision at the end of the journey, one sees "One Man Jesus the Saviour, wonderful!" (42.11). The seeing function of prophecy also appears in other ways. The prophetic act of revealing eternal truth is the goal of many events in the poem. Palamabron calls the assembly to reveal the truth (8.46), and Milton has come to reveal self-righteousness for what it really is (38.43). The ending of the poem is a series of revelations of the true nature of the selfhood. The covering cherub, Satan, and Rahab are distinguished from Milton (37.6–12). The evils of Milton's shadow, the twelve Gods and twenty-seven churches (37.20–38.4), appear from out of the shadows of rationality. The corrupted seven angels of Satan are distinguished from their eternal identities as the starry seven appear in opposition to the appearance of Satan's retinue (38.55–39.4). The connection between the teachers of natural religion and Rahab-Babylon appears as Ololon discovers the delusive work of her feminine portion (40.9–16; 41.30). Thus revelation of the eternal nature of things is the work of the prophetic imagination. And such a revelation is also a view into the individual's unconscious, for there lies the eternity of impulse, energy, and desire, ever struggling for expression. The rational faculty, which ignores the unconscious, ignores a truth sayer in the largest sense. Reason's spectrum is narrow compared to the full rainbow of impulse and image from the unconscious. The truth does not necessarily appear in the white neon lights of reason.

Nor is the revelation of eternal truth merely the vision of an individual for his own spiritual insight. The individual identity and the divine identity are, after all, the same, and as the individual imagination bodies forth the truth from within, it is embodying a truth from the same deity that is the essence of all others. Consequently, the prophetic truth can be of use to others in their own struggles against the selfhood. Prophecy is for the eternal salvation of all. The words "Mark well my words! they are of your eternal salvation" (7.16; 7.48) are spoken by the bard, of course, intending to emphasize the importance of his prophetic truth to Milton, who is moved to action by the words (21.33–34). But the words also reach from the page to the reader, letting him know that the bard William Blake feels that his prophetic message is not merely a fiction in a narrative but a statement of profound importance. The revelation of the poetic or prophetic truth is the prelude to real, human action.

There are also hints in the poem that mental creativity demands physical creativity. Los's function in forming the instruments of harvest (6.8–13) is to embody the spirits, allowing them to put off the indefinite. Los wishes to give Urizen a "Definite form" (3.9). His sons labor at "putting off the Indefinite" (28.4). This putting off the indefinite is part of the formation of thought, and it requires activity as well as vision. Los's workshop is a symbol suggesting that the artist, the artisan, the workman must produce form. The act of mental creation must take physical manifestation in a poem, a picture, a ploughshare, or a plowed field. And creativity requires industry. It is the industrious who find the moment that is uncontrolled by Satan's watch fiends, turning that moment into eternal creation:

> the Industrious find
> This Moment & it multiply & when it once is found
> It renovates every Moment of the Day if rightly placed.
> (35.43–45)

Industrious creativity renovates both the interior of a man and the exterior world. The central symbol of exterior creation appears in Milton's struggle with Urizen. As Urizen attempts to corrupt him,

Milton took of the red clay of Succoth, moulding it with
  care
Between his palms; and filling up the furrows of many years
Beginning at the feet of Urizen, and on the bones
Creating new flesh on the Demon cold, and building him,
As with new clay a Human form. . . .
                (19.10–14)

Milton, like Los, is giving definite form, and indeed a
human form, to Urizen, through the symbolically creative
act of molding with clay. This single act continues throughout the journey of Milton until the final moment when Ololon sees Milton striving with Urizen "In Self annihilation
giving thy life to thy enemies" (40.8). This act of putting off
the indefinite is one method of self-annihilation; it is also a
creative act that represents the definite embodiment of
thought.

To see the truth is not the duty of an isolated prophet. It
belongs to each man. Blake makes this clear in the poem's
epigraph: "Would to God that all the Lords people were
Prophets" (I. Preface). This allusion to Numbers 11:29 has
been shown to refer to the problem of hunger in Blake's
day, but it also refers to the duty of prophecy. Moses'
words, spoken of the elders who went to the people to
prophesy, are followed by Moses' bidding the other elders
from the tabernacle to join the people. Moses' injunction
symbolically enjoins the duty of prophecy on all men. In his
annotations to Watson, Blake might have written: "Every
honest man . . . [can be] a Prophet [if] he utters his opinions both of private & public matters."[15]

The great antagonist to Blake's notion of inspired,
prophetic imagination was John Locke. Blake's bard's radical statement, "I am inspired I know it is Truth" (13.51), is
more than a departure from the empirical tradition. It flies
in the face of all that Locke and his followers held. To see
how Blake becomes Locke's contrary, we must examine
briefly Locke's theory of knowledge. Locke had made sen-

sation the exclusive inlet of knowledge. For him all ideas in the mind originate in sensation and are stored in the memory. Ideas are built up from simple to complex, by such mental operations as comparison, composition, naming, and asbstraction.[16] There are three degrees of knowledge that this process may develop: intuitive, demonstrative, and sensitive. Sensitive knowledge is essentially a conviction that an object exterior to the perceiving mind exists. Demonstrative knowledge proceeds by reasoning to discover the agreement or disagreement of ideas. But intuitive knowledge is the basis of the demonstrative process because it consists of an immediate perception of the agreement or disagreement of two ideas. "This part of knowledge is irresistible, and like bright sun-shine forces itself immediately to be perceived."[17] Locke's intuition thus is a matter of immediate perception that conveys conviction, but the materials of perception are always the ideas that are ultimately derived from sensation. Knowledge is limited to perception and can never reach the full extent of perceptions that are always based on sensation.[18] Yet Locke feels that man is intuitively certain of God's existence, though man has no innate ideas of perceptions of God, because "it is an evident demonstration, that from eternity there has been something."[19] In other words, Locke relies on the ontological argument for the existence of God. His proof is demonstrative. Though Blake would not deny Locke's conclusion, he would certainly reject the rational method of argument.[20]

Locke, however, goes somewhat further. Reason is "the faculty which finds out the means and rightly applies them to discover certainty."[21] Reason is the connection and the form of the intuitive discernment. Moreover, it is the implicit judge of faith, which is "nothing but a firm assent of the mind: which, if it be regulated, as is our duty, cannot be afforded to anything but upon good reason; and so cannot be opposite to it."[22] Revelation itself cannot communicate to man, except through ideas, which are based on sensation. Revelation is "natural reason enlarged."[23] Though

Locke admits of revelation, he does not approve of enthusiasm. Enthusiasm is the mistaken impulse that tells a man his "groundless opinion," settled in his fancy, "is an illumination from the spirit of God."[24] The "strength of persuasion" of its truth is no proof.[25] Enthusiasm is a flight from that truth which can be found only by reason. Revelation itself must be judged by reason, the final arbiter.[26]

Blake reverses Locke's whole process. The perception of truth, that is, the agreement or disagreement of ideas, which for Locke is intuition, is for Blake dependent on spiritual vision, untrammeled by sensation or reason. The enthusiast's firm persuasion of truth for Blake has the accuracy that Locke attributes to intuition. In *Milton* the Bard's justification of the truth of his story "I am Inspired! I know it is Truth" (13.51) is then a contradiction of Locke's reason. In *The Marriage of Heaven and Hell* Blake had made Ezekiel speak against Locke's distrust of enthusiasm by Ezekiel's confirmation of the "firm persuasion [that] removed mountains"[27] as justification for his prophetic writings. In his annotations to Reynold's *Works*, Blake had written "Meer Enthusiasm is the All in All."[28] For Blake, Lockean rationalistic demonstration is opposed to self-evident truth. He writes: "Self-Evident Truth is one Thing and Truth the result of Reasoning is another thing. Rational Truth is not the Truth of Christ but Pilate."[29] Self-evident truth, the truth of "Inspiration, needs no one to prove it; it is evident as the Sun & Moon."[30] Blake's inspired Bard, summing up Blake's long-standing attitude, is defying the reasoning of Locke in favor of the enthusiasm that Blake called inspiration. At the end of *Milton* Blake replaces rational demonstration and memory with faith, inspiration, and imagination. In doing so he has replaced John Locke with John of Patmos. Blake's connection of imagination with the faculty of spiritual vision is implicitly a mockery of Locke's making the fancy the place of the enthusiast's misguided impulse.

But one asks if Blake's connection between imagination and prophetic inspiration is original. Morton Paley has

given a brief summary of several conceptions of the imagination that seem relevant to Blake's concept, though in
most cases he finds the conception only somewhat analogous. He does find in Thomas Taylor's *Restoration of the
Platonic Philosophy* a notion similar to Blake's idea that the
imagination is the essence of human existence.[31] Paley also
finds Blake's "characterization of the world as 'One continual Vision of Fancy or Imagination' " as part of the "development of the [eighteenth-century] sublime tradition towards an idea of a symbol-making constructive imagination."[32] For the connection between imagination and
prophecy, he finds only Plato's *Timaeus*, the prophets of
the Old Testament, Pico, and Hartley, but in no case does
he find a similarity that puts Blake in line completely with
any of them. But the connection of prophetic inspiration
and imagination for Blake really does not need a source to
explain it. It follows logically from Blake's equation of man
with God and identity with imagination.[33] The imagination
is the human existence itself. It is not slave to the exterior
world of sensation, and, in fact, is necessary for the perception that, from an empiricist's view, is merely sensation.
Thus the world about man is vision. Moreover, the individual is really a part of collective humanity, which is God;
and since the individual's essence is his imagination, the
collective imagination is God. Therefore, the individual
imagination has the sanction of divine inspiration, for the
source of its vision is ultimately divine.

One is tempted to see Blake's insistence on the truth of
imaginative vision as similar to Berkeley's *esse est percepi*,[34] but there are important differences. For Berkeley all
existence is an idea in the mind. God's mind thinks the
cosmos. Man, God's idea, but still a spirit as distinct from a
passive idea, perceives the ideas of God. Matter, as a third
thing, a mechanically contrived set of atoms, working without being perceived, does not exist. Indeed, this seems like
Blake's notion of spiritual vision. For what man can conceive is, for Blake, truth. However, Berkeley, insisting on a
difference between ideas produced by the imagination and

ideas produced by sensation, feels that reality lies with the idea of sensation. "There is a mind which affects me every moment with all the sensible impressions I perceive."[35] The imagination can be distinguished from sensation because "these creatures of the fancy are not altogether so distinct, so strong, vivid, and permanent, as those perceived by my senses." Imagination forms images that are faint, indistinct, and dependent on the will.[36] Thus Berkeley makes the distinction between sensation and imagination an intuitive one, dependent on the relative difference in the qualities of distinctness, strength, vivacity, and permanence of the idea. Herein is the essential difference between Blake and Berkeley. Blake claims that the imagination makes the stronger impression on our intuitive judgment. Berkeley's assumption, that the ideas perceived are real, limits perception essentially to the combinations of ideas that God has created. Blake would break those barriers and find in the imaginative vision the same reality that Berkeley finds in "sensible impressions." Blake seems indeed to be unique in his view.[37]

There are several symbols in *Milton* for the prophetic creativity that reveals truth. Many of these symbols are contraries to the forces of the selfhood; for instance, removal of delusion is symbolized by images of removal of false coverings, images that are the contrary of the covering cherub. Images of removal of coverings throughout the poem culminate at the end with the removal of the last vestiges of the selfhood. This imagery is parodied when Satan, imitating God, promises to remove from his covering all who disobey his laws:

There is no other! let all obey my principles of moral individuality
I have brought them from the uppermost innermost recesses
Of my Eternal Mind, transgressors I will rend off for ever,
As now I rend this accursed Family from my covering.
(9.26–29)

The act of removal is performed without parody by Los when he removes his left sandal (8.12), and thereby refuses to enforce rigid justice between Palamabron and Satan.[38] The next image of removal occurs when Milton "took off the robe of the promise & ungirded himself from the oath of God" (14.13). Milton here removes the promise of worldly dominion, in the promise given to Abraham that Israel would possess the land of Canaan (to be discussed later). Further on, when the Shadowy Female announces her intention to clothe herself in the delusory clothing inappropriate for the female, Orc, in his rage against this false covering,

Burns to the top of heaven against thee in Jealousy & Fear.
Then I rend thee asunder, then I howl over thy clay & ashes
When wilt thou put on the Female Form as in times of old
With a Garment of Pity & Compassion like the Garment of
    God?
                    (18.32–35)

The image of removal again occurs when the insects around the winepress "throw off their gorgeous raiment: they rejoice with loud jubilee" (27.23). I conjecture that the insects symbolize, among other possibilities, the thinkers and writers who, in their delusion, have shrunk to become "armies of disease" (27.17), that is, the disease of rationality. But infused with the wine of prophetic truth, they are able to remove their gorgeous, but delusory covering. The final, stupendous act of removal is a culmination of these images. The appearance in their true identity of Satan, Rahab, Ololon, and Milton at the end of the poem is the prelude to the removal of the false coverings. After Milton's shadow, which contains the evil of Satan, appears, Milton "collecting all his fibres into impregnable strength/ Descended down . . . " (38.5–6). Here Milton has removed the ultimate covering of the selfhood, Satan. Furthermore, the virgin Ololon also has a false covering removed. Once Rahab-Babylon has appeared;

the Virgin divided Six-fold & with a shreek
Dolorous that ran thro all Creation a Double Six-fold Wonder!
Away from Ololon she divided.
(42.3–5)

This is the symbolic act of removal of covering that Milton
explains so eloquently in his long peroration. He will "cast
off," "take off," or "cast aside" the clothing of the corrupted selfhood (41.3–20). The removal of the false covering is thus a symbolic statement representing the removal of
some aspect of the selfhood (hood of the self), principally
that of delusion.[39] As such it is an act of revelation of the
true, eternal nature of man, a revelation coming from
imaginative vision, faith, and inspiration, as Milton himself
points out.

Another group of images suggesting victory over delusion is that of awakenings. The images of sleeping, couches
of various sorts, and awakening form a symbolic picture of
delusion and its removal. In Blake's mythic cosmos, sleep
can represent either a state of rest from the mental struggle
in eternity or a delusory state in time. This distinction is
suggested when Satan is said to have transformed sleep into
death (29.32–3), that is, Satan deludes man into believing
that life here (that is, sleep in eternity) is without any possibility of spiritual existence (that is, death). There is the
golden couch of eternity where Milton's humanity resides
throughout the first part of his journey (15.13). But this
same couch can be the couch of death (15.10) if the sleeper
becomes appropriated to Satan's realm. The couches then
become "sepulchres" (14.21), "Deaths vales" (17.6),
or the "graves of the dead" (14.34), where Milton,
the "awakener" (21.33), goes to bring his message
that will remove the delusion. The sleepers in the
aggregate are called Albion, who reclines on the rock
of eternity (15.38). He is "embalmed, never to awake"
(19.57), according to the lying Tirzah. But Los knows

that Albion will arise from sleep (23.54), and calls for
him to do so (23.3). Albion is called to awake again
by the seven eyes of God when Milton arrives at the end of
his journey (39.10):

Then Albion rose up in the Night of Beulah on his Couch
Of dread repose seen by the visionary eye; his face is to-
    ward
The east, toward Jerusalems Gates: groaning he sat above
His rocks, London & Bath & Legions & Edinburgh
Are the four pillars of his Throne; his left foot near London
Covers the shades of Tyburn: his instep from Windsor
Of Primrose Hill stretching to Highgate & Holloway
London is between his knees: its basements fourfold
His right foot stretches to the sea on Dover cliffs, his heel
On Canterburys ruins; his right hand covers lofty Wales
His left Scotland; his bosom girt with gold involves
York, Edinburgh, Durham & Carlisle & on the front
Bath, Oxford, Cambridge Norwich; his right elbow
Leans on the Rocks of Erins Land, Ireland ancient nation.
His head bends over London: he sees his embodied Spectre
Trembling before him with exceeding great trembling &
    fear
He views Jerusalem & Babylon, his tears flow down
He movd his right foot to Cornwall, his left to the Rocks of
    Bognor
He strove to rise to walk into the Deep, but strength failing
Forbad & down with dreadful groans he sunk upon his
    Couch
In moony Beulah. Los his strong Guard walks round be-
    neath the Moon.
                            (39.32–52)

Here Albion is a giant flat on his back atop the British isles,
then a rising man sitting up on the isles and supporting his
giant form by placing his limbs in the various geographical
locations, next rising and facing west, and finally relapsing
upon his "couch" of eternal rest where he is yet in a state
of delusion. The picture symbolizes the attempts of the
British nation collectively to arise from the delusion of the

selfhood. It is tragically unsuccessful. The successful awakening seems delayed for some reason, but indeed that reason is not hard to find. The reader, who must mark well Blake's words, is part of that as yet unawakened giant and his own awakening is necessary for the completion of Milton's task. The incompleteness of this action suggests that there is yet more to be done. Indeed, the poem ends on a note of expectancy, not completion. It is not a history. It is a prophecy that enjoins the reader and all men to awaken. Albion cannot rise completely until all delusion, the reader's included, is removed. The potential for personal awakening is the essence of the meaning. Even though all Britons do not rise, the individual may. Albion, Urizen, and the Zoas may remain in their sleep (34.43–46), but the reader can awaken to his own vision of eternity, and, by so doing, aid Albion.

Another symbol related to the removal of delusion is mental war, the contrary of the physical war waged by the world-rulers of the selfhood. The distinction between mental and corporeal war is announced in the ringing call of the Preface, to "Rouze up O Young Men of the New Age! set your foreheads against the ignorant Hirelings! For we have Hirelings in the Camp, the Court & the University: who would if they could, for ever depress Mental & prolong Corporeal War" (I. Preface). In the ensuing song, the bow, arrow, spear, chariot, and sword are instruments of mental warfare. In *Jerusalem* a similar section describing the instruments of mental warfare shows the bow to represent sexual distinction and mercy, the arrows to represent love, and the wars mutual benevolence (*Jerusalem*, 97.12–14). In *Milton* the same kind of symbolism, but of slightly different meaning, seems to emerge. The symbolic meaning of writing perhaps adds to the love imagery, making the spear a pen, the chariot a paper, and the sword possibly a burin. The astute reader will find other possible meanings. But the distinction between kinds of war is insisted on: "I will not cease from mental fight" (1.13).[40]

The distinction is called upon in the description of Beulah, where it is said that creativity takes place in "the great Wars of Eternity" (30.19). And it is made explicit in the passage concerning the lamentation of the living creatures of the four elements, since element against element is "opposed in War/ Not Mental, as the Wars of Eternity, but a corporeal strife" (31.24–25). Ololon discovers the difference when she looks into Ulro and sees how the wars of eternity, which appear "in the Eternal Spheres of Visionary Life" (34.51), are corrupted in the lower realm. The visionary war—the mental war, the war of eternity—is one of the creative imagination to clear away the delusion that turns the individual's energy to "War the Wars of Death" (41.36).

The opposition of corporeal and mental warfare suggests a way of looking at the imagery of wine and blood. Wine and blood in the symbolism of the poem represent the same thing, but the individual's point of view determines how he will perceive each. Blake suggests this identification when he says: "The Wine-press is call'd War on Earth, it is the Printing Press/ Of Los" (27.8–9). The blood of war and the wine of the press are the same thing, but the destroyer sees blood, while the mental warrior sees the wine of prophecy. It is the "wine of wildest power" (12.43), making one "Wild with prophetic fury" (12.45) that ironically reverses its effects on Satan.

The winepress has different significance for different points of view.[41] The war seen here can be corporeal strife, but Blake insists on its connection with the printing press to illustrate its potential for higher meaning. The press is the conveyor of Los's spiritual wisdom. He "lays his words in order above the mortal brain" (27.9). Moreover, in suggesting that the struggle of mental war can be a creative, productive struggle that produces the wine of prophecy, not the blood of destruction, Blake connects the imagery of harvest with the positive aspect of mental warfare.

The harvest can be one of joy: "O when shall we tread

our Wine-presses in heaven; and Reap/ Our wheat with shoutings of joy, and leave the Earth in peace" (23.45–46). Los enjoins the reapers to go forth "with rejoicing" (25.44) because it is a "glorious spiritual/ Vegetation" (25.60–61). The poem ends with the human harvest imminent, and the note of wrath introduced at that point is the wrath against the oppression that has produced poverty (42.34–43.1). The wrath of the winepress is wrath only to those enthralled by the power dynamics of the selfhood.

> The Wine-press on the Rhine groans loud, but all its central beams
> Act more terrific in the central Cities of the Nations
> Where Human Thought is crushd beneath the iron hand of Power.
> (25.3–5)

The destruction of thought by power in the exterior world is really the attempted repression of human thought by those like Pitt who attempted to control the press. But it is to no avail, for thought cannot be crushed, and oppressor and oppressed, both of whom are tossed in the winepress (25.6–7), receive their own kind of harvest. The oppressed are merely victims of worldly power, the oppressors of their own selfhoods. Blake's play on the meaning of press here suggests how each individual views the press as he himself is fitted to view it. It can be oppression, corporeal war, or mental war, just as blood and wine are the same thing seen from different points of view. Blake has altered the connotation of the imagery of harvest and wine press, taken from Revelation 14, where John of Patmos envisions the wine as the harvested wrath of God:

> And another angel came out of the temple, crying with a loud voice to him that sat on the cloud, Thrust in thy sickle, and reap; for the time is come for thee to reap; for the harvest of the earth is ripe.
> And he that sat on the cloud thrust in his sickle on the earth; and the earth was reaped.

And another angel came out of the temple which is in
heaven, he also having a sharp sickle.
And another angel came out from the altar, which had
power over fire; and cried with a loud cry to him that
had the sharp sickle, saying, Thrust in thy sharp sickle,
and gather the clusters of the vine of the earth; for her
grapes are fully ripe
And the angel thrust in his sickle into the earth,
and gathered the vine of the earth, and cast it into
the great winepress of the wrath of God
And the winepress was trodden without the city, and
blood came out of the winepress, even unto the horse
bridles, by the space of a thousand and six hundred
furlongs. (Rev. 14:15–20)

Here the harvest seems a punishment for those who have
the mark of the beast (Rev. 14:9–10), who are said to have
drunk of the wine of God's wrath. Those who are harvested
are thrown into the winepress, which exudes blood, but
Blake has dropped the notion of punishment in his adaptation of the image.

The wine-blood-printing press symbol is embroidered
upon even further in an obscure passage that places the
press "before the Seat of Satan" (27.1–2). This location
suggests that it is on the outer reaches of the mythic landscape where the struggle with Satan occurs. It is surrounded by the sons and daughters of Luvah, who laugh
and shout "drunk with odours" (27.4), or who are "drownd
in the wine" (27.5). These are the children of love, who are
filled with the prophetic vision. Distinct from these are the
low and creeping animals and insects surrounding the
winepress, who cast off their garments in a symbolic act of
removing delusion. This occurs when they are "Drunk with
wine" (27.24). They become thus capable of seeing truth.
The oppressive aspect of the press is shown in the human
grapes. There the instruments of torture produce a suffering
that surprisingly is identified with "the sports of love & the
sweet delights of amorous play/ Tears of the grape, the

death sweat of the cluster" (27.39–40). Sexuality, introduced here somewhat discordantly with the theme of mental warfare, seems to be its own punishing oppression. One can only conclude that sexuality for its own sake, or for the selfhood's pleasure, is an oppression. The song of Luvah is the sexual impulse in man, and it can be as selfish and oppressive as any other form of tyranny, for "Affection or Love becomes a State, when divided from Imagination" (32.33). The winepress is then a symbol of struggle, which, inevitable for all individuals, is potentially a spiritual harvest, but can be experienced as sexual turmoil or oppression. That the slaves at Satan's Mill can rejoice in Palamabron's spiritual wine indicates that the freedom from selfhood can come from the attitude toward mental war. But the individual's duty is not to cease from mental fight until Jerusalem has been built in one's native land (1.15).

The image of building Jerusalem (who in the cosmic myth of Albion is Albion's emanation, or the exterior world of freedom for all men to love and to create) suggests one further anti-delusory symbol in the poem, the building of Golgonooza. Golgonooza is the interior mental vision that results from the creativity of the individual encased temporarily in the physical body. It is both a place of creation to which the individual journeys, and the mental creation itself of the individual. Golgonooza is characterized as a spiritual place, or, in other words, a place of mental activity. It is the "spiritual fourfold London, in the loins of Albion" (20.40), which exists behind "Satan's Seat" (20.39). It can be entered through different gates of the body. Satan's seat is the exterior physical world in this instance, from which the individual travels into his own interior world, for "Golgonooza cannot be seen till having passed the Polypus" (35.22); here the polypus represents the bodily nerves of sensation that are *not* connected to true vision. Golgonooza is built by Los and his children (3.39), as a place to form the instruments of harvest. This purposeful act symbolically stands for the creation of mental forms.

Golgonooza's exterior manifestation is seen as art and manufacture (24.50) because it is a place of exterior productivity that comes from creativity. Golgonooza is also the place of salvation from Satan's rules, for Los directs the spirits to be vegetated into Golgonooza (29.48). Its "mighty Spires & Domes of ivory & gold" (35.25), the mental creations of the interior mind, constitute true vision, opposed to the exterior world of sensation that is Satan's seat (17.29). It is that vision which is the beginning of removal of the selfhood's delusion. It is the beginning of regeneration.

Golgonooza, the winepress, mental war, the removal of covering, and awakening all symbolize an aspect of that anti-delusory activity of the mind which leads the individual away from the selfhood's tyranny to the acts of spiritual salvation. Golgonooza is the created vision. The winepress is the activity in which potential for vision exists. Mental warfare is the focusing of that activity in its struggle against delusion. The removal of covering is the actual removal of delusion, and awakening is the opening of the interior mind to the vision that is Golgonooza. This mental activity completed then leads to a release from selfhood's control, which release is symbolized in still further ways.

II. RELEASE FROM THE SELFHOOD

At the risk of being repetitious I shall review the psychic mechanisms of the selfhood to see how release from its tools comes about; release from the selfhood's interior controls can be seen as freedom from the oppressive bondage of the self-centered urges of the individual. The selfhood's guiding strings are all the rules, morals, and roles acquired from parents and teachers, that direct the activity of the individual. Its controlling power, however, resides not in the individual's wish to obey its moral rules, but in the individual's anxiety about the consequences of disobedience of those rules. That anxiety may be stated in several forms—fear of loss of security or loss of personal esteem—but the ultimate cause of that fear, and the thing that the fear wishes to avoid at any cost, is death. Indeed, the development of personality is ultimately rooted in the individual's desire for survival, and the selfhood's ropes are guidelines, the breaking of which may lead to failure in the struggle for survival.

Frequently the controlling wires of the selfhood cut off feelings that are not related directly to survival, such as altruistic sympathy, self-sacrifice, or love, a feeling that in its desire for another leads the individual to forget self-interest. This extreme separation manifests itself in a tightening of control over both the inner urges and the threatening exterior world. But in becoming so rigid, the individual becomes a shrunken organism, a constricted, mean, fear-driven creature whose empty life is not really worth its sustenance. When this occurs, man must be released from the rigid rules of the selfhood, lest his life become merely a nightmarish life-in-death. He must be released from the oppressive anxiety that denies all selfless activity. To accomplish this the controls of the inner and outer world must be slackened. One method of slackening is to alter the individual's conception of morality, and it is here that Blake substitutes more lenient doctrines than the rigid teachings of the selfhood. Blake substitutes rules of mercy for justice, rules that release the individual from fear of punishment and ultimately of death. He inculcates doctrines that remove guilt, the inducer of anxiety, thereby loosening the selfhood's inner and outer controls.

Blake counters the rules of retribution and guilt with the doctrine of classes and the doctrine of states, which teach mercy, and brotherhood.[42] He further represents these conceptions in his symbols of the great consummation, freedom or loosening of bonds, willing unity, the journey, and, strangely, the subordination of the female.

Blake's doctrine of states, like the symbol of the polypus, works both on the cosmic and on the individual level, and its purpose is to provide a theory of existence that releases man from the necessity of retribution, thereby releasing him from the anxiety-produced controls of the selfhood. The doctrine appears fully articulated by Hillel, who is Lucifer, one of the seven eyes of God, as he converses with the aspect of Milton that remains in eternity. Hillel instructs Milton about the fate of the seven eyes and how they became druidic, and in so instructing, articulates the doctrine:

We are not Individuals but States: Combinations of
    Individuals   (10)
We were Angels of the Divine Presence: & were Druids in
    Annandale
Compelld to combine into Form by Satan, the Spectre of
    Albion,
Who made himself a God &, destroyed the Human Form
    Divine.
But the Divine Humanity & Mercy gave us a Human Form
Because we were combined in Freedom & holy
    Brotherhood   (15)
While those combind by Satans Tyranny first in the blood
    of War
And Sacrifice &, next, in Chains of imprisonment: are
    Shapeless Rocks
Retaining only Satans Mathematic Holiness, Length:
    Bredth & Highth
Calling the Human Imagination: which is the Divine Vision
    & Fruition
In which Man liveth eternally: madness & blasphemy,
    against   (20)
Its own Qualities, which are Servants of Humanity, not
    Gods or Lords.
Distinguish therefore States from Individuals in those
    States.
States Change: but Individual Identities never change nor
    cease:
You cannot go to Eternal Death in that which can never
    Die.
Satan & Adam are States Created into Twenty-seven
    Churches   (25)
And thou O Milton art a State about to be Created

Called Eternal Annihilation that none but the Living shall
Dare to enter: & they shall enter triumphant over Death
And Hell & the Grave: States that are not, but ah! Seem to
  be.
Judge then of thy Own Self: thy Eternal Lineaments
  explore   (30)
What is Eternal & what Changeable? & what Annihilable!
The Imagination is not a State: it is the Human Existence
itself
Affection or Love becomes a State, when divided from
Imagination
The Memory is a State always, & the Reason is a State
Created to be Annihilated & a new Ratio Created   (35)
Whatever can be Created can be Annihilated Forms cannot
The Oak is cut down by the Ax, the Lamb falls by the Knife
But their Forms Eternal Exist, For-ever. Amen Halle
[1]ujah.

(32.10–38)

States are defined as exterior combinations of individuals
(10) which contain, but are not the eternal essence of individuals (22–23). They are created conditions symbolized by
the various mythic characters, for example, Satan and
Adam, or the angels of the Divine presence (11, 25). But
they are further defined as parts of the internal psychological makeup of an individual; for example, love divided from
imagination, memory, or reason are states (33–34).[43] The
two definitions of states, as aggregations of individuals and
as divided parts of an individual, seem confusing at first.
But, if seen properly, a state is understood as an individual
mental condition caused by a propensity in the personality,
which condition is held in common with other individuals
and can therefore be said to characterize a whole group of
individuals. As groups they are mental conditions of collective humanity, or Albion. A segment of men, the deists for
instance, has the same effect on collective humanity in general that excessive rationality has on the individual, deism

being a product of excessive rationality. The common de-
nominator of rationality joins the individual to the aggregate.

Blake complicates the doctrine of states by adding the
term *form* (12) to represent *state* (10). And in one sense
form and state are different aspects of the same process.
Each individual has an eternal essence (called the imagination or the human form) and various subordinate parts
(reason, love, or sexual form). That human essence in
psychological terms is the imagination, which is indestruc-
tible (32). Love, reason, and memory are parts of the personality, not the essence, and when divided from the essence become mental attitudes of varying degrees of
moribundity. In cosmic terms the human essence in eternity is the human *form,* but when the individual is in the
temporal world, he takes a lesser, impermanent form, like
female or male. This is the sexual existence, which is not its
essential identity. The word *form* is used frequently in *Milton,* but it usually appears as human form, meaning eternal
essence (for example, 18.19; 18.31; 19.14; 24.37) or female
form, meaning a nonessential part (for example, 18.28;
18.34; 36.15). It is the inner form of the generated body
(26.31), the material shape given by Antamon (28.17), or
other aspects of bodily shape (for example, 3.2; 3.36; 5.19;
14.37; 15.38). Thus form is the material shape of an identity,
except, of course, when it is the human form, which is the
eternal and immaterial essence. The form is not, however,
the material object, merely its shape. Thus forms exist
apart from material existence and eternal essence, and have
their own permanence (32.36), though they are not the essence of the individual. Theoretically, the individual can go
through many forms. Indeed Ololon changes form, and the
angels of the divine presence change form. And the individual can exist in several forms at once, as Milton does.
This condition is the same as that of the state. States are
series of mental conditions through which the eternal essence may pass, though that it can be a multiple condition
at one time, as the forms potentially are, is not spelled out.

The tendency to work on both cosmic and individual level is also seen in Blake's doctrine of classes. The individual contains within himself the three classes but in the aggregate he is a member of one class. As aggregates of individuals the three classes are the elect, the redeemed, and the reprobates (6.35–7.2). They are general categories created by Los and everything that takes form selects one of these classes, "For in every Nation & every Family the Three Classes are born And in every Species of Earth, Metal, Tree, Fish, Bird & Beast" (25.40–41).[44] On the other hand, Milton, though said to be one of the elect class (23.56), nevertheless contains the three classes within his total identity. As he struggles with Urizen, Blake tells us that:

> His Mortal part
> Sat frozen in the rock of Horeb: and his Redeemed portion,
> Thus form'd the Clay of Urizen; but within that portion
> His real Human, walkd above in power and majesty
> Tho darkend; and the Seven Angels of the Presence attended him.
>
> O how can I with my gross tongue that cleaveth to the dust,
> Tell of the Four-fold Man, in starry number fitly ordered
> Or how can I with my cold hand of clay! But thou O Lord
> Do with me as thou wilt! for I am nothing, and vanity.
> If thou chuse to elect a worm, it shall remove the mountains.
> For that portion named the Elect: the Spectrous body of Milton:
> Redounding from my left foot into Los's Mundane space,
> Brooded over his Body in Horeb against the Resurrection.
> (20.10–22)

Thus Milton's total identity seems to be composed of four parts, the human, elect, redeemed, and mortal. The elect and redeemed are names of classes, and the name "mortal" stands for the class of the reprobate. The fourfoldness of complete identity is stated early in the poem: "the Three Classes of Men take their Sexual texture. Woven/The Sexual is Threefold: the Human is Fourfold" (4.4–5). The three classes are conditions of material and temporal existence, but complete and eternal existence contains a fourth class, the human. Here the double meaning of class as a category of individuals and as an individual part becomes clear.[45] The sexual garment is the bodily form, and the three classes are the sexual garments in that they are parts of the bodily form. His propensity for one class or another causes the individual to fit into one of these aggregates when he takes bodily form, but the individual is indeed more than merely a part of a class. He contains the propensity of all the classes in this total being, which can never be complete in any combination of the three temporal, sexual classes, but only in the eternal humanity, the fourfold. However, even as the concept of form complicates the idea of state, the concept of classes is complicated by the introduction of the related idea of the contraries and reasoning negative. Early in the poem Blake states that the "three Classes of men . . . are the Two Contraries & the Reasoning Negative" (5.14). These are equivalent to the classes of the redeemed, reprobate, and elect, the elect being the reasoning negative. Like state and class, they are constituents of an individual as well as general categories.

Emerging from this complicated set of concepts is the notion that the essence of the individual exists above any part of the temporal world. The human form, the imagination, the fourfold man, exist eternally. The temporal conditions of the individual's existence are states in which he exists in part, but they are not his essential identity. This is the key concept that unlocks the anxiety produced by retribution and guilt.[46] For Blake places guilt on the state, not on the individual in the state. The individual therefore has nothing to fear from retribution. Indeed, the endurance of man's existence in state, form, or class is for Blake a mercy to insure eternal existence. Time is the mercy of eternity

(25.70) in that the identity of those fallen from eternity is continued by mercy (23.34). The temporal world was created to allow existence for the mistaken, such as Satan, who reject eternity (13.13). And those mistaken cannot be asked to justify themselves by deeds or to atone for guilt, for their gilt *would* cause them to be condemned to eternal death (11.15). It is by mercy alone that one lives (23.34). The innocent alone may satisfy justice, for they cannot be destroyed. For strict justice demands of the guilty what strict mercy would prohibit, and for Blake mercy, not justice, is the divine virtue.[47] The concept of classes is deeply concerned with the simple statement that guilt does not cause punishment. The elect, the class of Satan, are to be saved. In the final consummation, the material form of the reprobate and redeemed may be destroyed completely, for they have never rejected eternity and will not lose eternal existence. The elect, however, require special treatment.[48] They cannot be consumed lest they truly die, for they, like Satan, have rejected eternity.

The Elect is one Class: You

Shall bind them separate: they cannot Believe in Eternal
    Life
Except by Miracle & a New Birth. The other two Classes;
The Reprobate who never cease to Believe, and the Re-
    deemd,
Who live in doubts & fears perpetually tormented by the
    Elect
These you shall bind in a twin-bundle for the Consumma-
    tion—
But the Elect must be saved [from] fires of Eternal Death,
To be formed into the Churches of Beulah that they destroy
    not the Earth.

(25.32–39)

It is by mercy that the elect live (13.33). Though they cannot be redeemed, they are created continually by the offering and atonement of others (5.10–11). Christ is of the class of the reprobate (13.27) for none of the elect, who have rejected eternity, could atone. The ironic discovery of the elect that they are saved by the death of the reprobate (13.27), besides being a satiric attack on the pride of those who feel they are among the elect, is a doctrinal statement of divine mercy. To avoid punishment for the crime of slaying Thullough, the judgment is put not on Satan the guilty but on Rintrah (9.10), just as Christ must put on sin to save the guilty (5.3). One may speculate skeptically on how clearly this displacement solves the problem of justice being arbitrary, but it does help ease the anxiety produced by guilt.

It is perhaps needless to suggest how this doctrine effects the controls of the selfhood. Blake's doctrine teaches that there is no death or punishment for the essential identity. This doctrine therefore removes the fear that submits to the thunderings of moral retribution, and the excess of the selfhood can no longer bind a motivating force to bind the man. The danger of total anarchy is never stated or denied by Blake, but one surmises that in a religious sense Blake would have felt that the potential anarchy of this life was no cause to grant the rigid morals of prudence a complete death-grip on the basic emotions and imaginative creations of man, for only in those emotions could he find eternal life.

The release from the selfhood's grip is symbolized in several ways. One of the primary ways is in the symbols of loosening from bondage. There are scattered hints that binding represents the desire of the selfhood. Scofield is bound in iron armor (19.59). Milton would be bound in bonds of war if Rahab had her wish (20.5). The freeing from bondage, however, is one of the clearest motifs. Milton's purpose includes the freeing of Satan from hell (14.31), which Enitharmon mistakenly fears (17.33). The freeing of Satan, however, changes into the freeing of Orc, who seems chained in the brief view we get of him with the Shadowy Female (18.44–45). Later Los sees the purpose of Milton's journey as the fulfillment of the prophecy

That Milton of the Land of Albion should up ascend
Fowards from Ulro from the Vale of Felpham; and set free
Orc from his Chain of Jealousy.
                    (20.59–61)

Here the unloosing of Satan, announced as Milton's intention, and the prophecy of his freeing Orc, are in accord.
Rintrah fears mistakenly that Milton "will unchain Orc . . .
& let loose Satan, Og, Sihon, & Anak" (22.33). Freedom
from bondage will have been accomplished when the children of Jerusalem are saved from slavery (40.31). The
image of Orc being freed and the fear inspired by the possibility of his freedom make a perfect symbol for the freeing
of the unconscious urges, the feelings and emotions, the
impulses of the body (i.e., nerves of the body) from the
restriction of the superego. The fear inspired in Enitharmon
and Palamabron is the fear of anarchy inherent in such
freedom.

Another symbol related to release is joining, to become
as one.[49] Satan's purpose has been one of separation, but
Milton's journey begins a process of joining that repairs
Satan's separation. The family divine begins the process by
uniting "as One Man" (21.41). Ololon is united with the
One Man (21.60). Milton seems to join Blake when he falls
on Blake's left foot (15.49), and Blake joins with Los: "and
I became One Man with him arising in my strength"
(22.12). The resolution of the action is the joining of Milton
(and the starry seven who have accompanied Milton) with
Ololon: "with one accord the Starry Eight became/ One
Man Jesus the Saviour wonderful! round his limbs/ The
Clouds of Ololon folded as a Garment dipped in blood"
(42.10–12). To become one man is to submerge the selfhood in the individual so that the true identity may unite
with the true identity of all others. The place of unity is in
the source of identity, that is, in the One Man, the eternal
great humanity divine, Jesus.

Joining is accompanied by another somewhat puzzling

symbolic action, the return of the female to her proper sphere. Other than Satan and Urizen, the principle factors of evil are female in *Milton*. Milton's wives and daughters are in conflict with him (17.7), the Shadowy Female wishes to sidetrack Milton from his purpose (18.18), and Rahab and Tirzah attempt to seduce him to their own purposes (19.36ff). Leutha, of course, is one of the root causes of the fall into selfhood. These females are attempting to dominate. The divine voice, however, suggests that the female's jealous desire to dominate must cease. She must be relegated to the proper dependency: "Thy love depends on him thou lovest & on his dear loves/ Depends thy pleasures" (33.8–9). The female, to return to her proper sphere, "shall relent in fear of death: She shall begin to give/ her maidens to her husband: delighting in his delight/ And then & then alone begins the happy Female joy" (33.17–19). This freeing is symbolized in the return of Jerusalem. For the female to give her maidens to her husband is to "bring Jerusalem in thine arms in the night watches" (33.21). The cessation of female domination represents freedom, for Jerusalem never attempts to dominate, is always lovingly submissive. Jerusalem, both woman and city, represents past freedom driven away by agents of the selfhood, and the promise of the future when the selfhood is annihilated. Her foundations began before the druids in "Lambeth's Vale" (6.14) and she will return and "overspread all the Nations" (6.18). Once the mate of Albion, she is now driven from his side and Satan hungers to devour her (12.27). Her children will be saved in the act of self-annihilation (40.30–31).

It is important to see that the subordination of the female is in no sense meant to be a social phenomenon of this world. The separation of the sexes for Blake is a sign of a fallen state, and further struggle between them cannot afford any benefits. Certainly the female is to be taken as an aspect of the psychic structure.[50] I would suggest that she represents the condition of servitude or freedom from the superego's restrictive rules and the relationship between subject and object. She represents servitude when, like Rahab and Tirzah, she attempts to dominate. She is then the objective world dominating the subjective perception. Jerusalem signifies the return of the condition of mental freedom and imaginative vision. The unconscious impulse, the desire, the imagination of Albion and of the individual man are free to carry on the mental war of creativity when Jerusalem returns to Albion. It is significant that, at the end, Ololon has surrounded Milton as a "garment of war" (42.15), for it is spiritual war, allowing the creativity associated with freedom.

The symbols of joining and of release are goals of still another symbolic process, the journey. Blake himself is involved in a journey in the poem, which reaches the goal at Felpham. The epic invocation of the poem suggests the central place this symbolic process plays. The recording of "the journey of immortal Milton" (2.2) is the recording of the central action of the poem. Just as Satan has journeyed away from eternity, Milton, by his journey, will win back eternity. His journey is matched by Ololon's, who follows Milton to eternal death. I shall discuss the journey in detail in the next chapters.

The goal of the journey, seen as freeing, joining, and the return of the female, is given another symbolic meaning of central importance, self-annihilation. Milton's purpose is to perform the "unexampled deed" (2.21), to go into the deep to redeem his emanation and "himself perish" (2.20). He announces: "I will go down to self annihilation and eternal death" (14.22). Self-annihilation is the "Universal Dictate" (21.53; 38.53) that "each shall mutually/ Annihilate himself for others good" (38.35–36). Ololon learns the dictate and decides to obey it when she says "Let us give/ Ourselves to death in Ulro among the Transgressors" (21.45–46). Milton's deed of self-annihilation will become a state "Called Eternal Annihilation that none but the living shall/ Dare to enter: & they shall enter truimphant over Death" (32.27–28). Milton strives with Urizen and the other Zoas "In self annihilation giving thy life to thy enemies" (40.7). The object that must be annihilated is identified as "the Reasoning Power in Man . . . a False Body: an Incrustation over my Immortal/ Spirit: a Selfhood, which must be put off & annihilated alway (40.35–36). These varying statements about self-annihilation define the act. It is an internal act of the mind. To put off the incrustation is to remove an aspect of mind from its dominant position. The individual, in short, must rearrange his internal hierarchies. The rearrangement consists in denying the "rational power" complete sway. As we have seen, the rational power is but one manifestation of the selfhood. In annihilating the rational power, the selfhood is annihilated. This act is to become a typical act, or state, which Milton's act symbolizes and exemplifies. Thus Milton's act is the creation of a state.[51]

All individuals enter that state when they perform the act. They are not asked to die in actuality, but to die to the controls of the selfhood. But it is not an easy act. It is one of selflessness, the antithesis of self-interest. In fact, the motivating force is altruistic care for others, a care that insists that no coercion of others, even for their good, can be associated with self-annihilation. Even the selfhood must be treated properly:

> Satan! my Spectre! I know my power thee to annihilate
> And be a greater in thy place, & be thy Tabernacle
> A covering for thee to do thy will, till one greater comes
> And smites me as I smote thee & become my covering.
> Such are the Laws of thy false Heavns! but Laws of Eternity
> Are not such: know thou: I come to Self Annihilation
> Such are the Laws of Eternity that each shall mutually
> Annihilate himself for others good, as I for thee.
>   (38.29–35)

The danger of the use of force, here symbolized by the use of force against Satan, the grand symbol of the selfhood, lies in the implication about the motive for action. Power, not love; fear, not kind regard; stealth, not openness are the motives and characteristic of the selfhood. To use force, even against the selfhood's force, is to submit to the self-hood. In a deeper sense, man cannot, by simply willing, by exerting his desire, make his superego relax its grip. He must learn the art of gently opening the mind, in a relaxed, defenseless attitude, to the promptings from below. The voice of the unconscious is not stentorian or frightening. Man must listen, feeling the whispers. To love the selfhood seems a radical statement, but that is indeed Blake's injunc-tion. Collective man is freed by Christ's self-annihilation, the elect being the object of love. Individual man must love himself to be set free. For when the superego denies his pleasure, his instinctive urges, his creative instinct, man is in chains internally, and, being self-deceived, becomes an unwilling slave of the unperceived fear of the superego. To love himself by releasing the superego's control, by awak-ening the superego to the voice of the instincts, by remov-ing the false garments of delusive fear, by reaching inwards and outwards in brotherly affection, freeing his love, in-creasing the potential for love, he annihilates the selfhood. Pointedly, Milton performs no act of force against the Satanic symbol of selfhood. His only strife is the act of giving human form to Urizen.

Self-annihilation, then, is the individual's mental act of removing the dominance of his selfhood, which is only part of his psyche, the servant who has made himself into a God (32.21). But the selfhood itself is a state, which does not pass out of existence. The individual passes out of the state of the selfhood into self-annihilation. The selfhood, like all other states, remains permanent.

Blake was not the first to use the term *self-annihilation*. Though his concept is closely related to Boehme's turning again to God ("Here the whole Life of Christ resigned itself into the Father's Desire, *viz.*, into the will of the Eternal Nature, and fully gave in the Will of his Self-hood, *viz.* his creaturely will again into the Center. . . . The self-will must again enter into Nature's End, so that the selfishness may wholly die."[52]) and to Swedenborg's reliance on God rather than the proprium, or selfhood, the terminology for self-annihilation is Hartley's. In *Observations on Man* Hartley had conceived of self-annihilation as a mental condition wherein the individual persona, seen as a cause of sin, must be humbled by recognition that all powers come from God. The will must be subjected to the divine will.[53] Man must be rid of sin, which arises from self.[54] But Hartley believed in the form of predestination called necessity, and the process of self-annihilation is forwarded, paradoxically, by the progressive and inevitable substitution of purer degrees of self-interest, until self-annihilation and self-interest are reconciled[55] in the recognition that all comes from God.[56] Blake, in his usual dialectic, has taken the concept of the opposition and put it in a context that alters the implications of the concept. For Blake causation is not material or necessitarian. It is spiritual and free. The act of self-annihilation, instead of being an inevitable, almost predestined mental condition, takes on the exalted quality of free spiritual act. Hartley and Blake are at variance also in their ideas about the constituents of the self, for Hartley sees the extinction of imagination amid the extinction of the various pleasures.[57]

The concept of self-annihilation may also help to account for the choice of the dragon form of Satan to symbolize the selfhood. For in Revelation, when casting out of the great dragon, the followers of Christ "overcome him by the blood of the Lamb, and they loved not their lives unto the death" (Rev. 12:11). Blake's "dragon red . . . which John of Patmos saw" (40.22) is the object of self-annihilation because in self-annihilation the impulse to fear for oneself cannot hold sway. To love not the life unto death is part of self-annihilation, and therefore the symbol of selfhood is the red dragon, the enemy of those who overcome him.

Self-annihilation is an individual's internal act. But there is also the external, collective manifestation of the selfhood that must and will be annihilated.[58] Although the evil of the individual and of the aggregate of individuals is represented in the same symbol, the selfhood, self-annihilation in the aggregate is symbolized by the great "consummation," The consummation is forecast when Milton descends to Sinai (20.23). In temporal terms it will occur six thousand years from the time of the beginning of material existence (22.18). Only the classes of the reprobate and redeemed, however, can be consumed (25.37), for the class of the elect is an aggregate of the selfhood, and consummation for them would be equivalent to the use of force against the individual manifestation of the selfhood. The consummation will be a purging by fire (41.27) of all the temporal and material manifestations of the self. In short, all but the spiritual essence must be consumed at the end of time. This symbol, perhaps meant literally as a forecast of the end of creation, seems more acceptable to us if we assume that Blake means to annihilate the social and cultural phenomena of the selfhood, which will be consumed in the individual's self-annihilation. The interior change will bring a change in the exterior world.

The journey to this change, the journey of immortal Milton (of Blake, and of every man) is the act that becomes the state of self-annihilation. We must now follow that journey.

5

The Journey: Background

I. JOHN MILTON, THE FALLEN GUARDIAN

In examining Milton's journey we shall see that the journey, the keystone of the narrative structure of *Milton,* is the symbol of the departure from the toils of the selfhood.[1] There have been past attempts to perform this journey, but they have all failed. From the past patterns of failure on the journey, symbolized in the cyclical recurrence of corruption in the myth of the seven eyes of God, Milton's journey differs in that it is a step toward a new act; the state of annihilation is about to be created. Blake's choice of Milton to partake in this new process, and thereby to become its symbol, puts Milton surprisingly in the company of Jehovah and Jesus. But to Blake, John Milton the man was an example, similar to the corrupted seven eyes of God, of a prophet who had also become corrupted. John Milton the man had been subverted by the selfhood. Therefore Blake selected him to undertake the journey in which he must struggle against agents of the selfhood and that ends in the act of self-annihilation. Thus Blake uses Milton's journey to sym-

180

bolize an archetypal antidote to the fall of Satan, which represents the selfhood's growing influence and dominance.

For Blake Milton's journey is an eighth manifestation of the same purpose that called forth the seven eyes. The seven eyes are described as guardians, though it is made clear that they themselves become prey to the selfhood:

> they ratify'd
> The kind decision of Enitharmon & gave a Time to the Space,
> Even Six Thousand years; and sent Lucifer for its Guard.
> But Lucifer refus'd to die & in pride he forsook his charge
> And they elected Molech, and when Molech was impatient
> The Divine hand found the Two Limits: first of Opacity, then of Contraction
> Opacity was named Satan, Contraction was named Adam.
> Triple Elohim came: Elohim wearied fainted: they elected Shaddai.
> Shaddai angry, Pahad descended: Pahad terrified, they sent Jehovah
> And Jehovah was leprous; loud he call'd, stretching his hand to Eternity
> For then the Body of Death was perfected in hypocritic holiness,
> Around the Lamb, a Female Tabernacle woven in Cathedrons Looms.
>
> (13.15–26)

The seven eyes are guards, who, either through their own self-centeredness or the power of the preceding eye, as in the relation of Jesus to Jehovah, fail to carry out their guardianship. Their journey to the world of death has ended not in guardianship but in the growing power of the selfhood.[2] But the seven eyes also have double states of existence, and just as Milton's immortal human essence resides in eternity, so the seven eyes also have a human essence existing in eternity. The earthly manifestation of the seven eyes is the selfhood's work. In fact, the earthly aspects of the seven eyes have been appropriated to Satan's retinue. They have become the "Seven angels [who] bear my [Satan's] Name & in those Seven I [Satan] appear" (38.55). But the immortal aspects of the seven eyes remain in Eden with Milton, where they join him.

> With him the Spirits of the Seven Angels of the Presence
> Entering; they gave him still perceptions of his Sleeping
>   Body;
> Which now arose and walk'd with them in Eden, as an Eighth
> Image Divine tho' darken'd; and tho walking as one walks
> in sleep; and the Seven comforted and supported him.
>   (15.3–7)

Blake's linking of Milton with the seven to become the starry eighth suggests a good deal about his choice of Milton. In the seven eyes we see that the function of guardianship has been corrupted. This corruption is manifested in the Satanic dominance of an ecclesiastical organization that elevates a particular guardian to Godhead. This process is clearest in the case of Jesus, where the body of his religious doctrines is taken over by the female tabernacle, which is the organization of an ecclesiastical hierarchy. Thus each eye has been diverted from his primary function of guardianship and has thereby become an agent of the selfhood. The legacy of each has been a further permission for the selfhood to dominate the mind of man. Ecclesiastical domination, elevation of self to Godhead, and love of power, are then the characteristics that Blake saw as the things to be annihilated in Milton's journey. But why had Blake picked Milton to stand the charge of ecclesiastical domination, elevation of self, and power-hungry grasping?[3] The reason lies in the disparity between Milton's life and his work. This disparity lies behind the dramatic situation at the end of the poem, when Milton is facing Satan, who is his selfhood. All worldliness, all love of domination, all hypocrisy, ecclesiastical power, and usurpation of Godhead are seen in Milton's selfhood. But the selfhood exists only in man's temporal existence, while man's imagination is eternal. Milton at this moment may stand for the ideas and poetic creations of the imagination of John Milton, while the selfhood may stand for the actual John Milton's moral, wordly performance, and the legacy of that performance. This contrary character of the final opposition of Milton and Satan constitutes Blakes comment that Milton's moral performance in his public life was at variance with the ideas in his art. His actual life displayed the selfhood's syndrome of morality, worldly domination, and retribution. Now, in Blake's garden at Felpham, Milton views his selfhood much as a hypocrite looks at his own behavior for the first time.

If we see Milton's actions from a sympathetic point of view, much that is implied here will bewilder us. We might search the *Life of Milton* of Hayley, Blake's patron, in vain to find such criticism. But it is possible to see Milton, not through Hayley's eyes, but through those of Sam Johnson.[4] The devastating attack on Milton in Johnson's *Life of John Milton* is the focus for much of Hayley's defense, and Blake, perhaps taking the antagonist's side to aid in "progression," espoused a critical point of view to clarify his concept. For Johnson, Milton's life at various intervals exhibited instances of savageness of manners, malignity, servile flattery, depredation of the church, a desire to destroy, severity, arbitrariness, and "something like a Turkish contempt of females."[5] Much of Johnson's vitriolic character assassination is not clearly related to any specific quality in Blake's picture of Milton's selfhood; but Johnson's treatment of Milton's attitude toward the rebellion can be seen to constitute an accusation of exactly the same sort of activity that earned Bishop Watson Blake's strictures as a "state trickster."[6] As an apologist for the protectorate and its acts, Milton, according to Johnson, became an abettor of tyranny. His position as Latin secretary was that of an apologist for Cromwell. Johnson writes:

> Cromwell had now dismissed the Parliament by the authority of which he had destroyed monarchy, and commenced monarch himself, under the title of Protector, but

with kingly and more than kingly power. That his authority was lawful, never he pretended; he himself founded his
right only in necessity; but Milton, having now tasted the
honey of publick employment, would not return to hunger
and philosophy, but, continuing to exercise his office
under a manifest usurpation, betrayed to his power that
liberty which he had defended. Nothing can be more just
than that rebellion should end in slavery; that he, who had
justified the murder of his king, for some acts which to him
seemed unlawful, should now sell his services, and his
flatteries, to a tyrant, of whom it was evident that he could
do nothing lawful.[7]

Indeed, even for Johnson, Milton never stands under censure of advocating state religion, but his motives for defense
of the protectorate included, according to Johnson, the
emolument of two hundred pounds a year, and an estate of
sixty pounds a year belonging to Westminster Abbey.[8] Milton, the surly and acrimonious republican was, in short, a
self-serving man. But the venality of self-service is superseded by a motive much more serious. The driving force of his
activity was "his predominant desire . . . to destroy rather
than establish, and he felt not so much the love of liberty as
repugnance to authority."[9]

That Blake saw Milton through Johnson's eyes is not my
contention, but that he saw him in a similar, though less
stringent, way. Blake saw in Milton a fallen guardian whose
prophetic message was greater than his own acts, which in
several instances were more like those of Satan in *Paradise
Lost*. If Blake saw Milton as Johnson saw him, a destroyer,
then the irony of Satan's speech "For onely in destroying I
find ease/To my relentless thoughts" (9. 129–30) as a characterization of John Milton's behavior becomes the central
point of Blake's having Milton face Satan, his self-hood, at
the end of his poem. John Milton's denial of the value of war
in Christ's speech in *Paradise Regained,* wherein heroic
acts are set below the "winning words to conquer willing
hearts/And make persuasion do the work of fear" (*P.R.*

1.222–23) is much like Blake's own emphasis on mental warfare; but the Latin secretary had been able to urge General Monk to take the final solution for "freedom" in his own hands: " . . . your excellency once more declaring publicly this to be your mind, and having a faithful veteran army, so ready and glad to assist you in the prosecution thereof."[10] Milton's remark that he wrote his prose tracts with his left hand suggests more than his merely writing in prose rather than poetry.[11] The impulse of Milton the destroyer is malignity, according to Johnson. We may see that in *Paradise Lost* God allows Satan freedom so that "he might/Heap on himself damnation. . . " (1.214–15). Milton's God argues strongly that He is merciful, as Christ's redemption of man indicates, but where is mercy in the future Latin secretary when he writes in 1641:

> But they contrary that by the impairing and diminution of the true *Faith,* the distresses and servitude of their *Countrey,* aspire to high *Dignity, Rule,* and *Promotion* here, after a shamefull end in this *Life,* (which *God* grant them,) shall be thrown downe eternally into the *darkest* and *deepest Gulfe* of Hell, where, under the *despightful controlle,* the trample and spurne of all the other *Damned,* that in the anguish of their *Torture,* shall have no other ease, than to exercise a *Raving* and *Bestiall Tyranny* over them as their *Slaves* and *Negroes,* they shall remain in that plight for ever, the *basest,* the *lowermost,* the *most dejected,* most *underfoot,* and *downtrodden Vassals* of *Perdition.*[12]

Is there not a strong malignity in this vision? John Milton was hardly a man of forgiveness and mercy. But in *Milton* Blake's depiction of Milton's refusing to use force against Satan pointedly annihilates those overpowering, moralistic, destructive urges that inspired the rebel John Milton.

What of John Milton's "Turkish contempt of women"? Blake's symbol of the female returning to her appropriate

role is hardly Turkish. Neither is Milton's poetry so completely contemptuous of the female. Blake's return of the
female to her proper sphere is suggested in this speech of the
subordinate Eve, shedding the evil of her vanity and desire
for self-sufficiency in her chastened plea for Adam's pity:

> Forsake me not thus, Adam, witness Heav'n
> What love sincere, and reverence in my heart
> I bear thee, and unweeting have offended,
> Unhappilie deceav'd; thy suppliant
> I beg, and clasp thy knees; bereave me not,
> Whereon I live, thy gentle looks, thy aid,
> Thy counsel in this uttermost distress,
> My onely strength and stay: forlorn of thee,
> Whither shall I betake me, where subsist?
> While yet we live, scarse one short hour perhaps,
> Between us two let there be peace, both joyning,
> As joyn'd in injuries, one enmitie
> Against a Foe by doom express assign'd us,
> That cruel Serpent: On me exercise not
> Thy hatred for this miserie befall'n.
> On me alread lost, mee then thy self
> More miserable; both have sin'd, but thou
> Against God onely, I against God and thee,
> And to the place of judgment will return,
> There with my cries importune Heav'n, that all
> The sentence from thy head remov'd may light
> On me, sole cause to thee of all this woe,
> Mee mee onely just object of his ire.
>   (*P.L.* 10. 914–35)

Ololon's recognition of her guilt and her repentance is not
unlike this repentence. Eve has submitted to the station she
must take at Adam's side. But when John Milton met resistance from Mary Powel, it was in the divorce tracts that he
eased his restless thoughts. And his daughters were left ill
educated, forced to assist their father in their ignorance by
reading languages to him that they could not understand.
Even Hayley does not enjoy the apologetic task of discuss-

ing Milton's daughters, and he hurries over Johnson's "prejudices" that he might "have occasion to speak of them no more."[13] The return of Jerusalem, the uniting of Milton and Ololon, and the Shadowy Female's return to pity and compassion are exemplary actions that Milton could have imagined but did not experience, and his attitude to living women must account for the sixfold emanation "which in blood & jealousy/Surrounded him, dividing and uniting without end or number" (17.7–8).

The aspect of John Milton's life that seems to make him a choice example for the selfhood is stated most vigorously by Johnson. Milton's political motives were "an envious hatred of greatness, and a sullen desire of independence; a petulant impatience of control, and pride disdainful of superiority."[14] This indeed is the malice of Satan in *Paradise Lost*. It is the drive of the inflated pride of the selfhood giving man the delusion of divinity. It is John Milton in history who in Blake's poem is "that Evil One" (14.30). Milton, the corrupted guardian of liberty who served the satanic Cromwell, the warmongering, moralistic Latin secretary, the domestic tyrant, had led himself to the abomination that in his poetry belongs to the forces of evil.

However, if there is any doctrine of John Milton that Blake might have singled out as error, that doctrine is moral retribution. Despite Johnson's inference that Milton did not adhere to strict morality, Hayley, undoubtedly to the dislike of Blake, had defended Milton as a pure examplar of the Socratic morality. For Hayley, Milton's purity kept him from indulging in the excesses of Geneva.[15] Hayley is displeased that Johnson sets up an opposition between Socrates and Milton on education, "since no man appears to have embibed the principle of Socratic wisdom more deeply than our poet."[16] Milton taught "the familiar and useful doctrine of the Attic philosopher."[17] Blake may indeed have found the disparity between man and poet less significant on the question of morality, for though Milton certainly sees grace triumphant over works in the gaining of salvation, he yet never relinquished a love and respect for natural virtue in his poetry. In *Paradise Regained,* despite Christ's placing Greek thought below the teachings of Hebrew literature, he nevertheless accepts the possibility that the Greeks, though not inspired, may yet receive truth "where moral vertue is express't/By light of Nature not in all quite lost" (*P.R.* 4. 351–52). Moral virtue's other form, divine justice in *Paradise Lost,* demands that man die in order to fulfill justice.[18] Morality is seeking destruction in Milton's poetry, and, in this regard, Blake has reason to correct Milton's doctrines. As we shall see in examining the details of Milton's journey, it is particularly the destructive element in John Milton's character that made Milton the choice for Blake. *Milton* implies that John Milton is responsible for self-righteousness, and, in a way, for natural and state religion.[19] We need not judge Blake's historical accuracy on these points. It is sufficient to see that for Blake Milton's life had become a symbol of the selfhood's domination; and as symbol, Milton thereby became responsible for the outcome of the selfhood. Historical accuracy is the field of scholars; prophetic vision is the universe of the poet.

II. BLAKE'S ASSOCIATION WITH THE JOURNEY

If the question, Why John Milton? is appropriate, then the question, Why the connection of Blake, Milton, and Los in Milton's journey? is also appropriate. Blake actually participates in the action of the poem from the beginning of Milton's journey to the vision of the uniting of Milton and Ololon at the end. The answer to the question may be found in the close personal meaning the idea of a journey had for Blake, and in the way Blake viewed that personal meaning as a token of the authenticity of the poem.

Blake's attitude toward the journey appears in letters written during the time of his stay at Felpham. Blake's letters deal with his real journey to Felpham (Letter to Flaxman, Sept. 12, 1800; to Hayley, Sept. 16, 1800; and to Butts, Sept.

23, 1800).[20] But by 1802 the idea of a determined, heroic journey had become symbolic for Blake. He writes to Butts on January 10, 1802; "Temptations are on the right hand & left behind the sea of time & space roars & follows swiftly he who keeps not right onward is lost & if our footsteps slide in clay how can we do otherwise than fear & tremble."[21] Later that year he writes: "but I have traveld thro Perils & Darkness not unlike a Champion I have Conquerd and shall still Go on Conquering Nothing can withstand the fury of my Course among the Stars of God & in the Abysses of the Accuser" (Letter to Butts, Nov. 22, 1802).[22] The journey has become an epic of immense psychological meaning. Still another projected journey was in Blake's mind. The long-delayed peace between England and France, brought into actuality by the Treaty of Amiens, had led Blake to rejoice in the possibility of traveling to Paris. He had written to Flaxman Oct. 19, 1801:

> I rejoice to hear that your Great Work is accomplish'd. Peace opens the way to greater still. The Kingdoms of this World are now become the Kingdoms of God & his Christ, & we shall reign with him for ever & ever. The Reign of Literature & the Arts Commences. Blessed are those who are found studious of Literature & Humane & polite accomplishments. Such have their lamps burning & such shall shine as the stars.

> Now I hope to see the Great Works of Art, as they are so near to Felpham, Paris being scarce further off than London. But I hope that France & England will henceforth be as One Country and their Arts One, & that you will Ere long be erecting Monuments In Paris—Emblems of Peace.[23]

It is significant that Blake associated his journey with peace, for the long-delayed respite from war had become a frustrating condition for Englishmen. The journey and peace are also tied up in Milton's journey, in that Milton comes to rid England of that selfhood whose destructive impulses were binding Albion in eternal war.

The journey also becomes associated with spiritual duty in Blake's letters. He writes to Butts Jan. 10, 1802:

I find on all hands great objections to my doing any
thing but the meer drudgery of business & intimations
that if I do not confine myself to this I shall not
live. this has always pursud me. You will understand by
this the source of all my uneasiness. This from Johnson
& Fuseli brought me down here & this from M^r H will
bring
me back again for that I cannot live without doing my
duty to lay up treasures in heaven is Certain & Determined
&
to this I have long made up my mind.[24]

Blake's journey from London to Felpham, and his return to London, are thus said to be motivated by his spiritual duty.

Later that year (Nov. 22, 1802) in another letter to Butts Blake writes a poem, beginning "with happiness stretch'd accross the hills," symbolizing his condition, and insisting that he, Blake, serves a spiritual, not a natural master.[25] Los is imagined threatening Blake with poverty if Blake should return to London. Los appears in all his power as the sun, but Blake defies Los. This defiance becomes mental warfare, which is followed by Blake's fourfold vision. Thus the projected journey to London is associated with a dramatic change in mental attitude. Blake had achieved fourfold vision, which is, in essence, the vision of Milton in his fourfold aspect. In *Milton* fourfold vision is the ability to see four levels of mental perspective, which consist of Milton's existence in eternity, his spectre, shadow, and vegetable body (pl. 20). A new dimension is added to this perception by the ending of Blake's short poem, which suggests that threefold vision is associated with Beulah, and single vision with Newton. To see the eternal completeness of anything is to see with fourfold vision. To see a threefold level of existence, above the mundane and close to eternal but essentially not eternal, is to see the realm of Beulah, which in the poem is close to eternity but not eternity itself. To see with single vision in the mathematical rationalism of Newton is to see only Ulro. In a sense Blake's defiance of Los leads Blake, as he insists on proceeding on his journey to London, to the fourfold vision mentioned in his poem to Butts.

Moreover, his joining with Los in *Milton* is suggested by the short poem where, after his correct defiance, Blake seems to achieve a working coalition with Los, just as Milton refuses to submit to Los's resistance and subsequently joins with Los.

When I had my Defiance given
The Sun stood trembling in heaven
The Moon that glowd remote below
Became leprous & white as snow
And every Soul of men on the Earth
Felt affliction & sorrow & sickness & death
Los flamd in my path & the Sun was hot
With the bows of my Mind & the Arrows of Thought
My bowstring fierce with Ardour breathes
My arrows glow in their golden sheaves
My brothers & father march before
The heavens drop with human gore.
(11.71–82)[26]

Blake illustrates the joining with Los on plate forty-three of *Milton*.

The connection between Blake's references to his own journey, his place in *Milton*, and Milton's journey, suggests the possibility that personal allegory plays a large part in *Milton*.[27] But, as I have observed, Blake's allegory is sublime, not topical. The likely significance of his involvement lies in another direction. The placement of himself in the poem as actor, and the obvious parallels of events in the poem to events in his own life (see chap. 3) are Blake's signs of authenticity, a quality that Blake thought important for a prophet.[28] Blake wrote to Butts April 25, 1803:

> But none can know the Spiritual Acts of my three years Slumber on the banks of the Ocean unless he has seen them in the Spirit or unless he should read My Long Poem descriptive of those acts.[29]

Here, the double potential of seeing the spiritual act as an immediate witness or of reading an inspired poem is suggested as Blake's way of seeing truth. This double potential is mentioned also in Blake's commentary on Bishop Watson. The problem of authenticity was a special topic for Watson since Paine's *Age of Reason* had devoted much of its invective against the authenticity of the Bible, using dating methods to point out inconsistences between dates of the stories and the stated authors of the story. Watson's defense was that the facts of the stories may be true, copied from public records, after the stated author has passed on. Blake's wonderful comment, "of what consequence is it whether Moses wrote the Pentateuch or no," puts both Paine and Watson in perspective, and his ensuing comment, "Public Records [!] as if Public Records were true Impossible for the facts are such as none but the actor could tell, if it is True Moses & none but he could write it unless we allow it to be Poetry & that poetry inspired."[30] Again Blake is showing the double potential of the immediate, actual witness or the inspired vision as measures of authenticity. Earlier in his commentary on Watson he wrote with the same double possibility in mind: "If Moses did not write the history of his acts it takes away the authority altogether it ceases to be history & becomes a poem of probable impossibilities fabricated for pleasure as moderns say but I say by Inspiration."[31] Again the measure of authenticity is found in either a witness of the event or in inspiration. This double potential seems to explain Blake's presence in *Milton*. The two segments of the poem, the

Bard's Song and Milton's journey, are given authenticity by inspiration and by actual witness. The Bard's Song is inspired, according to the Bard, and Blake himself had witnessed the ensuing events. Blake does not enter the poem after the invocation until the Bard's Song is complete, and when the Bard is called upon to prove the truth of his song,

The Bard replied. I am Inspired! I know it is Truth! for I
  Sing
According to the inspiration of the Poetic Genius
Who is the eternal all-protecting Divine Humanity
To whom be Glory & Power & Dominion Evermore Amen.
  (13.51–14.3)

Almost immediately after the Bard's statement Blake becomes a present witness of the events when he first sees Milton entering the zenith: "Then first I saw him in the Zenith as a falling star/ Descending perpindicular, swift as a swallow or swift" (15.47–48). And from this point on Blake witnesses virtually all the events of the poem. Blake therefore, like Moses or John of Patmos, is the witness of the spiritual event, or actor in a spiritual event. The truth of his witnessing is different from, but of equal value with, the inspiration of the Bard. Blake saw himself as a witness particularly after the manner of John of Patmos. He too beheld the "Dragon red & hidden Harlot which John in Patmos saw" (40.22). John's attack on Babylon strongly parallels Blake's attack on state religion. Both Revelation and *Milton* are prophetic revelations of a present evil. But Blake is also using his reference to Revelation to suggest the prophetic quality and therefore authentic nature of his vision. The echo of John's statement "and I stood upon the sand of the sea and saw a beast rise up out of the sea" (Rev. 13:1) is heard in the final vision of Milton:

The Spectre of Satan stood upon the roaring sea & beheld
Milton within his sleeping Humanity! trembling & shuddring

He stood upon the waves a Twenty-seven-fold mighty
  Demon
Gorgeous & beautiful: loud roll his thunders against Milton
Loud Satan thunderd, loud & dark upon mild Felpham
  shore
Not daring to touch one fibre he howld round upon the Sea.
                    (38.9–14)

This vision of the inspired poet is an authentic vision of true spiritual acts. Thus Blake is involved in the poem, like John of Patmos in Revelation, to illustrate the authenticity of his vision. The spiritual acts he has viewed are true in a profound sense for him. When questioned by such people as Crabb Robinson or William Hayley about the truth of his vision, both Blake and Bard can say, without any loss of composure, "I am inspired" and "I have witnessed."

III. PARALLELS TO MILTON'S JOURNEY

How is Milton's journey to be taken? The purpose of equating Milton with the seven guardian eyes is to show that Milton's acts are parallel to actions of the past. But since Milton is to create the new state of self-annihilation, his actions differ from those of his predecessors, and he has several predecessors in the spiritual journey. His journey's parallels to those of his predecessors have as their general purpose the differentiation of Milton's act and those which have preceded it. There are at least five journeys behind Milton's; hints, parallels, and allusions to those journeys, intentionally worked in by Blake, help the reader focus on the significance of Milton's journey. Those past journeys are those of Christian in *Pilgrim's Progress*, of Dante in the *Commedia*, of Christ to Golgotha, of Satan in *Paradise Lost*, and of Moses to the promised land.[32]

Pilgrim's Progress is more of an exemplary parallel than a contrast to *Milton*. Christian's journey is recalled most clearly in the allusion of Beulah. Blake has borrowed the idea of Beulah from Bunyan (discussed in chap. 2). The basic structures of *Pilgrim's Progress* is the story of Christian's journey to salvation and the various attempts made to stop him. Christian learns to distrust the doctrine of legality and to rely on faith, as the episode of the interpreter makes so clear to Christian. Blake is borrowing the paradigm for his own purpose, but Bunyan's basic doctrine of reliance on faith is Blake's, with expanded meaning. The journey for Blake is a change in the mental state. The progress of Christian and the journey of immortal Milton are changes of the interior state. Both Christian and Milton are followed on their journey by their female counterparts, Christiana and Ololon. Other possible connections may be found in the sword of Blake's introductory song, "and did those feet," which may well be taken from the two-edged sword given to Christian; in the common use of the symbol of the harvest; and in Appolyon's rage, which is much like Satan's.

Dante provided Blake with the notion of accompaniment by a related mirror image on the journey. E. J. Rose has pointed out the parallel between the relationship of Milton-Blake-Los and Statius-Dante-Virgil in the *Purgatorio*. As Virgil is the master of Dante and Statius, Los is the master of Milton and Blake. Virgil, belonging to another age, is shut out from heaven just as Los, belonging to another existence, has fallen from eternity. Statius, close to Dante in time, is ridding himself of sins, just as Milton, close to Blake in time, is ridding himself of error. Dante is author and actor, conductor and conducted, just as Blake is. Both Blake and Dante are experiencing a vision during their mortal existence.[33] Florence Sandler, though finding the parallel in the *Inferno*, sees Dante's revelation of Satan at the nadir of hell parallel to Blake's revelation of Satan at the end of *Milton*.[34] That Blake had Dante in mind is suggested by Crabb Robinson's note that Blake declared Dante to be a mere politician and atheist "busied in this world's affair: as Milton was, til in his old age he returned back to the God he had abandoned in his childhood."[35] The essential reason for the parallels between Blake and Dante no doubt lies in this point. A change in religious feeling, in mental state, that Blake found in Dante and Milton, is the theme of *Milton* and the purpose of his journey.

The analogy to Christ's journey to Golgotha is hinted in several places, though the sequence of the hints does not coincide with the sequence of events in the New Testament.[36] In general, Milton is seen in several parallels to Christ, which add light to the specific hints of his journey to Golgotha. At the beginning of Milton's journey, the statement "I go to eternal death. . . . I will arise and look forth for the morning of the grave" (14.14–20), and Milton's consequent appellation as Milton "the Awakener" (25.22) who will awaken Albion, are allusions to Christ's statement about Lazarus: "I go, that I may awake him out of sleep" (John 11:11). The point of the allusion is that Milton and Christ are both awakeners. Just as Christ miraculously called Lazarus from death, so is Milton to call all mankind from the death of delusion. In fact, the domination of the selfhood after Christ's time on earth (he is the seventh eye surrounded by hypocritical holiness) has required Milton's coming. Los says:

When Jesus raisd Lazarus from the Grave I stood & saw Lazarus who is the Vehicular Body of Albion the Redeemd Arise into the Covering Cherub who is the Spectre of Albion.
                    (24.26–28)

Christ's raising of Lazarus has been to no avail. The selfhood has usurped his vehicular form. As we have noted, the vehicle is something like the small entity that is the material essence, which can pass from one condition of material existence to another. Here Lazarus is the form of the redeemed identity that becomes, in a larger sphere, Albion, who stands for collective man. To see it in a less confusing way, we may say that Lazarus is the symbol for, and predecessor of, Albion. He is usurped by the Covering Cherub, or hypocritical religion, just as the spectre of Albion usurps the redeemed aspect of Albion. Milton then, another Christ, has the task of reawakening Lazarus-Albion.

Another allusion that parallels Milton and Christ occurs in Milton's struggle with Urizen.

> with cold hand Urizen stoop'd down
> And took up water from the river Jordan: pouring on
> To Miltons brain the icy fluid from his broad cold palm.
> (19.7–9)

Milton ignores Urizen's gesture and responds by molding Urizen a completely new form with clay. One cannot escape the connection with Christ's baptism by John. The rite of baptism in the New Testament might seem more appropriately administered to John by Jesus, as John the Baptist himself points out (Matt. 3:14), but Christ insists on receiving the rite, "for thus it becometh us to fulfill all righteousness" (3.15). Righteousness for Blake was a quality of the selfhood, and Milton's refusal to acknowledge Urizen's proferred rite, in contrast to Christ's seeking it, represents Blake's denial of the formalistic ritual that the selfhood's righteousness requires. But another allusion in the Urizenic baptism episode is Milton's molding Urizen with clay, which again parallels Milton and Christ. Remembering that in the *Book of Urizen* Urizen is depicted as blind, and that on plate sixteen of *Milton* Urizen appears a vague, unseeing visage, one is tempted to think of Urizen as blind. If so, Urizen's blindness is spiritual, a symbol of the spiritual blindness of Ulro. Milton's shaping of Urizen with clay is like Christ's use of clay upon the blind man. Christ "spat on the ground, and made clay of the spittle, and he anointed the eyes of the blind man with clay." (John 9:6). The spiritual blindness of Urizen, a more profound defect than physical blindness, calls for a complete remolding by Milton, just as the physical resurrection of Lazarus, insufficient in itself, leads to the necessity for the greater, spiritual reawakening of Albion. Thus Milton performs a Christ-like act, but the point of the act is slightly different.

The allusions paralleling Christ and Milton in general found in the brief episode of the Milton-Urizen episode, have one further possibility that ties the whole episode into the parallel of Christ's journey to Golgotha and Milton's journey to self-annihilation. Urizen is a particular aspect of the selfhood, which, as we have seen, is manifested in both the internal mind and the external phenomenon of history. The present external phenomenon, constituting the selfhood politically, is state religion, which, for Blake, is represented by Watson and Pitt. In Christ's day it was represented by Caiaphas and Pilate. Though it is not directly suggested by Blake, Urizen, in the baptism episode, could readily represent the church-state relationship that existed in the relationship between the Jewish high priest and the Roman governor. As a parallel to Christ, Milton would be struggling against the attempt to dominate and the inevitable force of destruction that characterizes the selfhood. Christ, when questioned by Caiaphas, at first answers nothing. Eventually he admits to being the son of God, and the alledged blasphemy leads to his crucifixion. The symbolic gesture of Milton's Satan ("I am God") is the gesture of Christ: "And the high priest arose, and said unto him, Answerest thou nothing? what is it which these witness against thee? But Jesus held his peace. And the high priest answered and said unto him, I adjure thee by the living God, that thou tell us whether thou be the Christ, the Son of God. Jesus saith unto him, Thou hast said: nevertheless I say unto you, Hereafter shall ye see the Son of man sitting on the right hand of power, and coming in the clouds of heaven" (Matt. 26:62–64). (Christ is also said in Matthew to have remained silent before Pilate, a motif that is picked up, but not consistently, by the other evangelists.) Milton, however, standing before Urizen, utters nothing. "Silent Milton stood before/ The darkend Urizen" (20.7–8). Christ's admission that he considered himself the son of

God allowed him in Blakean terminology to become a covering for the Satanic selfhood, manifested in the ecclesiastical organization that grew after his death. Milton's
complete silence symbolizes his refusal to give in to the
domination of state religion and also his refusal to become
a covering through which the selfhood may work. The
meaning of his silence is articulated when Milton faces Satan
at the end of the Poem:

Satan! my Spectre! I know my power thee to annihilate
And be a greater in thy place, & be thy Tabernacle
A covering for thee to do thy will, till one greater comes
And smites me as I smote thee & becomes my covering.
Such are the Laws of thy false Heavns!
(38.29–33)

If one can accept the Urizenic baptism episode as parallel
to Christ's responses to Caiaphas and Pilate, it will not be
difficult to see Blake's point in the finale of the poem. Milton's self-annihilation is parallel to Christ's crucifixion. The
magnificent oratory of Milton's self-annihilation speech is
carried by the metaphor of the removal of garments, as we
have noted. But Christ's clothes were stripped from him.
"And when they had crucified him, they parted his garments, casting lots upon them, what every man should
take" (Mark 15:24), a grisly scene that Blake illustrated
elsewhere. Milton willingly removes the rotten rags that
have become symbols of delusion. Another allusion to the
crucifixion scene occurs when, at the finale, Ololon, the
Greek root of whose name suggests wailing, cries for "the
Children of Jerusalem/ Lest they be annihilated in thy annihilation" (40.15–16). As Jesus carries the cross to Golgotha "there followed him a great company of people, and
of women, which also bewailed and lamented him. But
Jesus, turning unto them, said, "Daughters of Jerusalem,
weep not for me, but weep for yourselves, and for your
children" (Luke 23:27–28) because they will be made mis-

erable. Again the allusion points to a difference. As Christ predicts destruction to the children of Jerusalem, Milton, on the other hand, can only save them by willing self-annihilation: "All that can be annihilated must be annihilated/ That the Children of Jerusalem may be saved from slavery" (40.30–31). The difference in the fate of the children of Jerusalem is the allusion's point. As we discriminate between their fates, the causes also differ, and that difference is Milton's willing act of self-annihilation. Christ's act, according to the teaching of the covering cherub, was atonement. But Blake remarked to Robinson some years later: "It is a horrible doctrine; If another pay your debt, I do not forgive it."[37] This statement follows Robinson's note that Blake digressed "into a condemnation of those who sit in judgement on others."[38] The doctrine of the atonement, for Blake, simply reinforced the laws of retribution which, for Blake, were delusion. The sacrifice of one man for another in the law of retribution is required ("Dye hee [man] or Justice must"; *P.L.* 3.210). This is the meaning put on Christ's death by the church. But self-annihilation takes place in a context where man annihilates himself for another willingly, without constraint, for self-annihilation is really the removal of barriers from the true essence of each man. It is not required as atonement. It is simply given. Thus the allusive parallels between Milton's journey to self-annihilation and Christ's journey to Golgotha suggest a discrimination in purpose. Milton, the eighth eye of God following Jesus, has, as part of his task, the correction of the doctrine of atonement, the ultimate absurdity of the law of retribution. His act is certainly an "unexampled deed" (2.21).

The parallels between Milton's journey and Satan's in *Paradise Lost*, working by contrast principally, suggest Milton's desire to transform the results of Satan's destruction. Satan's journey is repeated in order to be changed. The larger outlines of the two journeys are the same, but the episodes are contraries. Where the parallels become allusions, they work on the reader by contrast, thus causing Milton's repetition of Satan's journey to lead to a very different end. In the broad pattern of *Milton*, Milton travels from eternity through a kind of chaos, through the visible world where he meets his female emanations, and eventually arrives in Blake's garden, where he effects a change for the good in Blake, and potentially in all men. Satan leaves hell, where he meets his female counterpart, Sin, travels through the void of Chaos, through the newly created universe to earth, arrives at the garden of Adam and Eve, causes their corruption and that of all mankind, leaving a legacy of sin and death behind. Both Satan and Milton are followed to earth by their female counterparts, Sin and Ololon. Both Satan and Milton meet resistance in their journey from spiritual powers, Satan meeting Ithuriel, Zephon, and Gabriel (as well as Sin and Death), Milton meeting Los, Urizen, Rahab, and Tirzah. The purpose of Satan is destruction of others; the purpose of Milton is self-annihilation.

Suggestions of the parallel begin early in *Milton*. As Milton leaves eternity, following a course to the mundane world, he appears "in a trail of light as of a comet/ That travels into Chaos" (15.19–20). While the puzzling placement of the shadows of hell just within the realms of Beulah suggests the psychological closeness of different attitudes of mind, it also ties Milton to Satan who, upon encountering his son, Death, "like a Comet burn'd/ That fires the length of Ophiucus huge" (*P.L.* 2.708–9). The encounter of Satan with his daughter-wife, Sin, is another parallel to Milton's discovery of the true nature of "those three females whom his Wives & those three whom his Daughters/ Had represented and contain" (17.1–2). The subsequent passage of Sin and Death along the causeway from hell to earth in the later books of *Paradise Lost* is also parallel to the passage of Ololon to the mundane creation. Sin informs Satan:

Hell could no longer hold us in her bounds,
Nor this unvoyageable Gulf obscure
Detain from following thy illustrious track.

                    (*P.L.* 10.365–8)

In *Milton*:

But Ololon sought the Or-Ulro & its fiery Gates
And the Couches of the Martyrs: & many Daughters of
    Beulah
Accompany them down to the Ulro with soft melodious
    tears
A long journey & dark thro Chaos in the track of Miltons
    course.

                    (34.19–22)

Milton's track parallels the "stupendous Bridge" (*P.L.*
10.351) stretching over "the dark Abyss" (*P.L.* 10.371).

There are many other parallels between the two journeys, and the strongly contrasting counterparts of the journeys point to the difference in means and purpose between
Satan and Milton. Satan's method of journeying past his
opposition is one of deceit. His changing appearance to a
toad (*P.L.* 4.800), a cormorant (*P.L.* 4.196), and eventually
to a serpent in Book 9, are suggested by the deceitful appearances of the covering cherub in *Milton*. The contrary of
this deceit is Milton's open meetings with the opposition. In
fact, the hypocrisy of those who oppose Milton's journey is
the hypocrisy of the selfhood, who is indeed Satan, as Milton has let us know at the very beginning of his journey: "I
in my selfhood am that Satan" (14.30). The Satan of
Paradise Lost and *Milton's* Satan being manifestations of
the same spiritual evil, Milton must undo the work of Satan
to achieve self-annihilation. Against Urizen Milton uses no
wiles, but silently begins the work of renewal. To the siren
song of Rahab, Milton responds not. Satan's disguises in
the garden parallel negatively Milton's plain garb when Milton, separating from the covering cherub,

Descended down a Paved work of all kinds of precious
stones
Out from the eastern sky; descending down into my Cottage
Garden; clothed in black, severe & silent he descended.
(38.6–8)

Milton's silent refusal to use the deceits of the covering
cherub is akin to another negative parallel between Satan
and Milton. When Satan is caught by Ithuriel and Zephon
and taken before Gabriel, a battle between the evil and
good forces becomes imminent. But a sign in heaven informs Satan of his ultimate defeat should he use arms (*P.L.*
4.1000ff.). Satan's refusal to do battle, motivated by his
desire for triumph and power, differs markedly from Milton's refusal to use power (38.29–35). Milton's refusal is an
open denial of the efficacy of force. Milton's refusal lacks
the hypocrisy of Satan's boasting and Satan's motivation
for dominion. In fact, his refusal implies that force locks the
individual in a cycle of endless struggle for domination.
Milton's journey thus exemplifies the openness and passivity that destroy deceit and aggression. It is the removal of
the rotten rags of the selfhood that Milton wishes to bring to
man. The rotten rags are the clothing of Adam and Eve, the
delusion of sin, that Satan left as his legacy to man, the
legacy of man's own selfhood.

The parallels between Milton and Moses, like those of
Milton and Satan, also involve a difference, but the explanation of those parallels will require a look at Watson and
Paine again. Milton's struggle in the lands around Canaan
has long been recognized as parallel to Moses' proceedings
through the desert, leading the Israelites to the promised
land.[39] In fact, Milton's descent from eternity to Blake's
garden is also related to Moses' journey. Milton's leaving
eternity is generally parallel to the Jews leaving Egypt. Just
as the Israelites crossed the Red Sea, Milton crosses the sea
of time and space. The Israelites were led by a pillar of

cloud by day and of fire by night. Milton appears as a falling star, a rough equivalent of the fire, and then as a black cloud, when he descends to Blake. Not long after they have crossed the Red Sea, Moses and the Israelites receive the decalogue at Sinai. In his descent to the desert, Milton first lands on Sinai, where he writes the cruelties of Ulro, which would include the delusion of the moral restrictions of the decalogue. In their journey the Israelites meet resistance from the king of Edom, but they manage to circumvent his kingdom. Milton in his journey meets resistance from Los, but he manages to pass. The Israelites struggle with kings Og and Sihon, who are slain as the Israelites proceed to the Jordan. Milton meets Urizen, with whom he struggles, but without violence or physical conquest. The Israelites are aided in their invasion of Canaan by the prostitute Rahab, who protects the spies of Joshua, the Israelite general. As Milton struggles with Urizen he is beckoned across the Jordan into Canaan by Rahab and Tirzah. They invite him to partake of the pleasures of Canaan by coming in conquest. Milton seems to ignore them. These rough parallels give shape and meaning to the theme of war in *Milton*.

We have already noted the weariness of the English war effort and Blake's association of peace with his own projected journey, as well as the numerous references in *Milton* denouncing the evil of war. It is Satan who musters to war (10.11). It is Rahab who is revealed as religion hidden in war (37.43).

The evaluation of the journey of Moses, who is marching to conquest, throws light on the meaning of Milton's parallel journey. Blake is following the evaluation of Thomas Paine, whose *Age of Reason*, attacking the morality of Moses, was attacked in turn by Bishop Watson. Paine is a violent opponent of Moses. He disapproves particularly of the warmongering of the Israelites under Moses' leadership. The invasion of the promised land for Paine is merely rapine and murder.

There are matters in that book [the Bible], said to be done by the *express command* of God, that are as shocking to humanity and to every idea we have of moral justice as anything done by Robespierre, by Carrier, by Joseph le Bon, in France, by the English government in the East Indies, or by any other assassin in modern times. When we read in the books ascribed to Moses, Joshua, etc., that they (the Israelites) came by stealth upon whole nations of people, who, as history itself shows, had given them no offense; that they put all those nations to the sword; that they spared neither age nor infancy; that they utterly destroyed men, women and children; that they left not a soul to breathe—expressions that are repeated over and over again in those books, and that, too, with exulting ferocity—are we sure these things are facts? Are we sure that the Creator of man commissioned these things to be done? And are we sure that the books that tell us so were written by His authority.[40]

Besides, the character of Moses, as stated in the Bible is the most horrid that can be imagined. If these accounts be true, he was the wretch that first began and carried on wars on the score or on the pretense of religion; and under that mask, or infatuation, committed the most unexampled atrocities that are to be found in the history of any nation, of which I will state only one instance. When the Jewish army returned from one of their plundering and murdering excursions, the account goes as follows [Here Paine quotes Numbers 31:13].

Among the detestable villains that in any period of the world have disgraced the name of man, it is impossible to find a greater than Moses, if this account be true. Here is an order to butcher the boys, to massacre the mothers and debauch the daughters.

After this detestable order, follows an account of the

plunder taken, and the manner of dividing it; and here it is that the profaneness of priestly hypocrisy enters the catalogue of crimes.[41]

this book, said to have been written by Joshua, reference to *facts done* after the death of Joshua, it is evidence that Joshua could not be the author; and also that the book could not have been written till after the time of the latest fact which it records! As to the character of the book [Joshua], it is horrid; it is a military history of rapine and murder, as savage and brutal as those recorded of his predecessor in villainy and hypocrisy, Moses; and the blasphemy consists, as in the former books, in ascribing those deeds to the orders of the Almighty.[42]

These two books [Kings 1 and 2] are little more than a history of assassinations, treachery and wars. The cruelties that the Jews had accustomed themselves to practise on the Canaanites, whose country they had savagely invaded under a pretended gift from God, they afterward practised as furiously on each other.[43]

Paine's violent dislike of the Israelite's invasion of Canaan is part of his attack on the authenticity of the Bible. Now, it is clear that Blake thought the Bible to be the authentic word of God, and neither Paine nor Voltaire, nor any other deist, could dissuade him. But it is also clear that Blake saw the Israelite's invasion of Canaan just as Paine saw it. Paine's opinions were attacked by Bishop Watson in 1797, and Blake's annotations to Watson illustrate how Blake assimilated Paine's point of view. Blake writes:

To me who believe the Bible and profess myself a Christian, a defense of the Wickedness of the Israelites in murdering so many thousands under pretense of a command from God is altogether Abominable & Blasphemous. Wherefore did Christ come was it not to abolish

the Jewish Imposture Was not Christ murderd because
he taught that God Loved all men & was their father &
forbid all contention for Wordly prosperity in opposition
to the Jewish Scriptures which are only an example of
the wickedness & deceit of the Jews & were written as
an Example of the possibility of Human Beastliness in
all its branches.[44]

Farther on Blake writes: "the destruction of the Canaanites
by Joshua was the Unnatural design of wicked men To
Extirpate a nation by means of another nation is as wicked
as to destroy an individual by means of another individual
which God considers (in the Bible) as Murder & commands
that it shall not be done."[45] Blake makes other remarks that
indicate that at least on the point of the morality of the
Israelite's invasion of Canaan, Blake and Paine were
agreed. With this knowledge, we may begin to understand
what some of the parallels between Milton and Moses
mean.

One of the first of Milton's acts is the denial of the intention of the journey to Canaan. After hearing the Bard's
song, Milton rose in eternity and removed the "robe of the
promise & ungirded himself from the oath of God" (14.13).
The oath of God is no other than the oath made to Abraham. In Deuteronomy Moses explains to the Israelites
that "because the Lord loved you and because he would
keep his oath which he had sworn unto your fathers, hath
the Lord brought you out [of Egypt] with a mighty hand"
(Deut. 7:8). This is the oath made to Abraham in Genesis
12:7 and repeated in Genesis 15:7. It occurs again in
Exodus 3:17 and 6:4: "and I have also established my cov-
enant with them, to give them the land of Canaan, the land
of their pilgrimage, wherein they were strangers." Thus
Milton's removal of the robe of the promise is really a
pointed denial of the whole intention of the Israelites to
take Canaan. The precise reason for the denial is made
clear in allusions to later parts of the Israelite's journey.

Paralleling Milton's struggle with Urizen to the journey of the Israelites in Arabia and the western side of Jordan, Blake writes:

Silent they [Milton and Urizen] met, and silent
   strove among the streams, of Arnon
Even to Mahanaim, when with cold hand Urizen
   stoop'd down
And took up water from the river Jordan: pouring on
To Miltons brain the icy fluid from his brood cold palm.
But Milton took of the red clay of Succoth, moulding it with
   care
Between his palms; and filling up the furrows of many years
Beginning at the feet of Urizen, and on the bones
Creating new flesh on the Demon cold, and building him,
As with new clay a Human form in the Valley of Beth Peor.
                  (19.6–14)

This passage covers the territory stretching from Succoth, one of the sites where the Israelites rested at the beginning of their journey, to Beth-Peor, where Moses was buried, a spot close to Jordan. The Arnon is a river flowing westward into the Dead Sea, a spot midway in the Israelite's journey in the lands east of the Dead Sea. Struggling with various opposing tribes, the Israelites finally encamped in the area of east Jordan until they were led into Canaan by Joshua's armies. In this area occurs the struggle between Urizen and Milton. Urizen represents, on one level, the resistance of the various tribes to the Israelites, which elicited from the Israelites the warlike response that destroyed them. But Milton does not destroy Urizen, for that would be to fall into the trap of the selfhood. Rather, he reforms him. On another level, Urizen's attempts to baptize Milton repre- sent an attempt to assimilate him into a state religion for the purpose of conquest, just as Moses as leader and Aaron as priest forged the war machine that conquered Canaan. Mil- ton, however, resists the attempt and, instead of resorting to war, responds with a humane effort to create Urizen

anew, an effort symbolically encompassing the whole journey of the Israelites. For Blake this act represents the alternative to the destruction resulting from a warmongering
state religion. Moses and Aaron are still with man in the
persons of Watson and Pitt. "The Beast & the Whore rule
without control."[46]

A third episode in the parallel occurs while Milton reforms Urizen.

> The Man [Milton] and Demon [Urizen] strove many
> periods. Rahab beheld
> Standing on Carmel; Rahab and Tirzah trembled to behold
> The enormous strife. one giving life, the other giving death
> To his adversary. and they sent forth all their sons &
> daughters
> In all their beauty to entice Milton across the river,
>
> Saying. Come thou to Ephraim! behold the Kings of Ca-
> naan!
> The beautiful Amalekites, behold the fires of youth
> Bound with the Chain of Jealousy by Los & Enitharmon;
>
> Come then to Ephraim & Manasseh O beloved-one!
> Come to my ivory palaces O beloved of thy mother!
> And let us bind thee in the bands of War & be thou King
> of Canaan and reign in Hazor where the Twelve Tribes
> meet.
>
> So spoke they as in one voice! Silent Milton stood before
> The darkend Urizen; as the sculptor silent stands before
> His forming image; he walks round it patient labouring.
> Thus Milton stood forming bright Urizen.
>
> (19.27–20.10)

Rahab is the prostitute who conceals Joshua's spies in
Jericho in return for protection when the Israelites invade.

In effect, she has become a traitor to insure her own survival. To Blake she seems to be inviting the Israelites. Her
intention in *Milton* is to lure Milton across the Jordan, that
is, to entice him to an act of aggression that would pervert
his intentions. She offers the lure of dominion and power if
he will partake of the militarism that stifles freedom (the
Amalekites are chained). Her final allurement, that Milton
will be bound in the bonds of war, simply reinforces the
point. To enter Canaan is to enter into a war of conquest
that will perpetuate itself. John Milton, and the England of
Blake's day, needed to avoid the promise of victorious
dominion. Thus the analogy between Blake's Milton and
Moses is really meant as a contrast. Moses' failure to enter
Canaan was not of his own will. Milton, however, stead-
fastly refuses the enticements, and in essence has corrected
the error of Moses. Later in the poem, when Milton refuses
to strike at Satan on the grounds that the use of force
merely necessitates the use of force again when another
aggressor comes, the contrast of Milton to Moses helps
explain what Blake saw as the wearisome and endless
struggle that victory of arms always seems to extort from a
nation. But we shall now examine Milton's journey more
closely.

6

The Journey

I. GENERAL STRUCTURE OF THE JOURNEY

Blake organized Milton's journey in such a way as to demonstrate the relationship of the individual episodes to the central act of self-annihilation at the finale of the poem.[1] One of his principles of organization is that of incremental revelation: with each episode he reveals more and more of the cause of evil, until, at the finale of the poem, the whole truth stands open to Blake's and the reader's gaze.[2] We shall see how Milton's journey proceeds in two stages, the first representing the resistance by, and Milton's discovery of, the selfhood and its spiritual causes, in the exterior world, and the second stage representing the discovery of the external world of expanded vision. We shall see how Ololon follows Milton to discover her own selfhood, and how, at the finale of the poem, self-annihilation occurs as Milton and Ololon join, after their selfhoods have been revealed for what they really are and have been shuffled off.[3] The stages of Milton's journey are complicated by the division of *Milton* into four separate "portions." Blake attempts to delineate this fourfold division by summarizing on plate twenty the fourfold distinction as (1) the "redeemed" portion traveling in the mundane shell; (2) a "Mortal" part as physical death; (3) the "Real Human," which exists in eternity; and (4) the elect, or shadow Milton redounding from Blake's left foot, in essence the selfhood in its exterior manifestation (20.7–29). The redounding black cloud from Blake's left foot represents the effects of the selfhood on Europe. The shadow aspect of Milton remains in this situation (the cloud over Europe) until the "redeemed" portion of Milton, (which is the same as Milton's "Human Shadow") completes its journey.

Milton's "redeemed" portion's journey, a dream of the "Real Human" Milton, takes place in the mundane shell, thus carrying over the distinctions between divisions of Milton's identity into Blake's distinctions of place. Milton's shadow travels through chaos, past Beulah and Albion, through the sea of time and space, ending in Blake's foot. His shadow has journeyed through part of Blake's cosmic world to become momentarily fixed as a black cloud in time and space, recognizable from Ulro only as a black cloud. The redeemed portion of his shadow, however, continues the journey in the realm of the Mundane Shell, encountering Blake's spiritual entities: the Four Zoas, the Shadowy Female and her biblical descendents, and Urizen. The mundane shell is a realm distinct from the world of time and space, though the spiritual entities there are the symbolic spiritual causes of the events in time and space. In this section of the journey, parallels between similar though vastly separated temporal events suggest that these separate events are results of the same spiritual causation. For instance, biblical characters (e.g., Rahab and Tirzah) are seen as symbols of the spiritual cause (shadowy female) that has created the phenomenon of the eighteenth century (Rahab creates Voltaire, Tirzah creates Rousseau). The journey of the "redeemed" portion of Milton continues in this realm until Milton encounters Urizen. Once Blake has advanced the story of the "redeemed" portion's journey to this culminating episode, he leaves the "redeemed" portion struggling with Urizen outside of time, and continues his narrative with the "Real Human" portion of Milton, Milton's shadow, Los, and Blake all joined, moving through an even more greatly expanded vision, which is the realm of eternity or Eden. At the finale, Milton separates into two, final, opposing sections—the real human and shadow—the latter of which is revealed as the Satanic selfhood. Ololon must be conceived as Milton's counterpart, or emanation, and just as Milton's selfhood is Satan, the Dragon, and Urizen, so Ololon's selfhood is Leutha, Rahab, and Tirzah. The symbolic meaning of Blake's female is that of mental expression or creation. She is the objective counterpart of subjective perception by the human, here symbolized by Ololon. When she attempts to become independent, that is, is under domination by the selfhood, she takes on various delusory appearances such as Rahab, Tirzah, or Leutha. All the manifestations of Milton's sixfold emanation share the quality of delusion. It is the revelation of the true delusive nature of those females that Ololon finds at the end of her journey, and her discovery allows her to undergo the act of self-annihilation, just as Milton's discovery allows him to do the same. Throughout the poem, Blake has used the female to represent delusion, and we can see how Ololon connects virtually every female in the poem by her discovery of her own delusory selfhood. The delusion of Leutha is working within Satan throughout the Bard's Song. Satan is said to be in a feminine delusion of false pride (11.26), and Leutha admits that she desired Palamabron and caused Satan's deluded love, because Elynittria's jealousy prevented her from having Palamabron (11.35–12.8). This check to her impulse led her, in dragon form, to attack Elynittria. To prevent this impulse, she employs secretive means that lead to Satan's delusion. This is the first of the connections between female jealousy, delusion, and female control of the male, that is, the hermaphroditic delusion. After Leutha has been driven from Satan's brain, and Satan has had a space created for him, Leutha and Elynittria reconcile as Leutha flies to Satan's space and is brought to Palamabron's bed "in moments new created for delusion" (13.39). She becomes the mother of Rahab, who is the mother of Tirzah. Delusion thus mothers delusion. Moreover, at the end of the work, it is Ololon who claims Rahab and Tirzah as a portion of herself. Ololon is then the true "human" counterpart of the whole delusory female part of the selfhood. It is the selfhood of Ololon that is the hermaphroditic shadow Milton finds as he enters the verge of Beulah. It is Ololon who stands behind the alluring speech of Rahab and Tirzah as Milton struggles with Urizen. But just as Milton's real human portion remains briefly in eternity as his redeemed portion proceeds on its journey in the mundane shell, so Ololon is the real, human portion of the females working to delude Milton. Ololon, like Milton, must discover these truths about her selfhood, and reunite with Milton before the act of self-annihilation is complete.

But we must focus more narrowly on the details than this general view permits.

II. JOURNEY OF MILTON'S SHADOW

Milton's partial identity and his ensuing journey are forecast even in the Bard's Song when Palamabron says: "prophetic I behold/His [Satan's] future course thro' darkness and despair to eternal death" (7.24–25), a statement that describes not Satan's but Milton's journey.[4] Milton, motivated by the Bard's Song, begins his journey in Eden, as the bard brings his story to a close. The bard, terrified at the resistance to his song suggested by the murmuring in the heavens of Albion, which represents the church-dominated, fallen world that had emerged from the fall into selfhood, takes refuge in Milton's bosom (14.4–9). Psychologically, the Bard's taking refuge symbolizes the influx of inspiration that Milton has experienced from hearing the song. Milton rises, showing in his countenance "the shades of Death & Ulro" (14.12), indicating that John Milton has yet to annihilate the selfhood's delusion, which he still retains and which is still affecting the England he has left behind. Seeing Milton, the divine assembly weeps, thereby suggesting that the separation between wrath and pity, begun at the fall, is about to be healed (14.10–12). Then Milton ungirds himself from the oath of God (14.13); on the individual level he is denying the destructive impulse to conquer, and on the cosmic level he is abandoning the promise of dominion offered by state religion.[5] Milton's ensuing speech gives the key to the meaning of the entire journey. He begins by focusing on the present state of life in the fallen world. Separated from eternity, which is the imagination, life is eternal death, or delusion. That life in chains of the selfhood is warlike, contradictory, and blasphemous, because the selfhood is ultimately delusive and destructive (14.14–16). Milton suggests that there is potential freedom from the selfhood's chains when he alludes to images of resurrection, of awakening, and of morning, all of which represent the removal of delusion; Milton expects Jesus' coming (14.17–18), which is really that of Milton himself, the eighth eye, and this expectation is a foreshadowing of the finale of the poem when Milton and Ololon join, appearing as Jesus.[6] Milton then announces his intention to go to the "sepulchre," and "self annihilation" (14.20–4). In other words he announces his intention to make the journey to remove himself from the dominion of his selfhood, which has given him his worldly delusion and drive for domination. He sees Christ dimly (14.25–28), but this is a forecast of Christ's full appearance at the end of the poem, when he will be seen with the clear vision of imagination that has removed the mists of rationalism. Milton focuses next on the separation between himself and his emanation (14.28–9). He suggests that his journey is to reclaim his emanation, which is Blake's way of saying that Milton must remove the selfhood's delusions that have controlled his perception of reality; at the moment he is locked in a materialistic world of memory without vision or inspiration. Milton then identifies himself as Satan, the spectre, the selfhood, stating that he goes to free him from the furnace (14.30–32), which is the selfhood's endless round of domination in this world. The purpose of Milton's journey, to go to self-annihilation, is thus to be accomplished by the release of Satan and the uniting of Milton with his emanation. These two symbolic gestures, freeing Satan and redeeming the emanation, which constitute self-annihilation, like leitmotifs throughout the journey, remind the reader of Milton's purpose.

Milton begins his journey on "the outside course" (14.34). In terms of the poem's cosmos, Milton has entered the physical world without taking bodily form in a womb. He is only on the "verge of Beulah" (14.36). He has not been lured through Beulah down the river Storge (34.30) by amorous delight of the separate male and female, as the Neoplatonist imagines the soul drawn into the body; rather he has entered the physical world without the sexual garments. It is this outside course among the graves of the dead that causes eternity to shudder (14.35). Milton's act, which has never been known before (23.56–58), allows Milton's identity to be diffused into different aspects during his journey, for it is not bound into the physical body.

Milton's descent to his shadow (15.2) marks his reentrance into the selfhood that must be annihilated. As he takes his shadow form, he is beginning the process of revealing the shadow's true outlines. His is a voyage of discovery, as he announces at the finale (38.43–46), both for himself and for all men, for the act of self-annihilation requires true vision. His descent into the vegetated shadow is the beginning of the fourfold division of Milton, though at first he exists only in the dual state of shadow and of real human in eternity. Milton's shadow, which is "vegetated" (15.9), symbolizes the results in the exterior world of those delusions exemplified by John Milton. The shadow is the twenty-seven churches of state-controlled orthodoxy and the hermaphrodite of state religion. Later it is revealed that the shadow is the polypus of the material body, the materialistic delusion stemming from rationalism (15.8–10). As Milton enters the shadow here, one may feel bewildered by the mysterious identification of the shadow as twenty-sevenfold, or as hermaphroditic, or as a polypus. But the mystery is purposeful. As Milton journeys, the question of the identity of these symbols becomes more important to the reader, and in the finale, Milton's discovery is an answer to the reader's questions. Just as Milton has come to discover for himself, the truths are discovered for the questioning reader too.

The division of Milton into the duality of journeying shadow and immortal spirit residing in eternity emerges from the picture of the seven eyes of God surrounding Milton's couch in eternity (15.3–8). As his shadow part journeys, his immortal or "real human" part resides in eternity for a short interval. His "real and immortal" self, though asleep in eternity, is aware, as in a dream, of his journeying part. This double awareness suggests that this is a journey of self-discovery in which one delves into his roots and examines his motives and productions. It is self-examination, recollection of things past, psychoanalysis, anamnesis, or whatever general name one chooses for the process of sorting out things of the individual's inner world. It is a psychic journey. The emanations that feed the sleeping Milton (15.13–15) are the creations of the starry seven to help Milton to his own discovery, just as the prophet's word or artist's work help the individual to find the truths of the world and of himself.

The shadow part of the man, the selfhood, experiences the discovery, however, as an actor in a dream. The awakened man in eternity is able to see that the dream world has meaning that he could not comprehend in the actual dream experience. But his shadow feels, in the dream, as a "wanderer lost in dreary night" (15.16). Blake does not deal with the state of doubting uncertainty where man does not know if he wakes or sleeps. The sleep of doubt produces only a weary dream of life where man wanders only to find the cold repose of materialistic certainty. He must awaken from this mere dream of life, and must leave behind the flying shadow world for the radiance of imaginative vision.

The shadow part of Milton therefore travels into a chaos, which is purposefully reminiscent of Satan's journey in *Paradise Lost*. But the journey into this gulf is a guarded one for Milton, whose "real human" is surrounded in eternity by the seven eyes (15.20). His shadow's journey is described in a universe of vortices that are the centers of each material being, but also a universe where time and space are not the ultimate reality (15.21–35). As the individual moves in this universe, he goes from vortex to vortex on an infinite plane, almost from mental state to mental state. The vortex, Blake's reworking of the Cartesian concept, thus marks sequence, not space.[7] It introduces Milton's particular meeting with one part of the chaos in the material world, the giant Albion asleep on the rock in eternity (15.36). Milton's meeting with Albion is explained in the vortex passage, for the passage describes events of an individual's journey through life as if they were the same as celestial bodies in a journey through space. Milton's passage through the vortex of Albion becomes a fall into the sea of time and space. Albion from the point of view of eternity would appear to the descending Milton as a dead man, but when Milton enters into him, as though into past existence, he finds the causes of that dead appearance, which is really only profound slumber. Milton bursts into the physical universe as it is perceived by earth dwellers, and appears to Blake "in the Zenith as a falling star/ Descending perpendicular" (15.47–48). This wonderful appearance brings the world of spirits and the phenomenological world into focus for the reader. The physical manifestation of the spiritual event is the falling star, which all men would recognize with their limited senses, yet its momentary flight is part of a spiritual epic of immense moment.[8] Milton lands on Blake's left foot, and "enter'd there" (15.49). Milton is beginning the assimilation with Blake that will continue to grow as poem and journey progress. Milton's shadow's journey from eternity to Blake's foot is also the creation of an outside course, or a track that will be followed later in the poem by the immortal part of Milton and by Ololon.

III. JOURNEY OF THE REDEEMED PORTION OF MILTON

But the shadow aspect of Milton's identity must be assumed to become threefold at this point in the poem, though Blake does not note the division. Milton's shadow now exists as (1) the redeemed portion, "human shadow" (17.18) journeying in the mundane shell, (2) the rock Sinai, and (3) the shadow cloud redounding from Blake's left foot. Only the first of these divisions is now active in the poem, and the redeemed portion continues the journey until the "real human" part of Milton joins with Blake later in the journey. Milton's "redeemed" portion, traveling in the "Mundane Shell," first encounters Milton's three wives and daughters, who are, like Milton, divided between a "real human" existence in eternity and their physical, delusory existence. His "redeemed" portion is "in conflict with those Female forms" (17.7), as he will be in conflict with the at-first-mistaken Los, and with Urizen. Milton's wives and daughters, who are the Shadowy Female, Rahab, and Tirzah, attempt to stop his journey or corrupt his purpose by seducing him into the purposes of the selfhood. Their existence is essentially on three levels, though only one is really active. Like Milton, they have a human form (17.4) in eternity, and a twofold portion existing in the mundane shell. Their "mortal" portion is symbolized in the barren mountains of the deserts of Midian (Hor, Peor, etc), which is also Ulro, the delusion of physical materiality that deadens the spirit. Though given biblical names and places in the rocky mass of the mundane shell, this portion takes no action throughout the poem. The other portion of these females in the mundane shell are Rahab and Tirzah, as well as the rest of the daughters of Zelophehad, the first two acting symbolically for the six. When he encounters them, Milton is said to see "the cruelties of Ulro," which he "wrote . . . down/ In iron tablets" (17.9–10). His iron tablets, parallel to the decalogue that Moses accepted on Sinai, contain the dictate said to be copied by his daughters (17.13–14), recalling the legend of Milton dictating to his daughters. However, the iron tablets of this dictation are far different from stone tablets of the decalogue. Milton is writing down the cruelties he is discovering about the ethic of the selfhood; he is writing the divine dictate, mentioned later, that explains the rule of self-annihilation, and this dictate is producing his daughters' resistance in thunder, smoke, and fire. The thunder, smoke, and fire also suggest the resistance to Milton's journey that is to follow. (Los's obstruction of roots is parallel to the thunderous complaint of Milton's six females, and to the freezing of Milton's feet in marble in the succeding episode with Urizen. This resistance is stiffened with each character trying to obstruct or pervert Milton.) Milton's "redeemed" portion proceeds in regions of the mundane shell, specifically the deserts of Midian, leading up to the Jordan, thus repeating the passage of Moses. But Blake tells us that travelers from eternity pass outward to Satan's seat. Milton has left eternity on the outside path and proceeds to Canaan, Satan's seat. That is to say, if Milton does repeat Moses' journey by being perverted into the designs of the selfhood, he has gone to Satan's seat. His "redeemed" portion must repeat the journey, dramatically changing the final step that would be the culmination of the seductions into the selfhood.

The first overt resistance Milton's "redeemed" portion encounters is that of the mistaken Los, putting up obstructive roots because of Enitharmon's fear that Milton would "unloose my bond . . . Satan shall be unloos'd upon Albion'' (17.32–33). In psychological terms, one may say that the superego fears the unloosing of the id. But this indeed is precisely what Milton intends (he has come ''to loose Satan from my hells''). Enitharmon's fear of the freeing of Satan is a mistaken, selfhood-induced fear of impulse. The results of that freeing, however, are different from those imagined by the anxious Enitharmon or the other members of Los's family. Their purpose has been to restrict in order to save. But they have unwittingly aided the selfhood by creating physical form, which can never be a permanent residence of the spirit. Milton's fear-destroying act of self-annihilation will remove the anxiety of Enitharmon which, while it is the very chain that holds Satan, is also the chain with which Satan holds the world. That Los's resistance is mistaken is dramatized in the next section, when Los comes to realize that Milton's journey is to free Orc. The equation of Orc and Satan is not the point of the discovery, but that the act of freeing frees both the binder and the bound. Satan's being unloosed will not give him license to destroy the sleeping Albion as Enitharmon fears, but will free men from the reactionary fear that gives the selfhood license to invoke the rules of power. In the historical world of time and space Enitharmon's fear would be manifest as the conservative reaction against the principles of the French Revolution. Pitt, the lover of English liberty, had called for ''gagging'' bills. Burke, the supporter of the rights of the American colonies, had denounced the French revolutionaries. Watson, a guardian of the church, had called for increased taxes to support the war against France. For fear drives them all to use power to maintain the status quo, which itself is the work of the selfhood. The endless cycle of domination can stop only when the dominator is totally free from fear. Milton's nonthreatening actions on his journey are the antithesis of the syndrome displayed by Enitharmon and Los.

Milton's journey is beheld by the other zoas: Urizen, Tharmas, and Luvah, who is Orc, though Tharmas takes no action in the poem and Orc only passive action. In fact, the mention of the two zoas, Orc and Tharmas, seems Blake's artificial transition from the resistance of Los to the plans of resistance of the Shadowy Female, who is in company with Orc. Though Blake implies that all the zoas are resisting, his purpose is to connect the Shadowy Female with Milton's journey. Plate eighteen, which contains the episode, is an added plate; Blake, needing a transition to the episode, used the connection between Los and the other zoas to introduce the Shadowy Female and Orc. It is possible to read from plate seventeen to plate nineteen without losing the thread of Milton's redeemed portion's journey to the culminating episode with Urizen. But the insertion of plate eighteen fulfills another purpose. It furnishes a contrast to the actions of Milton on the ensuing plate, and it informs the reader of the purpose of Rahab and Tirzah. As Los, inspired by Enitharmon's fear, resists by trying to block Milton, the Shadowy Female, more than resisting, intends to pervert his purpose; and perversion rather than obstruction is the purpose of the resistance of Rahab, Tirzah, and Urizen. The Shadowy Female outlines the method of perversion that the seductive Rahab and Tirzah attempt to put into practice. She is, in fact, the spiritual essence of Rahab and Tirzah, who are biblical manifestations of the delusion she represents.

The speech of the Shadowy Female (18.5–25) brings together, in Blake's best manner, elements of the phenomenological world and Blake's spiritual cosmos. The Shadowy Female says that she will take the human form and clothe it, but her clothing will be the covering of the selfhood. Symbolically her statement means that she (who is a spiritual cause) will manifest her delusive power in the living men of the eighteenth century, these men being human forms, images of God; but she will clothe them in a garment that is a picture of two classes of men, the oppressor and the oppressed. The oppressed are kept in a condition of servitude characterized by unhappy families, suffering, poverty, pain, woe, starvation, sick fathers, prisoners, slaves, and the delusive teaching of the ethic of the selfhood. Those in this condition have only broken hearts, anxiety, cares, desperation, death, repentance for sin, sorrow, punishment and fear. Blake has here created a Swiftian catalogue of evils almost as extensive as those appearing in the final book of *Gulliver's Travels*. His catalogue of the oppressors is smaller: kings, councillors, and mighty men, who employ famine, pestilence, and war to maintain their oppression. To entice Milton from his path to self-annihilation, the Shadowy Female is going to offer Milton power, power to become an oppressor, and that power is economic, psychological, political, and military: the realms of the exterior world where the selfhood manifests its domination most clearly. This offering, identical to the power offered by Rahab and Tirzah, explains the relation of the Shadowy Female to these two, for she intends "to divide into Rahab and Tirzah" (18.18). Her purpose in this offering is to defend herself from the terror of Orc (18.25). Thus she intends to pervert Milton's journey, which has as its purpose the breaking of the selfhood's restrictions. Her intention is to maintain dominance over Orc, and her putting on the human form is a hermaphroditic act of female domination. Psychologically, it is a form of sexual restriction. Historically, it is the same reactionary fear evinced from Enitharmon.

The hermaphroditic nature of the act is pointed out by Orc, who asks the Shadowy Female to take a female, not a human form. He would have her in her proper sphere, not in that of the usurping hermaphrodite. And the domination of the Shadowy Female seems to be defeated after the appearance of the temptresses Oothoon and Leutha, whom Orc woos in vain, and the appearance of the jealous darkness of the Shadowy Female, and earthquake and thunder rend "the Immortal Females limb from limb" (18.49). But this rending is no victory for Orc. On the contrary, it represents the success of the domination of the Shadowy

Female. For Orc has only remained locked in the cycle of domination, and he is doomed to repeat the process eternally until he is freed from the selfhood:

When thou attemptest to put on the Human Form, my wrath
Burns to the top of heaven against thee in Jealousy & Fear.
Then I rend thee asunder.
(18.31–33)

Orc's description of the process also marks the separation between wrath and pity. Previously the Shadowy Female had worn the garment of pity, but now she wears cruelty. Pity has been usurped by cruelty, and Orc's wrath is left only to consume in its own flames. In this separation lie the dynamics of the interminable repetition of Orc's wrathful rending, and the female's delusive covering of pity that is really the tyrant's cruelty. Ironically, Orc is chained on his couch throughout the episode. He can only stretch his hands to woo. The chain, of course, is the chain of the cycle, but a chain permitted and induced by Orc himself. It must be assumed that Orc's action is representative of the way *not* to respond to the female delusion. His wooing, his anger, and his destruction are part of the selfhood's dynamics of domination.

It is partly for this reason that Blake had inserted plate eighteen. It is a picture of successful female domination that contrasts sharply with the failure of the females on plate nineteen to dominate Milton. Both Orc and Milton face two women associated with the Shadowy Female as a source. Oothoon and Leutha are within "the Shadowy Female's bosom" (18.43) and the Shadowy Female intends "to divide into Rahab & Tirzah" (18.18). Rahab's and Tirzah's glorying in the "fires of youth/Bound with the Chain of Jealousy by Los & Enitharmon" (19.37–38) suggests their connection as causes with the fiery Orc of the previous plate. Tirzah is said to put on "all beauty/And all perfection" (19.44–45), just as Oothoon and Leutha mingle "in interchange of Beauty & Perfection" (18.40). Rahab and Tirzah, "shining in darkness, glorious upon the deeps of Entuthon" (19.35), are almost mirror images of Oothoon and Leutha "shining glorious/In the Shadowy Female's bosom. Jealous her darkness grew" (18.41–42). Just as Orc is lured into wooing and wrathfulness, so Rahab and Tirzah intend Milton to be seduced from his purpose. It is the contrast in results that is Blake's point. Orc's submission and wrath are pointedly different from Milton's silent refusal to respond. Milton's purpose is fulfilled not by rending Rahab and Tirzah or invading Canaan in military triumph, just as his purpose is not to destroy Urizen. The inserted plate, showing the intention of the Shadowy Female to pervert Milton's purpose, and her method of attack in the luring of Orc into wrath, thus serves to explain the intention of Rahab and Tirzah in the following episode and to furnish a contrast to Milton's "unexampled" action.[9]

The next episode in the journey of Milton's "redeemed" portion through the mundane shell forms a central symbol for the poem. I have already pointed out how the action represents a united symbol of creativity, and serves as a parallel to both the action of Christ before Caiphas and the action of Moses in leading Israel to Canaan. The episode also suggests, in the imagery of marble, the selfhood's love of controlling power. At first Urizen causes Milton's path to freeze, to become marble, thus making Milton's feet bleed. The change of clay to marble represents the distinction between the poor and the wealthy, like the distinction of the Shadowy Female between the oppressors and oppressed. The image of marble, recalling the marble of Greek temples and of Christian churches, suggests the cold, resplendent display of ecclesiastical power. It is the temptation of power that causes Milton's pain, making him labor in his journey.

The action has a further meaning directly related to self-annihilation.[10] Milton and Urizen then strive along the eastern borders of Jordan. This strife, besides being an allusion to Moses' journey, is mental strife, Urizen attempting to assimilate Milton through baptism, Milton to give Urizen a new form. Urizen's attempt to induce Milton to submit to an ecclesiastical order is interpreted as "giving death/To his adversary" (19.29–30). Milton is "giving life" (19.29). The paradox of self-annihilation is clarified somewhat here, for self-annihilation is not an act of destruction, which is the selfhood's way of enslavement of the destroyer as well as the destroyed. Rather it is a positive act of love requiring forgiveness. The act has internal implications, Urizen and Milton being the symbols of the defensiveness of the drive for survival and the altruism that gives man a comprehensive love and identification with all life. Psychologically, man forgives himself for his own defensiveness. This forgiveness implies truth and faith, requires openness and honesty. When one attempts the violence of psychological control of the defense mechanisms, a more sinister, malevolent, unconscious desire for domination and destruction result. Man must forgive himself, not control himself. His defensive gestures must not cause a guilt-ridden attempt to cease from being defensive. He must recognize the inevitability of his defense mechanisms and forgive himself for them. The defenses will not cease, but the feelings of guilt, which always call for retribution, must cease.

The act of forgiveness coincides with the image of building a new man with clay.[11] The image, suggesting the first building of man with the red clay of Adam's flesh, as well as the removal of blindness by the clay used by Christ, represents a life-giving act that transforms mere wordly existence into spiritual vision. This act suggests itself as the way to comprehend the idea of giving life to the selfhood. Love and openness imply a willingness to accept physical death, which the defense mechanisms of survival directly oppose. By giving the selfhood life, man implies a willingness to lose his life, even though selfhood, paradoxically, wishes to remain living. But selfhood is a part of identity, not the whole of it, and its blindness to spiritual existence must be forgiven.

A recapitulation of the relationship between the four zoas, Albion, and the fall follows (19.15–26), and is intended to suggest the significance of Milton's journey. It suggests first that the announced goal of the journey, eternal death, is now a journey to Golgonooza. The location of Golgonooza is later placed within the realm of the polypus or beyond Satan's seat (35.18–25), which is to say within the deepest recesses of the physical manifestation of man, or in eternity where the selfhood is inoperative. Milton is traveling toward Golgonooza, but must travel through chaos, time, and space, and the polypus of the body to reach it. Eternal death is the mental condition of the self-hood. Golgonooza is the creative and created world within each man that can bring salvation from eternal death. Second, complete return to the state of the universe before the fall, clearly referring to the departure of Urizen and the slaying of Albion, and reemphasis of the point that Urizen opposes Milton's journey are Blake's means of suggesting the enormous implications of the act of self-annihilation. It is not merely John Milton who is at stake, but Everyman. The reversal of the original fall is about to become exemplified before all mankind, and Urizen, the dark angel of the selfhood, opposes.

The hermaphroditic counterpart of Urizen, Rahab and Tirzah, introduced while Milton and Urizen struggle, appear before Milton just as Leutha and Oothoon appear before Orc, tempting him, alluring him, all for the purpose of controlling him (19.27–20.6).[12] Urizen and the two females, working together here to dominate Milton, exemplify and forecast the discovery of the hermaphroditic nature of the selfhood, "the dragon red and hidden harlot." Rahab and Tirzah here represent the delusion of power that lures man to conquest. The history of the biblical harlot Rahab who aided Joshua in the conquest of Canaan lies behind the allurement. Rahab is the delusion justifying the Israelite's notion that the possession of Canaan was divinely sanctioned, and thus she is the delusion of state religion, which ultimately is used to justify war. But this delusion is present in Blake's day in the form of natural religion; here Blake implies that natural religion is another attempt to furnish the delusion that reinforces the power structure of the world, thus merely another manifestation of the same force that lies behind state religion. Tirzah is Rahab's daughter. Natural religion is the cold learning, streaming from the Cambridge of Blake's day (Paley's crowning work, *Natural Theology*, was published in 1800), fulfilling the same need to grasp power that underlay the binding of the Amalekite youths in the chains of jealousy. Rahab's and Tirzah's delusory aspect appears in their lies. This ascription of the binding of the Amalekites to Los and Enitharmon is a half truth. Time and space are locations, not the causes, of the restriction. The separation of Enion from the fallen Tharmas, and Ahania from the fallen Urizen, are the effects of the fall into the selfhood, not real justification for the triumph of natural religion. The statement that Tirzah has power to enchain the spirit in the body's brain, heart, and loins, is a delusion. Later Blake illustrates the true spiritual causes of material creation, and Tirzah's claim to triumph here is an attempt to delude. She claims that the physical body, the "image" of the "Lamb of God," is born for war and sacrifice, thereby suggesting the power she possesses and can give to Milton. She invites him to the cities of Canaan (Ephraim, Manasseh, and Hazor), where he will be established as a king over the divided nations, and thus become the reigning symbol of political power sanctioned by religious delusion.[13]

The silent Milton, like Christ before Caiaphas and Pilate, and unlike the bound Orc or the conqueror Joshua, ignores the hermaphroditic temptation and patiently continues his symbolic gesture of forming a "new image." Blake then describes the four divisions of Milton, the mortal, redeemed, human, and elect parts. The elect ("selfhood," or "spectrous portion") broods over the mortal part of Milton. It then appears as the "cherub on Sinai," glowing in fear of the resurrection about to come, thus revealing, for the first time, how the delusive nature of state religion (the covering cherub) has its source in the individual's selfhood, and forecasting the success of Milton in achieving self-annihilation.

Until the end of the poem, Milton's redeemed portion remains, struggling to rebuild Urizen and avoiding the temptation of worldly power. His redeemed portion's journey, so far, has been "straight onward," to use Blake's phrase in his letter to Butts, and Milton's not wavering on the path begins the process of reawakening that has been forecast. "Albions sleeping Humanity began to turn upon his Couch/Feeling the electric flame of Miltons awful precepitate descent" (20.25–26). Thus Blake summarizes the accomplishment of Milton so far. His departure from eternity was marked by his descent through Albion, and his progress is marked by Albion's turning. The picture of Albion at this point thus recapitulates the accomplishment of Milton, and is summarized briefly once again: "Thus Milton fell thro' Albions heart, travelling outside of Humanity/Beyond the Stars in Chaos, in Caverns of the Mundane Shell" (20.41–42).

IV. JOURNEY OF MILTON'S HUMAN PORTION

At this point of the poem, a new section of the narrative begins, one that is potentially confusing on two accounts. First of all, Milton's location is in some measure confused by Blake's later insertion of plate thirty-two, which places Milton in eternity; although this plate has as its purpose the explanation of the doctrine of self-annihilation, it is not made entirely consistent with the location of Milton's human portion on his journey, for from this point in the poem, Milton's human part, who is the starry eighth in eternity, leaves eternity and joins with Blake to move onwards toward the discovery of the selfhood at Felpham. In broad terms, the complete departure from eternity suggests the complete act of self-annihilation. All of Milton must go to eternal death. But a second confusing element is introduced when Blake suggests that Milton is forced out of eternity, rather than departing willingly.[14] I wish to suggest, however, that Milton's departure is not forced, rather that the conditions of eternity are such that Milton must indeed depart in order to heal the split between wrath and pity that seems to exist even in eternity.[15] Part of the meaning of the reconciliation of Milton and Ololon lies in the healing of the split between wrath and pity. At this point, Ololon makes her first entrance into the poem, and she is characterized by wrath. As an eternal, she appears as a sexless group filled with rage, apparently directed against the human portion of Milton. These eternals are filled with wrath and "rend the heavens round the Watchers in a fiery circle/And round the Shadowy Eighth" (20.46–47). The eight, which includes Milton's human portion, "flee with cries down to the Deep. . . . They soon find their own place & join the Watchers of the Ulro" (20.48–50).[16] Yet we learn later that this descent has been willed because Milton knew the divine dictate (21.52–53). His act of obedience to the dictate is discovered later by the wrathful eternals who themselves, at the moment of discovery, shift from wrath to lamentation. At that moment, as wrath joins again with pity and love, the wrathful eternals appear as the river Ololon, and begin the process of descent into a female form, by which they may rejoin with Milton. Thus Milton's exemplary acceptance of the dictate, mistaken by the eternals for a forced eviction, leads to the healing of the split between wrath and pity. Milton's human portion's descent is seen by Los, who now recollects the prophecy that Milton will set Orc free. This recollection elicits from Los action distinctly different from his previous resistance to Milton, and his present reaction, after his seeing the human aspect of Milton and understanding its true implication, is also to be contrasted with the fear-inspired and mistaken resistance of Rintrah and Palamabron to come. Los recalls the prophecy that Milton will free Orc from his chain of jealousy, which brings into the reader's mind Milton's original statement of purpose—to loose Satan from his hells. Thus Blake reinforces the intention of the journey, which will be complete when the restricting forces of the selfhood are removed. Following the "vast breach of Milton's [shadow's] descent" (21.7), Milton's human portion now enters Blake's foot. Milton's human portion's entrance to Blake's foot and his joining the watchers of the Ulro are the same act, for to watch Ulro is to be in time and space. Blake, however, is still limited by the Ulro vision. He is ignorant of the entire spiritual meaning—only Los has a hint of the significance of the events. For the revelation of the full significance, it is necessary that Los, the force of imagination, Milton, the prophet of self-annihilation, and Blake, the vegetated man laboring to bring eternal creation to light, join in a harmonious relationship so that Blake may "reveal the secrets of Eternity" (21.10).[17] And Milton's entry to Blake's foot symbolizes the first glimpse of the true spiritual nature of reality to Blake. Previously, Milton has appeared only as a falling star, a physical manifestation. Now Blake binds on the whole vegetable world as a sandal, thus putting in perspective the view of physical reality as his spiritual vision expands so that he may join the journey "to walk forward thro Eternity" (21.14).[18] At this point Blake shifts the focus of the narrative to Ololon to illuminate another kind of recognition, that recognition by Ololon that she too must completely depart from eternity (21.15–60). Not only is the name Ololon now given to the wrathful eternals who surrounded Milton in a fiery circle, but their character has undergone a change: "There is in Eden a River of milk & liquid pearl/Nam'd Ololon, on whose mild banks dwelt those who Milton drove/Down into Ulro" (21.15–17).[19] Milton's opponents now weep for their deed; Fisher long ago pointed out that the Greek root for Ololon suggests lamentation,[20] an appropriate name for the eternals at this point, when they are shifting from wrath to mildness and sighing. But now Ololon is no longer identifiable as a group of eternals. Now Ololon has become a female, an emanation of Milton himself. This surprising shift of identity from eternals to emanation, however, can be explained if one recalls that earlier in the poem Milton's sixfold emanation is said to have a human (i.e., eternal) portion (17.3–4) just as Milton had. The fiery circle of wrathful eternals has always been Milton's emanations. Their sudden change here indicates that the split is about to be healed. But the split between the contraries of wrath and pity that began with Satan's fall can be completely healed only with the joining of the masculine, prophetic wrath of Milton with the feminine, emanative pity of Ololon. Ololon's shift toward pity, her becoming, in fact, a lament at this point, gives her the potential to fulfill her journey's major purpose, the discovery of the truth about the female hermaphrodite that is working in the world of time and space.

Ololon laments that they had driven Milton into Ulro, "for they knew too late/That it was Milton the Awakener: they had not heard the Bard/Whose song call'd Milton to the attempt" (21.32–34). They had not known that Milton's shadow had gone of its own will. The inference from their ignorance is that failure of knowledge leads to an aggressive attempt, and as such fits the selfhood's shift from delusion to destruction. Ololon's lament is for the wrath that they think has driven Milton down, though Milton's motive indeed is not fear but love. The Divine Family, the total brotherhood of eternity that is Christ, now sympathizes with the lamenting Ololon, who decides to "descend also. Let us give/Ourselves to death in Ulro among the Transgressors" (21.45–46). Ololon has decided on the same act that Milton attempts. But she also asks a key question: "Is Virtue a Punisher?" and answers it from within with the inevitable No. Her answer is also a reflection on the wrath she has previously shown. The driving of Milton from eternity has been motivated by self-righteous wrath, the "virtue" of the selfhood, and Ololon has discovered here the importance of her own shift in attitude. The note of discovery is continued as she begins to perceive the "unnatural refuge" (21.49) that is the world of time and space, which, paradoxically, is "unnatural" from the point of view of eternity. Here again the escape from delusion is suggested by the way dawning recognition and opening knowledge are beginning to lead Ololon to proper action. The Divine Family points out that Milton had understood the divine dictate (21.52–53), that is, "one must die for another throughout all Eternity" (11.18), the mercy and love of which is to be contrasted to the rigid retribution of its negative side: "if the guilty should be condemmed he must be an Eternal Death" (11.17). Now the Divine Family and Ololon, feeling the dictate, symbolically unite, their unity marking the importance of the discovery and change for they appear as Jesus. Ololon's divinely sanctioned journey is to discover the delusory aspects of her selfhood that have manifested themselves in time and space, and, by discovering them, to reveal the eternal lineaments of the human emanation. After Ololon has decided to follow Milton, Los descends to Blake, appearing as a flaming sun. Los too binds on the sandal of expanded vision.[21] Los's realm is Udan Adan, a spiritual equivalent to the fallen and usurped existence of Blake in Lambeth. The placing of Blake in Lambeth is not accidental. Later in the poem he refers to his journey from Lambeth to Felpham and its purpose. That journey to the discovery at Felpham is the earthly manifestation of the spiritual journey of Milton to discover and reveal the selfhood. The combining of Los at this point with Blake-Milton is the mark of prophetic inspiration that is the agent of the revelation leading to self-annihilation. The unity of the two is emphasized by the speech that follows Blake's announcement that he "arose in fury & strength" (22.14), for the speech, though spoken by Los, could well stand for the prophetically inspired speech of Blake with his present view of eternity. At the end of the speech, which announces the prophetic capability of seeing the world of time and space from an eternal view and the essential eternality of all identities, Blake and Los are said to be traveling, like Milton, whose human part is now in Blake, to Golgonooza, Los's "supreme abode" (22.26), when they meet the mistaken resistance of Palamabron and Rintrah.[22] Their request to Los to destroy Blake-Milton hints much about the way the spiritual forces of the selfhood, to which John Milton was subject, have caused the events ensuing in the eighteenth century.

Rintrah's spiritual resistance to Milton's journey results from his mistaken conception of Milton's intention, a dramatically ironic picture of Rintrah, actuated by wrath, attacking the supposed wrath of Milton.[23] His speech (22.29–23.20) also contains a sequential picture of the events in religious history since Milton's time. These events appear in references to Milton's religion, the churches at their period, Voltaire, Rousseau, Swedenborg, Whitfield, and Wesley. Los's answer (23.32–24.43) fills in even more history, and uses the analogy of the far past of the Hebrew nation to the recent past of Christian Europe to illustrate his injunction against wrath. At first Rintrah points out that a new religion is being woven from the new jealousy of Theotormon because of Milton's religion. Rintrah, like the other spiritual forces, except Los, is mistaken. Indeed, new religion is always being woven from new jealousy. Although Rintrah's conception of church history is based on a Swedenborgian pattern of cyclic change in religious organization, in this specific instance the religion that Milton brings is an exception that Rintrah does not perceive. Remembering the John Milton of the seventeenth century and his religion of destruction, he thinks that the dismal sign on Blake-Milton's left foot signifies the coming of even further destruction. He does not know that Milton has learned the universal dictate of self-annihilation, and therefore that the destruction he brings is of a completely new and final kind that will destroy the old destruction. His mistake leads him to recount the history of religion since the time of John Milton, pointing out how the old religion of Milton, the religion of wrath, vengeance, and destruction, had led to the apparent end of the churches in the eighteenth century.[24] When the fierce religious wars of the seventeenth century had threatened the end of the ecclesiastical hierarchies, Rahab and Tirzah found substitutes for the old ecclesiastical organization in the form of deism and natural religion, whose leading lights were Voltaire and Rousseau. While they apparently attacked the churches ("Mocking the Confessors & Martyrs"), an act more appropriately attributed to Voltaire than to Rousseau, both Voltaire and Rousseau asserted self-righteousness, or virtue, and accepted a notion of retribution. And not only did they keep the key doctrine of vengeance, but they also believed in the necessity of state religion. Thus, though the orthodox church was weakened, Rahab and Tirzah still triumph in their doctrine of vengeance. Rintrah also claims that Rahab and Tirzah have perverted Swedenborg, both in his imaginative vision (in Beulah) and in the reporting and handling of that vision (in Ulro). Swedenborg's imaginative vision is perverted in that he himself had submitted to the doctrine of vengeance when he had shown hell as under punishment in his work *Divine Providence*, but the formation of churches around his doctrine (i.e., New Jerusalem Church) perverted his teaching even further. Swedenborg is shorn by the delusive female just as Samson was shorn by Delilah.

To counter the growing tide of the religion of vengeance, Rintrah and Palamabron rightly raised up a doctrine of faith by the preachers Whitfield and Wesley. But the doubting establishment, hearing the doctrine of faith of these two, demanded miracles as testimony for the doctrine of faith. However, the rationally deluded churches are ironically blind to the miracle of the two witnesses who have devoted "Their life's whole comfort to the entire scorn & injury &

death" (23.2). The churches cannot receive the doctrine of faith, and therefore, like the two witnesses of Revelation, Whitfield and Wesley are said to "Lie dead in the Street of the Great City" (22.59), an allusion inferring that the present church is also dominated by the hermaphroditic whore and dragon of Revelation. "No Faith is in all the Earth" (22.60). In this passage the "cries of the churches" (22.56) are not voiced immediately, but delayed until the fate of the witnesses is announced. Then the substance of the cry "Shew us Miracles" (22.62) is given. This is Blake's attempt to suggest the tragic cry of Rintrah, and an oral rendering of the passage will hold the hearer spellbound through the seven lines, exploding in the ironic "shew us Miracles." Here the oppressive weight of eighteenth-century doubt, with Hume, Paine, Rousseau, Voltaire, Gibbon, *et al.* in the balance, dramatically presses out Rintrah's anguish over the terrible loss of faith that has occurred since Milton's day. Rintrah sees the dismal state of Albion and the triumphant covering cherub—combining with the powerful sons of Albion, Hand, Hyle, and Coban, and the combination of war and religion, the work of the hermaphrodite—being forwarded. Yet he is ignorant of the true cause, and the true remedy remains ironically undiscovered as he himself calls for vengeance and justice: "Let us descend & bring him chained/To Bowlahoola" (23.17–18). Rintrah's intention is sufficiently clear from his characterization of Los, whom he sees as "pitying and permitting evil/Tho strong and mighty to destroy" (23.19–20). Rintrah wishes to invoke the destruction he himself wishes to end. The selfhood's delusion and dominion still remain in him. Undoubtedly there is a hint that Milton's being thrown into Bowlahoola represents also Blake's being thrown into a court of law by Privates Scolfield and Cock. Blake's own experience furnishes an analogy to that of Milton here, but both are illustrations of the way the doctrine of vengeance perpetuates itself.

Los's answer to Rintrah and Palamabron is a warning

against the very wrath which holds Rintrah in the same chain that holds Orc. Los informs him of the prophecy of Milton setting forward from Felpham (thus symbolically joining Blake and Milton just as they are already joined in Blake's foot) to free Orc from the chain of jealousy. He excuses the daughters of Los, the lovely females (23.39), whom Rintrah had accused of weaving new religion (22.38), in that they protect man from the law of retribution, hiding him from Satan's watch fiends (23.40). The protection seems to be the embodiment in flesh carried out by the work of Enitharmon. In this, Los is showing that the law of vengeance is at odds with the law of mercy, as Satan's accusations are stopped by souls being embodied in vegetative form. Los's warning becomes quite specific when he points out that the wrath of Calvin and Luther led to war and division. The "fury premature" (23.47) of these two is the same fury associated with the old religion of John Milton. Los points out Rintrah's failure of understanding in his warning that one cannot know the mystery of redemption until Albion has arisen (23.53–54), that is, until Milton has completed his journey. However, the end is imminent, for it has been signaled by the unique act of Milton, one of the elect, returning to earth. Now the only virtue Los can suggest is patience.

But Los delves into the far past for further examples of the evil of divisive wrath. The wrath and fury of the original fall outlined in the Bard's Song had led to the division of the twelve tribes of Israel, which division is symbolized in the fancy that the twelve tribes were twelve sons of Los who left the spiritual realm and were generated in bodily form under the influence of Tirzah (23.63–24.4). Only seven are mentioned: Reuben, Manazzoth, Gad, Simeon, Levi, Ephraim, and Judah. Los remarks that Rintrah, Palamabron, Bromion, and Theotormon remain with him, as yet undivided, though Rintrah and Palamabron are in serious danger. Again Los finds warning examples in Amalek and Canaan, who under Tirzah had become "Nations" (24.16),

which is Blake's concept of the result of the divisive process. A nation is that which is born *(natus)* into selfhood,
and is less than the total identity of all men. The sale of
Joseph to the Amalekite, which led to Israel's enslavement
in Egypt, illustrates the desire for domination preceding the
divisive process. Los then warns once more against the
wrath that would pull Rintrah and Palamabron away from
the spiritual world of Los (24.22–25) and points out a
further instance of divisiveness in the work of the covering
cherub (24.26–33). Lazarus's raising, the prophetic symbol
of Albion's rebirth, was countered by the covering cherub's
division of Christianity into the four churches of Paul, Constantine, Charlemagne, and Luther: The covering cherub's
action had been a defensive one, for the raising of Lazarus,
like the raising of Whitfield and Wesley and the raising of
Milton, had presaged the awakening of Albion. The covering cherub is following a course of action that causes divisiveness, a reaction against the hoped-for awakening that
will constitute a rejoining with eternity. In psychological
terms, the defense mechanisms of the ego begin to force the
division of the total man through repression and rejection,
when an act is misperceived as threatening, even though
that act is really for the health of the total man. Los then
finishes his reply with a plea to his sons to give all their
strength against eternal death, and not to throw Milton into
Bowlahoola, for Milton is the sign of the last vintage.

At this point one must assume that Blake-Los-Milton has
arrived at Golgonooza, where Palamabron and Rintrah
have met them (22.27).[25] The description of Bowlahoola,
Allamanda, the winepress, the spiritual causes that are
known as the sons of Los, and the perverting influences of
Tirzah, constitute Los-Blake-Milton's discovery of true
spiritual causation, and the natural world as a symbolic
"Vision of the Science of the Elohim" (29.65).[26] This discovery is profoundly important for the message of self-
annihilation, for once one understands that this world is
only a limited vision of a vast spiritual existence, the delu-

sive, survival-oriented fear of the selfhood cannot affect the individual so powerfully as it needs to carry out its mistaken purpose. Undoubtedly the extended length of Blake's descriptions in this revelation indicates joy in the release from anxiety. Like a newly discovered universe, this eternal world of spiritual causation holds seemingly infinite possibilities for the new man, and the details of that world, though perhaps more fully depicted here than some readers enjoy, must be infinitesimally sparse compared to what Blake saw as the possibilities of vision.

V. LAMENTATIONS AND OLOLON'S DESCENT IN TIME AND SPACE

As Los-Blake-Milton walks in the realm of spiritual vision, and Milton's "redeemed" portion struggles with Urizen, the narrative now focuses on the journey of Ololon, which had already begun in the previous section. Ololon's journey is picked up at the beginning of Book II as Ololon descends to Beulah (30.4), just as Milton had descended. But instead of revealing aspects of the selfhood in the form of resistance to her journey, the descent of Ololon to Beulah is characterized by a choric lamentation and an openness that has been prepared by Milton's track.[27] Consequently her journey functions as a characterization of loving aspects of Ololon rather than elements of selfhood to be overcome. Blake's method of development in this first step of Ololon's journey is derived from the lamentation for Tyre in Ezekiel, and as such is an allusion pointing to that which is to be put aside. In Ezekiel the prophet announces a lament for the coming destruction of the rich, prosperous, merchant city of the proud prince of Tyre. It is to be destroyed; Tyre is said to be the covering cherub. The lamentations of Beulah for Ololon are likewise heralds of destruction, but destruction of the delusive aspect of Ololon. The lamentation of Beulah is divided into four sections. The first section reveals the threatened aspect of the emanated world that will be annihilated in the completed act of self-annihilation. The first aspect is called the nations (31.12). The nations have been generated by Tirzah (24.16) and are said to be perversions caused by Rahab and Tirzah (29.55–56). To become a nation is to be divided and cut off from the universality of human brotherhood. As results of Rahab and Tirzah, the nations are the ultimate degenerate form of Ololon herself. Their awareness of her intention to obey the divine dictate causes their "bitter wailing" (31.18). But the nations are only one aspect of the division caused by delusion. Another is the four elements, which are said to be not capable of regeneration (i.e., not capable of a spiritual return to eternity). The four elements (fairies, nymphs, gnomes, and genii), which cannot be regenerated, have become the gods of the earth, opposed in corporeal strife. The connection between nations and elements also reveals something about the nature of the Ulro vision. They are both conceptions that derive from the rational faculty that makes distinctions. Mankind is divided into nations; the physical beauty of earth is reduced to struggling elements—all by the reason, the agent later identified as the spectre or selfhood. The point here is that both nature and element are aspects of emanation from the human imagination that have become corrupted and fixed by the selfhood's rationality.[28] Ololon in her greatest degeneration is the rationalist, Democritan view of the physical world, which, if seen with imagination, is really a coalesced, spiritually caused vision. In this analyzed and rationally divided conception lies the mistaken view that is materialism. The four elements are indeed gods insofar as they are rationally derived concepts used to delude men. The gods of materialism are the same mental weapons used by the priest in old times. Their wailing is the wailing of fear.

The second and third sections of the lamentation are of different quality. The second section (31.28–45) consists of a magnificent description of the continuous song of birds, and especially of the lark at sunrise. Differing from the fearful lamentation of the four elements, this is rather a lamentation of love, one not for the evil to come, but for the wasted past. The rational faculty has reduced the vision of nature to four elements, but the imaginative faculty can see the lark's song as a natural symbol of a spiritual event. What the reason sees as corporeal strife is really an act of awe and love between the momentarily pausing sun and the choir of day. It is a lament of joy at the promise of love.

The third lamentation (31.46–63) is much like the second in general intent and it reinforces the sense of love. Both passages deal with the vision of nature in a particular literary fashion that Blake uses to suggest a vision of nature above the rational view. Nature is personified, giving it a human quality that separates it from the analytical, scientific, rational view, revealing it as alive, as participating in the divine brotherhood of the imagination. The birds are a choir, the sun an awed, yet powerful king filled with love at the sudden song of the lark; the flowers revel in a universal dance. These personifications are nature, or emanation, perceived with imagination, and that perception is one of love, opposed to the bitter strife of the four elements and the nations.

The final lamentation of Beulah focuses on a different kind of consciousness from that of imaginative vision. It is still the song of Beulah comforting Ololon, but the comfort comes in the form of an explanation of the relationship between human and emanation (33.1–34.7). In the form of an address to Rahab (the daughter of Babylon), the selfhood aspect of Ololon, the divine voice informs Ololon that emanative jealousy has led to the necessity of Milton's act of self-annihilation. The continuous redemption of Ololon by Milton's self-annihilation is the unhappy fate of Ololon if she should remain in the toils of her own selfhood. But the passage really brings the message of hope, for the promise of Ololon's redemption from her selfhood's jealousy is given. Ololon will relent; she will bring Jerusalem, no longer to be called a harlot, to her husband. This act is the act of openness and trust, not of the selfhood's jealousy.

The four lamentations thus furnish a view of the eternal state, unknown to Ololon's selfhood. Freedom will replace jealousy, and imaginative vision will replace the analytical reason of the selfhood. Ololon has heard comfortable notes indeed from the songs of Beulah.

Just as Milton has proceeded first through the verge of Beulah to the world of time and space, Ololon now passes into a lower world. She beholds four states of humanity in repose, Beulah, Allah, Al Ulro, and Or Ulro (34.8–23). Blake does not explain these states, and does not employ them again.[29] But they are certainly arranged hierarchically, and Ololon's choice of the lowest form of Ulro indicates her change from terror to pity (34.7) since she is following Milton's track (34.22). Arriving at this stage, Ololon views the Ulro as a vast polypus, which is here equated with physical embodiment in the time-space world (34.24–31). It contains the sixfold emanation that is Ololon's own selfhood, and acts as the delusion that may trap one into the belief that material existence is total existence. At this point Ololon momentarily resides, and a separation of the sons and daughters of Ololon apparently occurs, for the sons of Ololon are said to reside in the space of Ulro awaiting the time to awaken Urizen (34.40–48). Some of the daughters return, apparently to Beulah. The myth is here somewhat perplexing, for the distinction between the male and female aspect of Ololon seems a notion that is actually meant to clarify the coming sexual manifestation of Ololon as a female, but its added weight to an already heavily detailed mythic structure does not help the reader to see more clearly.

The important act at this stage of Ololon's journey is the act of discovery that is part of the revelation of Ololon's selfhood (34.49–35.17). She discovers the terrifying effects of the selfhood's transformation of eternity's mental warfare to the vicious struggle for survival that occurs in the selfhood-limited world of time and space. The fixing of form in the material world is the creation of decay and death. The law of retribution in that world changes difference of opinion to the hypocrisy of the curse and flattery. It is the emanation's selfhood that creates that fixed and deadly form (deadly if perceived as fixed) through the freezing of form in the loins of the emanation's selfhood, the sixfold Miltonic female. Ololon discovers this horror "in reminiscence astonished" (35.18), thus suggesting that Ololon had indeed forgotten some dreadful thing in her past. Indeed, since she is the eternal form of Leutha (as Milton's immortal part is the eternal form of the fallen Satan), the point of her reminiscence is that of discovery of her own selfhood. She remembers because she is that selfhood.

But she cannot behold Golgonooza (35.18–19). This failure suggests that her journey of discovery is yet incomplete. To fully destroy the selfhood's work in time and space, she must enter it completely; thus she must take on physical form, she must "become mortal & Vegetable in Sexuality" (35.24). To perceive (to see Golgonooza), one must make the act of faith by accepting the complete experience of the selfhood (become mortal). But before Ololon takes this step she makes a gesture that is part of the return of the emanation to its proper sphere.[30] Examining the couches of the dead (i.e., the resting place outside of Eternity, or Beulah, of the fallen eternals), Ololon discovers Milton surrounded by the starry eight (35.29–33). She falls down prostrate before the eight, asking forgiveness. This act counters the pride, jealousy, and self-righteous wrath of the selfhood that led Ololon to attempt to drive Milton from eternity. It is the return to proper relationship. The implied meaning of this act is important psychologically. The separated emanation in the toils of selfhood wishes to remain separate, and therefore creates the delusion that it has an existence entirely separate from the human imagination that created it. For the emanation to remain separate and to attempt to convince the man that she is indeed independent, is to delude, and thus the separate, independent emanation, striving for dominion, is delusion. Since the emanation represents in part a misguided view of the world, the meaning emerges that the physical world as conceived as independent of mind is delusion. Berkeley is chosen over Locke. Separated from the perceiving mind, the exterior world is delusion. Truth can be gained only when the subject dictates the way the object is to be perceived. When one becomes convinced of the independence of the exterior world, one is deluded. The return of Ololon, as symbol of emanation or objective reality, is a sign of the proper valuation of the objective world. The objective world cannot control the perception that gives it meaning, but must be subservient to it. Time and space must obey Los's will. Ololon must repudiate the delusion of Rahab and Tirzah.

Ololon must enter the polypus, that is, take a physical, sexual form, in order to complete her journey to self-annihilation. The danger of this step, hinted at earlier in the reference to the perverting influence of Tirzah (29.53–54), can be avoided by selection of the correct "moment" (35.42). Ololon, in this moment, descends to Los and Enitharmon (35.46). Here Blake describes a physical setting that extends into the world of eternity in a way that defies the rational perception of time and space, but that suggests the spiritual perception resulting from the subordination of Ololon to Milton (35.48–36.12).[31] The physical details include a fountain in a rock that flows in two directions, one straight to Golgonooza, the other through the physical universe to Golgonooza, where the two streams meet again. The spatial relationships are inconceivable in terms of length, breadth, and height, but they may be seen as symbols of two ways to reach eternal vision—by going inwardly directly to the imagination, or by going outward, transcending the narrow spatial view of the physical universe. Since either way reaches the eternal vision of Golgonooza, both become symbols of ways of perception. The double stream of the fountain is an allusion to "the river of water of life," which is part of the heavenly city of

Jerusalem in Revelation.[32] It is the river of the divine imagination that is in every man. The scene also contains the
wild thyme[33] and the lark, both said to be "messengers" of
Los who travel the separate paths to eternity. The lark's
flight through the path of the physical universe, like the
thyme's roots going down into the underworld path, are
ways of conveying messages to eternity. These two are
allusions, but allusions that begin to fit Ololon into the biblical pattern of Mary Magdalene. The messengers are
angels at the tomb of Christ. The rock from whence the
fountain flows is the rock removed when Christ is resurrected. At this key moment in time, Ololon, like Mary
Magdalene, is about to discover the truth of resurrection
from eternal death. As Milton, the starry eighth, is another
Christ, Ololon is his Mary Magdalene, the redeemed prostitute, discovering the divine purpose at that dawn when she
was met by the two angels (Luke 24:4). The moment of
Ololon's descent is the moment of the revelation of the true
immortality of the divine Milton. It is the twenty-eighth lark
that meets Ololon, which is Blake's indication of the possibility for the newest manifestation of the divine. The
twenty-seven churches have succeeded each other in hermaphroditic delusion; now the twenty-eighth, which will
have been formed on the divine dictate, offers new hope, so
long as the repentant Ololon avoids the processes of Rahab
and Tirzah. For she is now, safe from Satan's watch fiends,
able to complete the act of self-annihilation.

When Ololon steps into the polypus, she becomes a virgin of twelve years (36.13–17). This transformation allows
her to be a manifestation of that false chastity that is merely
another hypocritical side of the "Virgin Babylon Mother of
Whoredoms" (33.20). Ololon is seen here as a virgin so that
her virginity can be annihilated, just as Milton's selfhood
appears in order to be separated from his true self. The
deceitful "loom of generation" of Tirzah, the corruptions
of natural religion, are hidden in the pure virgin form. Blake
perceives Ololon at this point and, appropriately courteous,

asks her to comfort Catherine, his "Shadow of Delight" (36.31). As Blake is associated with Milton, Ololon is associated with Catherine, and the act of self-annihilation is both Blake's and Catherine's.[34] At this point in the poem all of the active characters have been introduced, and have journeyed in their own way to Blake's cottage at Felpham. Milton and his shadow's existences, Ololon and her shadowy females, Los, and Blake, and Catherine, are now ready to share the momentary vision that will reveal the new dictate of self-annihilation.

VI. FINALE OF THE JOURNEY

Blake has brought Milton's journey to its final destination when he refers to his own journey to Felpham (36.21–25). The passage of Blake-Los-Milton to Golgonooza has been the spiritual journey, and Blake's journey to Felpham has been its material manifestation. Los had joined with Blake in Lambeth (22.4–14) and Blake had finally arrived in Felpham. The purpose of his journey is quite explicitly the earthly manifestation of Milton's spiritual journey, for he was put in Felpham to write out his "Visions/To display Natures cruel holiness, the deceits of Natural Religion" (36.24–25), which is the discovery that Milton announces in the pages to come. Here Blake's vision of truth is part of the discovery that allows the action of self-annihilation. The causes of natural religion have been stated briefly. Now the full revelation is at hand, as is the solution that neither Los nor any of the mortals had been able to discern.

In this finale there are several moments of revelation. As each speaker ends his speech a further revelation occurs, until the finale ends in the uniting of Milton and Ololon. The finale begins with Ololon's appearance before Blake's cottage at Felpham (36.26–27). Her inquiry about Milton seems to bring about the manifestation of Milton, who is revealed during the whole finale in his two aspects of personality that obtained at the beginning of his journey, the shadow and real human. The first moment, in response to Ololon's questions, reveals Milton's shadow and all that it represents:

That Miltons Shadow heard & condensing all his Fibres
Into a strength impregnable of majesty & beauty infinite
I saw he was the Covering Cherub & within him Satan
And Raha[b], in an outside which is fallacious! within
Beyond the outline of Identity, in the Selfhood deadly
And he appeard the Wicker Man of Scandinavia in whom
Jerusalems children consume in flames among the Stars.
(37.6–12)

The equation between the shadow, covering cherub, Satan, and the selfhood is complete here. The selfhood has the exterior aspect of hypocrisy (covering cherub) and an interior Satanic drive. Milton's total selfhood now becomes the object of Blake's description, for Blake is describing the phenomenological manifestation of the selfhood throughout history, the revelation of which constitutes the goal of the journey of discovery. As Milton's shadow descends into Blake's garden, it is said to be a "Cloud & Human Form" (37.14): The cloud is the selfhood, or shadow, that was the black cloud over Europe redounding from Blake's left foot. Joined to it is the "human," the aspect of Milton that had at first remained in eternity but had since left with the starry eight. At this point both are revealed together. Within this vision Blake discerns the gods and churches that have become the delusions of human history, stemming from the individual's selfhood (37.20–43). Blake details the gods, equating them with the spectre sons of the druid Albion, thereby inferring that they are the rigid hypostatizations of the imagination, used by the ecclesiastical organizations of the past for domination.[35] The cries of the victims, the pestilence, the dark tabernacles and pomposity, assasinations, and secrecy, that characterize these gods, are the real moral qualities of the selfhood. Blake's description of the churches, equated with the twenty-seven heavens, characterizes them as hermaphroditic, thus indicating that the delusion represented by the female dominance of hermaphroditism, lies behind the history of ecclesiastical organizations. Blake's relating church and heaven by placing the churches in the twenty-seven layers of the sky may confuse us somewhat, but the general analogy allows him also to include the Levites, the tribe of priests, as the center of control of the churches.

At this point there is a formal separation of the human form of Milton from the selfhood, which is the first step of self-annihilation. The cloud and human form have appeared as one before Blake, reaching from heaven to earth. Blake, like John of Patmos, who stood "upon the sand of the sea and saw a beast rise up out of the sea" (Rev. 13:1), beholds the selfhood of Milton as Milton's human portion separates from the selfhood:

And Milton collecting all his fibres into impregnable strength
Descended down a Paved work of all kinds of precious stones
Out from the eastern sky; descending down into my Cottage
Garden: clothed in black, severe & silent he descended.
The Spectre of Satan stood upon the roaring sea & beheld
Milton within his sleeping Humanity! trembling & shuddring
He stood upon the waves a Twenty-seven-fold mighty Demon
Gorgeous & beautiful: loud roll his thunders against Milton
Loud Satan thunderd, loud & dark upon mild Felpham shore
Not daring to touch one fibre he howld upon the Sea.
(38.5–14)

This separation is the result of that exploration of the "eternal lineaments" of man which must be discovered before the selfhood and all its temporal ramifications can be annihilated. The revelation of the historical selfhood now allows Blake to discern the works of the selfhood clearly. Blake beholds the desolations of Satan (38.15–27), describing them as a ruined building, planes of burning sand, mountains of marble, pits of molten ore, pitch and niter, ruined palaces and cities. This picture of sterility is touched with hints of a landscape that is part of the industrial mess of England and the corruption of church and state. The landscape remains visionary in that it is not clearly fixed in spatial relationships nor given detail. The mountains of marble are visions of church dominance, not visual depictions of marble hills. But the vision dips farther down into the experience of the Ulro vision available to man's limited senses. The angels and emanations of the vision, like time-and-space men and women, "Labour with blacken'd visages among its stupendous ruins" (38.21). The spiritual evil of the selfhood is manifested for Blake in the exploitation of labor by the industrialist. But it is not capitalism or industrialism *per se* that is the cause. The place of the cruel labour is the secret place of Babylon, the female component of the selfhood, the delusion of the churches.

Blake has made the discovery because Milton is now separate from his selfhood. The redemptive act of self-annihilation can now proceed. Milton confronts the selfhood with an announcement that he knows the law of the use of power (38.29–49). To use power against the selfhood will produce only another Orcan chain of domination, with Milton the new covering for the Satanic impulse. But Milton goes by the eternal law of self-annihilation, a mutual annihilation of self for other's good, "as I for thee" (38.36). Milton takes no action, lifts no finger, no weapon. To love is to bring about the destruction of the law of domination. Milton simply reveals the doctrine. The law of the selfhood is the law of self-preservation, the supreme fear of death and its consequent behavior. The law of self-annihilation is to despise that fear in the symbolic act of death to self. The law of the selfhood discovered by Milton entails the law of retribution and the reliance on moral virtue, which Milton now sees as hypocrisy.

Milton's revelation at this point calls Satan into the second revelation, that of the selfhood's hypocritic nature. Satan is suddenly revealed as the hellish parody of the eternal humanity divine. With the law of retribution on his lips: "I am God the Judge of all, the living & the dead" (38.51), he demands worship and obedience. He mentions the seven angels who bear his name. These are the seven eyes who, in their corrupt form, are Moloch, and so on, but who in their divine form are the starry seven to whom Milton has become the eighth. They are part of Satan's corrupted retinue of display for the purposes of delusion. As Blake points out on the next plate, the delusive retinue of Satan is "permitted/(Lest he should fall apart in his Eternal Death)" (39.25–26). The force of destruction is permitted by the force of mercy. Just as Los has the power of mercy and wrath, but enacts only mercy, so does the divine humanity. Ironically, Satan attacks the notion of mercy, claiming that Jesus is a delusion, which he pretends to be able to destroy.

Satan's pretense to this power elicits a third revelation of truth. He has claimed the starry seven as his own, but now they appear as a column of fire around Milton in opposition to Satan (39.3–13), in a symbolic statement representing the true nature of their allegiance. The eternal guardians are on the side of love and mercy, not on the selfhood's payroll of retribution. Their sounding trumpets are the clarions of the last judgment, calling collective man, Albion, to awake, which is the symbolic act of shunting off delusion. The delusion, the reasoning spectre, the aspect of selfhood that produces the Ulro view, is to be cast off.

The rebuff of Satan's claim now leaves Satan in a state of frustration. The techniques of delusion have failed. The desire to dominate, left unsatisfied by his failure, turns to the rage of destruction; but, since Milton has not submitted to the struggle for domination (as Orc had previously), Satan is now powerless to inflict any damage or control.

The frustrated impulse leaves Satan trembling, astonished, howling, hungering to "devour/But fearing the pain, for if he touches a Vital/ The torment is unendurable" (39.20–22). Milton's refusal to take Satan's delusory gambit has forced the cathexis of Satan's rage only back on Satan himself. The destructive impulse turns ultimately to the selfhood. Mustering, however, one final delusion, Satan manifests himself now as an imitation of the divine humanity, with his retinue of cherubim, chaos, sin, death, and night (39.16–31). But it is to no avail. The trumpets of the starry seven have begun their work. Albion rises now and attempts himself the act of self-annihilation. But the time is not ripe. The revelation of the selfhood has brought the true state of humanity into view, but the act of self-annihilation is not complete. For all Albion to be redeemed, not only must every individual undergo the process, but the separation of emanation and man must be healed. Albion relapses, but his relapse must be understood as temporary.

The act of self-annihilation proceeds.[36] The long-enduring struggle between Urizen and Milton on the banks of the Arnon now appropriately reaches an end. Not downcast or destroyed, but reduced from his position of power by Milton's refusal to indulge in the power of domination, Urizen faints. His power is at an end, for Milton and, because of the revelation at Felpham, potentially for every man who comes to the knowledge of the true nature of the selfhood. The Urizenic priest can no longer delude with his teaching of obedience, of future rewards and punishments, of fear.

Once Satan has been revealed with all his hypocritical retinue, Ololon too must discover her complete selfhood. As she views Milton's struggle with Urizen, as she sees the whole circumstance of the four zoas, she also beholds the work of her own "Feminine portion" (40.10). Those who condemn religion have become in their feminine or emanative portion the cause and promoter of the religions. They are manifested in Voltaire, Rousseau, Hume, Gibbon, and

Bolingbroke, whom Blake lumps together as representatives of natural religion. Ololon is the cause. Ololon, the separate emanation in her selfhood, wishing to dominate by delusion, has generated the doctrine of natural religion that Blake associates with eighteenth-century culture. She is Rahab and Tirzah, the doctrine of materialism, of rationality, of doubt, of retributive justice, of state religion. Her discovery precipitates the mythical form of her selfhood, Rahab-Babylon. The earthly delusion of natural religion has been the harlot Rahab and the harlot Babylon, who are also Mary Magdalene. The delusory prostitution of the eternal imagination's creation is now perceived in its corrupt selfhood, the hidden harlot, the female of the hermaphrodite. Moral virtue, the doctrine of natural religion as well as of the church, is the hidden harlot of delusion lying in the corruption. The terror of the shadowy female that had displaced the eternal pity is revealed. Ololon's pity now is distinguished from the terror masquerading as moral virtue. The retribution that breeds war can be distinguished in the religion that subscribes to the doctrine of divine justice rather than divine mercy.

As Ololon begins to discover her own selfhood in Rahab and Tirzah, she questions Milton's act. She sees his struggle with Urizen and recognizes the act of life-giving, and a further question, prompted by her fear for the children of Jerusalem—the common men of England and all the earth—elicits from Milton his supreme peroration, stating the nature of the act (40.28–41.28). In short, it entails the abjuration of all that can be annihilated, that is, all that is temporal, not essential to the eternal man. The reasoning power is not the imagination, which is the true eternal identity of the individual. The long series of acts that follow are the acts of removal that constitute the denial of validity to natural religion, empiricism, rationalism, and hypocrisy, all the cultural manifestations of the selfhood in the eighteenth century. These phenomena, being temporal manifestations of the selfhood, are therefore merely "Sexual Garments"

(41.25), which must be "put off."[37] The revelation of evil is almost complete. The final stage of self-annihilation is at hand.

Milton's speech to Ololon, outlining the act of self-annihilation, introduces the final symbolic act of Ololon. She recognizes now that her selfhood, the "Six-fold Miltonic Female" (41.30), has arisen because the sexual, or material form, could not sustain the mental strife of eternity, that is, the emanation of the physical world is not equal to the human imagination's energy, but a contrary to it, that is, a projection that is opposite but dependent. Ololon sees that her selfhood has led to the creation of a state of mind whereby physical existence (a womb) becomes separated from eternity. Separate from Milton, she is a delusion. She is the cause of natural religion.[38] She now separates her true self from the virgin selfhood of Ololon, which joins the Satanic shadow, the selfhood of Milton.[39] Like Milton opposed to Satan, Ololon stands opposed to the sixfold, virgin emanation.

Then as a Moony Ark Ololon descended to Felphams Vale
In clouds of Blood, in streams of gore, with dreadful thun-
    derings
Into the Fires of Intellect that rejoic'd in Felphams Vale
Around the Starry Eight; with one accord the Starry Eight
    became
One Man Jesus the Saviour. wonderful! round his limbs
The Clouds of Ololon folded as a Garment dipped in blood
Written within & without in woven letters: & the Writing
Is the Divine Revelation in the Litteral expression:
A Garment of War, I heard it namd the Woof of Six
    Thousand Years.
                    (42.7–15)

Ololon has joined completely with Milton, both now purified in the act of self-annihilation. Milton now appears with the starry eight as Jesus. He is the human imagination freed of the selfhood. Ololon, the emanation of the imagination, surrounds Milton as the divine revelation.[40] No longer the delusive natural religion or holiness of state religion, Ololon is the divine revelation that is the Bible, the word of God, the emanation of the divine imagination.[41] The delusion of orthodoxy, of materialism, of deism, of natural religion, all of which mediate between a supposed God and man through a form of priesthood, is now removed for the true light, the Bible, which is to be read literally[42] and interpreted individually as inspired history, the woof of six thousand years. No Catholic priest, no Swedenborgian symbol, no Bishop Watson, no deist Paine, no scoffer Voltaire, no atheist, will interpret the Bible for anyone else, but the Lord's people themselves will be their own prophets, and, avoiding the delusion of any form of mystery, will read the "litteral" expression with individual vision. All the Lord's people can be prophets.

Ololon is thus a temporal emanation, Milton's or any man's, which as temporal emanation has become corrupt, and in delusion deludes man. She is eternal truth in the Bible, but in earthly form is misread by the selfhood, a form permitting delusion. She is that created vision which, in the infection of the selfhood, can become hypostatized delusion, striving to control the imagination that has created it. She is redeemed by Milton's self-annihilation. In the gradual discovery of the truth about her own delusion and about the delusion she has caused, she grows in vision until she understands her true relationship to Milton. She must be subservient. As a symbol of objective nature triumphant, she is the sixfold emanation Rahab, Tirzah, and so on. As a symbol of the subservient emanation she is the redeemed saved by the transgressor. She is Mary Magdalene, saved by Jesus.

On the psychological level, the corrupted emanation has been part of the psychodrama. Delusion as knowledge, and restrictive jealousy as behavior, are indeed an emanation of every mind. These are generated in each individual, and, when made into symbols, can be seen as emanations of the essential consciousness. They may be seen as the concept of the physical world surrounding man, a physical world whose chief characteristic is the fact of physical death. The individual struggle for survival is never sure, is always threatened. The individual develops a fear that he will be destroyed, and begins to delude himself and to control others. The individual can only be convinced by refusing the testimony of the senses that death will not be his lot. The conception of the physical reality of the world as a sole and independent existence is the cause of that fear. But the transcendence of the sense's data demands some power that removes the fear, and for Blake that power is the imagination, which transcends time and space, the very conditions of death. The delusion of death can be removed only by imagination, or, in its religious form, faith. Once one has this faith, he need not fear physical death. He can endure true self-annihilation. He can ignore all the frightening teaching of the importance of morality, of virtue, or retributive justice, and by faith expect mercy, not in vain. Thus the psychodrama of everyman has the female representing the conditions of existence, the male the creative aspect of mind. Since the conditions of physical existence mean death, the creative aspect of the mind must transcend the delusion of the female.

With the final vision of Milton and Ololon purified of selfhood and united, Blake shifts the focus to himself and Catherine (42.16–43.1). He has himself experienced the journey to self-annihilation and his attitude to Catherine has clearly undergone a change. He himself now perceives the vision of the coming awakening of all men. The vision is the same as that of John of Patmos. The twenty-four elders around the throne divine of Revelation 7 are the twenty-four cities of Albion. The four zoas are the four beasts around the throne. The trumpet announces the resurrection of Blake himself, just as the trumpets of the starry seven had announced the redemption of Milton in self-annihilation. The messenger lark mounts to bring the news to eternity, just as the lark had taken the news of Ololon's descent. Los and Enitharmon, Milton and Ololon, William and Catherine are joined now, ready for the coming harvest, the last judgment, the redemption of all men. The fallen Albion is about to be, but is not yet, risen.[43]

Notes

1. The structure of *Milton* is generally seen in two distinct ways, as a three- or two-part structure. E. J. Rose sees the poem as divided into Bard's Song, Milton's descent and ascent in the world of Los, and the journey of Ololon ("Blake's *Milton*: the Poet as Poem," *Blake Studies* 1 [Fall 1968]: 32). This view is shared by Florence Sandler ("The Iconoclastic Enterprise: Blake's Critique of Milton's Religion," *Blake Studies* 5 [Fall 1972]: 16–21). Both Sandler and Rose, of course, have their own contributions to the articulation of the details of this structure. Northrop Frye (*Fearful Symmetry: A Study of William Blake* [Princeton, N.J.: Princeton University Press, 1947], p. 336) sees a two-part structure conforming to the two books of the poem. Susan Fox ("The Structure of a Moment: Parallelism in the Two Books of Blake's *Milton*," *Blake Studies* 2 [Fall 1969], pp. 26–33) follows Frye's two-part theory, seeing each part divided into three major sections that parallel each other. W. J. T. Mitchell ("Blake's Radical Comedy: Dramatic Structure as Meaning in "*Milton*," *Blake's Sublime Allegory*, ed. Stuart Curran and Joseph Anthony Wittreich, Jr. [Madison, Wis.: University of Wisconsin Press, 1973], pp. 281–307. This collection of excellent essays will be referred to as *BSA*) follows the two-part-structure thesis, interpreting the poem as radical comedy. My agreement with Rose and Sandler here is only part of my debt to their illuminating studies. All of these critics of course agree with Rose that the work is a unity ("Blake's *Milton*," p. 83).

Scholars tend to make a distinction between the sequential events of the poem and a single, instantaneous event that constitutes the whole of the poem. Foster Damon (*A Blake Dictionary* [Providence, R.I.: Brown University Press, 1965], p. 280) sees the events as simultaneous but the poem without "logical sequence."

Harold Bloom (*Blake's Apocalypse* [Garden City, N.Y.: Doubleday, 1963; rpt. 1965], p. 340) sees the crucial events of *Milton* as simultaneous and "existent in the continual present of Eternity." Susan Fox seems to follow Bloom. Peter Alan Taylor ("Providence and the Moment in Blake's *Milton*," *Blake Studies* 4 [Fall 1971], p. 52) sees aspects of providence converging at the moment in Blake's garden. E. J. Rose insists that the poem cannot be read as narrative ("Blake's *Milton*," p. 17), seeing the structure (as distinct from the sequence) as the "thematic and mythic content of the poem" ("Blake's *Milton*, p. 34). Sandler perhaps suggests this dichotomy in her view that the poem, following the technique of the *Apocalypse*, makes successive unveilings (p. 15). It is wise to let Blake reveal the events of the poem, which indeed have a sequence, and the sequence is connected in such a way as to give a sense of order, development, and passing time. Certainly there is an order and experience behind the poem that may be grasped in a moment, as Blake perhaps grasped it, but the sequence of events in the poem is clearly connected and focused.

In *The Prophetic Writings of William Blake,* ed. D. J. Sloss and J. P. R. Wallis, 2 vols. (Oxford: Clarendon, 1925), Sloss and Wallis make more serious objections to the poem's unity. They see the poem principally as "a succession of exemplary episodes emphasizing the fundamental obligation to unconditional and unremitted abstinence from judgment, and especially from moral censure . . ." (1: 345). For them, *Milton* comes near to achieving unity (1: 342), but the Bard's Song has "no organic connexion with the rest of the work" (1: 344) and the distinction between the Milton-Urizen struggle and Milton's journey to self-annihilation is evidence of revision without excision (1: 344). From my point of view, the poem's unity is achieved by the depiction of the fall into, and the release from, the selfhood. Blake makes the structural unity of the poem clear in two ways. He divides the poem into the Bard's Song, recounting the action that motivates Milton, and the journey of Milton, which includes the journey of his emanation, Ololon, and concludes with the uniting of Milton and Ololon in Blake's garden at Felpham. Blake also separates the poem into two books, which tends to separate the journey of Milton from the journey of Ololon, though not entirely. Thus Blake arranges the poem in three parts: Bard's Song, showing the fall into selfhood; Milton's journey; and Ololon's journey, which joins the emanation to the true man, thereby completing the escape from selfhood.

2. All quotations of Blake's poetry and prose, except for Blake's letters, are from *The Poetry and Prose of William Blake,* ed. David Erdman, commentary by Harold Bloom, 4th printing, rev. (Garden City, N.Y.: Doubleday, 1971). Quotations from *Milton* are given by plate and line number. Erdman's text retains Blake's original punctuation and includes all of the plates, the meanings of which all have some relevance to the theme of the poem. References to other work of Blake will be to Erdman's text, as E., and to Geoffrey Keynes, ed., *William Blake Complete Writings*, 3rd printing, rev. (Oxford: Oxford University Press, 1971), as K. Quotations from Blake's letters are from K.

3. J. A. Wittreich, Jr. expresses this notion somewhat differently as "inversional

transformation," in "Opening the Seals: Blake's Epics and the Milton Tradition," *BSA*, pp. 36, 55.

4. K 825.

5. " 'Sublime Allegory': Blake's Epic Manifesto and the Milton Tradition," *Blake Studies* 4 (Spring 1972):22.

6. The traceable references in *Milton* conform to Erdman's conjectural dates for the poem, 1804 being the date for Blake's completion of the main body of the composition, 1808–1810 the dates for the completion of the engraving. Certainly the poem could not have been totally engraved until after Blake had been attacked in John Hunt's *Examiner* on August 7, 1808. If Erdman's conjecture that Blake's mythic character, Hand, is derived from the hand with pointing finger used by Hunt to sign his essays, then the appearance of Hand on plate 23 of *Milton* suggests that at least that plate was not engraved until after Hunt's attack. In Blake's Public Address note of (circa) 1810, he writes that his poem about his three years at Felpham (1800–1803) will root out the nest of villains who are represented principally by the work of the *Examiner*. He also remarks that he "will soon publish" his poem. It seems to me that Blake saw that his poem had special relevance to Hunt, who had recently attacked Methodism for relying on exactly the qualities that Blake extolled in *Milton*. Hunt favored the state-established church (May 7, 1808, p. 301); he scoffed at the Methodist belief in present miracles and divine inspiration: "the Methodists are divinely inspired, and are therefore like the Apostles. A pious and modest conclusion! . . . [they can always] take refuge in a miracle" (May 22, 1808, p. 334); he attacked the Methodist rejection of reason (7 May, 1808, p. 302); and he attacked the belief in salvation by faith (May 15, 1808, p. 317). Blake saw *Milton* as a direct answer to Hunt's attack, and when the *Examiner* attacked Blake, Blake had a double reason for seeing *Milton* as an answer to the "nest of villains."

7. "Sublime Allegory," p. 35.

8. Ibid., p. 39.

9. Hazard Adams, *Blake and Yeats: The Contrary Vision* (Ithaca, N.Y.: Cornell University Press, 1955; revised 1968), p. 22.

10. *To the Palace of Wisdom* (Garden City, N.Y.: Doubleday, 1964; rpt. 1965), p. 431.

11. Price, p. 429.

12. Ibid., p. 431.

13. Sandler, p. 14.

14. The "traditions" of *Milton* have thus received some important recent illumination. Not all agree on the precise nature of Blake's "tradition" in general. Kathleen Raine, *Blake and Tradition*, 2 vols. (New York: Bollingen, 1968), places Blake in the tradition of the perennial philosophy, which subsumes Neoplatonism, Hermeticism, mystics such as Boehme and Swedenborg, some Hindu philosophy, and other subjects. Though sometimes Raine forces Blake's meaning, her work does not deserve to be summarily dismissed as it is by F. R. Leavis in "Justifying One's Valuation of Blake," *The Human World* 7 (May 1972): 58. I am not sure that Joseph Wittreich is entirely correct when he suggests that Blake is in a tradition of

the revolutionary, "Blake and Tradition," *Blake Studies* 5 (Fall 1972): 7–11, but he is quite correct in his strictures on T. S. Eliot's failure to recognize any tradition at all in Blake. Eliot, though admitting Blake to the rank of poets of genius, found him no classic, such as Dante, because Blake lacked the traditional framework of theology, philosophy, and mythology available to Dante. For Eliot, Blake's philosophy was like "an ingenious piece of home-made furniture." Indeed Eliot, the guardian of tradition, turning his "flaming sword" every way "to keep the way of the garden of the tree of life," accurately detected the eclectic nature of Blake's thought, though Eliot's taste for the Eden of his own tradition left him a stationary archangel when faced with the *terra incognita* of Blake's extended prophecies. But Eliot cannot be condemned for his desire to keep to his familiar paradise, for the modern scholarly study of Blake had not yet opened the many ways out to Blake's golden realms of complex and startling reality. Modern scholarship would have allowed Eliot to explore that new world with much less anxiety. Yet, even if Eliot had had such light, I suspect that his taste for Blake would not have grown. For Eliot's love of a particular form of tradition seems born of a mental attitude diametrically opposed to that of Blake. Attachment to the very basis of tradition, the uniformity of assumption that makes for harmony between poet and audience, is a condition that does not admit of the need for rebellion, of the urge to scream *non serviam,* which brings man into conflict with the establishment of his intellectual world. The beauty of establishment in Eliot's traditionalism is frequently an imprisoning and fruitless gorgeousness for the man whose hunger for new light, new worlds to explore, is starved on the stale fruit of the routine. In Eliot's Eden there can be starvation; and starvation of the mind, when there is a fatal injunction against the search even for manna, is a double frustration. Let the fruit of Eden be ever so varied, there is not variety enough to satisfy the hungry spirit if there is a single caveat against newness. Men like Blake have always wished to change the concept of Eden from that of a garden to the idea of an endless universe, a limitless expanse of mental action that satisfies their yearning for more. But the difference between the love of fixity in Eliot and of newness and change in Blake reflects only a difference in taste. There is an intellectual discrimination to be made between Blake and the tradition that Eliot loved, for it is unfair to see Blake outside of tradition. He is only outside of Eliot's tradition. Blake belongs to the tradition of the prophet, of the spiritual visionary, of the intellectual rebel, who is ever cast out of the enclosing limits of a "traditional" Eden, who is ever seeking a limitless world where he can create and re-create a paradise out of his own discoveries. If Blake's furniture was homemade, his house was the vast desert of Sinai, not an abandoned churchyard.

15. Price, p. 434.

16. A parallel example of the method can be found in Bishop Berkeley's *Three Dialogues,* where Philonous, after reducing the arguments of Locke's empiricism to absurdity, begins to use the term *substratum* in an ironic fashion that demolishes these abstractions. See *Works of George Berkeley, Bishop of Cloyne,* ed. A. A. Luce and T. E. Jessop, 9 vols. (London: T. Nelson, 1948–1957), 2: 260–61. Martin

Nurmi demonstrates Blake's technique in "Negative Sources in Blake," *William Blake Essays for S. Foster Damon,* ed. A. Rosenfeld (Providence, R.I.: Brown University Press, 1969), pp. 303–20.

17. *Thomas Taylor the Platonist: Selected Writings,* ed. Kathleen Raine and G. M. Harper (New York: Bollingen, 1969), p. 166.

NOTES TO CHAPTER 1. THE SPIRITUAL WORLD

1. Voltaire, Blake's target for other reasons, had extolled men of reason, who penetrate the hidden secrets of nature and the universe, far above the warrior or the divine. He singles out for praise "the Bacons, the Lockes, and the Newtons," *Essay on Chancellor Bacon* in *The Works of Voltaire,* trans. W.F. Fleming, 22 vols. (New York: Dumont, 1901), 19: 27. Frye recognizes the connection in the similarity of Locke's substratum of nature, the atomism of Democritus and Epicurus as found in Bacon, and Newton's corpuscular theory of light (*Fearful Symmetry,* p. 17). Asloob Ansari, *Arrows of Intellect* Aligarh, India: Noya Kilabghar, 1965) devotes a chapter to the "infernal trinity," pp. 1–34.

2. Francis Bacon, *Novum Organon,* (trans. unknown), ed. Joseph Devey (New York: P. F. Collier, 1902), p. 29.

3. Ibid., p. 30

4. Israel Levine, *Francis Bacon* (London: Parsons, 1925), p. 121.

5. Isaac Newton, *The Mathematical Principles of Natural Philosophy,* trans. Andrew Motte, 2 vols. (London, 1729; rpt. London: Dawson, 1968), 2: 202–5.

6. *Essay Concerning Human Understanding,* 2: 8.17. In *The Works of John Locke,* 10 vols. (London: Otridge, 1812).

7. David Hartley, *Observations on Man,* 2 vols. (London, 1749: Gainesville, Fla: Scholars' Facs. rpt. 1966), 1: 58–64.

8. Joseph Priestley, *The Theological and Miscellaneous Works of Joseph Priestley,* ed. J. T. Rutt, 25 vols. (London: Hackney, 1817–32), 3: 181–82.

9. (London, 1751), pp. 12–25 and throughout.

10. *The Light of Nature Pursued,* 7 vols. (London, 1768–1778; rev. London: Foulder, 1805), 3: 384–400.

11. *Selected Writings,* p. 138.

12. Ibid., p. 159.

13. Ibid., p. 147.

14. *Principles of Human Knowledge,* Part I, par. 9, in *Works* II.

15. Ibid., par. 23.

16. Ibid., par. 3.

17. Ibid., par. 7.

18. Ibid., par. 26.

19. *Three Dialogues, Works,* 2: 246.

20. Ibid., pp. 212–13.

21. Ibid., p. 216.

22. In considering Blake's conception of matter we can find two distinct ideas which, superficially similar, logically lead to different conclusions affecting the meaning of parts of *Milton*. The conceptions are (1) that material existence is purely delusion, and (2) that material existence separate from mind does not exist. From the first, followed by Hazard Adams, (*Blake and Yeats: the Contrary Vision*; see, e.g., pp. 25, 30, 33, 37), it follows that all things exist only in man's mind. Past time and memory are not the result of passing experience, but an illusion contained in the mind alone. In the second proposition, real experience, memory, and physical objects such as flowers, constellations, etc. are real insofar as they can exist without the thought of an individual. According to Berkeley, who follows this second proposition, these things exist in the archetypal perception of God. Blake, it seems to me, is much closer to the second proposition. The difference between Blake and Berkeley, however, is that in Blake the perception of the individual mind is not constrained by the archetypal world, which in fact is highly modified by the shaping imagination of the perceiver. But the thing perceived has an archetypal existence, not an existence independent of mind. Raine, *Blake and Tradition*, 2: 102, 119, and 145 (incorrectly), and Frye, *Fearful Symmetry*, p. 14, have suggested Blake's "debt" to Berkeley. T. W. Herzing correctly claims, without giving any treatment of eighteenth-century philosophy, that Blake only rejects the "Urizenic assumption that materiality is everything," in "Book I of Blake's *Milton:* Natural Religion as an Optical Fallacy," *Blake Studies* 6 (Fall 1973): 29.

23. Raine finds *Milton* Blake's best expression of the ideas of "space and time and all appearances as creation of mind" (2: 142). See T. W. Herzing for a similar view, p. 32.

24. In Leutha's words: "Till two Eternities meet together" (13.11). Boehme sees diversity as unity manifested temporally as two opposites; "it goes from Eternity to Eternity into Two Essences." These two eternities are evil and good, the two making an eternal enmity. Only when the individual turns from the evil to the good can he return to God (Signature of All Things, XVI. 20), *The Works of Jacob Behmen,* 4 vols. [London, 1763–81], 4: 135.

25. Cf. Emanuel Swedenborg, *Earths in the Universe,* par. 126, in *Miscellaneous Theological Works* (New York, 1928). All references to Swedenborg, except where noted, are to the standard editions of the Swedenborg Foundation. References are made to Swedenborg's works always by paragraph number.

26. In *Three Dialogues* Berkeley conceives of the creation in a way that Blake might accept. Since God has eternally perceived all things, then creation seems to have had no beginning. Berkeley answers this point by suggesting that "things, with regard to us, may properly be said to begin their existence, or be created, when God decreed they should become perceptible to intelligent creatures." *Works,* 2: 253.

27. Cf. Boehme: "the Self-Will of Man rent itself off from the Will of the Word; . . . and was thereupon weak and blind as to God, and fell down into sleep, and laid between God and the kingdom of the World" (Mysterium Magnum, LXXVI. 14), *Works,* 3: 487–88.

28. Cf. Raine, 2: 78, who finds this source of opacity and contraction in Fludd's *Mosaicall Philosophy.*

29. For an extended discussion of Blake's use of the term *limit* as borrowed from Boehme, see Raine, 1: 404.

30. It is notable that, in Renaissance studies of the art of perspective in drawing, the trick of depicting spatial relationships depended on the postulation of a horizon, which is a line drawn across the picture. This line is labeled variously *orizon* or *ourizen;* see e.g., Erwin Panofsky, *The Codex Huygins and Leonardo DaVinci's Art Theory* (London: Warburg Institute, 1940), plates 49, 50, 51, 54. It is the basis for the illusion of the spatial, three-dimensional world. It also limits the possibility of the picture to a single view of reality. Only one spatial world fits the picture. This suggests that Urizen, perhaps derived from orizon, is a limiter who causes the delusion of the spatial world. It is single vision, Newton's sleep.

31. Cf. Susan Fox, p. 34, who points out the change of this scheme from its form in the *Four Zoas.*

32. R. L. Grimes ("Time and Space in Blake's Major Prophecies," *BSA,* p. 64) expresses this notion clearly when he writes that Blake's concern is "not creation but creativity."

33. Boehme writes of God's creation: "The Creation is the same sport out of himself" (Signature, XVI. 2), *Works,* 4, which recalls the "Divine Vision/and . . . the sports of Wisdom in the Human Imagination" of *Milton* (3.3–4). J. J. McGann, without reference to Boehme, suggests the same thing in "The Aim of Blake's Prophecies and the Uses of Blake Criticism" *BSA,* p. 14.

34. *Observations,* 1: 18.

35. Cf. Frye, *Fearful Symmetry,* p. 349.

36. *Heaven and Hell,* par. 94–95.

37. *Earths In the Universe,* par. 125n.

38. Cf. Raine, 2: 145–46.

39. Cf. Frye, *Fearful Symmetry,* p. 348. Rose equates the mundane shell with inner space, in "Los, Pilgrim of Eternity," *BSA,* p. 92.

40. Cf. Raine, 2: 202.

41. *Essay,* p. 12.

42. *Lt. of Nature,* 3: 384–97.

43. Cf. Boehme: "Thou must learn to distinguish well betwixt the Thing, and that which only is an image thereof . . . . But if thou have left the *imaginary* Life, and quitted the low imaged condition of it; then art thou come into the super-imaginariness, . . . which is a State of living *above Images,* Figures, and Shadows" ("Of the Supersensual Life"), *Works,* 4: 75.

44. Raine finds sources for Blake's concept of the moment in Locke, Boehme, and Swedenborg. See 2: 144, 147, 154–55.

45. Berkeley mentions the telescope and microscope in *Three Dialogues, Works,* 2: 211, 245.

46. Cf. Frye, *Fearful Symmetry,* p. 343.

47. Cf. ibid., p. 18. Frye traces the spectre to Locke's "reflection." Also see Raine, 1: 25, 237. I feel that in *Milton,* as in the other epics, Blake refers to an

aspect of identity as the spectre. Indeed, he equates the spectre with reason (see Damon, *A Blake Dictionary,* p. 380), but he is using the term to represent the visible form of man that is perceived by sensation. *Spectre* was the term used by the Epicurean school (mentioned in Thomas Reid, *Essays on the Intellectual Powers of Man* [Edinburgh, 1785; rpt. New York: Garland, 1971], p. 26) to represent images or semblances that emanate from corporeal things. Each object gives off continuous images, or spectres, of itself, through its fluxile atoms, which are received by the senses. In places in *Milton,* the word *spectre* seems to mean only *aspect.*

48. *Selected Writings,* p. 309.

49. Ibid., pp. 310–11.

50. The numbers of Sotha and Theotormon, as well as the sons of Ozoth, indicate that they are an aggregation of spiritual causes having a vast field in which to work, but the precise numbers (7,007,700 and 8,000,008) seem unimportant as specific numbers.

51. Raine, 1: 253, points to a passage in McPherson's *Introduction to the History of Great Britain and Ireland* dealing with the crested cock of Odin who calls the heroes to war. It is interesting that the spectres in *Milton* are terrified by the cock and flee (28. 24–26).

52. Raine, 1: 242.

53. *Selected Writings,* p. 304.

54. Ibid., p. 305.

55. Cf. Eve Teitelbaum, "Form as Meaning in Blake's *Milton,*" *Blake Studies* 2 (Fall 1969): 56.

56. Cf. ibid., pp. 55–56.

57. Raine (1: 250) sees Udan Adan as space-time.

58. Raine, 2: 296.

59. Entuthon Benython seems much like Berkeley's definition of matter: "nothing but the general abstract idea of entity" of "those miserable refuges, whether in an eternal succession of unthinking causes and effects, or in a fortuitous concourse of atoms . . . in a word, the whole system of materialism" (*Works,* 2: 213).

60. Cf. Adams, *Blake and Yeats,* p. 111.

61. Cf. Sandler, p. 21.

62. Cf. Adams, *Blake and Yeats,* pp. 5, 25.

NOTES TO CHAPTER 2. FALL INTO SELFHOOD

1. Paul Henri Thiery, Baron de Holbach, *The System of Nature,* 3 vols. (trans. unknown) (London: G. Kearsley, 1797), 1: 91–92.

2. *A Vindication of the rights of men in a letter to Edmund Burke* (London: J. Johnson, 1790), p. 28.

3. *The Romance of the Forest,* 2 vols. ed. A. L. Barbauld (London: T. Hookham, 1810), 2: 65.

4. Burton R. Pollin, *Education and Enlightenment in the Works of William Godwin* (New York: Las Americas Publishing Company, 1962), p. 48.

5. Adam Smith, *Essays*, ed. Joseph Black and James Hulton (London, 1872), pp. 279–81.

6. *An Enquiry Concerning the Principles of Morals* (London, 1777; rpt. Chicago: Open Court, 1912), p. 138.

7. Ibid., p. 143.

8. Henry St. John, Viscount Bolingbroke, *The Works of Lord Bolingbroke*, 4 vols. (London, 1844; rpt. New York: A. M. Kelly, 1967), 3: 224. Pope varies the idea slightly: "Self-Love and Reason to one end aspire" (*Essay on Man*, 1: 87).

9. *Observations on Man*, 2: 271–82. See proposition 67.

10. *The Social Contract and Discourses*, trans. G. D. H. Cole (London: Everyman, 1913; rpt. 1946), p. 182.

11. Raine, *Blake and Tradition*, 2: 214–16, sees Swedenborg's *proprium* and Blake's selfhood as what is now called *ego*. Morton Paley, *Energy and the Imagination: A Study of the Development of Blake's Thought* (Oxford: Clarendon, 1970), p. 154, sees Blake and Boehme using the term to represent the "unregenerate ego" that isolates the individual from the human community.

12. (Baltimore, 1812), par. 556. The translation, however, is the same one annotated by Blake around 1790.

13. *Heaven and Hell*, par. 557.

14. *Works*, 3: 109.

15. Ibid., 4: 124.

16. S. H. Fraiberg, *The Magic Years* (New York: Scribners, 1956), p. 247.

17. In dealing with the Bard's Song one must recognize the apparently disorganized material in plates 3 to 6. Since it is not dramatic symbolism, but symbolic doctrine, it may be best to give here some account of its relationship to the poem. The material was incorporated apparently at different times as Blake felt the need to amplify different themes of the poem. The material is roughly focused on four distinct themes: (1) the actual narrative of the Palamabron-Satan quarrel; (2) an attempt to establish an association between materialism and retribution; (3) an added set of details to amplify the cosmology of the poem; (4) the introduction of the concept of classes of men, whose different classification gives their actions a temporal value without eternal punishment. The additions to the Palamabron-Satan quarrel consist of Los's shaping of Urizen (plate 3) which, failing to restore Urizen completely, causes Los to separate into a female emanation and a male spectre (3.28–36). Los, his emanation Enitharmon, and the spectre, begin the work of creative activity; during this time progeny are born to Los and Enitharmon, all of whom share in the work of creation, even Satan, their latest born, whose function is that of a miller (3.37–43). Los is dramatized in a reproof against Satan for wishing to forsake his function and usurp the task of Palamabron (4.6–19). Satan's fainting beneath the "artillery," i.e., the unbearable and striking vision of Palamabron's return with his harrow (5.1–2), suggests the strength of Satan's desire for usurpation. (It also forecasts Urizen's fainting later in his strug-

gle with Milton (39.53), for Satan is Urizen drawn down into a lower manifestation (10.1–2).) The details lead logically into the dramatic narrative beginning on plate seven, giving an explanation of the origin of Satan's relationship to Los and Palamabron. But Blake wished the opening part of the Bard's Song to expose more meanings as groundwork for later episodes and passages in the poem. The linking of materialism and the doctrine of retribution is engrafted onto the narrative at several points, but without complete success. The doctrine of materialism is represented essentially by Lockean Empiricism, though the Newtonian universe is also involved. The language used in epistemological discussions, and the symbolic act of the creation of the senses of Urizen, are Blake's suggestions that empiricism is a degenerative and delusory doctrine. Though Los is forming Urizen, rescuing him from complete chaos, his attempts are not totally successful. After he forms the senses of Urizen, Urizen's gesture is one of refusing to turn to the east, i.e., turn to the place of God (3.6–27). Urizen's destructive urges are not regenerated, and his refusal of form (3.9), echoed by Satan's refusal of form (3.41), has continued in the compromise of his endowment with senses. Moreover, Urizen is an abstract horror (3.9). Not only does he refuse form (3.9), he is also associated with doubt and reason (3.8). Los's spectre is subdued from particulars to generals (3.37–38). Abstraction, form, reason, particulars, and generals are terms used in Locke and Berkeley. When Satan, who is Urizen, is identified as Newton's pantocrator (4.11), which Raine describes as "a universal ruler of a phenomenal universe" (Raine, 2: 168), a concept that differentiates Satan from a qualitive and nonspatial deity, and then is said to weave the woof of Locke (4.11), the association of the scientific-empirical tradition (materialism for Blake) with Satan is established. Satan's mills symbolize a rationalistic, nonspiritual conception of the universe. Blake then attempts in several segments to tie the enclosure in the senses (empiricism, materialism) to the doctrine of retribution (retribution in its manifestation as atonement). The enclosure in the senses is symbolized by the weaving of the daughters of Albion and by the furnaces around which a fierce dance by a group of males occurs. The dancing males lament the inadequacies of the "narrow doleful form" (5.19) of the senses that enclose the spirit. But the spirit is called a victim (5.15), who is prepared for the furnace by the females. From the deluded point of view of the singing males and females, these "victims" are carrying out an atonement. Other examples of atonement are mentioned: Christ (5.3); and in an obscure passage, "Charles calls on Milton for atonement" (5.39). It may be suggested that Milton, who justified the regicide of Charles I, was involved in the assent to the doctrine of retribution. The fact that "Cromwell is ready" (5.39) suggests that Cromwell is ready to carry out the doctrine. James (James II), calling for fires, is himself also seeking an atonement in a form of retribution. The historical sequence suggests that atonement or retribution becomes an endless process of sacrifice. This pessimistic view gives light to the picture of Tyburn, the site of legal executions, which is seen as "Calvary's foot" (4.21), the site of Christ's atonement. Tyburn is described as a place where naked beauty mocks Druidic, mathematical proportion, a symbol in the poem for rationalism, which again unites the materialistic and retributive doctrines. These segments seem to imply that Blake was attempting to give introductory material to the themes expounded later in the work. They are tied in also to his conception of the elect, the first of the three classes mentioned so frequently early in the poem. The atonements taking place are atonements for the elect who are unable, as they see it, to attain eternal salvation. They "cannot be redeemed, but [are] Created continually/By offering & atonement in the cruelties of Moral Law" (5.11–12). The process of atonement is apparently required by the elect, who mistakenly see their lot as one requiring sacrifice. But Blake suggests that the act of creation is itself the atonement, for the Daughters of Albion and the males, as well as Los's whole family, are engaged in the process of giving form to the inchoate spirits, i.e., building "the looms of Generation" (3.38). From Blake's point of view this process is mercy, a point of view expanded later in the poem. But the elect see it as atonement, because of their own delusions. I shall discuss the elect in further detail in a later chapter. Clearly, in these plates, Blake was attempting to introduce explanatory material, but its mass of surprising references and unexplained connections has not helped his purpose.

18. Northrop Frye, *Fearful Symmetry,* sees the plowman traditionally symbolizing the visionary, p. 335. Raine sees the harrow as symbolizing energy, irrationality, and the mysterious (2: 224). W. J. T. Mitchell sees the plow as a revolutionary instrument (*BSA,* p. 291). I cannot agree with Raine's connection of the mysterious with John Milton's notion of the conscience (Raine, 2: 220).

19. Cf. Boehme: "So Lucifer also would be as a God and Creator . . . and would *domineer over the Meekness* of the Heart of God" (*Threefold Life,* viii. 44).

20. *Arcana Coelestia,* 12 vols. (New York, 1933–1938), 1, par. 1060.

21. Frye sees Canaan as symbolizing the garden in *Paradise Lost* and eighteenth-century Europe. "Notes for a Commentary on *Milton,*" *The Divine Vision,* ed. Vivian de Sola Pinto (New York, 1957; rpt. N. Y.: Haskell House, 1968), p. 122.

22. Cf. Boehme: "But the Devil's Kingdom, after which he longed and laboured, stood in the *Wrathful* Fire's might" (Mysterium Magnum, XXII. 32), *Works,* 3: 93. William Law, in *The Spirit of Love,* following Boehme, also associates wrath with the condition of the fall:

> Whereever Christ is not, there is the wrath of nature, or nature left to itself and its own tormenting strength of life to feel nothing in itself but the vain restless contrariety of its own working properties. This is the one only origin of hell and every kind of curse and misery in the creature. It is nature without the Christ of God or the Spirit of Love ruling over it. And there you may observe that wrath has in itself the nature of hell; and that it can have no beginning or power in any creature but so far as it has lost the Christ of God. (*Selected Mystical Writings of William Law,* ed. Stephen Hobhouse [London: Dawson 1938] p. 144)

In Boehme, Law, and Blake the nature of evil is associated with the isolation or separation of wrath, not wrath *per se.* Blake, however, had adopted the concept in psychological terms, not merely cosmic.

23. Frye, *(Fearful Symmetry,* p. 335) sees Leutha as the begetter of the Antichrist, "a combination of Tirzah, Vala, and Rahab," who represents "objective nature." Sandler (p. 17) points out her parallel to the dragon of Revelation 12: 1–3.

24. Cf. Boehme's reference to fire in n22. Again the fall is imaged in Boehmenistic imagery.

25. Sloss and Wallis (1: 346) see the Palamabron-Satan episode as an illustration of the iniquity of moral judgment and the cruelty of retributive justice. Sandler (p. 17) points out parallels of the episode and the dragon's war with the saints in Revelation.

26. "Vision of the Last Judgement," E 551/K 612.

27. 1: 381.

28. Robert Hindmarsh, *Rise and Progress of the New Jerusalem Church,* ed. Rev. Edward Modely (London: Hodson, 1861), pp. 23–26. For a discussion of the possibilities of Blake's early relation to the New Jerusalem Church, see my "Audience for *The Marriage of Heaven and Hell,*" *Blake Studies* 3 (Fall 1970): 19–52.

29. Raine has pointed out the way in which Boehme has made man a similitude of God, a microcosm. The analogy between individual man and the cosmos is the analogy Blake is implying between the fall of Albion, which represents England, and the cosmos, to the fall of any individual. Raine interprets this cause of the fall of Albion as the "loss of world through the belief that the phenomenon possesses a substantial existence independent of mind" (2: 254). Price seems to agree (p. 432). This interpretation fits well with the conception of Albion as England, for it makes the sickness of Albion the sickness of Lockean empiricism. Berkeley had pointed out the sickness in *Three Dialogues.* But the total archetypal meaning requires more detail, and must be seen in relation to the fall in *Milton.*

30. Cf. Boehme:

When the Soul brought its Imagination from that [Divine *Essence* or Substance] out of and into the Astral Property, then also its Body, wherein the three-fold Spirit Worketh, became wholly earthly, gross and *beastial;* for into whatsoever the Imagination of the Spirit bringeth itself, such a Body also is, through the Impression of the Spiritual Desire. (Treatise of Baptism, I. 20, *Works,* 4: 169)

Blake's phrase summarizes Boehme's concept. Both see the process as relating to the fall.

31. E 527/K 571.

32. E 523/K 567.

33. Erdman suggests the following parallels: (1) Satan's usurpation of Palamabron's place is parallel to Cromwell's domination of Parliament; (2) Palamabron's solemn assembly is parallel to Parliament; (3) Palamabron's prayer for protection (9.5–6) is parallel to Parliament's need for protection from Cromwell; (4)

Palamabron's Harrow levels as a revolutionary. As it is abused by Satan, so does Cromwell abuse his revolutionary function; (5) Satan's assumption of Godhead (9.25) is parallel to Cromwell's; (6) Satan's mills are parallel to the mills that produced Cromwell's artillery; (7) Los's initial support of Satan is parallel to Milton's support of Charles's execution; and (8) Satan begins as elect and ends as reprobate, as does Cromwell. *Blake, Prophet Against Empire,* rev. ed. (Princeton, N.J.: Princeton University Press, 1969), p. 424.

34. At the time of the composition of *Milton,* Blake had been working with Hayley, who was completing the *Life and Posthumous Writings of William Cowper* (London: Swords, 1803). The invitation to Mary Unwin and Cowper from John Newton to come to Olney after Mr. Unwin's death came at the end of a term when Cowper wrote of his "singularly peaceful and devout life" (*Life,* 1: 37). After his move to Olney and the influence of Newton, who was a Calvinistic follower of Whitfield, Cowper began a decline in spirits. "In his sequestered life he seems to have been much consoled and entertained by the society of his pious friend, Mr. Newton, in whose religious pursuits he appears to have taken an active part, by the composition of sixty-eight hymns. Mr. Newton wished and expected him to have contributed a much larger number" (*Life,* 1: 49). Though Hayley does not suggest that Newton's influence caused Cowper's derangement, he writes that "in 1773 he sunk into . . . severe paroxysms of religious despondency" (*Life,* 1: 51). Cowper emerged slowly from the sickness, but, though again Haley does not say it, the strong Calvinist flavor of the Olney hymns shows the influence of Newton. See Maurice J. Quinlan, *William Cowper: A Critical Life* (Minneapolis, Minn.: University of Minnesota Press, 1953), pp. 78–88. It is possible to imagine Cowper as Palamabron and Newton as the usurping Satan, the selfhood of Newton usurping the creative effort of Cowper.

35. The historical manifestations of the archetype should not be seen as merely sources, either. Indeed, they may illuminate the sublime allegory, but the attention must move from the world of history to eternal and sublime truth. The source is only a manifestation of the archetype, not the intended meaning. It is too easy to confuse the material and the final cause. Blake's statement in his letter to Butts, April 25, 1803 (E 698/K 822), that Hayley is his spiritual enemy and corporeal friend, for instance, does not necessitate the identification of Palamabron as Blake and Satan as Hayley simply because the Bard repeats the same words (4.26). The insight that Blake gained from his experience with Hayley needed to be sublimated into a grand archetypal myth, not made into a nasty covert attack under a hidden allegory. The nature of the insight Blake obtained implies self-knowledge, and Blake was probably aware that the principles of motivation that he discerned in Hayley had to exist in all men, including William Blake.

36. The more cautious scholars always demur somewhat. Fyre, (*Fearful Symmetry,* p. 325) sees Hayley as Satan, but he recognizes too that the Satan of the second half of the poem is not related to anything like Hayley. Sloss and Wallis (1: 347) recognize the possibility of seeing Satan as Hayley but cannot be certain. Stuart Curran wisely attacks this identification as it is reflected in the work of Frye,

Bloom, and Erdman ("Blake and the Gnostic Hyle: A Double Negative," *Blake Studies* 4 [Spring 1972]: 120). James Rieger, agreeing with Curran, attacks the identification on the same grounds in " 'The Hem of Their Garments': The Bard's Song in *Milton*," *BSA*, p. 260.

37. W. J. T. Mitchell sees Satan primarily as Blake's Selfhood, *BSA*, p. 293.

38. For Blake's letter, see E 682/K 803. For Butts's reply, see G. E. Bentley, ed., *Blake Records* (Oxford: Clarendon, 1969), p. 76.

39. E 687/K 811.

40. E 697/K 822.

41. *Blake Records*, p. 105.

42. See Blake's Memorandum, E 700-702/K 437-39.

43. *Blake Records*, p. 89.

44. E 681/ K 803.

45. E 685/K 808.

46. E 612/K 399. Blake would not have been alone in seeing Pitt as the cause of destruction. Fuseli blamed the ills of England on Pitt. See the listing for July 20, 1807, in *Farington Diary,* ed. James Grieg, 8 vols. (London: Hutchinson, 1923–28) 4: 180–81.

47. It should be noted that the Satan-Palamabron myth in *Milton* is a combination of the Satan-Palamabron episode (at the end of Night Eight of the Four Zoas [Night 8, p. 115], written after Blake left his residence at Felpham) E 738, and the story of Luvah's assuming Urizen's horses (written before Felpham). (See Night 3, p. 39. 11.2–5). The story of usurpation probably existed *in ovo* before Blake went to Felpham, and may have been intended by Blake to reflect the events of his time. Clearly the Hayley-Blake meaning does not exhaust its possibilities. Erdman *(Prophet Against Empire)* has explored the possibilities of the Bard's Song's relationship to Milton's own career, seeing Cromwell's domination over Parliament as Satan's usurpation of Palamabron's function. This domination could as well have been seen in Pitt. The characters appearing in *Europe,* whom Erdman has shown to reflect actions in Europe of that time, reappear in the Bard's Song. It is not incorrect to look for Blake attempting consistency.

48. *History of the Reign of George III,* 2 vols. (London, 1803; rpt. 1816), 2: 347. As Bisset points out, Burke and Pitt were associated in the radical mind as warmongers; consequently what was said of Burke's attitude to France, by a kind of semi-logic, could have been applied to Pitt. The split between pity and wrath, associated with Satan, may have derived from Blake's remembrance of Paine's devastating attack on Burke's fulsome lament for Marie Antoinette:

Not one glance of compassion, not one commiserating reflection . . . has he bestowed on these who lingered out the most wretched of lives, a life without hope, in the most miserable of prisons.

It is painful to behold a man employing his talents to corrupt himself. Nature has been kinder to Mr. Burke than he is to her. He is not affected by the reality of distress touching his heart, but by the showy resemblance of it striking his imagination. He pities the plumage, but forgets the dying bird. (*The Life and*

Works of Thomas Paine, ed. William M. Van der Weyde, 10 vols. [New Rochelle, N.Y.: Thomas Paine National Historical Assoc., 1925], 4:38–39) The uselessness and deception of pity without wrath can be applied no better than Paine has done. (See also *Prophet Against Empire,* p. 184)

49. Bisset, 2: 484.

50. Ibid., p. 394.

51. *Dictionary of National Biography,* ed. Leslie Stephen and Sidney Lee, 22 vols., 15: 1261.

52. Bisset, 2: 459.

53. Draper Hill, ed., *Fashionable Contrasts, Caricatures by James Gilray* (London: Phaidon, 1966), p. 147.

54. *DNB,* 15: 1262–63.

55. M. D. George, *English Political Caricature to 1792* (Oxford: Clarendon, 1959), p. 198.

56. George, p. 215.

57. Hill, p. 137.

58. *DNB,* 15: 1261.

59. The story of Luvah's usurpation of the horses of Urizen in the *Four Zoas* has been interpreted by Erdman as follows: "censorship [Urizen's iron laws] has been introduced in England too late to be effective. Urizen once having permitted ideas of freedom to enter the thought processes of his kingdom (having allowed Luvah to drive the horses of instruction) has had poor luck with his 'curbes of iron & brass' " (*Prophet Against Empire,* p. 303). Remembering that Satan is Urizen drawn down into generation, one can translate Erdman's notion to the Palamabron-Satan quarrel, seeing Satan as attempting to introduce restriction.

60. Bisset, 2: 393.

61. *DNB,* 15: 1259. Erdman shows how Blake describes the same event in relation to *Europe* (*Prophet Against Empire,* p. 217), though Erdman relates the source of animosity to Thurlow's resistance to Pitt's Sinking Fund bill.
The connection between Thurlow and Thullough suggests further historical episodes behind the Bard's Song. Gillray's famous print of Pitt, Thurlow, and Queen Charlotte as Satan, Sin, and Death, is a political satire that suggests that Queen Charlotte had "interests . . . favourable to Pitt" (George, p. 216). Gillray's practice of using literary allusions for topical satire fell on Pitt more than once (see, e.g., Hill, pp. 138, 141–42, 147–48). Blake *may* be using the method in his allegory of Leutha and Satan. Leutha has a dragon "forth issue from" (12.2) her limbs when she enters Satan's brain (12.4), and, at the time of the resting of the horses, she "came forth from the head of Satan! back the Gnomes recoil's/And call'd me Sin, and for a sign portentous held me" (12.36–83). When Milton's Sin sprang from Satan's head, "amazement seiz'd/All the Host of Heaven; back they recoil'd afraid/At first, and call'd me *Sin,* and for a Sign/Portentous held me" (*Paradise Lost,* 2: 757–60); further, Sin's incest-born and incestuous Death "Forth issu'd" from Sin (*P.L.,* 2: 785). The obvious allusions of Leutha to Sin, however, may also

be intended to recall Gillray's famous print and his identification of Sin as Queen Charlotte. Of course, Blake would have revised Gillray's assignment of Pitt as Death to Satan. This allusion to Gillray would not be surprising, for the caricatured attacks on the Queen had accused her of secret relations with Germany, concealing the state of the King's health, and of concealment of "things" at Kew (George, p. 199). It is possible that Leutha's delusion was seen by Blake behind these actions of Queen Charlotte.

But Leutha is more representative of symbolic delusion, and would stand for no single person. One episode from the final days of Marie Antoinette may illustrate this point. When new guards at Versailles were entertained, "in the course of their festivity, when both hosts and guests were heated with wine, the king and queen, with the infant dauphin, visited the banqueting room. The royal mother carried the infant prince completely around the table. Meanwhile the music played an air which the ladies of the court accompanied with the appropriate stanzas pathetically describing the feelings and sufferings of a captive king . . . [the officers were inspired to throw off the red cockade, to take royal colored cockades]" (Bisset, 2: 220–21). Such proceedings might constitute the "blandishments" (12.37) that Leutha attempted on the gnomes. When one realizes that the gnomes, the genii, and even the horses of the Bard's Song are really living people whom the world rulers control as automatic functionaries with their function their only right to existence in the selfhood's mind, then one begins to see the trenchant and ironic satire in *Milton.* The way of the selfhood forces the reduction of human beings to automatons.

NOTES TO CHAPTER 3.
THE BLOSSOMING OF THE SELFHOOD

1. The comprehensive connections of evil are suggested by E. J. Rose in his discussion of the Female Will, *BSA*, p. 90.
2. Cf. Raine, 2: 218.
3. Frye, (*Fearful Symmetry,* p. 337) found Puritanism the ancestor to Deism. Peter Fisher (*The Valley of Vision* [Toronto: University of Toronto Press, 1961], p. 158) demonstrated Blake's equation of Druidism and Deism. Fisher sees moralism and a remote God as the connecting link.
4. *Works,* 8: 50.
5. Ibid., pp. 44–45.
6. Ibid., p. 85.
7. Ibid., p. 54.
8. Ibid., pp. 54–55.
9. Ibid., pp. 84, 81.
10. Ibid., p. 101.
11. Cf. Teitlebaum, p. 43; Raine, 2: 275.
12. *Works,* 3: 396.
13. *Principles of Morals,* p. 14.
14. Blake's remarks about the talk of benevolence and virtue refer to the theme

of benevolence in the moral philosophy of the eighteenth century. The philosophy was adopted by the Cambridge Platonists and by Hutchinson, who, according to Adam Smith, was its greatest exponent (*Essays*, p. 268). In a way it is apparent in some form in Hume, Smith, and Godwin. Benevolence is to be defined as the human motive, opposed to self-interest, that constitutes a necessary factor in a morally good action. Hutcheson saw benevolence as the essential factor in moral action, and imagined self-interested motives as negative values. (Utilitarianism, in which a moral action's value is determined by the greatest good for the greatest number, is merely the objective side of benevolence. Rather than looking at the motive, Utilitarianism looks at the result.) Hume's notion of man's sympathy with his fellow man as distinct from self-interest is in the same general category of benevolence, but the notion of utility generally makes self-interest the underlying motive for action. Godwin's theory of moral action saw "reason" as the sole guide to virtue, but the motivating force of virtuous action was clearly not self-interest. The reason that could force one to consider all mankind before one's own intimate friends or family is clearly a nonselfish, benevolent motivation. Blake seems to be attacking the philosophy that he himself advocates, but his real point is that he deplores the hypocrite who preaches but does not follow the philosophy.

    15. Sloss and Wallis, 1: 348.

    16. Tucker, *Lt. of Nature*, 3, Sec. 21 sees the vehicle as rational which, upon its extinction, frees the soul from rationality.

    17. The meaning of the polypus is suggested by Paul Miner, "The Polyp as a Symbol in Blake," *Texas Studies in Literature and Language* 2 (Summer 1960): 202, as a "mass of growing, endless, unpurposeful life." Adams suggests its "delusory physical existence" (p. 97). Damon suggests its connection with materialism, *Blake Dictionary*, p. 33, as does Raine, 1: 241. As far back as the *Hieroglyphics of Horapollo Nilous* the polypus was a symbol that would have sinister meaning for Blake; speaking of iconographic imagery, Horapollo writes: "When they would symbolise a man the ruler of his tribe, they depict a crayfish and a polypus" (*Hieroglyphics*, trans. Alexander Cory [London:Pickering, 1840],p. 151). It is generally assumed that the polypus is a sea animal, but Blake certainly remembered its meaning as a cancer. See, e.g., John Arbuthnot, *An Essay Concerning the Nature of Aliments* (London: J. Tonson, 1732), p. 265, and Rousseau's fear for the "polypus" on his heart in *The Confessions of Jean-Jacques Rousseau: The Anonymous Translation into English of 1783 to 1796*, rev. and completed by A. S. B. Glover (New York: Limited Editions Club, 1955), p. 223.

    18. *Works*, 3: 62.

    19. *Christianity as Old as Creation* (London, 1730; rpt. Stuttgart: Fromann, 1967), p. 13.

    20. Tindall, p. 13.

    21. *Observations*, 2: 45–7.

    22. Cf. Sloss and Wallis, 1: 344.

    23. Cf. Sandler, p. 27; Teitelbaum, p. 57.

    24. *Confessions*, 2: p. 622.

    25. Cf. Sandler, p. 23.

26. *Works,* 3: 18102.

27. Cf. Sandler, p. 45; Bloom, *Blake's Apocalypse,* p. 360.

28. The possible confusion between Tirzah's looms and Enitharmon's probably lies behind Blake's deletion of the line "By Enitharmon's Looms and Spun beneath the Spindle of Tirzah" from plate seven (see E 729). The original implication is that the "Web of Life" (6.34) is woven by Enitharmon and Tirzah working cooperatively, but Blake really uses Tirzah to represent delusory aspects of the material form and Enitharmon as merciful and kind. For an extended discussion of weaving and the garment woven, see Morton Payley "The Figure of the Garment in *The Four Zoas, Milton,* and *Jerusalem,*" *BSA,* pp. 119–32.

29. Cf. Frye, "Notes," p. 113.

30. Richard Watson, *An Address to the People of Great Britain,* 4th ed. (London, 1798), p. 12.

31. Ibid., p. 13

32. Ibid., p. 28

33. Ibid., p. 29

34. Ibid., p. 30

35. Ibid., p. 28

36. E 601/K 383.

37. Cf. Raine, 1: 328, who sees distinctions in kinds of hermaphrodites. See also Jean Hagstrum "Babylon Revisited, or the Story of Luvah and Vala," *BSA,* p. 114.

38. Cf. Sandler, pp. 19–20.

39. Cf. Raine, 1: 327.

40. See *True Christian Religion* (New York, 1873), Appendix, par. 2.

41. *Heaven and Hell,* par. 59.

42. Cf. Sloss and Wallis, 2: 344.

43. Frye has pointed out that there are biblical allusions to the costume of Aaron, illustrating the fact "that priests always worship a female will" ("Notes," p. 123).

44. See also Irene Taylor's discussion of Blake's view of chastity in "Say First! What Mov'd Blake? Blake's *Comus* Designs and *Milton,*" *BSA,* pp. 243–44.

45. Cf. Bolingbroke, who agrees here with Blake, *Works,* 3: 62.

46. Cf. Sandler, p. 20; Frye, "Notes," p. 116.

47. Cf. Adams, pp. 26, 64.

48. Cf. Sandler, p. 37.

49. Ibid., p. 22.

50. Ibid., p. 14.

51. *Works,* 3: 238–39.

52. Ibid., p. 239.

53. *Works,* 8: 5.

54. Ibid., p. 278.

55. Sandler agrees, but finds the deist sources in Boulanger and Dupuis, pp. 47–57.

56. Cf. Raine, 2: 230.

57. *Paradise Lost* suffers also from its biblical ambiguity. See Naseeb Shaheen, "Of Oreb, Or of Sinai," *ELN* 9 (Sept. 1971): 25–28.

58. E 604/K 388.

59. E 607/K 393.

60. *Works*, 3: 399.

61. *Christianity Not Mysterious* (London, 1696; rpt. Stuttgart, 1964), p. 60.

62. *Works*, 5: 103.

63. See notes to chap. 2, n40.

64. E 685/K 809.

65. *DNB* 15: 1267.

66. See Frye, "Notes," p. 122.

67. Bisset, 2: 392–93. Also see Erdman, *Prophet*, p. 311.

68. William E. H. Lecky *A History of England in the Eighteenth Century*, 6 vols. (New York: Appleton, 1887), 6: 203.

69. Ibid., p. 206.

70. Rose puts it well: "Satan is the state of the world, psychologically, politically, economically, and in every way" ("Blake's *Milton*," p. 20).

71. (*Signature of All Things*, XVI. 10), *Works*, 4: 136.

72. (*Signature of All Things*, XVI. 35), *Works*, 4: 140.

73. Par. 322.

74. Par. 203, et al.

75. E 599–601/K 131–33.

76. *Essays*, p. 144.

77. Ibid., p. 150.

78. 2: 428.

79. *Works*, 4: 306.

80. *Works*, 2: 113.

81. *Works*, 4: 251.

82. *Works*, 8: 270.

83. Jean Jacques Rousseau, *Emilius and Sophia: or, A New System of Education* (trans. unknown) 4 vols. (London: R. Griffith, 1767), 3: 40.

84. 3: 59.

85. 3: 76.

86. 3: 80.

87. 3: 70.

88. 3: 103.

89. Ibid.

90. 3: 152.

91. *Confessions*, p. 375.

92. *Emilius*, 3: 70.

93. *Ibid.*, p. 72.

94. *Ibid.*, p. 69.

95. Mark Schorer, *William Blake: the Politics of Vision* (New York; Holt, 1946; rpt. Vintage, 1959), p. 118.

96. *Philosophical Dictionary*, trans. Peter Gay, 2 vols. (New York: Basic Books, 1962), 2: 479.

97. 2: 447–48.

98. D. C. Somervell, *English Thought in the Nineteenth Century* (New York: Longmans, 1929), p. 19.

99. *The Works of William Paley* (Philadelphia: Woodward, 1831), p. 271.

100. *Works*, p. 386.

101. *Works*, p. xiii.

102. *Works*, p. 145.

103. Ibid.

104. *Works*, p. 149.

105. Edward Gibbon, *The History of the Decline and Fall of the Roman Empire*, ed. Rev. H. H. Milman 6 vols. (London, 1776–1788; rpt. Boston: Aldine, 1845).

106. Rev. Canon John H. Overton and Rev. Frederick Relton, *The English Church from the Accesession of George I to the End of the Eighteenth Century* (1714–1800), (London, New York: Macmillan, 1906), p. 158.

107. Ibid., p. 228.

108. Leslie Stephens, 1: 385.

109. *English Church*, p. 257.

110. Edmund Burke, *Reflection on the Revolution in France* (London: Everyman, 1910), p. 96.

111. *English Church*, p. 281.

112. Watson, p. 11.

NOTES TO CHAPTER 4. REGENERATION

1. Cf. Frye, *Fearful Symmetry*, p. 27.

2. Cf. Rose, "Blake's *Milton*, p. 20.

3. Cf. Sandler, p. 20.

4. 1: 509.

5. 1: 528.

6. 1: 552.

7. 1: 562.

8. 1: 539.

9. 1: 543.

10. Stephens, 1: 340.

11. Cf. Sandler, p. 20.

12. Cf. Frye, *Fearful Symmetry*, p. 212.

13. *Works*, 8: 197–98.

14. Blake relies on the concept of eternal vision when he remarks that "a Prophet is a Seer not an arbitrary Dictator" (E 607/K 392). Here Blake is concerned to distinguish between absolute statements about futurity and opinions about consequences.

15. E 607/K 392.

16. Frye (*Fearful Symmetry*, p. 135) develops the relationship between Blake and Locke further.

17. *Human Understanding* IV. ii. 1.

18. Ibid., iii. 6.

19. Ibid., x. 3.

20. Blake's rejoinder to Locke has been given in *There Is No Natural Religion*, where he argues that the limitation of knowledge to sense perception could lead to no knowledge of God, but since there is indeed knowledge of God, then man's knowledge is not limited to sense perception.

21. *Human Understanding* IV. xvii. 2.

22. Ibid., xvii. 24.

23. Ibid., xix. 4.

24. Ibid., xix. 6.

25. Ibid., xix. 11.

26. Ibid., xix. 14.

27. *M.H.H.*, pl. 12; E 38/K 153.

28. E 634/K 456.

29. E 610/K 396.

30. E 603/K 386.

31. *Energy and Imagination*, p. 208.

32. Ibid., p. 227.

33. Cf. Frye, *Fearful Symmetry*, p. 30; Raine, 2: 249.

34. Cf. Adams, p. 24.

35. *Three Dialogues, Works*, 2: 215.

36. Ibid., 2: 235.

37. Cf. Adams, p. 32.

38. See Harold Fisch, "Blake's Miltonic Moment" *William Blake: Essays for S. Foster Damon*, p. 40.

39. Cf. Bloom, *Blake's Apocalypse*, p. 396.

40. Raine, 1: 347 mistakenly sees Blake as indifferent to war.

41. Cf. Teitelbaum, p. 57, and McGann, *BSA*, pp. 14–15.

42. See E. J. Rose "Blake's Metaphorical States," *Blake Studies* 4 (Fall, 1971): 19.

43. Behind Blake's doctrine of states lies Boehme's conception that the eternal, fixed, spiritual entity is manifested in time, but remains permanent:

> all Things stand in the Seed and Procreation; and there is not any Thing but has a Fixity in it, be it either hidden or manifest, for it shall stand to the Glory of God.
> Whatever is risen from the eternal Fixity, as Angels and the Souls of Men, remains indestructible in its fixt Being; but whatever is risen in the unfixt Being, *viz.* with the Motion of Time, that does again enter into the first Motion from whence it has taken its Original, and is a Map of its Form which it had here, like a Picture, or as an Image in a Glass without Life; for so it was from Eternity before the Times of this World. (*Signature of All Things*, XIV. 3–4) *Works*, 4: 111–12

Blake's use of the word *form* as almost synonymous with *state* is suggested by this passage. Blake's idea of states also contains the Swedenborgian concept of state (cf. Raine, 2: 240). For Swedenborg, *state* refers to a condition of spiritual life, a man's spiritual attitude. Swedenborg also conceived of an inner and outer state, changes in the outer state being simply indications of changes in the inner state. The outer state has the appearance of spatial existence, and changes in space are symbols of the change in the interior state: "Motions, progressions and changes of place, in the other life, are changes of the state of the interiors of life and neverthe-less it really appears to spirits and angels as if they actually existed" (*Earths in the Universe*, 2: 125n). The notion that the state is the spatial world and changes of state progression through space, combined with Boehme's notion of eternal fixity being manifested in time only to return to fixity, makes up the essence of Blake's doctrine. But Blake adds his own characteristic thought to the idea, using it to explain God's mercy.

44. Cf. Rose, "Blake's Metaphorical States," pp. 19–31 for discussion of the extent of Blake's development of the three classes.

45. Blake may have been following Boehme, who writes: "Man has indeed all the forms of all the three worlds lying in him; for he is a complete image of God, or of the Being of all beings; only the order is placed in him at his incarnation; for there are three work-masters in him which prepare his form [or signature], viz. the threefold fiat, according to the three worlds; and they are in contest about the form, and the form is figured according to the contest; which of the masters holds the predominant rule, and obtains it in the essence, according to that his instrument is tuned, and the other lie hid, and come behind with their sound, as it plainly shews itself" ([*Signature of All Things*, I. 10], *Works*, 4: 6). Here the notion of three categories contained within man is clear. Though Boehme does not use this for the idea of election or reprobation, William Law, following Boehme, makes the categories internal elements of each personality. Election and reprobation are in a man insofar as he has an external personality united to earth and destruction and an internal one united to divinity. However, Frye notes that Blake may have found the idea of a tripartite personality in the Bhagavad Gita's concept of gunas (see Frye, "Notes," p. 132). I cannot agree with Damon, *Blake Dictionary*, pp. 87–88, or Raine, 2: 223, who traced the notion to Milton. The concepts of election and reprobation can be found in St. Paul, Revelation, and Calvin, but not in a tripartite or internalized form.

46. Cf. Raine, 2: 243.

47. Cf. Algernon Charles Swinburne, *William Blake: A Critical Essay* (London, 1868; rpt. N. Y.: B. Blom, 1967), p. 264.

48. Blake's reversal of the value of the elect to suggest their lower state in the creation is possibly satirical. Zealous Calvinism, which included the rigid belief in election held by Dr. John Gill, characterized many ministers of the Baptist sects (Joseph Ivimey, *History of the English Baptists*, 4 vols. [London: Burditt, 1811–30], 3: 272–73, 290). Blake's father may have belonged to the Grafton Street Baptist Church from 1769–1772 (*Blake Records*, pp. 7–8), and Blake *may* have been remembering some unhappy associations from his early life. But, if Sandler is correct, Blake was also particularly interested in following Nicholas Antonine Boulanger, *Recherches sur l'origines du despotisme oriental* (1761), who con-

ceived of an ancient group of men, believing themselves particularly favored by the Deity, who became scourges to mankind, striving to establish a universal rule of the elect. It was this group of elect who led the Hebrews to invade Canaan (Sandler, pp. 48–49). If Blake is following Boulanger, the idea of election becomes a category of those who possess power over others and strive for conquest, which would include men like Pitt and Watson.

49. Cf. Adams, p. 33.

50. W. J. T. Mitchell suggests something like this when he talks of the masculine imagination contemplating its own creation (*BSA,* p. 300).

51. Cf. Raine, 2: 247.

52. (*Signature of All Things* XI. 87), *Works,* 4: 96.

53. 2: 405–15.

54. 1: 509.

55. 2: 281–82.

56. 2: 269–82.

57. 2: 282.

58. Cf. Peter Alan Taylor, "Providence and the Moment," p. 47.

NOTES TO CHAPTER 5. THE JOURNEY: BACKGROUND

1. Cf. Sandler, p. 18.

2. Cf. Taylor, "Providence and the Moment," pp. 46–48.

3. Crabb Robinson's note that Blake said that Milton had come to him to correct his error in *Paradise Lost* that sexual intercourse arose from the fall (*Blake Records,* p. 544) was the beginning of much speculation on the errors of Milton that Blake intended to correct. S. F. Damon sees Milton's elevation of reason as his error (*Blake Dictionary,* p. 276). Bernard Blackstone sees the error as Milton's making woman the cause of the fall in *Paradise Lost* (*English Blake* [Cambridge, 1949, rpt. Hamden, Conn.: Archelon, 1966], pp. 139–40). Sandler, p. 43, sees Milton's religion as the cause of a religion of chastity and revenge. Paley (*Energy and Imagination,* p. 246) sees Milton's task to be to redeem his inspiration and his female emanation. Erdman (*Prophet Against Empire,* p. 426) sees Milton as responsible for the failure of the seventeenth-century revolution. Sloss and Wallis (1: 349) see Milton's errors as the cause, and his greatest error as the identification of the creator of the world and of moral law with God. Bloom sees Milton as coming, not to correct *Paradise Lost,* but to make Milton a savior (*Apocalypse,* p. 339). Raine says Milton was chosen because he was an apt symbol of poet as prophet. P. A. Taylor sees the error in *Paradise Lost*'s separation of wrath and mercy in the character of father and son ("A Reading of Blake's Milton," *Blake Studies* 1 [Spring 1969]: 208). There are others. My addition to this heap is certainly not meant to stop speculation.

4. This is a purely rhetorical hypothesis.

5. Samuel Johnson, "Milton," *The Works of Samuel Johnson,* ed. Arthur Murphy, 2 vols. (New York, 1859), 2: 38.

6. E 602/K 384.

7. Johnson, 2: 29.

8. Ibid., p. 37.

9. Ibid., p. 38.

10. "The Present Means," in *The Works of John Milton*, ed. F. A. Patterson et al., 18 vols. (New York: Columbia University Press, 1931–1938), 6: 109.

11. William Hayley, *The Life of Milton* (London, 1796; rpt. New York: Garland, 1971), p. 53.

12. *Works*, 3: 79.

13. *Life of Milton*, p. 201.

14. Johnson, 2: 37–38.

15. *Life of Milton*, p. 51.

16. Ibid., p. 56.

17. Ibid., p. 57.

18. McGann points out Milton's commitment to moral law (*BSA*, p. 8).

19. Wittreich suggests that Cowper and Hayley saw Milton as a shaper of new Christianity (*BSA*, pp. 27–28).

20. E 679, 681/K 799, 801, 803.

21. E 688/K 812.

22. E 691/K 815.

23. E 686–87/K 810–11.

24. E 688/K 812.

25. E 692–94/K 816–19.

26. E 693/K 818.

27. See also Mitchell, *BSA*, p. 282.

28. Cf. Taylor, "A Reading," p. 208.

29. E 697/K 823.

30. E 607/K 392.

31. E 606/K 390.

32. Harold Bloom (*Blake's Apocalypse*, pp. 400–402) compares *Milton* to the Book of Job and *Paradise Regained* as studies in gathering self-awareness. The parallels are convincing, but the journey motif, in particular, is not part of the parallel. Milton's depiction of the journey of Christ is one of wandering and musing that passively reacts to the aggressive Satan by nonaction, whereas Blake's Milton makes a positive act. Blake's Milton seems to have direction and purpose. In *Milton* the journey is the narrative structure. In *Paradise Regained* it is a symbol for a state of mind. In all three, of course, Satan is the evil to be overcome. See also Wittreich, *BSA*, p. 49.

33. "Blake's *Milton*," pp. 21–22.

34. P. 22.

35. *Blake Records*, p. 543.

36. M. L. Johnson suggests a general parallel between Jesus and Milton in "Separating What has been Mixed: A Suggestion for a Perspective on *Milton*," *Blake Studies* 4 (Fall 1973): 11–17.

37. *Blake Records*, p. 548.
38. Ibid.
39. Bloom, *Blake's Apocalypse*, pp. 361–63; Frye, *Fearful Symmetry*, p. 337.
40. *Works*, 8: 112–13.
41. Ibid., pp. 133–35.
42. Ibid., p. 140.
43. *Works*, 8: 154.
44. E 603–4/K 387.
45. E 604/K 388.
46. E 601/K 383.

NOTES TO CHAPTER 6. THE JOURNEY

1. T. W. Herzing sees the poem as a discovery of natural religion in "Book I of Blake's *Milton*," *Blake Studies* (Fall 1973): 26. Also see Fox, p. 23.

2. See also Wittreich, who shows how Warburton's "Dissertation of the Second Book of Virgil's Aeneis" provides a framework for *Milton* (*BSA*, p. 57n).

3. Mitchell would seem to agree with the general structure (*BSA*, p. 286), but he sees Ololon's function as distinctly different from Milton's (p. 301).

4. Cf. Teitelbaum, p. 54.

5. Cf. Frye, *Fearful Symmetry*, p. 312.

6. Mitchell also equates Milton with the eighth eye of God (*BSA*, p. 296).

7. See Martin K. Nurmi's conception of the negative source for the vortex, in "Negative Sources in Blake," *Essays for S. Foster Damon*, p. 311.

8. The motif of the falling star, illustrated frequently in the engravings, may come from Revelation 8:10–11 or 9:1, where falling stars suggest the beginning of the end.

9. Cf. Rose, "Blake's *Milton*," pp. 18–19. See also Mitchell, *BSA*, p. 295.

10. Cf. Rose, "Blake's *Milton*," p. 19.

11. Ibid.

12. Cf. Sandler, p. 45.

13. Cf. Frye, "Notes," p. 119.

14. See Mitchell, p. 295.

15. It is true that this implied split in eternity does not accord with eternity's general symbolic meaning of imagination. But one can only recall Blake's remark to Crabb Robinson that his conception of eternity did not include the notion of God's omnipotence (*Records*, p. 543) to see that eternity, or in psychological terms, the imagination, need not have traditional completeness or power. But certainly this has a redeeming implication. The inevitability, the finality, the necessity of future events, in the Calvinistic or Hartleyan necessitarian view of omniscience and omnipotence are done away with. The action of the individual is insignificant in a fatalistic world. But when even the eternal world is fallible, then the individual, though not predetermined to success, has a tremendously important role. The struggle of life becomes real, not a charade played against a backdrop of predestination. Human life has indeed a great race to be won or lost, and easy solution,

comfortable reliance on God's knowledge, are delusion. After all, the existence of an eternity did not preclude the coming into being of evil. Eternity, therefore, is either not omniscient or not omnipotent. Milton must take action, even in eternity.

16. Cf. Fox, pp. 29–30.

17. Cf. Rose, "Blake's *Milton*," p. 33. Sandler, p. 21, suggests that Los is the mighty angel of Revelation 10:1.

18. Cf. Teitelbaum, p. 56.

19. Cf. Sandler, p. 21.

20. Fisher, *Valley of Vision*, p. 248.

21. Cf. Fox, p. 24.

22. Cf. Frye, *Fearful Symmetry*, p. 337.

23. Cf. Frye, "Notes", pp. 130–31.

24. McGann asserts Rintrah's correctness on this point (*BSA*, p. 9).

25. There is a brief discussion of Milton and the starry eight on plate 32. They repose on the death couch, conversing about the nature of self-annihilation. The death couch is now in eternity, although, earlier, Milton's death couch had been transformed into a tabernacle as he and the starry seven departed from eternity. The death couch and the tabernacle are the same thing, seen from different perspectives. Blake's return to the eternal perspective here is perhaps a slight mistake, since the plate is a later addition. The location, of course, does not affect the action of the journey.

26. Cf. Mitchell, *BSA*, p. 299.

27. Cf. Taylor, "Providence and the Moment," p. 53.

28. Cf. Raine, 2: 222.

29. Cf. Fox, p. 28.

30. Cf. ibid., p. 29.

31. Cf. Taylor "Providence and the Moment," p. 54.

32. Cf. Bloom, *Blake's Apocalypse*, p. 387.

33. Cf. Taylor, "Providence and the Moment," pp. 56–57.

34. Ololon is also like the New Jerusalem's descending in Revelation 21:2. See Sandler, p. 21.

35. McGann also points out (*BSA*, p. 10) Blake's awareness of the danger of art's becoming an abstraction, a system.

36. Mitchell (*BSA*, p. 305) suggests that self-annihilation has begun with Milton's shedding of the role of the promise and continues beyond thepoem.

37. Cf. Sandler, pp. 34–40.

38. Cf. ibid., p. 46.

39. Cf. Frye, *Fearful Symmetry*, p. 354.

40. That Ololon represents Divine Revelation has several suggestive connotations. The change of Ololon from a fiery circle to a garment of blood is a change from the Bible interpreted by state religion as a justification for wrathful vengeance, to the Bible of divine mercy. Ololon's track opens the way to eternity, quite appropriately, since she is the true revelation.

41. At the end of *Milton*, Ololon is revealed religion, just as her corrupt or elect

portion, Rahab, is state religion, Tirzah natural religion. Blake is making Ololon, Milton's emanation in 1800, annihilate the effects of selfhood by overthrowing the evils of the eighteenth century. Revealed religion, the Bible, is true, while natural religion and state religion are false incrustations.

This implies, of course, why Ololon must make her journey, why she is analogous to Sin of *PL* in her opening a track between eternity and Ulro. As sin went one way, Ololon goes the other. She is reversing the devastating effects of natural religion.

42. The "litteral" meaning of the word is a Swedenborgian concept involving what Swedenborg calls "simultaneous order which is a spiritual order arranged from center to circumference," inner to outer (*True Christian Religion*, par. 210). Now this is a concept Blake uses in *Milton*. Ololon is the literal sense of the word and there is the whole notion of inner and outer.

43. McGann (*BSA*, pp. 5–7) explains the necessity for the reader's response to Blake's vision. R. L. Grimes (*BSA*, p. 74) also discusses the sense of an open-ended ending.

Selected Bibliography

Adams, Hazard. *Blake and Yeats: the Contrary Vision*. Ithaca, N.Y.: Cornell University Press, 1955; rpt. New York, 1968.

Ansari, Asloob. *Arrows of Intellect*. Aligarh, India: Naya Kitabghar, 1965.

Arbuthnot, John. *An Essay Concerning the Nature of Aliments*. London: J. Tonson, 1732.

Bacon, Sir Francis. *Novum Organon*. Trans. unknown. Edited by Joseph Devey. New York: P. F. Collier, 1902.

Bentley, G. E., Jr. *Blake Records*. Oxford: Clarendon Press, 1969.

———, and Nurmi, Martin K. *A Blake Bibliography*. Minneapolis, Minn.: University of Minnesota Press, 1964.

Berkeley, George. *Works of George Berkeley, Bishop of Cloyne*. Edited by A. A. Luce and T. E. Jessop. 9 vols. London: T. Nelson, 1948–1957.

Bisset, Robert. *History of the Reign of George III*. London: Longman, 1803; rpt. Albany, N.Y.: Packard, 1816.

Blackstone, Bernard. *English Blake*. Cambridge, England, 1949; Hamden, Conn.: Archelon, 1966.

Blake, William. *Complete Writings*. Edited by Sir Geoffrey Keynes. 3rd printing, revised. Oxford: Oxford University Press, 1971.

————. *The Poems of William Blake*. Edited by W. H. Stevenson. Text by David Erdman. London: Longman, 1971; New York: Norton, 1972.

————. *The Poetry and Prose of William Blake*. Edited by David Erdman. Commentary by Harold Bloom. 4th printing. Garden City: Doubleday, 1971.

————. *The Prophetic Writings of William Blake*. Edited by D. J. Sloss and J. P. R. Wallis. 2 vols. Oxford: Clarendon, 1925.

Bloom, Harold. *Blake's Apocalypse*. Garden City, N.Y.: Doubleday, 1963; rpt. 1965.

Boehme, Jacob. *The Works of Jacob Behmen: the Teutonic Philosopher*. Translated by J. Sparrow, *et al.* Edited by G. Ward and T. Longcake. 4 vols. London: M. Richardson, 1763–81.

Bolinbroke, Henry St. John, Viscount. *The Works of Lord Bolinbroke*. 4 vols. London, 1844; rpt. New York: A. M. Kelly, 1967.

Burke, Edmund. *Reflections on the Revolution in France*. London, 1790; rpt. London: Everyman, 1910.

Clayton, Robert. *Essay on Spirit*. London: J. Noon, 1751.

Curran, Stuart. "Blake and the Gnostic Hyle: A Double Negative." *Blake Studies* 4 (Spring 1972): 117–33.

————, and Wittreich, Joseph Anthony, eds. *Blake's Sublime Allegory*. Madison: University of Wisconsin Press, 1973.

Damon, S. Foster. *A Blake Dictionary*. Providence, R. I.: Brown University Press, 1965.

Erdman, David. *Blake: Prophet Against Empire*. Revised. Princeton, N.J.: Princeton University Press, 1969.

————. *The Illuminated Blake*. Garden City, N.Y.: Doubleday, 1974.

————, ed. "The Romantic Movement: A Selective and Critical Bibliography." *English Language Notes* 3–12 (Supplement, 1965–74).

————, and Grant, John, eds. *Blake's Visionary Forms Dramatic.* Princeton: Princeton University Press, 1970.

The Examiner. London, 1808–1881.

Farington, Joseph. *Farington Diary.* Edited by James Grieg. 8 vols. London: Hutchinson, 1923–38.

Fisher, Peter. *The Valley of Vision.* Toronto: University of Toronto Press, 1961.

Fox, Susan C. "The Structure of a Moment: Parallelism in the Two Books of Blake's *Milton.*" *Blake Studies* 2 (Fall 1969): 21–35.

Fraiberg, Selma H. *The Magic Years.* New York: Scribner's, 1956.

Frosch, Thomas R. *The Awakening of Albion: The Resurrection of the Body in the Poetry of William Blake.* Ithaca, N.Y.: Cornell University Press, 1973.

Frye, Northrup. *Fearful Symmetry: A Study of William Blake.* Princeton, N.J.: Princeton University Press, 1947.

George, M. D. *English Political Caricature to 1792.* Oxford: Clarendon, 1959.

Gibbon, Edward. *The History of the Decline and Fall of the Roman Empire.* Edited by the Rev. H. H. Milman. 6 vols. London, 1776–88; rpt. Boston: Aldine, 1845.

Gilchrist, Alexander. *Life of William Blake, "Pictor Ignotus."* Edited by Ruthven Todd. London and New York: Everyman, 1945.

Hartley, David. *Observations on Man.* 2 vols. London, 1749; rpt. Gainesville, Fla.: Scholar's Press, 1966.

Hayley, William. *The Life of Milton.* London, 1796; rpt. New York: Garland, 1971.

————. *The Life and Posthumous Writings of William Cowper.* 2 vols. New York: Swords, 1803.

Herzing, T. W. "Book I of Blake's *Milton*: Natural Religion and the Optical Fallacy," *Blake Studies* 6 (Fall 1973): 19–34.

Hill, Draper, ed. *Fashionable Contrasts: Caricatures by James Gillray.* London: Phaidon, 1966.

Hindmarsh, Robert. *Rise and Progress of the New Jerusalem Church.* Edited by the Rev. Edward Madely. London: Hodson, 1861.

Hirst, Desirée. *Hidden Riches: Traditional Symbolism from the Renaissance to Blake*. London: Eyre and Spottiswoode; New York: Barnes and Noble, 1964.

Holbach, Paul Henry Thiery, Baron de. *The System of Nature*. Translator unknown. 3 vols. London: Kearsley, 1797.

Horapollo. *Hieroglyphics of Horapollo Nilous*. Translated by Alexander Cory. London: Pickering, 1840.

Howard, John. "An Audience for the *Marriage of Heaven and Hell*." *Blake Studies* 3 (Fall 1970): 19–52.

Hume, David. *An Enquiry Concerning the Principle of Morals*. London, 1777; rpt. Chicago: Open Court, 1912.

Ivimey, Joseph. *History of the English Baptists*. 4 vols. London: Burditt *et al.*, 1811–30.

Johnson, M. L. "Separating What Has Been Mixed: A Suggestion for A Perspective on *Milton*." *Blake Studies* 4 (Fall 1973): 11–17.

Johnson, Samuel. *The Works of Samuel Johnson*. Edited by Arthur Murphy. 2 vols. London: Honsard, 1801; rpt. New York: Harper, 1859–1873.

Law, William, *Selected Mystical Writings of William Law*. Edited by Stephen Hobhouse. London: Dawson, 1938.

Leavis, F. R. "Justifying One's Valuation of Blake." *The Human World* 7 (May 1972): 58.

Lekcy, William Edward Hartpole. *A History of England in the Eighteenth Century*. 8 vols. New York: Appleton, 1887–1890.

Levine, Israel. *Francis Bacon*. London: Parsons, 1925.

Locke, John. *The Works of John Locke*. 11th ed. London: W. Otridge, 1812.

Milton, John. *The Works of John Milton*. Edited by F. A. Patterson *et al.* 18 vols. New York: Columbia University Press, 1931–1938.

Miner, Paul. "The Polyp as a Symbol in Blake." *Texas Studies in Literature and Language* 2 (Summer 1960): 198–205.

Murray, John Middleton. *William Blake*. London and Toronto, 1936; rpt. New York and Toronto: McGraw Hill, 1964.

Newton, Sir Isaac. *The Mathematical Principles of Natural*

Philosophy. Translated by Andrew Motte. 2 vols. London, 1729; rpt. London: Dawson, 1968.

Overton, John H., the Rev. Cannon and Relton, the Rev. Frederick. *The English Church from the Accession of George I to the End of the Eighteenth Century.* London and New York: Macmillan, 1906.

Paine, Thomas. *The Life and Works of Thomas Paine.* Edited by William M. Van der Weyde. 10 vols. New Rochelle, N.Y.: Thomas Paine National Historical Association, 1925.

Paley, Morton D. *Energy and the Imagination: A Study of the Development of Blake's Thought.* Oxford: Clarendon, 1970.

Paley, William. *The Works of William Paley.* Philadelphia: Woodward, 1831.

Panofsky, Erwin. *The Codex Huygins and Leonardo Da Vinci's Theory of Art.* London: Warburg Institute, 1940.

Pinto, Vivian de Sola, ed. *The Divine Vision.* New York, 1957; rpt. New York: Haskell House, 1968.

Pollin, Burton R. *Education and Enlightenment in the Works of William Godwin.* New York: Las Americas Publishing Company, 1962.

Price, Martin. *To the Palace of Wisdom.* Garden City, N.Y.: Doubleday, 1964; rpt. Anchor, 1965.

Priestley, Joseph. *The Theological and Miscellaneous Works of Joseph Priestley.* Edited by J. T. Rutt. 25 vols. London: Hackney, 1817–31.

Quinlan, Maurice J. *William Cowper: A Critical Life.* Minneapolis, Minn.: University of Minnesota Press, 1953.

Radcliffe, Anne. *The Romance of the Forest.* Edited by A. L. Barbauld. 2 vols. London: T. Hookham, 1810.

Raine, Kathleen. *Blake and Tradition.* 2 vols. New York: Bollingen, 1968.

Reid, Thomas. *Essays on the Intellectual Powers of Man.* Edinburgh, 1875; rpt. New York: Garland, 1971.

Rose, E. J. "Blake's Metaphorical States." *Blake Studies* 4 (Fall 1971): 9–31.

_____. "Blake's *Milton: The Poet as Poem.*" *Blake Studies* 1 (Fall 1968): 16–38.

Rosenfeld, Alvin, ed. *William Blake: Essays for S. Foster Damon.* Providence, R.I.: Brown University Press, 1969.

Rousseau, Jean-Jacques. *The Confessions of Jean-Jacques Rousseau: The Anonymous Translation into English of 1783 and 1790.* Revised and completed by A. S. B. Glover. New York: Limited Editions Club, 1955.

————. *Emilius and Sophia: or a New System of Education.* Translator unknown. 4 vols. London: R. Griffiths, 1767.

————. *The Social Contract and Discourses.* Translated by G. D. H. Cole. London: Everyman, 1913; rpt. 1946.

Sandler, Florence. "The Iconoclastic Enterprise: Blake's Critique of Milton's Religion." *Blake Studies* 5 (Fall 1972): 13–57.

Schorer, Marc. *William Blake: The Politics of Vision.* New York: Holt, 1946; rpt. 1959.

Shaheen, Naseeb. "Of Oreb, Or of Sinai." *English Language Notes* 9 (September 1971): 25–28.

Smith, Adam. *Essays.* Edited by Joseph Black and James Hulton. London: A. Murray, 1872.

Somervell, D. C. *English Thought in the Nineteenth Century.* New York: Longman, 1929.

Stephens, Leslie. *History of English Thought in the Eighteenth Century.* 3rd ed. 2 vols. New York: Putnam's, 1902; rpt. 1927.

————, and Lee, Sidney, eds. *Dictionary of National Biography.* 22 vols. London: Spottiswoode, 1882–1901; rpt. London: Oxford University Press, 1959–60.

Swinburne, Algernon Charles. *William Blake: A Critical Essay.* London, 1868; rpt. London: B. Blom, 1967.

Swedenborg, Emanuel. *Arcana Coelestia.* Translated by the Rev. John Clowes. Revised by the Rev. John Potts. 12 vols. New York: Swedenborg Foundation, 1933–1938.

————. *Miscellaneous Theological Works.* Translated by the Rev. John Whitehead. New York: Swedenborg Foundation, 1928.

————. *A Treatise Concerning Heaven and Hell.* Translator unknown. Baltimore, Md.: Miltenburger, 1812.

————. *True Christian Religion.* Translated by John Ager. 2 vols. New York: Swedenborg Foundation, 1928.

————. *Angelic Wisdom Concerning the Divine Providence.* Translated by John C. Ager. New York: Swedenborg Foundation, 1938.

Taylor, Peter Alan. "Providence and the Moment in Blake's *Milton.*" *Blake Studies* 4 (Fall 1971): 43–60.

————. "A Reading of Blake's *Milton.*" *Blake Studies* 1 (Spring 1969): 208–9.

Taylor, Thomas. *Thomas Taylor the Platonist: Selected Writings.* Edited by Kathleen Raine and G. M. Harper. New York: Bollingen, 1969.

Teitelbaum, Eve. "Form as Meaning in Blake's *Milton.*" *Blake Studies* 2 (Fall 1969): 37–64.

Tindall, Mathew. *Christianity as Old as Creation.* London, 1730; rpt. Stuttgart: Fromann, 1967.

Todd, Ruthven. *Tracks in the Snow.* London: Grey Walls, 1946.

Toland, John. *Christianity Not Mysterious.* London, 1698; rpt. Stuttgart: Fromann, 1964.

Tucker, Abraham. *The Light of Nature Pursued.* 2nd ed. Revised and corrected by John Mildmay. 7 vols. London: Faulder, 1807.

Voltaire [François Marie Arouet]. *Philosophical Dictionary.* Translated by Peter Gay. 2 vols. New York: Basic Books, 1962.

————. *The Works of Voltaire.* Translated by W. F. Fleming. 22 vols. New York: Dumont, 1901.

Watson, Richard. *An Address to the People of Great Britain.* 4th ed. London, 1798.

Wittreich, Joseph Anthony, Jr. "Blake and Tradition." *Blake Studies* 5 (Fall 1972): 7–11.

————. " 'Sublime Allegory': Blake's Epic Manifesto and the Milton Tradition." *Blake Studies* 4 (Spring 1972): 15–44.

Wollstonecroft, Mary. *A Vindication of the Rights of Men in a Letter to Edmund Burke.* London: J. Johnson, 1790.

Index

291

OXFORD GEOGRAPHICAL AND
ENVIRONMENTAL STUDIES

Editors: Gordon Clark, Andrew Goudie, and Ceri Peach

CLASS, ETHNICITY, AND COMMUNITY IN SOUTHERN MEXICO

ALSO PUBLISHED BY
OXFORD UNIVERSITY PRESS
IN THE OXFORD GEOGRAPHICAL AND
ENVIRONMENTAL STUDIES SERIES

The New Middle Class and the Remaking of the Central City
David Ley

Culture and the City in East Asia
Woe Bae Kim, Mike Douglass, Sang-Chuel Choe, and Kong Chong Ho (eds.)

Energy Structures and the Environmental Futures in Europe
Torlief Haugland, Helge Ole Bergessen, and Kjell Roland

Homelessness, Aids and Stigmatization
Lois Takahashi

Island Epidemics
Andrew Cliff, Peter Haggett, and Matthew Smallman-Raynor

Pension Fund Capitalism
Gordon L. Clark

Cultivated Landscapes of Native Amazonia and the Andes
William M. Denevan

Cultivated Landscapes of Native North America
William E. Doolittle

Indigenous Land Management in West Africa
An Environmental Balancing Act
Kathleen Baker

Class, Ethnicity, and Community in Southern Mexico

Oaxaca's Peasantries

Colin Clarke

OXFORD

UNIVERSITY PRESS

Great Clarendon Street, Oxford OX2 6DP

Oxford University Press is a department of the University of Oxford.
It furthers the University's objective of excellence in research, scholarship,
and education by publishing worldwide in

Oxford New York

Athens Auckland Bangkok Bogotá Buenos Aires Calcutta
Cape Town Chennai Dar es Salaam Delhi Florence Hong Kong Istanbul
Karachi Kuala Lumpur Madrid Melbourne Mexico City Mumbai
Nairobi Paris São Paulo Shanghai Singapore Taipei Tokyo Toronto Warsaw

and associated companies in Berlin Ibadan

Oxford is a registered trade mark of Oxford University Press
in the UK and in certain other countries

Published in the United States
by Oxford University Press Inc., New York

British Library Cataloguing in Publication Data

Data available

Library of Congress Cataloging in Publication Data
Clarke, Colin G.
Class, ethnicity, and community in Southern Mexico: Oaxaca's peasantries / Colin Clarke
p. cm.—(Oxford geographical and environmental studies)
Includes bibliographical references (p.) and Index.
1. Peasantry—Mexico—Oaxaca (State) 2. Oaxaca (Mexico: State)—Economic conditions.
3. Social classes—Mexico—Oaxaca (State) 4. Ethnicity—Mexico—Oaxaca (State)
5. Community—Mexico—Oaxaca (State) 6. Peasantry—Mexico—Oaxaca
(State)—Political activity I. Series.
HD1531.M6 C58 2000   305.5′633′097274—dc21   00–035696
ISBN 0–19–823387–6

1 3 5 7 9 10 8 6 4 2

Typeset by Hope Services (Abingdon) Ltd.
Printed in Great Britain
on acid-free paper by
Biddles Ltd.
Guildford and King's Lynn

*To Silvana Lévi and the
memory of the late Cecil Welte*

EDITORS' PREFACE

Geography and environmental studies are two closely related and burgeoning fields of academic enquiry. Both have grown rapidly over the past two decades. At once catholic in its approach and yet strongly committed to a comprehensive understanding of the world, geography has focused upon the interaction between global and local phenomena. Environmental studies, on the other hand, have shared with the discipline of geography an engagement with different disciplines, addressing wide-ranging environmental issues in the scientific community and the policy community of great significance. Ranging from the analysis of climate change and physical processes to the cultural dislocations of post-modernism and human geography, these two fields of enquiry have been in the forefront of attempts to comprehend transformations taking place in the world, manifesting themselves in a variety of separate but interrelated spatial processes.

The new 'Oxford Geographical and Environmental Studies' series aims to reflect this diversity and engagement. It aims to publish the best and original research studies in the two related fields and in doing so, to demonstrate the significance of geographical and environmental perspectives for understanding the contemporary world. As a consequence, its scope will be international and will range widely in terms of its topics, approaches, and methodologies. Its authors will be welcomed from all corners of the globe. We hope the series will assist in redefining the frontiers of knowledge and build bridges within the fields of geography and environmental studies. We hope also that it will cement links with topics and approaches that have originated outside the strict confines of these disciplines. Resulting studies will contribute to frontiers of research and knowledge as well as representing individually the fruits of particular and diverse specialist expertise in the traditions of scholarly publication.

Gordon Clark
Andrew Goudie
Ceri Peach

PREFACE

Most of the world's peoples are peasants—small-scale farmers or artisans, whose ancestors were geared to self-sufficiency. Yet everywhere peasant household production and peasant lifestyles are being transformed (in some cases destroyed) by the capitalist world economy. In North-West Europe, the historical core area of capital accumulation on a global scale, nineteenth-century industrialization generated a strong process of urbanization, and peasantries were substantially eliminated between 1800 and 1950. In Latin America, however, a long history of colonial and post-colonial dependence on the capitalist cores, which now number the US, the European Community, and Japan, has ensured that urbanization has not been led by industrialization. Capital accumulation in the Third World city has been, and remains, more modest; and capital's penetration of the countryside is uneven, especially where the resources are few or the risks are high.

Mexico is among the more economically developed of Latin American countries (and Mexico City is one of the world's largest urban agglomerations), yet its rural communities often remain isolated and attached to their indigenous roots. Oaxaca, one of the most southerly and impoverished of Mexico's states, has a population of three million inhabitants, most of whom are peasants. Spatially concentrated, historically, into nucleated settlements, isolated from one another and the outside world by high mountain ranges into which rivers have incised deep valleys, Oaxaqueños are divided among 570 administrative units (*municipios*), where most of them control their own government and land.

Oaxacan peasants are among the least 'integrated' Mexicans from a sociolinguistic perspective. Although bilingualism is now widespread, linguistic groups whose formation pre-dates the Spanish Conquest provide the basis for many potential identities. In addition to Spanish, now the common language, a fraction less than 40 per cent of the population speak a pre-Columbian language, of which Zapotec, Mixtec, Mazatec, Chinantec, and Mixe are the most widespread. Lack of natural resources, and the sheer impenetrability of the high-level terrain, protected Oaxaca's peasant communities from Hispanization, but not from domination.

Oaxaca's geographical position in a remote, poorly endowed, mountainous region has accounted for the stability—but not stasis—of its peasant communities. The significance of change in these peasantries merits attention, since a visitor might envisage Oaxaca as colonial, traditional, rustic, pre-industrial— and to some extent it is all those things. On closer scrutiny, change, superficial or more fundamental, is occurring everywhere in Oaxaca: indeed, much that looks ancient in the Oaxacan countryside has been created or reinforced by the role of the state since the end of the Mexican Revolution (1910–17).

Oaxaca's peasantries, while dating back to the pre-Hispanic period, were fortified by the state, through its land-reform programme, for a period of seventy years following the Revolution. That policy ended in 1992, with the reform of Article 27 of the constitution of 1917, which preceded the entry of Mexico into the North American Free Trade Agreement (1994). The reform has concluded the policy of land redistribution to iron out the previous monopolization of land by large estates. Land-reform property, or *ejido* land (see glossary), which had been invested in the state, may now be privatized by individuals, once certification and titling has been completed by PROCEDE and the *ejidal* community has voted in favour of the change (Pisa 1994).

Although the process of titling is well advanced, individual control and sale of land-reform plots is comparatively rare, especially in Oaxaca and other southern states (Pisa 1994; Stephen 1998*a*). Irrespective of this stasis, peasantries are being transformed by increased commercial activity, out-migration and circulation, ethnic movements, changing community structures, and people's possibility to reject the political dominance of the party of perpetual government, the Partido Revolucionario Institucional (PRI). Having constructed Oaxacan (and Mexican) society in its own image, and having rejected wholesale repression in the 1980s, the PRI has been compelled, by a broad-based resistance to its monopoly of power, to yield up space to many of the social groups it once controlled.

This thumb-nail sketch of Oaxaca raises a number of key social questions relating to peasantry that will be explored in the text. Can peasantry be construed as a distinctive mode of production in the context of Mexico, one of the most capitalist of Third World countries? How has peasantry survived (in this instance become reinforced and reconstituted) within the framework of capitalism? Assuming continuance is possible, as the Oaxaca evidence suggests, does peasantry become differentiated under capitalist accumulation or at least shift into petty-commodity production? Is petty-commodity production (or rural petty industry) a stepping-stone to capitalism?

Does peasantry change uniformly, or do innovations take place in specific places and in response to different (local and non-local) markets? Is capital accumulation feasible within peasantry? How does social stratification occur within the peasantry, and does it create polarization between classes? Does urbanization of the peasantry produce proletarian conditions in the towns, and does the urban commercial élite of these towns exploit peasantry? Is migration and circulation (including an international dimension) consistent with peasantry and the persistence of peasant communities?

The second set of ideas to be investigated relates to community, ethnicity, and politics, and here the issues are more specific to Mexico. In Oaxaca, small-scale political units, *municipios* (municipalities), have provided the basis for local self-government, civil–religious hierarchies, and control of land held in common. Hence, community is reinforced by common access to resources and a shared politico-religious (superficially Catholic) existence, in

which classlessness is (allegedly) given priority. These circumstances of equivalence are consistent with peasantry, but not with class differentiation. So, do they inhibit class differentiation? Or are they modified by it?

If community is constructed at a small scale, does it preclude a sense of identity based on language at a larger but sub-national scale? Is language ethnicity? Are language groups contained within the class structure? Do they have their own capacity to organize? How do language groups relate to community, class, and capitalist development? Are Oaxaca's language groups collectively or individually an under-class? How does the small-scale traditional community relate to national power structures? Is it subordinate, or can it challenge PRI dominance at the municipal, state, and federal levels? How do class and ethnic difference mesh with PRI or opposition politics in Oaxaca? How much room for manœuvre do dissident groups have, given the historical dominance of the PRI?

Structure of the Book

In an attempt to capture the evolutionary history and complexity of Oaxaca's peasantries, the book is divided into three parts and a conclusion. Part I deals with the historical foundations of Oaxaca's peasantries, and discusses their survival in the context of society, landholding, and the state in the colonial and early independence periods (Chapter 1). The Mexican state and its post-revolutionary development strategies, as manifest in the Oaxacan socio-economic mosaic for 1970, are the focus of Chapter 2. Here it is shown that the twentieth-century land reform provided the basis for the reconstitution of peasantry in tropical areas from which it had disappeared. However, it went hand in hand with an urban-industrial policy that used peasantry as a labour reserve, much as the landed estate had done in former times.

The two subsequent parts of the book are largely contemporary, and concentrate on the period since public discord broke out in Oaxaca (and Mexico City) in 1968. Peasants, commercialization, and urbanization are the foci of Part II. The diversified economic activities of Oaxaca's peasantries are explained and discussed in relation to the natural environment (Chapter 3). This provides the prelude to an account of the recent expansion of traditional markets, the commercial exchange of agricultural and artisan products, and the development of urban capitalism (Chapter 4). Migration from rural to rural and rural to urban areas, including locations in the USA, and the processes of urbanization and proletarianization in Oaxaca City are then discussed (Chapter 5); they involve, and have enormous implications for, Oaxaca's peasantries.

Part III concentrates on ethnicity, community, and politics, and builds on the findings of Part II. The role of language in constructing ethnic identities at the Oaxaca state level is discussed, with particular reference to class structures and contemporary ethnic movements (Chapter 6). Attention is then

given to rural community structures, their transformation by class, and their association with the *municipio* in the context of the federal government's policy of administrative decentralization (Chapter 7). Lastly, the roles of class, ethnicity, and community are evaluated in the construction of political alliances in opposition to the PRI and its associates in the Oaxacan élite (Chapter 8).

The Conclusion (Chapter 9) brings together the findings about peasantry, class, ethnicity, community, and migration and re-examines them in the context of social theory. It is argued that the role of the post-revolutionary Mexican state has been crucial in the creation and balancing of the disparate socio-economic forces of capitalism and peasantry, and in the definition and contextualization of class, ethnicity, and community in Oaxaca. The pressure for greater formal democracy from all social groups, however, is spilling over from politics into other arenas, such as the spheres of ethnic and community organization.

These issues are discussed with reference to the Zapatista uprising in neighbouring Chiapas in 1994, which was aimed at the Salinas's administration's neo-liberal policy and the sham democracy (as the Zapatistas saw it) of the PRI. Oaxaca emerges as more flexible and negotiable than Chiapas, and explanations for this are advanced. Oaxacan identities are increasingly constructed not only at the local community level, but also regionally through language, and transnationally through migration to the USA. These contexts are dynamic and highly interactive.

C.C.

ACKNOWLEDGEMENTS

During fieldwork and the writing of this book, I have incurred many debts. I first went to Oaxaca in 1966, during a study I was making of the Mexican land reform. But it was not until 1976, after a decade and a half devoted to study of the Caribbean, that I seriously considered carrying out detailed research in Oaxaca. During my 1976 visit I had the good fortune to meet Cecil Welte, who gave me permission to use his *Oficina de Estudios de Humanidad del Valle de Oaxaca,* and to consult his excellent library on the archaeology, history, and anthropology of the state. I was rapidly deflected from my aim to concentrate on the social geography of Oaxaca City. This was partly because research had already been carried out by John Chance, Michael Higgins, Art Murphy, and Alex Stepick. Moreover, the peasantries of rural Oaxaca were compelling and materials about them rich.

In 1978, I spent five months in Oaxaca, on sabbatical leave from my post at Liverpool University; this fieldwork was funded by the Nuffield and Astor Foundations. Once more I was the recipient of Cecil Welte's generous hospitality and of his detailed academic advice. I met, and learned a vast amount from, experienced researchers, notably Michael Higgins, John Chance, Scott Cook, and Ross Parmenter. I also made friends with a host of committed Mexican researchers, including Margarita Dalton, Manuel Esparza, Ángeles Romero, and South American anthropologists in exile in Oaxaca, Stefano Varese, Alicia Barrabas, and Miguel Bartolomé.

Subsequent shorter trips in 1982, 1984, 1986, 1988, 1990, 1992, 1993, 1996, and 1998, were variously funded by the Nuffield Foundation, the British Academy, Jesus College, Oxford, and the InterFaculty Committee for Latin American Studies, the Anthropology and Geography Faculty Board, and the Hayter Committee of Oxford University. During these visits I was able to travel widely throughout the major regions of Oaxaca. I also had the opportunity to discuss my research with an ever-increasing circle of social scientists. For their interest and advice, I am grateful to the late John Paddock, Art Murphy, Martha Rees, Salomón Nahamad, Gloria Zafra, Henry Selby, Jack Corbett, Ron Waterbury, Carol Turkenik, and Jane Howell, and helpful friends—Lowell and Ursula Greenberg, Patsy Welte, and the late Marie Veghte. A brief examination of the bibliography will indicate the extent to which I have been informed by the research of my academic colleagues—Mexican, American, and European—in many disciplines.

Although this book is rooted in Oaxaca, the gateway was always Mexico City, where I received the full support of the directors and staff of the Instituto de Geografía at the Universidad Nacional Autónoma de México. I should like to mention, in particular, María Teresa Gutiérrez de MacGregor,

who gave me generous backing and advice at the beginning of the project, and Silvana Lévi and Alberto López, who have entertained me and my family in their home on numerous occasions. I have greatly valued their professional assistance, kindness, and unstinting support.

I wish, also, to express my gratitude to Oxford doctoral students who, in recent years, have greatly stimulated my interest in Latin American societies. In particular, I thank Katie Willis for the insights she shared with me during her research on women's work and social network use in Oaxaca City (1994). I am also grateful to Sarah Howard, whose thesis on the Miskito and regional autonomy in Nicaragua (1993) has informed my treatment of ethnic issues in Oaxaca. Alina Darbellay completed a study (1995) of the highland area around Sucre in Bolivia, and has given me a more thorough appreciation than I had before of the complexities of rural–urban interactions. David Howard's thesis on race, colour, and identity in the Dominican Republic (1997) has reminded me of the historical appeal of whiteness in an allegedly mixed-race society. Additionally, he has given me a great deal of help with the bibliography.

I have benefited from the enthusiasm and advice of members of the small British-based group of *aficionados*, who have held three Oaxaca workshops since 1989—Brian Hamnett, Jutta Blauert, Paul Garner, Jean Starr, and our 'adopted' colleague, Guy Thompson, who works on the neighbouring state of Puebla. Most of the statistical and automated cartographic analysis of Oaxaca census data was carried out by my colleague at Jesus College, Dr Patricia Daley (based on preliminary work by Dr Miska Guzkowska and Dr Hilary Winchester), while she was a postgraduate assistant completing her own doctorate. I am also pleased to record my gratitude to the cartographers in the Department of Geography at Liverpool University and the School of Geography at Oxford, who have been responsible for the illustrations.

Special thanks are due to a number of highly supportive colleagues who read sections of the book while it was being written. Ángeles Romero, Brian Hammett, and Paul Garner commented on the historical chapters (1 and 2). John Gledhill criticized the chapters on ethnicity and community (6 and 7). Katie Willis evaluated the chapter on migration and urbanization (5), and Ron Waterbury provided a detailed commentary on the chapters on peasants (3 and 4) and on ethnicity and community (6 and 7). I am indebted to Bryan Roberts for reading the entire text and encouraging me to think about Oaxaca's circumstances in the broader context of Mexico.

I am grateful to Jesus College, Oxford, for grants in two successive years to enable me to reduce my tutorial stint and thus to start to write this book, and to the University of Oxford for a Special Lecturership in 1993–4, during which much of the first draft was completed. It is a pleasure, once more, to acknowledge the support I have received from Gillian Clarke, my wife. She has accompanied me on most of my trips to Oaxaca, and her gentle good humour and steadfastness have sustained me during the fieldwork and the

period over which the book has been written. In appreciation of their warm friendship and patient, academic advice given over many years, I dedicate the book to Silvana Lévi and the late Cecil Welte.

C.C.

CONTENTS

LIST OF ILLUSTRATIONS

LIST OF FIGURES

LIST OF TABLES

GLOSSARY

acaparador	monopolizer or profiteer
adobe	sun-dried brick
agarrando cosecha	taking in the harvest
agencia de policia	police agency
agencia municipal	municipal agency
agente	mayor of *agencia municipal*
aguardiente	distilled alcohol
alcalde mayor	Spanish official in charge of a district
alcalde	judge
alcaldía mayor	district under jurisdiction of *alcalde*
alguacil	policeman or messenger
almud	equivalent to 5 litres
ambulante	itinerant vendor
anciano	elder, in Indian community
apertura democrática	democratic opening (of early 1980s)
arando	ploughing
artesania	handicraft
atole	soft drink made of maize
aviador	merchant
ayuntamiento	local community council, town council
baldio	wasteland
barrio	district of a town
bienes comunales	communal land or propery
bracero	farm labourer
cabacera municipal	municipal centre
cabecera	head settlement or community
cabildo	council
cacicazgo	estate of *cacique*
cacique	hereditary Indian ruler or chief; now often translates as local boss
caciquismo	chieftainship; leadership regime
caja de comunidad	community chest
cal	quicklime
cambio de indumentaria	clothing change from traditional Indian to Western
campo	open countryside
canícula	hot dry period in midsummer
cargo	post or obligation
carro completo	PRI candidates elected *en masse*, a car load
casa grande	great house
casta	mixed socio-racial category, such as black-Indian
caudillo	local leader or boss
cerro	mountainous terrain
chapulin	fried grasshopper

científico	literally scientist, here politician motivated by scientific theory
ciudad	city or town
coa	wooden-handled curved steel blade
cofradía	lay brotherhood
colonia popular	irregular or informal settlement
colonia	colony or colonial period
comerciante	businessman or trader
comida	meal
comisariado de bienes	committee of management of communal resources
commadre	godmother
compadrazgo	fictive kinship
compadre	godfather
comunal	communal
comunero	communal land participant
comunidad agraria	agrarian community
congregación	concentration of scattered Indian settlements, usually to assist religious conversion
corregidor	Spanish official in charge of Indian district
corregimiento	jurisdiction of *corregidor*
coyote	border crosser
criollo maize	native maize
criollo	American-born white
curandero	traditional healer
de labranza or *de labor*	worked land
derecho de monte	royalty on cut timber
desconocimiento	repudiation
deshierbo	weeding
desmontado	levelling or clearing
dialecto	dialect
distrito	district, for administrative purposes
echando orejera	secondary furrows
ejidatario	holder of land reform unit
ejido	land reform unit
encomendero	possessor of *encomienda*
encomienda	grant of an Indian town with right to exact tribute
enganchador	labour recruiter
expendio	shop or store
fandango	party or celebration, often associated with marriage
fiesta	religious festival (usually a saint's day)
fraccionamiento	private subdivision
garbanzo	chickpea
genres de vie	lifestyles
gente de razon	Mexican expression defining 'civilized' people
gobernador	governor
guardano cosecha	storage
guelaguetza	reciprocal work or exchange
gusano	worm

hacendado	estate owner
hacienda	landed estate, based on agriculture and ranching
hermanidad	brotherhood of fraternity
horno	oven
huaraches	sandals
huipil	woman's tunic or top
humedad propia	containing natural moisture
idioma	language
indigenismo	policy of the post-revolutionary period, emphasizing non-coercive integration of the Indians into Mexican society.
ixtle	fibre made from maguey (*mezcal*) cactus
jacal	one-room shack
jefe político	political boss of a district
jornalero	(day) labourer
jugo propio	naturally moist land
junta de bueyes	pair of oxen
labor	small landed estate in agriculture
ladino	Hispanized non-white
lama-bordo	terrace farming
latifundia	large estate
leña	firewood
Ley de Baldios	Law of uncultivated wasteland
Ley de Colonización	Colonization law
lienzo	linen canvas with pictorial history of community
limpiado	fields cleared or prepared prior to the onset of April rain
lingua franca	common language
localidad	locality
locatario	fixed-location trader or middleman
los gitanos	gypsies
macehual	Indian commoner
maguey	cactus from which *mezcal* is distilled
mandadero	those who follow orders; messenger
mano	roller
maquiladora	make-up industry (assembly of components)
mayeque	Indian of lower class
mayorazgo	entailment (legal device to prevent splitting of property through inheritance)
mayordomía	office responsible for supporting a particular saint's *fiesta*
mayordomo	holder of above office
mezcalero	producer of *mezcal*
mediero	sharecropper
mercado	market
mesquite	cactus and thorn scrub
mestizaje	race mixing
mestizo	person of mixed white and Indian origin

metate	grindstone
mezcal	Oaxacan alcoholic beverage made from agave plant
milpa	maize field or plot
minifundia	small properties
mojonero	stones used as community boundary markers
molino chileno	grindstone driven by animal
monte	pasture
municipio libre	free municipality
municipio	municipality, basic unit of local government
natural	member of an indigenous group
nopalero	*nopal* cactus grove
nuestros antepasados	our ancestors
Oaxaqueños ausentes	*Oaxacan absentees (political figures based in Mexico City)*
obligaciones de la iglesia	church duties
obraje	workshop (for textiles)
ocote	pitchpine
otate	wood for brooms
palacio municipal	municipal office or town hall
palenque	small distillery
panela	cake of brown sugar
paracaidista	parachutist
paraje	precisely named location in a community
patria chica	little homeland
patrimonio primitivo	original traditional lands
patrón	patron or master
peninsular	Spanish-born white
pequeño propietario	owner of 'small' post-reform estate
periferico	ring-road (around Oaxaca City)
petate	woven mat for sleeping on
piña	pine or head of *mezcal* cactus
pintando surcos	preparing furrows
piscando	harvesting maize
plaza	market-place
pleito	dispute, often over land
político	politician
Porfiriato	period of Porfirio Díaz's presidency
porfirista	supporter of Porfirio Díaz
presidente municipal	municipal president
priísta	PRI supporter
principal	Indian upper class, men who have held leadership roles, such as priests and administrators; now means elder, implying man who has held leadership roles in community
promotor	instigator or prime mover in development projects
propietario	office-holder
propio	producer-vendor
pueblos de ciudadanos	communities of citizens

pueblo conurbado	rural settlement (village) now incorporated into city
pueblos de Indios	small and medium-sized Indian communities
pueblo	village
puesto	stall
pulque	fermented drink
quiote	flower of *maguey*
rancheria	hamlet
rancho	ranch, small landed property
rayando	harrowing
regatón	travelling trader, who buys and sells for profit
regidor	councilman
repartimiento	labour draft; or monetary advance made to Indians during the colonial period which they re-paid with cochineal and cotton goods
representante de los bienes comunales	elected official of local community council responsible for communal land
república de Indios	Indian community
restauredor	restorer
revistido	an Indian who has given up traditional dress
riego a brazo	hand watering
riego	irrigation or irrigated
rurales	irregular rural police during Porfiriato
sembrando	planting
serape	woven blanket
serrano	mountain
sexenio	six-year term of office
shaman	cult priest
sierra	mountain
síndico	trustee
solar	yard or compound
suplente	alternate (for whatever office)
susto	fright
tela deshilada	loose weave
tela tupida	tight weave
temporada	season of year
temporal	seasonal rain-fed land
tepetate	calcareous layer in the earth
tequio	an obligatory labour draft levied on adult able-bodied men
tercermundista	Third World demagogue
terreno de labranza	worked land
terreno del santo	land whose produce is used to raise funds to celebrate a particular saint
terreno labrado	tilled land
terrenos enmontado	land overgrown with weeds
testigo	witness
tianguis	market
tierra caliente	tropical lowland

tierra comunal	communal land
tierra fría	cold highland
tierra templada	temperate upland
toma	water take-off at beginning of canal system
topil	village policeman; messenger boy
tortilla	flat maize bread
traje tradicional	traditional clothes
trueque	barter
tumba-roza-quema	slash and burn cultivation
usos y costumbres	traditional usages and customs
vallistocracia económica	economic élite of the Central Valleys
vallistocracia política	political élite of the Central Valleys
vecindad	rented tenement or block of flats
viajero	travelling middleman
villa	small town
zócalo	main square

Part I

Historical Foundations of Peasantries

1

Peasantries in Colonial and Post-Independence Oaxaca (1520–1920)

A salient feature of Oaxaca's peasantries is their history of subjugation to Spanish imperialism, and, after the independence struggle between 1810 and 1821, their continuing subordination to white and *mestizo* (mixed race) society. The Spanish conquest, though largely peaceful in Oaxaca, destroyed many aspects of Indian social structure and political organization and disrupted traditional religion; led to cataclysmic population decline; and disturbed agricultural production, imposing trade to Europe—especially in cochineal—on to a subsistence-with-market base. Nevertheless, more than elsewhere in Mexico, Indian peasants in Oaxaca clung on to their lands (and their subsistence crops and animals), not only in the mountains, but in the Oaxaca Valley, too (Chance 1989; Taylor 1972).

Failure of the *hacienda* (landed estate) to develop in Oaxaca was due to the high-level, accidented nature of the terrain, and to the fact that wealth resided in cochineal production (cochineal is an insect which, when dried and crushed, produces a red dye), rather than in land ownership and use. Crucial to the cochineal industry was the persistence of the peasantry, and the requirement that the Indians had to pay tribute to the Spanish crown. Moreover, the system of *repartimiento* (labour draft), together with debt peonage, secured labour and its application to the *nopaleros* (cactus groves) which were the natural habitat of the cochineal insect (Taylor 1972, 147). Oaxaca City (Antequera) emerged as the regional–mercantile hub of the cochineal trade to Vera Cruz and Cádiz, and its townscape became studded with magnificent religious houses, which, collectively, became the largest Spanish landowners in Oaxaca by the end of the colonial period (Taylor 1972)

Current Oaxacan peasantries have their origins in ethnic-linguistic groups of the pre-Hispanic period, which were subjected, collectively, to differential incorporation into the colonial state of New Spain as Indians. They also experienced an enhanced degree of fragmentation, enjoined by the Spanish system of civil jurisdictions, though it has been claimed that, even prior to the conquest, the Zapotecs had already undergone a high degree of fission into small-scale communities (Carmagnani 1988, 68). Despite their domination by the

Catholic Church, the indigenous population sustained many of their religious beliefs and practices—Carmagnani associates the seventeenth and eighteenth centuries with the return of the pagan gods (1988)—and enjoyed their own distinctive forms of community organization (*pueblos de Indios*). Pre-Columbian religion and political organization, instead of being abandoned, were syncretized with European institutions and values, and practised by populations that retained their pre-conquest languages (Spores 1984*a*).

Almost three centuries after the conquest, the War of Independence swept away the regional economy based on cochineal (and textiles), for which Oaxaca City had been the pivot (Dahlgren 1990). Nevertheless, Oaxaca City became the state capital and seed-bed for the Liberal programme of national reform that was to lead to the break-up of landed corporations and the freeing of factors of production under the Presidencies of two of Oaxaca's most illustrious sons, Benito Juárez and Porfirio Díaz. The Porfirian project of state-led capitalism produced infrastructural and economic developments of only modest proportions in Oaxaca compared to the rest of Mexico.

Oaxaca's peasantries, though undoubtedly dominated socially and politically and exploited economically during the Porfiriato, retained much of their land and maintained their spatial distribution more or less intact. It was Church-held property that was sold to private individuals during the Porfiriato, especially that located in the Oaxaca Valley, rather than land belonging communally to the isolated peasant communities of upland basin and highland Indians. When Indian-owned property was privatized, it was in the tropical lowlands or on the mountain slopes adjoining them that the incursions were concentrated. Unlike the colonial *haciendas*, which had produced grain and meat for the domestic market plus some cochineal, the later nineteenth-century plantations concentrated on tropical crops for export.

The main themes of this chapter are the status of Oaxaca's Indian peasantries in relation to the colonial regional society, the various systems of land holding and production that operated, and the nature and role of the colonial and post-colonial state. Nevertheless, some preliminary appreciation must be given of the physical geography, which has played such a large part in the evolution of human activities in Oaxaca. The hostile environment goes a long way to explain both the nature and persistence of Oaxaca's peasantries, as well as the generally low levels of living they have achieved over time.

Physical Environment

Physiography

Oaxaca covers an area of 95,000 km.^{2}. Most of the terrain is mountainous, with over 60 per cent of the state located at heights of more than 500 m. Elevations in excess of 2,000 m. are recorded in the Mixteca Alta (the Mixteca

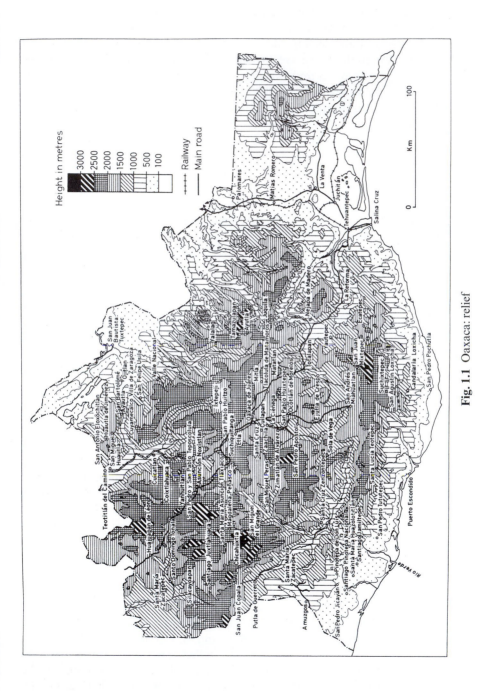

Fig. 1.1 Oaxaca: relief

Baja and de la Costa are accidented but generally lower areas) in the west. Similar heights also characterize the Sierras Zapoteca and Mixe in the north, and the Sierra Madre del Sur, which borders the Pacific, to the south (Figs. 1.1 and 1.2). Within these east–west trending mountain complexes of metamorphic and igneous rocks and—in the Mixteca Alta—tertiary volcanics (Fig. 1.3), ridges and valleys run parallel like ramparts, and the highland areas are extremely inaccessible (place-name spellings follow Bradomin 1980).

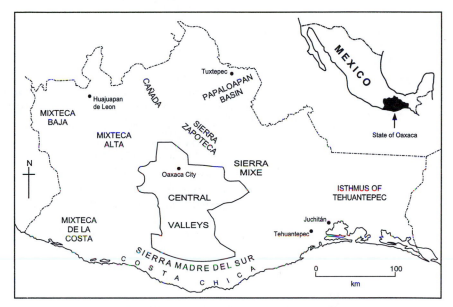

Fig. 1.2 Oaxaca: regions and major towns

For example, 'until fairly recently, a journey from the interior of the Mixe region required several days to reach the nearest paved road. For the Mixe, travelling means fording swift streams and flooded areas fraught with venomous snakes, traversing muddy trails leavened with mule excrement and urine' (Lipp 1991, 195). While these circumstances are extreme, they could be matched, in modified form, by similar age-old obstacles to communications throughout the deeply dissected, high altitude zones of Oaxaca.

Three peripheral lowlands fringe Oaxaca's mountain mass. These are—the narrow coastal plain adjoining the Pacific (the *Costa Chica*), the broad and rolling Isthmus of Tehuantepec, and the Papaloapan Basin around Tuxtepec (Fig. 1.2). In addition, the extensive highland masses are separated from one another by *los valles centrales de Oaxaca*, called here the Central Valleys. As their name implies, the Central Valleys—of which the Oaxaca Valley in the Upper Atoyac Basin is the core (Fig. 1.4)—lie at the geographical heart of the state (Moguel 1979).

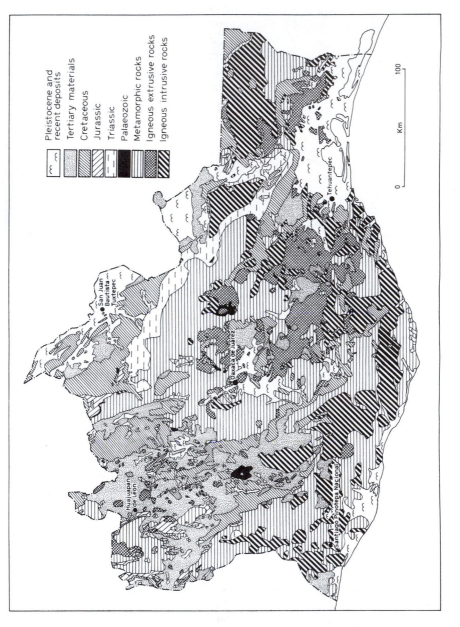

Fig. 1.3 Geology

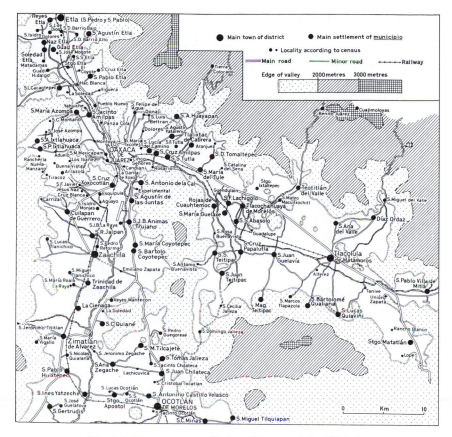

Fig. 1.4 Place-names in Valley of Oaxaca (after Welte)

These major physical units have been used by Tamayo as the basis for his division of Oaxaca into eight regions: the Central Valleys, the Mixteca Alta and Baja, the Cañada (the trench separating the Mixteca from the Sierra), the Sierra, the Istmo, the Pacific Coast, and the Papaloapan Basin (Fig. 1.2). However widely used in Oaxaca, this topographic scheme makes the Mixteca Alta too extensive (to the west), does not identify the Mixteca de la Costa, and fails to include the very substantial range (the Sierra Madre del Sur) that divides the Central Valleys from the Pacific (Moguel 1979; Tamayo 1950).

The Oaxaca Valley features a great deal in this book and comprises three linked troughs—each 20 to 30 km. long, named after the main towns located within them. The Etla Valley is in the north-west, Tlacolula in the south-east, and the two-pronged valley (or Valle Grande) focusing on Zaachila and Zimatlan in the south-east and Ocotlán in the south (Fig. 1.4). Each valley was formed by Tertiary down-faulting, and the steep-sided boundary slopes have developed across hard, metamorphic rocks; the valley bottoms are broad and

flat and filled with alluvial deposits of Quaternary age (Escalante Lazúrtegui 1973).

The arms of the valley system are shaped like the blades of an aeroplane propeller, the hub of which is provided by an up-standing rock, capped by Monte Alban, a Zapotec ruin perched about 300 metres above the valley floor overlooking Oaxaca City, the state capital. Oaxaca City is situated where the Rio Atoyac is joined by its tributary, the Rio Salado, before draining south to the Pacific, and it occupies a central place that has been the key social, political, and economic location in Oaxaca since before the Spanish conquest of Mexico began in 1519.

Temperature and Vegetation Zones

Oaxaca state, though tropical in location, is characterized by three major temperature zones, each calibrated with altitude and giving rise to a distinctive vegetation: the *tierra caliente*, up to 1,000 m., the *tierra templada*, from 1,000 to 2,000 m., and the *tierra fría*, from 2,000 to 3,000 m. (Fig. 1.1). The original vegetation of the peripheral, hot lowlands was tropical rain forest, but that has mostly been stripped out for pasturage and cultivation (Aceves de la Mora 1976). The process has been going on for centuries. However, in the case of the plains to the north of the Sierra Mixe, the forest has been systematically cleared only since the late 1970s.

The most extensive temperate area (*tierra templada*)—so attractive to Spanish urban and rural settlement—is located in the Oaxaca Valley at about 1,500 m. An analogous intermontane basin occurs around Nochistlan in the Mixteca Alta, and many of the incised river valleys in the mountain areas share similar climatic conditions. These areas have been cleared of natural vegetation for many centuries, and have been cultivated intensively since pre-Hispanic times (Earle Smith Jr. 1976 and 1978).

In the cold mountains of the *tierra fría*, above the *tierra templada*, the temperature declines to low levels with altitude, and gives rise to pine and oak woodlands, and, above that, to mist forest (Bravo 1960). It is in these areas that the Indian populations have concentrated, and it is here, at high altitude, that much of their communal land is concentrated. Both the Zapotec and Mixtec were known as 'Cloud People', and many Indian communities continue to be located at or above the cloud line (Flannery and Marcus 1983).

Rainfall and Aridity

The Cañada, the Coixtlahuaca Valley (in the Mixteca Alta), the Oaxaca Valley, and the north-west to south-east trench running from Oaxaca City down to the Isthmus can be thought of as semi-arid, with rainfall averaging less than 800 mm. per year (Fig. 1.5). Here, a *mesquite* vegetation (cactus and thorn scrub) is characteristic irrespective of the temperature zone (Bravo 1960). The

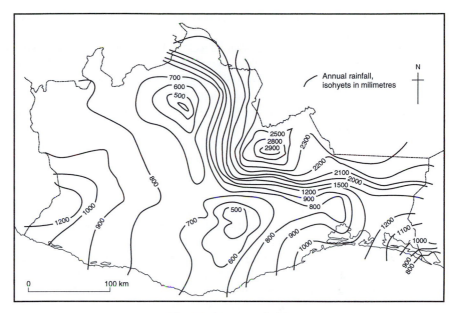

Fig. 1.5 Oaxaca: rainfall

remainder of the state receives up to twice this amount of precipitation, though the highest peaks on the northern boundaries of the state record up to 2,000 mm. per year, and the plains adjoining the northerly state of Vera Cruz are wetter still.

The entire state of Oaxaca experiences a dry winter season and a wet summer. The latter is often punctuated by a hot dry spell, or *canícula*, which starts in early August and may run into September. However, the *canícula* can be short-lived, and when depressions coincide in the Pacific and the Gulf of Mexico, as they frequently do in August, Oaxaca can be buffeted and drenched by intense tropical storms, and flooding of the lowland areas can be a problem (Alvarez 1983). It was in part to control seasonal flooding of this kind, following the inundation of Tuxtepec in 1944, that the Papaloapan project was initiated from the 1950s onwards (García Hernández 1994).

Travel everywhere in Oaxaca can be hazardous in the wet season; afternoon storms rapidly displace clear sunny mornings, producing flash floods and setting landslides in motion. In the Sierra Madre del Sur, where constant bulldozing is necessary to keep open the highway to the coast, the Chatino communities, many of which are eight hours walk from a road, are particularly difficult of access until the autumn drought sets in. Similar treacherous conditions beset the traveller in the northern Sierra Zapoteca and Sierra Mixe, too.

Varied altitude and aspect give rise to important differences in rainfall over short distances. Additionally, at any one location, there is great variability from year to year, both with regard to total precipitation and its periodicity.

This applies not only to distinctions between peaks and valleys in the northern mountains, which are generally wet, but also to the comparatively homogeneous Oaxaca Valley. For example, Oaxaca City has an annual average precipitation of 650 mm., while Etla, with 662 mm., is wetter and Ocotlan, with 750 mm. is wetter still. The driest area is around Tlacolula, where the rainfall drops below 600 mm., surface drainage is sporadic, and the bed of the Rio Salado has been used for salt making. Higher parts of the Oaxaca Valley and the interfluves and valley sides have moderate frosts in January and February, but no snow, unlike the mountain ridges, where spring blizzards are a hazard (Lorenzo 1960).

Human Implications

Oaxaca's physical environment has provided more than the stage on which its human history has unfolded. Many aspects of the environment are deeply implicated in the *genres de vie* of the Oaxaca peasantry, as well as influencing modern development. For the Zapotecs of the first centuries BC and AD, the dryness of the Oaxaca Valley was mitigated by the possibility of organizing irrigation from the rivers and tapping the high water table of the valley bottoms, much as Oaxacan peasants do nowadays. A hydraulic civilization developed under the Zapotecs, which, though it eventually declined and was superseded by Mixtec rule, was to spawn one of the key elements among Oaxaca's peasantries (Blanton 1978; Blanton, Kowalewski, Feinman, and Appel 1981; Flannery and Marcus 1983; Marcus and Flannery 1996; Spores 1967 and 1984*a*).

Oaxaca's river valleys also provide routeways through what would otherwise be almost impenetrable highland terrain. North–south routes across the sierras have always been perilous, though the north-west to south-east alignment of the physiography has facilitated the link from Mexico City, via Puebla, Oaxaca City, Tehuantepec, and Chiapas to Guatemala (Fig. 1.1). A major problem is that the northern sierras form part of the continental divide, so that the drainage network is unintegrated and north or south flowing, and thus rarely conducive to easy state-wide communications.

Stony and eroded soils in the highland areas, together with thorny vegetation and cactus in the lower zones, means that only about 15 per cent of the land area of Oaxaca is cultivated, and, in recent years, the figure has been declining, largely because of out-migration. Of the portion tilled (much of it in shifting cultivation to permit a fallow period), only 6 per cent is irrigated and another 6 per cent is moist enough to use without dry farming (Ortiz Gabriel 1992). About 70 per cent of the cultivated area is under subsistence crops, notably maize, beans, and squash, though specialization does occur with altitude and by locality. Even in the Oaxaca Valley, the aridity of the Tlacolula arm has had a differentiating impact on human activity: this is the area in which artisan activities have been most intensively developed to supplement the agricultural cycle.

The rocks of the highland areas are, in places, rich in minerals, such as silver and copper, which have, from time to time over the centuries, been exploited commercially. On a more modest scale, in certain villages of the Oaxaca Valley, carefully selected metamorphic rocks are quarried and fashioned into the *metate* and *mano* (grindstone and roller) used to de-husk maize by Oaxacan peasants from Zapotec times to the present day (Cook 1982*a*). So arid, stony, and steep is the Oaxacan landscape, in general, that it is possible to travel tens of kilometres without seeing any sign of rural activity, let alone habitation. However, historically, during the *colonia*, the hardy *nopal* cactus, with its insect, the cochineal grub, was the key to Oaxaca's prominence as a source of red dye that created great wealth for its merchants.

Oaxaca's Language Groups

Although much of Oaxaca looks traditional and impoverished, it would be wrong to assume that it has always been a lagging region and 'culturally backward'. When the Spaniards had consolidated their conquest of the Aztecs and penetrated southwards in 1521 to what is now Oaxaca, they found the sites and artefacts of Zapotec and Mixtec 'high cultures'. The Oaxaca Valley contained the ceremonial centres at Monte Alban (by then in ruins), Zaachila, Mitla (in ruins), Lambityeco, Yagul (in ruins), and their satellite settlements. This political core region had developed over a period of more than two millennia.

Based on irrigation from the rivers and ground-water supplies of the valley floors, Monte Alban's complex exchange economy, which involved jewellery, woven goods, and pottery, had given rise to commercial tentacles that extended throughout Meso-America. Many scholars have sifted the archaeological evidence for the Zapotecs (Blanton 1978; Flannery and Marcus 1983; Marcus and Flannery 1996; Paddock 1970 and 1983). They show that the Oaxaca Valley was studded with semi-independent townships, linked by warfare, tribute, and trade. These townships were divided into two estates: a noble estate of *caciques* (rulers) and *principales* (tribute collectors, administrators, and priests); and a lower estate subdivided into *macehuales* (commoners), *mayeques* (lower class), and slaves (Chance 1986*a* and 1990*b*).

In the Mixteca Alta, however, there were no population clusters that would warrant the designation 'urban', although Coixtlahuaca, Teposcolula, Yanhuitlán, and Tlaxiaco had dispersed populations of around 10,000 each, distributed in nucleations with or without hamlets (Lind 1979; Spores 1967). Mixtec society before the conquest consisted of 'local kingdoms grouped into several semi-discrete valley or regional subcultures'; codices reveal that the royal families were highly interrelated (Romero Frizzi 1996), and that the rulers of Tilantongo represented the most honoured of the lineages (Spores 1967, 184).

After the fall of Monte Alban and its occupation by Mixtecs, the lord of Zaachila came to dominate much of the Oaxaca Valley, receiving tribute from Teitipac, Tlacolula, Mitla, Macuilxóchitl, Tlalixtac, and Chichicapa. However, a town could be subject to two different independent units; Ixtepei, in the Sierra Zapoteca, owed tribute to a local lord, as well as to the Zapotecs of Tehuantepec and the Mixtecs of Tututepec (Whitecotton 1977, 127).

Linguistic reconstruction provides the most precise guide to the entire set of ethnic groups in Oaxaca, their distribution and historical evolution prior to 1520. Eight of the major languages of Oaxaca belong to the Otomangean family, and they were (and are still) located in the centre, north, south, and west of the state (Fig. 1.6). Those that were concentrated solely in the east constituted separate families, such as the Chontal (Tequistlatec–Jicaque group), the Huave, and the Mixe and Zoque (Mixe–Zoque group) (Flannery and Marcus 1983; Josserand, Winter, and Hopkins 1984; and Suárez 1983). Five Otomangean language groups are of importance in Oaxaca: (1) Zapotecan (Zapotec and Chatino); (2) Mixtecan (Mixtec, Cuicatec, and Triqui; (3) Chinantecan (Chinantec); (4) Popolocan (Mazatec); (5) Amuzgo. The languages that were most closely related were located spatially adjacent to one another, and their proximity suggests that their separation from one another has been comparatively recent (Jossrand, Winter, and Hopkins 1984).

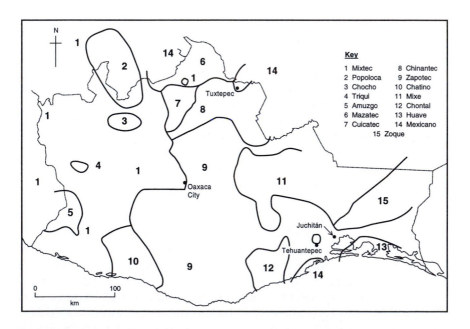

Fig. 1.6 Oaxaca: language groups

Swadesh has pointed out that linguistic communities tend to develop regional variants; greater similarity can be seen between neighbouring dialects, but less similarity is evident when the geographical distance is increased or the degree of social interaction is reduced (1967, 79). This is the point of departure of glottochronology, a lexicostatistical method of classification that takes into account the fact that language affinity and similarity depend not only on how recently two languages were separated, but also on the amount of contact maintained during the period of separation and differentiation.

Marcus (in Flannery and Marcus 1983, 6) has compared the glottochronological evidence for the divergence of the Otomangeans with the archaeological record and recognized eight stages. Stage 1, around 10,000 BC, was a Paleoindian period in which it is possible that everyone spoke the same language—an antecedent of Otomangean, Mayan, and Utoaztecan. During stage 2, from 8000 to 5000 BC, proto-Otomangean—a tonal language—evolved, and was spoken by hunter-gatherers in Oaxaca and the states to the north. In stage 3, from 5100 to 4100 BC approximately, the Chinantec split off from the Mixtec–Zapotec group, and may have moved southwards to their present location in northern Oaxaca. Archaeologically, the Chinantla went on to diverge from the rest of the Otomangean area, with formative affinities to the Gulf Coast lowlands of Mexico.

Stage 4, from approximately 4100 to 3700 BC, was a period of major language change. The Popoloca-Mazatec group separated from the Mixtecan. As glottochronology suggests that Mixtec and Chatino are separated by fifty-seven minimum centuries, Marcus concludes that the Mixtec–Cuicatec and Zapotec–Chatino stems had begun to diverge by 3700 BC. The initial separation of the ancestors of the Mixtec and Zapotec took place during a period of preceramic hunting and gathering, with some slow evolution towards agriculture.

Stage 5, from 2100 to 1300 BC, was another period of linguistic change. Cuicatec is believed to have split off from Mixtec by 1300 BC, as did Amuzgo as early as 1700 BC, and speakers of both moved south. Triqui separated from the Costa Chica dialect of Mixtec by 2100 BC, but it is not known, archaeologically, when the Mixtecs reached the Pacific. The neighbouring Mixe and Zoque had begun their linguistic divergence by 1500 BC—thirty-five minimum centuries ago. Suárez (1983), however, comments that some researchers have assumed a relationship between Mixe–Zoque and Mayan, and that Huave is possibly linked to Mixe–Zoque rather than to Otomangean. It is probable that many of these linguistic separations were related to increasing population and to migratory shifts to new environments that accompanied the development of sedentary agriculture.

Stage 6, 400 BC to AD 100, witnessed the separation of Mazatec from Chocho-Popoloca between 400 and 300 BC and the divergence of Chatino from Zapotec in approximately AD 100. At about this time, the Chatino may have moved towards the Pacific coast. Internal divergences within Zapotec contin-

ued during stage 7, from AD 500 to 1000, perhaps correlated with the decline of Monte Alban, and the Miahuatlan and Sierra dialects separated from that of the Valley of Oaxaca. During the final stage, from AD 1200 to 1400, Isthmus Zapotec separated from Valley Zapotec (six to eight minimum centuries). This may reflect the Postclassic Zapotec expansion to the Isthmus of Tehuantepec, displacing the Huave and perhaps the Mixe as well, though Marcus observes that archaeological data suggest that the Zapotec had been there many centuries earlier. Marcus therefore underscores the glottochronologists' insistence that their dates represent 'minimum' centuries for separation.

The major ethnic-linguistic groups in Oaxaca have occupied their present approximate locations since before the conquest. Spanish *congregaciones* (concentrations of Indians to facilitate proselytization and conversion), where they occurred, plus the decimation of the population during the first century of the *colonia*, adjusted that pattern at a local scale without disturbing it in any fundamental way (Miranda 1968; Spores 1984*a*). Hence, social isolation at various scales has been crucial for linguistic splitting, for maintaining the geographical coherence of the major language groups, and for generating language differences over very small distances. In view of the enormous diversity of pre-Hispanic tongues, it is hardly surprising that the language of the conquerors, Spanish, became the common language—but very gradually, and, until the second half of the nineteenth century, only in the urban centres.

Conquest and Racial Stratification

Spanish expeditions and conquest, which, as elsewhere in Mexico, produced a racial stratification of whites over Indians, went largely uncontested by the Zapotecs and Mixtecs in and around the Central Valleys (Romero Frizzi 1996). However, Zapotecs, Chinantecs, and the Mixe in the northern sierras were not brought under control until the 1550s (Chance 1989, 16). Outright Indian resistance occurred at Tututepec near the Pacific, where the Mixtecs fought a fierce battle with the Spaniards (Fig. 1.7). One of the reasons for the alleged peaceful nature of the conquest was the fact that the Zapotecs were already paying tribute to the Aztecs, whom the Spaniards had defeated. The Aztecs had maintained a small garrison close to what became, under the Spaniards, Huaxyacac, later to be known as Antequera de Oaxaca and, more recently, as Oaxaca City (Chance 1986*a*).

One consequence of the peaceful conquest was that Zapotec and Mixtec nobles who accepted Roman Catholicism were incorporated into the white ruling class. *Caciques* (hereditary rulers or chiefs) became highly acculturated, dressed in a European, aristocratic manner, and spoke perfect Spanish. Unlike neighbouring Chiapas in the then Captaincy-General of Guatemala, culture and class in Oaxaca could transcend the barrier of race. So it was the non-noble Indians who composed the basis for Oaxaca's colonial peasantries.

Fig. 1.7 Late eighteenth-century place-names (with property of Cortes inset)

From the outset, the densely populated, fertile Valley of Oaxaca was a bone of contention. In 1532 a royal cedula was issued recognizing the urban status of Antequera, located on the eastern side of the Rio Atoyac, but much of the Oaxaca Valley on the west bank of the Atoyac was engrossed by the (absentee) Conquistador, Cortés. He established the Marquesado del Valle, with its four main settlements (the *cuatro villas del marquesado*) in San Pedro Apóstol Etla, Oaxaca del Marquesado, Cuilapan, and Santa Ana Tlapacoya (Fig. 1.7). Control of grants of land in this fertile strip running beneath the ruins of Monte Alban was to remain for three centuries a matter of dispute between Cortés and his heirs, the Spanish crown, and the city of Antequera (which was anxious to acquire cattle pastures). Cortés, however, was more concerned to collect tribute from the Indian villages of the Marquesado, than to develop the land commercially (García Martínez 1969), though a highly lucrative business was eventually developed on his cattle estates in Tehuantepec (Brockington 1989).

Outside the Central Valleys, the Zapotec, Mixtec, and other ethnic groups, such as the Mixe and Chatinos, were subordinated to the Spanish *peninsulares*. Spaniards began to take up land in the isthmus—where indigo became an important crop, the more fertile interior valleys, and the coastal plains, and to acquire *encomiendas* (land grants, with the right to assess tribute) and *repartimientos* (labour drafts) (Gerhard 1972). Relatively few *encomiendas* were granted to individuals, and the crown quickly recovered most of them (Olivera and Romero 1973). Cattle and sugar estates became established, depending on the potentialities of the environment. However, unlike other parts of Mexico, the great *hacienda* did not become a major feature of the colonial landscape of Oaxaca, and the Indian population retained most of its traditional lands (Taylor 1972). The highland areas of the Mixes and Chatinos were too deficient in resources and too isolated to attract Spanish settlement on a substantial scale. But, where agricultural land was of good quality, as in the Oaxaca Valley and the smaller valleys in the Mixteca Alta, the Indians held on to it with tenacity (Taylor 1972).

Indian Demographic Decline and Partial Recovery

Despite the endurance and tenacity displayed by the Indians, especially with regard to their occupation and control of land, the encounter between them and the Spaniards in New Spain, in general, and Oaxaca, in particular, was intensely traumatic. This is clearly demonstrated by the excessive mortality suffered by the population, estimates of which were put as high as 3 million (Miranda 1968) or 4 million (Münch 1978) at the conquest, though recent regional figures aggregate to approximately half of Spores's estimate of 1.5 million inhabitants (1967, 72). Epidemics of European diseases, especially measles and smallpox, coupled to forced labour and enforced cultural change,

lay at the root of the decimation of the Indian population, a demographic collapse of continental proportions, and one with severe social and economic consequences in Oaxaca.

Taylor records that the Oaxaca Valley, with an estimated Indian population of 350,000 on the eve of conquest, had suffered a decline to 150,000 inhabitants after the first fifty years of the colony. The population dropped further to between 40,000 and 45,000 at the end of the first century of Spanish settlement (Taylor 1972, 17–18). An even more cataclysmic decline for the indigenous population of the Mixteca Alta has been computed by Cook and Borah (Fig. 1.7), who estimated a population of 700,000 for 1520 and 57,000 for 1590 (1968, 32). More recent archaeological work suggests a lower figure for the Mixteca Alta of 250,000 to 300,000 at the conquest, and therefore a drop more consistent with that in the Oaxaca Valley (Spores 1984a, 96). It is likely that the pre-conquest population of Tehuantepec plummeted from about 50,000 to 6,000–7,000 in 1560 (Brockington 1989; Zeitlin 1984). Population decline in the remote northern sierras occupied by the Zapotecs, Chinantecs, and Mixe was less precipitate, and the Indian population fell from 96,000 in 1548 to 32,000 in 1568 and 21,000 in 1622 (Chance 1989, 62).

The Indian population began to recover, numerically, during the eighteenth century. Taylor provides Oaxaca Valley estimates of 70,000 for 1740 and 110,000 for the 1790s (1972, 18); and Cook and Borah calculate that the Mixteca Alta had about 50,000 inhabitants in the 1740s rising to 76,000 in 1803 (1968, 54–5). But it was not until the 1970s that the Oaxaca Valley was to record a population equivalent to that achieved before the conquest—and this figure took into account the rapid demographic expansion of Oaxaca City (Cook and Diskin 1976, 13). Even in the northern sierra, where the demographic collapse of the post-conquest period was less severe, the recovery was so slow that it was not until 1960 that pre-conquest population was once more matched (Chance 1989, 63). In Oaxaca as a whole, the likely population total as of 1520 was reached again in the late nineteenth century. So, labour was in short supply throughout the colonial and early independence period, especially on the estates, and black and mulatto slave labour was frequently used, especially in the tropical lowlands (Brockington 1989).

Colonial Population and Race Distribution

A guide to the size, distribution, and racial composition of the entire population of the Oaxaca Intendancy (Fig. 1.7) during the late colony is provided by the Revillagigedo census of 1793. Out of a total population of 411,336, 88 per cent were Indian, 6 per cent were Spanish/Creole, and 5 per cent mixed (*castas*), presumably mostly *mestizo* (Indian-white), but with some black elements (Hamnett 1971a, 188). Taylor mentions 16,767 free blacks and mulattoes in Oaxaca in the 1790s, with a small concentration of them in the Oaxaca Valley

(1972, 21). There were also slaves on the Pacific Coast's cotton and sugar plantations (Spores 1984; Rodríguez Canto 1996), and on the cattle ranches of the Marquesado del Valle at Jalapa del Estado in Tehuantepec, where race mixing was common (Brockington 1989). Racial exclusivity was more marked in Oaxaca than in Mexico as a whole at this time, since race mixing typified about 40 per cent of the population of New Spain according to the Noriega census of 1810, by which time blacks were disappearing as a recognizable category (Aguirre Beltrán 1984).

By far the largest settlement in 1793 was Antequera (Oaxaca City), which, with 19,069 inhabitants, was the third largest urban centre in New Spain after Mexico City and Puebla. It had just under 5 per cent of the Intendancy total, though almost half of all the Spaniards and white Creoles were located there— absentee landowners, administrators, doctors, lawyers, clergy, artisans, and manual labourers (Chance 1978). The segregation of whites from Indians, based on the urban residence of the former and the rural location of the latter, must account for the comparative absence of miscegenation in Oaxaca. Very different circumstances existed in the capital, Antequera, where Indians made up approximately one-quarter of the population and race mixing was common, but insufficient to undermine the rigidity of racial stratification and segregation (Chance 1978 and 1981).

Major concentrations of Indians occurred at Villa Alta, in the Sierra Zapoteca, where cochineal and textiles were produced (Chance 1989), and at Huajuapan and Teposcolula in the Mixteca Alta, where the cochineal industry was well developed (Romero Frizzi 1990*a*). Spaniards were thinly scattered throughout the rural areas, and numerous only in Teposcolula, Jicayán, Tehuantepec, and Juslahuaca (Juxlahuaca). These were the very same localities where the mixed population concentrated (Fig. 1.8). There was a strong association between the white Spanish and Creole population and the supply and marketing of cochineal or the development of ranching in the tropical lowlands. Likewise, the overall distribution of population coincided with the diagonal line of communication running from north-west to south-east across the Intendancy from Huajuapan via Antequera to Tehuantepec.

Indian Landholding

One of the consequences of the exploitation of the *nopales* (and the Indians that cropped them) was that land acquisitions were not needed to create *haciendas*. So Indian *caciques* retained, with royal assent, both their status and, to a large extent, their landholdings throughout the colonial period (Taylor 1972, 65). Although *caciques'* holdings were usually fragmented, they were often vast, protected by primogeniture (Spores 1984*a*), and retained their attached *mayeques* (serf-like peasants) (Waterbury 1975). The *cacicazgos* of Etla and Cuilapan were the largest estates owned by individuals, Indian or

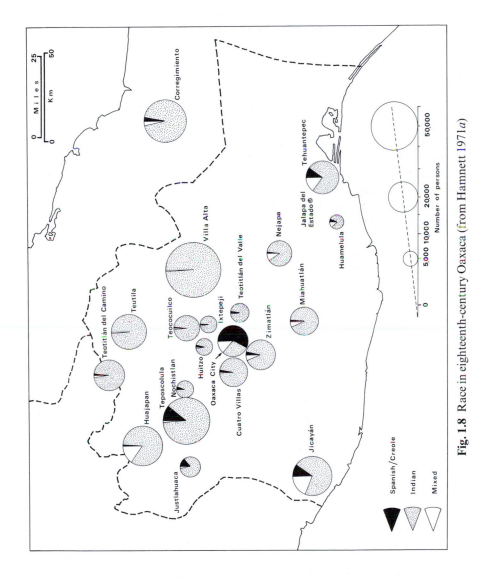

Fig. 1.8 Race in eighteenth-century Oaxaca (from Hamnett 1971*a*)

Spanish, in the Central Valleys, and the sixteenth-century Mixtec *caciques* of Yanhuitlán, Tlaxiaco, Teposcolula, and Nochixtlan (Fig. 1.7) were valued at hundreds of thousands of pesos, much of it held in property (Spores 1984*a*).

Indian communities and individual peasants, while dominated politically and economically by the Spanish, also remained important landholders. This was universally the case in the arid highlands of the Mixteca Alta, where the *nopaleros* for cochineal were concentrated and small stock numbering 100,000 head were recorded—particularly sheep (Miranda 1990). However, Indian landholding also persisted in the valleys of the Mixteca Alta (Spores 1984*a*), as well as in the Central Valleys. Indians produced maize, beans, and squash for subsistence, and stock for skins and tallow (Chance 1986*a*). The Spanish government granted the Indian communities legal title to their original lands (*patrimonio primitivo*), and also gave them the right to receive additional grants from the crown (Waterbury 1975).

Indian peasants worked the best of the Central Valley's cropland in the sixteenth century—using oxen and the Spanish plough. In general, most Indians were still self-sufficient farmers on the eve of the independence movement in 1810 (Taylor 1972, 107). Indigenous communities were retained under crown administration, and only a handful became dependent on lands they did not own; three or four towns relied on Spanish *haciendas* for their basic needs; and the residents of several others sharecropped.

Taylor argues that the Indian peasant in the Oaxaca Valley in the eighteenth century had more individual and communal land at his disposal than his descendants were to have in the late twentieth century (1972, 107). This was largely because of the limited possibilities for land redistribution after the Revolution of 1910—due to population increase and the right of the 'small' owners (*pequeños propietarios*) to retain rump estates. A crucial factor influencing Indian retention of property was the existence, throughout the period of the colony, of an imperial legal system that recognized Indian land rights. Also important was the determination of the Indians to defend their individual and communal property at law, and the economic role they played in providing food, especially maize and wheat, for Antequera.

Haciendas

The development of *haciendas* in the Oaxaca Valley was a slow and fluctuating process, and involved a shift from cattle production in the sixteenth century to the more diversified output of cattle, maize, and wheat during the seventeenth. Smaller estates, known as *labores*, became common in the seventeenth century and expanded in the eighteenth, as a result of purchase by Spaniards from Indian nobles and the Indian community. Estate ownership was quite unstable, except where entailment (*mayorazgo*) applied. Property changed hands through sale rather than by inheritance (Taylor 1972).

Most Spanish landholdings in the Oaxaca Valley remained not only small, but also widely dispersed throughout the colonial period. Spaniards owned more valley lands in the seventeenth century than they did in the eighteenth: at most 'Spanish estates accounted for one-third of the land in Oaxaca, and the largest holdings were suited only to grazing' (Taylor 1972, 163). Outside of the Oaxaca Valley, extensive activities were also the norm among the Spaniards (Romero Frizzi 1990a). In the Mixteca Alta herds with thousands of head of small stock were moved across vast areas in the form of 'floating *haciendas*', the net result of which was the devastation of an already fragile and eroded environment (Pastor 1987).

The comparatively small scale of the private Spanish landed estate in the Oaxaca Valley was partly offset by the presence of the Catholic Church, which was the principal non-Indian landowner. Engrossing about one-fourth of the productive rural property in the Oaxaca Valley, the various Church groups between them controlled more land than all the other Spanish landholders combined. The monastery of Santo Domingo in Antequera was the largest single landowner, with over 20,000 acres spread across seven estates, while the convent of Santa Catalina de Sena owned 210 houses in Antequera and more than 70,000 pesos' worth of the best grazing and arable land. Although much ecclesiastical land was in fact underused, Church holdings in Oaxaca remained undisturbed into the independence period (Taylor 1972).

A similar situation obtained in the Mixteca Alta, where there was little evidence of Spanish usurpation of Indian land (Romero Frizzi 1990a). It was far more common for Indians to rent, rather than sell, farming or grazing land to Spaniards; and sales tended to involve house plots in Yanhuitlán, Teposcolula, Tlaxiaco, and Tamazulapan. If there was land acquisition by the Spaniards, it was the Dominicans in Yanhuitlán who were guilty (Spores 1984a). The overall pattern is faithfully captured in data compiled in 1810 that showed there were only 83 *haciendas*, 269 ranches, and 5 cattle estates in Oaxaca at that time, compared to 928 *pueblos* with peasant cultivators and artisans (Reina 1988).

Spanish Political and Religious Domination

The white conquerors imposed the political and religious institutions of Spain on to the indigenous population (Spores 1984a). Antequera became the centre of Spanish power, with an *alcalde mayor* and *corregidor*, who were magistrates and had the contradictory remit to collect Indian tribute (when *encomenderos* died without heirs) and impart justice to the indigenous population (Olivera and Romero 1973). Holders of these offices were also eventually located in the smaller settlements that the Spaniards had inherited from the pre-colonial period, many of which had, before the 1520s, been given Nahuatl (Aztec) names (Gerhard 1972). Nahuatl was widely used by scribes and, in the Indian

settlement of Jalatlaco, adjacent to Antequera, by Indians of all language-ethnic groups until the shift to Spanish was complete in the late eighteenth century (Chance 1978).

During the colonial period, a *pueblo de Indios* needed eighty tributaries (or about 360 inhabitants) to form an autonomous government (Pastor 1987). According to Taylor:

The Crown encouraged the economic and social organization of colonial life around towns and villages. Peasants were required to form local governments to respond to royal orders, to collect taxes, to provide labour service, and to maintain a church, a community treasury, and sometimes a hospital. All of these institutions encouraged local people to think of themselves as a distinctive, separate community. Oaxaca is notorious for the atomization of social life in this period, with each little hamlet struggling to achieve the status of an independent head town. (1979, 23)

From the sixteenth century onwards, the Spaniards in Oaxaca set up *cabildos* (councils) in the indigenous communities to govern the locality under a system of indirect colonial rule (Carrasco 1963; Romero Frizzi 1975, 1). Each *república de Indios* (community) was turned into an inward-facing entity, divided off from its neighbours and separately integrated into the colonial system of administration via the *alcaldías mayores* and the *corregimientos*, located in the major settlements, such as Oaxaca City, Teposcolula, or Villa Alta. In the early years of the colony, the Indian *caciques* were in charge of local administration, but, later in the sixteenth century, they were replaced by elected officials, following Spanish usage (Romero Frizzi 1975). By the eighteenth century, *caciques* were often elected to *cabildos*, not because of their lineage, but because of their socio-economic standing.

As recognized social units under Spanish auspices, Indian villages were re-modelled to have a rectangular grid of intersecting streets and building alignments, with the central plaza occupied by the Catholic church and the civil offices, plus their own inalienable communal lands and their own political organization based on colonial models. In 1810, 928 *pueblos de Indios* were enumerated within the Intendancy of Oaxaca, with an average population of 600 in each one (Hamnett 1971*b*, 52 n.). Community income and expenditure (the *caja de comunidad*) were recorded in an account book, and audited by Spanish officials; periodic scrutiny was essential, since it was from the village treasuries that tribute payments were made. These nuclear settlements, often with outlying dependencies, plus 'resource areas and farmlands, constituted the functioning native community in colonial Oaxaca' (Spores 1984*a*, 168).

The composition of the *cabildo* varied from place to place, but the most common form involved a *gobernador* (governor), with two *alcaldes* (judges), two *regidores* (councilmen), and a number of *alguaciles* or *topiles* (police and messengers) (Olivera and Romero 1973). By the late colonial period, the *caciques* remained socio-economically important only in the Central Valleys. Among Rincón Zapotecs, *principales* had usurped the political influence of the

caciques, but were under pressure from upwardly mobile *macehuales*, who gradually became prominent office-holders in local *cabildos* (Chance 1986*b*). It was not uncommon for different *cargo* duties to be ascribed to nobles and commoners (Chance 1989).

Reflecting on the colonial past in an essay published more than thirty years ago, de la Fuente linked community closure to boundary disputes with neighbours, almost always conceived as hostile. 'Each village is, as a matter of fact, like a small republic, at odds with the others because of various disputes—among which predominate disputes related to questions of land' (1965, 32).[1] In a similar vein, Chance has argued that his research in Villa Alta confirms that 'the landholding village—the pueblo—gained importance in the colonial period at the expense of ethnic and regional ties' (Chance 1989, 124). As early as the sixteenth century, Yanhuitlán, in the Mixteca Alta, was beset with boundary, resource, and market-day disputes involving its neighbours (Spores 1984*a*). Most enduring of all was a dispute with the subject community of Tecomatlán, which attempted to break away in the 1550s, giving rise to boundary and land conflicts that ran into the 1970s (Spores 1984*a*, 214).

Spanish imperial control was religious as well as political. Oaxaca was one of the great episcopal sees of New Spain, established with Antequera as its seat in 1535. The origins of the state of Oaxaca may be traced to the diocesan boundary of the bishopric (which extended north to the Gulf of Mexico), though the Intendancy boundary of 1786 (associated with the Bourbon reforms), accords even more precisely to the current federal unit (Fig. 1.7 and Fig. 1.1). In 1592, the Dominicans, who had first entered the area in 1528, established a province, also based on Antequera, overlapping to a large extent with the see. During the late sixteenth and seventeenth centuries Oaxaca came under the spiritual control of the Dominican Order, which, 'from its Baroque convents and churches, exercised a theocratic authority that virtually excluded the power of the Crown' (Hamnett 1971*a*, 1).

Accordingly, Oaxaca was a region where 'Castilian authority influenced and permeated already well-formed indigenous cultures, and where, gradually, not without resistance, and often by means of symbols and demonstrations, the religion brought by the friars exercised a mystical fascination . . .' (Hamnett 1971*a*, 1). The culture-contact of conquest and colonialism in this phase of the first encounter between Europeans and non-Europeans outside Europe, was, however, complex and syncretic. Superficially, the Indians fitted in with the requirements of the Spanish, supporting *cofradías* in the late seventeenth and eighteenth centuries to cover the food, supplies, and ritual costs (managed by a *mayordomo*) of Catholic feast-day celebrations (Chance and Taylor 1985). By 1802 there were around 800 confraternities in Oaxaca, many of them with large holdings in cattle and cochineal (Lavrin 1990, 225). According to Spores, 'the church more than any other institution served to integrate society across

---

[1] This and all subsequent Spanish quotations have been rendered into English by the author.

geographical, social and ethnic boundaries. Christian ideology offered an acceptable body of explanation, a psychological palliative, and hope and security in a life hereafter' (1984*a*, 149–50).

However, the Indians' isolation left them considerable discretion in social organization. They were subject to a certain amount of resettlement (*congregaciones*) in the *sierras*, though they tended to slip back to their original locations; in the Oaxaca Valley a major resettlement of Mixtecs took place around the open church at Cuilapan, which the Dominicans built for the specific purpose of conversion. But in reality, in Oaxaca, Indian rural communities held on to their lands from which they subsisted by producing the God-given triad of maize, beans, and squash; and they clung to their old gods (Carmagnani 1988), later grafting them on to the Catholic saints (Spores 1967, 25–6). In the mid-sixteenth century, the *cacique* of Yanhuitlán and several *principales* were brought before the Holy Inquisition for idolatry, heresy, human sacrifice-murder, cannibalism, clandestine burial, polygyny, and related crimes. There was at least some substance to the charges, even though no conviction was obtained (Spores 1984*a*, 150).

Greenberg's field experience in southern Oaxaca in the 1970s testifies to the enduring significance of the Indians' pagan beliefs and practices. 'It was only after extensive work that I realized that what I had perceived as "bones" were the flesh and blood of Chatino belief and that "Catholicism" had been completely reworked and resynthesized in terms of the pre-existing nexus of ritual and doctrines' (1981, 82). The links between land and subsistence cultivation, landscape features and belief systems, community and the Catholic fiesta system were created in the intercultural zone between Spaniard and Indian during the 300-year period of the colony. In Oaxaca, this nexus persists, despite many changes, to this day (Carrasco 1966; Marroquín 1989).

Cochineal and Textiles in the Mercantile Economy

Key contributions of the Indians to the mercantile economy of colonial Oaxaca were the production of silk, which dominated the output of the Mixteca, notably around Yanhuitlán, between 1540 and 1580 (Spores 1967; Chance 1986*a*), and cochineal, which was first exported to Spain in 1526 (Hamnett 1971*b*). Cochineal developed very rapidly as the European textile industry took off in the eighteenth century. In 1745, the Spanish crown awarded Oaxaca a monopoly over cochineal production; annual output between 1760 and 1810 oscillated in weight between 500,000 and 1,000,000 pounds (Hamnett 1971*a*, 169–70). At the mid-point of that period, 1786, Oaxacan cochineal accounted for about 6 per cent of the value of the entire Spanish–American trade registered at Cádiz (Hamnett 1971*a*, 174).

Early in the eighteenth century, more than half the agricultural labourers of Oaxaca were engaged in cochineal production. Major concentrations of

cochineal extraction were in the arid areas of the Mixteca, such as the Coixtlahuaca Valley, Tamazulapan, Yanhuitlán, Teposcolula, Juxlahuaca, and Nochistlan (Nochezli), around Ocotlán in the Central Valleys, and at Villa Alta in the Sierra Zapoteca. Cultivation of cochineal insects, which involved supervising their breeding, feeding on the *nopal* cactus, and harvesting by hand, was a labour-intensive activity and more likely to be carried out by Indian peasants and their families than by employees on *haciendas*. But the spread of cochineal production had negative consequences for the Indian population, since the cultivation of the *nopaleros* (cactus groves) led to the neglect of Indian subsistence crops—with dire consequences for nutrition.

In Oaxaca City, the focal point of cochineal exchange, merchants made up the majority of the élite (most of them *peninsulares*), though it also housed high government officials, senior clergy, and owners of the large estates. The demand for cheap cotton goods from Indians and the urban poor throughout New Spain also stimulated the city's clothing industry: by 1792, Oaxaca's *obrajes* had more than 500 cotton and silk looms. 'Oaxaca, because of these activities, was often considered by the Spanish Peninsular merchants and the Royal administrators there to be next in importance to the silver-mining regions of Guanajuato and Zacatecas' (Hamnett 1971*a*, 1–2).

Many of the indigenous crafts of the pre-conquest period continued in rural Oaxaca, notably the cotton-mantle industry of Villa Alta in the Sierra Juárez and Teotitlán del Valle in the Oaxaca Valley. But, after the expansion and subsequent decline of the silk industry during the sixteenth century, the cochineal, cotton, and cotton-mantle trades became the central activities of the indigenous population 'upon whose labours the Spanish element depended for their prosperity and political supremacy' (Hamnett 1971*a*, 1).

Indians were, however, the victims of trade monopolies, coercion, and exorbitant prices at the hands of the *alcaldes mayores*, who emerged as crucial middlemen between Indian suppliers of commodities and the local urban-based merchants. *Alcaldes mayores* issued cash, equipment, or supplies, also known as *repartimiento*, to the Indians on the account of merchants, or *aviadores*; in return, the Indians would repay their debt in goods such as cochineal, cotton, and cotton mantles. According to Hamnett (1971*a*, 6), 'this form of trading always denounced by the Crown and clergy (at least at the level of the episcopacy) and contrary to the Laws, occurred frequently in the province of Oaxaca, because of the demand for its products'.

An alternative interpretation has recently been advanced by Baskes, who concludes that 'Alcaldes Mayores did not have nor did they need, sufficient power to coerce Indians to participate in the market. Indians accepted *repartimientos* voluntarily, because that was the only way they could obtain credit in a high-risk situation' (Baskes 1996, 28). An even more unlikely scenario is advanced by Carmagnani. He suggests that traditional community leaders were able to adjust between the resources available to the community and the domestic units of which it was composed using the *caja de comunidad* and

cofradías (lay brotherhoods)—thus protecting the Indian communities from the logic of mercantile exploitation (Carmagnani 1988, 178).

However, at Villa Alta, cochineal was bought from the Indians for half the price that the *alcaldes mayores* could later command; likewise, cotton mantle fetched only half its ultimate market price, and two *repartimientos* had to be woven per month. In the face of such blatant forms of exploitation, a series of rebellions broke out in Oaxaca, following a peasant rising in Tehuantepec in 1660, where the Indians killed the *alcalde mayor* (Díaz-Polanco 1996). 'The movement spread across to Nejapa against the Alcalde Major's *repartimiento* for cochineal and cotton mantles. In Ixtepeji, the *alcalde mayor* was forced to flee as a result of a rising against his *repartimiento* for cochineal. Similar outbreaks occurred in Teutila and Teococuilco, in Villa Alta, and across to Huajuapan' (Hamnett 1971*a*, 13; Chance 1989).

Investigation by an imperial agent sent from Mexico City revealed the abuse; but putting a permanent stop to it was beyond the capacity of absentee authorities. *Repartimientos* limped on beyond the introduction of the Bourbon reforms at the end of the eighteenth century (Hamnett 1971*a*), although it was recognized that the lack of provision within the administrative system for payments to *alcaldes majores* encouraged their coercive tactics. Hamnett, in his exhaustive study of administration and trade in Oaxaca, added to the list of their misdeeds: 'the Alcaldes Mayores were in the habit of seizing Indian lands, planting them, and using the rightful owners as the labour force, paying them at a miserable rate. They appropriated the water supply—sparse enough in any case—for their own irrigation needs, to the detriment of other cultivators' (1971*a*, 51).

The cochineal trade, imposed on Oaxacan Indian peasants by Spanish merchants and officials, disturbed the original pattern of cyclical peasant markets (Spores 1984*a*), and replaced them with a dendritic system. A dendritic market system is characterized by peasant producers, who control their own means of production, but are subordinate to a commercial class that monopolizes the supply of manufactured goods (Greenberg 1981). Typically, an élite monopolizes the commercial centres (here notably Oaxaca City) and transport, and peasant participation as middlemen is low. This dendritic system was destroyed with Mexican independence, and the pre-Hispanic subsistence-orientated cyclical pattern, which had persisted among the peasantry, resurfaced (Feinman, Blanton, and Kowalewski 1984).

Sovereignty: Political and Economic Crises

The War of Independence broke out in 1810, and within just over a decade transformed New Spain into Mexico, the Oaxaca Intendancy into a state of the federal republic, and Antequera into Oaxaca City. An immediate consequence of the war, in Oaxaca, was that the cochineal trade was threatened, the white

peninsular merchants and administrative élite quit Antequera, and capital flight began.

The catalogue of Oaxaca's woes during the independence wars and after sovereignty in 1821, though by no means unique in Mexico, was a long one. Oaxaca's trade links to Spain and Europe via Vera Cruz were severed, and Oaxaca City's functions contracted to the level of the state, where the ecclesiastical role of the see continued, although there was no bishop between 1827 and 1842. The city was reduced to providing business and service functions for the slender number of urban residents and the impoverished and disheartened peasantry of the rural areas.

In the 1820s Guatemala replaced Oaxaca as the main supplier of European cochineal, though output continued at a reduced level, notably in Ocotlán and Ejutla, before disappearing at the end of the nineteenth century. Free trade virtually destroyed Oaxaca's textile industry; and manufacturing contracted to a narrow range of products destined for the local market—*aguardiente* (distilled alcohol), *pulque* (a fermented drink), and soap. In Oaxaca City, weaving, pottery, woodcarving, cabinetmaking, and metalworking survived, but at levels of productivity lower than in the eighteenth century (Berry 1981). Oaxaca's peasantries retrenched into an isolated world characterized by near self-sufficiency, and *haciendas* survived as producers of maize and wheat for the state capital.

Newly independent Mexico was essentially weak. Racked by political crises throughout its first fifty years of sovereignty, in 1848 the fledgling state suffered the calamity of losing half its territory to the USA. The main accomplishment in Oaxaca during the first two decades of independence was the creation, by the state legislature, of the Instituto de Ciencias y Artes, which opened in 1827, and was to become a training ground for local professional men and a seedbed of Mexican liberalism, federalism, and anticlericalism. Oaxaca's two most famous sons, and Mexico's most outstanding nineteenth-century presidents, Benito Juárez and Porfirio Díaz, held posts at the institute (Hamnett 1994).

Juárez became Governor of Oaxaca between 1848 and 1852, and concentrated on state infrastructure, such as bridge building and improvements to the road to Tehuacan via the Cañada, which led to Mexico City (Berry 1981). This was also the period in which the white-*mestizo* stratum began to exercise renewed control over the Indian population, which still made up almost 90 per cent of the Oaxaca total. As an expression of this reconfirmation of power, 300,000 hectares out of the 1,097,000 belonging to Indians were allegedly transferred to members of the dominant group around the middle of the century (Carmagnani 1988, 236).

Porfirian Political Control, the Economy, and the Revolution

Dying in office as president in 1872, Juárez was succeeded by Lerdo, but in 1876 Porfirio Díaz seized power, thereby initiating an elected dictatorship that lasted more than thirty years. Extensive fraud was used to maintain his permanent domination of elections; between elections, *rurales*, answerable directly to Díaz, controlled the countryside, using strong-arm tactics, and 'pacified' *haciendas* characterized by labour troubles—though debt peonage seems to have operated in a rather benign way in the Oaxaca Valley (Cassidy 1981). After the 1890s, compromise and conciliation provided a veneer for the more brutal aspects of the regime.

During the Porfiriato, Oaxaca's *municipios*, which, from the 1870s, had been grouped into twenty-five administrative *distritos*, were placed under *jefes políticos* loyal to Díaz. This did not stop their multiplication, as the 874 villages that operated systems of communal land tenure in the mid-nineteenth century attempted to secure administrative status in defence of their territory, but more from one another than from the *hacendados* (Ruiz Cervantes 1988*b*, 354). As early as 1822, there were 232 acknowledged *ayuntamientos constitucionales,* yet even settlements with fewer than 1,000 inhabitants—the demographic threshold for municipal recognition (Pastor 1987)—were reported to aspire to this status (Hensel 1997, 232). Their success may be judged by the fact that there were 452 *municipios* in 1883, 465 in 1891, and 1,131 in 1910 (Ornelas López 1987*b*), though the majority of the latter seem to have been *agencias municipales*. So the *pueblos de Indios* of colonial times gave way to *pueblos de ciudadanos* (communities of citizens) in independence.

Meanwhile, with the abolition of corporate property, *cofradías* lost control of their land, and the formerly separate civil and religious offices of colonial times were joined to form a ladder of esteem which adult men were expected to ascend during their lifetime. Chance and Taylor argue that 'the modern civil-religious hierarchy in peasant villages . . . is more a product of the 19th century than a colonial adjustment that crystallized in the early period of Spanish-Indian contact' (1985, 22).

During the Porfiriato, the colonial system of municipal government was elaborated into a more dictatorial process of regional control through the *jefes políticos*, though some isolated and resource-deficient communities at high altitude were able to seal themselves off from outside control. Other communities, especially those in the tropical lowlands, were opening to economic influences from the outside. Irrespective of locale, the principle of the *municipio libre* became an important plank of revolutionary reform after 1910, the main thrust of which was to outlaw re-election to the federal presidency.

Díaz was a devotee of the idea of material progress. Surrounded by a cabinet of *científicos*, he embarked upon a policy of state involvement in infrastructural improvements, often in partnership with foreign engineers and

investors. Even backward and isolated Oaxaca was eventually drawn into the programme of modernization, and Oaxaca's regional economy improved after the 1870s. Expansion of landed estates was modest by Mexican standards of the day, but improved communications and peaceful circumstances led to a general improvement in the economic climate (Chassen 1986).

Mines in the Sierra Juárez, principally La Navidad, at Chichicapan near Ocotlán, and near Tlacolula, some of which had been opened up in the late colonial period to break up the monopolies of the *alcaldes mayores*, received a new impetus during the Porfiriato. Investments came from both the USA and Britain, especially after the railway broke Oaxaca's isolation in the 1890s, and some local capitalists switched from cochineal to mining gold, silver, copper, and lead. Approximately half the Oaxacan bourgeoisie at the beginning of the twentieth century was of European origin and predominantly Spanish (Chassen1990a and b; Chassen and Martínez 1990).

The major achievement, and symbol, of the Porfiriato in Oaxaca, was the railway between Mexico City and Oaxaca City, via Puebla, which opened in 1892 (Fig. 1.1). The line was later extended to Tlacolula and to Ejutla via Zimatlán and Ocotlán. For the first time in almost 400 years, the isolation of Oaxaca, or at least its state capital and the Oaxaca Valley, had been broken. Cash cropping increased, *haciendas* expanded, and maize, beans, and beef began to be exported to other parts of Mexico. Oaxaca's peasantries, particularly those at high altitude, however, remained largely untouched (Chassen 1986).

The pace of economic growth in Oaxaca increased with the turn of the century. There was substantial foreign investment in mining and commercial agriculture, to the extent that Oaxaca ranked fifth out of the Mexican states as a recipient of US investment in Mexico in 1902. Between 1902 and 1907, US investment in mining (especially silver) in Oaxaca reached $10 billion, second only to the state of Guanajuato. In addition, a wide range of tropical cash crops was produced for the export market—coffee, tobacco, sugar, cotton, and India rubber (Garner 1995). By the outbreak of the Revolution in 1910, Oaxaca had 100 mines, mostly American owned, employing a substantial Indian labour force, and a metal foundry was on the point of opening in the state capital (Murphy and Stepick 1991a).

Improved economic conditions characterized Oaxaca City by the end of the nineteenth century. Foreign-owned enterprises manufactured beer, cigarettes and cigars, glassware, soap, hats, shoes, and matches, and there were sufficient numbers of American and British residents at the end of the Porfiriato to warrant publication of an English-language newspaper. With a population approaching 40,000, Oaxaca contained the local Porfirian élite of *hacendados*, mine-owners, lawyers, administrators, and *políticos*, who dominated an urban mass, engaged in marketing, manufacturing, and the provision of petty services, including domestic work. In Oaxaca City there was even a *fin de siècle* theatre (now the Teatro Macedoneo Alcalá) and casino (Esparza 1988).

Of great national significance, but of lesser importance for Oaxaca City, was the opening of the Port of Salina Cruz and the inauguration of the Ferrocaril Nacional de Tehuantepec in 1907 (Fig. 1.1). Completed by Pearson (later Lord Cowdray), a British engineer, more than twenty-five years after the first stretch of track had been laid, the trans-isthmus railway promised to become a lucrative inter-oceanic trade route under Mexican state-ownership. Moreover, it provided national control of a sensitive geopolitical gateway between the Gulf of Mexico and the Pacific. At the outset, 'every two hours a train entered or left with goods from all parts of the world' (Esparza 1988, 279). This rail link, however, was to be undermined within a decade by the outbreak of the Mexican Revolution (1910), and, even more devastatingly, by the opening of the Panama Canal under US protection (1914).

Despite the arrival of the railway in Oaxaca City via Etla, Oaxaca remained one of Mexico's states least affected by the Porfirian project of modernization. There was simply an insufficient material base on which it might operate; and such developments as did occur were barely in hand before the Revolution broke out. 'The numerous predictions in the 1860s and 1870s of a harvest of untold bounty were never fulfilled, and at the end of the Porfiriato both promoters and government were still speaking in terms of the potential rather than the proven wealth of the state's resources' (Garner 1995, 8). It is not surprising, therefore, that Oaxaca stood aloof from the 1910 Revolution against Díaz, as much as was possible, and in 1915, following a liberal, anti-centralist policy that had been tested and abandoned almost a century earlier—it seceded from Mexico.

The Oaxaca Sovereignty Movement was a loose coalition of urban *porfiristas*, *serrano caudillos*, and disaffected revolutionaries. In 1916, the Movement was defeated by the forces of President Carranza. The post of *jefe político* was abolished, and the land reform, enacted at the federal level in 1915 to return land to the communities, was enforced (Ruiz Cervantes 1988*b*, 390–1). The secessionists, mostly peasant *serranos*, withdrew into the Sierra Juárez and the Mixteca, from which they prosecuted a guerrilla war until 1919 (Garner 1985, 1988). In 1920, García Vigil was elected Governor of Oaxaca. Although Oaxaca was not completely pacified, he rewrote the state constitution, continued land redistribution to the landless, and attempted a tax reform, which brought him into conflict with the *caudillos* of the northern mountains who had led the secession (Ruiz Cervantes 1986).

Disgusted with the corruption of the post-revolutionary federal government, García Vigil withdrew recognition of it, thereby restating Oaxaca's sovereignty. In 1924, abandoned by the secessionist *caudillos*, he was executed, and Oaxaca was reabsorbed into Mexico as one of its least significant states. Lacking spokesmen with clout, and with no local issue of sufficient national importance to require attention, Oaxaca failed to excite the concern of the centralizing federal authorities for almost fifty years.

Population and Race in Independence

Oaxaca's demographic record reflected the economic setbacks of the post-independence decades. Its population of 417,000 in 1820 was barely more than in 1793, and a good deal less than in 1810, when the census recorded 596,000. By 1850, it was close to 500,000, yet it took another half-century to rise to one million. If demographic changes after independence may be described as gradual, alterations to the race hierarchy, too, were slight.

Independence abolished the formulaic socio-racial distinctions (*castas*) of the colonial period, which, anyway were collapsing nationally, if not in Oaxaca, under the increasing impact of miscegenation. It also abolished nobility among the Indians. What it did not do, however, was to eradicate the race- or colour-class stratification (although the presence and influence of whites clearly diminished—in 1857 there were only 156 Europeans in Oaxaca). Nor did it extend civil rights to the bulk of the Indians (87 per cent in 1857) or *mestizos* (12 per cent), who remained socially marginal, though numerically in the vast majority (González Navarro 1990*b*). The independence struggle had not involved a radical restructuring of society. It had been essentially a conflict between two white élites; between the *criollos* (American-born whites) who wanted independence from Spain, and the Spanish-born *peninsulares*, who were loyal to, and frequently officers of, the crown.

An example of the way in which race affected public life in the early independence period is provided by the Liberals, who dominated the Conservatives, politically, in Oaxaca throughout the first half of the nineteenth century. They were divided into radical and moderate factions, loosely associated with socially mobile *mestizos* and established white *criollos*, respectively. However, the fact that both Benito Juárez (a Zapotec from Gelatao) and Porfirio Díaz (of part Mixtec descent) were prominent in Oaxaca's politics and later became Presidents of Mexico, suggests that, as during the colony, educated and upper-class 'Indians' were able to advance. Both men subscribed to the liberal view that Indians were fundamentally obstacles to progress and needed to 'modernize' and become citizens—like themselves.

In short, a class stratification was emerging among Spanish speakers, from which monolingual Indian-language speakers (the majority in Oaxaca) were excluded. In 1878 it was judged that 76 per cent of the Oaxaca population spoke Indian languages, and that only one-third could communicate in Spanish (González Navarro 1990*b*). By 1890, 78 per cent of Oaxaqueños were Indian, while the 1910 census reported that 49 per cent were Indian-language speakers (Chassen 1986).

It followed that the obligations of the upper and lower classes to the independent state were markedly different. The burden of taxation fell on the upper classes, while *mestizos* and Indians suffered from recruitment into the

army and various work-gangs (Berry 1981). Poverty, land disputes, and struggles over access to the salt ponds gave rise to Indian rebellions in the Isthmus in the 1830s and 1840s, while vagabondage, overlapping with armed uprisings in Tlaxiaco, Putla, and Juxtlahuaca, was a major problem in the Mixteca in the 1840s and 1850s (Reina 1988*c*). Indian oppression persisted until the Revolution, when new political dispensations affected Oaxaca's indigenous population and its peasantries. The indigenous population then became a marginal population to be integrated, the peasants a sector to be reinforced and expanded.

Indian Landholding during the Porfiriato

In general, the Oaxacan Indian communities at high altitude kept control of such lands as they needed after 1810. This generalization also applied, but to a lesser extent, in the Oaxaca Valley, where just over one-third of all proprietors established between 1889 and 1903 (37,533 for the entire state) were concentrated, though the new units in the Oaxaca Valley were comparatively small properties, averaging only 47 hectares (Cassidy 1981). The largest privatizations of property occurred in the Cañada and Tuxtepec (2,493,000 ha.) and in the Isthmus and on the Pacific (1,714,000 ha.), giving rise to vast estates and medium-sized or small *ranchos* (Esparza 1988, 290). Elsewhere, but especially in the *sierras*, the Indians maintained their traditional economy; in the Central Valleys they continued to focus on the Oaxaca City market.

By the early 1900s, the social and economic contradictions associated with the large landed estate and its converse, landlessness, were not so extreme in Oaxaca as elsewhere in Mexico. Nevertheless, a substantial number of peasants were employed as day labourers or debt peons, especially at the sowing and harvest seasons, and sharecropping in the Oaxaca Valley was common (Cassidy 1981). The physical isolation of the state and its lack of resources meant that the expropriation of land had not reached such extreme conditions as it had in Mexico as a whole, where more than 90 per cent of the rural population were said to be landless. For example, in the notorious sugar-producing state of Morelos, *haciendas* averaged 5,000 hectares by the early 1900s and accounted for 44 per cent of all agricultural units. In Oaxaca, there was no land monopoly on this scale. Waterbury calculates that only 14 per cent of landholding units were in *haciendas* in 1910, and less than 15 per cent of the population resided on them (compared to 24 per cent in Morelos) (1975).

The Reform of Corporate-held Land

One of the objects of the Liberal Reform was to free the factors of production from 'colonial' constraints. Corporations, notably the Catholic Church and

communal landholders (though neither Lerdo nor Juárez had anticipated that Indian communities would be affected), were to conform to the Ley Lerdo of 1856, and to divest themselves of real estate. In central Oaxaca in the early 1860s, more than 1,400 properties—mostly ecclesiastical—were released for sale, but they were predominantly urban, and by 1867 half still remained on the market. Half the ecclesiastical properties sold off in central Oaxaca went to professionals, bureaucrats, and merchants, one-third to persons of unknown social origin, and one-third to Indians (Berry 1981).

In localities more distant from the state capital, it seems that the process of disamortization was weak (Esparza 1988). Berry mentions that at least 647 properties were disentailed outside the Central District but within the state of Oaxaca by 1876, several of which were owned by ecclesiastical institutions and located near Teposcolula, in the Mixteca Alta (Berry 1981). But the pace of sales was slow. The depressed national economy, the shortage of local capital for investment, the heavy taxes imposed on land to sustain the various wars, and the isolation of Oaxaca, whose roads were notoriously treacherous and unfrequented, were major reasons for the lack of investors.

Disentailment of civil properties outside the Central District numbered 604 between 1856 and 1876. The principal concentrations were in Zimatlán (180), Ocotlán (94), Miahuatlan (30), Etla (22), Ejutla (19), and Tlacolula (10) in the Central Valleys, followed by Teposcolula (83), Tlaxiaco (15), and Jamiltepec (61) in the Mixteca Alta and Baja, and Villa Alta (28) and Ixtlán (27) in the Sierra Zapoteca. Few sales were noted for Yautepec (10) and Tlacolula (10), and virtually no sales were recorded in the isolated districts of Huajuapan, Choapan, Tehuantepec, Pochutla, Cuicatlán, Coixtlahuaca, and Juquila. None whatsoever was registered in Juchitán, Silcayoapan, Tuxtepec, and Nochixtlan (Berry 1981, 182–3). So, Indian communities at high altitude in Oaxaca kept their lands. Isolated and lacking in resources, their property held few attractions for the capitalist class, whether Mexican or foreign, in the second half of the nineteenth century.

Although the Porfiriato did not transform rural landholding in the *sierras* after 1880, there was penetration by large and medium-sized properties into the tropical lowlands of the state. This occurred especially around Tuxtepec and in the Cañada, where half of Oaxaca's land redistribution of the period 1889 to 1903 took place. But the process also affected the Isthmus of Tehuantepec and the Pacific Coast, which, together, accounted for a further one-third of land appropriations, and the Central Valleys, where one-tenth of the total reallocation by area during this period was located (Esparza 1988, 290).

Following the Ley de Baldíos (1863) and the Ley de Colonización (1875), incentives were offered to foreigners willing to invest in idle or abandoned land. In response to this legislation, nine substantial coffee estates were set up near the Pacific Coast from the 1880s, the specific intention being to replace cochineal as an export crop (Hernández Díaz 1992*a*). These expropriations, which involved Chatino communal land, coupled to the imposition of high

personal taxes, led to Chatino revolts in 1875, 1879, and 1896 (Hernández Díaz 1992*a*).

The most notorious example of foreign investment in the tropical lowlands of Oaxaca occurred in the tobacco plantations at Valle Nacional near Tuxtepec. One estate, cut out from communal property belonging to the Chinantec, was the focus of an investigation in 1911 (Turner 1969, 54–67). Here the imported labour, organized by the *jefe político* and allied recruiters (*enganchadores*), included Yaqui Indians from the north of Mexico. 'The slavery of Valle Nacional is merely peonage, or labour for debt, carried to the extreme, although outwardly it takes a slightly different form—that of contract labour' (Turner 1969, 57). Circumstances such as these were widespread in southern Mexico at the end of the Porfiriato, though Valle Nacional, with over 15,000 debt peons in its neighbourhood, was an extreme case within Oaxaca (Chassen 1986).

Esparza estimates that, by the end of the Porfiriato, more than half of the land area of Oaxaca, most of it in the *tierra caliente*, had been privatized along lines encouraged by the Reforma, but less than 8 per cent was cultivated. Most redistributed land was valued at one peso a hectare, and only 8 per cent went to *hacendados* (1988, 290). As late as 1913 there were only 225 *haciendas* in Oaxaca (92 in the Central Valleys, 56 at Tuxtepec, 22 in the Isthmus, 30 in the Cañada, and 14 on the Pacific) (Ruiz Cervantes 1988*b*, 348). Six of the *haciendas* of over 5,000 hectares were concentrated in the Isthmus of Tehuantepec near Juchitán, where cattle and a variety of tropical crops were produced, 7 were around Tuxtepec, and 10 in the Oaxaca Valley (Ruiz Cervantes 1988*b*, 347–8). Some *haciendas* in the Central Valleys had major concentrations of population, such as Santa Gertrudis and San José la Garzona (Progreso), each of which housed more than 1,000 residents (Welte 1978).

Oaxaca lacked 'land and labour' revolutionaries and reforming capitalists. But this must not obscure the fact that labourers on the *haciendas* suffered long hours of work and poor pay, sometimes doled out in kind—as maize (Ruiz Cervantes 1988*b*, 348–9). Conditions were particularly exploitative on the new tropical plantations (many of which were owned by foreigners), where the export crops, especially tobacco, coffee, cotton, and sugar, were competing on volatile world markets. Even in the Oaxaca Valley, where there was the largest concentration of *haciendas*, many communities undergoing population increase were becoming land hungry. It was there that the great houses of the landed estates were almost universally destroyed during the revolutionary struggle.

Conclusion

The history of the Oaxaca peasantry during the colonial and immediate post-independence periods is one of demographic collapse and slow recovery; of

peasant persistence and struggle against the large estate in the face of the Spanish conquest, the Ley Lerdo, and the Porfiriato. If peasantries persisted, it was, however, as a dominated Indian category, in which their subordinate position was maintained by tribute and tithes during the colony, and, subsequently by taxes, tithes, debt peonage, sharecropping, and poor wages, to which were added racial and cultural discrimination.

Oaxaca City had played a key role in the extraction of surplus value from the Indian hinterland through the cochineal trade to Cádiz and the colonial *repartimiento*. Independence destroyed both tribute and the *repartimiento*, and released Oaxaca's peasantries from those particular forms of domination. Gradual population recovery, coupled to the slow pace of estate-formation during the late nineteenth century, enabled the peasantries of Oaxaca to remain somewhat intact—though isolated, self-sufficient, and politically and economically dominated—at the end of the Porfiriato. Oaxaca's small farmers had survived long enough to become the local and substantial basis for the reinforcement and reconstitution of peasantry promised by the Mexican Revolution.

2

Peasantries in Post-Revolutionary Oaxaca

The State and Development (1920–1970)

Oaxaca is among the most backward states in Mexico. Forty years after the tumultuous Mexican Revolution ended, authoritative international agencies recorded that Oaxaca had the second highest rate of morbidity in Mexico, and, according to the 1960 census, was seventeenth—among the thirty-two federated entities—with respect to per capita wheat consumption. It was twentieth with regard to consumption of meat, fish, milk, and eggs. Twenty-first in the ranking in respect of dwellings constructed of adobe or wattle and daub. Twenty-seventh with reference to the number of persons per room; and in the last place based on the index of families with radios, television sets, electric irons, and sewing machines. Oaxaca was in second place with respect to the highest rate of illiteracy (UNDP/FAO 1972, 53).

Social deprivation was due to economic backwardness: it also reflected the failure of the state to address medical and educational issues. In 1968 there were only 324 doctors in Oaxaca, 1.5 to every 10,000 inhabitants. Only twelve doctors were located in the rural areas, although infant mortality did drop from 100 per 1,000 live births in 1950 to 59 in 1967. Almost 80 per cent of the Oaxaca population aged 6 and over was illiterate in 1940, improving to 60 per cent in 1960, but only the neighbouring states of Guerrero and Chiapas recorded worse figures (UNDP/FAO 1972).

Despite its isolation, Oaxaca was drawn increasingly into the ambit of the 'centralized' federal state during the 1920s and 1930s; as in the Porfiriato, the Oaxaca governorship remained a gift of the president. The Partido Nacional Revolucionario (1929) gradually set about creating the Mexican state in its own image. In doing so, it had to balance two major interest groups that had collaborated to win the revolution and now controlled the PNR. The agrarian pro-peasant lobby that wanted land reform, and the capitalist class that looked to the state for improved infrastructure and cheap labour, and was geared to industrialization and urbanization.

This chapter explores the institutionalization of the Revolution, and concludes

with a suite of statistical analyses that underline the impact, in Oaxaca, of the two long-term government preoccupations between 1920 and 1970—land reform and urban-based capital accumulation. To this end, population and agricultural data from the census have been correlated to measure the changing relationship between key variables at selected dates both for Oaxaca state and the Oaxaca Valley. These analytical–descriptive techniques confirm that Oaxaca was transformed after 1930, and especially after 1950. With the passage of time, land reform and urban-based economic activities became ever more powerful agents for change at the regional scale; but change did not necessarily lead to higher levels of living, except where superior services were supplied. In short, a peasantry was consolidated by guaranteed access to small parcels of generally poor quality land. Land reform provided the basis for peasant survival rather than the development of capitalized commercial agriculture.

'Hegemony' of the PRI

The main, direct, impact of the Revolution in Oaxaca came about through the application to the state of policy formulated in Mexico City. After the Mexican Revolution ended in 1917 (though pacification was not complete until 1923), the role of the state followed two contradictory paths that reflected the interests of the northern and southern power blocks that were victorious. Their goals were to modernize and industrialize the nation, while outlawing personal rule; and to break up the *haciendas*, transfer property to the landless (or those short of land), and thereby create a stable landholding peasantry.

Oaxaca was not, in 1910, notable (by national standards) for landlessness nor an outstanding example of modernization. But major changes to Oaxaca's peasantries have none the less been brought about by the land reform; by the government's Indian policy; and by the role of the state as funder and builder of infrastucture and purveyor of services. The latter have impacted on the processes of migration and urbanization and on the administrative and commercial role of Oaxaca City.

Before looking at each of these themes it is essential to consider the role of the victorious revolutionaries in pacifying Mexico and centralizing it within the framework of a federation. It was not until 1925, one year after the death of García Vigil, that Oaxaca was returned to civilian government. During the late 1920s, national political authorities gradually established control over Oaxaca and the rest of Mexico through the consolidation of a *de facto* one-party system: in 1935 the PNR was renamed the Partido de la Revolución Mexicana (PRM), later transformed (in 1946) into the Partido Revolucionario Institucional (PRI).

The PRM/PRI spawned a host of affiliates through which it penetrated different sectors of Oaxacan—and Mexican—labour. These bodies included the

Confederación Revolucionaria Obrera y Campesina (CROC), Confederación Revolucionaria de Obreros de México (CROM), Confederación de Trabajadores de México (CTM), Confederación Nacional Campesina (CNC), and the Confederación Nacional de Organizaciones Populares (CNOP). After the war-torn nineteenth century and the devastation of the Revolution, the PRM/PRI was to provide stability and direction for the state—but within the framework of a constrained, one-party democracy.

The PRI claims that Mexico is a federal democracy, with elections, on various territorial scales, held on regular cycles since the 1920s. But, from the PRM/PRI's formation to the end of the 1980s it did not lose a single presidential, gubernatorial, or senatorial election. Through the centralization of government, despite the national federal structure, the PRM/PRI was able to control most local governments. For example, in Oaxaca City, no one other than a PRI candidate was president of the municipality for more than sixty-five years after 1929; unpopular figures were simply replaced by other PRI nominees.

Both at the national scale and in Oaxaca, the PRI and the state are one—with identical colours, and apparently a united destiny. To balance the contradictions in PRI policy, and to satisfy its diverse clientele, has required skill, management, manipulation, and rhetoric; at worst it has involved co-option, fraud, imprisonment, violence, and assassination. Different presidential regimes have gravitated more to the agrarian and popular sectors—for example, Cárdenas in the 1930s (Knight 1994), while others have been pro-business —such as Díaz Ordaz, de la Madrid, and Salinas de Gortarí in the 1960s, 1980s, and 1990s, respectively. Echeverría and López Portillo attempted (unsuccessfully in the longer run) to appeal on a range of issues to Mexican society as a whole.

All presidents have been prepared to draw on an established repertoire of manipulation or coercion, as required. Much of this is reminiscent of the Porfiriato, except that the PRI has been more enduring: the issue of 'no re-election' can damn a man, but hardly a party. Even at the level of the *municipio*, conventional wisdom is based on the assumption that candidates of the PRI, or, more accurately, candidates validated by the PRI, have been elected *en masse* in Oaxaca—the *carro completo*.

While conforming, in general terms, to PRM/PRI policy during the process of consolidation after the Revolution, Oaxaca suffered the fate of its political and economic irrelevance—it was ignored (Murphy and Stepick 1991*a*). Lacking a sound local tax base, Oaxaca's authorities—state and municipal— were systematically underfunded for half a century. As recently as the early 1960s, the state budget was no more than 4 million US dollars or just over 2 dollars per head (Martínez Vásquez 1990, 80). The state governor, though Oaxacan by birth, was almost always a Mexico City resident before gaining the incumbency, on the say-so of the president; and even representatives of Oaxaca to the national House of Deputies were selected in the federal capital.

Nevertheless, the post-revolutionary federal state did begin to reconstruct

the national economy and society, and these changes were manifest in Oaxaca. The first state interventions began soon after the Revolution ended, and involved the breaking up of estates by the land reform and the development of an integrationist policy towards the Indians.

Land Reform

The major rural change resulting from government policy in Oaxaca after the Revolution, which it shares with the rest of rural Mexico, was the break up of large landed estates. Land reform units, or *ejidos*, were formed as nuclear groups of twenty landless labourers or more petitioned for 'surplus' land in their vicinity. Owners were allowed to retain land up to a certain limit, depending on its quality, with 50 (later 100) hectares of irrigated land as the norm (Leyes y Codigos de Mexico 1966).

The process advanced in fits and starts with the passing of presidential *sexe-nios* (Ornelas López 1988; Segura 1988), but, in the period 1917 to 1964, all ex-districts into which Oaxaca was divided experienced land reform, except the *sierra* areas of Ixtlan, Pochutla, Teposcolula, and Villa Alta (Fig. 1.7). These last four districts were areas in which Indian communities held on to most of their communal lands throughout the colonial period and the Porfiriato, though parts of other districts experienced similar continuity. According to the 1960 census, 1,128,000 hectares had been redistributed to 590 *ejidos* in Oaxaca since the Revolution, approximately 90 per cent since 1935 (Segura 1988, 252–3).

The lion's share of *ejido* land, by 1960, was concentrated in the districts in which the Porfirian redistribution of land had been most pronounced—the *tierra caliente* of Tuxtepec (226,959 ha.), Jamiltepec (270,121 ha.), and Juchitán (172,666 ha.) (Fig. 1.7). However, if the districts that cover the Oaxaca Valley are combined (Centro 34,399 ha., Etla 11,467 ha., Zaachila 5,583 ha., Zimatlán 5,366 ha., Ocotlán 41,520 ha., and Tlacolula 40,579 ha.), the total reformed area of 138,914 hectares makes this the fourth largest block of land redistribution (Segura 1988). The Oaxaca Valley, of course, contained the crumbling ruins of the major concentration of *haciendas* in Oaxaca, the origins of which were rooted in colonial times. The remains of some of these *haciendas* were, in some cases, incorporated into the buildings of the *ejidos* that superseded them (Pl. 2.1).

So, a reconstituted peasantry, occupying much of Oaxaca's most fertile intermontane basin and part of the tropical lowlands, was added to the peasantry that survived at higher altitude (Pl. 2.2). Among the long-established peasantries, the federal government was active in giving formal recognition to *tierras comunales*, and 506 units of 1,864,900 hectares were designated by presidential decree between 1940 and 1960. Additionally, the low-lying Isthmus of Tehuantepec was also prominent among the regions affected by this legislation

Pl. 2.1 Hacienda Blanca in the Etla arm of the Oaxaca Valley: the estate was turned into an *ejido*, and many beneficiaries and their families were living in the ruins of the *casa grande* in 1978

(Segura 1988, 244). By 1960, 67.5 per cent of Oaxaca was in *ejidal* (13.5 per cent), communal (38 per cent), or municipal, state, or federal (15.8 per cent) hands (Segura 1988, 248).

Between 1962 and 1986, over 500 acts of agrarian reform benefited Oaxaca, with more than 420,000 hectares distributed to *ejidos* and 2,700,000 hectares confirmed as *tierras comunales* (Piñón Jiménez 1988, 313). It is noteworthy that 40 per cent of this entire reallocation took place in the socially calm years between 1962 and 1970, with another substantial tranche after 1978; barely 11 per cent was distributed during the turbulent years 1970–7 (Piñón Jiménez 1988, 313). Clearly, the Mexican state has been at pains to exercise its rights over communal lands, and to deny the communities' independent title to them. Once the communal lands have been subtracted from the proportion of the land that is in state control, the impact of the reform is considerably muted.

Despite the land reform, private land ownership has remained significant in Oaxaca. Almost one-third of the state was still in private control in 1970, since the reform leaves prescribed amounts of irrigated, non-irrigated, and pasture land in the hands of the original owners. However, the land limits set can be circumvented by registering surplus land in parcels attached to the names of other people. Within these privately owned lands (numbering 90,700 units), there was the same pattern of polarization that had occurred prior to the

Pl. 2.2 Dessicated fields on a steep highland mountain side during the dry season: Yalálag, Sierra Zapoteca

Revolution. More than 88 per cent of properties had access to 34 per cent of the privately owned land area of Oaxaca in units of less than 5 hectares. Nine per cent controlled 23 per cent of the area in units of from 5 to 25 hectares; and 2 per cent had access to 43 per cent of the private hectarage in units of more than 25 hectares (Piñon Jiménez 1988, 308). These *pequeños propietarios* (so-called small proprietors) are a well-endowed and potentially powerful lobby.

Nevertheless, only two northern states of Mexico have a larger *ejidal* and communal land area than Oaxaca, so the role of the state in establishing and confirming the peasantry on the land—even if the land has remained technically government property—has clearly not been negligible. By 1970, there were over 1,000 *ejidos* and communal beneficiaries of the land reform in Oaxaca, most of the latter with substantial Indian populations.

The Indians

Turn-of-the-century and later non-Mexican social scientists termed Oaxaca's ethno-linguistic groups tribes (Beals 1945; Starr 1900, 32), though it is clear that they have lacked organizational capacity and coherence since pre-conquest times. Nevertheless, peasant lifestyles, set within the territorial framework of the *municipio*, have produced striking commonalities among Indians. Sororal polygamous marriage may characterize wealthy families among the Mazatec (Boege 1988), but there is comparatively little differentiation in family organization, marriage rules, kinship terminology, religious organization, or belief systems among the various ethnic groups (or between them and Oaxacan *mestizo* society).

Since the conquest, the major ethnic issue in Oaxaca has not been the interrelationships between the various pre-Columbian language groups or the distinctiveness of their cultures, but their common subordination to Hispanic—more recently *mestizo*—Mexico. Europeanized, late nineteenth-century Mexican liberals had 'dismissed the Aztecs as mere Barbarians and viewed contemporary Indians as a hindrance to their country's modernization' (Brading 1988, 75). But the Mexican Revolution destroyed the obstacles to the creation of a *mestizo* national identity, and *mestizaje* (a cultural rather than a racial project) launched the policy of *indigenismo*.

Others, considering themselves Indianists, opposed the *indigenista* movement. Some urban extremists of Indianist persuasion advocated the extirpation of all Spanish and foreign influences and the autonomous development of the Indian communities. There were also those on the political left who identified Indians as peasants, merely suffering the common oppression of their class. However, the mainstream *indigenista* viewpoint, associated with the PRI, and running throughout the period covered by this chapter and beyond, adhered to the principle of enlightened, planned, non-coercive integration, and rejected all other approaches, including Indianism, as heresies.

Incorporation of the Indian groups into national life meant, among other things, that they had to speak Spanish. For several years after the Revolution, the use of native languages was forbidden in schools. This measure acquired additional weight after 1921, when no special education was provided for Indian groups—other than the training of bilingual teachers. As a consequence, the period from the beginning of the Revolution to the 1930s was marked by the expansion of Spanish.

Mexican educational policy *vis-à-vis* the Indian began to change in the mid-1930s: Indians were to be encouraged to adapt culturally, while preserving their ethnic identity as much as possible. The object, then, was that:

Education should be bilingual, starting with literacy in the native language with a progressive shift to Spanish. This approach is the one that has prevailed, at least in theory, until now, and although no objective evaluation (in fact, no evaluation at all) has been

made of its effects, very little seems to have been achieved. No group has become literate in its own language, and the progressive spread of Spanish has probably been independent of these programmes. (Suárez 1983,168)

A major tool of post-revolutionary educational policy was the rural school.
This institution became the centre not only of education in the narrow sense—
literacy in the Oaxacan context—but of technical diffusion, agrarian reform,
political mobilization, and nationalist propaganda (Kowalewski and Saindon
1992). According to Knight, 'Indian customs, music, dance and rituals were
rehabilitated and woven into a new tapestry of folkloric nationalism; revolutionary martyrs, like Zapata, were claimed for the *indigenista* cause' (1990, 82).
As a reinforcement of this policy of integration, an Instituto Nacional
Indígena (INI) was inaugurated in 1948. The intention was to stimulate and
manage socio-economic change. A number of centres were subsequently
located among the major ethno-linguistic groups in Oaxaca, co-ordinated
from Mexico City and, later, from Oaxaca City.

By 1970, Oaxaca's 680,000 indigenous language speakers were concentrated
in high altitude areas lying peripheral to the Central Valleys—in the Mixteca,
Sierra Mazateca, Sierra Juárez, Sierra Mixe, and the Sierra Madre del Sur. In
many zones they accounted for 90 per cent or more of the population (Fig. 2.1).
A separate and quite distinctive concentration of indigenous language speakers also occupied the Isthmus of Tehuantepec.

At the geographical heart of this 'Indian' distribution were located the
Valley and Sierra Zapotec, with Mixtec and Chatino speakers to the west,
Chinantec, Mazatec, and Cuicatec speakers to the north, the Mixe to the east,
and Huaves, Chols, and Zoques occupying 'islands' among the Isthmus
Zapotec (Fig. 2.2). This pattern was strikingly similar to the distribution of
Indians at the end of the eighteenth century (Fig. 1.8) and, even earlier, at the
conquest (Fig. 1.6).

Segregation among the language groups was considerable at regional level,
yet only the Mixe, among the larger groups, were concentrated almost entirely
in one ex-district. All eight of the ex-districts of the Mixteca were substantially
Mixtec speaking; a similar degree of linguistic homogeneity typified the two
ex-districts where the Chatinos concentrated, seven out of the eleven which
were Zapotec dominated, and one out of the three where the Mazatecs were
prominent. Notably heterogeneous, so far as indigenous languages were concerned, were the Isthmus, the district surrounding Oaxaca City, and the north-
ernmost sierras and plains of Oaxaca, where Mazatecs, Chinantecs, and
Cuicatecs lived in close proximity.

In all but a few *municipios*, mostly in the remote *sierras*, the majority of
Oaxaca's population spoke some Spanish by 1970 (Fig. 2.3). However, mono-
lingualism in an indigenous language was quite widespread in the sparsely
populated areas where the Indian population was concentrated. Conversely,
Spanish speaking was common in the corridor, following the Pan-American
Highway, cutting from north-west to south-east across the state.

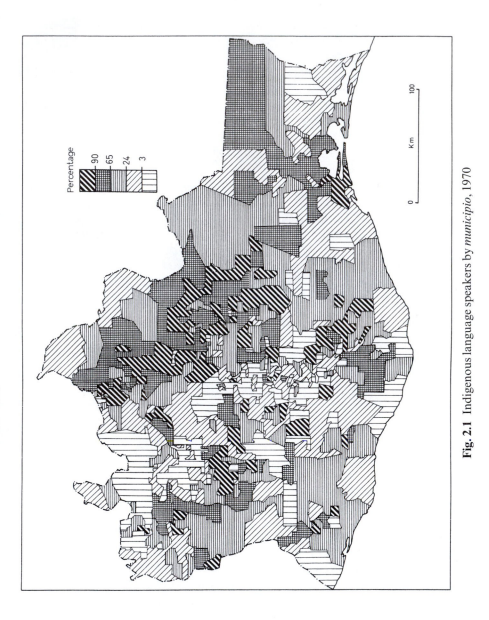

Fig. 2.1 Indigenous language speakers by *municipio*, 1970

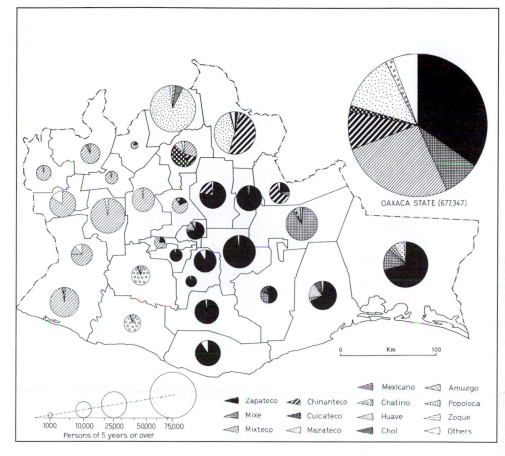

Fig. 2.2 Indigenous language speakers by ex-district, 1970

Federal Projects

Undoubtedly one of the major improvements initiated by the federal government has been the extension of the network of paved and unsurfaced roads.
Many Oaxacan peasants still refer to the road as 'a gift from God'. The crucial
period in Oaxacan post-revolutionary infrastructural development began during the 1940s, when the state was connected to the Pan-American Highway. In
1943 it reached Oaxaca City from Mexico City via Puebla and Huajuapan de
Leon. This section was finally paved in 1948, the year in which the road was
extended right across the state to Tehuantepec and on to Chiapas. The Pan-
American Highway was the only secure long-distance route through the state
until the 1970s, when the surfaced roads from Oaxaca City to Puebla via the
Cañada and to Tuxtepec via the Sierra Juárez were opened up.

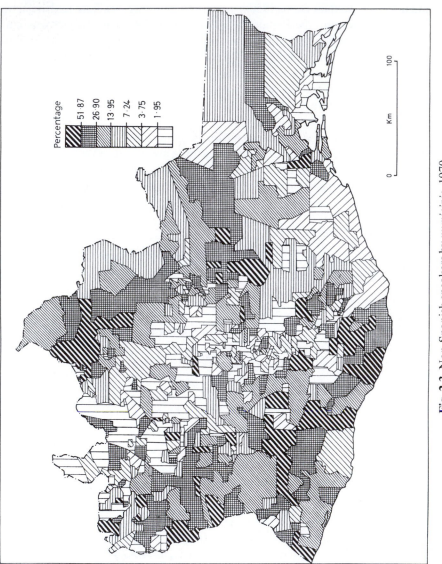

Fig. 2.3 Non-Spanish speakers by *municipio*, 1970

Two regional concentrations of large, federal projects of national concern have been located in Oaxaca to take advantage of site-specific natural resources, notably near Tuxtepec and in the Isthmus of Tehuantepec. Small in number, but massive in scale and cost, they were developed after 1950, and included the Alemán Dam (1950s), to control flooding, generate hydroelectric power, and develop the Papaloapan Basin (Fig. 2.4). This project was later expanded by the construction of the Cerro de Oro (Miguel de la Madrid) dam (inaugurated in 1988). Additional developments included paper processing and sugar manufacturing at Tuxtepec, the former based on Oaxaca's forest resources (1950s); and oil refining and exporting at the port of Salina Cruz (1970s), where there is also a massive container facility for trans-Isthmus trade.

In each of these cases, it has been the low-lying peripheral regions that have been affected, rather than the peasant-farming areas of the Oaxaca Valley and the high *sierras*. However, several of the infrastructural developments have impacted deleteriously on neighbouring Indian communities, especially where

Fig. 2.4 Papaloapan Basin and the Aleman Dam

population displacements were involved, as they were, notoriously, in the dam projects near Tuxtepec. Substantial Mazatec communities were dislodged from their natural habitat by the Alemán Dam, under conditions that have been described as ethnocide (Barabas and Bartolomé 1973).

Improvements associated with electricity generation took some time to filter into the more remote rural areas because of the difficulty of cabling. Although Oaxaca City was electrified at the end of the nineteenth century, the contrast between town and countryside persisted: as late as 1970, only 333 out of Oaxaca's 2,000 recognized communities had electricity (UNDP/FAO 1972). Lack of supply adversely affected the majority of peasant households, so traditional utensils and methods of food storage continued well into the 1970s.

To summarize, the Revolution, institutionalized politically in the PRM and the PRI, impacted on Oaxaca during the period 1920–70 in several ways. The land reform was put in hand, Indian policy evolved, and infrastructural projects were initiated, especially after the Second World War. But these developments were not synchronized, and they were not implemented at the same time in the same place. Heterogeneous in topography, but homogeneous, comparatively, in peasant lifestyle, how did Oaxaca change socio-economically? Before answering this question directly, the changed demographic circumstances of the post-revolutionary decades must be addressed.

Population: Growth and Distribution

Although Oaxaca was a revolutionary backwater, the state population of 1,040,000 in 1910 dipped to 976,000 in 1920. This decline reflected the disruption and death associated with the war and it was not until 1930 that the population recovered to its pre-revolutionary level. In 1940, the population was only 1,192,800, but thereafter it increased to 1,421,100 in 1950, 1,727,300 in 1960, and 2,015,000 in 1970. With mortality declining quite markedly after 1940, (and life expectancy rising from 40 to over 50 years between 1950 and 1970), the later figure clearly reflects the depletion of the Oaxaca population through out-migration (UNDP/FAO 1972).

By 1970, more than half of the state (at high and low altitude) was characterized by population densities of less than 15 persons per km.^{2} (Fig. 2.5). Seven areas of greater population density stood out, reaching more than 40 (in a few instances more than 100) persons per km.^{2} in the Oaxaca Valley, the Mixteca, the Papaloapan Basin, the Sierra Juárez, the Isthmus of Tehuantepec, the southern mountains, the Costa Chica, and Jamiltepec. Densely populated areas, though occurring in the *tierra fría, templada*, and *caliente*, were all located in comparatively favourable environments for agricultural development. The major exception was the high-density area of the Mixteca Alta, many of whose communities, between 1960 and 1970, experienced absolute population decline.

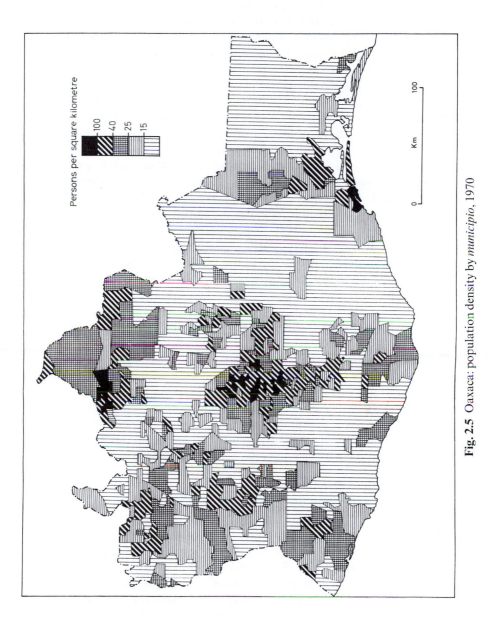

Fig. 2.5 Oaxaca: population density by *municipio*, 1970

All the major urban settlements—Oaxaca City, Tuxtepec, Huajuapan, Juchitán, and Tehuantepec, were located in these population clusters, giving rise to marked urban/rural differences at the local scale, as well as at the state level. Excluding the towns and focusing on the rural areas which had experienced land reform, high densities of more than one *ejidatario* or *comunero* per hectare of cultivated land in 1970 characterized the Sierra Zapoteca, the Oaxaca Valley, and the Mixteca Alta (Fig. 2.6). These were already exceptionally densely populated and intensively farmed; after 1970 they were the main source areas of out-migration to the US border region and the USA itself.

Distinctive demographic trends were recorded in Oaxaca City, where the population was only 27,792 in 1920 and 33,420 in 1930. A year later, the city was devastated by an earthquake that destroyed one-fifth of the buildings and severely damaged half the remainder. The élite, depleted by the events of the Revolution, was further diminished by out-migration to the security of Mexico City. Property values plunged, and a few families, including one of recent Spanish origin, accumulated huge urban estates. Oaxaca City remained within its colonial boundaries until 1940, by which time it had 29,300 inhabitants. Thereafter, under the influence of natural increase and cityward migration, it grew very rapidly to 46,700 in 1950, 72,300 in 1960, and 99,530 in 1970.

Population growth in Oaxaca, as elsewhere in Mexico, was essentially unplanned throughout the period 1920 to 1970. It was not until the late 1970s that the Mexican government, alarmed at the national rate of increase of more than 3 per cent per annum, began to disseminate information about birth control. The government began to realize that it was a major disadvantage to have an overflowing reservoir of cheap labour that was absorbing services and reproducing poverty, often to the detriment of the state's developmental projects.

With the population pressure imposed on small-scale agriculture and urban commerce clearly in focus, it is now necessary to return to the issue of socioeconomic and spatial change. These topics have been examined statistically, using data from the censuses of population and agriculture for the twenty-nine ex-districts of Oaxaca in 1950 and 1970. Attention is then directed to the core area of the state, and a second set of statistical analyses are carried out for the 111 *municipios* that comprise the Oaxaca Valley, at the centre of which is located Oaxaca City itself. Similar variables to those used for the ex-districts are employed, except for 1930, when only demographic data were available. The analyses are carried out for the years 1930, 1950, and 1970, thus giving a longer longitudinal span to the analysis than is possible for the ex-districts—as well as greater detail at small scale. These *municipio* results nest within the framework of the ex-district data, and identify and reflect similar processes to those picked out at the state scale. They also permit a comparison between the post-revolutionary period and the decades following the Second World War.

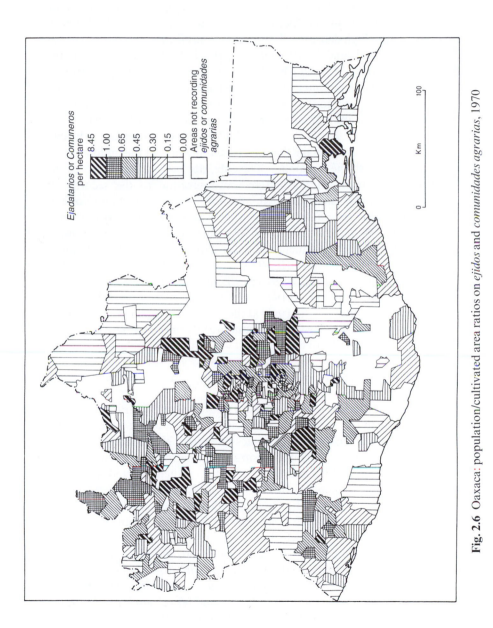

Fig. 2.6 Oaxaca: population/cultivated area ratios on *ejidos* and *comunidades agrarias*, 1970

Oaxaca State, 1950 to 1970

Urban Employment and Agriculture

An attempt has been made to measure intergenerational socio-economic change in Oaxaca, using the 1950 and 1970 censuses. As indicated above, 1950 marks the end of the first phase of highway penetration. Moreover, the 1950 census is the first for which appropriately diagnostic data were compiled at the ex-district level. The 1970 census completes the generational range of the analysis.

The relationships between land reform, peasantry, capitalist development, and urbanization have been examined using data from the 1950 censuses of population and agriculture. The units of analysis are the twenty-nine ex-*distritos* into which the state was divided at that time for statistical purposes (*Censo General de Población*, 1952; *Censo Agrícola, Ganadero y Ejidal* 1956). Fourteen variables used in the statistical analysis are set out in Table 2.1, and a full description of their composition is appended as footnotes to the correlation matrix. These densities, ratios, and percentages have been ranked from high to low for each ex-*distrito* and intercorrelated to produce a matrix of Spearman rank coefficients.

The highest and second highest coefficient in each column of the square correlation matrix have been underlined (Table 2.1), and a linkage diagram constructed to show the nature, strength, and direction of the major statistical bonds (Fig. 2.7). Four nodes are identified in the diagram: in each case they are the focus of a number of correlation bonds—agricultural employment (5 bonds), commercial employment (4), owner farmers (4), and farms over 5 ha. (4). These nodes produce two groups, which I have labelled employment and agriculture: they are not linked together. Within the employment group, the most important feature is the negative direction of the high correlations between agricultural employment, on the one hand, and commerce (wholesaling, retailing, and peasant marketing), transforming (industry and *artesanias*), and service employment (ranging from the bureaucracy to domestic service), on the other. Moreover, service employment correlates positively with commerce. It seems safe to conclude that by 1950 the major geographical differentiation at the state level involved urban–rural distinctions generated by the development of commercial, transforming, and service activities. These modernizing activities were located in urban places that were otherwise set in a sea of agricultural activity.

Examination of the additional linkages in the employment group shows that the ratio of female to male literacy was generally low in rural areas, but distinctly higher where transforming was located. Speaking Spanish, as opposed to non-Hispanic monolingualism, was associated with female literacy and *ejido* land; and *ejido* land with irrigation. Irrigated land was also positively linked with commerce. Shoe wearers were employed in commerce; people who went barefoot or wore sandals (Indians) were engaged in agriculture.

Table 2.1 Oaxaca by ex-district: Spearman rank correlation 1950

	1	2	3	4	5	6	7	8	9	10	11	12	13	14
1 Agriculture[a]	1.00	-0.41	-0.80	-0.69	-0.66	-0.33	-0.49	-0.51	-0.02	-0.28	0.15	-0.16	0.39	-0.19
2 Extractive[b]	-0.41	1.00	0.25	0.32	0.25	0.17	0.20	0.35	-0.27	0.03	-0.29	0.47	-0.44	0.18
3 Transforming[c]	-0.80	0.25	1.00	0.41	0.39	0.36	0.49	0.09	-0.09	0.16	-0.12	0.21	-0.45	0.10
4 Commerce[d]	-0.69	0.32	0.41	1.00	0.63	0.30	0.24	0.59	-0.42	0.38	-0.01	0.31	-0.38	0.54
5 Service[e]	-0.66	0.25	0.39	0.63	1.00	0.11	0.37	0.49	0.04	0.20	0.07	0.05	-0.14	0.24
6 Spanish-speaking[f]	-0.33	0.17	0.36	0.30	0.11	1.00	0.43	0.25	-0.11	0.39	-0.34	-0.08	-0.28	0.16
7 Literacy-ratio[g]	-0.49	0.21	0.49	0.24	0.37	0.43	1.00	0.27	-0.02	0.31	-0.36	0.07	-0.25	0.21
8 Shoe users[h]	-0.51	0.35	0.09	0.59	0.49	0.25	0.27	1.00	-0.20	0.25	-0.32	0.13	-0.10	0.40
9 Average farm size[i]	-0.02	-0.27	-0.09	-0.42	0.04	-0.11	-0.02	-0.20	1.00	0.05	0.29	-0.78	-0.55	-0.50
10 *Ejido* (land reform)[j]	-0.28	0.04	0.17	0.38	0.20	0.39	0.31	0.25	0.05	1.00	-0.09	-0.32	0.13	0.53
11 Cultivation[k]	0.15	-0.29	-0.12	-0.10	0.07	-0.34	-0.36	-0.32	0.29	-0.09	1.00	-0.42	0.51	-0.15
12 Owner farmers[l]	-0.16	0.47	0.21	0.31	0.05	-0.08	0.07	0.13	-0.78	-0.32	-0.42	1.00	-0.75	0.27
13 Units over 5 hecatres[m]	0.39	-0.44	-0.45	-0.38	-0.14	-0.28	-0.25	-0.10	0.54	0.13	0.51	-0.75	1.00	-0.09
14 Irrigation[n]	-0.19	0.18	0.10	0.54	0.24	0.16	0.21	0.40	-0.50	0.53	-0.15	0.26	-0.09	1.00

Notes:
[a] % economically active population engaged in agriculture
[b] % economically active population engaged in extractive industry
[c] % economically active population engaged in transforming industry
[d] % economically active population engaged in commerce
[e] % economically active population engaged in services
[f] % of population able to speak Spanish
[g] % of population able to read and write ÷ % males able to read and write
[h] % population wearing shoes
[i] average size of farm units (hectares)
[j] % of units of land in *ejidos*
[k] % of land cultivated (hectares)
[l] % of owner farmers among tenancy types
[m] area of holdings over 5 hectares
[n] % of agricultural land irrigated

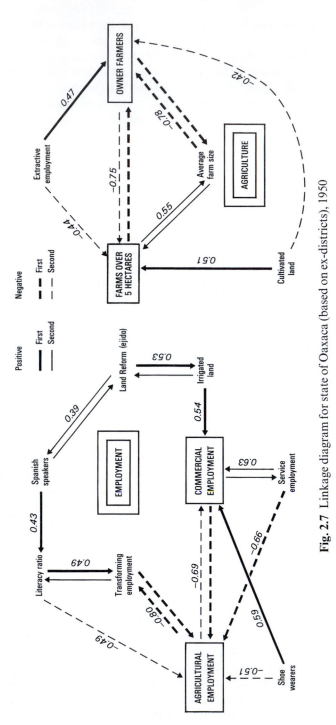

Fig. 2.7 Linkage diagram for state of Oaxaca (based on ex-districts), 1950

The second group in the linkage diagram reveals the nature of Oaxacan agriculture. Most *Oaxaqueños* in 1950 were peasants—hence the importance of owner farmers. But three out of the four linkages to it are negative and describe what owner farmers *are not*. They are not large landowners; they have a small average farm size (less than 5 hectares); and they are poorly endowed with cultivated land. They are, however, positively correlated with extractive employment—mining and forestry. In contrast, owners of farms over 5 hectares are more purely agricultural in their pursuits than peasant farmers, and they have access to substantial amounts of cultivated land. In short, the 1950 diagram expressed the contrast between *minifundia* (small properties) and *latifundia* (large estates), although the former had been bolstered by the Mexican land reform.

Intergenerational Change

To look at intergenerational change, data for the same twenty-nine ex-*distritos* have been compiled from the 1970 censuses of population and agriculture (*Censo General de Población* 1971; *Censo Agrícola, Ganadero y Ejidal* 1975). The twenty-two variables selected have been intercorrelated (Table 2.2), and their composition is defined in the accompanying footnote. Fourteen of them are identical, or almost identical, to the variables used in 1950, and eight more have been added to reflect the richer data in the 1970 census, especially with regard to levels of living and development. Once more, the highest and second highest coefficient in each column of the correlation matrix has been underlined (Table 2.2), and a linkage diagram constructed (Fig. 2.8). Six nodes are identified in the diagram: in rank order of the number of correlation bonds that focus on them, they are: agricultural employment (7), commercial employment (5), average farm size (4), dwellings with electricity (4), land reform (3), and farm units over 5 hectares (3). These nodes form three groups (Fig. 2.8): employment differences; levels of development; and variables of an agro-demographic nature. The agro-demographic system is linked to levels of living via owner-occupiers, and to employment via population density (towns). Employment differences and levels of development are joined together by the possession, or otherwise, of radios and televisions. The employment and agro-demographic groups are similar to the two major components identified in the smaller set of variables for 1950.

The linkage diagram reveals an employment group that is structured very much as it was in 1950. But key negative correlations between agricultural employment and urban commercial, service, and transforming employment were larger than before; and the typically urban occupations were even more closely associated with one another in 1970 than previously. Levels of development were depicted in the relationship between dwellings with electricity and radio ownership, piped water and irrigated land. Spanish *vis-à-vis* non-Spanish speaking linked negatively to tenants and positively to transforming

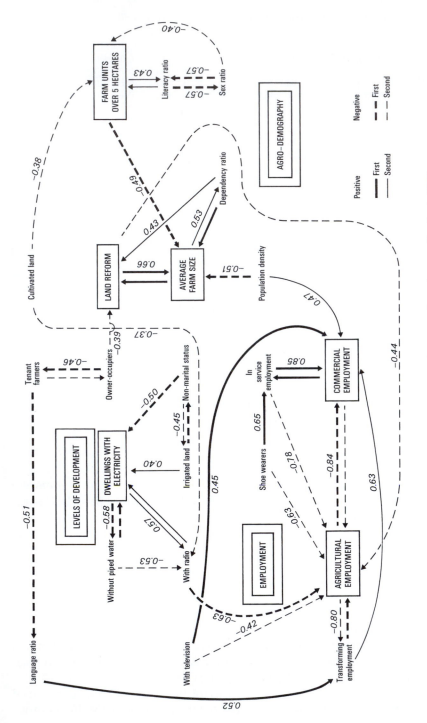

Fig. 2.8 Linkage diagram for state of Oaxaca (based on ex-districts), 1970

Table 2.2 Oaxaca by ex-district: Spearman rank correlation 1970

	1	2	3	4	5	6	7	8	9
1 Population density[a]	1.00	0.12	−0.13	0.17	−0.03	−0.07	−0.07	−0.35	0.29
2 Sex ratio[b]	0.12	1.00	−0.10	−0.13	0.19	0.10	−0.57	0.00	0.06
3 Dependency ratio[c]	−0.13	−0.10	1.00	0.30	−0.12	−0.10	0.24	−0.21	0.10
4 Shoe wearing[d]	0.17	−0.13	0.30	1.00	−0.24	0.40	0.43	−0.63	0.41
5 Non-marital status[e]	−0.03	0.19	−0.12	−0.25	1.00	−0.33	−0.31	0.31	−0.26
6 Language ratio[f]	−0.07	0.10	−0.10	0.40	−0.33	1.00	0.25	−0.49	0.52
7 Literacy ratio[g]	−0.07	−0.57	0.24	0.43	−0.31	0.25	1.00	−0.23	0.17
8 Agriculture[h]	−0.35	0.00	−0.21	−0.63	0.32	−0.49	−0.23	1.00	−0.80
9 Transforming[i]	0.28	0.06	0.10	0.41	−0.26	0.52	0.17	−0.80	1.00
10 Services[j]	0.44	−0.05	0.17	0.65	−0.09	0.19	0.25	−0.78	0.53
11 Commerce[k]	0.47	−0.04	0.17	0.57	−0.02	0.24	0.19	−0.84	0.63
12 With electricity[l]	0.18	−0.22	0.23	0.47	−0.50	0.16	0.35	−0.51	0.33
13 Without piped water[m]	−0.09	0.08	0.15	−0.39	0.36	−0.51	−0.36	0.48	−0.46
14 With radio[n]	0.17	−0.05	0.40	0.57	−0.36	0.36	0.29	−0.63	0.53
15 With television[o]	0.20	0.32	0.00	0.10	−0.21	0.24	0.02	−0.42	0.32
16 Average farm size[p]	−0.51	0.01	0.53	−0.02	0.10	−0.28	0.03	−0.05	−0.13
17 Land reform[q]	−0.03	0.16	0.43	0.27	−0.04	0.01	0.10	−0.44	0.24
18 Cultivated land[r]	0.27	0.32	−0.34	−0.15	0.34	0.02	−0.30	0.20	−0.10
19 Farm unit over 5 hectares[s]	0.23	−0.40	−0.05	0.23	−0.41	0.39	0.43	−0.26	0.29
20 Tenant[t]	0.28	0.19	0.00	−0.21	−0.01	−0.51	−0.20	0.08	−0.12
21 Owner occupiers[u]	−0.01	−0.09	−0.04	0.06	−0.09	0.30	−0.08	0.07	−0.05
22 Irrigation[v]	0.10	−0.26	−0.06	0.26	−0.45	0.00	0.14	−0.27	0.11

Notes:
[a] density of population per km.²
[b] males ÷ females
[c] children under 15 + old people over 65 ÷ adults 15–65
[d] population wearing shoes aged over 1
[e] % population aged over 12 not married
[f] Spanish speakers (and bilinguals) ÷ non-Spanish speakers
[g] % females able to read and write ÷ % males able to read and write
[h] % economically active population in agriculture
[i] % economically active population in transforming industry
[j] % economically active population in services

employment. Electricity and irrigation correlated negatively with non-marital status (cohabitation). Parallel to these 'cultural' associations were the dissociation of both television and radio ownership from agricultural employment.

Agro-demographic variables clustered around the positive relationship between average farm size and land reform, and the negative link between average farm size and units over 5 hectares. Additionally, average farm size increased with declining population density and increases in the dependency ratio. Large (but probably reformed) properties of more than 5 hectares recorded relatively small male/female majorities and comparatively high ratios of literacy for women compared to men. Finally, land reform was negatively associated with owner-occupiers (since *ejidal* land as well as communal property is government owned and, strictly speaking, inalienable), and positively correlated with high dependency ratios.

Comparison of the correlation matrices for 1950 and 1970 can be simplified by leaving out the variables introduced for the first time in the 1970 census.

10	11	12	13	14	15	16	17	18	19	20	21	22
0.44	0.47	0.18	−0.09	0.17	0.20	−0.51	−0.03	0.27	0.22	0.28	0.00	0.10
−0.05	−0.04	−0.21	0.08	−0.05	0.32	0.01	0.16	0.32	−0.40	0.19	−0.10	−0.25
0.17	0.17	0.23	0.15	0.40	0.00	0.53	0.42	−0.34	−0.05	0.00	−0.04	−0.06
0.65	0.57	0.47	−0.39	0.57	0.10	−0.02	0.27	−0.15	0.23	−0.21	0.06	0.26
−0.09	−0.20	−0.49	0.36	−0.36	−0.21	0.10	−0.04	0.34	−0.41	−0.01	−0.09	−0.45
0.19	0.24	0.15	−0.51	0.36	0.24	−0.28	0.01	0.02	0.39	−0.51	0.30	0.01
0.25	0.19	0.35	−0.36	0.29	0.02	−0.03	0.10	−0.30	0.43	−0.20	−0.08	0.15
−0.78	−0.84	−0.51	0.48	−0.63	−0.42	−0.05	−0.44	0.20	−0.26	0.08	0.07	−0.26
0.53	0.63	0.33	−0.46	0.53	0.32	−0.13	0.24	−0.10	0.29	−0.12	−0.05	0.11
1.00	0.85	0.48	−0.49	0.46	0.35	0.01	0.34	−0.10	0.01	0.14	−0.10	0.24
0.85	1.00	0.52	−0.40	0.47	0.45	−0.02	0.39	0.01	0.00	0.18	−0.17	0.19
0.48	0.52	1.00	−0.58	0.57	0.16	0.01	0.32	−0.31	0.06	0.26	−0.07	0.40
−0.49	−0.40	−0.58	1.00	−0.53	−0.25	0.30	0.10	0.27	−0.23	0.03	−0.09	−0.22
0.46	0.47	0.57	−0.53	1.00	0.25	−0.05	0.19	−0.37	0.30	−0.19	0.17	0.03
0.35	0.44	0.16	−0.25	0.25	1.00	0.02	0.40	0.29	−0.13	0.26	−0.36	0.19
0.01	−0.02	0.01	0.30	−0.05	0.02	1.00	0.66	−0.28	−0.49	0.16	−0.20	−0.03
0.34	0.39	0.32	0.10	0.19	0.40	0.66	1.00	0.07	−0.34	0.31	−0.39	0.13
−0.10	0.01	−0.31	0.28	−0.37	0.29	−0.27	0.07	1.00	−0.38	0.10	−0.23	−0.22
0.01	0.00	0.06	−0.23	0.29	−0.13	−0.49	−0.34	−0.38	1.00	−0.38	0.28	0.25
0.14	0.18	0.26	0.04	−0.18	0.26	0.16	0.31	0.10	−0.38	1.00	−0.46	0.05
−0.10	−0.17	−0.07	−0.09	0.17	−0.36	−0.20	−0.39	−0.23	0.28	−0.46	1.00	−0.06
0.24	0.19	0.40	−0.22	0.03	0.19	−0.03	0.13	−0.22	0.25	0.05	−0.06	1.00

k % economically active population in commerce
l % houses with electricity supply
m % houses without piped water
n houses with radio
o houses with television
p average size of farm units (hectares)
q % agricultural units held as *ejidos* or communal land
r arable land as % of total agricultural area
s area of holdings over 5 hectares
t % tenants among tenancy types
u % owners among tenancy types
v % agricultural land irrigated

Four themes stand out: employment, farm size, ethnicity, and women's status. Major changes in employment between 1950 and 1970 were embodied in the seven large negative increases (with commerce, services, Spanish, shoe using, land reform, cultivation, and irrigation) which linked agriculture to the remaining twelve variables. Positive increases of great significance were recorded by transforming (6 cases—with commerce, services, Spanish, shoe using, land reform, and irrigation), services (4—with transforming, commerce, literacy ratio, and shoe using), and commerce (3—with transforming, services, and shoe using). All had only one negative increase—in each instance with agricultural employment. Generally, urban–rural differentiation continued apace.

Imbalanced increases (3) and decreases (6), with only two changes of sign, characterized the correlations with average farm size for 1950 and 1970. In addition, many sign changes typified cultivation (7) and owners (7), with several coefficients declining. For units over 5 hectares, all twelve correlations

Table 2.3 Oaxaca Valley by *municipio*: Spearman rank correlation 1930

	1	2	3	4	5	6	7	8	9	10	11
1 Population density[a]	1.00	-0.12	-0.08	-0.09	-0.23	-0.08	-0.10	-0.02	-0.08	0.11	-0.19
2 Sex ratio[b]	-0.12	1.00	0.11	-0.05	-0.03	0.19	0.25	0.03	0.01	-0.49	0.05
3 Dependency ratio[c]	-0.80	0.11	1.00	0.13	0.24	0.11	0.13	0.02	0.11	-0.08	0.19
4 Literacy ratio[d]	-0.90	-0.05	0.13	1.00	0.45	-0.33	-0.32	0.59	0.58	-0.10	0.14
5 Language ratio[e]	-0.22	-0.03	0.24	0.45	1.00	-0.02	-0.31	0.51	0.41	0.06	0.34
6 Non-marital status[f]	-0.08	0.19	0.11	-0.33	-0.02	1.00	0.27	-0.17	-0.33	-0.24	0.03
7 Agriculture[g]	-0.10	0.25	0.12	-0.32	-0.31	0.27	1.00	-0.54	-0.40	-0.59	-0.21
8 Transforming[h]	-0.02	0.03	0.02	0.59	0.51	-0.16	-0.54	1.00	0.63	-0.11	0.19
9 Commerce[i]	-0.08	0.01	0.11	0.58	0.42	-0.33	-0.40	0.63	1.00	0.02	0.22
10 Services[j]	0.11	-0.49	-0.08	-0.01	0.06	-0.24	-0.59	-0.11	0.02	1.00	0.07
11 Extractive[k]	-0.18	0.05	0.19	0.14	0.34	0.03	-0.21	0.19	0.22	0.07	1.00

Notes:

[a] density of population per km.²
[b] males ÷ females
[c] children under 15 + old people over 65 ÷ adults 15–65
[d] % females able to read and write ÷ % males able to read and write
[e] Spanish speakers (and bilinguals) ÷ non-Spanish speakers
[f] % population over 12 not married
[g] % economically active population in agriculture
[h] % economically active population in transforming industry
[i] % economically active population in commerce
[j] % economically active population in services
[k] % economically active population engaged in extractive industry

Table 2.4 Oaxaca Valley by *municipio*: Spearman rank correlation 1950

	1	2	3	4	5	6	7	8	9	10	11	12	13	14
1 Sex ratio[a]	1.00	0.08	-0.01	-0.03	-0.23	0.02	0.01	-0.19	-0.04	-0.08	-0.06	-0.09	-0.04	-0.18
2 Dependency ratio[b]	0.08	1.00	-0.02	0.18	0.02	0.11	-0.11	0.07	0.00	0.01	-0.05	-0.03	0.02	0.13
3 Non-marital status[c]	-0.01	-0.02	1.00	-0.16	-0.16	0.07	0.01	-0.16	-0.01	-0.28	0.05	-0.16	0.00	-0.04
4 Spanish speakers[d]	0.03	0.18	-0.16	1.00	0.36	0.16	-0.26	0.27	0.15	0.28	0.07	0.27	0.22	0.10
5 Literacy ratio[e]	-0.22	0.02	-0.16	0.36	1.00	0.34	-0.29	0.40	0.24	0.57	0.21	0.15	0.16	0.00
6 Protestant[f]	0.02	0.11	0.07	0.16	0.34	1.00	-0.07	0.12	0.16	0.27	-0.02	0.31	0.28	-0.01
7 Agricultural employment[g]	0.01	-0.11	0.01	-0.26	-0.29	-0.07	1.00	-0.55	-0.81	-0.47	-0.05	-0.23	-0.32	-0.11
8 Commercial employment[h]	-0.19	0.07	-0.16	0.27	0.40	0.12	-0.55	1.00	0.39	0.43	0.24	0.37	0.14	0.23
9 Transforming employment[i]	-0.04	0.00	-0.01	0.15	0.24	0.16	-0.81	0.39	1.00	0.44	0.02	0.19	0.35	0.08
10 Service employment[j]	-0.08	0.01	-0.28	0.28	0.57	0.27	-0.47	0.43	0.44	1.00	-0.02	0.29	0.30	0.09
11 Shoe wearers[k]	-0.07	-0.05	0.05	0.07	0.21	-0.02	-0.05	0.24	0.02	-0.02	1.00	0.02	0.02	0.03
12 Exclusive tap[l]	-0.07	-0.03	-0.16	0.27	0.14	0.32	-0.23	0.37	0.19	0.29	0.02	1.00	0.45	0.18
13 With communal tap water[m]	-0.06	0.02	0.00	0.22	0.16	0.27	-0.32	0.14	0.35	0.30	0.02	0.45	1.00	0.08
14 No tap water[n]	-0.18	0.13	-0.04	0.09	0.00	0.01	-0.11	0.23	0.08	0.09	0.03	0.18	0.08	1.00

Notes:

- [a] males + females
- [b] children under 15 + old people over 65 ÷ adults 15–65
- [c] % of population over 12 not married
- [d] % of population able to speak Spanish
- [e] % females able to read and write ÷ % males able to read and write
- [f] % of population Protestant
- [g] % economically active population engaged in agriculture
- [h] % economically active population engaged in commerce
- [i] % economically active population engaged in transforming industry
- [j] % economically active population engaged in services
- [k] % population wearing shoes
- [l] % households with exclusive access to tap water
- [m] % households with access to communal tap water
- [n] % households without access to tap water

Table 2.5 Central Valleys by *municipio*: Spearman rank correlation 1970

	1	2	3	4	5	6	7	8	9	10
1 Population density[a]	1.00	−0.16	0.15	0.20	−0.40	−0.09	0.18	−0.26	0.14	0.19
2 Indigenous language speakers[b]	−0.16	1.00	−0.51	−0.33	−0.01	0.05	−0.41	0.11	0.09	−0.01
3 Dependency ratio[c]	0.15	−0.51	1.00	0.36	−0.04	0.00	0.34	−0.26	0.13	0.10
4 Literacy ratio[d]	0.20	−0.33	0.36	1.00	−0.23	−0.38	0.70	−0.53	0.12	0.41
5 Non-marital status[e]	−0.40	−0.01	−0.04	−0.23	1.00	0.00	−0.12	0.02	−0.04	0.01
6 Sex ratio[f]	−0.09	0.05	0.00	−0.38	0.00	1.00	−0.07	0.26	0.01	−0.24
7 Shoe wearers[g]	0.18	−0.41	−0.34	0.70	−0.12	−0.07	1.00	−0.44	0.23	0.34
8 Agricultural employment[h]	−0.26	0.11	−0.26	−0.53	0.02	0.26	−0.44	1.00	−0.28	−0.67
9 Extractive employment[i]	0.14	0.09	0.13	0.12	−0.04	0.01	0.23	−0.28	1.00	0.11
10 Transforming employment[j]	0.19	−0.01	0.10	0.41	0.01	−0.24	0.34	−0.67	0.11	1.00
11 Service employment[k]	0.19	−0.38	0.25	0.63	−0.09	−0.20	0.57	−0.60	0.14	0.45
12 Commercial employment[l]	0.39	−0.31	0.29	0.60	−0.26	−0.13	0.52	−0.60	0.16	0.59
13 Workers[m]	0.22	−0.27	0.30	0.57	−0.10	−0.10	0.69	−0.62	0.29	0.37
14 Agricultural workers[n]	0.19	−0.14	0.16	0.13	−0.09	0.07	0.07	−0.08	−0.01	0.17
15 Unpaid workers[o]	−0.25	0.30	−0.22	−0.34	0.05	0.14	−0.30	0.39	−0.10	−0.20
16 Land reform[p]	0.20	−0.32	0.25	0.16	0.03	−0.14	0.10	−0.09	−0.05	−0.01
17 One room[q]	−0.22	0.13	0.01	−0.22	0.15	0.13	−0.09	0.07	0.08	−0.10
18 Electricity[r]	0.29	−0.25	0.25	0.58	−0.21	−0.05	0.60	−0.47	0.10	0.47
19 With radios[s]	0.30	−0.41	0.29	0.53	−0.22	−0.05	0.56	−0.44	0.01	0.35
20 With television[t]	0.35	−0.10	0.07	0.20	−0.25	0.01	0.33	−0.26	0.14	0.25
21 Average farm size[u]	0.16	−0.20	0.13	0.20	−0.04	−0.05	0.15	−0.18	0.31	0.21
22 Cultivated land[v]	−0.39	0.30	0.07	−0.07	0.16	0.16	−0.05	0.12	0.09	−0.16
23 Irrigated land[w]	0.42	−0.14	−0.02	0.12	−0.37	−0.11	0.12	−0.13	0.00	0.15

Notes:

[a] population density per km.^{2}
[b] % population > 5 years speaking indigenous language
[c] children under 15 + old people more than 65 ÷ adults 15–65
[d] % females > 10 years able to read and write ÷ males > 10 years able to read and write
[e] those in free union ÷ those married
[f] males as % of total population
[g] % population > 1 year wearing shoes
[h] % population economically active aged > 12 years in agriculture
[i] % population economically active aged > 12 years in extractive industry
[j] % population economically active aged > 12 years in transforming industry
[k] % population economically active aged > 12 years in services
[l] % population economically active aged > 12 years in commerce

changed sign: the land reform transformed the rural scene, and there were more small units and smaller big ones. The significance of the polarization between urbanization and agricultural development was confirmed and reinforced by the variables 'shoe users' and 'land reform'; in each instance there were five increases in positive correlations and three changes of sign.

The correlations revealed enduring discrimination against non-Spanish-speaking Indians, but with some marginal improvement in conditions because of the land reform—especially government confirmed access to communal

11	12	13	14	15	16	17	18	19	20	21	22	23
0.19	0.39	0.22	0.19	−0.25	0.20	−0.22	0.29	0.30	0.35	0.16	−0.39	0.42
−0.38	−0.31	−0.27	−0.14	0.30	−0.32	0.13	−0.25	−0.41	−0.10	−0.20	0.30	−0.14
0.25	0.29	0.30	0.16	−0.22	0.25	0.01	0.25	0.29	0.07	0.13	0.07	−0.02
0.63	0.60	0.57	0.13	−0.34	0.16	−0.22	0.58	0.53	0.20	0.20	−0.07	0.12
−0.09	−0.26	−0.10	−0.09	0.05	0.03	0.15	−0.21	−0.22	−0.25	−0.04	0.16	−0.37
−0.20	−0.13	−0.10	0.07	0.14	−0.14	0.13	−0.05	−0.05	0.01	−0.05	0.16	−0.11
0.57	0.52	0.69	0.07	−0.30	0.10	−0.09	0.60	0.56	0.33	0.15	−0.05	0.12
−0.60	−0.60	−0.62	−0.08	0.39	−0.09	0.07	−0.47	−0.44	−0.26	−0.18	0.12	−0.13
0.14	0.16	0.29	−0.01	−0.10	−0.05	0.08	0.10	0.01	0.14	0.31	0.09	0.00
0.45	0.59	0.37	0.17	−0.20	−0.01	−0.10	0.47	0.35	0.25	0.21	−0.16	0.15
1.00	0.61	0.52	0.08	−0.30	0.19	−0.11	0.37	0.51	0.20	0.31	−0.22	0.20
0.61	1.00	0.47	0.23	−0.31	0.02	−0.19	0.51	0.57	0.31	0.26	−0.23	0.28
0.52	0.47	1.00	0.15	−0.50	0.08	−0.08	0.61	0.41	0.21	0.23	−0.06	0.12
0.08	0.23	0.15	1.00	−0.68	0.15	0.07	0.07	0.17	0.08	0.07	−0.05	0.02
−0.30	−0.31	−0.50	−0.68	1.00	−0.31	0.01	−0.25	−0.28	−0.16	−0.16	0.20	−0.04
0.19	0.02	0.08	0.15	−0.31	1.00	−0.08	0.03	0.11	−0.02	0.26	−0.09	0.01
−0.11	−0.19	−0.08	0.07	0.01	−0.08	1.00	−0.22	0.00	−0.12	0.08	0.25	−0.31
0.37	0.51	0.61	0.07	−0.25	0.03	−0.22	1.00	0.53	0.34	0.09	−0.21	0.23
0.51	0.57	0.41	0.17	−0.28	0.11	0.00	0.53	1.00	0.29	0.19	−0.29	0.25
0.20	0.31	0.21	0.08	−0.16	−0.02	−0.12	0.34	0.29	1.00	0.08	−0.14	0.13
0.31	0.26	0.23	0.07	−0.16	0.26	0.08	0.09	0.19	0.08	1.00	−0.05	−0.08
−0.22	−0.23	−0.06	−0.05	0.20	−0.09	0.25	−0.21	−0.29	−0.14	−0.05	1.00	−0.77
0.20	0.28	0.12	0.02	−0.04	0.01	−0.31	0.23	0.25	0.13	−0.08	−0.77	1.00

[m] % population economically active aged > 12 years employed as workers
[n] % population economically active aged > 12 years employed as agricultural workers
[o] % population economically active aged > 12 years employed as unpaid workers
[p] % agricultural units held as communal land or as *ejidos*
[q] % houses with only 1 room
[r] % houses with electricity supply
[s] % houses with radio
[t] % houses with television
[u] average size of farm unit (hectares)
[v] arable land as % of total agricultural area
[w] % arable land irrigated

land, the major element in the reform by 1970. Correlation increases (5) and decreases (3), both positive and negative, reflected the increased association of Indians with agriculture and commerce, and their declining involvement in transforming activities and services as these activities modernized. Eight decreases in the size of correlations were recorded (6 positive) with the female/male literacy ratio. Women's literacy *vis-à-vis* men's was rising in almost all contexts, though from a very low base.

Oaxaca Valley, 1930 to 1970

To explore a similar range of socio-economic relationships at a smaller scale, variables have been selected from the censuses of population for 1930, 1950, and 1970, and agriculture for 1950 and 1970. Intercorrelations have been calculated for the 111 *municipios* that cover the Oaxaca Valley (Fig. 2.9). The

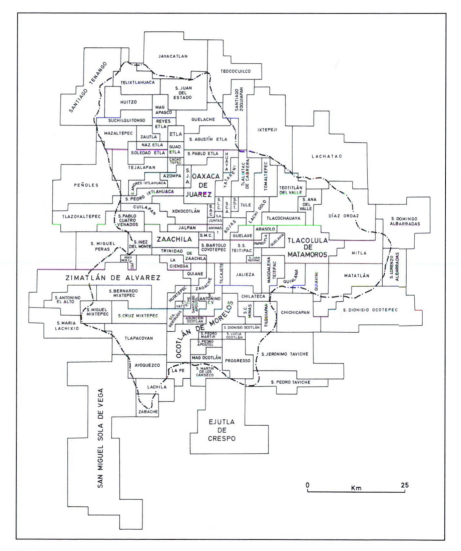

Fig. 2.9 Cartogram of *municipios*, Valley of Oaxaca (after Welte): size of units proportional to area reported in 1960 census

sophistication and the reliability of the census undoubtedly increases over time, and the data for 1930 are sparse and probably inaccurate.

1930

As in the case of the state-wide variables, those for the Oaxaca Valley are described at the bottom of each table (Tables 2.3, 2.4, and 2.5), and each data set has been subjected to Spearman rank correlation and linkage analysis. In 1930, the eleven variables selected (Table 2.3) formed five nodes, transforming employment (4 bonds), commercial employment (4), literacy ratio (4), agricultural employment (3), and the language ratio (3). The linkage diagram produced three groups, which have been labelled employment, located between demography 1 and demography 2 (Fig. 2.10). Within employment, the outstanding features were the large negative correlations between agriculture and services (services were associated with the presence of women, as revealed by the sex ratio); and between agriculture and transforming and commerce. Commerce and transforming were also positively linked.

Examination of demography 1 shows that the ratio of women's literacy to men's was high where transforming and commercial activities were present. Women's literacy depressed the frequency of non-marital unions. Demography 2 focuses on the ratio of Spanish to non-Spanish speakers, which correlated with transforming, commerce, a high female literacy rate compared to men, and involvement in extractive activities (probably mining and quarrying).

The correlation matrix and the accompanying linkage diagram display the low correlations one might expect in a rural and rather undifferentiated economy such as that of the Oaxaca Valley after the Revolution. However, even at this early date, urban–rural differences were marked, though services were largely domestic, and only weakly associated with commerce and transforming. Major social distinctions followed gender lines, with men in agriculture and women (working outside the home) in domestic work. Ethnicity was also important, since it may be inferred that non-Spanish speakers lived at low population density, were engaged in agriculture, and markedly dissociated from urban and modernizing influences, including literacy. However, isolated cases ran against this trend, as Leslie's study of Mitla shows. Here Zapotec-speaking merchants replaced *hacendados* as the persons with greatest authority in local affairs (Leslie 1960).

1950

For 1950, fourteen variables were analysed (Table 2.4), and they produced four nodes, but with a simpler overall set of linked components labelled employment and demography. In relation to the number of correlation bonds, the nodes were more firmly defined than in 1930: commercial employment

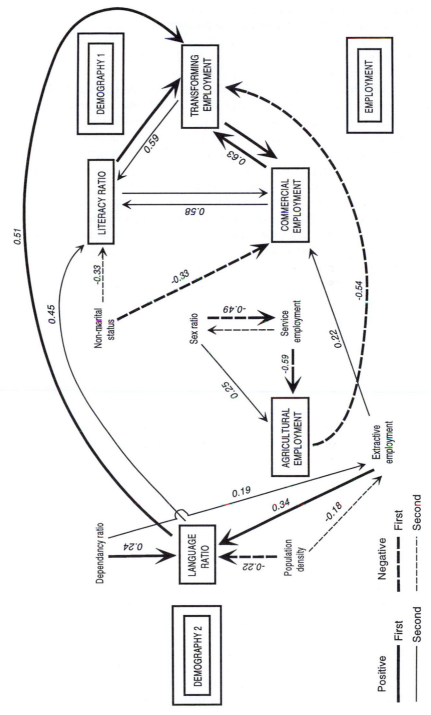

Fig. 2.10 Linkage diagram for Oaxaca Valley (based on *municipios*), 1930

recorded 6 correlations loading on to it, services (5), the literacy ratio (5), and agricultural employment (4) (Fig. 2.11). The major change, since 1930, was the disappearance from the nodal structure of transforming, though it remained an important satellite variable, negatively correlated with agriculture. In the 1950 analysis the term 'Spanish speakers' was used; it had declined in significance as a differentiator, but facility in an Indian language remained as an impediment to women's literacy and to access to service employment, which had emerged as a major node in the system after 1930.

An important aspect of the period 1930 to 1950 in the Oaxaca Valley was the close interrelationship that was starting to develop between commerce, service employment, and transforming, and their joint distinctiveness from agriculture. Commerce was the clearest indicant of urbanization, its satellite variables suggesting a female presence, shoe wearing (*mestizo* culture), and the social-class implication of the polarization between tap water and no water. Services, by 1950, had become urban, professional, and governmental, and this change is reflected in the association both with Spanish speaking and a high female-to-male literacy rate. The latter was strongly linked to commercial and service employment, to Spanish speaking, shoe wearing, Protestantism, and a female majority in the population.

Comparison of the correlation matrices for 1930 and 1950 shows that sign changes occurred in only 19 per cent of cases, but that in an additional half of the instances the size of the correlation declined—notably between agriculture and services, though the coefficient remained negative. Taking services, commerce, and transforming, and correlating each with the other pair at the two dates produces a uniform pattern of larger correlations in 1950, thus showing how this assemblage of occupations had created a distinctively urban scene. This is confirmed by the change in sign between services and transforming. Leaving aside the question of urbanization, there is evidence for a decline in social differentiation under the impact of government policy.

1970

The number of variables used in 1970 was twenty-three (Table 2.5), and the richer data produced new and more complex sets of relationships. To the earlier identified components of employment and demography were added agriculture and levels of living. Four of the nodes in the 1970 linkage diagram were the same as in 1950—the literacy ratio (with 5 correlations), agricultural employment (4), commercial employment (4), and service employment (3). New nodes were workers (5), shoe wearers (4), population density (4), and irrigated land (4) (Fig. 2.12).

While agricultural employment became more differentiated from services and commerce than before, its correlation with transforming declined. But commerce, services, and transforming were even more highly and positively correlated and associated with the new variable (urban) workers, which, in

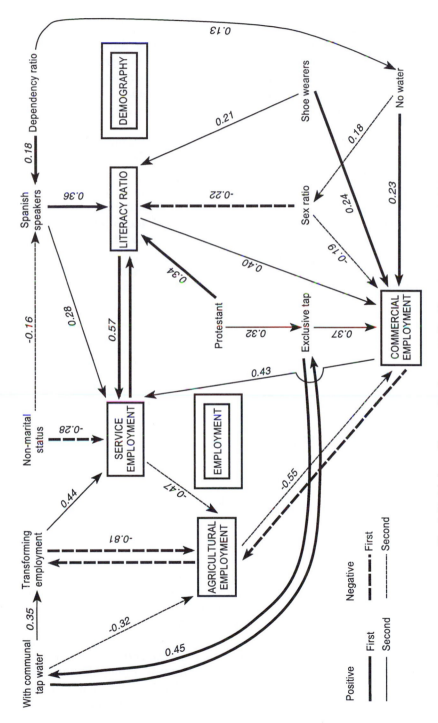

Fig. 2.11 Linkage diagram for Oaxaca Valley (based on *municipios*), 1950

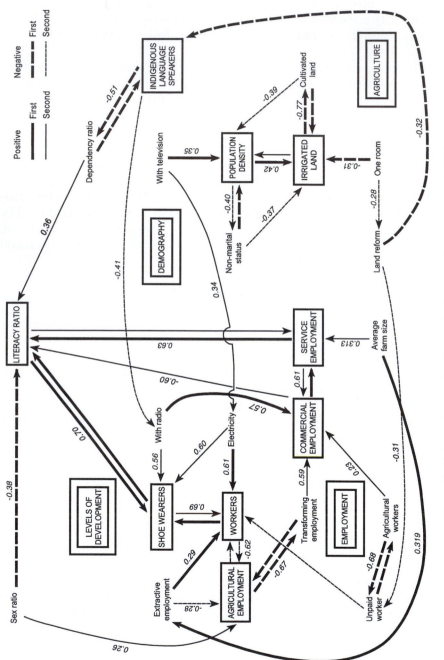

Fig. 2.12 Linkage diagram for Oaxaca Valley (based on *municipios*), 1970

turn, was linked with shoe wearing. Within the agricultural sector, irrigated land was intensively cultivated and gave rise to high densities of population. Electricity correlated with the 'urban' employment variables, and with the ownership of radios and televisions. Electricity had yet to be distributed to the rural areas.

Indigenous language speakers, though few in the Oaxaca Valley, had a low dependency ratio, lacked radios and shoes, and were dissociated from the land reform, probably because of land retention, and from urban-based commerce, services, and transforming. Their position remained marginal, as their low ratio of female-to-male literacy confirms. An improvement in female literacy was key to social advancement for women throughout the Oaxaca Valley.

Once more there were few sign changes in the correlation matrix over the generation (13 per cent), but half the correlations that can be compared for 1950 and 1970 increased, implying the emergence of greater social differentiation. That this differentiation was being driven by urbanization is implied by the increasing number of positive correlations particularly associated with commerce, services, and transforming activities, which then had an impact on the literacy ratio and Spanish.

Spatial Pattern

One way of capturing, spatially, these urban/rural contrasts is by examining population density, and the proportions employed in agriculture and transforming activities in the Oaxaca Valley. These 1970 census variables have been mapped for the *municipios*, the areal size of which accords with the hectarage recorded in the 1960 census. Oaxaca City emerges as the only population cluster of urban size, though the market centres, Etla, Zaachila, Ocotlán, and Mitla also stand out (Fig. 2.13). Population densities of more than 150 per km.² were associated either with these settlements, or with rural dwellers clustering along the Atoyac and Salado valleys. Population density thinned out towards the valley walls.

Agricultural employment, though ubiquitous, was particularly characteristic of the valley bottoms, the wetter sides of some of the valleys, and the southern, better-watered Ocotlán and Zimatlán arms of the Oaxaca Valley to the south of Oaxaca City (Fig. 2.14). The dry Tlacolula valley recorded fewer than 64 per cent of the labour force in agriculture and a correspondingly high proportion in transforming employment, notably in Mitla, Matatlán, Tlacolula, Díaz Ordaz, Santa Ana, and Teotitlán del Valle (Figs. 1.4 and 2.15). Other villages and small towns with transforming activities were San Augustín Etla and Atzompa in the Etla Valley, and Ocotlán and Santo Tómas Jalieza in the Ocotlán arm.

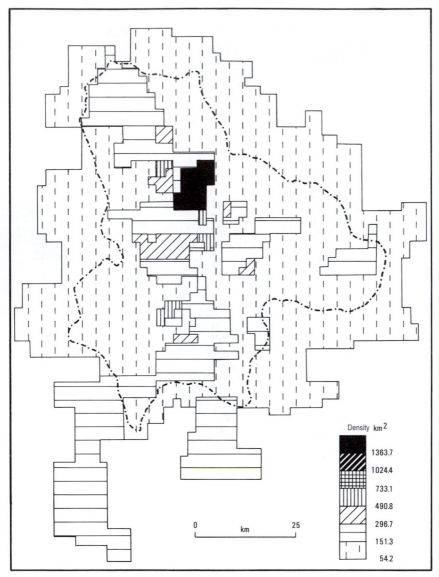

Fig. 2.13 Population density in the Valley of Oaxaca, 1970

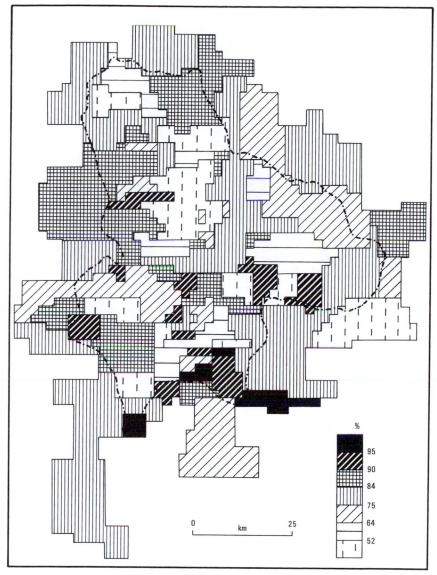

Fig. 2.14 Agricultural activities in the Valley of Oaxaca, 1970

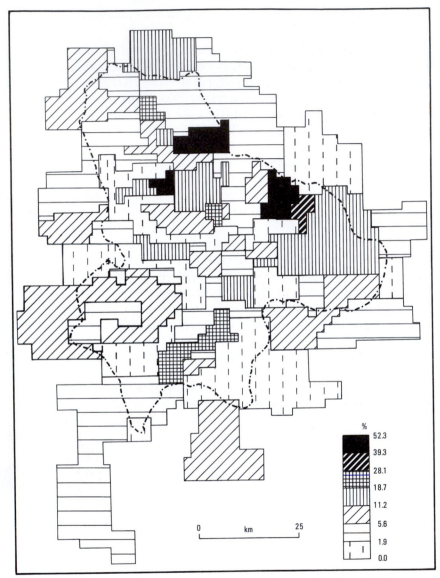

Fig. 2.15 Transforming employment in the Valley of Oaxaca, 1970

Conclusion

The statistical results for the Oaxaca Valley are essentially consistent with the correlation analysis for Oaxaca state as a whole. Where identical pairs of variables are used, the coefficients are larger at the state level simply because the smaller number and larger size of the spatial units (the ex-*distritos*) traps more of the variability within them than do the *municipios*. One item of comparison between the data for the Oaxaca Valley and the state warrants comment: when the time period 1930 to 1970 is examined for the Oaxaca Valley, the pattern of change is reminiscent of that recorded for the state as a whole for 1950 to 1970. The implication of this may be that the changes that were initiated in the Oaxaca Valley after 1930, especially those associated with urbanization and modernization, eventually diffused throughout the entire rural interior of the state.

The quantitative data are also of a piece with the qualitative materials produced in earlier sections of this chapter. Urban–rural differentiation was the major change in Oaxaca over the period 1950–70, though it remained one of the most backward states of Mexico. Urban modernization was expressed in shoe wearing and in greater facility in Spanish; improved education was also reflected in greater female literacy. However, urbanization—focused largely on Oaxaca City—was driven not by industrialization, but by state services, commerce, and transforming industry. The two latter were of a small-scale and artisanal type, often based on the small towns and specialized villages.

The second major change has been agrarian, and has hinged on the breaking up of large estates and the granting of communal title to the remote Indian communities. It has been spatially concentrated rather than universal, and has been less effective than urbanization in bringing about transformation at the regional scale. This has been so because the land reform has created peasantries that have only partly evolved towards commercial farming. Peasantries have modernized only where ecological circumstances and communications have been favourable. In the most isolated *sierras* change has been slight: communities have been confirmed in their traditional lands, and the road has been the major agent triggering spontaneous but gradual development.

What the statistical analyses do not show is that Oaxaca's peasantries, currently, are not only environed by regional capitalism, but are strongly interactive with Oaxaca City and the smaller market centres, where levels of living are markedly higher, and the employment structure is more diversified, than in most rural areas. Cityward migration has clearly taken place on a substantial scale, as the doubling of the population of Oaxaca City between 1950 and 1970 indicates.

The Mexican Revolution and the state it created, under the aegis of the PRM and the PRI, reconstructed Oaxaca—and Mexico—to their own ends. The peasantry, while an established and enduring part of the social structure of

Oaxaca during the colonial and independence periods, has been fortified and expanded rather than reconstituted from scratch, as in other states of Mexico, through the land reform. Urbanization created an alternative environment to the *campo*. Within the urban settlements, most notably Oaxaca City, were now located the state élite—mostly *comerciantes* and *políticos*, as well as a mass of workers assembled through population growth and migration. Standing outside this *mestizo*-dominated urban context, was the Indian population, which was mostly located in the highland regions, though slowly beginning to move to city and town destinations. This Indian population was the backbone of the peasantry, which, by 1970, still accounted for the vast majority of all Oaxacans.

With a focus on the period since 1970, Part II concentrates on the material and environmental circumstances of Oaxaca's peasantries. The transformations that are taking place within peasantries in marketing, artisan production, capital accumulation, and class differentiation are then addressed. Finally, attention is given to the role of out-migration that has led to the partial depopulating of many of the rural districts, and the processes of urbanization and proletarianization that are so typical of, but not exclusively concentrated in, Oaxaca City. Oaxaca City remains the control-point of the regional economy of the state of Oaxaca in which the peasantries are embedded.

Part II

Peasants, Commercialization, and Urbanization

3

Peasant Production and the Environment

Peasants are frequently portrayed as engaged in a distinctive mode of production, but, in the context of Mexico's capitalist economy, it is more logical to regard them as penny-capitalist rather than pre-capitalist. Cook and Binford argue convincingly that the notion of 'a separate but subsumed peasant economy, or petty commodity mode of production, dissolves' in the light of their empirical evidence from households in the Oaxaca Valley (1990, 27). They note:

In its place, emerges a concept of a single, complex, regionally and locally segmented commodity economy encompassing a variety of domestic units, including those of producers for own use as well as petty commodity producers in various socio-economic circumstances, of capitalists, and of wage labourers (usually paid by piece rate). It is obvious that all these subjects act within the same economy. It is also obvious that there are differences in their modes of involvement in that economy, as well as in the aims and material results of their material participation. (1990, 27)

In short, the Oaxaca peasantry is not only persistent; it is also highly differentiated—hence peasantries.

Most of Oaxaca's peasants—and virtually all at high altitude—live at a near-survival level, which they achieve through supplementing their cash-cropping agricultural activities by artisan production and migrant labour. In the Mixteca Baja, for example, almost 70 per cent of households had members who engaged in off-farm labour, payment for which 'formed a critical supplement to farm income' (Roberts 1982, 313). Even so, levels of living are low—80 per cent of Oaxacan people do not consume meat, eggs, or milk (Ortiz Gabriel 1992).

Subsistence levels of living are the outcome of peasant activities carried out in an unyielding environment. In 1960, for example, only 21 per cent of the surface area of Oaxaca was cultivated (and it has subsequently declined), 22 per cent was in pasture, 5 per cent was fallow, 9 per cent was unproductive, and 43 per cent was in forest (UNDP/FAO 1972, 8–9). Peasant agriculture is set in a wilderness of thorn- and cactus-scrub, rough grazing, and forestry, so that, to the outside observer, it frequently seems that the countryside is useless and empty. Indeed, activities outside the Central Valley and tropical lowlands are usually extensive, and even so are highly concentrated to take advantage of favourable small-scale environments.

The first part of this chapter is devoted to an overview of peasant agricultural activity and peasant material culture. Although Oaxaca's peasants are divided into miniature class hierarchies at the local scale, depending largely on differential access to land and other resources (Turkenik 1975), the vast majority live close to subsistence, and almost all share a peasant non-material culture. Attention is then given to the extensive *ejidos* and *tierras comunales*, and to the way in which they are cultivated. Traditional systems of land tenure, inheritance, and husbandry are examined. The role of climate in the seasonal agricultural cycle is discussed. Oaxaca's peasants live in close harmony with nature and enjoy an intimate knowledge of their immediate environment.

Oaxaca's physical geography is complex and some of its more 'extreme' environments require careful management, involving the age-old practices of soil conservation, flood control, and irrigation. But, because Oaxacan peasants are also open to the present as well as to the past, they are faced with the challenge of adopting modern fertilizers and mechanization and other innovations characteristic of the 'green' revolution. The penultimate section of this chapter is devoted to Oaxacan peasants' staple crops and their use of natural products, as well as to the hunter-gatherer activities in which a few engage. The chapter ends with a discussion of local crafts manufactured for the person, the home, and for tillage. A conclusion joins this chapter to the next, Chapter 4, which discusses the evolution of peasant markets, the production and exchange of speciality crops and crafts, and the role of urban commerce in the economic functioning of the Oaxaca region.

Oaxaca's peasantries are not disappearing under the corrosive influence of capitalism, but they are changing under the impact of population pressure. In particular, they are being affected by the absence for long periods of time of able-bodied migrants, especially men. These issues are referred to briefly in this chapter but are taken up in detail in Chapter 5.

Peasant Material Culture

Shanin characterizes peasants as living by *family labour* (my italics) applied to the *land* they farm—usually their own. Their culture and values are *traditional*, and, in the Oaxacan case, derived from the syncretism of Hispanic and pre-Columbian cultures, notably, but not exclusively, those of the Zapotec and Mixtec. Finally, they are *subordinate* politically and economically to higher social strata. Each of these defining criteria merits further consideration in the Oaxaca context.

Among Oaxacan peasants, both in the high mountains and the interior basins, the nuclear family is the main unit of production and reproduction, though residence usually takes place in family groupings on *solares*, or compounds, located in nucleated villages (Cook 1969). As is typical of peasants, the gender division of labour is sharp. Men till the soil, using digging sticks,

hoes, spades or ox-drawn ploughs, depending on the nature of the terrain, though much of the preliminary ploughing each year on the flatter land is now done by tractor. Women raise the children, prepare the daily quota of *tortillas*, or flat maize bread, and engage in handicrafts and the marketing of surplus produce. Hand labour is the essence of the productive system, and involves *guelaguetza*, or reciprocal work, at seed-time and harvest, when the women, too, are employed in agricultural tasks. Children are pressed into service—the girls as cooks and artisans, the boys as goatherds (Beals 1975).

Oaxacan peasants, whether on *ejidos* or more traditional holdings, rarely have individual legal title to their land. It is common for informal ownership to exist in the cultivated zone adjacent to the nucleated settlements, but pasturage and woodland are held and used in a truly communal fashion throughout Oaxaca's 570 *municipios*. Marriage within the community produces alliances that militate against the intense fragmentation of cultivated units (Downing 1977), though population increase since the Second World War has necessitated the cultivation of more and more poor quality former pasturage in most *municipios*.

Cultivation of the three Meso-American staples—maize, beans, and squash—is the lifeline of the Oaxacan peasantry, irrespective of the altitude at which they live. It is common for all three staple crops to be grown together and literally inter-cropped to provide ground cover and intensify output per unit area (Innis 1997). Oaxacans, like peasants the world over, are risk minimizers; if one crop fails—for example, maize yields depend on the onset of the summer rains, which is highly unpredictable—then others may survive (Kirkby 1973).

Maize, beans, and squash are cultivated for auto-consumption on all but the best and worst land. In the Oaxaca Valley, where ground water can be tapped by wells or irrigation is feasible by constructing channels or controlling flood water, profitable speciality crops are grown—alfalfa for stall-fed cattle, vegetables, chillies, and flowers (Turkenik 1975). Stony or parched land—the norm throughout most of the interior of the state—is used for extensive pasturage, though basin edges are often planted with the maguey cactus, the juice of which is distilled to produce mezcal, a popular alcoholic beverage. Many resource-deficient communities supplement their diet by culling the natural environment for insects and berries, and increase their cash income by collecting wood (*leña*) for sale as firewood or charcoal (Messer 1978).

Oaxacan peasants do not confine themselves to agricultural activities on their own account. Although the peasant household is a useful starting-point in discussing farming activities, it is neither isolated nor self-sufficient. Peasants interrelate with one another as renters–tenants, sharecroppers, *guelaguetza* exchangers, and day labourers, largely because so few of them have adequate or good enough land to practice auto-consumption, let alone self-sufficiency. Moreover, large numbers share in the production of some of the crops and other natural items discussed above. Some peasants operate mixed

farms; others sell their labour, often locally, frequently as migrant labourers in the tropical lowlands of Oaxaca or other states. As many as one-quarter of peasant-artisan households in the Central Valleys in the late 1970s relied on wage labour for between 20 and 30 per cent of their income (Cook and Binford 1990). In other, less endowed regions, the figure is much higher, and in recent years, under the influence of migration to the USA, is higher still.

It is unlikely that the figure of 75 per cent of households engaged in craft production, achieved in parts of the Central Valleys (Cook and Binford 1990), would be approached in any other major region of Oaxaca, except the agriculturally devastated Coixlahuaca Valley. In the case of the Central Valleys, it has arisen from ecologically based specialisms, reflecting comparative advantage, plus a deep involvement in the age-old marketing system. Nevertheless, similar craft activities also pervade the highland peasantries.

Artisan production has given rise to place-specific specializations geared to household survival. The exchange of these commodities is arranged, not as between households at the village level, because village specialization is the norm, but between settlements at a regional scale—the peasant market is an essential organizing focus. Petty-commodity production requires family labour—often by women and children semi-to-full time, and by men in the dry season or during those hours of the day when their cultivating or stock-rearing commitments are over.

As the state of Oaxaca extends across the entire climatic-altitude range from *tierra caliente* (up to 1,000 m.) via the *tierra templada* (1,000 to 2,000 m.) to the *tierra fría* (above 3,000 m.), there is a corresponding diversification into tropical and temperate fruits and vegetables (Beals 1975 and Cook and Diskin 1976). Moreover, the length of the fallow period increases with the drop in altitude, as shifting cultivation adapts to dry farming (Watters 1971). At a smaller scale (not involving altitude), shortages of rainfall and peculiarities of the geology are responsible for a host of non-agricultural specializations. These are particularly noteworthy in the more agriculturally-impoverished sections of the Oaxaca Valley, where textile weaving is important, and in the more eroded areas of the Mixteca Alta, such as the Coixtlahuaca Valley, where palm weaving and hat making have a long history (Velasco Rodríguez 1994).

Over the centuries, villages in the Central Valleys have developed weaving (Teotitlán del Valle, Díaz Ordaz), woodcarving (Santa Cecelia Jalieza), pottery making (Santa María Atzompa (Pl. 3.1) and San Bartolo Coyotepec), stoneworking (San Juan Teitipac), and brick-making specialisms (San Augustín Yatareni). These are paralleled by production in the agro-pastoral system based on the exploitation of favourable ecological niches—cheese (San Pablo Etla), pecan nuts (Cuilapan de Guerrero), tomatoes (Donají), castor beans (Ejutla de Crespo), flowers (San Antonino Castillo Velasco), and wool thread (Guendulain) (Beals 1975) (Fig. 1.4).

Specialities of the *sierras* include *huaraches* (sandals), peaches, quince, and walnuts (San Juan Analco), coffee (Alotepec), potatoes (Coixtlahuaca), bread

Pl. 3.1 Woman, throwing pot on rotating disc: Atzompa, 1990

and meat (Ixtlán de Juárez), *ixtle* (fibre) (Pl. 3.2), oregano, pitch pine, peas, and wood products (Laxopa), pottery and clothing (Macuiltianguis). Baskets, chilli, and palm-leaf hats are important products of the Mixteca, and apples, avocados, beans, coffee, and peaches are grown throughout the Sierra Mixe. The inland parts of the Isthmus of Tehuantepec produce tropical specialities such as bananas, coconuts, mangoes, and sesame, while the Huave-speaking villages on the Pacific Coast sell fish, shrimps, and salt (Beals 1975). A wide variety of crops, such as cotton, coffee, sugar, castor oil, coconuts, plus cattle are produced in the lowlands flanking the Pacific Coast (Rodríguez Canto 1989).

Whereas maize, beans, and squash are virtually ubiquitous and consumed by peasants at home or sold in local markets, speciality products, whether vegetables, spices, fruits, and flowers or household goods, clothing, and agricultural equipment are traded via a rotating market system. This system covers at least half the state and has at its hub Oaxaca City, the state capital. Subsidiary markets in this system take place in smaller towns—such as Tlacolula (Pl. 3.3), Ocotlán, and Etla—on a regular day each week, with Friday and Saturday reserved for the peasant market in Oaxaca City, probably the largest of its kind in southern Mexico and Central America (Beals 1975). Subregions of the Oaxaca marketing system focus on the Isthmus of Tehuantepec, the Sierra Mixe, and the Sierra Juárez, in addition to the Central Valleys. Somewhat independent markets are located in the Mixteca, such as those in Tlaxiaco, Nochistlan, and Putla (Warner 1976), and on the Pacific in Pochutla and Pinotepa Nacional (Cámara Barbachano 1966; Eder 1976).

Pl. 3.2 *Ixtle* ropes and muzzles, Tlacolula market: bag is advertising a firm from the state of Vera Cruz, 1996

Pl. 3.3 Tlacolula market: fruit section, 1996

Insights into the working of the rural economy of communities in the Oaxaca Valley are provided by a sample survey of just over 1,000 households drawn mostly from the drier sections of the Tlacolula and Ocotlán arms (Cook and Binford 1990, 36). These data, assembled between 1978 and 1981, provide a clear indication of peasant differentiation, including small-scale class distinctions based on land units and farm equipment. The largest category was that of peasant-artisan (57 per cent), followed by peasant (19 per cent), artisan (19 per cent), and other (5 per cent), that is, employees, including the rural proletariat (Cook and Binford 1990, 42).

Minifundismo was a major feature of this sample, with 60 per cent cultivating 3 hectares or less of seasonal (*temporal*) land, and 24 per cent landless. Barely 16 per cent of households had more than 3 hectares, and among them only 5 per cent held more than 5 hectares and could be thought of as being on the fringe of the category of *pequeños propietarios*. Most cultivated land was rainfall dependent (the survey largely neglected the comparatively well-watered Etla Valley) in a ratio of 10 hectares of rainfed to 1 hectare of irrigated land.

There was a marked landholding and production hierarchy among the peasants of the Oaxaca Valley. Among households with 1 hectare or less, fewer than 20 per cent had ox teams and only 5 per cent had a cart. Households owning 1–3 hectares were more likely to have an ox team (46 per cent) and a cart (15 per cent). Ox teams and ox carts were particularly concentrated among those households with more than 3 hectares, which accounted for only 16 per cent of all landed households but one-third of the ox teams and 56 per cent of the ox carts (Cook and Binford 1990, 45). Peasants in this top category alone were able to control sufficient animal power and equipment to plan their production process in a logical fashion. The rest (84 per cent of households) had to rent ox teams and land or offer their labour to others via sharecropping or cash arrangements (Cook and Binford 1990, 44–5), so that their own-account activities had to be fitted in between these other commitments.

Self-sufficiency in maize among peasants in the Central Valleys is rare. Cook and Binford imagined, originally, that all households with an ox team and more than 3 hectares of seasonal land would produce enough maize for themselves. But even the best-endowed households (with more than 5 hectares and owning an ox team and oxcart, of which there were only 2.6 per cent in the sample) produced a median of only 1,000 kilos of maize in 1979 or half their annual requirement. So the norm is for peasants to produce a small and annually variable proportion of their maize requirements and to purchase the remainder through cash-cropping of other commodities and artisan work—as the peasant-artisan and artisan categories imply.

The *Ejido*, Land Tenure and Inheritance

All the *hacienda* great houses in the Central Valleys were left in ruins after the Revolution. Nevertheless, a surprising 30 per cent of Oaxaca as a whole

was still in private units of 5 hectares or more in 1960, compared to 67.5 per cent which belonged to the state in the shape of communal, *ejidal*, and government holdings (Segura 1988, ii. 248). By 1988, there were 1,488 *ejidos* and *comunidades agrarias* in Oaxaca, almost 60 per cent of which were spread equally between the Mixteca, the Papaloapan, and the Central Valleys. They covered 7,400,000 hectares or 77.7 per cent of the state (Encuesta Nacional Agropecuaria Ejidal 1988). Three million hectares were divided between 330,000 *ejidatarios* and *comuneros*, with more than 90 per cent having access to parcels. The area devoted to agriculture was similar to the subdivided hectarage—giving on average 10 hectares per recipient, but the lion's share was under woodland or scrub (29 per cent) or categorized as pasture and mountain land (26 per cent) (Encuesta Nacional Agropecuaria Ejidal 1988).

Despite environmental constraints, 1,365 *ejidos* and *comunidades agrarias* (92 per cent of the state total) were agricultural, while only 79 were devoted to cattle, notably in the deforested lowlands of the Papaloapan and the Isthmus, 15 to forestry, and 8 to culling the environment for natural products. Maize cultivation was the main crop for 1,167 *ejidos* and *comunidades agrarias*, 115 specialized in coffee (in the Papaloapan and the Sierra Norte), 21 concentrated on beans (in the Sierra Sur, Central Valleys, and the Mixteca), and 19 on wheat (in the Mixteca). Other lesser specializations were recorded: 6 units concentrated on horticulture (Isthmus), 4 on rice (Papaloapan), 3 on sorghum (Isthmus), and 3 on alfalfa (Central Valleys). Less than 5 per cent of the *ejidal* area was irrigated, though the proportion increased to 27 per cent in the Isthmus, or more than twice the percentage in the Central Valleys (Encuesta Nacional Agropecuaria Ejidal 1988).

Peasant agriculture in Oaxaca is notorious for its low levels of investment, innovation, and technology. Mexico's land reform has been literally a redistribution of land, without adequate thought given to extension services or marketing. Indeed, 21 per cent of *ejidos* and *comunidades agrarias* declared that they employed no modern technology whatsoever. In general, it appears that the highlands are the most backward agricultural regions. In only 300 out of 1,488 reform units, were improved seeds recorded; 750 used herbicides or insecticides; 1,000 applied some fertilizer; and 450 received technical assistance. Almost three-quarters of land-reform units lacked tractors, credit, and services; only 29 had silos for storage; 144 (of which 54 handled coffee) had facilities for processing agricultural, pastoral, or forest products. Fewer than half the reform units received credit, of which only 36 (mostly in the Papaloapan) benefited from non-governmental sources. With regard to other forms of infrastructure, the situation was much more satisfactory, largely because of federal expenditure during the years after 1970. Eighty-five per cent of reform units had electricity; 52 per cent had drinking water; but fewer than 20 per cent were connected to the outside world by paved roads (Encuesta Nacional Agropecuaria Ejidal 1988).

The land reform has underpinned Oaxaca's peasantries, but it has been sadly deficient in providing the inputs that alone would have transformed that peasantry into successful commercial farmers. Given the environmental constraints on getting adequate returns on investment and innovation, coupled to the enduring isolation of most communities, it is not surprising that Oaxaca's peasant agriculture is backward and orientated to subsistence levels of living (Clarke 1986).

Leaving aside the land-reform *ejido*, where, until 1992, state legislation had forbidden individual alienation of property—though it has been widespread unofficially, there are two traditional types of land tenure in rural Oaxaca: communal and private. All non-cultivated land in each *municipio* is considered communal property (*bienes comunales*) and access to it is regulated by an elected official of the *ayuntamiento* (local community council), the *representante de los bienes comunales*. Also in communal ownership are the *terrenos del santo*, which support the local *fiesta* and are worked by *tequio* (an obligatory labour draft levied on adult able-bodied men). All adult male members of the community (usually the *municipio*) or tax payers are considered *comuneros* and have usufructory rights to the common land, involving a written permission that can be bequeathed but not sold.

Private ownership is exercised over agricultural land as well as house plots in the *pueblo*, and may be transferred by inheritance or purchase. Private owners possess written documents, such as wills or formal bills of sale, to substantiate property claims. There is usually a description of the plot, giving its *paraje* (precisely named location in the community), a description of the quality of the land, its metric measurement and number of furrows, and the names of adjacent plot owners. Inter-plot boundaries are often a cause of bitter interpersonal disputes.

Peasants, typically, have several non-contiguous plots of land scattered across various *parajes*. In San Sebastian Teitipac, for example, Cook's informants reported ten separate plots dispersed among seven *parajes* (1969). This has come about through the system of partible inheritance, by which a single patrimony is divided up among several heirs. According to Parson's account of Mitla in the 1930s, 'only those children or grandchildren living at home at the death of the parents inherit house or lands. These heirs inherit equally and irrespectively of sex' (1936, 67). She continued, 'sometimes a dying man makes an oral testament, but it usually carries little weight. Families quarrel a good deal about questions of inheritance, especially about land' (1936, 68).

There are four basic means by which property may be partitioned in Oaxaca—by (1) authorized document; (2) unauthorized document; (3) unwritten and unauthorized document; (4) post-mortem division by the testator's heirs. The first two options are exercised prior to the testator's death, usually when a substantial amount of property is involved. Legitimation or authorization usually involves the participation of community officials, such as the *alcalde*, or lawyers and government representatives as well as of witnesses

(*testigos*). The system of partible inheritance in Oaxaca is, in reality, fluid and variable, and the testator is less bound by law than by local tradition or personal evaluation and prejudice (Cook 1969).

None the less, certain generalizations hold. There is a tendency for the last-born male offspring to inherit his father's house and plot; for male offspring to take precedence over females; and for women with grown sons to receive only a minor share of their dead husband's estate. This patrilineal preference comes into operation only when the peasant is senile or dying. Although he may have made a pre-testament apportionment of his lands, he retains legal ownership of all his plots (even if his heirs are already cultivating them), and appropriates half the harvest in sharecropping arrangements. This situation is, of course, vexing for sons of mature age, who, despite their family commitments, find themselves tied into a dependency relationship with their father (Cook 1969).

Land tenure in the *comunidades agrarias* is, in practice, akin to the one described above, largely because it has evolved over the centuries, with minimal government intervention until recently. *Ejidal* land, until 1992, was supposed to remain government property in perpetuity, and even *ejidal* parcels, though individually allocated, carried with them right of usufruct, not of transfer. In practice, peasants have been able to pass them on to their descendants, with or without official approval, and—unofficially—even to rent or sell them; and there has been a marked convergence over time between the transfer of peasant property in the reform and non-reform sectors.

Land Husbandry

The rhythm of land husbandry in Oaxaca is dictated by seasonal changes in the climate. These operate irrespective of altitude, and may be divided into three discrete seasons (*temporadas*), an elaboration of the wet–dry dichotomy (Chapter 2). A cold-dry season begins in November and lasts through January or February; a dry-windy-hot season which starts in February or March and ends in April (Pl. 2.2); and a rainy season which usually has its onset in April or May and finishes in October. There is also a short dry period (the *canícula*) during the rainy season which runs from about 20 July into August and may herald a drought.

Land tillage fits into this annual cycle via three sets of operations: preparing the fields and planting; caring for the crop as it grows; and harvesting and storing. The maize cycle on rain-fed land exemplifies the most prevalent pattern, though it is not the only one. In the first phase, the fields are cleared or prepared (*limpiado* or *desmontado*) prior to the onset of the April rains. Secondly, ploughing (*arando*, *rayando*, or *pintando surcos*) and planting (*sembrando*) are carried out, often in a speculative fashion, since the rainy season begins in an unpredictable way and runs through until mid-July. Thirdly, weeding (*deshierbo*) of the fields takes place three weeks after planting, to be followed five weeks later by the ploughing of secondary furrows (*echando orejera*) to promote the absorption of moisture by the soil. Finally, four months after

planting and six months after the tillage cycle began, harvesting (*piscando* or *agarrando cosecha*) and storage (*guardando cosecha*) of the desiccated maize is completed. During the post-harvest dry season, November to March, a range of non-tillage operations is carried out: fattening cattle and hogs with alfalfa and maize; manufacturing *adobe* bricks from mud and straw; digging wells; repairing dwellings and other buildings; manufacturing brooms, baskets, or more sophisticated *artesanias* (handicrafts) (Cook 1969).

This tillage schema applies particularly to the comparatively flat lands of the Central Valleys and the peripheral plains of Oaxaca. Prevalence of steep mountain slopes in the *sierras* and on the edge of the intermontane basins sets a firm topographic and pedalogical limit to cultivation, and most uplands are tilled only when they are of exceptional quality or the need is great. Steep slopes at high altitude are sometimes cleared and cultivated for a year or two, but they must rapidly be returned to fallow if their nutrient base is to be replenished, and even so it will take many years before they recover. Ploughing is often impossible, and trees and brushwood must be cut with a machete and cultivation carried out with a *coa* (a wooden-handled curved steel blade) and a sharpened stick for planting. On the highly visible shoulders of the rainiest mountains, slash and burn cultivation (*tumba-roza-quema*) is widely employed by peasants who set up temporary huts high above their native villages but within the boundary of their communal lands (Watters 1971).

Peasants 'In' or 'Over' Nature

Oaxaca's peasantries have been attuned to the environment, at the small scale, to produce low levels of living with negligible resource depletion. The collective will of the community has been to defend itself against outsiders—whether they may be neighbouring *municipios* that will steal its lands or capitalist predators who will usurp its resources. The community seeks to guard its environmental and technical secrets, especially if they relate to artisanal activities whose knowledge brings exceptional rewards, as in some of the pottery or weaving villages.

Oaxacan peasants 'show an attachment to the native soil' (Berg 1974, 5). Whereas commercial farmers are generally characterized as dominating nature, peasants try (theoretically, at least) to conserve their environment by harmonizing with it. Of course, agriculture is an organized interference with nature, but peasants usually attempt to live 'in' nature, since that is the safest way of securing their future husbandry and that of succeeding generations. It is part of their risk-minimizing strategy.

A distinction has often been made between peasant cultivators, using hand tools and animals, and mechanized farmers (Berg 1974). The former alone have reverence for the land, so it is claimed—though to what extent they continue to do so under the influence of either mechanization or population increase is a moot point. Reverence for the land, as a trait, is particularly

marked among Oaxaca's Indian populations. In Shgosho, a Zapotec-speaking peasant community in the Sierra Norte, the inhabitants, both male and female, describe themselves as people who work the land. For them land is an extension of self (Berg 1974).

Zapotec peasants of the Central Valleys are noted for their understanding of the different qualities of the environment. For example, all land that lies beyond the *pueblo* of San Sebastian Teitipac—in the Zapotec-speaking arm near Tlacolula, is called the *campo* (Cook 1969). This in turn is divided into (1) *terrenos labrados, de labranza,* or *de labor* (worked land); (2) *terrenos en bruto, terrenos enmontados, monte* (land overgrown with weeds, thorn bushes, brush, and scrub) or *baldío* (wasteland); and (3) *cerro* or mountainous terrain.

Cerro is unsuited to agriculture, but is exploited for *leña* (firewood), *otate* (for making brooms), wood for charcoal-making and house construction, and as a source of medicinal and food plants. The mountain is also a source of spring water, pasturage for sheep and goats, and small game to be hunted. *Monte* or *terreno enmontado* is cultivable when cleared of brush and stones, but produces only low yields of beans and maize. If the population is increasing in the *pueblo* or there is factionalism that leads to the creation of a nuclear offshoot, it is more likely than not that cultivation will take place. Otherwise, *monte* is reserved for the same extensive purposes as the *cerro*. *Terrenos de labranza* are subdivided into three categories: *humedad propia* (containing natural moisture), *riego* (irrigated), and *temporal* (seasonal).

Based upon topography, soil quality, crop yield, and use, the community is divided into cultivated land of different grades—in San Sebastian Teitipac there are four. First-class land can be naturally moist (*jugo propio*: due to the high water table), have a high retention of precipitation (*de humedad*), or be irrigated (*de riego*). It has a thick fertile topsoil (often black) with very few rocks, and yields a heavy crop of maize, alfalfa, and beans, often producing two harvests per year. The moist, non-irrigated land is cultivated by hoe; ox-drawn ploughs are used on the irrigated type (Cook 1969).

Second-class land is low and flat but may have some slopes. Topsoil is thinner and less fertile than in the case of the first-class variety, and animal fertilizer is crucial to improved harvests. Only with exceptional rains is it possible to reap two crops. Maize, beans, squash, and chickpeas (*garbanzos*) are grown, and are frequently intercropped. Third-class land is typically hilly and rocky, with a thin and sterile topsoil. It produces a good harvest of maize and beans only when there have been heavy rains and some manuring. During fallow years, peasants often use this land for pasture. Even more unattractive circumstances apply to fourth-class land, which has a thin, rocky topsoil (*delgado, pedregoso, pedregal*), but may also be clayish (*arcilloso*), sandy (*arenoso*), or contain gravel (*cascajudo*). This land is usually confined to pasture, unless rains make it feasible for maize and beans (Beals 1975).

Peasants divide their intimately evaluated landscape into a series of localities called *parajes* (Schmieder 1930), identified by natural objects such as rocks,

trees, arroyos, flats, caves, or springs, and man-made markers such as dams, wells, mines, and quarries. They use small-scale elements in the landscape to identify sub-*parajes,* and to pinpoint a location within them. The only map of *parajes* is that which each peasant carries in his head: 'it is so indispensable to the San Sebastiano that he is unable to conceive of a situation in which it does not exist' (Cook 1969, 84). Almost a third of the 140 *parajes* in San Sebastian have land unsuited to cultivation and first-class land is confined to only a quarter. Just under 30 per cent of *parajes* record more than one type of land, and of these 70 per cent contain a combination of *cerro, monte,* and fourth-class land. So, an egalitarian system of land tenure and inheritance is vital to household survival, given the diversity of the physical environment even on a small scale.

While the riverine sections of the Oaxaca Valley and favoured valley bottoms in the *sierras* have first-class land, the remainder of the Oaxaca Valley and the *sierras*, are second, or more likely, third class. The vast majority of the state of Oaxaca comes into the fourth category set out above, partly because it is stony and steep, partly because it is arid and covered with thornbush and cactus (Beals 1975).

Environmental Management and Mismanagement

Soil Erosion

At a regional scale, Oaxaca is characterized by having numerous fragile, high-altitude environments (Fig. 1.1). One recent estimate suggests that 30 per cent of the surface area of the state has lost its soil, and that an additional 40 per cent is subject to moderate-to-accelerated erosion (Aragón 1980 cited in Nahamad, González, and Vásquez 1994). A great deal of the pastureland in Oaxaca's *tierra fría* has been eroded through overgrazing by small stock, especially goats, and communal ownership doubtless encourages selfish individuals to mine the land. In the Sierra Zapoteca and the Mixteca Alta, in particular, vertical channels gash the hillsides, and if unremedied lead to sheet erosion (Cook 1949).

The northern sections of the Mixteca Alta around Yanhuitlán are a byword for environmental devastation. Its origins lie in its fragile shales and clays, which are overlain by calcareous layers of easily breached *tepetate* (Kirkby 1972; Williams 1972). These materials were used intensively and misused in Mixtec times, and the region was deforested through seasonal grazing by 'floating' *haciendas* of small stock during the colonial period (Pastor 1987) (Pls. 3.4 and 3.5).

Historic Mixtec use of the Yanhuitlán beds was less destructive than this suggests, however, for it gave rise to a new system of farming known as *lama-bordo.* Some time after 1000 AD, Mixtec peasants realized that the red soil washing down into the lower parts of the Nochixtlan-Yanhuitlán Valley was

Pl. 3.4 Eroded landscape at Yanhitlán, Mixteca Alta, with maize plots on the made ground below

Pl. 3.5 Rill erosion in the Mixteca Alta: the aridity is indicated by the cactus and agave plants

more alkaline, fertile, and moisture retentive than the soils *in situ*; unusable V-shaped gullies were becoming farmable U-shaped valleys. Whether land pressure on hillside fields started erosion—and terracing was the only way to mitigate its effects—or erosion was deliberately started in order to provide material for terraces, is not known. Nevertheless, the combination of erosion and terracing proved to be a positive advantage for agriculture (Kirkby 1972).

According to earlier collateral work by Spores:

> these dikes, built of coursed stone and rubble, were 1 to 4 meters high and from 10 to 200 meters long. Modern farmers, who continue to construct these terrace systems, find that in 2 to 3 years sufficient soil (*lama*) can be accumulated in a new terrace . . . (*bordo*) to form level and quite fertile farm plots, and they produce excellent yields of corn, grain and vegetables. The plots, which range from a few hundred square feet to 10 hectares, can be worked for as long as the system is maintained, and many terraces have been worked since antiquity. (1969, 563)

The problem is that rapid out-migration from the Mixteca Alta since 1950 has led to such a reduction in the adult male population that it is no longer possible to maintain the terraces, and a new and unregulated phase of erosion has now been entered.

Over much of the rural landscape of the Mixteca Alta subsoil or bedrock outcrops at the surface. At Yanhuitlán the red clay is exposed in vermilion-coloured hill slopes. In the Coixtlahuaca Valley, the hillsides are covered with the white concretion, *tepetate*. Calculations for the late 1950s and early 1960s show that Oaxaca had the second highest erosion in Mexico after Tlaxcala. Furthermore, the district of Coixtlahuaca (adjoining Yanhuitlán) had the worst rate of erosion in Mexico; at such a rate, desertification was likely to extend throughout the entire Mixteca within fifty years (Tamayo 1950). By the late 1970s, erosion in the Mixteca was already affecting neighbouring areas; sediments carried by rivers leading down to Vera Cruz had made the Rio Santo Domingo unnavigable.

There have been some important grass-roots responses to these environmental problems in the Mixteca stimulated by NGOs such as CETAMEX (Centro de Estudios de Tecnología Apropiada para México) in Yodocono. The aim of this project, which started in 1982, is to draw on the knowledge of local peasants and thus improve deteriorated soils through soil and water conservation techniques. These involve contour bunds and ditches; hedging with mixed fruit, fuelwood and fodder plants; mulching, composting, and animal manuring; crop rotation, reforestation, and organic vegetable production. The long-term aim is to increase production with only minimal external inputs such as fertilizer, machinery, and pesticides (Blauert 1990, 458–60; Blauert and Guidi 1992*a* and *b*).

In San Juan Mixtepec, local teachers and returned migrants from the USA and northern Mexico have combined since 1986 to undertake a project entitled 'improvement of the environment and production for the reclamation of our

culture'. First guided by a *promotor* from the CETAMEX scheme, it has been headed by a woman agriculturist and administered by a woman anthropologist, supported by the local authority and a European development agency. Environmental innovations include water- and soil-conservation measures, such as contour-bench terraces and water diversion drains, using stone walls and planting perennial plants such as agaves and prickly pear (Blauert 1990, 463–6). Initial results seem encouraging, but much effort will be required before these achievements are established at a regional scale in the Mixteca Alta (Blauert 1988; Blauert and Guidi 1992*a*), since Oaxaca's peasants rely on extensive techniques of cultivation that have evolved in the context of low population densities (Kearney 1972).

Irrigation

Rainfall run-off is a major erosive problem at altitude and on fragile soils; but well-watered valleys provide opportunities for irrigation, most notably in the Oaxaca Valley, where the Zapotecs developed a maize-dependent hydraulic civilization that reached its apogee around 1000 AD (Flannery, Kirkby, Kirkby, and Williams 1967). Flood waters from the Rio Atoyac and Rio Salado and perennial flows from small tributaries form the main sources for irrigation water (Kirkby 1973; Lees 1973). On the valley floor, a water table of 1 to 6 metres and particularly at 2 to 4 metres provides a further source of water for agriculture, both directly through the soil and via surface application. Where irrigation is not feasible, dry farming is practised (Downing 1974; Kirkby 1974). Weeding reduces transpiration, while infiltration is encouraged immediately around plants by making shallow basins around each seed. Barriers are constructed to curb overland flow, check soil erosion, and reduce moisture loss. So dry farming merges into floodwater farming.

The history of water use in the Central Valleys is one of increasing abstraction at the outer edge of the drainage network leading to a decrease in water availability downstream in the Atoyac itself. More and more water has been taken from the perennial tributaries at their points of entry into the valley. Water has been used upstream of Oaxaca City in the Etla Valley by increasing the use of the high water-table zone and extending and modernizing canal systems. Abstraction has been multiplied many times over by the increasing number of wells with mechanical pumps, to the point that groundwater reserves are threatened (Waterbury 1999).

Four types of irrigated farming have been identified in the Oaxaca Valley—floodwater farming, water-table farming, well irrigation, and canal irrigation (Kirkby 1973). Floodwater farming is used where the frequency of controllable floods is about once a year—usually involving fields close to perennial or ephemeral streams. In some instances a *lama-bordo* type of terrace system is used; in others, canals have been constructed to draw off the excess water created by a sequence of dams—as on the Rio Salado near Mitla.

The presence of a high water table of from 0.25 to 1.0 metres below the surface is necessary for water-table farming. Crops may abstract water continuously by capillary action from the zone of high moisture content that lies above the water table itself. Known as *tierra de humedad*, this type of land is usually able to support crops during the winter dry season. With fertilizers, two to three maize crops a year can be grown, but it is more usual to ensure a heavy summer crop of maize by growing legumes such as chickpeas or beans during the winter. Wheat and alfalfa—for stall-fed cattle—are also common crops (Iszaevich 1973). Water-table farming is usually located on the low alluvium near stream courses, so the area of highest productivity varies from year to year with fluctuations in rainfall and flood size.

Irrigation is practised especially when high-value horticultural crops are planted, as they used to be at San Antonino Castillo Velasco (Turkenik 1975), though this has changed with depletion of the water table. The most distinctive water-table crop is alfalfa, a phreatophyte that abstracts from the water table itself, thus producing a vigorous growth which can stand 10 to 12 cuttings per year. In Guadeloupe Etla, so productive is this system that each family has only 0.25 to 0.75 hectares, yet achieves levels of living superior to all other agriculture-based communities; alfalfa is cut for stall-fed cattle that produce milk for cheese making (Iszaevich 1973).

Well irrigation is practised all over the valley floor where a high enough water table exists. Two main techniques are used today: pot irrigation (*riego a brazo*) and well-and-furrow irrigation, the latter increasingly using mechanical pumps. The method of pot irrigation is simple but laborious and requires from one to eight wells to be dug so that no part of the field is more than 10 metres from a well. The water is drawn by hand and tipped into circular hollows or rectangular boxes. Fields irrigated by this time-honoured method rarely exceed 0.1 hectare, and *riego a brazo* is found only on isolated plots (Kirkby 1973).

Where pumps are used to feed a carefully set pattern of furrows, one well may serve 100 hectares. Most wells are 4 to 15 metres deep, but a few tap aquifers located 30 to 60 metres below the surface. Well-and-furrow irrigation is widely used to supplement other types: the same system of furrows—set up and down slope at right angles to a master furrow—can distribute well and flood water; and the practice of having minimal pumping equipment permanently available means that there is a reliable back up. Kirkby provides a telling example of the impact of mechanization on alfalfa farming. To achieve ten cuttings a year a farmer drawing water by hand would spend three to four days per week to irrigate 0.5 hectare; another with a pump can irrigate more than 5 hectares in one day (Kirkby 1973, 45).

Streams provide the water for all canal systems, and in most cases the water is removed and used immediately without being stored in a reservoir. Schemes are generally small scale and controlled by one village or by co-operation between two or three (Lees 1973). A *toma* (take-off) is constructed behind a

low dam, usually made with boulders, branches, and earth. The dam is designed to raise the level of the water and, at the same time, to allow part of the water to flow over or through it; the *toma* is the beginning of the canal system and for its first few metres it may be concrete lined. Wooden boards that act as sluice gates control the flow of water in the main canals. Further out in the distributory system temporary dams of earth and vegetation are common. The absence of large, perennial streams and the tendency for tributaries to peter out as surface flow before they reach the Atoyac and Salado have given rise to two features of canal irrigation. Namely, a large number of small-scale and independent systems, and a high proportion of canals located on the less fertile piedmont rather than on the main valley alluvium.

Technological Change

The use of time-honoured irrigation systems, now usually operated by petrol-driven pumps, contrasts with the partial absence of a modern 'green' package of agricultural innovations so typical of the more progressive, commercially orientated rural areas of Mexico. These innovations—notable for their absence from the *ejido* sector in Oaxaca, as was seen above—involve hybrid grains, the use of fertilizers, herbicides, and pesticides, and the deployment of labour-saving mechanical equipment, notably tractors.

Generally speaking, Oaxacan peasants still plant *criollo* maize, and many Indians at high altitude breed their seed grain from carefully selected stock (Lipp 1991). Four main types of maize are recognized in the Central Valleys: 3-month (*violento*) Indian corn; 4- to 5-month *tardon*; 6-month *cajeta*; and hybrid varieties. Hybrid maize has been promoted around Ocotlán, but it is claimed that its yield is no better than the *criollo*. The advantage of the hybrid varieties is that their growing period is 3, not 4, months and they have greater resistance to weather changes.

In contrast, artificial fertilizers have been quite rapidly adopted since the 1970s, replacing or supplementing animal manure and waste vegetable matter from the mezcal distilleries. Fertilizer 18-46-00 and a pesticide known as *volanton* are widely disseminated. Estimates suggest that 29 thousand tons of fertilizer, particularly sulphate of ammonia, were used in Oaxaca between 1979 and 1982. During that period about half the output of the major crops was produced with fertilizer. Commercial output of watermelons, tomatoes, tobacco, and green peppers was mostly grown with fertilizer; subsistence crops of maize, beans, castor oil, and chickpeas received lesser inputs (Nahamad, González, and Rees 1988).

Very few Oaxaqueños are owners of draught bullocks or tractors, as has been seen, and rental is the norm. Tractor ploughing is widely used for clearing and preparing the land before sowing; weeding is still carried out by a *junta de bueyes* (pair of oxen) yoked to a Mediterranean plough. Twenty-five years ago, when tractors were rare, Kirkby estimated that their use cost a little less than

an ox-plough per hectare if the land was in large enough units—a situation which rarely existed. An impediment to co-operative ploughing between peasants with adjacent plots was disagreement about the best time to plant maize in relation to the rains. Kirkby concluded that the alternative methods of maize cultivation open to peasants were the *coa* (a curved metal blade) and ox-plough; average profits from a *coa*-worked holding were calculated to be 30 per cent higher, yet almost all peasants preferred the least-work solution of the plough (1973, 74–5). In the highland sections of the state, however, peasants frequently use the *coa* because the terrain is so steep that there is no alternative.

Staple Crops and Other Natural Products

Crops

Maize is Oaxaca's major crop, since it is the staple diet in every peasant household and is a basic food in urban areas. Maize is part of the life of every Oaxacan family, but it is not solely a crop; in the Indian communities it is considered a means of life and God given. Maize is grown in a variety of environments, from the irrigated areas of cash-crop production to the dry-farming hillsides and rain-fed high mountain shoulders. In the Oaxaca Valley, it occupies between 30 and 50 per cent of the agricultural land. Away from the intensively farmed valley bottoms, cultivation involves lengthy periods of bush fallowing and mixed cropping, usually involving the other two staples, beans and squash, or castor oil. Mixed cropping correlates closely with subsistence agriculture; single-crop cultivation with marketing of the produce (Beals 1975).

Wheat is grown at higher altitudes, notably in the flatter uplands of the Mixteca Alta where it is more ubiquitous than maize. Here mechanization is feasible because of the level terrain and the large size of the fields—in those areas where the *lama-bordo* system still operates.

In the tropical lowlands, particularly in the Isthmus and around Tuxtepec, rice has developed as a major irrigated crop, especially since the Second World War. Much of this is on larger holdings, though peasant producers are important in both areas. Other tropical crops of commercial significance are sorghum, coffee, and sugar. Sorghum, for vegetable oil, is a speciality of the Isthmus and is a highly lucrative cash crop. Coffee is grown commercially in the Sierra Juárez, the Mixteca Baja, and the Sierra Madre del Sur. Sugar plantations congregate around Tuxtepec, where the Mexican government built the López Mateos factory as part of its Papaloapan project in the 1950s. A further concentration of sugar estates occurs in the Isthmus of Tehuantepec, adjacent to the factory named after López Portillo. Sugar is also a major crop for peasants throughout the *tierra caliente*. They manufacture it into *panela*, or cakes of brown sugar, which are used for sweetening food and drink in poor urban and rural households (Binford 1992).

Livestock

Large and small stock are reared by peasants throughout Oaxaca. They are central to the mixed-farming system of the peasant, who usually has a few goats, pigs, and sheep, which are taken out to the communal pasture by his children. If he is wealthy, he may keep a *junta* of bullocks for draught as well as a cow or two for milking. At high altitude, in the *tierra fría*, the pastures are given over to goats and sheep and tethered cattle. Specialized stock-farms are a feature of the tropical lowlands of the Costa Chica, the Isthmus, and the recently deforested and colonized *ejidal* area to the north of the Sierra Mixe. In the two latter instances, there is a commercially orientated 'peasantry' evolving into a *hacendado* class, with horses giving way to pick-up trucks.

Commercial and subsistence agriculture are carefully calibrated to the environmentally prescribed pattern of advantages and disadvantages at both the state-wide and local scales. But beyond the cultivated and pastoral areas there are other activities in which Oaxacans engage: forestry, at high altitude, and hunter-gathering, wherever there is the prospect of gleaning something from the restricted environment.

Forestry

A very substantial part of highland Oaxaca is forested, with much of the *tierra fría* given over to pine and oak. Most Oaxacan communities, irrespective of altitude, have some communal woodland that can be exploited for *leña* (firewood) and construction timber, but it is only at high altitude that there are sufficient stands of timber for it to be considered a major exploitable resource. Virtually all this forest is located on *tierras comunales*. The experience of the Oaxacan forestry *ejidos* has been 'very variable, and on the whole not very successful' (Halhead 1984, 167), and much of the recent commercialization (cash trading) of the forest has hinged on the development of the Tuxtepec paper mill (FAPATUX: Fabricas de Papel Tuxtepec) in 1954.

In 1956, a presidential decree gave FAPATUX access to 250,000 hectares of temperate (pine-oak) and tropical forest in Oaxaca. The tropical forests have rarely been worked, and extraction of the temperate woods has been confined to the Sierra Juárez (65,000 ha.) and the southern Sierra Miahuatlan adjacent to Juquila (103,000 ha.). Misunderstandings and conflict punctuated relations between the *comunidades* and FAPATUX until the concession ran out (it was not renewed) in 1981 (Halhead 1984).

Initially, the area under concession in the Sierra Juárez involved twenty-two *comunidades*, but only eleven were active by the early 1970s. FAPATUX, faced with a shortage of timber for the paper mill, set out to improve relations with the communities by creating a medical service; upgrading working conditions; and constructing four sawmills, two of which were to be community ventures. Participation rose to sixty-four *comunidades* in 1976 and employment doubled to 3,500.

Community qualms focused on a number of social and economic issues. Social facilities did not improve to the degree expected. Roads were constructed to extract timber, not to connect villages. Wages were low and the work often dangerous. People felt that they had lost control over their environment and resources. Finally, the royalty set (the *derecho de monte*) was based on the value of pulp, whereas much of the wood was saw-timber or suitable for plywood. To compound the financial problem, 70 per cent of the *derecho de monte* was paid to the Fondo Nacional de Fomento Ejidal, and was essentially outside community control (Halhead 1984).

By the early 1980s, only thirty-two communities were still active in the scheme. A group calling itself La Organización en Defensa de los Recursos Naturales y Desarrollo Social de la Sierra Juárez (ODRENASIJ), with support from the major *municipios* in the area, argued that control and management of forestry should be in local hands (Halhead 1984). FAPATUX was boycotted, and court cases found in favour of the communities. Since the concession ran out in 1981, forestry in the Sierra Juárez has been essentially in community hands (Winder 1992), though community rivalries over continued cutting, admittedly at a reduced level, and the location of a bio-reserve have bedevilled sustainable forest management (Bray 1991).

Hunter-gathering and Herbalism

Oaxaca's forests have, of course, a wide variety of non-forestry purposes. They are cleared for cultivation, often with slash-and-burn techniques, provide pasturage for animals, and are used for hunting and gathering (Browner 1985*b*; Lipp 1971). The latter activity they share with other non-cultivated and cultivated landscapes. Oaxacan peasants have an encyclopaedic knowledge of edible animals, plants, and insects, as a visit to any major market-place reveals—fried grasshoppers (*chapulines*), in season, are a delicacy (Messer 1978). This information is an extension of their detailed knowledge of the landscape, as expressed in the *parajes*. In this way peasants have supplemented their diet, and built up a repertoire of traditional cures (Browner 1985*a* and *b*; Ortiz de Montellano and Browner 1985; Rubel and Gettelfinger-Krejci 1976). Oaxaca's peasants have their own definition and interpretation of illnesses, such as *susto* (literally fright). *Susto* implies imbalances between hot and cold circumstances (not temperature related), and cures require the intervention of a *curandero*, who alone has access to the appropriate folk (usually herbal) remedies (Rubel, O'Nell, and Collado-Ardón 1984).

Conclusion

This chapter is by no means an exhaustive account of farming and rural petty industry in Oaxaca. It has deliberately omitted new activities that have sprung

up in response to tourism and out-putting systems that sometimes bind communities together. And it has not explained in any detail how rural artisan activities have responded to modern technology, the opportunities represented by tourism, and the 'export' of certain *artesanias* to distant destinations, either in Mexico or abroad. These themes are taken up without more ado in the next chapter, which discusses the evolution of the peasant marketing system over the last fifty years; the commercial sale of agro-pastoral products; the production and exchange of a selected range of crafts; and the development of modern commercial activity in Oaxaca City.

4

Peasant Markets, Commercialization, and Urban Capitalism

The Changing Socio-Economic Context

Oaxaca's peasantries are not being destroyed by the inroads of capitalism—especially in remote mountain areas, though many communities are changing, some at a rapid rate. However, peasantries are becoming increasingly differentiated internally. This is either because the economic value of what they control has been altered by government investment, perhaps in the form of new roads, improved access to electricity, technology, or the market, or because they are influenced by improved education and health provision, once again largely state financed.

However, peasants in favourable agricultural niches in the Central Valleys are fully capable of conducting their own development by obeying market forces, as Waterbury attests in his detailed account of San Antonino over the period 1970 to 1998. Here over-pumping of groundwater for flower and vegetable production for the Oaxaca City market has reduced output, but producers have adapted by moving into dress embroidery, extending their trading connections to the tourist centres of the Pacific coast, and by out-migration (Waterbury 1989, 1999).

A measure of the changes that occurred in Oaxaca in the decade 1970–80, at the end of which oil wealth began, briefly, to lift the Mexican economy, is provide by the extension of roads of all kinds from 4,200 to 11,700 km., a near tripling of the network. However, travel to the Pacific through the Mixteca via Tlaxiaco, Putla, and Pinotepa, and through the Central Valleys to Puerto Ángel via Miahuatlan and Pochutla, became reliable only after the roads were properly surfaced in the early 1980s (Fig. 4.1). Prior to that, wet season travel was feasible only for heavy lorries and four-wheel-drives, and the main routes, excepting the Pan-American Highway, were often cut by landslides, despite continuous bulldozing.

Since the early 1990s, two new toll roads have been engineered across the state, following the alignments of the federal roads from Puebla to Oaxaca via the Cañada and the Mixteca Alta (Fig. 4.1). These roads run across

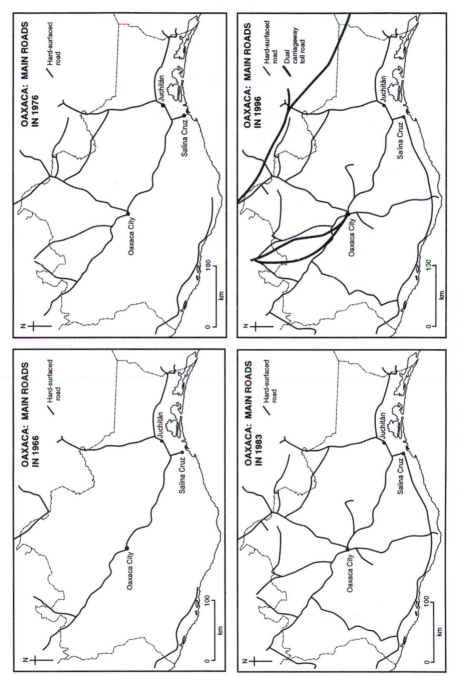

Fig. 4.1 Oaxaca: extensions to hard-surfaced roads, 1966–96

inhospitable country, and are empty for much of the time (since the toll fee is considerable by Mexican standards). However, they facilitate the government's drive to tap the tourist potential of Oaxaca City and the Pacific Coast, where a new resort was built at state expense in the late 1980s at Huatulco. The release of factors of production from their formerly circumscribed territorial bases, particularly through the capacity of paved highways to speed up the circulation of capital and commodities, has, within the last thirty years, changed those space–time relationships, which, in previous decades or centuries, had remained so immutable.

Although most Oaxacans still go to traditional healers or *curanderos* (or *supercuranderos*, who prescribe modern pharmaceuticals) when they are ill, formal medicine has been made accessible through state hospitals and health clinics. These facilities, like qualified doctors, who are mostly hi-technology specialists, are heavily concentrated in the urban settlements, especially Oaxaca City. None the less, the number of persons covered by the government's Seguro Social expanded almost four times to just under a quarter of a million between 1970 and 1980, while members of the state employers' social security scheme increased more than five times to 150,000 over the same period. In 1995, Oaxaca's basic healthcare centres numbered about 350, more than ten times the figure a decade earlier.

Similar changes have taken place in education. For example, the number of school children and students doubled to just under 900,000 between 1970 and 1980, the latter figure being similar to the entire Oaxaca population at the end of the Porfiriato. The federal government has also had a high-profile policy of electrification in recent years, often using community labour on Sunday mornings (the traditional *tequio*), to which all able-bodied men are expected to contribute. Nowadays electricity cables are strung through almost impassable mountains, so that some communities have more radios and televisions than flush water closets or taps with drinking water.

Oaxaca Valley 1980

Most of these changes are captured in a correlation analysis of 1980 census data for the Oaxaca Valley. The analysis is restricted to the population census (the agricultural census data were, allegedly, destroyed in the 1985 earthquake in Mexico City). The variables selected and manipulated numbered sixteen (Table 4.1), giving rise to three components in the linkage diagram, employment, levels of living, and demography. Five nodes were identified—agricultural employment (9 correlation loadings), workers (6), commercial employment (4), and unpaid workers (3) (Fig. 4.2).

The Oaxaca Valley emerged as increasingly urbanized, and most of the correlations with agriculture were negative. While the association between agriculture and services declined, agriculture's negative correlations with transforming (manufacturing) and commerce increased to -0.72 and -0.74,

Table 4.1 Oaxaca Valleys by *municipio*: Spearman rank correlation 1980

	1	2	3	4	5	6	7	8	9	10	11	12	13	14	15	16
1 Sex ratio[a]	1.00	-0.11	0.03	-0.22	0.08	0.20	-0.09	-0.13	-0.19	-0.11	-0.22	-0.08	0.20	-0.06	-0.13	0.03
2 Dependency ratio[b]	-0.11	1.00	-0.07	-0.08	-0.17	0.24	-0.31	-0.26	-0.23	-0.11	-0.17	-0.04	0.23	0.00	-0.18	0.24
3 Non-marital status[c]	0.03	-0.07	1.00	-0.03	0.06	0.05	-0.03	0.06	-0.09	-0.11	-0.06	0.13	-0.03	0.14	-0.08	0.10
4 Literacy ratio[d]	-0.22	-0.08	-0.03	1.00	-0.42	-0.66	0.43	0.38	0.55	0.49	0.60	0.00	-0.46	-0.35	0.62	0.19
5 Indigenous language speakers[e]	0.08	-0.17	-0.03	-0.42	1.00	0.27	-0.04	-0.10	-0.13	-0.24	-0.35	-0.09	0.33	0.11	-0.41	-0.11
6 Agricultural employment[f]	0.20	0.24	0.05	-0.66	0.27	1.00	-0.72	-0.56	-0.74	-0.49	-0.35	-0.09	0.70	0.36	-0.61	-0.15
7 Transforming employment[g]	-0.09	-0.31	-0.03	0.43	-0.04	-0.72	1.00	0.43	0.65	0.47	0.57	-0.02	-0.50	-0.23	0.52	0.06
8 Service employment[h]	-0.13	-0.26	0.06	0.38	-0.10	-0.56	0.43	1.00	0.44	0.31	0.64	0.08	-0.49	-0.30	0.37	0.12
9 Commercial employment[i]	-0.19	-0.23	-0.09	0.55	-0.13	-0.74	0.65	0.44	1.00	0.58	0.65	0.04	-0.58	-0.29	0.47	0.02
10 Co-operative workers[j]	-0.11	-0.11	-0.11	0.49	-0.24	-0.49	0.47	0.31	0.58	1.00	0.50	-0.09	-0.42	-0.29	0.29	0.04
11 Workers[k]	-0.22	-0.17	-0.06	0.60	-0.35	-0.35	0.57	0.64	0.65	0.50	1.00	0.12	-0.78	-0.41	0.58	0.15
12 Own account[l]	-0.08	-0.04	0.13	0.00	-0.09	-0.09	-0.02	0.08	0.04	-0.09	0.12	1.00	-0.27	-0.02	0.06	-0.02
13 Unpaid workers[m]	0.20	0.23	-0.03	-0.46	0.33	0.70	-0.50	-0.49	-0.58	-0.42	-0.78	-0.27	1.00	0.23	-0.49	-0.05
14 Dwelling with no water[n]	-0.06	0.00	0.14	-0.35	0.11	0.36	-0.23	-0.30	-0.29	-0.29	-0.41	-0.02	0.23	1.00	-0.20	-0.21
15 Electricity[o]	-0.13	-0.18	-0.08	0.62	-0.41	-0.61	0.52	0.37	0.47	0.29	0.58	0.06	-0.49	-0.20	1.00	-0.05
16 Protestant[p]	0.03	0.24	0.10	0.19	-0.11	-0.15	0.06	0.12	0.02	0.04	0.15	-0.02	-0.05	-0.21	-0.05	1.00

Notes:

[a] males as % of total population
[b] children under 15 + old people more than 65 ÷ adults 15-65
[c] those in free union ÷ those married
[d] % females > 10 years able to read and write ÷ % males > 10 years able to read and write
[e] % population aged > 5 years speaking indigenous language
[f] % population aged > 12 years economically active in agriculture
[g] % population aged > 12 years economically active in transforming industry
[h] % population aged > 12 years economically active in services
[i] % population aged > 12 years economically active in commerce
[j] % population aged > 12 years working in co-operatives
[k] % population aged > 12 years employed as workers
[l] % population aged > 12 years working on own account
[m] % population aged > 12 years working without pay
[n] % houses with no tap water supply
[o] % houses with electricity
[p] % population Protestant

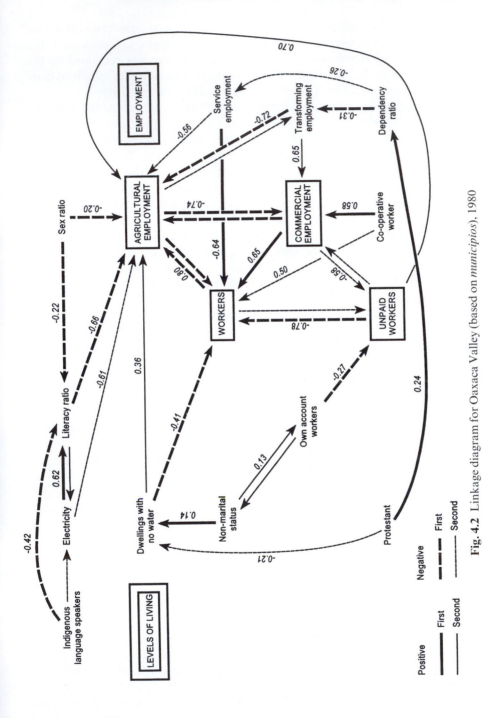

Fig. 4.2 Linkage diagram for Oaxaca Valley (based on *municipios*), 1980

respectively. By 1980, service employment had followed transforming (*artesanias*) into the periphery of the diagram, leaving workers and commerce as the touchstones of urbanization. Protestants and Indians, too, remained on the periphery of the linkage diagram; in the case of the Indians they remained marginal, and associated with female illiteracy and lack of electricity.

Comparing the census data for 1970 and 1980, 22 per cent of the variables common to both analyses for the Oaxaca Valley changed sign—those associated with the dependency ratio, non-marital unions, transforming, and services. But, taking the half-century from 1930 to 1980, 25 per cent of the variable pairings changed sign, notably those involving the sex ratio, dependency, non-marital unions, transforming, services, and commerce; neither agriculture nor Indian-language speakers recorded sign changes. Hence, urban economic activities created female majorities in Oaxaca City and the district towns. These same places also became characterized by high dependency ratios and marital unions. Indians remained impoverished and marginal throughout. Agriculture lacked the capacity to generate change in other variables, and it was still associated with unpaid labour (the essence of peasantry).

These statistical analyses give an impression of the socio-economic structure of the Oaxaca Valley, notably the increasing significance of urban commerce and employment in an overall context of agrarian stasis (Hernández Reyes 1994). Yet they provide no more than a backdrop to the rural–urban market interchanges that bind the rural areas into the urban network. To give a sense of the changing relationship between producer and consumer over time, taking into account the rapid growth of the Oaxaca population, the rotating peasant marketing system, which centres on Oaxaca City, is examined for three periods: the early 1940s, the mid-1960s, and the early 1990s. The production and commercialization of selected agro-pastoral products are then considered in detail, and compared to a range of handicrafts. Modern commercial exchanges outside the peasant market but centred in Oaxaca City are discussed. They reveal the existence of a modern commercial élite, with state-wide connections, that operates almost independently of peasantry.

Oaxaca's Markets in Space and Time

Many of Oaxaca's agro-pastoral and craft products can be traced, historically, to the colonial period. But few of the activities that now have the capacity for capital accumulation would have had this potential before the road system was improved or before the Revolution placed land resources in peasant hands. Many key commodities in capital accumulation are completely new (embroidery); others have been given new contexts (*mezcal*) by improved access to regional, national, and international markets. It is impossible, given space constraints, to trace marketing arrangements commodity by commodity over

time, but there are unique longitudinal data for the Oaxaca City market that enable its evolution over the last half-century to be depicted.

Oaxaca Markets in the Early 1940s

The first social-scientific account of the peasant market system which integrated settlements in the Oaxaca Valley and beyond in the early 1940s is provided by Malinowski and de la Fuente (Spanish edition 1957; English version edited Drucker-Brown 1982). Written from a functionalist standpoint, the book largely ignored the historical context—as well as the ongoing land reform, yet it provides an illuminating interpretation of a system where 'the function of the market is closely related to the hand-to-mouth existence of the poorest Indians'. They continued:

It is also related to the short-term budget of the majority of the inhabitants of the area, townsmen, villagers and mountain people alike. The regular flow of limited income from the sale of the producers' commodities and the small range of consumers' requirements combine to make the market in the Valley a well-adjusted mechanism for the satisfaction of most economic needs of the participants. (Malinowski and de la Fuente 1982, 68–9)

In many of the smaller towns there was 'a clear-cut distinction between the Westernized, indigent townsman and the peasant who may live beside him. There is a current Oaxaca expression defining the "civilized" people as *gente de razón* and the genuine indigenous group as *naturales*. . . . There is, moreover, a current expression in Oaxaca, which characterizes all the culturally indigenous Indians as *yopes*.' The peasants, though, resided 'predominantly in the many villages. . . . There is a high degree of uniformity in peasant housing and furniture, in domestic implements and clothes. The characteristic diet consists of coffee, chocolate or *atole* with tortillas in the morning, tortillas and occasionally meat or soup at midday; and in the evening a dish of black beans or soup with chillies and tortillas. Meat may be eaten once a week or more often, according to the wealth of the peasant. The poorer peasants may have a much plainer diet. Their clothes are more tattered or mended, and furniture is simpler. . . . Roughly speaking, people in the villages in the Valley live within a budget of between 25 centavos and 2 pesos a day per person' (1982, 125–6).

The interrelated notions of settlement hierarchy, market regions, nested functions, and weekly rotating markets were clearly understood by Malinowski and de la Fuente (1982, table 2, 105). 'The market system consists primarily of the big market place in Oaxaca, the capital, and of related dominant markets in Ocotlán, Tlacolula, Etla, Zimatlán, Zaachila, and Ejutla' (1982, 70); 'the centre of our system, Oaxaca, supplies its own inhabitants, numbering about 30,000. For this purpose there is not only the weekly large market on Saturdays, but daily markets in the main establishment and in three additional ones. As regards the hinterland, Oaxaca is important to all the adjacent

regions. We meet here the Indians from the northern Sierra Juárez, from the mountains of the Mixe, from the extensive ethnographic areas of the Mixtecas, and from the western ranges inhabited by a few Zapotec villages, but mostly by the Mixtec' (1982, 83). However, Oaxaca City did not monopolize the system. Ocotlán had control of its immediate neighbourhood, important because of its productivity in maize, vegetables, and as a centre for cattle. Through the commercial enterprise of some of its residents, 'many of the long-distance commercial journeys were undertaken from this centre' (1982, 84).

Tlacolula, Etla, and Ejutla, also, had considerable independence, but, as in Ocotlán, the days without markets in the district capitals, Oaxaca City excepted, were dead. The markets were also 'subject to a yearly cycle as regards intensity and specialization' (1982, 90), generated by agricultural activity and the weather. During the wet season, 'man, beast, ox-cart and motor car are often unable to move especially on the marshy grounds of Zaachila and Zimatlán. The only permanent roads run between Oaxaca and Ocotlán and from Oaxaca to Tlacolula and Mitla. The segment between Oaxaca and Etla is permanent, but inferior in quality, and at times cannot be used by bus' (1982, 90).

Malinowski and de la Fuente provided a detailed account of the Tlacolula, Ocotlán, Zaachila, Zimatlán, and Etla markets. Despite the great variety of goods and sellers, the market-places had a regular layout, so 'the fixity of configuration, the type of selling site, the class of transaction and the economic background of the vendor are all intimately related' (1982, 107). More importantly, they evaluated the role of middlemen, large buyers, and exporters in Oaxaca. 'These people scour the hostelries and attempt to purchase all the raw palm leaf, large quantities of maize, of perishable vegetables, of eggs or of charcoal in order to pool the produce and manipulate it on a large scale' (1982, 88). A few years later, similar monopolies were reported for the market at Tlaxiaco, where maize shortages from March to October drove up the price, and peasants had to sell their other produce cheaply to purchase this staple (Marroquín 1978, 208).

Exploitation could be even more direct in the Oaxaca market, and took the form of 'small-scale systematic exploitation and cheating of the less educated Indians by the various classes of middlemen, shopkeepers and even ordinary buyers and sellers. This cheating . . . may be plain petty thieving, *sub rosa*, of which the Mixe are especially afraid, and rightly so. Besides this are the differential handling of measures, cheating in quantity, in quality, in calculations and even in money. All this, once more, enters as an economic factor which affects certain transactions and not others' (Malinowski and de la Fuente 1982, 141).

Malinowski and de la Fuente contrasted peasant pottery production in Coyotepec and Atzompa with the more industrialized output of thrown and glazed ware manufactured in Oaxaca City. The latter supplied bowls, plates, and vases to the rural communities as well as modern articles for local and

national use and export to the USA (1982, 111–12). Another important section of their book analysed the network of intermediaries that linked Atzompa to the outside world and accounted for the doubling of product prices between Oaxaca City on the one hand and Puebla on the other (1982, 159). A third section described Mixtec palm hat weavers' abortive attempt to form co-operatives, purchase shaping equipment, and thus double the selling price of their products (1982, 160–1).

With regard to 'imported' goods, whether from other parts of Mexico or abroad, and Oaxacan products, Malinowski and de la Fuente agreed that the local goods characterized the peasant market, though English thread and foreign satins were present in addition to celluloid articles (1982, 134). In the middle-class orientated commercial establishments in Oaxaca City, however, 'we would find a great many articles not produced in the state of Oaxaca, or the republic of Mexico. Motor cars, sewing machines, gramophones and radios come principally from the USA. That country as well as Germany and, to a lesser extent, Great Britain and France, supply kerosene and gas lamps, electric torches and a whole range of articles connected with lighting, and heating and more elaborate cooking apparatus. Hardware pots and pans, very little used by the Indians and peasants, come principally from the USA and Germany. . . . We were impressed by the quantity of cheaper Japanese objects to be found in the region, excepting a few celluloid objects such as combs, mirrors and toys' (1982, 133–4).

Barter (*trueque*) was the standard form of exchange in Atzompa, where pottery was negotiated for a cash price, which was immediately converted into bread, cheese, cooked meat, sweetmeats, and fruit traded from Etla, Cuilapan, and Zaachila. Accounts are also given of *trueque* in Ocotlán (fruit for firewood and tortillas for *cal*—quicklime); but in these and other cases cited, barter took place 'on a firm monetary basis as regards the definition of value, although the transaction [was] principally carried out in goods' (1982, 152). Unfortunately, Malinowski died before he could quantify his results, and de la Fuente's career took him away to Mexico City. It was not for another generation that the Oaxaca market system would be systematically reinvestigated—by Beals and his graduate students from the University of California, Los Angeles.

Oaxaca's Markets in the Mid-1960s

By the mid-1960s several important contextual changes had occurred in Oaxaca. The Pan-American Highway reached Oaxaca City via Huajuapan in 1943, and the surfaced road ran right across the state to Tehuantepec by 1948. The population, which had been 1,192,800 in 1940, had increased to 1,727,300 in 1960, thus undermining the state's fragile capacity for feeding itself with maize. Out-migration to the cities, especially Mexico City, Puebla, and Oaxaca City, was gathering pace. Whereas Oaxaca City recorded barely 30,000 inhabitants in 1940, it had accelerated to 72,400 in 1960. All this had an enormous impact on the integration of the trading system, the volume of commodities exchanged, and the penetration of the market area by 'imported' factory-produced goods.

Beals's book refers from time to time to the market study of Malinowski and de la Fuente, citing the 1957 Spanish-language edition. It does not, however, construct a systematic comparison between the two pieces of research, which is unfortunate, since Beals had first visited the Benito Juárez market in central Oaxaca City in 1933, several years before Malinowski began his fieldwork. In general, it is true to say the two accounts are of a piece, though Beals's work involved a team of more than half a dozen postgraduate assistants, several of whom (notably Ronald Waterbury, 1968), wrote doctorates out of their contribution. Beals's book therefore contains much more detailed empirical evidence.

One of Beals's achievements was to classify the geographical and social contexts of commodity interchange in Oaxaca. Within the Oaxaca market area, exchange took place: between households and between households and stores; village to village, omitting the *plaza* (market-place); village to village via the market-place; inter-*plaza*; to and from the world outside. Trading in the market-place was in the hands of several actors. *Propios* (producer-vendors) sold their own goods to customers or intermediaries—both retailers and wholesalers. *Regatones* or *viajeros* (traders or travelling middlemen) travelled the markets and villages. *Locatarios* (fixed location traders or middlemen) were mostly based in the market towns. Storekeepers operated outside the peasant market, but sold to peasants as well as to townspeople. Finally, there were *ambulantes* (itinerant vendors), who sold on the streets, usually from stock obtained from a trader or storekeeper. Based on a census carried out in 1970, it was estimated that, in the farming and trading community of San Antonino, near Ocotlán, more than one-third of the inhabitants aged over 16, the vast majority of whom were women, were in market-place orientated occupations (Waterbury and Turkenik 1976).

Examining the linkages to which these various spatial transactions gave rise, Beals concluded that the Oaxaca marketing system covered the whole of the central and eastern parts of the state, involving most of the Zapotec-, Mixe-, and Huave-speaking areas. He calculated that the market system served about 741,000 people in 1960 and 900,000 in 1970—approximately half the population of Oaxaca. It contained four regional components or subsystems: the Valley, the Sierra Zapoteca, the Sierra Mixe, and the Isthmus (Fig. 4.3), though Chiñas has suggested that the latter was separate but linked (1976, 171). Within each subsystem, the primary market day rotated (Beals in Cook and Diskin 1976, 33–4).

Outside the Oaxaca market system there were others. On the Costa Chica, there were daily markets attended by black and *mestizo* marketeers (Eder 1976, 78). In the Mixteca, Putla, Tlaxiaco (Marroquín 1978), and Nochistlan (Warner 1976) were important, the latter having a market area that reached

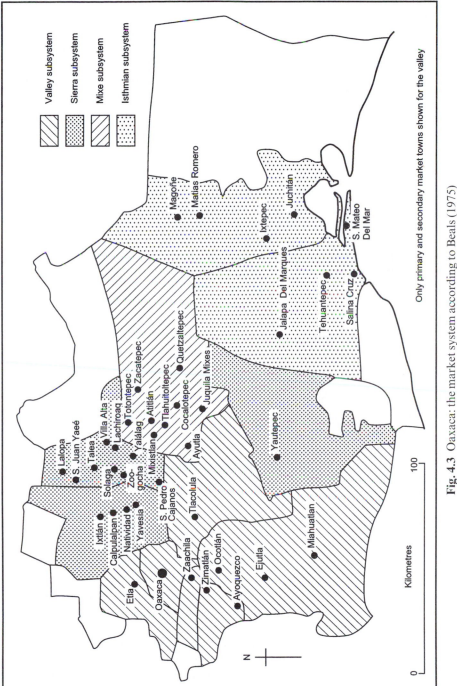

Fig. 4.3 Oaxaca: the market system according to Beals (1975)

towards the Etla Valley. Within each of these systems there was considerable village specialization by commodity, and some interchange with the Oaxaca system, for example, of cattle between the Costa Chica and Oaxaca City.

The Oaxaca Valley subsystem was divided into a hierarchy of market (central) places containing three ranks, at the apex of which was Oaxaca City. This Valley hierarchy was similar to the more complex one devised by Malinowski and de la Fuente, which (correctly) picked out Tlacolula and Ocotlán, for their commercial significance, from the rest of the district capitals (Fig. 4.3). The *sierra* subsystem was divided culturally and geographically into Zapotec and Mixe components, the latter linked into the Valley via Mitla—to which Malinowski and de la Fuente also alluded (1982).

Only seven out of seventeen basic food necessities were produced in every village in the Valley of Oaxaca—maize, beans, squash, greens, beef, pork, and herbs; three basic items came from other subsystems; and seven were supplemented from outside the system altogether (Beals 1975, 110). To obtain these items—and modern consumer goods—villagers had to work for cash or to trade. Beals calculated that, theoretically, peasants had eleven alternatives for disposing of their products, though not every one was available to each commodity.

Intermediaries were vital to this complex pattern of exchange, and Beals particularly underlined the importance of inter-*plaza* traders. 'Before the introduction of modern transportation it was possible for inter*plaza* traders in the Valley to visit a different *plaza* every day. Both the timing of the weekly *plazas* and the distances between them are such that, by traveling at night, a succession of *plazas* could be visited. . . . Even with modern transport, however, most inter*plaza* traders today find this too arduous. Few visit more than 5 *plazas* a week; the majority visit three or four' (1975, 149). Inter-*plaza* traders in the Valley tended to live in and work from Oaxaca City, and confined their circuits to that subsystem. Some, however, visited the markets at Nochixtlan and Tlaxiaco in the Mixteca Alta, and *sierra* traders may have used Tlacolula to buy goods.

If improved roads led to the speeding up of the circulation of retail goods, they had an even more dramatic impact on wholesaling. Malinowski and de la Fuente did not mention wholesalers of fruit and vegetables, but at the time of Beals's study, four produce wholesalers did the bulk of the business, though there were about twenty smaller dealers (1975). Most of these wholesalers were from Puebla and were previously drivers of their own trucks. With seasonal exceptions, such as the trade in watermelons, wholesalers concentrated on 'imported' goods—mostly from Mexico City markets or direct from growers of oranges in San Luis Potosí or of pineapples in Loma Bonita. Wholesalers from the Isthmus and Chiapas and inter-*plaza* traders in the Isthmus and the Valley were their major customers, followed by owners of *puestos* (stalls) in the *mercado* (market) Benito Juárez. Beals estimated that wholesalers operated with a 20 per cent mark-up above their basic cost price and would seldom go

below 5 per cent. But the general impression he gives is of fair transactions between buyer and seller at all levels of activity—except those involving moneylending, where monthly rates of interest of 5 to 10 per cent were common. Beals concluded that 'only rarely does the Oaxaca peasant feel he is exploited' (1975, 267).

Oaxaca City's market, located at the hub of the system in the *tierra templada*, where tropical and high altitude products could be easily concentrated, remained in the buildings (Benito Juárez and 20 de Noviembre) to which it had been removed from the *zócalo* (main square) towards the end of the nineteenth century. Since Beals visited the market in the early 1930s, permanent stalls had been constructed in Benito Juárez, which was given over to agricultural produce, fish, meat, and clothing, while 20 de Noviembre specialized in bread, chocolate, pottery, and food stalls (Waterbury 1970). The Saturday market spilled out on to the streets and footpaths surrounding twenty blocks adjacent to the covered market (Pl. 4.1). This Saturday emporium attracted 2,000 street vendors and 30,000 buyers according to a census Waterbury conducted in 1964–5. His plan (reproduced in Beals 1975, 124–5) is the sole extant evidence for the layout of that market, with its fine-grained pattern of segregation by commodity (Pl. 4.2).

One of the outstanding changes to take place after Malinowski and de la Fuente's work was the decline in barter. Beals's study recorded that barter between peasants and shopkeepers was widespread, and still commonplace

Pl. 4.1 Oaxaca City market: Saturday stalls in the street, 1966

Pl. 4.2　Oaxaca City market: Saturday street market, 1978

between peddlers and potters in Atzompa; in each case cash equivalence was established. But commenting specifically on what he interpreted as the reduced incidence of barter, Beals observed, 'it is also possible that Malinowski, with his early experience in nonmonetary exchange systems, made a special effort to find examples of barter, thereby exaggerating their relative frequency' (1975, 197).

Examining the fees paid by stall-holders, Beals calculated that between 1938 and 1966 the annual total income of the Oaxaca City Market Administration increased almost eleven times. The data showed the importance of Saturday compared to the daily *mercado*, and illustrated seasonal variations in activity associated with the agricultural cycle and the *fiesta* calendar. Beals argued that, when increased fees (through inflation) and population growth had been discounted, there were clear signs of 'an increased rate or level of economic activity' (1975, 242). This led him to his major conclusion: 'the data presented suggest that the traditional peasant economy not only is capitalistic but that its marketing system offers perhaps a much closer approximation to a "perfect" market situation than does the modern economy' (1975, 269).

Why, then, had so 'few peasants . . . made the transition into the modern sector of the economy' (Beals 1975, 272)? Beals argued cogently, that:

the continuing small scale of most peasant economic activities in Oaxaca cannot be attributed solely to the difficulty of accumulating capital. The explanation for it lies in other characteristics of the marketing system. Of these, perhaps the most important is

the relative stability of the amount of the more important peasant-produced goods absorbed in the market, the relatively small amounts of capital required for most productive and trading activities, and the existence of a large number of peasant or peasantlike competitors satisfied with a relatively low standard of living. (1975, 271)

Oaxaca City Market in 1990

The role of the federal state as a modernizing/urbanizing and land-redistributing agent accelerated greatly in the 1970s and 1980s, and not only reconstructed Oaxaca's space, but facilitated or intensified peasant differentiation in rural areas and encouraged capital accumulation in the towns. A major consequence was that, seventy years after the Revolution ended, Oaxaca City was being transformed from 'colonial jewel' into a minor metropolis with just over 300,000 inhabitants. At all spatial scales, including those involving urban–rural distinctions, socio-economic processes were giving rise to new patterns of social differentiation.

Between 1970 and 1990, the population of Oaxaca state had increased by 50 per cent. Hard surfaced roads had been built across the Sierra Zapoteca and down to the Pacific Coast, and a major beach resort had been constructed at Huatulco. The contribution of tourism to the economy of the state remained constant at just under 20 per cent. So an intensification of the processes identified when comparing the market system in 1990 with that in 1940 and 1965 might be expected. This has, indeed, been the case. The big district markets at Tlacolula and Ocotlán have maintained their vitality, though there have been minor adjustments in their layout and content; and despite predictions to the contrary, the new Oaxaca City market, opened in 1978, has continued to develop. It is now as crowded and bulging on Saturdays as was the downtown market twenty years ago, and its hinterland includes up to 1.5 million people.

After years of pressure from city-centre shopkeepers and prevarication on the part of the factionalized market-sellers' union, the Oaxaca peasant market was moved in 1978 to a purpose-built site, which had been ready for some years, on the Periferico (ring road) beside the recently opened second-class bus station. The Benito Juárez and 20 de Noviembre markets remained to service the city centre—and a suburban produce market was eventually developed for the inhabitants of the rapidly expanding Colonia Reforma to the north of the Pan-American Highway. The disappearance of the Saturday peasant market from the streets of downtown Oaxaca left the city centre to the 'respectable' urban classes—as the shopkeepers wanted. As a consequence, the city now has two major daily markets in Benito Júarez and the Centro de Abastos, and the peasant market takes place at the latter, on a specially laid out space—*tianguis* (market) 1 and 2—adjacent to the permanent stalls (Pls. 4.3 and 4.4).

Oaxaca City's Mercado de Abastos has been laid out so that the permanent, daily market, with separate sections for groceries (often with refrigeration facilities), dry goods, bread, crafts and cafes, is located at the heart of the

Pl. 4.3 Oaxaca City market: pottery section of new Mercado de Abastos, 1996

Pl. 4.4 Oaxaca City market: sugar skulls for sale for the Days of the Dead; Mercado de Abastos, 1978

development, opposite the bus station. Adjacent to it are *tianguis* 1 and 2, plus a line of shops and stores, and sections given over to fruit warehouses and wholesaling premises. The permanent market largely reproduces the content and zoning of the *mercados* Benito Juárez and 20 de Noviembre.

A survey carried out in the Centro de Abastos in August 1990 showed that more than 80 per cent of weekday vendors were residents of Oaxaca City and only 27 per cent produced the goods they sold. Of the items purchased, 70 per cent were obtained from wholesalers, 68 per cent of whom 'imported' them from outside the Oaxaca market system (Crumpton 1991). The Centro de Abastos, therefore, has been set up to serve the burgeoning city, and now substantially relies on food imports—not only of maize. Today's market also contains manufactured items not mentioned by Beals—jewellery, watches, a variety of electrical goods, and ready-made clothing.

Market statistics collected in 1990 suggest that there was a total of 2,670 stall-holders who had paid for their places in the Centro de Abastos; on Thursday, 2 August, the number of stall-owners present was 1,180, and on the following Saturday, 4,435 (Crumpton 1991). The first figure is consistent with the ebb and flow of the weekly market, but the second suggests that more than 1,700 Saturday sellers were illegal—probably peasant *propios*, and that the total number of Saturday sellers was at that time more than twice that recorded in 1965. The new Oaxaca market has two dimensions: one highly commercial and orientated to urban consumption; the other less commercial and an expression of the peasants' continuing need to exchange. This is borne out by the commodities in which the non-regulated sellers specialized—all peasant produce: fruit, beans, garlic, onions, tomatoes, chillis, herbs, vegetables, coffee, maize, lime, flowers, fish and shrimps, *tortillas*, bread and potatoes, plus *artesanías*—pottery, fibre products, hats and sandals, baskets and mats, and *metates*. Other illegal vendors specialized in 'modern' goods, such as jewellery, patent medicines, electrical goods, and records.

Such was the pressure on space created by the illegal sellers that by 1993 they had been banned from the market area of the Centro de Abastos, and the Saturday unregulated 'peasant market' was largely confined to the peripheral roads. Hence, the shape of the market is ever changing, though the component parts remain very stable. In July 1996, the peripheral road was crammed with vegetable and salad sellers; there were no *ambulantes* in the regulated market.

Commercialization of Agricultural Products

It is impossible to review the process of commercialization of all the major agro-pastoral products of Oaxaca. Selection is essential, and the products chosen for detailed consideration are significant in Oaxaca either for their volume or value. Maize, as has been seen, is the rural staple that is supposed to be eaten at home but is sold; coffee has local, national, and international markets; and

mezcal is a typically Oaxacan alcoholic beverage that has an expanding national and international clientele.

Maize

The first detailed account of Oaxacan maize transactions appears in Malinowski and de la Fuente's 1940–1 study of the Oaxaca market system. In this they discussed the case of a peasant who had brought 5 to 10 *almudes* (1 *almud* was equivalent to 5 litres) to sell in the market, hoping to realize 2 to 4 pesos. 'He takes out from his stock of corn an amount calculated to cover his weekly budget. In maize he has a staple commodity which is always negotiable and which he produces, if he is a typical, average peasant, in a quantity to cover all his needs all the year round' (Malinowski and de la Fuente 1982, 177–8).

Owing to the differential production of the staple grain in the Valley, some districts were richer in maize in certain seasons, while in others the supply would be deficient (Malinowski and de la Fuente 1982, 179). Thus, at times, even peasants would be purchasing maize in the markets. Most buyers were typified as 'Indians from the mountains', 'the industrial districts of the Mixteca', 'urban populations', and 'those half-peasants, half-artisans who, like the sarape makers of Teotitlán or Santo Domingo del Valle live mostly by their industries' (1982, 179). There were semi-permanent regional variations in price. Under normal conditions in mid-August, the cheapest price, that of 43 centavos, obtained in Ocotlán. In Etla and Oaxaca the price at the same time was 45 centavos per *almud* for the best product, 50 centavos at Ejutla and Tlacolula, and 55 at Miahuatlan. In a normal year this degree of regional price variation would occur whatever the level of prices. It would only change in an especially wet season (Malinowski and de la Fuente 1982, 180).

Malinowski and de la Fuente dealt specifically with the activities of middle-men and *acaparadores* (wholesale buyers) in the maize market. 'These purchase according to their own financial capacity directly from the producers, always paying a substantially lower price than would be paid elsewhere, and at times cheating' (1982, 179). However, they were uncertain how far the activities of a few larger capitalists in cornering and exporting the grain actually affected the retail price. 'We would have to study the manipulations of the wealthier mill owners, who were mostly of Spanish extraction. We would also need to observe the exporters and importers of maize, the various agents and the "regulating commission", which is a semi-official board, somewhat influenced by the interests of the larger merchants' (1982, 179).

Maize, according to Malinowski and de la Fuente, was the controlling factor in the marketing system. But by the time that Beals's Oaxaca market study was carried out in the mid-1960s, this situation had changed, 'modern communications permitting economical import or export of maize interregionally as well as its freer movement within the region' (Beals 1975, 57). Moreover, a system of government warehouses had been established in the meanwhile, with

minimum buying and maximum selling prices fixed annually from 1957 to 1973, though guaranteed prices were still being set by the government into the 1990s. The differences between buying and selling prices were essential to cover the operating costs of CONASUPO (Compañia Nacional de Subsistencias Populares), though the whole system was geared to a pro-urban, cheap food policy. But, as Beals remarked, even twenty-five years ago, price controls were not complete, since *criollo* maize fetched more than imported hybrids, largely because of its superior taste.

Beals argued that maize and its price no longer dominated the Oaxaca market system, yet it still played an important part because 'a variable amount . . . must be imported annually from elsewhere in Mexico to meet basic subsistence and livestock feed requirements' (1975, 57). This was largely because of population growth, since the area under maize doubled between the early 1940s and the late 1960s, and production increased rather more sharply (Sorroza Polo no date). Reporting on circumstances obtaining in the 1960s, Beals concluded that only two out of forty-three villages in the *sierra* ex-districts of Villa Alta and Ixtlán regularly produced a maize surplus, while ten more did so occasionally. Twenty tons of maize per month were being imported by Mitla merchants and truckers from the Isthmus and Chiapas alone, some of which was resold in the Mixe region. In the Oaxaca Valley probably no more than 25 per cent of villages produced a surplus in the best years (Beals 1975, 57–8).

At the village and household level, conditions were very similar to those described a generation before. Even villages with maize surpluses contained households with deficits. Households with or without maize surpluses often had to sell maize to pay off debts and meet household emergencies. Sellers at one season would become purchasers at a later date; surplus producers who stored their crop at home as a security against future deficits would find them eroded by insect and rodent damage. These findings, though more aggregate and optimistic, are essentially of a piece with those of Cook and Binford (1990).

Estimating household maize consumption for a family of four, Beals arrived at the figure of 730 kilograms per annum, and he believed that even the more affluent would not exceed 950 kilos (1975, 93). Using 1,000 kilos as their yardstick when collecting data in 1979, Cook and Binford drew attention to the 223 households in their sample of 1,008 drawn from the Oaxaca Valley that cultivated between 0.1 and 1.0 hectare and lacked both an ox team and ox cart. These households occupied the largest landed category in the survey, but produced a median of only 100 kilos of maize in 1979, or 10 per cent of their subsistence requirements. Another 243 households were described as landless and avoided total dependence on the maize market only by renting or sharecropping land, though their capacity to farm independently was severely restricted by a lack of animal-powered equipment (Cook and Binford 1990, 44–5, and table 2).

Generalizing across Cook and Binford's more detailed quasi-class categories, and focusing solely on the landed households, it can be shown that the

mean maize harvest in 1979 was 477 kilos, while for peasants it was 598 kilos and for peasant-artisans 435 kilos. These categories of households had to buy corn (including imports of subsidized maize from the USA) for a median of six, five, and seven months, respectively. Similar figures have been advanced for Yaitepec in the Sierra Madre del Sur (Greenberg 1981, 141–2). Using the figure of 672 kg. as the yield of maize per acre (the 1960 agricultural census figure for holdings of less than 5 ha.), and a per capita consumption figure of 164 kg. per annum, 0.24 hectare of land would be needed per person. But as only 0.1 hectare was planted per person, the deficit was 50 per cent, or 97 kilos of corn per capita. At prices prevailing in 1973, this would have cost 194 pesos, and for a family of five without other resources would have taken between 65 and 85 days' labour at a wage of 12 pesos a day with lunch or 15 pesos a day without *comida*. Similar figures, also for the Chinantec of the Sierra Madre del Sur, have been estimated by Bartolomé and Barabas (1982, 189), showing a maize deficit of about 50 per cent when comparing consumption with production

The case of maize is interesting and important because it shows how the impact of population increase (with shortening of the fallow period leading to reduced yields by 80–90 per cent: Hernández Díaz 1992*a*, 69) on a restricted resource base has undermined subsistence. Oaxaca ought to be able to support more than the same population that lived there in pre-colonial times, namely between 750,000 and 1.5 million. The latter figure is slightly above the number of inhabitants recorded in the 1940 census, at the time at which Malinowski and de la Fuente were implying that maize subsistence was achieved. The area under maize has contracted with out-migration since 1980 (and the trend for beans is even more marked) (Sorroza Polo no date). Without improved communications and maize imports from the USA, food shortages and starvation would ensue among the 82 per cent of the Oaxcan population who lack 4 hectares of arable land (Schejtman 1983, quoted Ríos Vázquez 1992, 29). The inability of the Oaxacan peasant family to feed itself is also associated with the development of *artesanias* as an adjunct of household agricultural activities— largely because of the development of international tourism; it is also linked to endemic migration of circular and more permanent kinds, all these factors being intertwined.

Coffee

The introduction and development of coffee in the Sierra Juárez demonstrates the complex interlocking changes that have taken place in the mountains in recent decades (Young 1976). Here, in the 1930s, most villages were to a considerable degree self-sufficient in basic foodstuffs, largely because of the small weekly market-places that integrated the two vertical climatic zones—the *tierra fría* with wheat and potatoes, and the *tierra templada* with beans and sugar. There was also village specialization in *artesanias*: some villages produced ixtle fibre products, others pottery, yet others leather goods and wooden

saddles. The local economy was based on barter, and coffee, *ocote* (pitch-pine), and salt served as the media of exchange.

Peasants have cultivated coffee on a limited scale since the 1880s, when it was bartered for simple manufactured goods brought in by traders. Generally, producers handled the marketing of their coffee themselves, and even those who specialized in coffee buying did so on a small scale and were also peasant-producers. In the mid-1930s, however, a new wholesale coffee buyer—a Spaniard—entered the area, offering cash advances and credit for the purchase of manufactured goods to muleteers who would re-sell them in the *serrano* markets. The muleteers were also engaged to carry his raw coffee beans down to his warehouses in the Central Valleys—a week's journey there and back.

Between 1938 and 1954 coffee prices rose steadily—the world market price increased by twenty-two times—and more and more peasants who could do so turned to coffee. Land was taken out of staple crops, and communal land was unofficially alienated. Coffee producers became more and more reliant on cash transactions, and in the *tierra templada* maize output was expanded to meet the demands of the coffee cultivators. Families without access to land for coffee planting became day labourers; bartering declined—and *ocote* and salt lost their convertibility, as the cash nexus was installed.

After the end of the Second World War, coffee prices accelerated and producers were able to command a range of manufactured consumer goods—domestic articles, ready-made clothes, foodstuffs, and drinks. These not only undercut or made redundant traditional *artesanias*, but also swamped the transport system based on mule trains. Local merchants and their modernizing allies, the increasing number of primary school teachers, lobbied the government for improved roads, which were constructed with local *tequio* (obligatory) labour. Coffee traders moved into truck purchase, often using deposits provided by the wholesalers (now solely buyers), thus displacing the muleteers after 1950. A single truck replaced 33 mules or 80 donkeys, 8 to 18 men, and cut the round trip to Oaxaca from 7 to 3 days using only 3 or 4 men (Young 1976).

In the mid-1950s, however, coffee prices fell sharply. By this time, inter-zonal exchanges had largely given way to regional integration into the national economy, as more and more traditional products—for example, those associated with muleteers—waned, and were replaced by imported food (including maize) and manufactured goods. Some coffee farmers tried to expand their holdings by buying up adjacent plots and reverting to family labour; but many peasants, especially the young women, lacking access to income-generating activities, started to emigrate.

The history of coffee in the Sierra Juárez shows how the commercial development of one export crop meshed with regional changes in transport to destroy the small-scale integration of the inter-zonal economy and to integrate the area into the national economy—but as an essentially subordinate,

peripheral component (Young 1976). Modernization has occurred, but at the expense of greater class differentiation and the transformation of the *sierra* into a reservoir of surplus labour (created by the decay in crafts on the one hand and population increase on the other), waiting for migration and marginal urbanization.

Similar events have occurred in the coffee-growing areas of the Mixteca and the Sierra Madre del Sur, but in each case exploitation of Indians by *mestizos* would be added (perhaps the ethnic dimension in the Sierra Juárez was deliberately omitted in Young's essentially Marxist analysis). Merchants' payments to Triqui coffee growers in the Mixteca Baja south of Putla de Guerrero have been underpriced by local standards and notoriously so when compared to international market prices (García Alcaraz 1973).

In the case of the southern *sierra*, 19,000 hectares of *tierras comunales* in one particular Chatino *municipio* were at risk of alienation, under the protection of a local *cacique* (self-appointed leader or boss), by powerful residents intent on making fortunes out of the late 1950s coffee boom. Illegal private land acquisitions were followed by extensive coffee planting in the 1960s and 1970s, capital accumulation, increased class differentiation and conflict, involving complex chains of vengeance which ran on into the late 1970s (Hernández Díaz 1987).

Mezcal

The last agro-pastoral product to be discussed in detail is *mezcal*, which is distilled from the *maguey* plant. This agave thrives on the drought-ridden piedmont in the Central Valleys, in districts such as Tlacolula, Etla, Ocotlán, Ejutla, and Miahuatlan, in Yautepec, in the drought-ridden area to the east of Tlacolula, and in Nochixtlan, in the Mixteca Alta. An estimate puts the number of families that depend economically on this plant at 25,000 (Sánchez López 1989, 8), but this included intermediaries as well as those who work with the *ixtle* fibre. There is a strong association between the *maguey* plant, which is cultivated by 19,000 households, the Zapotec-speaking population (more than 80 per cent of Oaxaca *mezcal* comes from the district of Tlacolula), illiteracy, and the persistence of very low levels of living. All these factors are exacerbated by the aridity of the environment.

There are 700 *palenques* (small distilleries) producing *mezcal* in Oaxaca, of which just over 500 are registered. So labour intensive is the fabrication, that 3,000 workers are directly engaged in the complex operations involved in cooking the *piña*, grinding the cured head, fermenting the fibrous sludge, and distilling the (pure *maguey*) alcohol (Sánchez López 1989). Output now runs at about 12 million litres per annum, of which the *municipio* of Santiago Matatlán in Tlacolula, with 161 *palenques*, accounts for half (Pl. 4.5).

A great variety of *magueys* grow in the wild and under cultivation in Oaxaca, but of increasing significance is *espadín* (*Angustifolia Haw*), which is carefully

Pl. 4.5 *Mezcal* distillery, Matatlán, 1996

propagated because of the high sucrose content of its *piña* and the fibrous quality of its spines. It is therefore ideal for the manufacture of both *mezcal* and
ixtle. Approximately 10,000 hectares are under cultivated *magueys* in Oaxaca.
They may be planted at 2 metre intervals to give a density of 2,000–2,500 plants
per hectare, or sown in lines at half that density and inter-cropped with maize,
beans, and squash. Sometimes *magueys* are distributed in small irregular
colonies, usually on steep and arid slopes. At Matatlán, the slopes are often
contoured into deep steps, with *magueys* and other crops on alternate treads.
A major problem for *maguey* cultivators is that the plant takes between six and
eight years for it to produce its *quiote* (flower), which is cut to force maturation
during the following year. It requires considerable skill to manage peasant
budgets on this time scale, and many have to sell their crop at a reduced price
before it is mature.

Most Oaxacan *mezcal* is produced using traditional artisanal methods and
implements, modified here and there to incorporate technological innovations. For example, clay stills have mostly given way to copper since the 1930s,
and breaking up the cooked *piña* is much more likely to be done by animal
power using a grindstone (*molino chileno*) than by hand—especially in
Matatlán (Díaz Montes 1982). As the industry has gradually modernized, the
work has become less family based and more dependent on wage labour. One
of the most specialized and time-consuming tasks involves the construction of
the *horno* (oven). An open pit is filled with wood and firestones and then covered with layers of *piña*, bagasse, *petates*, and earth. Cooking to release the

sugars from the *piñas* is a skilled job, and it takes upwards of three days before the pit can be reopened.

Mezcaleros are small-scale cultivators with agricultural holdings of less than 2 hectares; in Matatlán, they are mostly *ejidatarios*. Introduction of new technology and the increasing use of family members to oversee recruited labour and marketing has 'industrialized' the social relations of production. Nevertheless, the time-honoured system of sharecropping has also been adapted by peasants with capital, who establish new *palenques* managed by *medieros* (sharecroppers) on a commission basis. There is also an incipient hierarchy of wealth in Matatlán: 11 per cent of households had two or more stills, and 2 per cent processed fifteen loads of *maguey* per month, against three to six loads recorded by 84 per cent of households (Díaz Montes 1982, 75).

Three levels of producers have been identified. Household producers (including *medieros*, or share-producers) pay for their still on credit, buy their *maguey* on credit, and sell their *mezcal* cheaply to merchants who make them cash advances. Domestic units with a little capital use family and paid labour, consume about six loads of *maguey* per month and sell to an intermediary, while marketing some of their own produce. Large-scale *mezcaleros* with two or more stills administer their business and market their produce, often in their own *expendios* in Matatlán or elsewhere. Despite these internal differences, producers have organized the Unión de Productores de Mezcal de Matatlán and the Unión de Productores de Mezcal del Valle de Tlacolula. They collaborate to pursue their interests on issues such as government taxes and access to national and international markets.

There are two circuits of *mezcal* distribution. The first is in the hands of local merchants who are also producers. They go around the *palenques* twice a week, and, when they have collected 1,500 to 2,000 litres, sell it either to an urban merchant or directly to small shops or booths. More highly capitalized merchants may pay in advance and sell on credit. The mark-up associated with these transactions can be of the order of 50 per cent, and the whole operation is often shrouded in secrecy. This is because federal law requires alcoholic beverages to reach the customer in bottles of less than 5 litres and with the appropriate label. But there are insufficient bottling plants to cope with output, so merchants generally bribe inspectors, evade federal tax, distribute in Mexico in bulk, and pay only the nominal state tax.

Vendors who own general stores or *expendios de mezcal* in the smaller towns, notably Tlacolula, or Oaxaca City, comprise the second circuit. Some shopkeepers and merchants in Tlacolula and Oaxaca bottle *mezcal*, adding honey, colouring, or a worm (*gusano de maguey*). Most *mezcal* is retailed in unlabelled bottles, a clear indication that it, too, is free of federal tax. In recent years, however, *mezcal* has been legally defined. It is increasingly marketed in appropriate litre bottles, such as those of the firm Mezcal Benevá.

The *mezcal* industry runs the gamut from peasant–artisan production to the manufacturer–merchant type. One has evolved from the other, and may

regress or fail—the modern plant at San Augustín de las Juntas, just south of Oaxaca City, which was set up in 1972, went out of operation by the late 1980s. Yet it is the larger enterprises that are able to capture the greater part of the value added by cutting out middlemen. *Mezcal* from Etla, Miahuatlan, Sola de Vega, and Nochixtlan is drunk in the household in which it is produced or is sold locally for *fiestas*. The bulk of marketed *mezcal* comes from Yautepec and Tlacolula, Matatlán being the source of most national and international consumption. About half the production never leaves the state of Oaxaca; almost another 40 per cent is consumed in Mexico; and 10 per cent enters the international market, principally the USA and France, through bottling firms such as Mezcales Monte Alban.

Let us summarize. Maize is a peasant subsistence crop that can be, and usually is, marketed, even when production is below household consumption requirements. Paradoxically, Oaxaca, though a peasant state, is incapable of meeting its own requirements. But maize is one of the few crops that lacks exploitative connotations, largely because of government intervention in the market price of this vital staple—though there are large and small or even landless peasants. Coffee is essentially a cash crop, and the chains of commercialization associated with it give rise to local class differentiation, *caciquismo*, and exploitation. The manufacture of *mezcal* from *maguey* is the most capitalized of transformations discussed, and sometimes involves factories employing labour.

In each case the initial commodity is the product of small-scale, poorly capitalized farmers, who are identifiable as peasants or had their recent origins in the peasantry. But in the process of commodity transformation, peasant techniques may be replaced and new social relations of production begin to emerge. This is most true of *mezcal*. Where *mezcal* and coffee have similarities is in the hierarchical system of marketing, and the scope that it provides for mark-ups and for wholesaler retailing.

Commercialization of *Artesanias*

Peasant–artisan transformation of goods, at one degree removed, or totally separated, from the cycle of cultivation, as reflected in maize, coffee, and *maguey*, is now the focus of attention. Developments in weaving and embroidery are investigated, and an attempt is made to focus on specific communities, recent innovations, and products that embody heritage values (García Canclini 1993).

Weaving Wool

By far the best-known artisan village in Oaxaca is Teotitlán del Valle, located in the Tlacolula arm of the Central Valleys, and famous for its woven woollen

goods, including ponchos, *serapes*, bedspreads, and rugs. This industry has developed in tandem with weaving activities in the neighbouring community of Santa Ana, which is largely subordinate to it. In Teotitlán, more factory-made yarn (80 per cent wool content plus acrylic) is woven than hand-spun; the latter is largely home produced, the women taking two or three weeks to spin what a man can weave in a week. Hand-spun yarn is usually targeted at a specific weaving task, for which natural dyes such as cochineal may be earmarked (Cook and Binford 1990).

Almost half the households in Teotitlán are landless, which no doubt accounts for the village's long association with weaving. In addition, the proportion of households engaged as full-time farmers declined from 60 per cent in 1930 to 54 per cent in 1960 and 10 per cent in 1986. Crucial to the concentration on weaving was male migration to the USA in the 1950s and 1960s, followed, after their return, by investment in looms and raw wool. The intensification of weaving production was accompanied by an increased use of ethnic motifs. As Stephen notes, 'the Zapotecs of Teotilán have created their own locally defined ethnic identity in opposition to, *and* incorporating elements of, the commoditized Indian identity promoted first by the revolutionary Mexican state and later by U.S. and Mexican textile entrepreneurs' (Stephen 1991, 14). She continues: 'the brand of ethnic identity that merchants use to try to maintain an upper hand in the negotiating process with U.S. importers tends to project a vision of a kin-based community producing traditional crafts tied to a glorious past' (Stephen 1991, 252).

When local demand for woven goods in the Oaxaca City and Tlacolula markets declined in the face of competition from factory-produced items, merchants in Teotitlán switched their sales to the Mexican and US markets, portraying their goods as traditional ethnic blankets. The number of merchants increased five times between 1950 and 1985, and the class distinction between them and weavers (now female as well as male) became marked. Class relations, however, were mediated through ties of kinship and fictive kinship (*compadrazgo*), though the change involved a shift from mercantile to commercial capitalism (Stephen 1991).

By the late 1980s, in Teotitlán, out of just over 1,000 households, 10 per cent could be regarded as merchant households. Ten were large merchants, with operations in Santa Ana and San Miguel as well; thirty were medium merchants; and seventy were small merchants who purchased only a limited number of weavings and sold their own production in the local Teotitlán market. In addition, four types of weaver were recognized; household workshops consisting of independent weavers, and involving men, women, and children; merchant workshops with hired labourers, who were usually paid by the piece; merchant workshops with pieceworkers, who own their own equipment but are paid for the commodities woven; finally, there were households of pieceworkers, whose dyes and yarn are supplied by a merchant (Stephen 1991, 124).

Some master weavers specialize in reproducing paintings by world mas-

ters—Picasso was popular in the US market in the 1970s (Pl. 4.6), but the current style involves cochineal-based colour combinations to produce banded patterns in the range red, purple, grey. Densely woven floor coverings of high quality can fetch US 1,000 dollars in Oaxaca City stores, but many merchant-weavers have workshop exhibitions of their own in Teotitlán and offer credit card sales. One outstanding Teotitlán weaver, Arnulfo Mendoza, is now based in Oaxaca City, where his weavings, using innovative designs and gold thread, fetch enormous sums. The majority of Teotitlán weavings are now sold on the US market, where mark-ups of 250 to 600 per cent are reported (Stephens 1991, 136).

Pl. 4.6 Weaving a Picasso: Spanish treadle loom, Teotitlán del Valle, 1976

Santa Ana weavers use more synthetic dyes than their Teotitlán counterparts and have a smaller repertoire of designs. Much of their work involves simple pre-Columbian figures and the designs derived from the archaeological site at Mitla (Pl. 4.7). Teotitlán weavers have a longer history of weaving, stretching back to the colony (when their forebears wove cotton mantle); and they broke through into creative, ornamental styles before the weavers in Santa Ana. Furthermore, about 40 per cent of weavers in Santa Ana receive yarn on credit from local intermediaries, who not only buy the finished article, but also specify the design and type of product they want. Once they have the finished products in their hands, the intermediaries sell them to merchants in Teotitlán, and Mitla, who, in turn, retail them in the local markets, such as

Pl. 4.7 Pre-Columbian figures and designs, woven in Santa Ana and derived from the archaeological site at Mitla. On sale in the courtyard of the Catholic church, Tlacolula, 1990

Tlacolula (Pl. 4.7). Intermediaries aim to make a double profit; as purveyors of factory-made thread, and as resellers of woven goods.

Weaving Cotton

The hierarchical relationship between Teotitlán and Santa Ana is repeated in a more exaggerated way for Mitla and Xaaga, its neighbour 5 km. to the east. Cotton weaving, an established trade in Oaxaca City at that time, was extended to Xaaga in 1950, but transferred to Mitla in 1953: by the 1960s it was a 100-loom industry. It was from this Mitla training ground that the Xaaga workshops were refounded. Three main tasks are carried out in Xaaga; weaving, machine sewing, and shawl knotting. Weaving is men's work, while sewing is a task carried out by wives and daughters. The tying of the loose ends of shawls is also a female task, and is paid at piece-rates in outworking situations.

Xaaga weavers do not purchase thread on credit nor do they get their thread from buyers. Nevertheless, they are almost entirely dependent on their sales to Mitla merchants, since the latter control the highly lucrative market (frequented by tourists) situated adjacent to the famous archaeological site. The dependence of Xaaga on Mitla is largely 'invisible'; indeed a visitor to Xaaga could be forgiven for thinking that the spacious but drab village is isolated and moribund. The give-away to Mitla's affluence, however, are the satellite TV dishes on the roofs of merchants' houses.

Although loom and sewing-machine ownership go together in Xaaga, the industry is more complex than this suggests. In the late 1970s, one-in-five Xaaga weavers regularly employed loom operators on a piece-rate basis (Cook and Binford 1990, 97); some households had two machines, and out-seamstresses were employed; some households without looms had sewing machines for piece-rate work. A few weavers produce and sell cloth, but most prefer to make garments from the cloth and sell them. Clothes are designed, cut, and sewn in the parent weaving shop; pre-cut cloth is also put out to seam-stresses in other households who sew on a piecework basis. Xaaga weavers produce two types of cotton cloth: loose weave called *tela deshilada*, and a tight weave known as *tela tupida*. Both types are used to make dresses, short-sleeved shirts, and shawls.

An interesting feature of this new artisan industry at Xaaga is the way that it has been able to get access to a lucrative tourist market, but only by conforming to the requirements of Mitla gatekeepers. Furthermore, at the very time that it might be expected that women were beginning to free themselves from the home, they have found themselves drawn anew into domestic activities as adjuncts of their husbands' work. This has involved some rescheduling of household tasks, and many women find that they have to cope with a 'double day'.

Embroidery

As has been seen in the case of Santa Ana, when merchant capitalists not only buy up the finished products, but put out the raw materials, their relations to peasant-artisans approximate most closely the social relations of capitalism. This is repeated in an extreme form in another domestic activity that has become established in Oaxaca villages since the late 1960s—embroidery of dresses and blouses. Here the dispersal of female outworkers and the piece-rate system of payment have militated against operative co-operation.

The embroidery industry has been developed most intensively in the villages around Ocotlán, for example San Antonino, where the drop in the water table, through over-extraction plus contamination of the soil, has placed limitations on horticulture (Waterbury 1989). It involves Ocotlán-based merchants, who put out, either directly or through village-based commission agents, pre-cut pieces of cloth for sewing and embroidering in return for a lump-sum advance. Sometimes the thread is supplied; often the embroidery is divided up between different members of the household—including, occasionally, men, where land shortage is a problem.

Some villages work solely for absentee merchants—Santa Cecilia and Santo Domingo Jalieza, Magdalena Ocotlán, San Baltazar Chichicapan, and Santa Lucía Ocotlán; others, such as San Juan Chilateca, have outworker families living adjacent to households that manufacture quite independently, though the latter may operate their own outworking systems (Fig. 1.4). The outworkers' strategy for increasing earnings is to cease to accept materials on a putting-out

basis, purchase their own materials, enlist household help, and try to accumulate sufficient capital to convert the household production system into a buying-up or putting-out business. If such a change cannot be achieved, the returns to women seamstresses are no better than making *tortillas* (flat maize bread) for the market, which is one of the most poorly remunerated tasks. This is acceptable to the women only because they often have no alternative source of cash to supplement the household budget, and because embroidery can be picked up and put down within the framework of the day's domestic tasks.

Embroidery merchants, themselves often peasants, bakers, or tailors in, or around, Ocotlán (including San Antonino itself) locate at the centre of small networks involving a median of four outworkers. But Cook and Binford report that five entrepreneurs had between 150 and 400 embroiderers working for them, and one of Waterbury's San Antonino merchants mentioned having 900 outworkers (1989). By increasing the volume of what are otherwise low unit profits, some embroidery merchants generated incomes comparable to those of the wealthiest entrepreneurs in Oaxaca City. Most of the finished garments end up in the Oaxaca City stores, though one independent embroiderer sold her dresses in Mexico City, charging 300 pesos (in 1979) per dress, having paid her five outworkers 100 pesos per item. The Zona Rosa merchant in Mexico City charged, in turn, about three times the sum he paid for the dresses. It is little wonder that Oaxaca women embroiderers have been described as suffering *hyper*exploitation, the ratio of their payment to the value of the finished dress being 1:9 (Cook and Binford 1990, 207).

Petty-commodity, Petty-capitalist Production

Are these activities in weaving and embroidery to be considered petty-commodity or petty-capitalist production? Cook and Binford (1990) identify petty capitalism when the means of production are privately owned or controlled; when wage labour is regularly employed to the tune of half the value of unit output per turnover period; when the purpose is to produce profit, and individual proprietors spend as much time in management and marketing as in production. As market conditions change, so investment in labour and other means of production will change. They conclude that 'capitalist development is not occurring uniformly in the petty industrial sector and that in several industries it is not occurring at all' (1990, 149). Yet they add that the existence of a wage-profits nexus in the weaving and embroidery industries represents 'some form of capitalism rather than petty commodity production' (1990, 150).

The link between petty-commodity and petty-capitalist production is highlighted by Cook and Binford, who turn on its head Chayanov's (1966) argument about the cyclical effect of household expansion and contraction on capital accumulation and capital dispersal over time among peasants. They argue that accumulation of capital, by using unwaged family labour, can be a

positive stimulus to the shift from petty-commodity production to petty-capitalist production in the context of a national capitalist economy (Cook and Binford 1990, 151). The crucial factor must be the presence or absence of market stimuli. These stimuli are sufficient to account for petty-capitalist developments in some parts of the weaving and embroidery industries, and in *mezcal* production, too. It seems to require a national or international capitalist market to effect the change. This is conspicuously missing for most peasant products except coffee, for which the manufacturing process is minimal and non-peasant based, and pottery, the main attraction of which is its rustic and handmade nature (though it has a major marketing problem because of its weight and fragility).

It follows that those cheap goods that are produced for a comparatively inelastic peasant (or urban proletarian) market provide no scope for accumulation and the evolution of petty-capitalistic activities. This, of course, is the situation in which the vast majority of the Oaxaca peasantries find themselves. Nevertheless, being trapped in petty-commodity production for survival is more likely to apply to communities living in the comparative isolation of the *sierras* than to those in the Oaxaca Valley and tropical plains. Even in the Oaxaca Valley, which has a tourist industry with a national and international clientele, only a limited range of privileged activities has the capacity for undergoing change, and it is a comparatively narrow band of operatives who, through family accumulation, make the transition to petty capitalism.

Virtually no one moves into capitalism proper, though examples do occur in the weaving industry in Teotitlán del Valle. Here, 'most households that have achieved merchant status within the past fifteen years used a combination of unpaid household labour and accumulation of initial capital through migration to the United States to do so . . . In some cases this has been supplemented by cash from the sale of land or animals . . .' 'Most current merchant households began as pieceworkers or independent producers. This situation appears to be changing as the current merchant class is consolidating and beginning to pass on capital to its offspring to be used in starting new businesses' (Stephen 1991, 125–7).

Modern Capitalist Activity

There are clear signs of the penetration of the Oaxaca City market by capital—witness the operations of the largest wholesalers, and the sale of articles such as electrical goods. Nevertheless, the bulk of modern manufactures reaching the inhabitants of the state of Oaxaca is neither generated nor handled by the traditional system of exchange. Rather, they are 'imported' by urban-based merchants and storekeepers (as Malinowski and de la Fuente noted) who act as relay posts for the onward movement of manufactured goods produced outside the state. This group of intermediaries has developed in its present form in

Oaxaca since the Mexican Revolution. As the landholdings of the *hacendado* class were eroded by land reform, its members proceeded to relocate in the towns where their families would have been temporary residents during the Porfiriato. At the same time, the modernizing projects of Mexico's post-revolutionary governments encouraged urbanization, and, even in non-industrial Oaxaca, provided opportunities for capital accumulation through commerce and tourism.

Soon after the Revolution, non-market-based commercial houses—mostly located around the *zócalo* in Oaxaca City—operated three kinds of general stores selling: textiles and clothing; hardware, paint, and agricultural implements; groceries and processed food. The stores supplied essential goods to the various urban classes as well as to the peasantry. Among the owners there were several foreigners, notably Spaniards and Germans, and many of their enterprises have remained in their families until today. Out of the 24 most important dry goods and clothing stores, 18 belong to foreigners or their descendants; and 12 out of the 18 are owned by 3 Spanish families, among whom the most important historically is that of Vidal García, the founder of El Importador. In 1931 Oaxaca City was virtually destroyed by earthquake, and Vidal García began to purchase property at bargain prices, thus turning his family into owners of a massive real estate. One of his descendants now owns five clothing shops as well as having investments in the most important mixed-goods store in Ocotlán (Bailón Corres 1979, 181–4).

The three most important hardware stores in Oaxaca City, also, are in 'foreign' hands, one owner being German and two Spanish. Germans are significant in selling paint, Spaniards in agricultural implements. Only in groceries has the foreign presence been weak, and it remains so. The major change over the decades has been the concentration of local Oaxacan capital in urban commerce, especially in lines that are not related to the Spaniards or the peasantry—and for the latter reason, therefore, provide considerable scope for capital accumulation. This is so because valuable industrial products are involved, and because the purchasers are urban dwellers or rich peasant-artisans.

Currently, fifty-seven élite families dominate the business life of Oaxaca state, and most of them have Oaxaca City as their base of operations. By far the most important sector is trade in manufactured goods—especially consumer durables, since there is a substantial middle class in the state capital, and forty families are engaged in these lucrative activities. Provision of sophisticated services is the second ranking sector with thirty families, followed by nascent industries in which thirty-one are engaged. Some families have interests that bridge all three sectors; sixteen family firms do so, while seven families repeat the pattern through their involvement in companies. The family names with the greatest commercial import in Oaxaca are Hamilton (of US mining and *hacienda* origin), Gutiérrez Ruiz, Muro Castillo (of recent Spanish antecedence), Hampshire Franco, Audelo Galguera, and Cordova Brena (Basáñez 1987).

Among these élite families, the purchase and sale of foodstuffs is not important—the major exception being coffee, which in the southern *sierra* is handled by the Basilio Rojas family of Miahuatlan. Foodstuffs have been replaced by trade in motor cars and trucks, and spare parts, furniture, kitchen equipment, electrical goods, hardware and agricultural equipment, heavy machinery, and construction materials. In services, repair shops are important, and so are transport, property, tourism, consultancies, and accountancy. Manufacturing, though poorly developed, involves bottling of beer and soft drinks, metal construction, making electric fans, processing of wood and plastic, and the building industry.

These business activities evolved out of family firms, often based entirely in one or other economic sector. During the 1970s, some family members started to form companies with which to expand into new areas. But it has only been since the late 1970s that they have entered associated fields such as construction—a lucrative activity given government sponsorship of urban infrastructure, production of plastic goods, and the provision of heavy machinery.

Commercial activity, based in the Central Valleys, Tuxtepec, the Isthmus, and the Pacific Coast, has been key to the success of these families, though services developed in these very same regions have recently played an important part in their accumulation of capital. Industrial investment has been sparing, and has concentrated in products whose success was guaranteed, rather than in activities that would be labour absorbing—one of Oaxaca's greatest needs. Similar circumstances have applied in the construction industry, for which the federal government's public works have provided secure funding, though in this instance a great deal of casual work has been created.

One of the major achievements of the fifty-seven families has been to restrict access to Oaxaca by outside private capital. The nature of this closure was exposed in the late 1970s, when the supermarket chain Blanco tried to get a toehold in Oaxaca and was prevented from doing so. Later, in 1983, they bought out the supermarket, El Tostón, from the Grupo Montajes, the first example of a major national enterprise becoming established in the city (Basáñez 1987). In the early 1990s the business was transferred to another national chain—Gigante.

Fifty-five out of the fifty-seven families no longer make their profits out of the peasantry—unless the upper stratum in the peasantry is able to afford sophisticated consumer items. The other two families retain their contact with the coffee trade, which, as has already been seen, suffers many excesses. If the fifty-five families are to be described as exploitative, it is because of the near monopoly they have jointly achieved, and the rapacious way in which they have allegedly conducted their business (Basáñez 1987).

Conclusion

Oaxaca appears to be traditional and unchanging, but change is everywhere. Population growth and migration, improved roads, electrification, health, and education have all had a massive impact on the peasant–artisan population. Maize is ubiquitous, but does not form the basis for either self-sufficiency or capital accumulation among Oaxaca's peasantries. However, it has been shown that modest capital accumulation has been achieved in a selection of peasant–artisan activities, particularly those controlled by urban middlemen or by producers who have retained or captured certain middleman functions. Successful accumulation in peasant–artisan activities depends on a national or international—non-peasant—market for the product.

The Oaxaca market system has changed over the years; integration of its subsystems is greater, because of improved transport; and wholesalers' imports of fruit, flowers, and eggs from out-of-state sources are now important. The most significant change has been the spawning of the new market on the Periferico, so that Oaxaca City has two major permanent markets, both of which are essential to the feeding of a state capital with 300,000 inhabitants. The Saturday market, which is still the crucial hub of regional peasant interchange, is an adjunct of the new Centro de Abastos, to which it is attached in a semi-parasitic, illegal way and from which non-accredited vendors have recently been expelled. Although the Centro de Abastos shows signs of penetration by cheap manufactured goods, bulk sales of consumer durables are in the hands of city-centre enterprises owned by Oaxaca's commercial élite. For them the peasant Saturday market was both irrelevant and an eyesore by the 1970s; in 1978 they took their opportunity to engineer the market's removal to the new site.

Oaxaca City dominates its state hinterland, but more through administration, public services, and the supply of manufactured goods and private services than through the extraction of surplus value from a reluctant peasantry. That there is such extraction is clear from the accounts of the weaving, embroidery, and *mezcal* industries, but it involves other towns as well as Oaxaca, and, coffee excepted, it does not make a large contribution to the wealth of the élite. Their source of profits lies elsewhere—where the pickings are greater: in markups on manufactured goods and services for the urban middle class; and in the rapidly expanding tourist industry, which caters to both Mexican and foreign holidaymakers who come for the archaeological sites, the colonial buildings, and the peasant markets.

Both this chapter and the previous one have stressed the economic production of the Oaxaca peasantry. But urbanization has begun to have a massive impact on peasant Oaxaca, generating migration flows within and outside the state, depopulating some rural areas, creating middle-class and proletarian urban consumers, and flooding Oaxaca City's labour and housing markets.

Moreover, international migration to the USA, particularly since the late 1970s and the early 1980s, has created oscillations in the resident population of many Oaxacan villages, generated problems for the maintenance of cultivation, yet offered income security on a modest scale. It is to issues related to migration, urbanization, and proletarianization that the next chapter is devoted.

5

Migration, Urbanization, and Proletarianization

Migration in Oaxaca is ubiquitous, and has been a major stimulant to change among Oaxaca's peasantries. It has become the 'natural' means of peasant adjustment to rapid population increase in a context of limited land for cultivation, low technology, and incipient or substantial ecological degradation. Migration has become socially institutionalized in Oaxaca. Analysis of census data led Weaver and Downing to estimate Oaxaca's overall inter-decadal out-migration at 8 per cent in 1950, 11 per cent in 1960, and 15 per cent in 1970 (1976). In 1980 out-migration dropped back to 11 per cent, but increased again thereafter (Alcalá and Reyes Couturier 1994, 80).

In 1970, when Oaxaca had 2,194,000 population, the birth rate was 42.1, the death rate 14.5 (and the infant mortality rate 62.9 per 1,000 live births), giving a natural increase of 27.8 per 1,000 population (Alcalá and Reyes Couturier 1994, 76). Bearing in mind that fertility was declining less rapidly than mortality into the 1980s, the number of inhabitants ought to have more than doubled between 1970 and 1990. Yet it increased by only about 50 per cent—a clear confirmation of the high level of out-migration from the state to the tune of at least one million people between 1970 and 1990. During this period, Oaxaca's out-migration (to Mexico City, Puebla, and Vera Cruz, as well as to the USA) accelerated to take on national significance (Luque González and Corona Juapio 1992).

Taking the figure of 50 per cent increase between 1970 and 1990 as the Oaxacan norm, it is possible to pick out areas of heavy out-migration, where a decrease of more than 12.5 per cent was recorded. The Mixteca Alta, Sierra Juárez, and the Tlacolula Valley and adjacent northern mountains were all heavily drained of residents, some registering a population decline of more than 25 per cent (Fig. 5.1). Everywhere else recorded large increases of more than 50 or more than 100 per cent, notably the district headquarters and the state capital, plus the tropical lowlands in Tuxtepec, Tehuantepec, the Mixteca Baja, and parts of the Pacific Coast. Lesser population increases with some out-migration typified much of the Central Valleys and the adjoining highland areas.

Surveys have been invaluable in examining the macro-scale dimension of Oaxacan out-migration. A recent investigation by the Instituto Nacional

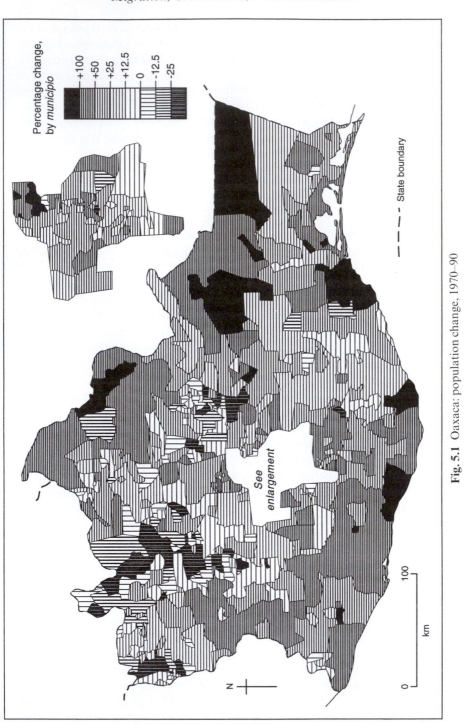

Fig. 5.1 Oaxaca: population change, 1970–90

Indigenista has shown that, while there are 600,000 Mixtecans (residents of the Mixteca, *not* Mixtec-language speakers) in Oaxaca out of a state population of 3 million, there is an equal number of Mixtecans (600,000) in the informal set-tlement of Nezahualcoyotl in Mexico City. According to the same source, an additional 27,000 are engaged as agricultural workers in Baja California (*Uno más Uno*, 11 August 1990, 13).

Not only do Oaxacans migrate to Mexico's capital city—and for temporary agricultural labour on tropical plantations, but they cross the Rio Grande as 'wet-backs' and are employed as undocumented and legal workers by US farms, factories, and restaurants. This chapter concentrates on population movements originating within Oaxaca, and, in particular, on their impact on town and country. Oaxaca's peasantries are being transformed by various forms of migration, most recently international movements of an oscillatory kind; and the peasant movers themselves are changing into proletarianized or semi-proletarianized workers, either on plantations or in the towns—in Oaxaca, the rest of Mexico, and the USA.

Oaxaca is one of the most backward of Mexican states; it is also among the least urbanized. During this century, Oaxaca City, the state capital, has plum-meted in significance compared to other Mexican colonial towns, and its recent demographic recovery has taken place under conditions of dependent urbanization. In short, Oaxaca City has lacked a powerful indigenous motor for economic growth and change, but rapid population increase among peas-antries with a very restricted resource base has resulted in mass migration. Population movement is neither confined to the state of Oaxaca (though 90 per cent of Oaxaca City's incomers are Oaxaqueños), nor is it a single and unre-peated action.

This chapter is divided into two parts. Peasant out-migration and its local consequences are examined first, before the emphasis is shifted to cityward movements and the internationalization of rural work-seekers through migra-tion. The second part is devoted to population growth and the economy in Oaxaca City, and the role of migrants in the labour force, class structure, and housing market.

Rural Responses to Out-migration

Rural out-migration to overcrowded cities—whether Oaxaca City or the much more distant and industrialized Mexico City, Puebla, and Vera Cruz—is diffi-cult to characterize. This is largely because the points of departure are infi-nitely more diverse than the Oaxacan destinations (though it should be repeated that the destinations may be national or international as well as within Oaxaca). Until recently, hardly any research has been devoted to out-migration at the regional scale, though Aguilar Medina (1979) commented that forty-three out of seventy-five *municipios* in the Mixteca lost population in

the period 1960–70. This pattern has persisted in the Mixteca since then, thirty-two *municipios* recording population decline in the decade of the 1970s (Alcalá and Reyes Couturier 1994). Referring to the state-wide catchment of rural migratory flows to Oaxaca City, Murphy and Stepick have drawn attention to 'near-empty villages barely able to sustain their permanent populations', that 'spring to life on days devoted to patron saints, when relatives . . . return to participate in the festivities' (1991*a*, 47).

As has been seen, three major areas of out-migration from Oaxaca may be identified: the Oaxaca Valley, especially the Tlacolula arm, the Mixteca Alta, and the Sierra Juárez (especially around Ixtlán and south of Villa Alta). These were first of all (in the 1950s, 1960s, and 1970s) labour reservoirs for migration to Mexican cities, notably Oaxaca City, Mexico City, Puebla, and Vera Cruz. During the last two to three decades, however, they have become export zones for long-distance migrant labour to the border region with the USA and across the border, particularly to California. It is likely that the harsh environment of these sending areas, coupled to the high rate of natural increase, has predisposed their populations to migrate. Important facilitating factors have been improved communications at the local and state level, and the dense social networks that characterize Indian communities in the high- and medium-altitude zones.

Oaxaca Valley

Migration from the Central Valleys has been calculated by comparing inter-decadal population change for *municipios* with life-table predictions derived from national-level data (Gregory 1986). Percentages of migration have been established for men and women for the age groups 20–9 and 30–4; every decade since 1890 has been examined, except the years of the Mexican Revolution. The average inferred migration throughout the period is 13 per cent for 20–9 year olds and 12 per cent for 30–4 year olds. Out-migration was negligible before 1930, except for women in the decade 1890 to 1900 (25 per cent). But it picked up for both age- and gender-specific groups between 1930 and 1940 (21 per cent for men aged 20–9 and 18 per cent for women aged 30–4) (Gregory 1986, table A, 30).

As the impact of the land reform began to be felt during the 1940s, and the Pan-American Highway was driven eastwards across the state, so out-migration declined, especially among the 30 year olds; among young women aged 20–9 there was even some in-migration (2 per cent). All this changed definitively after 1950, however. The small size of agricultural holdings in the land reform projects, coupled to the penetration of the countryside by improved communications and the achievement of higher levels of education, ensured that rural population increase would be transformed into migration towards more lucrative non-agricultural work. Between 1950 and 1970, migration increased first to levels previously reached only in the 1930s, and later exceeded

them. The highest rates of gender-specific out-migration were achieved by men aged 20–9 and women aged 30–4, the rates for each being 17 and 19 per cent in the 1950s and 35 and 24 per cent in the 1960s (Gregory 1986, table A, 30).

Gregory concluded that out-migration from the Central Valleys was due to scarce land and unreliable water supplies for irrigation. Craft production, especially around the market towns of Tlacolula and Ocotlán, limited the extent of out-migration, but rural transport encouraged it. These observations are generally consistent with my correlation analysis of 1970 census variables:

In the valley data, however, the low sex ratio provides clear evidence for female city-ward migration (and domestic employment) and male rurality. The dependency ratio is equally indicative of demographic shifts and increases in harmony with the fertility ratio: dependency is characterised by a superfluity of children rather than the aged, and this fits well with our knowledge of the high fertility and low life expectancy of Oaxaqueños (Corona 1979). However, the sex ratio also has an impact on dependency, and masculinity and large numbers of children are positively correlated in the rural areas . . . High rural natural increase coupled to cityward migration appears to be the valley norm. (Clarke 1986, 26–8)

Mixteca Alta

What has been happening in the highland areas of the state? A preliminary historical answer to this question is provided by evidence for Tilantongo, a settlement in the eroded Mixteca Alta, a region already referred to because of its strong association with out-migration. Tilantongo is typical of the Mixtecan *municipios* in that its population reached a steady state through migration as long ago as the post-war decades—the number of its inhabitants being 3,941 in 1950, 3,507 in 1960, 3,954 in 1970, 3,651 in 1980, and 4,272 in 1990). According to Butterworth's survey, conducted in the late 1960s, out of a sampled population of 248 adults, only 34 per cent had never migrated, 17 per cent had migrated and returned, 17 per cent were temporary migrants, and 33 per cent had settled permanently elsewhere (Butterworth 1975, 59).

There has been a clear relationship between wealth and migration in Tilantongo. The poorest inhabitants (53 per cent of the total) engaged in temporary, seasonal migration for agricultural work in the Central Valleys of Oaxaca and on the sugar plantations of Vera Cruz, or established themselves permanently in small settlements in these two states or in Mexico City. Wealthier residents avoided temporary agricultural work and migrated either to Oaxaca City or Mexico City. Indeed, they were the group most likely to have experienced migration; most likely to settle permanently elsewhere; and most likely to return eventually later in life to comparatively privileged positions in the Tilantongo community (Butterworth 1975, 177–89).

The link between wealth and migration is a part explanation why cityward migration has occurred 'without breakdown' (Lewis 1952), but it has also been due to the complex goals of migrants, who have sought paid employment while

anticipating improved education for their children and better healthcare for their family. In Oaxaca, urban residents enjoy superior living conditions in comparison to their rural counterparts; and migration, particularly in the 1960s and 1970s, was an obvious means of switching from one century to another in the space of a few tens of kilometres.

Migration may have inflated the cities, but static or declining population in the rural, sending areas has created unbalanced situations to which communities have found it difficult to adjust. The lack of youthful leaders, the abandonment or under-utilization of agricultural land, the potential shortage of eligible religious and civil *cargo* holders, and the lack of appropriate potential spouses, are among the factors leading to the decomposition of the traditional rural community in Tilantongo, as elsewhere. To some extent these problems are mitigated by the redefinition of the community as a more variegated, non-contiguous entity (Uzzell 1977), whose web, though anchored in Tilantongo, is woven around many other places, such as Oaxaca City, Mexico City, and various small *pueblos*. The consequence is that:

The emigrants make collections among themselves for the repair of the church, the construction of the basketball pitch, and for the school. Emigrants in Mexico City have their own board that meets every month and keeps an exact account of donations received for the improvement of Tilantongo. (Butterworth 1975, 203)

So, increased dependence on remittances goes hand in hand with the penetration of the countryside by urban values and technology—electricity, radios, and television. The urban–rural continuum is urbanized at both ends by the process of migration.

Sierra Juárez

Kate Young's research in the Sierra Juárez, north of Oaxaca City, has produced evidence consistent with Butterworth's findings. Using Bogue's formula for calculating out-migration, she estimated the rate to be 169 per 1,000 population in Copa Bitoo in the 1950s, rising to 292 in the 1960s. Butterworth estimated the rate to be 412 for Tilantogo in the 1960s, when it was 66 for the entire state of Oaxaca (Young 1976).

Young shows that even with these lower rates of out-migration, 55 per cent of the total population aged between 10 and 19 were missing. Similarly, 64 per cent aged between 20 and 29, and 60 per cent aged between 30 and 39 were out of Copa Bitoo at the time of her fieldwork (Young 1976, 85–8). Like Butterworth, she detailed the impact on the community, though she admitted that migration was but one of many changes that were influencing community structures—impacting in a disruptive way on *tequio* (communal labour), the *cargo* system, marriage, and politics, as well as the agricultural economy. She noted:

Since the 1940s the village population has become very mobile, and the rate of out-migration has grown each decade, with the result that in 1972 there were some 496

migrants (adults born in the village but living outside it) as compared to 587 villagers. ... Perhaps more significantly, of all the residents of over 20 years of age (337 in all) only some 108 women and 43 men (or 43 per cent) had never spent more than a few days outside the village. The village was thus characterised by out-migration, seasonal migration and return migration. (1976, 273)

The most important insight provided by Young's work relates to the relationship between migration and the Mexican version of dependent development (Young 1980). She showed that while male migration originally predominated, women joined fully in the movement from the 1950s, as the traditional Copa Bitoo economy was disrupted by capital penetration, and a relative surplus population was created. By 1971, male out-migrants barely outnumbered females (228 : 219). Twenty-nine per cent (based on a grand total of 447) were men in Mexico City, 18 per cent were locally resident men (in the *sierra* mines, or elsewhere in Oaxaca and Vera Cruz), and 4 per cent men in the USA, Baja California, and other destinations. Thirty-one per cent were women in Mexico City, 16 per cent local women movers, and 2 per cent women elsewhere (Young 1976, 288).

The pulling power of industrialization and urbanization in Mexico City, coupled to the expansion of domestic and construction jobs, was clearly exemplified by Young's data. Whereas 61 per cent had moved to local destinations in the 1940s, by the 1950s Mexico City was receiving 50 per cent of migrants, rising to 60 per cent in the 1960s—the *bracero* (farm labourer) programme ended in 1965. Simultaneously, migration to other destinations—especially to the USA, where wartime *bracero* work was the original lure, dropped from 14 to 10 per cent (1976, 291).

Migration in the 1980s and 1990s

More recent research on the Mixteca (Ortiz Gabriel 1980), and on different communities in the Central Valleys (Ornelas López 1980; Vázquez Hernández 1982) confirmed the conclusions reached so far. Ortiz Gabriel showed that land shortage in San Juan Mixtepec correlated with out-migration. Funds acquired during migration were expended on subsistence (46.4 per cent of households), purchase of land (12.0 per cent), house construction (10.8 per cent), agricultural investment (8.4 per cent), commercial activities (3.0 per cent), and religious and wedding costs (2.4 per cent).

Vásquez Hernández, working on Guelavía, argued against Ortiz Gabriel on one point, and suggested that landholding and migration did not correlate closely in that *municipio*. Migration in Guelavía is a universal strategy that fitted, in complex ways, into the fabric of the entire community, each potential migrant selecting migratory paths that conformed to his or her range of economic needs and cultural obligations.

Information for the Sierra Madre del Sur is rarer than for the better-known migrant source areas, though the evidence available confirms the general

nature of population out-movements. In 1980, about 12 per cent of the Chatino population had left their communities and were living in forty-three Oaxacan *municipios*; one-quarter were in Oaxaca City. Movers tended to be in the age groups 14–19. In addition, substantial numbers migrated on a short-term basis to Salina Cruz, to work in the construction industry, and to Pluma Hidalgo and Loma Bonita for agricultural labouring tasks (Hernández Díaz 1992*a*).

Circular International Migration

Oaxacan rural families are no longer moving *en masse* into Mexican towns, but maintain their rural residence as a base from which to seek work in distant localities. The men, and increasingly the women, too, migrate to the developed north of Mexico and the USA (California, Arizona, Texas, and Washington) for temporary (or more permanent) labour in urban or rural areas, thus earning the wages that enable their Oaxacan-based dependants to subsist (Ortiz Gabriel 1992).

A quarter of this international migration currently comes from the Central Valleys around Oaxaca City (Luque González and Corona Juapio 1992), though the Mixteca is probably the region with the most profound experience of emigration, since about 90 per cent of households are affected (Ortiz Gabriel 1992). In the early 1990s, about one-quarter of all dollar remittances to Oaxaca, running to many millions in total, were paid to recipients in the Mixteca (Ortiz Gabriel 1992). One estimate puts the proportion of the income of the Mixteca generated outside the region at 80 per cent, but not all of that is from the USA (Anguiano 1992).

Creation of this long-distance, pendular movement of Oaxacan migrants has involved the reworking and intensification of patterns that have their roots in temporary migration for agricultural labour in Mexico and in the US *bracero* programme of the Second World War. The cause of the current circular migrations is the Mexican economic crisis of the early 1980s. Mexico was no longer able to service its foreign debt out of rapidly declining oil profits, and unemployment and underemployment in Mexico City reached dire levels as structural adjustment created mass redundancies in factories formerly protected from import competition.

The US context, too, has changed, with the 1986 Simpson-Rodino Act making US employers responsible for not engaging undocumented workers, and the granting of an amnesty to formerly illegal Mexican residents. Part of the amnesty programme has involved the recognition of Special Agricultural Worker status, though the requirements are not particularly stringent and are open to fraud (Hulshof 1991, 20).

During the 1980s and 1990s whole villages in the Zapotec-speaking Central Valleys were depopulated of their able-bodied menfolk. This is not fully

expressed in census figures for 1990, since the census is a *de jure* enumeration, and reports on the population normally living there, not those actually in residence. A survey carried out in San Bartolomé Quialana (2,650 population), south of Tlacolula (Fig. 1.4), in 1988 showed that more than half the households participated in migration to the USA; a further 20 per cent had been involved in the past. The 420 migrants in California included twenty women; virtually all migrants worked in restaurants rather than in agriculture (Hulshof 1991).

Whereas migration prior to 1980 (to Tapachula, in Chiapas, and to the USA for agricultural work) had involved older married men, subsequent new migrants from San Bartolomé tended to be single and in the age range 15–35 years. Households lacking men in this age category were simply not involved in the migration. Greatest frequency in circular migration was recorded among heads of household, whose return visits coincide with the harvest season. Younger, single men in San Bartolomé return less frequently but usually manage to attend the village *fiesta* in August. As the migration system has developed over time, so it has expanded from the better-off families to encompass the entire village, since fares can be borrowed and the risk of failure has been reduced by the presence of neighbours at the points of destination (Hulshof 1991).

Similar circumstances have been recorded in the neighbouring community of San Lucas Quiavini (2,230 population). Here, by 1986, 60 per cent of households were participating in migration to the USA, and a further 28 per cent had done so in the past. Unlike San Bartolomé, however, most migrants in San Lucas come from large families, where the father stays behind and the younger sons migrate. San Lucas has *ejidal* land and a stronger agricultural base, including *maguey* cultivation, than San Bartolomé; hence the unwillingness to risk reducing production levels, which are maintained by hired labour (Hulshof 1991).

Santa Inés Yatzechi, east of Ocotlán (Fig. 1.4), provides yet another variant on the migration theme. This is a poorer village than the other two, and migration started only after 1985. Migration affects one-third of households, and only the wealthier families are involved in US destinations. The poorer ones work in Sinaloa as agricultural labourers. Return visits to Santa Inés coincide only incidentally with important village *fiestas* and peak seasons in agriculture (Hulshof 1991).

Oaxacan men migrate with experienced *coyotes*, border crossers, to whom payment for this illegal service is made only when their safe arrival in the USA has been confirmed. The *coyotes* may be contacted in the border area or in the sending community. Migrants send money (via cheques or telegraphic money orders) or bring back substantial funds to support the family. Evidence of such remittances is to be found in the banks in Oaxaca City, where country people, once rarely encountered, are now commonplace. Equally, the Oaxaca City airport is frequently jammed with peasant migrants and their families, returnees being conspicuous for their massive parcels of TV and stereo equipment.

As a result of remittances, the three villages in the Central Valleys mentioned above have improved diets (fruit and meat are used more frequently), better clothing, and medical care. However, the greater part of the remittances, notably from married men, are spent on consumer durables, such as refrigerators, gas stoves, washing machines, and brick houses, brick boundary fences, and iron gates (very much as in the successful *artesania* villages). Some invest in land, livestock, and irrigation or the purchase of a *yunta*, or pair of oxen. But there is little evidence for the greater application of fertilizer, pesticides, or higher yielding varieties of maize (Hulshof 1991, 72).

So far this evidence has related to the Central Valleys, but circumstances in the Mixteca Alta are essentially the same. Historically, migrants have been leaving San Juan Mixtepec for much the same reason as their Mixtecan neighbours in Tilantongo. With the termination of the *bracero* programme by the USA in 1965, Mixtepec migrants focused on Mexico City and the commercial farming areas of Morelos; a decade later, the target had shifted to temporary agricultural employment in northern Mexico and the USA. By the mid-1980s, 92 per cent of households in Mixtepec were surviving only through migration; 85 per cent of the migrants were in northern Mexico—especially Sinaloa and Baja California, and more than half had crossed into the USA at least once (Blauert 1990).

Migration from Mixtepec is seasonal and has two main peaks: from January to mid-March and from August to October. Migrants are mostly men aged 15 to 50, but migration of women has been increasing rapidly, as higher educational standards in rural Oaxaca have improved their Spanish, and migrant networks have been established in receiving areas. Blauert writes, 'from the early 1980s, whole families and single mothers have increasingly migrated, enhancing the desolate picture of villages where, for much of the year, only the old and very young remain. In some cases, families or couples stay in Tijuana with the men crossing the border while the women and children work in the town selling food or other goods' (1990, 268).

Most temporary migrants today are still from the poorest households. Erdinger (1985) found that it was the Mixtepec households that never had maize to sell (81 per cent) that had the highest frequency of migration (95 per cent). Blauert, reporting on the Mixtepec hamlet of Tejocotes, notes that one-third of the households and family farms were run by women, even though her survey was carried out in late March—traditionally a period of low migration because of local labour requirements in agriculture (1990, 270). Male migration has increased women's work commitment, but extended women's decision-making capacity in the family and agriculture.

The rationale for a strategy of migration on this scale and over these distances is based on the higher wages available; these may be up to twelve times larger on the Mexican border and in the USA than in Oaxaca (or Mexico City) (Ortiz Gabriel 1992). Work for men includes agricultural labour, gardening, driving, construction, and, for women, domestic service, street selling, and factory work in the *maquiladora* (assembly) industries.

Mixtec migrants to Hermosillo, Sonora, have set up a small settlement of 1,000 residents from which they work in the adjacent vineyards. In Nogales, also in Sonora, 500 migrants live in Colonia Oaxaca, from which the men travel to work in the construction industry, while the women are engaged as hawkers. The largest and oldest Oaxacan migrant settlement on the boarder is in Tijuana, where Mixtec migrants concentrate in six *colonias populares* and engage in marginal urban tasks. On the coast of Baja California there are several substantial Mixtec settlements where agricultural day labour is the norm. In both Nogales and Tijuana, there are unions specifically mentioning the Mixteca in their titles (Anguiano 1992).

Costs of travelling, border-crossing, living, and social security (in the USA) allow about one-third of a migrant's income to be remitted, but that permits the purchase of clothes, food, construction materials, fertilizers, animals, and land, and the discharge of *fiesta* obligations. Nevertheless, 80 per cent of this expenditure goes to producers outside the region, 49 per cent actually returning to the USA or going to European or Japanese enterprises—presumably in the shape of consumer goods purchased for the return trip (Erdinger 1985, 168, 220).

Although circular migration disrupts community life, it also strengthens community resolve to take command of socio-economic change at home. Political experience gained during migration has been deployed in community organization at the local level. At the same time, while away, migrants have maintained and strengthened their ethnic identity by living in Mixtec-speaking enclaves, where ties of family and community have been activated and reinforced. Whereas 1960s migrants returned with schemes for educational and infrastructural improvements, present-day returnees focus more on issues of marketing, production and ethnic identity at the *municipio* level.

Circular migration to the USA has become a crucial means of securing and improving the livelihood of peasant households in resource-deficient villages in the Central Valleys and the Mixteca. Remittances have enabled villages to continue their subsistence-orientated agricultural activities (often at a lower level of activity), and, occasionally, to strengthen the household's economy. Circular migration has not been a catalyst for rural development; nor has it reversed the economic stasis that lies behind migration in a context of population increase. But it has been an invaluable stand-by, given the unavailability of well-remunerated work in Oaxaca and most other parts of Southern Mexico (Hulshof 1991).

Cityward Migration

Although international migration has clearly come to dominate population movements in the Mixteca, the Central Valleys—and parts of the Zapotec Sierra—internal migration affects receiving as well as sending areas in Oaxaca.

Indeed, it is in places where population accumulates that it is most immediately noticeable. Clues about the level of migration within Oaxaca are to be found in the demographic record of population increase (Fig. 5.1). Oaxaca City, the state capital, had a population of less than 30,000 in 1940, a figure that it had already surpassed in the late nineteenth century. Since then, the city's population has increased very rapidly—by 4.8 per cent per annum between 1940 and 1950, 4.5 per cent between 1950 and 1960, 3.5 per cent between 1970 and 1980, and 9 per cent between 1980 and 1990. According to the 1990 census, greater Oaxaca City records 300,000 inhabitants, or more than ten times the number enumerated half a century ago.

Evidence for peasant in-migration is to be found in Oaxaca City's sex ratio. In 1930 there were 853 men to every 1,000 women, a figure which rose to 874 in 1970 and 878 in 1990. This persistent, but slightly weakening, female surplus appears only after the age of 15, and is explicable solely in terms of differential selectivity of migrants, either of female arrivals or of male departures. In either case the same reasons apply, since Oaxaca is able to absorb peasant women, rather than men, in domestic service and market selling. Female peasant in-migration has not only expanded the population, but also increased its reproductive capacity.

Sample surveys carried out in Oaxaca City show that only 30 per cent of male (and 26 per cent of female) household heads were born there (Rees, Murphy, Morris, and Winter 1991). So the vast majority of household heads are men of peasant origin. When their offspring are included, however, the total urban born rises to about 60 per cent (Murphy 1979; Nolasco 1981; Willis 1991). The vast majority of migrants are from rural areas of the state (68 per cent), or from other Oaxacan towns, notably the district head-towns (8 per cent). Only 11 per cent are from urban settlements in other states. Three-quarters have migrated only once. A study of San Juan Chapultepec, a poor neighbourhood in Oaxaca City, revealed that 80 per cent of household heads were in-migrants. However, source areas were so diverse and chain migration was so pervasive that three villages, each in different parts of the state, had sizeable populations of similar proportions living in San Juan (Graedon 1976).

Apart from Oaxaca City, the only towns that have been studied in any detail are Tuxtepec and Salina Cruz. Tuxtepec, located in the tropical lowlands of Oaxaca adjacent to the state of Vera Cruz, increased slowly in population from 5,360 in 1930, shortly after the railway line arrived from Vera Cruz, to 8,451 in 1960. With the completion of the Aleman Dam and its hydroelectric power installation in 1955, road improvements occurred, and the state constructed a paper mill, a rice mill, and a sugar factory in the vicinity. By 1970, 18,023 people were living in Tuxtepec, many of them enforced migrants from the flooded reservoir area, while others were former residents of the state of Guerrero, originally recruited by labour contractors (Rollwagen 1973).

Twenty-two thousand people, mostly Mazatecs, were displaced by the Aleman project to five rural resettlement schemes in the tropical lowlands of

Oaxaca and Vera Cruz below the dam (McMahon 1973). Large numbers also migrated on their own account to towns such as Tuxtepec and, over the border to Tierra Blanca in Vera Cruz (Barabas and Bartolomé 1973). By 1980, Tuxtepec's municipal population stood at 61,093, and it increased to 110,136 in 1990.

A similar history of rapid urban growth under the influence of state investment has been recorded in Salina Cruz on the Pacific Coast of the Isthmus of Tehuantepec. Salina Cruz was chosen by Pemex in the late 1970s as the refinery and transhipment port for Gulf of Mexico oil, transported across the isthmus and destined for Mexico's Pacific ports and the Japanese market. In a handful of years, the population more than doubled, from 30,000 to almost 70,000 (Rivière D'Arc and Prévot-Schapira 1984, 154), but very few Oaxacans benefited from the jobs created. Fifteen per cent of a sample of workers taken by Rodríguez (1984) were from Salina Cruz itself, but the lion's share of the Pemex refinery jobs (estimated at just over 3,000 in the early 1980s) were secured by in-migrants from the oilfield state of Vera Cruz.

While Oaxaca City has been the long-run focus of cityward migration within the state, and chain migration has brought neighbours from manifold points of departure into co-residence, inter-village feuds, so common to rural areas, have not been translated to the town. Peasant migrants have adapted with great flexibility to the urban scene, and taken on a comparatively homogeneous proletarian lifestyle into which their children have been socialized.

Oaxaca City's role has been to provide markets and administrative services to its hinterland and to absorb, within itself, the socio-economic shocks resulting from rural–urban migration. There is evidence, however, not only for the modernization and proletarianization of the peasantry in privileged rural areas, which was investigated in Chapter 4, but for the proto-proletarianization of rural migrants in Oaxaca City. This process parallels, under even more hazardous conditions, the experience of Oaxacan peasants in Californian towns.

Employment, Education, and Class

Occupation and Education

A strong urban economic base, in the developed world, has usually been equated with manufacturing; by these standards, Oaxaca City's is weak. The state capital musters barely a handful of modern factories—three soft-drink bottling plants, each employing thirty people, and a plywood enterprise owned by the Tuxtepec Paper Company with 300 workers. Oaxaca City's major sources of employment are in government administration and public services, wholesaling, retailing and marketing, handicrafts, petty manufacturing and repairing, transport and construction, and domestic service and tourism.

Comparison of occupational data in the census between 1940 and 1990 together with a 1977 sample survey reported in Murphy and Stepick (1991*a*, 80) shows, over the half-century, that agricultural work declined from just under 10 per cent of the urban labour force to 2 per cent. The service category (including domestic service, public services, and tourism) remained at just over 30 per cent. However, the public sector, which was separated out (for statistical purposes) from other services only in 1970, increased from just under 10 per cent to 28 per cent, and employment in construction doubled to 9 per cent. Commerce increased its share of employment from 14 to 18 per cent between 1940 and 1950, and thereafter held its own. The expansion of the public sector and construction work was matched by the declining share of employment in industry (where the drop was from 34 to 10 per cent), as modern manufactured goods made inroads into the local artisan economy (Willis 1994, 39).

Commensurate with these occupational shifts have been changes in Oaxaca City's educational levels. Improved literacy was particularly marked among women, whose level of illiteracy over the period 1960 to 1970 fell from 28 to 10 per cent. A sample survey carried out in Oaxaca City in 1974 revealed a very similar level of illiteracy (9.5 per cent). In addition, 45 per cent of residents had been to primary school for one to six years, 16 per cent had between one and three years at secondary school, 9 per cent had studied at the secondary, pre-university level, and 3 per cent had received a professional training at university or equivalent standard. While illiteracy has declined, fewer than 30 per cent of Oaxaca residents have had more than a primary education, despite the concentration of secondary and tertiary educational establishments—including the Universidad Autónoma 'Benito Juárez' de Oaxaca—in the state capital.

How do peasant migrants fit into the educational pattern? While migrants to Oaxaca City are more illiterate than the local born (13 per cent compared to 10 per cent), they are much less illiterate than the average for the state as a whole (42 per cent for adults in 1970) (Hendricks and Murphy 1981, 62). Natives of the capital had completed primary school more commonly than migrants, though 45 per cent of migrant household heads had received some primary education. In secondary schooling, migrant household heads fell far behind non-migrants, a mere 7.5 per cent of movers having attended. Only at the professional level did migrants out-achieve locals, and that was largely due to recruitment of out-of-state professionals for work in the expanding (especially federal) administration during the 1980s.

Peasant migrants to Oaxaca City have reduced educational levels at the bottom of the scale, while middle-class migrants have improved them at the top. But better levels of rural education, especially since the early 1970s, have meant that the discrepancy between town and country born has been reduced, and recent peasant migrants have arrived with far better educational credentials than their predecessors. This fact, coupled to recent migrants' ability to use networks established by already resident kin and friends, helps to explain the surprisingly swift adjustment of newcomers to the urban scene. Moreover,

recent migrants have a greater tendency than ever before to come from small town backgrounds rather than small peasant communities; the last place of residence before moving to Oaxaca dropped from 76.5 per cent rural in 1969 to 62 per cent in 1977 (Hendricks and Murphy 1981, 65).

Residents of Oaxaca City, both local born and migrants, are not educationally prepared to participate in an advanced industrial economy. But no economy of this type exists in the state capital nor in any other settlement, bar the industrial enclaves at Tuxtepec and Salina Cruz. Absorption of the economically active population—both local born and peasant migrant—into the labour market has been achieved by the expansion of activities with low-entry requirements in educational levels, especially in the commercial, industrial, and services sectors of the urban economy (Hendricks and Murphy 1981). It is to the labour force associated with these sectors that attention is now directed.

Formal and Informal Sectors

A convention of labour-market analysis in Third World cities is to divide employment into formal and informal sectors. Formal employment is regulated in various ways, and involves labour with large firms, a fixed workplace, negotiated wages, and a range of social security benefits. Informal activities are unregulated, more casual and uncertain, and the labour force is often self-employed or comprises non-waged family members; another characteristic is temporary incorporation into work crews for wages related to the task to be completed. In many ways this dichotomy between formal and informal is false, because linkage often exists between the two sectors; some products move from one to the other during the manufacturing process, and many workers straddle both sectors on a variety of timescales.

A detailed survey carried out in 1976 facilitates a rough categorization of the Oaxaca labour force. The formal sector comprised government employees (19.8 per cent), private employees (17.8 per cent), industrial workers (9.5 per cent), merchants (8.8 per cent), professionals (0.6 per cent), and entrepreneurs (0.2 per cent). In contrast, the informal sector was made up of service workers (15.7 per cent), construction workers (12.1 per cent), agricultural workers (4.5 per cent), artisans (4.5 per cent), and the unemployed (6.5 per cent). Thus approximately 57 per cent were in the formal sector and the balance in informal activities (Murphy 1979, 42).

These informal-sector activities merit more detailed investigation. They included domestic service, market selling, street vending, baking or plumbing, day labouring, and the cannibalizing of manufactured goods to make repairs. 'Many poor women make extra money by embroidering peasant blouses and dresses using materials provided for them by a middleman or representative of a retail firm' (Murphy and Stepick 1991*a*, 94). However, fewer than 10 per cent of informal-sector workers in Oaxaca City had been reported to engage in artisan production—and 'Oaxacan colonias populares are not loci of informal

activities' (Murphy and Stepick 1991*a*, 68). Few workshops have linkages to the formal sector in Oaxaca City, and they seem not to operate as counter-cyclical shock absorbers in times of economic crisis (Holloway 1998). The most recent national setback in 1994–5 saw workshops shed paid labour, and gravitate towards a system of unpaid family labour of the kind reported in the early 1970s (Chance 1973).

The Mexican economic crisis, which began in 1983, has shifted strongly the balance of employment in Oaxaca City in the direction of the informal sector. Whereas in 1977 43.5 per cent of male household heads were in the informal sector, the figure for 1987 was 66.2 per cent; the corresponding percentages for women household heads were 63 and 73 in 1977 and 1987, respectively. The main consequence of this restructuring has been to remove job security for men and even more dramatically for women (Murphy, Rees, French, Morris, and Winter 1990).

Informal sector employment does not seem to have been the route into the labour force chosen uniquely by peasant migrants. Migrants to Oaxaca City accounted for 66 per cent of all household heads in 1977, rising to 70.2 per cent in 1987. At each date, their contribution to the informal sector was 69.4 and 71.1 per cent—in both instances only modestly above the expected level for the city (Murphy, Rees, French, Morris, and Winter 1990). Most jobs in Oaxaca City are sufficiently unskilled for even the poorly educated rural migrant of peasant origin to cope with the tasks—at a very low level of remuneration and living.

In the construction industry, for example, it is common for informal sector *jornaleros* (day labourers) to gather on the *zócalo* between six and seven o'clock in the morning. 'They clump in groups of three to five, talking among themselves, perhaps smoking a cigarette, and shivering in the early-morning cold. Around 6.00 am, pickup trucks begin to arrive. A few drivers want ten to fifteen labourers, but most want one, two, or three for a day's work. They try to hire workers they know' (Murphy and Stepick 1991*a*, 91).

Class

Employment data can be used as a guide to present-day class structure (Murphy 1979). Professionals, senior bureaucrats, and merchants formed the Oaxaca City élite and accounted for about 10 per cent of the labour force. Below them were ranked a rather indefinite middle class of white-collar workers in the public and private sectors, who together made up about 40 per cent of workers. The rest, both formally and informally employed, comprised the lower class, and this stratum included the majority of people. As work in the public and private sectors was very poorly paid, it is certain that this estimate of the lower class is too small.

If a comparison is made between these data from Murphy's survey and a sample taken in 1974 by Nolasco (1981), it becomes possible to refine the strat-

ification in wealth terms. Nolasco regards 3 per cent of families as extremely rich; 23 per cent as rich; 29 per cent as living at a subsistence level; and 42 per cent as poor. Improvement in living standards over time may be detected by comparing Nolasco's results with Yescas Peralta's study carried out twenty years earlier. The latter noted 3 per cent rich, 28 per cent poor, and 69 per cent living in *miseria* (1958). But that was barely a decade after the surfacing of the Pan-American Highway to Oaxaca.

Nowadays there is a tiny élite containing 5 to 10 per cent of the population of Oaxaca City; a middle class with 25 to 35 per cent of the population; and probably up to 60 per cent in the lower class, notably, but not exclusively, located in the informal sector. As the mean household income for the city fell by more than half between 1977 and 1987 (as a result of national economic crises), it was the poorest 30 per cent who suffered most, experiencing declining levels of living, including a worsening diet (Murphy and Stepick 1991*a*). It is into this semi-proletarianized, increasingly impoverished lower class that most peasant migrants to the city have moved.

The most severe decline in living standards has been experienced by nuclear working-class households, especially households headed by women. These women are confined to menial service tasks and, because of marriage breakdown and their inability to find the time to create new contacts, lack support networks. Middle-class women in Oaxaca City are even more likely to head their own households, since they have the educational background to command reasonable jobs and salaries; however, they have the money to employ their own servants and to maintain contacts with kin and friends (Willis 1994).

Irrespective of whether households are headed by middle- or working-class women, they seem not to have been extended to bring additional workers and helpers into the unit to combat the influence of the post-1983 national economic crisis (Chant 1991). However, Pacheco Vásquez, Morris, Winter, and Murphy (1991) report a 10 per cent increase in proportion of households that were extended between 1977 (20 per cent) and 1987 (30 per cent). One reason for the lack of extension, as revealed by the history of households in her samples, Willis argues (1993; 1994), has been the absence of a manufacturing sector which could contract (in Oaxaca the contraction happened before 1980, not afterwards). Indeed, not only Willis's surveys, but also those of Winter, suggest that reciprocity is uncommon among the Oaxaca urban poor, and that 'the family is facing the economic crisis relatively alone, with only its own resources as the margin against disaster' (Winter 1991, 82).

Housing

Constraints of class and employment are reflected in the residential structure of Oaxaca City, the outstanding feature of which is the plethora of shanty towns, which climb the valley slopes ringing the old colonial core of the state

capital. However, it would be rash to categorize them as squatter settlements or to be so mesmerized by their scale that the city's range of housing types and tenures is obscured. No better guide can be had to the residential complexity of the city than Murphy's study of 1,452 households and his sixfold classification of them into: invasions, *colonias populares*, site-and-service projects, *pueblos conurbados*, the centre city, and middle-class housing (Murphy 1979, 22). Each category merits further consideration.

Settlements located on invaded land occupy only 1 per cent of the city's area, and involve plots of marginal value. Lacking title to land, the settlements house only 1.4 per cent of households, are essentially impermanent, and are liable to removal by the local authorities. The houses are predominantly *jacalitos*, one-room shacks with earth floors and flimsy walls; few homes have electricity, running water, or sewer connections.

Invasions by *paracaidistas* (parachutists) (Chance 1973, 191) are often thought of as the major basis for squatting in Latin American cities, following the pioneer work of Mangin in Lima (1967), though more recent research shows that illegal subdivisions may be just as important (Gilbert and Ward 1985). In Oaxaca City, at least, invasions are a very small feature of the residential scene and are occupied by the poorest of the poor. But, if the residents manage to hold on to the land and to attract infrastructure and gradually improve their homes, they do have the potential to approximate and merge with the poorest *colonias populares*.

Colonias populares cover more than 50 per cent of the land area of the city, and house just over 58 per cent of residents. Over 70 per cent of household heads are migrants, mostly of peasant origin. *Colonias populares* are 'irregular' settlements—sometimes involving the purchase of illegal subdivisions rather than outright squatting (Butterworth 1973, 212; Willis 1994), but they have been, or are being, up-graded by the local community often with government assistance. Almost 60 per cent of units have electricity, but only 10 per cent have water piped into the house and 7 per cent sewerage. Barely 30 per cent of households report regular ownership in the poorest settlements, rising to almost 60 per cent in the more affluent ones.

On the basis of the minimum wage, Murphy divided the *colonias* into those with very low incomes, those with low incomes, and those with moderate incomes. In general, he observed an increase in the quality of life in the *colonias populares* as one moved up the scale, although this was not always the case (1979). Topography also plays a part in up-grading: 'the most desirable land is that close to the highway. Families are increasingly poor as one goes up slope' (Butterworth 1973, 192).

Pueblos conurbados have a unique historical and political relationship with the city, since they have had an existence as settlements before their incorporation. They account for 11 per cent of the area of Oaxaca, and 8.9 per cent of households. Community spirit and the long period of their development have produced many good-quality—adobe and red-tiled—dwellings based on

autoconstruction. But the *pueblo* retains the flavour of a village and a residual association with agricultural work—a paradoxical situation since almost 60 per cent of household heads are from Oaxaca City or the immediate vicinity. Sixty-four per cent of households report security of tenure and over 80 per cent the availability of electricity, but only 43 per cent have a water supply and 12 per cent sewer connections.

Site-and-service projects were created in the 1970s under the aegis of INDECO (Instituto Nacional para el Desarollo de la Comunidad y de la Vivienda Popular), starting with a pilot project at Xoxocotlán in 1971 (Prince and Murphy no date). They occupy about 8 per cent of the urban area and house 6.9 per cent of households, and are different from the *colonias populares* only inasmuch as they have received, at the outset, some basic aid from the government. A consequence of this aid is that 67 per cent of households have electricity, 65 per cent have water, and over half have sewer connections.

The city centre or *centro* coincides closely with the boundary of the built-up area in 1940 (Fig. 5.2). At the end of the Second World War, the city's élite clustered around the main square, with the lower classes on the outer edge (Hayner 1966). It is a measure of Oaxaca's growth that, by the late 1970s, the city centre accounted for barely 20 per cent of the city's morphology and only 14.7 per cent of households. Much of the property here is in the form of rented *vecindades*, or subdivided patio-type houses, some of which are of colonial vintage. The worst have dilapidated rooms, a single source of water in the yard, and shared toilet facilities; the best have been renovated to a good standard and the accommodation is self-contained.

Two-thirds of the households in the *centro* have sewer connections, but 87 per cent report electricity and piped water. However, 68 per cent of residents are living in houses not rented apartments (27 per cent of households), and the centre stands in second place after the suburbs as the most desirable residential area in which to live. Its attractiveness is explicable by its centrality and its stability; almost half the household heads were born in Oaxaca City, and over 60 per cent of households have lived in their present location since they were formed.

Finally, middle-class housing is similar in appearance to the moderate-income *colonias populares* and the better-off site-and-service schemes, except that the residents have higher incomes and live in better-quality dwellings. These housing areas account for 9.8 per cent of households and may be divided into two types: private subdivisions (*fraccionamientos*) with groups of houses or vacant lots with services; and government-inspired mass housing projects destined for middle- and upper-level employees.

Government-subsidized housing is of two types known as INFONAVIT (Instituto para el Fomento Nacional de Vivienda) and ISSTE (Instituto de Seguro Social para los Trabajadores del Estado). INFONAVIT constructs for salaried workers in the private sector, and ISSTE for state and federal employees. Among these middle-class households only 38 per cent were born in

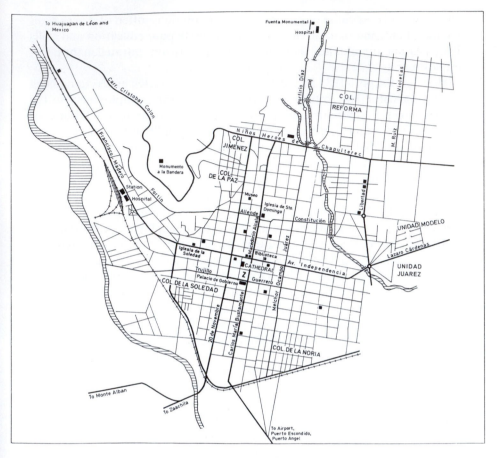

Fig. 5.2 Oaxaca City map

Oaxaca City, but an additional 15 per cent came from urban points of departure in other states. Eighty-five per cent of households have a regular title to
their land or are legally renting; 94 per cent have piped water, 93 per cent electricity, and 81 per cent sewerage connections.

If those living in moderate-income households in the *colonias proletarias*
(8.1 per cent)—the best off—are added to those in households in the city centre
(14.7 per cent) and in middle-class housing (9.8 per cent), then the remainder
can be described as poor. They occupy only partially upgraded property,
sometimes of insecure tenure. Thus, about 67 per cent of the households—and
a slightly larger proportion of the total residents, correcting for household
size—are living in informal housing. This figure should be compared to the 47
per cent whom Murphy estimated to be in informal employment in 1979.

Many in secure employment in 1979 were unable to acquire adequate
accommodation for their families. It may be inferred that informal sector

employment is the cause of informal housing solutions, often of a very rudimentary kind; and that, given their comparatively poor education and skills level, peasant migrants and their families are heavily concentrated in the poorest housing.

How has the post-1983 Mexican economic crisis affected access to housing in Oaxaca City? The shift in the labour force towards employment in the informal sector, especially among women, has already been noted, but even those who held on to formal sector jobs suffered badly in relation to house tenure. Households in the formal sector of employment recorded a drop in ownership from 77.5 per cent to 70.4 per cent between 1977 and 1987, while those in the informal sector experienced a decline in house ownership from 75.4 per cent to 70.2 per cent.

On the other hand, better access to higher quality housing seems to have occurred among both formal and informal sector employees, with some evidence for convergence between them. Formal sector employees living in shacks declined from 15.8 to 6.3 per cent of households between 1977 and 1987, while the proportion of informal sector employees in the same housing category fell from 28.9 per cent to 13.6. At the other end of the housing scale, formal sector workers living in houses increased from 69.4 to 85.7 per cent, and informal workers achieved an increase from 55.4 to 76.1 per cent.

Loans for house improvements from official agencies and household self-help lie behind these trends (Morris 1991), and show the determination of the household to continue to improve the fabric of the house, even in the face of the economic crisis. The net result is that housing of poor fabric—the shantytown—is located on lands 'whose legal statuses range from complete outlaw to official incorporation' (Butterworth 1973, 219). Shantytowns are not coterminous with *colonias populares*, and most *colonias* are not squatter settlements (or invasions).

Conclusion

More important than the peasantry as a social formation from which to extract surplus value, is the peasantry as a reservoir of cheap labour for use in the city or elsewhere. This reservoir can be tapped, through migration, to supplement plantation labour at harvest time, or it can provide the towns with cheap manual labour on a longer timescale. Whether in country or town, these peasants and ex-peasants are consumers, and it is in this capacity that they are so important for capital accumulation among the Oaxaca commercial class.

Peasants are a captive market for a wide variety of consumer goods ranging from manufactured clothes to household effects, notably sophisticated electrical items, including televisions. Oaxaca City merchants monopolize the supply of these high order goods (though migrants to the USA may bring back pur-

chases), and are able to manipulate prices and sales very much to their own collective ends.

As the tentacles of modernization reach into the countryside—often speeded up by circular migration, it is clear that the Oaxacan peasantry is being transformed. At the same time, of course, Oaxaca City is being altered by the arrival and incorporation into the labour force of a population whose characteristics are less deeply rural than was true of migrants in previous years. Peasants, divorced from the land, become a proletariat (or semi-proletariat) that has to sell its labour on an even more permanent basis than they did in the countryside.

Major shifts in residential patterns have taken place in Oaxaca City as urbanization has proceeded. The local élite has quit the city centre for residences to the north of the old colonial city, moving especially to Colonia Reforma or further north to San Felipe. But the peripheral growth of shanty towns has left the colonial centre as the second most desirable place in which to live. Elements of the pre-industrial city pattern continue side by side with others of an industrial kind. This epitomizes the hybrid quality of dependent urbanization in Oaxaca City, where shops selling sophisticated imported technology—such as microwave ovens and video recorders—coexist with the traditional peasant market in which some stall-holders display watches and cassettes.

International circular migration has, through remittances and transformed values, underpinned a degree of urban–rural convergence in some parts of Oaxaca—particularly in the Oaxaca Valley. While the Oaxacan countryside is definitely becoming more comfortable in terms of the levels of servicing, urban–rural differentials in living standards remain marked, especially for the more sophisticated indices of development.

So, cityward migration and circulation, much of which is now international, have become crucial to peasant survival and to the partial fulfilment of Oaxacans' aspirations to a better material life. Dependence on migration and remittances is especially characteristic of the Indian, backward, eroded areas, such as the Mixteca Alta—which at the same time sport the most obvious symbols of migrant advancement, the satellite dish! It is to the quest for ethnic identity in Oaxaca, most notably in the Mixteca Alta and other high-altitude regions of the state, that the following chapter is devoted.

Part III

Ethnicity, Community, and Politics

6

Ethno-Linguistic Groups
The Quest for Identity

Oaxaca's peasantries are diverse, not only in socio-economic terms, but also ethno-linguistically. Oaxaca is one of the most multi-ethnic states in Mexico, if language is taken as a cultural marker. A little under half the population speaks a pre-Columbian language, and there are sixteen different major linguistic groups. Chance, reporting on the Villa Alta area of the Sierra Zapoteca, notes, 'the district's five basic ethno-linguistic groups have of course persisted until the present time, but only as rather vague, language-based reference groups as far as the people themselves are concerned' (1989, 124). In addition there are, within some languages, such as Zapotec, which is spread across the various altitudinal zones in the centre of the state and the Isthmus of Tehuantepec, important dialect differences that make for mutual unintelligibility between adjacent communities (Rendón 1995).

As a consequence of linguistic pluralism and Spanish colonialism, coupled to state penetration since the Revolution, Spanish has become the common language and bilingualism has spread. Most Oaxacan Indian-language speakers have some facility in Spanish, and the younger generations are often fluent in both Spanish and their home language. Diglossia is common, with speakers moving between languages within the span of a sentence or two.

Indian-language speakers remain marginalized within the socio-spatial structure of Oaxaca society, both at the state level and in the Central Valleys (Chapter 2). They are among the poorest of Oaxaca's citizens in material terms, the least educated, the most rural, the most deficient in technical and mechanical development. Located at high altitude, they have been the last communities to be touched by modernization. However, they are not totally isolated; they are migrants to Mexico's cities and to the USA, where they perform both agricultural and industrial labour, and work in kitchens and on construction sites.

So, many migrants have developed multiple identities as, say, Mixtecs, Oaxacans, Mexicans; and their travels to the USA may have added some English to their language repertoire, yet reinforced, rather than diminished, their Indian identity. Even where migration has played a small role, as it has until recently among the Chatinos, neither the growth of the market economy nor social differentiation within the group has necessarily entailed loss of ethnic identity (Hernández Díaz 1992*a*).

The cultural difference between the ethnic groups, leaving aside language, is slight, though Mazatecs do practise polygamy, 20 per cent of men having had more than one wife at a time (Boege 1988, 63). Rather, it is the historical relationship between the language group and its territory that sets one ethnie apart from another. A core element in the construction of ethnic identity, within the framework of peasant maize cultivation, is the idea of work. Among the Mazatecs, for example, it is not a question of any kind of work but of 'work in the forest' which is crucial; it implies a special relationship between people and the environment. Cultivating the land is not simply an economic act; it synthesizes centuries of experience in the management of the particular region with which the specific ethnic group associates itself and is associated (Boege 1988). Echoes of this idea appear throughout the ethnographic literature on Oaxaca: 'the ever-recurring and eternal rhythms of planting and harvesting and of prayer and toil are the pulse that ticks in the veins of the Mixe' (Lipp 1991, 195).

Non-Indians, however, focus not on ethnicity but on national society. Since the Revolution, Mexicans have considered their country to be a *mestizo* society. The term *mestizo*, which in colonial and early independence years was used to designate offspring of mixed—white and Indian—race, has been used as a cultural category since 1920, implying an hispanized Mexican. Hispanized Mexicans are 'the nation of bronze', and while Indian historic figures are lauded, contemporary Indians stand outside the pale of national society.

The designation of Mexico as a *mestizo* nation, with an aspiration to a homogeneous national culture, has been a government project designed and implemented by anthropologists and archaeologists and presided over by the PRI. Speaking a pre-Columbian language is, therefore, usually a crucial cultural marker in Mexico: it is, in general, *the* key indicant of who is or is not an Indian. This alerts us to the peculiar nature of Oaxacan society, since almost 20 per cent of all Mexican indigenous-language speakers live in the state.

Although Indians, defined linguistically, are fewer than 10 per cent of the Mexican population, they account for almost 40 per cent in Oaxaca. There is, then, a distinction between the Mexican national social stratification, which is class based but has marked racial/cultural correlations (white/Indian) at the extremes of the social scale, and hinges on occupation, education, and wealth, and that of Oaxaca. About 60 per cent of the Oaxacan population is *mestizo*, in a cultural sense, but more than one-third form an enclave inside the class hierarchy because it speaks an Indian mother tongue. Ricardo and Isabel Pozas characterize Indians as having an *intraestructura* (intrastructure), based on language, the family, land, and community, which the remainder of Mexican society lacks (1978, 35). In Oaxaca, Indians form an ethnic segment, or more accurately a series of ethno-linguistic segments, which are not only inside, but also the bottom layer of, the class structure of *mestizo* society.

This chapter begins with the problem of defining who is or is not Indian in the context of colonial race mixing between whites, blacks, and the indigenous

population. Emphasis is given to contexts in which Oaxacan Indians have been able to redefine themselves, culturally, as *mestizos*, and to those in which an ability to speak an Indian language is, or is not, an indicator of Indian identity. The focus is then shifted to the distribution of the major pre-Columbian language groups of Oaxaca, and the role of landholding as an underpinning to ethnicity. Cityward migration is shown to hasten Indian acculturation, or 'passing', expressed in language shift and clothing change (*cambio de indumentaria*).

Indians are not only the bottom stratum of the Oaxaca peasantry, but are generally described as lacking a class structure. This classlessness is changing under the influence of economic development, especially where export crops such as coffee are involved. In some regions there is also an ethno-linguistic pecking order among the Indian groups, and, in the Isthmus of Tehuantepec, Zapotec is widely spoken among the commercial and cultural élite—against the expected trend. Where Indians have been subject to blatant exploitation, social movements have sometimes been launched against *mestizo* society in an attempt to redress the imbalance, often in the form of messianic movements.

Increasingly, Indians are taking the initiative and making demands for the recognition of their cultural difference, even if the objective measurement of that difference is fading in the face of Mexican modernization. Crucial recent changes have involved the founding of Indian organizations and journals as expressions of a resurgent identity. In 1992, on the 500th anniversary of the encounter between Columbus and the Indian population of the Caribbean, Article 4 of the Mexican constitution was reformed to express the ethnic plurality of the nation. This is an important, if belated and reluctant, response to a situation of '*mestizo*-conformity' which has existed throughout the PRI period of government. Article 4 affirms:

The Mexican nation has a multi-cultural composition sustained originally in its Indian communities. The law will protect and promote the development of their languages, cultures, usages, customs, resources and specific forms of social organization, and will guarantee to their members effective access to the jurisdiction of the state. In the judgements and agrarian procedures in which they take part, their legal practices and customs will be taken into account in terms established by law. (Clavero 1994, 189)

Article 16 of the Oaxaca constitution has recently been reformed to be consistent with Article 4. 'The state of Oaxaca is sustained in the presence of its 16 indigenous groups. The law will establish the means to preserve indigenous cultures' (Gijsbers 1996, 84–5).

Race and Ethnicity

The main social issue among Oaxaca's peasants is not racial, but linguistic or ethnic, though it does have race (and class) overtones. Describing parts of

Mexico reminiscent of Oaxaca, Aguirre Beltrán explored the names given to the two main cultural categories and concluded that the term *mestizo* is adequate for non-Indians, though local terms are more likely to be used in practice. The term *ladino*, so common in Guatemala and Chiapas, is not heard in Oaxaca.

In the inter-cultural regions of the centre and south of the country, Mexicans call themselves people of reason, respectable people, neighbours, toffs, well-manered, or some such designation. They give the Indians the name of natural ones, country people, mad ones, or some other that might make visible the difference between European ethnic origins and those of the original Americans. Like *ladinos* these Mexicans also consider themselves descendents of the Spaniards and take extreme care to make strangers aware that they are not Indians. In all cases when they are questioned explicitly whether they consider themselves *mestizos*, only the educated ones, that is the intellectuals or persons who have had contact with the large urban centres, agree that they are. But most are ignorant of the term or give it another name. (Aguirre Beltrán 1970, 140)

Mestizaje in Oaxaca is a metaphor for 'passing' from one linguistic–cultural category to another. Aguirre Beltrán notes that 'the Mexican of to-day says he is a *mestizo* and defines *mestizaje* not as a simple process of racial amalgamation, but essentially, as added processes of acculturation and social integration' (1970, 140). However, where black traits are prominent in the population, as they are in the fishing communities on the Pacific Coast, they have been treated neither like Indians as 'naturales' nor like other Spanish speakers as 'gente de razón', but as 'gente de media razón' (people of half-reason). Moreover, they are frequently stereotyped as violent (Flanet 1977).

In most parts of Oaxaca, none the less, ethnicity is transactional, in the sense that the boundary between *mestizos* and Indians is fluid. This is not everywhere the case in Meso-America, and Colby and van den Berghe have been at pains to contrast the rigidity of the boundary in Guatemala, its malleability in Chiapas, and its flexibility elsewhere in Mexico. They add, 'Mexicans . . . view the country's population as consisting of a culturally homogeneous group of hispanized mestizos' (1961, 788).

Remaining an Indian in Oaxaca, therefore, depends largely on the maintenance of a linguistic boundary marker by the individual and the community in which he or she lives, although there are other indicators of Indian culture. An obvious external expression of Indian cultural difference from the *mestizo* peasant is the clothing of the Indian populations. Typically, this involves the wearing of traditional garments (*traje tradicional*), such as white cotton shirts and trousers and leather sandals for men, and colourful woven and embroidered *huipiles* (tops) and cotton or wool skirts (depending on the altitude of the group) and going barefoot (or wearing plastic sandals) for women. In the *tierra caliente* on the Pacific, Mixtec women used to wear nothing over their breasts unless they went to market, in which case they would put on a cotton *huipil* (Tibón 1961 reissued 1981). Traditional garments are unique in colour and

design for each language group, but local variants may occur at the community level, much as a specific dialect is often peculiar to a *municipio*.

In the Oaxaca Valleys, assert Cook and Joo, 'the informed outside observer is hard-pressed to distinguish between mestizo and Zapotec non-language forms of ethnocultural expression' (1995, 36), though that hardly invalidates language as *the* vehicle for a specific ethnic identity. Ultimately, being Indian hinges on individual and group self-evaluation and its acceptance by others. *Mestizos* in Jamiltepec speak Mixtec to pursue commercial contacts with local Indians, but they do not conceive themselves, nor are they thought by others, to be Indian (Bartolomé and Barabas 1982; Hernández Díaz 1992*a*).

Zapotec speakers in the Tlacolula Valley do not consider themselves to be Indians, merely peasants (Cook and Diskin 1976). Here Zapotec speakers who also converse in Spanish refer to their mother tongue as *idioma* or *dialecto*, and think of their ancestors not as Zapotecs but as *nuestros antepasados* (Cook and Joo 1995, 37). Additionally, women from the communities around Tlacolula wear the traditional Zapotec blouse, but there seems to be a strong collective wish among them and their menfolk to differentiate themselves from the *sierra* Indians and the pejorative stereotypes attached to them.

Indian Language Groups

The proportion of Oaxaca's population (of 5 years or more) able to speak pre-Columbian languages declined from 54.9 per cent in 1940 to 41.6 per cent in 1980 and 39.1 per cent in 1990. Simultaneously, indigenous monolingualism dropped from 17.5 in 1940 to 11.1 per cent in 1980 and 6.4 per cent in 1990, and suggests that passing has taken place. In addition, the contraction in Indian-language speakers must, in part, be due to death or out-migration from Oaxaca. Against this trend, but as a result of population growth, the absolute number of Indian-language speakers in Oaxaca (just over 1 million) is now larger than the entire population of the state in 1900.

Pre-Columbian language speakers in Oaxaca may be divided into two groups on the basis of their size in 1990. The first has more than 20,000 speakers in each group aged over 5 years—Zapotecs, Mixtecs, Mazatecs, Mixes, Chinantecs, and Chatinos; the second fewer than 20,000 speakers—Cuicatecos, Huaves, Zoques, Triquis, Chontales, Chochos, Amuzgos. In addition, there are three very small groups—Nahuas, Ixcatecos, and Tacuates. Among the larger groups, bilingualism was most common among the Zapotecs (84.5 per cent) and the Mixtecs (77.8 per cent), and lowest among the Mazatecs (66.25 per cent) and Chatinos (63.95 per cent). In the small groups, bilingualism was most frequent among the Zoques (96.0 per cent) and Cuicatecos (88.0 per cent) and rarest among the Triquis (64.1 per cent). Both the Chatinos and the Triquis are unusual in their linguistic homogeneity, their greater sense of ethnic identity than is common among the other groups, and their history of oppression by *mestizos*.

While the Zapotecs occupy the Central Valleys adjacent to the ruined ceremonial city of Monte Alban, the neighbouring Sierra Juárez and Sierra de
Miahuatlan, and the Isthmus of Tehuantepec, the Mixtecs are confined to the
western sections of the state—the Mixteca Alta, Baja, and de la Costa (Fig.
6.1). Mazatecs, Chinantecs, and Mixes occupy the mountainous northern rim
of the state, the north-facing slopes, and adjacent plains—the outer arc to the
Sierra Zapoteca, though each group is spatially separated from the others, as
they are also from the Zapotecs.

Chatinos and Chontales are located in enclaves in the southern Sierra
Madre del Sur: Chatinos lie between the southern Zapotecs and the Mixtecans
of the Costa Chica; Chontales are islanded among Zapotecs. Enclavism also
characterizes the smallest language groups: Cuicatecos are sandwiched
between the Mixtecs, Mazatecs, Chinantecs, and Zapotecs; Huaves and
Zoques occupy Pacific Coast concentrations in the Isthmus of Tehuantepec;
Triquis, Chochos, Amuzgos, Nahuas, Tacuates, and Ixcatecs are islanded
among Mixtecs on the western limits of the state. There is a tendency for those
groups that are nearest spatially to be linked linguistically, though small differences in dialect may make communication difficult, even *within* linguistic
groups.

Information about three settlements close to Ocotlán in the southern portion of the Central Valleys clarifies the problem of mutual intelligibility among
Zapotec speakers (Fig. 1.4). 'Yatzeche can understand the variety of Ocotlán,
and speakers of Tilquiapan can understand the variety of Yatzeche, but speakers of Tilquiapan and Ocotlán do not understand each other' (Suárez 1983,
15). As a result of problems of mutual incomprehensibility of this kind, Suárez
proposes that Zapotec contains 38 subgroups of speakers, Mixtec 29,
Chinantec 14, Mixe 11, Mazatec 6, and Chatino 5 (1983, 18). As many as 100
mutually unintelligible linguistic varieties may be spoken in Oaxaca (Suárez
1983, 16).

Two further aspects of the major language distributions require underlin-
ing. First, there is a strong association between the retention of pre-Columbian
languages and peasant communities living at high altitude, though the altitudinal aspect breaks down among the lowland Isthmus Zapotec. Second, there
is comparatively little interdigitation among the groups. Although only the
Mixe are neatly enclosed within a single district, each major language or ethnic
group has 'its territory', and the larger ones, especially the Zapotecs, Mixtecs,
Mazatecs, Mixes, Chinantecs, and Chatinos, are able to live substantially
within their own communities. If they mix with outsiders, it is more likely to be
with *mestizos* than with other Indians.

Linguistic segregation on this scale has facilitated language retention, especially among the larger groups, for the Indian community forms, in the majority of cases, the unique social space for the circulation of the local language
and, in consequence, the sole possibility to legitimize its presence and func-
tionality (Lewin 1986). The smaller groups, in comparison, are under threat of

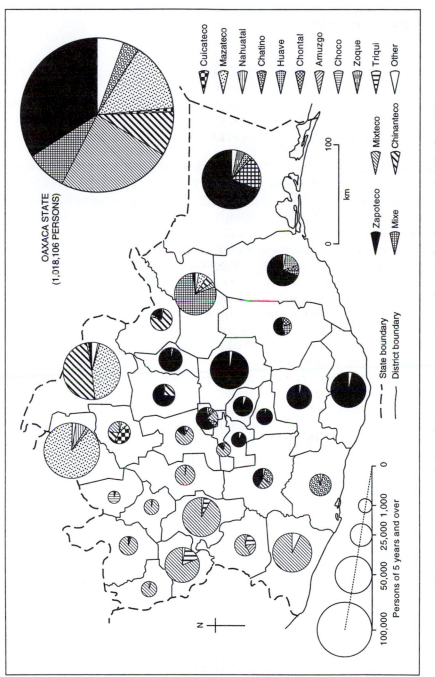

Fig. 6.1 Oaxaca: population of 5 years and over who speak an Indian language, by district, 1990

extinction unless bilingualism becomes the norm, or, like the Triquis, they isolate themselves, or are isolated, from the mainstream (Bartolomé and Barabas 1996; Ruiz López 1993).

'Usos y Costumbres'

In mid-1995, the Oaxaca government, under pressure from the indigenous groups, revised its electoral legislation to allow 408 (or just over 70 per cent) out of the 570 *municipios* to opt to carry out their elections to political *cargos* through community assemblies (Maldonado Alvarado 1996). This adoption of 'usos y costumbres' (traditional usages and customs), is distinct from having secret ballots for political parties, as did the other 162 (Fox and Aranda 1996, 20). Four *municipios* had their results annulled, in at least one instance because the PRI wanted a balloted election, while the community attempted to use its all-male assembly to keep the PRI out.

The introduction of 'usos y costumbres' has, in general, been a means of marginalizing the influence of party politics and other forms of factionalism at the level of the community. In addition, it can also be taken as an approximate guide to those communities that consider themselves to be Indian in a cultural sense. *Municipios* operating 'usos y costumbres' concentrate in the sparsely peopled, central highland areas of the state, surrounding the Central Valleys; in the Central Valleys, they congregate towards the valley sides (Fig. 6.2).

'Usos y costumbres' is an expression of an Indian, corporate, cultural, and material existence, which enjoins the sharing of language, land, male assembly, *cargo*, festival, and *tequio*. These features of Indianness are experienced and expressed at the community level, not at the scale of the language or ethnic group. Not surprisingly, 'usos y costumbres' characterize communities where, in 1970, more than 60 per cent of the population over 5 years spoke an indigenous language (Fig. 2.2). These indigenous characteristics coincide with areas occupied now, and in the past, by the Zapotecs of the Central Valleys and northern and southern *sierras*, by the Mixtecs of the Mixteca Alta, and by the Mazatecs, Cuicatecs, Chinantecs, Mixes, and Chatinos (Fig. 6.1).

Conversely, 'usos y costumbres' are not practised in the *tierra caliente*, and are notably absent from the Tuxtepec area, the Mixteca Baja and Mixteca de la Costa, the Pacific coastal plain, and the Isthmus of Tehuantepec. In short, 'usos y costumbres' do not typify the tropical lowlands, which once belonged to Indian communities but were distributed as large-scale properties after the nineteenth-century reform. However, these areas were reallocated to peasants under local pressure after the Revolution. In the Central Valleys, electoral ballot remains the norm in the modernized valley bottoms following the main roads. Electoral ballots are also held in communities along the principal regional routes leading out of Oaxaca City through the Etla Valley and running north-east towards Puebla via the Cañada or the Mixteca Alta.

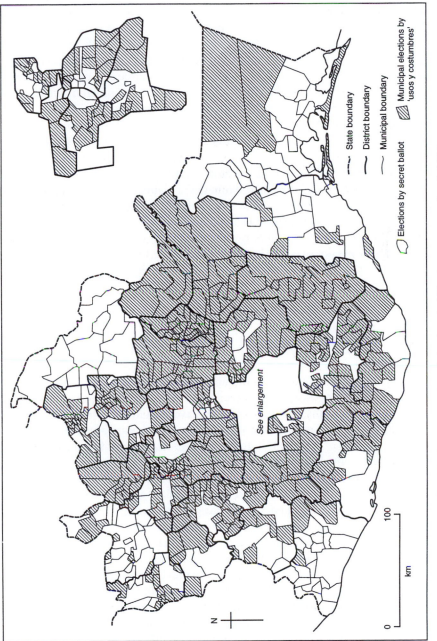

Fig. 6.2 Oaxaca: municipal elections held by 'usos y costumbres', 1995

A sample of twenty communities used by Cook and Joo to study 'Indian identity' was taken from the Tlacolula and Ocotlán arms of the Central Valleys, which, unlike the Etla Valley, do not have a long history of hispanization. Here, nine of the eleven Zapotec-speaking communities (defined by Cook and Joo 1995, 40, table 1) operated 'usos y costumbres' in 1995, as did five of the seven *mestizo* communities and both communities categorized as transitional. There is a strong tendency for communities that are Zapotec speaking to use 'usos y costumbres', while those that are *mestizo* or ambiguous may also adopt 'usos y costumbres' to redefine themselves as indigenous. That is totally consistent with current ethnic movements in Oaxaca, where the absence of traditional culture is by no means a handicap for groups that wish to reinvent themselves as Indian.

Most of Oaxaca's district head-towns are culturally *mestizo* and use the ballot, but there remain six—San Juan Bautista Coixlahuaca, Santiago Choapam, Ixtlán de Juárez, San Ildefonso Villa Alta, San Carlos Yautepec, and Santiago Zacatepec Mixe—where indigenous languages prevail and assemblies are still held. Moreover, 'usos y costumbres' characterize all the *municipios* except the head-towns in the districts of Tlacolula, Cuicatlán, and Nochistlan. A transitional stage applies in some *municipios*, such a Tlacolula, where town centres engage in electoral party politics, and Zapotec-speaking outlying settlements operate community assemblies (Fox and Aranda 1996, 20).

Language Shift and Clothing Change

An important factor in individual Indians passing into the *mestizo* population has been the role played by various agents of the government. Rural teachers, agricultural technicians, and state officials have all had an influence on interethnic interaction and on the linguistic–demographic balance between Indians and *mestizos*. The role of the INI, founded in 1948 and with fourteen co-ordinating centres in the Indian regions of Oaxaca since 1975, has been significant in mediating between *mestizos* and Indians. It has also played an important role in breaking down the isolation of the Indian groups through its programmes of road building and Spanish-language teaching (Infante Cañibano 1998). However, there is evidence to suggest that the INI has encouraged neither self-help nor participation, and that its benefits have, for a variety of reasons, favoured only a minority of the community (Infante Cañibano 1998).

The Indian marker to loose its significance most quickly in Oaxaca was ethnic clothing. In the late 1950s, Drucker discovered that only 11 per cent of the Indian families in Jamiltepec on the Costa Chica of the Pacific coast had members who had given up traditional costume (*revistidos*) in favour of *mestizo* dress. Most of them were literate and had a family history of bilingualism (Drucker 1963). Since Drucker's research, it is clear that the process of clothing change and assimilation to the *mestizo* stratum has become dissociated, as she herself predicted (Drucker 1963). The sheer numbers—especially of men—involved in clothing change in Oaxaca have rendered it of little social significance as a differentiator, leaving language (and, more recently, identity) as the vital—but increasingly fluid—boundary marker.

There has been a noticeable change since 1960 in the degree of commercialization among Indian peasants, especially in the high-altitude communities producing coffee. Commentators have drawn parallels between conditions among the Triqui and the Chatinos with regard to their integration into the cash economy, their reinforced social subordination, and loss of individual language and communal ethnic traits (Hernández Díaz 1992*a*). In the community of Tlacotepec, between 1930 and 1980, Chatino was virtually displaced by Spanish (Hernández Díaz 1992*a*). A less extreme situation has developed in Yalálag in the Sierra Zapotec, where only 3 per cent of the population spoke Spanish in 1900. Around 1940, a generation after the Revolution ended, the figure was only 20 per cent (de la Fuente 1977*a*); yet by 1990, the census showed that barely 20 per cent of Yalaltecos were unable to speak Spanish (high though that figure was by Oaxacan and Mexican standards).

Unless Indians accept that *mestizaje* is synonymous with proletarianization, a major challenge for them is not merely to cope with bilingualism followed by 'language shift', but to achieve sufficient socio-economic mobility to make the effort to cross into the *mestizo* population worth while. *Mestizos* place a high value on wealth and property, esteem commerce and denigrate manual labour, especially agriculture, and emphasize competitiveness and authoritarianism. All these orientations are totally at variance with values formerly held dear in Indian communities.

Why, on the other hand, would Indians wish to maintain their ethnic identity, when it carries the stigma of *natural*, and puts them at such an economic and cultural disadvantage? Indians live out a large part of their lives in isolated rural communities, at some distance from those who can exploit them. Speaking an Indian language is crucial to community membership, which determines a range of benefits (and obligations) of a corporate kind.

Equality, equivalence, and an emphasis on reciprocity characterize Indian communities, from which differentiation is—at least theoretically—banned. So, in aggregate, Indians prize agricultural labour in the *milpa* (maize field), and stress the community at the expense of the individual: they enjoy social security and eschew social mobility—assuming it can be obtained. Above all, they insulate themselves from social subordination to *mestizos* by orientating their lives towards involvement and co-operation with one another. At least, this is what they may once have done.

Ethnicity and Migration

If low rural educational standards have been no barrier to mobility and migrant absorption in the urban labour force (Chapter 5), nor have the plural ethno-linguistic categories of the Oaxacan population. Although almost 40 per cent of Oaxacans speak one of a great variety of pre-Columbian languages, they have never, since 1930, accounted for more than 15 per cent of the inhabitants in Oaxaca City (according to the census), and the vast majority of them are competent in Spanish. The proportion of the population of Oaxaca City aged over 5 who could speak a pre-Columbian language increased from 3.2 to 6.4 and 13.4 per cent in 1960, 1970, and 1980. This is a clear indication of the impact of rural–urban migration, though the proportion dropped to less than 10 per cent in 1990.

In 1980, there were 21,000 non-Spanish speakers in the *municipio* of Oaxaca de Juárez (the figure was 6,500 in 1970), but only 15,000 in 1990. Most used their Oaxacan tongue—predominantly Zapotec or Mixtec—only occasionally, so prevalent was language 'shift' to Spanish among migrants.

Spanish, even if it is only rudimentary and full of grammatical errors and slang, is taken up as quickly as possible and becomes the language of the home. Migrants want to be certain their children learn the city language, and their ethnic identity is saved for the trips back to the village. There they can speak their native tongue and enjoy their Indian heritage without suffering the condescension of urban Mexicans. (Murphy and Stepick 1991*a*, 129)

The definition of race and ethnicity in Oaxaca City is more elusive than that of class. Yescas Peralta claimed that, in the late 1950s, 90 per cent of the population were *indígenas*, 6 per cent *mestizos*, and 4 per cent white (1958, 771). He was clearly using these terms as racial not cultural categories. No one in recent years has attempted a racial classification of the city's population, but the proportion of whites has almost certainly declined under the influence of heavy cityward migration, while the same process has strengthened the Indian presence.

Writing about Oaxaca City in 1966, and drawing particular attention to the abandonment of 'Indian' clothing as a means to passing into the *mestizo* population, Hayner noted:

Although some of the 'Indians' in the suburbs and a few in the outlying villages have helped their children to advance through education, most of them retain a substantial proportion of pre-Columbian culture traits. Attitudes are so strong against fellow campesinos who change their ancient apparel or improve their living conditions that they are regarded as traitors to their class and are forced to leave their native villages. It is only in the towns that men of the lower class have been able to wear shoes, drill pants, sack coats, or European-style felt hats. (1966, 49)

Change of clothing (*cambio de indumentaria*) in the urban areas has often gone hand in hand with language shift, and the wearing of Western fashions is

now as widespread among the urban lower class as the speaking of Spanish. Working on San Juan Chapultepec, Graedon claimed that one-quarter of her sample of adults were bilingual, mostly in Spanish and Zapotec or Mixtec, but with a few speakers of Mixe, Chinantec, Mazatec, and Chatino as well. Yet, she concludes:

Household heads are almost never monolingual because of the necessities of making a living in a Spanish-speaking city. A handful of women speak little or no Spanish, relying upon their husbands to speak for the household when necessary. Few people speak Indian languages outside the household, except with close kin; only neighbours from one of the three well-represented villages are likely to use their common language in public, and even then may become embarrassed if they are overheard. Language is the most obvious marker of Indian ethnicity in the city, and most families do not encourage the children to learn and speak the lower-status language. The few who do attempt to teach the children the family tongue are unlikely to succeed in a nearly monolingual environment. Nine-tenths of the children are monolingual in Spanish, and bilingual children use Spanish with their peers in preference to the language spoken at home. (Graedon 1976, 133)

As the more impoverished environments are the major source areas of Oaxaca's out-of-state emigrants, it follows that the indigenous populations of the Mixteca and Sierra Zapoteca—Mixtecs, Zapotecs, Chinantecs, Mixes, and Triquis—are prominent in the current streams of migration to the US–Mexican border and to the USA. The movement focuses on the agribusiness activities and urban service centres of California, but also spreads north to Washington, Oregon, and the Pacific Coast of Canada, and east to Miami and New York. Many of these indigenous workers are, or have been, undocumented and liable to exploitation by Americans and other Mexicans. Moreover, they leave behind communities typified by a lack of male adults (though this is difficult to detect in the *de jure* census) and a decaying agricultural system.

One of the positive consequences of this migration, however, has been the formation of indigenous migrant organizations, some of which have drawn on their ethnic identity as well as their experience of labour disputes in Oaxaca and other parts of Mexico. Prominent among such organizations is El Comité Cívico Popular Mixteco, which was founded in Baja California in 1981 and is active in San Diego County and other parts of California. The Zapotec organizations, though ethnic at base, are more specific to the *municipio* in which the migrants originated. For example, Tlacolula, in the Central Valleys, has given rise to a migrant organization in Los Angeles. It has been active in support of the political 'left' in the parent *municipio*, and has lobbied the Mexican Consulate in Los Angeles as well as the governor of Oaxaca (Sarmiento Sánchez 1992).

Indian Subordination?

While Oaxaca's *mestizos* are stratified by class, Indians, almost all of whom are peasants, are often depicted as unstratified. *Mestizos* form a social and cultural section in the society that is superior to Indians; this distinction is especially marked if it involves the *mestizo* middle class and Indian peasants. However, there is no watertight barrier between *mestizo* peasants and Indian peasants in Oaxaca, though each group tends to occupy a different ecological zone. For example, the wetter, more affluent Etla arm of the Central Valleys is notably Hispanized and *mestizo*; so, too, are the tropical lowlands on the periphery of the state. However internally unstratified each Indian ethno-linguistic group has been, historically, there is nevertheless an ethnic pecking order in many regions of Oaxaca, with the Zapotec often playing leadership or brokerage roles.

The following section examines *mestizo* domination of rural Indians, but also shows that social movements have taken place among Indians to redress their status as an underclass. Against the stereotype of Indian subordination, the socially superior status of some Zapotecs has to be acknowledged, together with the privileged position of Zapotec as a language. The Zapotec language has been the basis for literary and political movements of a regional nature in the Isthmus of Tehuantepec, and Zapotec-speaking weavers in the Oaxaca Valley have drawn upon their ethnic identity as a source of artistic inspiration.

Mestizo Dominance

The sociological and anthropological literature on Oaxaca is replete with reference to *mestizo* dominance at all scales, whether the focus is Oaxaca City, where it is almost total, or small communities, whose *mestizo* residents are a mere handful. A typical observation is the following which refers to the Mazatec tropical lowlands, where, in the context of resettlement, 'mestizo shopkeepers have acquired control of the best land and dominate the economic life of the community' (Partridge, Brown, and Nugent 1982, 258). Given the complexity and fragmented nature of the community structures and ecology of Oaxaca, however, Hernández Díaz's observation bears quotation:

Even if it is certain that in general terms the relations which are established between Indians and non-Indians (*mestizos*, Spaniards, people of reason . . .) are asymmetrical, where the Indians are the social sector dominated, subjugated, exploited, marginalised, stigmatised, it is also certain that these processes are not by any means homogeneous. Very much to the contrary, they acquire their specificity through multiple and varied factors that intervene in the nature of the inter-ethnic contact. Thus we have communities where the contact with national society has not been with numerically important sectors, however, the effects of the contact have been highly complicated and totally transforming of Indian organization. (1986, 314)

A typical example of Indian exploitation is provided by the involvement of the Chatinos in the coffee industry of the Pacific Coast:

On the coffee estates the Chatinos together with *mestizos* share the same social position in terms of class. They are all peasants who temporarily migrate to work in the coffee estates. Hence there exists no difference up to this point between Indian and non-Indian peasants. But on arriving at the estate each has a different treatment. Non-Indians always have the possibility of eventually occupying positions a bit superior to the rest, such as that of watchman or yard boy. The Chatinos are exploited both because it is on their communal lands that the whites have set up their large estates, and because they are used as cheap labour. They are cheated both in the accounting of their work and in the payment made. (Hernández Díaz 1986, 314)

Sometimes the hierarchical relationship between *mestizos* and Indians is mitigated by ties of *compadrazgo* (ritual co-godparenthood), but these, too, invariably involve asymmetrical relationships, with *mestizos* making short-run, small-scale contributions to their *compadres* and *commadres*, but invoking substantial—often non-financial—support in return on a continuing basis.

Indian Protest

It is not surprising that those groups that have the longest and bitterest history of exploitation and abuse in Oaxaca—the Triqui (Amnesty International 1986), and the most violent experience of federal government interference—the Mazatec and Chinantec—should have been involved in social movements against authority. The state itself, rather than individual oppressors, was the appropriator of 50,000 hectares located to the west of Tuxtepec, adjacent to the Alemán Dam, leading to the forced resettlement of about 20,000 people between 1949 and 1952 (McMahon 1973). In the area to be flooded, Mazatecs, who accounted for 96 per cent of the population, owned 21,000 hectares. An additional 30,000 hectares were in the hands of *metizos*, who made up the remainder.

The failure of the Papaloapan Commision to acquire sufficient land and provide appropriate infrastructure and compensation led to a catastrophe for the Mazatec. Two thousand families struck out on their own and disappeared from the record. The remainder, despite the involvement of the Instituto Nacional Indigenísta, suffered hardship, community collapse, and class subordination in the resettlement zones, two of which were located in Oaxaca, close to Tuxtepec (Ballesteros, Edel, and Nelson 1970; Partridge, Brown, and Nugent 1982).

While many Mazatec protested by escaping, subsequent government action in the Papaloapan Basin has provoked a reaction of despair among the neighbouring Chinantec at Cerro de Oro (Miguel de la Madrid Dam). The Chinantec, fearful that another bout of forced resettlement to make way for a further dam project was but a euphemism for proletarianization and ethnocide, created a messianic protest movement in the 1970s to voice their fierce

opposition to the scheme (Barabas and Bartolomé 1973; Barabas 1977; Bartolomé and Barabas 1990).

On 12 December 1972, the Virgin of Guadelupe appeared in a cave on the hillside overlooking the dam; allegedly, she asked the president and priests of the *municipio* to speak with her. This apparition developed into a cult centred on pieces of wood found at the site. The pieces of wood have been carried in procession, and the cave in which 'God's engineer' appeared has become a centre for Chinantec pilgrims. 'The incipient messianic movement', wrote Barabas and Bartolomé, 'has accomplished what politicians, engineers, businessmen, and false mediators have tried to prevent; the unity of the Chinantec people in the face of pressures from the regional and national society' (1973, 15). The project was not completed until the end of the 1980s, and involved the displacement of more than thirty communities with 26,000 inhabitants. Most of them were resettled in the state of Vera Cruz, some of them hundreds of kilometres from their native villages (Bartolomé and Barabas 1990, vol. ii; 1996; 1997).

A rather more traditional form of oppression obtains among the Triqui in the Mixteca Alta and Baja. Here they are spread across the various climatic zones and three districts, but dominate only one *municipio*. The Movimiento de Unificación de Lucha Triqui (MULT) was founded in 1981 and has involved the three Triqui communities in the Mixteca Baja located around Putla. These communities have experienced intense population pressure. They are often at war with one another, and in semi-permanent conflict with the neighbouring market centres of Putla, Chicahuaxtla, and Tlaxiaco. They suffer depredations against their communal lands; exploitation through the price offered for their coffee, which they have traded for guns and liquor (Tibón 1981 originally 1961); and linguistic and cultural disparagement (though there is now a Triqui-Spanish dictionary (Good 1979))—all at the hands of their urban–*mestizo* neighbours (García Alcaraz 1973).

Many Triqui from the Mixteca Alta around Chicahuaxtla have migrated to the comparative safety of Oaxaca City since the late 1970s, where they weave and sell artisanal goods in a small open-air market. However, the majority of the small Triqui-speaking community (approximately 12,900) still live in Mixteca, where they maintain their struggle against their oppressors, occasionally breaking out in violence.

Zapotec Superiority

Relations between the various ethnic groups are in many cases slight and frequently egalitarian. This applies between Chatinos and Mixtecs and Chatinos and Zapotecs, the Chatinos referring to the latter as people of a different language, but without any pejorative qualification. Mixtecs and Chatinos mix at *fiestas* in the Mixteca Baja, while Mixtecs, Mazatecs, Cuicatecs, and Chinantecs meet at Catholic festivals and markets in the northern highlands.

The relations these groups develop are cordial, and in addition to the inter-change of goods, they function to transmit news and meetings between acquaintances and friends (Ravicz 1965).

In contrast, inequality characterizes the relations of highland Zapotec and the Mixe, as it does also the contact between Mixtecs and the Triqui. Nahmad reports that Zapotecs refer to the Mixe as idle, ignorant, and uncivilized (1965). Further information about the hierarchical relations between the Zapotec and Mixe are exposed by Nahmad:

Relations between Zapotecs and Mixes are equivalent to the relations that in other regions of refuge the Indians have with *ladinos*, *mestizos*, or people of reason. (1965, 91–2)

The characteristic method of exploiters in other Indian zones is naturally put into effect in this region: loans and advances in cash against the harvest, at prices previously fixed, the high prices of goods, switched scales, the use of co-godparenthood as a means to enlace emotionally relations that are apparently social and religious, and that are deep down economic. These subtle methods, that bind a person, operate daily between the Mixes in their relations with the Zapotecs. (1965, 53)

De la Fuente reports, in a similar vein, that Zapotec disparagement of Mixes was extended to Chinantecs (1977*a*).

In the Isthmus of Tehuantepec, Zapotecs control the production and con-sumption of the Huaves via the markets in Salina Cruz, Tehuantepec, and Juchitán, and the Zoques through Matias Romero and Niltepec. But Zapotec domination is not only economic:

The acquisition of Zapotec language, clothing and festivities by Zoques and Huaves is not merely an economic phenomenon, but one of cultural domination because of the role they play as reference points. (Hernández Díaz 1986, 307)

In fact, isthmus Zapotecs tend to consider themselves different from *mestizos* and 'indios', the latter being treated as poor and marginalized (Hernández Díaz 1992*a*).

Zapotec as a Prestigious Language

Zapotec's prestige as a language goes back to pre-colonial times. It has been remarkably well preserved in the Isthmus of Tehuantepec—notably in Juchitán, where it is still the everyday language of the local élite. It is also the vehicle for a substantial literature and for cultural protest movements involv-ing local history and poetry (de la Cruz 1984; Campbell *et al.* 1993)—much of it carried in the journal, *Guchachi' Reza*. Juchitán's neighbour and rival, Tehuantepec, is, in contrast, a typical *mestizo* town, and pitted against it on most issues, contemporary or historical. The inhabitants of Juchitán are mostly Zapotec speaking, proud to be Juchitecos, and resent Spanish-speaking officials whether from Oaxaca or Mexico City. Their distinctive eth-nic identity enabled an amalgam of radical groups, based on the Coalición

Obrero-Campesino-Estudiantil del Isthmo (COCEI), to supplant the PRI in the government of the *municipio* in the early 1980s, until they were driven from office in November 1983.

Class and Ethnicity

Ricardo and Isabel Pozas's (1978) contention that Mexico has a hierarchical class structure related to a capitalist mode of production typical of the Third World seems to apply well at the national level. However, I lay greater emphasis than they do on the phenotypical correlation between éliteness and whiteness or lightness, and vice versa. Their discussion of the Indians as an *intraestructura*, or an enclave, within the class structure conforms somewhat to my own interpretation, except that Indians are not simply peasants and culturally different. Rather they are culturally different and form an enclave in the peasantry, subdivided into ethno-linguistic categories. The situation appears caste-like, but turns out to be more malleable.

The Indians' position is determined first and foremost by their peasant status, but it is their cultural characteristics, that make them such prime targets for stereotyping and exploitation. Ethnic pluralism seems to be highly relevant to this discussion, since it separates class issues from those of culture and race, and enables us to envisage Oaxaca's Indians as class and culturally determined. However, they are often exploited in economic terms as well as being culturally dominated and disparaged, and so some aspects of their subordination take on class characteristics.

That ethno-linguistic pluralism in Oaxaca has broader social structural implications than simply being an expression of an individual's lifestyle is due to the corporate nature of the Indian communities and the way in which their social solidarity, as Indians, is expressed in the holding of, and access to, land. It is at the level of the *municipio,* therefore, rather than that of the entire ethnie, which is a linguistic category rather than a functioning group, that ethnicity is constructed.

Oaxaca's social structure is composed of two major socio-cultural sections: *mestizo* and Indian, the former being slightly the larger of the two and growing at the expense of the latter through modernization, migration, education, and the national language policy of Hispanization. The *mestizo* section is both urban and rural and is class stratified, with a rural peasantry and an urban middle class as well as a proletarian/marginal population. The Indian section is almost entirely rural, and is generally looked down upon by the *mestizo* section that controls the state capital and most of the smaller towns, notably the principal settlements of the ex-*distritos*. *Mestizos* dominate governmental and educational functions and the major commercial transactions that occur in towns and the larger villages. Nevertheless, levels of material life are little different among the Indian and *mestizo* peasantries, which, between them, account for over 80 per cent of the Oaxaca population.

The Indian section is not class stratified, except where Indian middlemen have emerged, though evidence for rich individual Indians goes back decades (Malinowski and de la Fuente 1982). In some areas there is an ethnic pecking order among the different language groups based on prestige and power, and expressed in commercial exploitation resembling that exacted by *mestizos*. That apart, the Indian section is not internally class stratified to any great degree, and the municipal components into which each ethnie is subdivided have, historically, emphasized ritual expenditure as a levelling device. It is the value of social equality lived out at low levels of living within landholding corporate communities that gives the linguistically defined Indian section its coherence and marks it off from *mestizo* Oaxacan—and national—society.

Clearly, most of these processes of cultural-linguistic domination and—among the *mestizos*—class differentiation, have their roots deep in the colonial period. Oaxaca City might be diagnosed as a *mestizo* control point for the entire state, surrounded by a Hispanized aureole in the Central Valleys and, at a greater distance, by an Indian hinterland or region of refuge (Aguirre Beltrán 1973)—mostly at high altitude. From this hinterland, it might be argued, surplus value is being extracted by the market mechanism. Indeed, there is evidence for this in the coffee industry and other profitable peasant activities. The failure of peasant markets to operate, in this simple way has, however, been discussed in Chapter 4. Here I want to concentrate on two topics only: the Hispanization of the Central Valley region, and the permeability of the *mestizo*–Indian barrier.

The Central Valleys have been Hispanized by contact with Oaxaca City and by the influence of the colonial Marquesado of Cortes, which spread from the western edge of the colonial capital into the Etla and Zimatlan arms of the valley system. It is here that modern developments—including education, land reform, and migration—have encouraged *mestizaje* in a rural context. The pottery-making village of Atzompa exemplifies this process (Hendry 1957). Here Zapotec was allegedly still spoken in 1940, but has now quite disappeared. However, information about 'usos y costumbres', shows that male elective assembly was used there in 1995, in preference to the ballot. So the argument about the adoption of 'usos y costumbres' as a means of recuperating ethnic identity in the Tlacolula and Ocotlán arms of the Central Valley may be applicable in Atzompa as well.

The net consequence is that Oaxaca City is surrounded by an aureole of *mestizo* communities that are extremely well integrated into the market and represent commercialized peasant communities that are certainly not culturally exploited (Cook and Joo 1995). But Oaxaca City functions in a dominant way *vis-à-vis* the highland Indian communities, either directly, through government, the law (Parnell 1988), and commercial transactions—often based on the sale of manufactured goods—or indirectly via smaller towns in the Oaxaca settlement hierarchy such as Putla or Tlaxiaco.

The permeability of the boundary between *mestizo* and Indian, expressed by language shift over time at the state level, and, in Oaxaca City, through migration followed by language change, has made the cultural sections more voluntaristic than ever before. Moreover, bilingualism among the Indians has made them more self-confident and able to fend off exploitation and more capable of expressing their identity beyond their municipal boundaries. The growth of ethnic organizations in the last decade or two is testimony to these changes, and, ironically, has been made feasible by the Indians' ability to read, write, and publish in Spanish—as well as by their experience of migration to distant border regions and the USA. Changes in the national political situation have also facilitated ethnic awareness among the linguistic-indigenous groups in Oaxaca.

Ethnic Organization

Revindications by Indians in Mexico (and throughout the Americas) were launched by the International Work Group for Indigenous Affairs' 'Declaration of Barbados on Native Rights' in the early 1970s (IWGIA 1971). This was followed in Mexico by the 1975 Patzcuaro Conference on indigenous issues. Presided over by President Echeverría, it was organized by the Secretaría de Reforma Agraria, the INI, and the Confederación Nacional Campesina (all essentially agencies of the PRI).

One of the principal achievements of Patzcuaro was the establishment of a Consejo Nacional de Pueblos Indígenas (CNPI), which at first was docile but then adopted an increasingly intransigent, anti-PRI stance at the 1977 and 1979 meetings. The CNPI promoted Supreme Councils to give a regional voice to each ethno-linguistic group. These developments spawned a number of ethnic movements in Oaxaca, and facilitated the publication of ethnic journals, such as the (Spanish-language) *El Topil*, voice of the Asamblea de Autoridades Zapotecas y Chintecas de la Sierra (AZACHIS).

Also founded during the Echeverría administration was the Alianza Nacional de Profesionales Indígenas (ANPIBAC), again with government involvement. This association of 2,000 bilingual teachers claimed to represent fifty-six ethnic groups at the national level, and took as its objective the development of a bilingual and bicultural educational project with an emphasis first and foremost on the culture of the group in question. Education was to be a means to reinforce ethnic identity. Although ANPIBAC argued that indigenous communities were being destroyed by capitalism, they did not seek to overturn it; rather they sought 'a place in the federal political arena, insisting that their objective was to maintain the specific forms of life, culture and identity of the indigenous population' (Hernández Díaz 1993, 49).

Important in the formulation of new strategies for the Indians was the *corriente crítica* (critical current) developed by certain anthropologists and intellec-

tual Indian leaders during the 1970s and 1980s. They have rejected (like the 'Indianists' before them) the *indigenísmo* of the anthropological and political establishment, who assumed the assimilation of Indians and their disappearance into national society. Rather, they have argued in favour of *indigenismo radical* or *indianismo*, according to which Indian ethnic groups will endure, and should be allowed to return to the civilizatory projects interrupted by the Spanish conquest.

Accordingly, they demand respect for the rights of Indians to be different, and recognition of Indian languages as official languages (Spanish, Zapotec, and English are now used to label the archaeological remains at major sites in the Central Valleys of Oaxaca). Acknowledgement and respect for ancestral cultures, and conditions for the technical maintenance of ancestral and/or traditional production are additional aspects of their platform (Hernández Díaz 1993, 45–6). Language, religion, history, and lifestyle have been deployed in various combinations to guarantee or extend ethnic rights at the state and federal levels. Ethnicity has been used to justify rights and claims, and as a motive for mobilization (Hernández Díaz 1993, 47).

In Oaxaca, during the 1980s, the most important ethnic organizations in Oaxaca were the Coalición Obrero Campesino Estudiantil del Istmo (COCEI) based on Juchitán, in the Isthmus of Tehuantepec, and the Movimiento de Unificación y Lucha Triqui (MULT) in the Mixteca Alta. Also of significance were the Comité Organizador y de Consulta para la Unión de los Pueblos de la Sierra Norte de Oaxaca (CODECO) in the Sierra Juárez, the Comité de Defensa y Desarrollo de los Recursos Naturales y Humanos de la Región Mixe (CODREMI) in the Sierra Mixe, and the Organización para la Defensa de los Recursos Naturales de la Sierra Juárez (ODRENASIJ) in the Sierra Juárez. ODRENASIJ, CODECO, and CODREMI were essentially regional organizations, representing twenty 'comunidades indigenas' in the case of the two former and thirteen in the case of CODREMI.

By 1996, ODRENASIJ was defunct (Maldonado Alvarado 1996), but two new new ethnic organizations had been created: the Frente Unico de Presidentes Municipales Indígenas de la Sierra Mazateca (FUPMISM) and the Organización de Autoridades Comunales y Municipales de la Triqui Alta (OACYMTA). Also formed in recent years have been the Asamblea de Autoridades Mixes (ASAM)—an adjunct of CODREMI, Servicios del Pueblo Mixe, the Unión de Comunidades de la Zona Norte del Istmo (UCIZONI) in the Isthmus of Tehuantepec, the Unión de Comunidades Indigenas de la Costa 'Cien Anos de Soledad' (UCI) on the Pacific Coast, the Union de Comunidades Indigenas de la Región Istmo (UCIRI) in the Isthmus, la Asamblea de Autoridades Chinantecas y Zapotecas de la Sierra (ASAZCHIS) in the Sierra Norte. There is scarcely an area of Oaxaca notable for the persistence of indigenous language groups that now lacks some form of ethnic movement.

Each group focuses on the issues that are most relevant to itself, and has alliances with either intellectuals (CODREMI, CODECO, and ODRENASIJ),

or peasants and proletarians (COCEI and MULT), or the rural poor (UCIRI and UCI). All envisage their struggle as part of the larger indigenous issue in Oaxaca and Mexico. Indeed, the demands are very similar from one group to the other. These include, accurate demarcation of territorial boundaries; regulation of the extraction of natural resources, especially forestry; expulsion of the Summer Institute of Linguistics, which has introduced Protestantism and schism to many communities (the Summer Institute was banned from Mexico in the late 1970s but never left).

Other preoccupations include recognition of traditional methods of electing municipal leaders (though this implies the disenfranchising of the female population); respect for municipal autonomy; provision of public services; and elimination of local and regional *caciques* (bosses). Removal of government employees who are dishonest or incompetent; provision of credit for agricultural workers; and freeing of indigenous political prisoners, are additional demands (Hernández Díaz 1993, 51).

FUPMISM, for example, was founded in 1993, and brings together the presidents of eleven *municipios* where Mazatec (and some Nahuatl) is spoken. Its objectives have been to improve public services and economic output, to consolidate the traditional *cargo* system, and to discuss the autonomy of the area—in the sense of wishing to exclude political parties from elections, which should, instead, be by 'usos y costumbres'. Realizing that, with the expiry of the (municipal) presidential period in 1995, FUPMISM would be in danger of disappearing, the Consejo Indigena Regional Autónomo de la Mazateca was formed in March 1995, in the presence of 600 delegates from nine *municipios* and fifty-five *agencias municipales* (Maldonado Alvarado 1996).

In 1995, OACYMTA was created by the Triqui communities of Chicahuaxtla and its four *agencias de policía*, in collaboration with Yosonduchi, an *agencia municipal* of Putla. In furtherance of the goal of achieving greater autonomy, through the reorganization of local government units along ethnic lines, a government official and the president of Putla were held hostage for several days in Chicahuaxtla. San Andrés Chicahuaxtla has become the centre for Triqui cultural revival: recovery of group historical memory and defence of traditional rights have been identified as key issues, together with what are seen as vital issues for the Triqui—communal assembly and the *cargo* system (Maldonado Alvarado 1996).

Conclusion

Oaxaca is divided socially into two cultural sections, the numerically larger *mestizo*, the smaller Indian. *Mestizos* are ranked by class and live in urban settlements, peasant villages, and the modernized rural areas, notably where there are large estates, sugar mills, or oil refineries, which give them access to many of the material benefits of modern life. They disparage Indian culture and values,

rurality and poverty, all of which are set in a context of physical isolation, often associated with areas of high altitude. Indians are essentially classless and emphasize the corporateness of their peasant lives at the municipal level.

Indians are not a cohesive group, but are subdivided linguistically in complex ways not only into many major languages, but also into dialect islands within those tongues. No language group has achieved internal organization, though several are well on the way to doing so. Whitecotton's observation about the Zapotec, that the term has been 'more of an artefact of external observers than a meaningful unit for the people to whom it has been applied' (1977, 271), was, until recently, applicable to all linguistic-ethnic groups in Oaxaca.

Indians endure peasant isolation as a collectivity, from which individuals can escape at will—but at their peril—into the *mestizo* section of society, a process which usually involves language shift, migration, urbanization, and proletarianization or marginalization. Only recently have ethnic movements developed with the intention of reconstructing identities at an ethno-regional level, seizing control of the management of local resources for their own benefit, and thus elaborating a proactive policy for the development of Indian Oaxaca. In some cases, migration to the USA has encouraged the sense of ethnic identity beyond the confines of the *municipio*.

Ethnic movements in Oaxaca are not free from problems. The only ethnic political boundary in existence is that surrounding the Mixe district, which has been notorious for its historic manipulation by *caciques*; otherwise, ethnic groups and district boundaries are by no means concordant. Even more problematic is the fact that, while the majority of Oaxacans are peasants, and the vast majority of Indians are peasants, not all peasants are Indians; many non-Indians have problems similar to those who consider themselves 'indigenous'.

Finally, the very isolation of the Indian communities in the past has ensured their survival. Yet the pro-development strategy adopted by many Indian groups may lead to their being drawn into the mainstream of Mexican life more rapidly and fully than under the PRI's indigenist policy, so that a new and more terminal process of de-Indianization may occur. An opposing argument can, however, be constructed. The determination of the Indian groups, and especially their young, educated leaders, to organize for their own benefit, and the speed with which they have responded, via 'usos y costumbres', to recover control over their community, where that has been necessary, suggests a different outcome.

Although Oaxaca's ethno-linguistic groups have begun to reclaim their regional identity and their capacity to act in an organized way, the fundamental social unit of peasant Oaxaca remains the *municipio*. Speaking about male migrants in Oaxaca City, Murphy and Stepick note that, if they 'have an identity other than Mexican, it is first with the village they come from and secondly with the language they speak—not as Indians' (1991*a*, 129). Accordingly, it is to social organization at the micro-level of the village or *municipio* that attention is turned in the following chapter.

7

Community, Class, and the Rural Municipio

Administrative fragmentation occurs to an extreme degree in Oaxaca, and this is a result both of its mountain and valley physiography and the insular nature of its settlements, the origins of which go back to early colonial or pre-Hispanic times. The current archipelago of towns, villages, and hamlets, set in a sea of near-uninhabited mountains and valleys, is reflected in the spatial pattern of *municipios*, the principal units of local government below the level of the state. There are 570 *municipios* in Oaxaca, about 24 per cent of all those in Mexico (Brito de Martí 1982), with an average of 5,200 persons per unit. Not only are these municipal jurisdictions much smaller and more numerous than elsewhere, but they are also relatively more autonomous (Fox and Aranda 1996).

Social fragmentation does not end with the *municipio*. Within each there is usually a miniature hierarchy of settlements, reaching down from the nucleated *cabacera municipal* (head settlement) to smaller offshoots, often having a recognized, but subordinate, legal status. In 1950, for example, 3,000 distinctive population aggregates (*localidades*) in Oaxaca were recognized by the census, ranging from *ciudades*, *villas*, and *pueblos* down to *rancherías* and *congregaciones*. Each of the two latter had less than 200 inhabitants, with *congregaciones* being typified by scattered populations: 79 per cent of the Oaxaca population at that date lived in places with fewer than 2,500 persons.

Since 1950, the number of *localidades* recognized by the census has increased with the expansion of the population. By 1970, the number had risen to 3,690 and 21 per cent of the inhabitants lived in settlements with fewer than 100 dwellers; by 1990, the number of *localidades* had increased to 7,200, 47 per cent of which recorded fewer than 100 inhabitants. While cityward migration has concentrated on Oaxaca City and the smaller district centres, rural population increase has been accommodated within the *municipios* by developing local pioneer zones.

It is at the level of the *municipio* that the peasant community, as a small-scale social collectivity, is constructed, lived, and expressed (Martínez Vásquez and Arellanes Meixueiro 1985). Most communities have their origins in the *republicas de Indios* (Indian communities) established by the Spaniards during the *colonia* (Chapter 2). In the *pueblos* of the Villa Alta area during the seventeenth and eighteenth centuries, endogamy was high, approaching 100 per cent in

some periods (Chance 1989, 124). The more isolated *municipios* tended to enjoy greater autonomy than did those close to the seat of Spanish rule in Antequera, but, during the Porfiriato, they were all grouped into administrative districts, each under a hand-picked *jefe político,* loyal to Díaz, who controlled a posse of armed *rurales.*

In direct contradiction of Díaz's dictatorial system of social control, Article 115 of the Mexican constitution of 1917 defined the *municipio libre* as the basic unit for the territorial, political, and administrative organization of the federated Mexican states, to be governed by an *ayuntamiento* (council) chosen by direct popular vote. Article 115 declared 'there shall be no intermediate authority between [the municipality] and the state government' (Perez Jiménez 1975, 18). The twenty-six districts were re-designated ex-*distritos* (former districts) and in Oaxaca were relegated to use by the census. Despite local community pressure in the opposite direction, the number of *municipios* in Oaxaca was cut drastically after the Mexican Revolution—from 1,131 (including *agencias municipales*) in 1910, when three-quarters had fewer than 1,000 inhabitants—to 618 in 1921 (Ornelas López 1987*b*). It was reduced further to 590 in 1930 and 571 in 1942, when the ex-districts were increased to twenty-nine. Since 1968 the number of municipios has been stable at 570, and the districts, which by then numbered thirty, have been legally restored (INEGI 1997).

Irrespective of the demotion of ex-districts, district headquarters retained important judicial and administrative functions associated with the federal and state governments. In Santa Catarina Juquila, a district capital, for example, located in the Sierra Madre del Sur, about 40 kilometres inland from Puerto Escondido on the Pacific Coast:

There is an office of the internal revenue service and the state tax collector; there is an office for the inspection of federal schools, a coordinating centre of the National Indian Institute; a post office, a telegraph office, a district jail, a state police post, and a small detachment of the army. There is also a district court. The magistrate of the district court hears appeals from municipal courts, felony cases, and a few civil suits. Working with the district court is a public prosecutor who may order arrests and is constitutionally empowered (as is the *presidente municipal*) to impose agreements and levee fines on transgressors. (Greenberg 1981, 59)

The *municipios* have provided the spatial framework for the evolution of high- and medium-altitude corporate communities, which not only elect their own political leadership through male-only communal assemblies, and thereby exercise control over local government, but manage their communal resources, notably land, water, and forests. These traditional political systems have recently been recognized by the Oaxaca legislature, which permits communities to run their political affairs according to 'usos y costumbres' (traditional usage and custom). Just as significantly, corporate communities have traditionally organized their unique Catholic *fiesta* system, and have operated

a series of religious *cargos* that parallel, and often interlace with, the secular system of local government posts. These posts have been closed to women, though women's assumed 'invisibility' in community affairs has been increasingly contested by female researchers, and notably so in the context of religion.

This chapter opens with a discussion of Oaxaca's rural settlement pattern, passing over the major city—Oaxaca City, known officially as Oaxaca de Juárez, which was considered in detail in Chapter 5. The spatial framework of the *municipios* is examined and the system of peasant local government explored. Attention is then focused on the civil–religious hierarchies and the closed or open nature of the peasant communities; both these themes require careful evaluation in the light of Oaxaca's recent history of out-migration and modest socio-economic differentiation. A further element of complexity is introduced by discussion of *municipio* boundaries and boundary conflicts, the emergence of the *ejido* communities, and the evolving role of women in community affairs. It is concluded that stasis-orientated models of communities are inadequate to capture the subtle changes that are, and have been, taking place in Oaxaca.

Irrespective of how open and class differentiated communities are becoming, the importance of the *municipio* as a self-governing entity is increasing. The final section of this chapter looks at the role of Oaxaca's *municipios* in the context of Mexico's recent policy of decentralizing public administration. The Mexican government has reduced its bias against sharing its revenue with poorer states, like Oaxaca, and the World Bank has established a Municipal Funds Programme that has targeted Oaxaca's *municipios* and encouraged local decision-making about the selection of development projects and the priority to be given to them. This represents a radical departure from the passivity of the *municipios* formerly encouraged by the PRI.

Settlement Pattern and Community

Traditionally, geographers have categorized settlement as either nucleated or dispersed. Using that dichotomy, most Oaxacan peasants live in nucleated towns and villages and only in the Mixtec areas are scattered farmsteads common (Luebke 1959). In the *sierras*, where the layout of the settlement may be disrupted by irregular terrain, it is quite normal for peasant households to maintain both a village house and a more flimsy hut at higher altitude from which cultivating or stock-rearing tasks can be carried out in the summer season. This latter pattern is particularly widespread among the Mixe.

Nucleated settlements that are located on flat sites, irrespective of whether they are *pueblos* or *rancherias*, are laid out on a common gridiron pattern, and are replicas, in miniature, of the archetypal Latin American colonial city—and therefore of Oaxaca City itself. Each block in the settlement is divided into substantial plots, or *solares*, surrounded by adobe walls or cane fences made from

reeds. Entry to the *solar* from the road system, which may be paved in the village centre and degenerate to a dirt track towards the edge, is through a gateway. This may be modest or imposing depending on the economic means of the occupants, but is always large enough to take bullock carts and other pieces of agricultural equipment.

Semi-concealed within the *solar* in villages in the Oaxaca Valley, are the reed or adobe houses, kitchens, and food stores of the nuclear or extended family; tethered under the shade trees or wandering in the open are glimpsed the draft stock and domestic animals—chickens, turkeys, goats, and pigs. House design and building materials are controlled by altitudinal/climatic factors: in the *sierras*, wooden houses with interdigitating logs at the corners and shingle roofs are the norm, as are wattle-walled and steeply pitched thatched houses in the tropical lowlands around Tuxtepec. Houses near the Pacific are different again, with circular walls and conical thatched roofs that some have attributed to the African heritage of its black plantation labourers (Tibón 1981).

At or near the centre of the settlement stands the Catholic church, dedicated to the patron saint, whose name is attached to the pre-Hispanic (often Aztec) settlement name, as in Santa María Atzompa or San Felipe Jalapa de Díaz. The stone church (often with a beautiful but deteriorated interior ornamentation of the Baroque period) is usually located on, or adjacent to, a small *plaza*, which, in the more affluent villages, is nowadays adorned by a bandstand and basketball court—symbols of modest 'urban' achievement. Also on the *plaza* are the main shops and the seat of local government, the *palacio municipal* (Pl. 7.1), all of which, together with the church, usually have loudspeakers over which competing messages of a secular or religious kind—or just simply pop music—may be broadcast.

More important than the settlement category or size-grouping into which each small town or village fits is its administrative status as *cabecera* (head place) of the *municipio* or as a subordinate *agencia municipal* or *agencia de policía*. Of course, all towns are *cabeceras*, and the major ones are heads of *distritos* that group together, on average, about twenty *municipios*. In the 1950s, for example, Oaxaca had twenty-nine districts (then called ex-*distritos*), 571 *municipios*, 589 *agencias municipales*, and 1,586 *agencias de policía*. An *agente municipal* or an *agente de policía*, each appointed by the *ayuntamiento* (council) of the *municipio,* administers these small units. The basic pattern has remained essentially the same since then; in 1990 there were 30 districts, 570 *municipios*, and 2,300 *agencias municipales* (Fig. 7.1) (Gijsbers 1996).

The spatial distribution of *municipios* faithfully reflects the distribution of rural population. Units are small where population density is high, for example in the Oaxaca Valley, Mixteca Alta, the Chinantla, and Sierra Juárez. *Municipios* are typically large in the sparsely populated and more remote *sierras*, for example in the Mixe area, and in the peripheral tropical lowlands adjoining Vera Cruz to the north, the Pacific to the south, and the Isthmus of Tehuantepec in the east (Fig. 7.1).

Pl. 7.1 Landscaping improvements are an expression of civic pride in the *municipio* of Tlacochahuaya: the *palacio municipal* (town hall) bears Mexico's coat of arms

In addition, with the exception of San Pedro y San Pablo Etla in the Oaxaca Valley, all the district head-towns are universally large *municipios*, and their size is almost certainly, in most cases, the result of their power *vis-à-vis* smaller and weaker neighbours (Fig. 7.2). Villa Sola de Vega and Miahuatlan de Porfirio Díaz are noteworthy for their contorted shapes as well as for their size; San Carlos Yautepec is the largest *municipio*, and accounts for about half the area of the district of Yautepec.

Large municipal units are more likely to have multi-nuclear settlement patterns, though population growth and pressure on the land may be a stimulus to internal migration and the creation of daughter hamlets in the smaller *municipios*. Generally speaking, however, it is the tropical lowlands, which have undergone land reform since the revolution, that record the *municipios* with the most rapidly growing number of small rural settlements.

Municipios in Oaxaca, as Luebke (1959) has shown, were, and probably in most instances still are, coterminous with communities—a conclusion which is perhaps not surprising, given their small average area—167 km.²—and population. Oaxaca's *municipio*-based corporate communities are 'the functional equivalents of the lineages and clans of tribal society; like descent groups, they have such marks of corporate identity as myths of how they came to be founded, rules of membership, and continuity over time' (Dennis 1987, 33). Intense loyalty to the community is expected of its residents: the renegade *par*

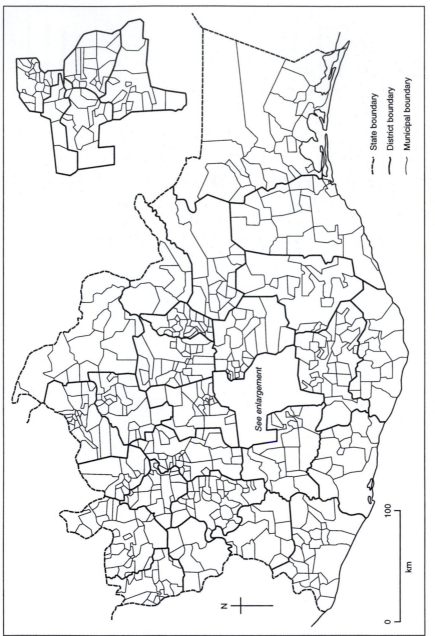

Fig. 7.1 Oaxaca: *municipios* and districts, 1990

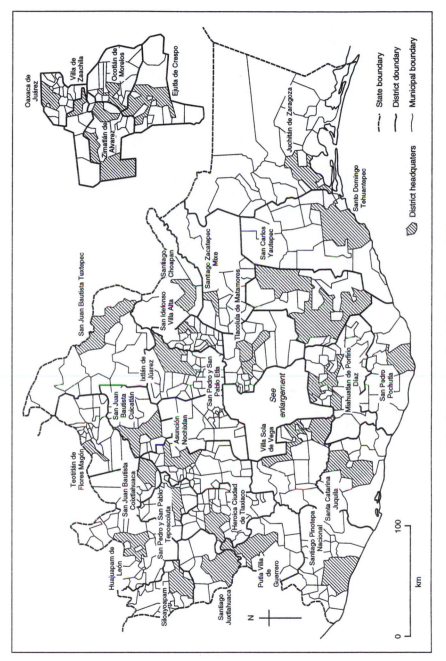

Fig. 7.2 Oaxaca: district headquarters, 1990

excellence is someone who conspires with the village's enemies (de la Fuente 1977*a*, 210).

The fierce sense of group identity and individuality that is shared within communities is often regarded as excessive by outsiders, as Lemoine Villicaña indicates:

An intricate mosaic of peoples, parceled out across a territory of varied physical contrasts, has been a cause, among others, that there, more than in the rest of the country, regionalisms, circumscribed by relatively small area, have impressed on each locality a specific character, reflected in most in an odd way, in an exaggerated notion of autonomy, in an almost atavistic aversion to any idea of subordination and collaboration, and in a marked wish to settle its domestic problems in its own way. (1954, 69)

In his study of inter-village conflict, Dennis goes so far as to propose that Oaxaca villages have their own micro-cultures:

Each microculture includes a panoply of saints and religious organizations (*cofradías* or *mayordomías*) for sponsoring fiestas, a strong local political system, a local dialect of the particular Indian language, and often a traditional costume distinctive to the village. Some of these visible markers of village identity are disappearing, in particular the beautiful and expensive home-made textiles worn mainly by women. The national language, Spanish, has also made inroads as the rural school system has gained a foothold in each community and as emigration to the cities has increased. Nevertheless, villages continue to pride themselves on their own particular variety of marriage and fiesta customs, and they patiently explain to outsiders that their version of Zapotec or Mixtec is clearer and easier to understand than versions of neighbouring communities. (Dennis 1987, 19)

In similar vein, and at an earlier date, de la Fuente inferred that micro-cultural differences confer on each community a distinctive personality, each considering itself superior either for its progressiveness or its traditionalism. As a consequence, difference, if not outright rivalry, means that inter-community relations are often unfriendly, if not fraught (de la Fuente 1965, 31). Juchitán, in the Isthmus of Tehuantepec, provides an outstanding example of a *patria chica* (little homeland):

For Juchitecos, the defence of village autonomy meant not only a fight to defend a piece of land and the right to be governed by local individuals, it touched on their very existence as a people with a distinct language, set of customs, and identity rooted in a particular centuries-old ecological and social adaptation. Indeed, in Juchitán, land, political autonomy and ethnic identity were indissolubly linked. Only people who had been born in the community and their placenta (doo yoo) buried there could qualify as Juchitecos. (Campbell 1994, 53–4)

Rivalry between *municipios*, given the Mexican government's opposition to Oaxacan particularism, has resulted in amalgamations. 'A given *municipio* eventually may attempt to extend its jurisdiction over weaker population clusters, incorporating into itself a number of villages and hamlets, both as part of the *municipio* and as tributary to the head village in the structural pattern of the

larger community' (Luebke 1959, 131). A classic example of municipal suppression is provided by the loss of *municipio* status by San Juan Copala, the Triqui centre, and its attachment as an *agencia municipal* to its rival Juxtlahuaca in 1948 (Parra Mora and Hernández Díaz 1994).

It was this very process of *municipio* suppression and amalgamation that reduced the number of units after the end of the Revolution, and it is likely to be the reason for the large size of those powerful municipal entities that are also district headquarters. Yet such was the demand for autonomy at the small-scale end of the continuum, that for a long time after 1920 Oaxaca's *municipios* rarely met the minimum population requirement of 2,000 inhabitants set by the federal government, and there are many that still fail to do so.

An attempt by the, then, governor of Oaxaca in 1980 to reduce the number of *municipios* to seventy-five, taking as a guide the 1974 state constitution which stated that a population of 10,000 was the minimum requirement, was utterly rejected by village presidents. The history of Oaxaca could not be removed from the map by the stroke of a pen (Ornelas López 1987*b*). This was not a surprising outcome, since many villages have *lienzos* (linen canvasses), some stretching back in a few instances to the conquest (Parmenter 1982) or maps showing community boundaries during the ensuing centuries (Instituto de Artes Gráficas de Oaxaca, 1997).

Where *municipio* and community boundaries are discordant, possibly through the establishment of interior satellite settlements created to cope with population growth, factionalism, or to secure disputed territory, *agencias* may bid for autonomy and the acquisition of facilities that are normally confined to *cabeceras*. If successful in the latter, they may obtain schools, churches, and cemeteries, but municipal status is clearly not on offer to aspirant communities from the Mexican state.

Municipal Government

Each of Oaxaca's 570 *municipios* is governed by an *ayuntamiento constitucional*, which is responsible for all administrative and judicial matters on a local scale. According to the constitution of the state of Oaxaca, government of all *municipios* is divided into three branches—executive, legislative, and judicial. Executive power is vested in the *presidente municipal* (who is either a Spanish speaker or bilingual) and his *suplente* (alternate), while the legislative branch comprises five *regidores* (councilmen) and their alternates. An *alcalde* and two *suplentes* make up the judicial branch of local government. In reality, although conforming somewhat to this pattern, each *municipio* has its own system of *cargos* (posts).

For example, while the larger district headquarters tend to have the prescribed number of offices, most rural administrations consist of only three *regidores*. Where the settlement is a small town, as in the case of Juxlahuaca, it

may be divided into neighbourhoods or *barrios*, each of which nominates a *regidor* (Romney and Romney 1973). The district headquarters are not quite so complex as Oaxaca City (which has commissions and departments), but their *regidores* are tied to specific offices (education, the gaol, public works) and may, in fact, number more than five (*Los Municipios de Oaxaca* 1987).

Tequios, or communal work projects, are a quintessential part of *municipio* life, and involve able-bodied males over the age of 18. They are expected to answer the roll-call on Sunday mornings. Organized by the appropriate *regidor*, *tequio* service involves building and repairing roads and bridges, clearing municipal boundaries, and other activities deemed to be of public benefit. Expansion of the federal electricity grid across Oaxaca's rural communities has largely depended on these labouring tasks carried out by adult males. Schools and health clinics are also built by 'voluntary' labour of this kind. Male absentees from communal work are liable to moral and financial sanctions. 'Obligatory work on community projects not only maintains the community physically but also reaffirms the legitimacy of the community authorities and strengthens community organization' (Dennis 1987, 26).

Crucial to the executive arm of the *municipio* are the *síndicos* (trustees), the treasurer, the *municipio*'s secretary and the *topiles* (police). The *síndicos* represent the *municipio*'s corporate personality in all fiscal, administrative, and judicial matters; they also by convention usually supervise public works. The treasurer administers the *municipio*'s funds, while the secretary (who must have competence in Spanish and in some Indian communities is a *mestizo* or a bilingual teacher—Hernández Díaz 1992*a*, 143) drafts all documents pertaining to the municipality, handles official correspondence, and provides information as requested by higher authority. The *topiles* (police) are required to maintain public order, but they also carry messages for the authorities and participate in public works (Greenberg 1981, 58). All these local government positions are (nominally) filled on the basis of election to posts that, like the religious ones, are referred to as *cargos* (offices).

Most young men begin their community service as *topiles*. In Chatino communities they are inducted by the *ancianos* (elders) using the following words:

It is an obligation that is imposed on us and permitted by our Saint Father Sun. You must serve, so that you can continue our laws and justice, to ensure that our organization does not end, to guarantee that our beliefs may continue, to ensure the continuation of our village, so that other authorities may be elected and safeguard the continuation of the Chatino people. (Hernández Díaz 1992*a*, 103)

Unofficially, most *municipios* recruit appropriately skilled persons to fill the important tasks of secretary and treasurer. Other vacancies are filled by consensus or by popular vote. The term is for three years, which expires on 31 December. Immediate re-election is proscribed. The president (almost always a man) is responsible for all civil matters within the community and between

the community and the state and federal authorities, and his associates assist him in these responsibilities. Additionally, in traditional communities in Indian areas, the council of elders (*ancianos* or *principales*), consisting of men who have already held leadership roles (in Yaitepec, the position of *alcalde* is the last stage of the civil hierarchy), advises the president on the course of action to be followed.

The committee of elders, whether in the Chatino, Mazatec, or Mixe areas, has its own president, secretary, and treasurer. Its members are ranked according to seniority based on time elapsed since serving as an *alcalde*. They are in charge of the communal lands, and no official can be appointed or elected to local government office without their consent—indeed, they have the power to remove civil *cargo* holders whose behaviour is considered detrimental to community interests.

Behind the formal power of municipal government in the Indian communities, then, there lies the informal system based on age-grades and consensus. 'While the constitutional government may hold the secular reins of power, sacred power which is achieved by participating in the civil–religious hierarchy is embodied in the elders' (Greenberg 1981, 66). This is important, because outsiders are continually attempting to subborn local governments, and the *ancianos* are (or expected to be) impervious to such influences. However, where local bosses are in control over a long period of time, as they have been in the Sierra Mazateca, it is common for the committee of *ancianos* to cease to function altogether (Boege 1988).

The Civil Hierarchy

How has the peasant civil hierarchy responded to the political and socio-economic changes that have occurred in Oaxaca since the Revolution (Corbett and Whiteford 1983)? Unlike recruitment to minor or *ad hoc* offices, election to the *ayuntamiento* is affected by external factors, notably state laws and political parties. Elections to the *ayuntamiento* take place every three years on the first Sunday in December, and the entire slate of candidates elected by Indian assemblies, prior to 1995, was usually portrayed as PRI affiliated. During the preliminary stage of selection, however, the PRI was not usually involved, and it moved in only at the point when a distinction was being made between the *propietarios* (office-holders) and the *suplentes* (substitutes). The approved list was then ratified in Oaxaca City as the PRI slate.

While elections, based on universal adult suffrage or male assemblies, recruit adult males to the *ayuntamiento*, allocation of specific offices depends on post-election manœuvring. Theoretically, the person receiving most votes becomes president, and so on down the hierarchy of posts. In some *municipios*, however, offices are allocated by age; in others a raffle is held. There is, however, a marked tendency for the highest level of the civil hierarchy to be occu-

pied by men with formal education, economic resources, and contact with the national society (Hernández Díaz 1992*a*, 133).

There is also considerable variation in the time spent in the various offices—the presidency being the crucial determinant of the system. The president may serve eighteen months and then switch with his *suplente*; or the three top officials—*presidente*, *síndico*, and *regidor de hacienda* may rotate in office once a year (Cervantes Cortés 1992). The precise method adopted is usually left to the elected officials to devise, and the method of office allocation may vary not only from *municipio* to *municipio*, but also from time to time within *municipios* (Corbett 1976, 169–70).

The municipal president is often described as 'the father of the village'; in the same vein, male citizens are 'sons of the village' (Dennis 1987, 25). District offices, and state and federal governments consider the *ayuntamiento*, and more specifically the president, to be the embodiment of the community, and hold him responsible for anything adverse that takes place in the *municipio*. Hence he has been described as a 'political middleman'. His 'citizens' regard him as a crucial intermediary with the federal government, especially in the case of land disputes with neighbouring *municipios*. 'He is expected to defend the lands by preparing and delivering official documents, bribing government officials, and gaining the favour of powerful *patrones* (patrons) outside the village. A good president should not be afraid to go into the highest offices, and he should be able to argue eloquently and convincingly on his community's behalf' (Dennis 1973, 422).

However, the president's office carries with it no political powers or sanctions. Within his own community, the president has no alternative to seeking co-operation and consensus from the *patria chica*. Consequently, many eligibles try to avoid presidential office altogether, either by absenting themselves from the community, or by involving themselves in lesser religious *cargos* (Krejci 1976). But even migration may not suffice to avoid senior office, since telephone calls to the USA can be, and are, used to summon 'citizens' to their communal duty—the ultimate sanction being the threat of ostracism.

Some presidents, whether reluctant or not to fill the office, find that diplomatic trips away from the community are a convenient way of coping when the situation they are in becomes untenable; later they can return and attempt to negotiate a solution once tempers have been restored. This seems to be the preferred strategy when land disputes take place and violence has occurred, 'because it preserves the president's integrity for the more important business of carrying on litigation through the government' (Dennis 1973, 425).

To carry forward the normal business of the community, the *ayuntamiento* holds sessions in the evenings in the *palacio municipal*, symbolically located on the main square of the *cabecera*. Special assemblies of adult men (aged 18 or over) are called when important issues have to be discussed. Women are essentially 'invisible' in public assemblies and in political affairs at the level of the *municipio*. Assemblies of adult males last many hours, since the object is to

reach a consensus, rather than to arrive quickly at a clear-cut decision that will only leave some aggrieved.

Stephen, writing about Teotitlán de Valle, reports that the separation of the religious and civil hierarchies, coupled to male dominance of formal politics, has increased women's marginalization from community affairs. Although women have achieved wealth through weaving, and ritual status via their sponsorship of *fiestas*, this has not led to increased political power. The only civil *cargo* posts held by women in Teotitlán in the late 1980s were in health and education, committees on which state officials expect their involvement (Stephen 1991, 230).

In contrast to women's experience in Teotitlán, women in Yalálag, in the Sierra Juárez, have made considerable headway, politically, largely because men have needed their support to break free from *caciques* who have dominated the community throughout much of this century. Yalálag women were prominent in the protests that followed an alleged fraudulent election in 1980. They took part in spontaneous occupations of buildings. They participated in discussions in Oaxaca City with the state Electoral Commission and the Justice Department, and successfully demanded that the Zapotec language should be permitted in the negotiations. They also engineered a meeting with the governor's wife stressing their demands for new democratic elections (Gijsbers 1996). In 1981, a Unión de Mujeres Zapotecas was founded. It has been active in community development projects, notably in the building of a technical secondary school and bilingual education centre; the establishment of a community corn mill; and the installation and running of a community store. As a result of its activities, women are allowed to participate in municipal meetings and political decisions (Stephen 1991, 232–4).

A similar situation (also arising out of oppression) exists among the Chatino in the *sierra* south of Miahuatan. Here bilingual teachers in Nopala, Lachao, and Tataltepec have challenged the authority of the *ancianos*, and have seized political leadership from them by demanding 'one vote for each individual' (Hernández Díaz 1992*a*, 128). An interesting outcome of these 'democratizing' processes is that they permitted a Chatino woman teacher to be elected to the presidency of a *municipio* (perhaps uniquely so in Oaxaca). Another, Cirila Sánchez, became a state and federal Deputy and, later, Director of the Office for the Defence of the Indian in Oaxaca (Hernández Díaz 1992*a*).

An adjunct of the *ayuntamiento* is the *comisariado de bienes comunales*, which consists of a separate body with its own president, secretary, treasurer, vigilance committee and members, and is responsible for the management of communal resources. The *comisariado* collects taxes from residents in return for grazing and irrigation rights and for permission (if the population is expanding) to cultivate the communal grounds. If the village has irrigation, the *comisariado* will organize it, and will set up communal labour projects to maintain the system. It also will manage the use by outsiders of local resources, such as timber and mineral deposits, and will charge for concessions, the proceeds

of which go into the public coffers. In view of the resources that may be at its disposal, the *comisariado* may have greater economic and political significance than the municipal organization itself (Hernández Díaz 1992*a*, 140).

Religious Cargos

Municipios find themselves, *de facto*, subordinate to the district centres, although, constitutionally, they are 'free' and self-governing. Spanish in structure, but with clear indigenous underpinnings, the Oaxacan *cargo* system involves the hierarchy of offices of municipal government on the civil side, paralleled in religious organization by the *cofradías* or *mayordomías* honouring the Catholic saints. All local men are expected to climb this ladder of achievement during their lifetimes, moving back and forth between civil and religious posts as they age and acquire greater moral worth. 'The acquisition of status and prestige runs in parallel with passage of time and the fulfillment of the *cargos*' (de la Fuente 1977*a*, 212). It has been remarked that 'the system of religious cargos . . . saturates the consciousness of the community. To a significant extent it forms the framework of much of the village's activity, and the charter of its leadership and socio-economic differentiation' (Webster 1968, 6).

Religious *cargos* operate largely independently of the Catholic priesthood. Many Oaxaca communities have no resident priest and practise a folk Catholicism imbued with indigenous traditions (Norget 1997*b*). Local catechists take the services, with clergy visiting for special events, notably *fiestas*. The community itself may perform many life-cycle events (El Guindi 1986); in Panixtlahuaca, in the Chatino area, the most important persons in the marriage ceremony are the civil authorities and the *principales*, who sanction the union according to ancient ritual (Hernández Díaz 1992*a*, 108).

Folk Catholicism is a synthetic and living faith; 'for most Mixe a distinction between Catholicism and paganism does not exist' (Lipp 1991, 24), and a similar situation applies among most other Oaxacan Indian groups, and, to a lesser extent, most *mestizo* peasants as well (Norget 1997*b*). When Chatino *principales* give thanks, they mention Mother Earth, Saint Father Sun, and Saint Mother Moon, but the Catholic Saint who occupies the main position on the altar may go unnoticed in the ritual (Hernández Díaz 1992*a*, 115). Many Indian communities have their own *shamans* (folk religious practitioners), who perform life-cycle and agricultural rituals, and several still operate their own calendrical systems, in addition to the Christian or Gregorian calendar (Lipp 1991). It is not uncommon for some Indian groups to retain 'a sacred, divinatory calendar and a more mundane calendar . . . utilized to regulate community festivals and agricultural activities' (Lipp 1991, 52).

Chance and Taylor have shown that a civil hierarchy, based on annual elections, separate from *fiesta* offices, existed in highland Indian zones in colonial times. The interlacing of the civil–religious hierarchy was achieved only in the

nineteenth century, after independence, as *cofradías* lost their access to communally held land and decayed (1985, 2). This change merely foreshadowed others that have taken place since the Revolution, such as the involvement of the PRI in municipal affairs, and the partial or complete separation of the civil and religious hierarchies (De Walt 1975). Additionally, the contraction in the number of *cargos* (de la Fuente 1977a), and the failure of *mayordomías* to cancel wealth accumulation are factors that have disrupted this 'democracy of the poor' (Chance and Taylor 1985, 2).

As long ago as the 1960s, in Guelaxé, a bilingual Zapotec- and Spanish-speaking *municipio* in the Tlacolula Valley near Oaxaca City, the hierarchy of *cargos* had become loosely integrated, and formed a 'Y', with 'regular reticulate crossing' between the upper arms (Webster 1968, 9). The stem was made up of *mandaderos* (those who follow orders), and comprised about twenty civil offices of a petty nature, which were held primarily by young unmarried men. The left and right arms of the 'Y' formed the administrative authorities and the *mayordomía,* or *obligaciones de la iglesia* (church duties), respectively. Very few men held a civil office beyond *suplente* before discharging one of the two most important and expensive *mayordomías* (the *grandes*).

Two factors ensured that *mayordomías* were taken up in Guelaxé: the prestige associated with their successful completion, and the sanctions that would be invoked by the entire community against anyone who shirked their responsibility. However, few *mayordomos* were able to afford all the ritual expenditures—especially for the 'big' *cargos*—without the help of kin, fictive kin, and friends. Their contributions were delivered as *guelaguetza* (reciprocal loans), and were recorded in each family's register of obligations; they were returned in cash or cash-related kind when the donors incurred their own expenditures for *mayordomías*, marriages, funerals, or other similar events requiring exceptional financial outlays. In this way, peasant *mayordomos* spread the expense of their *cargo* over many years; eventually, they would become sufficiently solvent to accept their next office.

Recalling her experience of government in Talea, in the Sierra Zapoteca over a period of thirty years, Nader observed, 'the cargo organization has been changing from a more perfectly-age graded system, which was also more egalitarian, toward a more hierarchical system, which now has elements of class built into the selection procedures. To age and experience, we can now add schooling and the ability to serve without compensation' (Nader 1990, 32). Concomitantly, payment for religious rites were shifted away from wealthy individuals to savings-and-loans organizations.

In a recent review of religious *cargo* systems, Chance confirms that the dominant opinion expressed in the literature is that communities maintain a hierarchy of public offices for the express purpose of serving the local saints, but that linked civil–religious hierarchies are now in the minority (1990a, 30). He perceptively notes that 'religious *cargo* systems . . . simultaneously constitute a recognition of decreased village autonomy and power relative to the state, as

well as an attempt to prevent yet further losses' (1990*a*, 38). Nevertheless, four other possibilities have also been identified. Religious *cargos* may disappear altogether or may be replaced by *cofradías*, fraternities that support the cult of a particular saint—a feature common in colonial times. Collections may be carried out, or the prestige and ritual of the *mayordomía* may be transferred to individual life-cycle rituals—as in Teotitlán del Valle (Stephen 1991, 158; Hernández Díaz 1992*a*, 112 n. 30).

In Teotitlán, the *cargo* system began to change under pressure from the precursor of the PRM in the 1920s, and the present situation took on its distinctive shape as the modern weaving industry developed in the 1960s and 1970s (Stephen 1991). Prior to the Revolution, there were forty *cargos* associated with nineteen *mayordomías*; after the Revolution, the civil hierarchy was expanded to accommodate offices concerned with education and the *ejido*, and a religious branch of the *cargo* system accepted responsibility for the ritual calendar (Stephen 1991, 161). By the late 1980s, only 20 per cent of Teotitlán households had sponsored one *mayordomía*, and 7 per cent two or more: the last *mayordomía* cost its sponsor an estimated US$24,000.

Generally speaking, women are invisible in the *cargo* system. For example, in Mathews's study of pseudonymous San Miguel, in the Oaxaca Valley, she found that of the 138 religious offices to be filled during the period of her fieldwork only nine involved women (1985, 291). The post-revolutionary Mexican constitution excluded women from voting and holding elective office until 1953, and, despite some pressure for greater female involvement in community politics, these gender distinctions have remained entrenched at the level of the *municipio*. During Mathews's study period, of sixty-one civil offices filled, only two were occupied by women, and both were nominated rather than elected (1985, 292). Mathews comments that women are less educated than men, on average, less travelled, and often lack fluency in Spanish—all important criteria for managing the *municipio* in its relations with the outside world. So women seem even more insignificant in the civil than in the religious hierarchy in Mathews's village.

Two pieces of evidence mitigate the rule of gender exclusion from peasant municipal affairs. The first comes from Mathews. She shows that religious *cargos* are allocated to households on the basis of wealth, and that male and female sponsors are given joint title to office and have parallel roles and duties. The second is provided by Browner, in her work on a Chinatec community in the Sierra Juárez. Here political office, as elsewhere in rural Oaxaca, is exclusively invested in men, but women have organized themselves to co-operate with healthcare agencies of the federal government, despite the opposition of the *ayuntamiento*. The key issue here has been mothers' identification with the childcare benefits facilitated by teachers, doctors, and nurses, whom the municipal authorities thought were merely interfering (Browner 1986*a* and *b*).

Levelling, Population Growth, and Class

Traditionally, ritual expenditure was a means of circulating cash within the community, redistributing it from the comparatively wealthy *mayordomos* to the poor, who sold the ritual articles, food, and drink required in the celebration of the *fiesta*. Moreover, these items, especially food and drink, were consumed by participants and their guests, and, in times when the community was relatively closed, may have provided vital elements of nutrition for a population normally constrained in its access to food.

Population growth in Oaxaca's *municipios*—many, despite migration, now have twice the number of residents they recorded at the end of the Second World War—means that by no means all adult men must now serve the community in the civil–religious hierarchy and its adjunct bodies (Mathews 1985). Even out-migration has not necessarily disrupted the community; three-quarters of the twenty-four *municipios* studied in the course of an investigation into migration reported that they continued to receive support for public works and religious *fiestas* from those no longer living in the community (Ríos Vásquez 1992).

Moreover, the changes in socio-economic structure at the community level brought about by road construction, by improvements in marketing, schooling, health, by electrification and the provision of potable water, have created much more entrenched class divisions. These are not easily eradicated by the levelling potentialities of ritual expenditure via the *fiesta* system. Forces that give rise to stratifying have now largely replaced others conducive to levelling. 'Rather than being wholly contradictory, [they] are better viewed as states in a complex system of adjustment (between *cargo* positions, amounts distributed, and population) that Indian communities make as part of their adaptation to different political situations' (Greenberg 1981, 158–9; see also 1972, 3).

More controversial is Greenberg's contention that 'increasing socio-economic differentiation has been bought at the expense of social cohesion' (1972, 3); in other words, that class hierarchy tends to undermine community. This line of argument represents a rejection of Cancian's revisionist assessment of *cargo* levelling mechanisms (1965). Cancian noted, for Zinacantan, Chiapas, that the *cargo* system may also legitimatize wealth accumulation in certain families, while allocating prestige to the very same people, apparently in accord with community-wide consensus. In the context of Oaxaca, it is likely that levelling still takes place in the most isolated and least modern of communities. But the civil and religious hierarchies are more likely to have separated—and the religious sector to have decayed—where urbanization and modernization—and new settlement formation—are most advanced, notably in the *tierra caliente*, but also in the Central Valleys.

However, one of the most detailed (though dated) accounts of the civil–religious hierarchy for the Central Valleys points to the power of Cancian's hypothesis at that time. Writing more than thirty years ago, Webster reported

that the apparently homogeneous community of Gualaxé split into an upper–lower class division, with those in the superordinate stratum character-ized by their having accomplished the two most prestigious *cargos*. Within the two major classes there was further socio-economic differentiation associated with relatively more respectable or disrespectable achievement in the hierar-chy, once age was taken into account. Webster concluded:

If the upper strat[um] indeed represents a loose upper socio-economic class, distin-guished by relative wealth (which, fairly clearly, is a prerequisite for such accomplish-ment in the system, and even to some degree a result of it), and prestige (very probably accumulated in proportion to the advance of one's career, and to some degree a pre-requisite for it as well), one might say that Guelace [*sic*] is slightly top-heavy with upper class. (Webster 1968, 39)

Guelaxé's lower class was smaller, because it consisted of landless day labour-ers, whereas landholding peasants (who formed the majority of the so-called upper class) occurred most commonly.

Mathews reaches a similar conclusion in her study relating religious *cargo*-holding to class in another community in the Oaxaca Valley, this time with a *mestizo* population of Zapotec and Mixtec descent. Once more there was a marked correlation between household socio-economic status and participation in *mayordomías*. Seventy-four per cent of those in the highest stratum (92 households) held *cargos*, as did 71 per cent of those in the middle stratum (84 households). But involvement fell away dramatically in the lower stratum (178 households), where only 6 per cent were active in the religious domain (Mathews 1985, 292).

Civil–Religious Hierarchies, Government, and Lay Religious Associations

With the growth of national culture, the spread of state institutions, and the increased level of commercial activity in some favoured communities, Oaxaca's formerly somewhat homogeneous communities have become loosely inte-grated, voluntary, class-based entities. These changes have caused the separa-tion of the two intertwined civil and religious hierarchies; *mayordomía* has undergone readjustment, even loss in some cases. The most effective agents of change are those that undermine the authority structure behind *mayordomía*, and those providing adequate alternatives. The constitutional civil govern-ment with its emphasis on the separation of church and state, and the forces of socio-economic modernization (many of which have been initiated by the state) come into the first category; in the second are lay religious associations with their voluntary, permanent membership.

Imposition of municipal civil government has had its biggest disruptive effect in communities where non-Hispanic mother tongues are spoken and

Indian elders have traditionally controlled the religious *cargo* system. Under these circumstances it is common for the Indian hierarchy of religious *cargos* to function side by side with the civil government, though in some instances there remains a traditional *ayuntamiento* which shadows the *ayuntamiento constitucional* (as in the case of Yaitepec). The former situation is most likely to develop if the community is split into Indian and *mestizo* segments and *mestizos* commandeer the civil posts. This has occurred in the Mixteca de la Costa, where, additionally, blacks have been traditionally excluded from local government (González Circedo no date). It is also not uncommon, where class structures are beginning to emerge, as they are among the Chatino, for the rich to pay the poor to serve their lesser *cargos* for them, though the prestige acquired is attached to the payer not the server (Hernández Díaz 1992*a*, 132).

Lay religious associations are structurally quite different from *mayordomía* groups. In many respects they are much more similar to true *cofradías* and *hermanidades* (fraternities), and in fact sometimes bear these terms in their official title. Membership is voluntary and frequently for life. They are sex segregated, with women's organizations far outnumbering men's. Groups that are ostensibly open to both sexes are segregated internally. Youth associations occur, as do auxiliaries of religious orders. They are closely linked to the—usually absent—clergy, and headed by a president, secretary, and treasurer.

In many places, lay associations have absorbed functions that once were invested in *mayordomías*, and at Yalálag religious aspects of all *fiestas* have, for more than forty years, been the responsibility of the feminine *hermanidad* (de la Fuente 1977a). Under these circumstances, *fiestas* are increasingly secularized and managed by the civil authorities (as in Santa Ana, near Tlacolula), often with the support of wealthier emigrants and/or a levy imposed on all residents.

Let us recapitulate. As *municipios* have stabilized as spatial units since the 1930s, so have they changed internally through the establishment of municipal constitutions, the encroachment of modernization, and the growth of population and its shift to non-*cabacera* settlements. Furthermore, civil hierarchies have been strengthened and given constitutional precedence, and socio-economic differentiation has usually outstripped the operation of traditional levelling mechanisms.

The acceptance of *mayordomos* has become more voluntary; in some places it has been replaced by *hermanidades* that seek subscriptions from the entire community. *Fiesta* obligations may have become more streamlined, but they have not entirely disappeared, and most Oaxaca communities, irrespective of the trimming of the *fiesta* cycle, still support at least a patronal feast as an expression of a semi-secularized civic consciousness (Brown 1977).

While it is true that the *municipio* breaks up the potential sense of regional or ethnic identity in Oaxaca, there is very little evidence for the operation of civil–religious hierarchies as pumps for extracting surplus wealth within the framework of internal colonialism (Greenberg 1972, 2). Moreover, Greenberg's contention that 'increasing socio-economic differentiation has

been bought at the expense of social cohesion' may be true (1972, 3); but only relatively so, since the civil authorities, *hermanidades*, and emigrants have provided a countervailing reinforcement of community pride at the level of the *municipio*.

This pride has been further expressed, for example, by the establishment of local museums, where are displayed archaeological remains, artefacts, and photographic or archival information relating to such events as the community's involvement in the Mexican Revolution and the subsequent land reform. There is now a network of more than ten *municipios* in the state of Oaxaca, each with its own proposal for a community museum, of which nine had been established by the mid-1990s. While assistance for these projects has been given by the INAH, the collections are housed by the *municipio* and curated by voluntary workers, often with mixed results (Necoechea Gracia 1996).

Protestant–Catholic Tensions

Although Protestants make up fewer than 10 per cent of the Oaxaca population, they are marginally more numerous among indigenous-language speakers, largely because of the proselytizing activities of the Summer Institute of Linguistics (Instituto Lingüístico de Verano). Based in the USA, it has worked on the grammatical structure of the pre-Columbian languages as a prelude to, and pretext for, Bible translation. Indeed, much of what is known about many of Oaxaca's languages has been derived from this controversial source (Turner 1973). In 87 of Oaxaca's *municipios*, Protestants account for 10 per cent of the population, in 24 for 25 per cent, in 13 for 33 per cent, and in 5 for the majority (Marroquín 1992).

Protestants are noteworthy in the three major cities, Oaxaca City, Salina Cruz, and Tuxtepec, and among the Zapotec (15 per cent), Huave (17.4 per cent), Chontal (20.7 per cent), Chinantec (21.6 per cent), Mixe (27.9 per cent), and Zoque (35.1 per cent). It has been claimed that, with 500 Evangelical ministers (Gijsbers 1996), Oaxaca is the state which records the largest number of cases (about fifty per year) of violations of human rights against Protestant groups (Gijsbers 1996). 'This process of rapid religious conversion has, in certain instances, resulted in considerable intra-family tension as well as factional struggles on the community level' (Lipp 1991, 25).

Protestants, whether Evangelical groups (mostly of US origin) or Brooklyn-based Jehovah's Witnesses, are seen as emphasizing individual salvation and opting out of the Catholic community with its system of *cargos* and *fiestas*. They almost invariably refuse to comply with collective labour on community projects. Moreover, Protestants are anti-drink (alcohol is widely—and sometimes excessively—used in *fiestas* and in folk rituals), many choosing conversion to remove themselves from the drinking culture that typifies male bonding in both rural communities and urban neighbourhoods (Marroquín 1995).

Examples of Catholic–Protestant conflict are numerous: in 1987, three people died at Santiago Atitlán in the Sierra Mixe; in the Central Valleys, Santo Domingo Tomaltepec experienced violence, and so did San Sebastián Dulce, Zimatlán, where Protestants were coerced into contributing to the Catholic *fiesta*. Three highland indigenous communities provide similar evidence—Yaganiza in the Sierra Juárez, Tlahuitoltepec in the Mixe, and San Juan Piñas, Juxtlahuaca, in the Mixteca, from the last of which thirty Pentecostal families were expelled in 1992 (Gijsbers 1996).

In many rural communities Protestants are allowed to withdraw from their obligations to the Catholic *fiesta* cycle, provided they comply with communal secular obligations. This is facilitated where the civil and religious *cargo* systems have already separated, as in Yalálag (Gijsbers 1996), though, where they have not, adhesion to 'usos y costumbres' has often increased Catholic–Protestant tensions. Tiltepec, a Chatino community in southern Oaxaca, is interesting because bilingual teachers have mediated the conflict between Catholics and Protestants. The most senior offices of president and *regidor* are held by bilingual teachers, with mandates to reconcile the warring parties. Catholics and Protestants share the lesser civil *cargos* (Hernández Díaz 1992*a*, 130–1).

Significant changes have also affected the Catholic Church in Oaxaca over the last twenty-five years. In 1975, the recently appointed Archbishop, Carrasco, introduced New Evangelization, stressing spiritual rebirth, an abrupt change of life, and abandonment of ideas and vices standing in the way of an individual's spiritual and social development and self-empowerment (Norget 1997*b*). These ideas are close to Protestantism, and have set up tensions with orthodox Catholics as well as with the mass of Oaxacans, who are followers of syncretic folk Catholicism (Norget 1997*b*). In addition, at a regional scale since 1963, the Salesian Order has spearheaded the 'second spiritual conquest' of the Mixe, establishing Ayutla as its base (Kuroda 1993).

Locally, it is not uncommon for adjacent communities to be led by priests with very different orientations. Norget, however, wisely observes that popular Catholicism in Oaxaca 'celebrates traditional values and positive sociality related to collectivism, communalism, and social equilibrium, thereby affirming the virtues of poverty and the world of the autochthonous and traditional' (1997*b*, 78). Hence, 'church-motivated class-based utopian struggle is intertwined with an indigenous grassroots fight for local autonomy' (Norget 1997*a*).

Closed and Open Communities

Municipios provide the basic framework for Oaxacan communities; but the nature of those communities has changed over time, so far as their civil–religious hierarchies are concerned. Can a similar claim be made about their degree of closure to the outside world? Wolf has distinguished between two

types of Latin American peasant community, closed and open, both of which are germane to Oaxaca.

Closed corporate communities exist at high altitude where Indian culture and marginal land have, historically, sealed off the settlements from direct interference (probably domination) from large landed estates and other inimical outside influences. The corporate structure of these communities is expressed in, and maintained by, the civil–religious hierarchy: it entails equal access to communally held resources, especially land (the commons), which are crucial for self-sufficiency (Wolf 1955, 456–60). These corporate communities operate with 'usos y costumbres', and it is here that political officers are selected by male public assembly and open debate (Fig. 6.1).

Open communities are located in humid low uplands and tropical lowlands, where the peasantry engage in cash cropping, often for the world market. In contrast to the closed community, the open community 'emphasizes continuous interaction with the outside world and ties its fortunes to outside demands'. It 'permits and expects individual accumulation and display of wealth during periods of outside demand and allows this new wealth much influence in the periodic reshaping of social ties' (Wolf 1955, 462).

Most of Oaxaca's high-density lowland populations, on the Pacific Coast, in the Isthmus of Tehuantepec, and in the fringes adjoining Tuxtepec, conform to the open type of peasant community, interactive with plantation systems. Moreover, under the forces of political, economic, and social change that have already been identified, the closed corporate highland communities have gravitated towards greater openness with commercialization and wealth accumulation. The 'opening' processes have been especially marked in the Central Valleys, notably in the settlements adjacent to the main roads.

Of course, there is still a tendency for the closed corporate communities to record high levels of endogamy (in Yaitepec, for instance, Greenberg (1981) recorded 75 per cent endogamy in each of the two main *barrios*). In-marrying remains particularly marked wherever crucial artisanal skills have to be protected from outside knowledge. In Zautla, in the Etla Valley, a survey in 1970 showed that only 5 per cent of spouses had come from outside, and the people involved all seemed to be marginal to the active social life of the community and interested in remaining inconspicuous. In no case had an elaborate formal marriage (*fandango*) taken place (Dennis 1987, 32–3). Municipal endogamy, with exogamy among extended patrilocal families, is the norm among the Mazatecs (Boege 1988).

Endogamy ensures that intra-village ties based on common residence are greatly reinforced by kinship. Related for generations in the past, community members consider themselves to be sons of the village: within the community, local issues generate a moral tone that goes far beyond the ties of common residence. Stereotypes of outsiders, on the other hand, describe them as being of another race, animals, people without reason—terms similar to those used by *mestizos* about Indians (Dennis 1987, 33).

Ayuntamientos husband resources traditionally held in common by the entire community. But education, migration, and the cash economy (including remittances) have opened up communities as never before. Only the most isolated, high-level, Indian-language communities can be thought of as closed, and then merely relative to the *mestizo* settlements. In the Etla Valley, for example, the recent improvement in the relations between Zautla and Mazaltepec has resulted in several intermarriages, *fandangos* have been held, and ties of kinship are being spread across the two formerly hostile communities.

The openness or otherwise of formerly closed communities hinges on their rejection of outside domination and exploitation by sealing themselves off, and their ability to practise ceremonial redistribution through participation in the *cargo* system. 'Specifically, the adaptation of Indian communities rests on ideologies of reciprocity and redistribution contained in native religion' (Greenberg 1981, 193). Non-capitalist modes of production and exchange can be maintained only if the ideology by which they are organized is also maintained (Greenberg 1981, 193).

Another factor in the maintenance of the *cargo* system and the closed community it supports is demographic growth; a high proportion of offices to households is essential if participation in the *cargo* system is to be maintained at an intense level. In Yaitepec, the arrival of coffee in the 1950s, followed by the decline of mule transport, signalled by road improvements, introduced outside influences and stimulated the cash economy; simultaneously, rapid population growth has taken place. Demography has not driven the expansion of the *cargo* system, but neither has capital accumulation led Yaitepec men to refuse office, though the coffee growers seem to spend only the bare minimum required by their posts (Greenberg 1981, 198–9). However, in Yaitepec, individualism is in conflict with the egalitarian norms of the community, and often leads to violent interpersonal quarrels (Greenberg 1989).

At the level of the peasant community, a whole series of developments are taking place in concert. Development—in the broadest sense—is leading to modest wealth accumulation. The wealthier are bearing civil and religious *cargos* or are allowing the latter to be hived off to sodalities; in neither case is *cargo*-induced indebtedness giving rise to levelling. Nor is the change destroying community solidarity. Rather, the latter is being restated in a more secular context, itself the product of the greater openness of the community. The costs and benefits of this greater openness are extremely difficult to assess, but certainly cannot be collapsed to a single dimension labelled 'exploitation'.

The most likely outcome is one of greater socio-economic differentiation at the municipal level, but with higher levels of living enjoyed by all, provided access to community resources is maintained for the poor (Chapter 3) or the poorest have access to migration. Migration may not disrupt the *cargo* system too severely; in Zoogocho in the Sierra Zapoteca in the late 1980s, migrants to Los Angeles, California, supported nine out of the sixteen *mayordomías* and filled all the major municipal offices in the community (Hernández Díaz 1992*a*, 147).

Community Boundaries and Conflict

Sharing municipal resources among themselves—at least in theory—and stressing the linguistic differences between them and their neighbours, even if it only involves a variant of Zapotec or Mixtec, most communities are at loggerheads with adjacent settlements. Indeed, Selby has shown that Zapotec suspicion (of witchcraft) characterizes attitudes towards all non-proximate neighbours, even those living within the same settlement as themselves (1974); the anathematizing of outsiders is a logical extension of the principle. So, too, are land conflicts, which are endemic in Oaxaca, unless there is some basis for accommodation: for example, Luebke noted that sparsely populated Juquila rented land to farmers from its poorly endowed neighbour, Yaitepec (1959, 74; see also Greenberg 1981, 76, for a contradictory view).

Municipios are invariably surrounded by other municipal entities, the precise boundaries between them being marked on the ground by *mojoneros*, large rocks or even rock-and-cement structures. Older men in each community will be able to recite all the boundary markers in order (Dennis 1987, 46). San Miguel Tulancingo, in the district of Coixtlahuaca, for example, has seven other municipalities on its perimeter, and its circumference is defined by thirty *mojoneros* (Nieto Angel 1984). When amicable relations exist, sporting events, such as basketball or football, take place between the communities, and *cargo* holders from each may attend one another's patronal feast as honoured guests.

Many years ago, when Mazaltepec and Zautla in the Central Valleys were friendly, even the saints visited one another during *fiestas*. Another indicant of good relations is the exchange of brass bands, although, so far as the bandsmen are concerned, it is the payment of fees rather than the expression of goodwill that is important. Yalálag's relations with other villages in the Sierra Zapoteca are often tense after violent clashes and killings, but the exchange of bands usually marks the return to normal—but distant—relations.

Land conflicts in Oaxaca seem to have been endemic in colonial (Taylor 1972; Spores 1984*b*) and post-independence times, and individual cases often have histories going back for decades or centuries (Dennis 1976*b*). They may involve long-established *municipios* that try to move their borders against one another, or satellite settlements that want to separate from a parent community and achieve municipal status on their own. Whatever their origin, they have served the dominant sectors in society by fragmenting ethnic identity and channelling antagonisms into inter-communal, instead of inter-class, strife.

An example of the first type of dispute is provided by the conflict between San Martín Huamelulpan and Santa María del Rosario in the Mixteca Alta near Teposcolula. Land disputes with its neighbours have been recorded for

San Martín since the eighteenth century, though they may stretch back to the early colonial period. Conflict with Santa María began in 1851, and continued until 1944, when Huamelulpan's lands were finally settled by presidential resolution (Romero Frizzi 1975).

Greenberg describes a similar case. He reports Chatino Yaitepec's *conflict* with Juquila, the district headquarters, which seems to have taken a sizeable portion of the *municipio*'s northern lands as a result of the decision made by the *jefe político* in 1863 (Greenberg 1981, 72–4). Moreover, Greenberg shows that Yaitepec was not only in conflict with Juquila, but also with adjoining Temaxcaltepec and Yolotepec; once again, the basis for the disagreement was the 1863 decision, of which Yaitepec's leaders seem to have remained ignorant for many decades. These disputes, with peaks and troughs, ran from the 1920s to the early 1970s, when, after much petitioning in Mexico City, involving the Instituto Nacional Indigenista and the Confederación Nacional de Campesinos, Yaitepec acknowledged that it had lost its battle with the neighbouring *municipios*.

The second type of land and boundary struggle is exemplified by the hostility between Tlacochahuaya and Abasolo, and San Juan Teitipac and Guelaxé, in the Tlacolula Valley, east of Oaxaca City (Fig. 1.4). Both Abasolo and Guelaxé are daughter villages (of Tlacochahuaya and San Juan Teitipac, respectively), and each remains part of the larger historic parish named after the parent settlement. Abasolo was founded in early colonial times to cultivate the fertile valley of the Río Salado. To counter Tlacochahuaya's colonization plans, Teitipac sent families to settle Guelaxé (Taylor 1972, 87–8).

Strife between Tlacochahuaya and Abasolo dates from 1878, when Abasolo was granted the status of a *municipio*. Through ties to the *jefe político*, Abasolo received title to 1,200 hectares of communal land in 1908, though Tlacochahuaya later claimed that it had been coerced into signing away what it had always regarded as its land. After the Revolution, Tlacochahuaya was riven into two factions—Protestant (Adventist) and favourable to land reform, and Catholic and anti-reformist. So it was not until the 1940s that the land struggle with Abasolo was resurrected.

In 1954, much to Abasolo's amazement, a presidential decree placed all their lands within Tlacochahuaya's boundaries, based in its 'primordial titles' (Dennis 1987, 104–5). After more than ten years of inter-communal violence, which sucked in the army and the police, the Departemento de Asuntos Agrárias y Colonización brokered a non-aggression pact; in 1966 the Supreme Court ruled in favour of Abasolo. Twenty years later the line of separation had still to be marked on the ground (Dennis 1987, 106), though Abasolo appeared as a separate *municipio* in the census.

No sooner had the Abasolo–Tlacochahuaya non-aggression pact started to take effect, than Guelaxé entered the scene. Guelaxé had received *ejidal* land expropriated from Hacienda de Santa Rosa. The *hacendado* was a priest—it was not uncommon for priests to be land owners or even *caciques* (Marroquín

1992), who used his pulpit the attack the *ejidatarios*. Adjacent villages which also had claims on the *hacienda*'s land began invading Guelaxé and stealing crops, but federal land-reform authorities backed the original distribution of *ejidal* property.

Although Gualaxé had maintained good relations with Tlacochahuaya, it had a history of conflict with Abasolo. This flared up immediately after the non-aggression pact between its neighbours, since the communal land ceded to Abasolo was the object of a counter-claim by Guelaxé. Trespass, gunfire, and murder ensued in the late 1960s and early 1970s, and Abasolo's president and secretary were seized and shot. Eventually the state authorities intervened and forced Guelaxé and Abasolo, also, to sign a non-aggression pact (Dennis 1987, 107–8).

A variant of this type of inter-municipal rivalry is provided by the case of Ixtepeji and Ixtlán in the Sierra Zapoteca north of Oaxaca City. Dispute over pieces of land or over the control of offshoot villages were not at the root of the conflict, which, instead, focused on their rivalry to be the political and economic centre of the *sierra*. During the Mexican Revolution, each *municipio* aligned itself with a different national faction, Ixtepeji with the pro-peasant movement led by Zapata, and Ixtlán with government forces that in 1912 sacked Ixtepeji (Kearney 1972), leaving Ixtlán in the ascendance as district headquarters.

Pleitos (disputes) between adjacent communities enhance the isolation inherent in the cellular nature of the network of *municipios*, and thus break up larger potential ethnic blocs, as well as giving vent to *mestizo*–Indian stress (as in the case of *mestizo* Juquila and Yaitepec, as discussed above). In the case of inter-municipal conflicts, they also line the pockets of the legal profession and outside political arbiters, whether they are individuals or agencies. Divide and rule has many dimensions to it, all of which may facilitate external social control by government agencies or alleged political protectors, and deflect rural communities from jointly confronting their subordinate socio-economic status as peasantries (Dennis 1973).

Ejidos and Communities

Creation of the land-reform *ejido*, so common in rural Oaxaca, has had a substantial impact on the internal structure of the *municipio* as a community sharing common interests. *Ejidos* usually cover only part of a pre-existing *municipio*, and introduce new systems of landholding, which have distinct leadership structures and vertical links to the federal political hierarchy. Oaxaca records 800 *ejidos*, and the progress of the land reform has undoubtedly been an important factor in the expansion of *localidades*. So *municipios*, as communities, may be segmented internally, as well as islanded among hostile neighbours. Luebke warns that, 'any given *ejido* may qualify as a fully-fledged

community, may be merely part of a larger community, or may constitute a closely-knit neighbourhood' (1959, 140).

However, *ejidos* are not ubiquitious, and concentrate in the tropical lowlands, especially around Tuxtepec, in the Isthmus of Tehuantepec, in the Mixteca Baja and Mixteca de la Costa, and at higher altitude in the Central Valleys and the northern Mixteca Alta (Fig. 7.3). In general, *ejidos* in Oaxaca are associated with open communities, rather than with communities practising 'usos y costumbres' (Fig. 6.2). 'Where large, contiguous tracts were acquired for *ejido* settlement, strong, well-integrated communities developed; and where *haciendas* were acquired in small, non-contiguous tracts over an extended period, a number of problems have developed in regard to economic activity and social integration' (Luebke 1959, 142).

The *ejido*, in general, lacks the broad political powers and religious institutions that serve as integrative factors in other communities, notably the *municipios*. Where the *ejido* covers roughly the same area as the *municipio* with which it is affiliated, the interests of both may be well integrated in the community matrix. Yet, if the *municipio* is divided into two or more *ejidos* or into a mixture of *ejidos* and other forms of land tenure, community cohesion may suffer accordingly.

The *ejido* has been accorded special status by the Agrarian Department of the Federal Government, equivalent in some respects to political status. Through the *comisariado* (executive committee) and the vigilance committee, the Agrarian Department exercises its authority over *ejidatarios vis-à-vis* the land and other community property. Administrators of the *ejido* enjoy no powers other than those in the land and the general welfare of the inhabitants, so they are obliged to work closely with the government of the *municipio*. Where most community members are *ejidatarios*, they may, of course, come to dominate the government of the *municipio*. Even where they do not, the *ejido* may gain unofficial political power through its external links to the Agrarian Department or the National Ejido Bank.

The *ejido* is specifically forbidden to participate in religious activities, since it is expected to conform to the values of the secular state as defined by the Revolution. The Agrarian Law forbids the *ejido* to expend its funds for religious purposes, to build churches, or support religious *fiestas*. And so the *ejido* is potentially a long way from becoming coextensive with the community—if conceived as a municipal-religious entity, though, as we have seen, this is breaking down in many *municipios*.

However, the *ejido* is permitted to carry out activities that may tighten secular bonds. An *ejido* may engage in co-operative processing, selling, and buying of commodities for its members; it may fund education for children living on the *ejido*; and it may engage in welfare programmes. In these ways, the *ejido* may strengthen a sense of community (or diminish it). An *ejido* may be in competition with other *ejidos* or with other landholding groups or persons or with its own *municipio* government. Land interests may spark internal conflict

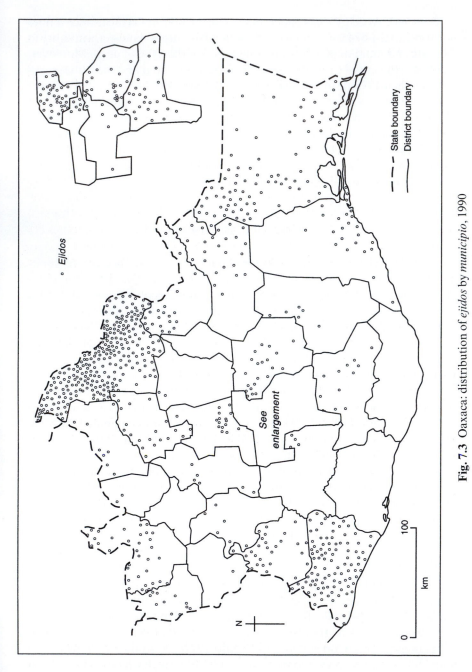

Fig. 7.3 Oaxaca: distribution of *ejidos* by *municipio*, 1990

between the two entities, and power struggles may ensue for the loyalty of the inhabitants.

Reform of Article 27 has had a muted effect so far in Oaxaca, since it does not apply to the 674 communal landholdings (the largest land-reform entity in the state and more than half the national total of this type of unit). Moreover, barely 40 per cent of the state's *ejidos* have been surveyed and their titles certified (Stephen 1998*a*). In the Sierra Madre del Sur and the Costa, the proportion is below 24 per cent and only in the Sierra Norte does it reach 80 per cent (Stephen 1998*a*). Moreover, there has been little trade in land, even where the formal procedures of the PROCEDE titling process have been complied with at the community level (Stephen 1994). It seems safe to conclude that the *ejido* will continue to play a major role in landholding, land use, and community structures in Oaxaca for many years to come.

Role of Caciques

Díaz Montes claims that forty 'Indian' municipalities in Oaxaca are dominated by *caciques* or local bosses (Fox and Aranda 1996, 9 n. 2). Communities objected (in 1980) to the PRI's approving, as municipal officers, candidates selected by *caciques* in Santiago Chazumba, Huajuapan, Pochutla, Santa Catarina Ticuá, Tlaxiaco, Tuxtepec, Zaachila, Valle Nacional, Nochixtlan, and Yalálag. In 1983, Juquila, Yalálag, and San Francisco Telixtlahuaca (Etla) were also mentioned as under the sway of *caciques*. The best-documented examples of *caciques* come from the Sierra Mixe, the Sierra Mazateca, and the Isthmus of Tehuantepec, all indigenous areas, though it is clearly a widespread phenomenon, and one that is by no means at an end.

At the beginning of the twentieth century, two *caciques* dominated the Mixe area of Oaxaca, Daniel Martínez, based in Ayutla, and Manuel Rodríguez, in Zacatepec (Nahmad 1965). After 1914, Martínez extended his control over the other bosses and the Mixe-speaking population, and became a colonel in the forces of the *sierra*-led sovereignty movement (Beals 1945). Subordinate to Martínez were Manuel Rodríguez and his son, Luis Rodríguez Jacob, Martínez's lieutenant. Luis Rodríguez, who spoke good Spanish, established his power base in Zacatepec, of which he was the municipal secretary during the 1920s, and wrested the local *cacicazgo* from his father in 1926 (Laviada 1978).

Before the end of the 1930s, war broke out between Martínez and his henchman, Luis Rodríguez, for control of the Mixe region. In 1938, the state governor acceded to pressure from the Mixe, exerted by the *caciques*, for the formation of a new district to be carved out of Ixtlán, Villa Alta, Choapan, Tehuantepec, and Yautepec (de la Fuente 1977*a*; Kuroda 1993). Martínez found himself outmanœuvred by his more youthful rival, who used his links to state and federal authorities to name the insignificant and more isolated

Zacatepec as the district head-town in preference to Martínez's base, Ayutla (Laviada 1978).

Luis Rodríguez set up a private army led by his brother, cousin, and José Isabel Reyes. They fought Martínez's forces, attacked the major Mixe settlements, and destroyed the telephone system and road that Martínez had brought into the *sierra*. With the complicity of the Oaxaca civil and military authorities, José Isabel Reyes killed Daniel Martínez on a visit to Oaxaca City on Luis Rodríguez's orders, and Rodríguez took over as the overlord of the Mixe. By this time Luis Rodríguez was also secretary of the Confederación Nacional Campesina in the Mixe and an honorary inspector of schools. His dominance persisted until 1959, when the victims of his tyranny in Alotepec, Cacalotepec, Estancía, and Quetzaltepec rose up against him, but he died of natural causes before his enemies could exact their revenge (Laviada 1978).

Three of Rodríguez's relatives inherited the *cacicazgo*, and developed it into a commercial and moneylending enterprise of substantial proportions. This three-generational line of *caciques* dominated and despoiled the Mixe Indians and cost hundreds of people their lives. It was ended only when an association of Mixe authorities, bringing together all nineteen *municipios* of the district, was formed in the late 1970s (Gijsbers 1996).

Most of the money extracted from the Mixe found its way into the pockets of urban bureaucrats in the form of bribes. The *caciques*, particularly those of the first two generations, lived at levels little different from those of the people they terrorized, but they had the power to command economic exchanges and select the municipal presidents they wanted. Seen from the perspective of the PRI, *caciques* in the post-revolutionary period secured order, cohesion, and allegiance from otherwise poorly integrated regions of the state, very much as *jefes políticos* had during the Porfiriato.

Many of the isolated communities of the Sierra Mazateca have fallen under the control of *caciques*, to such an extent that the 'consejos de ancianos' have disintegrated. Mazatlán Villa de Flores has been dominated by *caciques* since the 1930s, and, in this instance, their activities have run on into the 1990s. In the early 1930s, Teódoro Zaragoza was *presidente municipal* of Mazatlán. His family wiped out the rival teaching family of Cliserio Torres in 1933 and established a *cacicazgo*. The federal government sent in the army under General Cuéllar, who tortured Mazatec Indians and rustled stock. Under his tutelage, other *caciques* followed until, in 1965, the García González family, also prominent in the field of education, started to take control. By 1970, they had a presence in the municipal council (Gijsbers 1996).

Filigonio García González was elected municipal president in 1980 and remained in office (unconstitutionally) until 1991, with the support of the PRI deputy for that area. In 1990 Filigonio's brother was installed, with PRI blessing, though the community believed that his opponent had won the election. Soon after, there was an uprising in the community and the new president was driven out. The Mazatlán Mazatecs complained about the lack of services, and

maintained that the former *caciques* had kept them impoverished and subordinate. They expressed their determination to hold elections in future by public assembly in order to minimize interference by the PRI. To this the PRI has responded with false imprisonment and armed intervention, which has given rise to public protest locally and in Oaxaca City (Gijsbers 1996).

These two cases, between them covering almost the entire twentieth century, illustrate the role of *caciques* in the subordination and social fracturing of communities; and their mediation between the community—and region—and the broader political system represented by the PRI. Force has been used, in an almost colonial fashion, to terrorize isolated rural communities of Indian language speakers and to bring them into submission to the *caciques* and their political allies.

That these cases are not isolated is confirmed by the Charis *cacicazgo* in Tehuantepec, which lasted from the 1930s to the 1960s. It was based on Charis's exceptional military endeavours during and after the Revolution, his Zapotec credentials, his violence and rapaciousness, and his ability to broker his way into the political system at local and national levels. After 1930, he controlled Juchitán's politics, and eventually became a PRI federal deputy and senator. It was during his ascendancy that the Isthmus got its first roads, schools, library, hospital, electricity, and irrigation (Campbell 1994).

Municipal Funds

An international dimension has been introduced into Oaxaca's peasant communities through an early-1990s agreement between the Mexican government and the World Bank to boost municipal funds. By taking advantage of the 'social capital' that had already been built up through local government and community development at the level of the *municipio*, it was proposed to introduce a grass-roots, anti-poverty package that would benefit the largest number of the poorest people (Fox and Aranda 1996). Of the four states that were selected for participation in the programme, Oaxaca, with its dense network of 'democratic' *municipios*, was thought most likely to benefit from the decentralization of decision-making and organization that the scheme entailed (Rodríguez 1997).

The governor allocated approximately US$17,000 dollars to each *municipio* in Oaxaca, no account being taken of area or population. In 82 per cent of cases, the funds were turned over directly by the *presidente municipal* to the Municipal Solidarity Councils, comprising the *presidente municipal*, agents of the outlying settlements, the municipal treasurer and councillor for public works, plus representatives of community-level Solidarity Committees. These were supposed to be responsible for dividing up the funds, but met in barely half the cases, decisions otherwise being left to municipal assemblies and to smaller social groupings within the *municipio*. Fifteen per cent of the fund

could be allocated as the community wanted, but of the remaining 85 per cent, only 25 per cent could be spent on the *cabecera*, with 75 per cent going to out-lying settlements. Where over two-thirds of the *municipio*'s population lived in the *cabecera*, 40 per cent of funds could be spent there.

In Oaxaca, in 1991, 77 per cent of the expenditure was on social infrastructure (urbanization, education, and drinking water), 18 per cent on support infra-structure (rural roads and crop storage and marketing), and only 5 per cent on productive infrastructure. As funds had to be expended within a year, it is likely that Councils opted for easily identified and implemented 'urbanization' pro-jects, such as paving the roads in the village centres or installing park benches or fountains (Pl. 7.1). One way in which the shortage of funds was managed was by Councils suggesting that outlying communities might take it in turn, in subse-quent years, to have a substantial part of the budget (Fox and Aranda 1996).

An interesting aspect of Municipal Funds in Oaxaca is the light it sheds on relations between *cabeceras* and outlying settlements. In many *municipios*, the *presidente* is, in fact, chosen only by residents of the principal settlement, and the *agentes* of the *agencias municipales* are either nominated by him or (more likely, in the case of Oaxaca) elected by their own subcommunities. There is considerable scope for intra-municipal conflict, and it is interesting that Fox and Aranda comment that the cap on the sum that could be expended in the *cabecera* did empower local *agencias* by giving them a sense of entitlement to public development funds for the first time (1996). However, there is some evi-dence from the Chatino area to suggest that *agencias* are often semi-indepen-dent from, or more politically powerful than, the municipal authorities in the *cabacera*. In Ixtlán, in the Sierra Juárez, *agencias* protested their exclusion from decision-making in the Municipal Funds initiative by temporarily taking the Oaxaca governor hostage.

Conclusion

Oaxaca's peasant communities elude easy generalization. With 570 *municip-ios*, the vast majority of which contain several potentially competitive nucle-ated settlements, spread through more than fifteen major language groups, complexity and differentiation are to be expected. Nevertheless, the *municipio* still provides the spatial framework within which the majority of *Oaxaqueños* live out their lives; it is the unit within which most marriages are contracted and resources (especially land) are managed and allocated; it is the basis for com-munity self-government and collective religious celebration. These observa-tions apply especially in the high-altitude Indian communities which practise 'usos y costumbres', but are less appropriate to the hot, lowland communities. Here open communities with-land reform *ejidos* are common, *mestizos* and Indians interact intensively with plantations, and individual competitiveness is more marked.

However, it is not possible to argue that the closed corporate community based upon the levelling mechanism of the civil–religious hierarchy is the norm. *Municipios*—even those at high altitude—are ever more open. Socio-economic differentiation is continually increasing by overriding levelling—where it persists. Proportionately fewer people (out of the field of eligibles) have to serve in the *cargo* system. Religious offices are allocated via queuing, taken over by sodalities, or replaced by individual sponsorships attached to life-cycle events. Civil and religious hierarchies, which became entwined as recently as the nineteenth century, are once again becoming separated under the secularizing influence of the Mexican state.

Although openness is more common, and corporateness is declining, the drive to effect administrative decentralization and poverty alleviation by the Mexican government is making the municipal community ever more relevant to public life in Oaxaca. PRI domination of Oaxaca, in part through its 'control' of the municipal system and its monopoly of the peasant vote in state and federal elections, is, therefore, examined in the next chapter. It also explores the social bases for electoral and non-electoral challenges to PRI 'hegemony' over the last thirty years.

8

PRI 'Hegemony' and Political Dissent

A major thrust of the argument so far has been that the Mexican state, under the aegis of the PRI, has been responsible for the reconstitution and reinforcement of Oaxaca's peasantries. It has also played a major role in the post-revolutionary construction of weak peasant ethnicities, and of subordinate, but quasi-autonomous, peasant communities. By delaying, until the late 1970s, the implementation of a population policy based on modern methods of contraception, the state has contributed to the creation of potential surplus population throughout the rural and urban communities of Oaxaca.

However, in conjunction with its pro-peasant policy, the Mexican state has simultaneously pursued a strategy of urban-capitalist development, especially since the Second World War. It has used peasant production as a source of cheap food, and precipitated peasant migration to the towns and other economic growth points as a cheap labour supply. In addition, the state has improved communications and the provision of electricity, and thus enabled some privileged peasant producers to evolve towards capitalist production for profit, creating, as a consequence, minor class structures within peasantries.

It is a contradiction that, as peasant communities have modernized and their youth has become more fluent in Spanish, so demands for ethnic recognition have grown, stimulating demands for more ethnically controlled economic and social development. This has resulted in the state's recognition of pluri-ethnicity and the right of indigenous communities to their own democratic procedures—'usos y costumbres'. The latter system of elections existed, *de facto*, at community level throughout the post-revolutionary years, but is now (allegedly) to be without PRI interference.

The politically controlled nature of social relations, which was instituted by the PRI in the 1930s, has progressively collapsed since 1968, as student radicalism has challenged the nation's rigged democracy. PRI policy towards democratic opposition has softened over the years, and outsider groups, and left-wing elements that were formerly repressed and marginalized, have been allowed a political platform, especially since 1980.

An important factor in the shift towards greater PRI accountability and transparency has been the entry of Mexico into the North American Free Trade Area (in 1993). This has been a logical extension of its pro-capitalist

stance, but with the twist that manufacturing will no longer be protected and geared to the national market, as in the past, but will be unprotected and for export. This neo-liberal shift, which was so closely associated with the Salinas administration (1988–94), was accompanied by the US's requirement that its trading partners, Mexico as well as Canada, should be patently democratic. How could this demand for democracy be made compatible with the PRI's intention to remain Mexico's party of government in perpetuity?

This chapter has a more national focus than the last two, and looks at the role played by peasants and non-peasants (the urban poor, the urban middle class, students, and the socio-economic élite) in the recent politics of Oaxaca. More specifically, the question is asked to what extent has the PRI been able to maintain its hegemony? The brief answer is that Oaxaca's peasantries (and economic élites) have stayed loyal to the PRI. It has been students, in the 1960s and 1970s, and, more recently, the urban middle and lower classes that have rejected the PRI.

An examination of the relationship between the Oaxaca élite and the PRI from the post-revolutionary period to 1967 provides the opening to the chapter. It then charts the subsequent rise of radicalism among students, peasants, and workers, both nationally and in Oaxaca, following the student massacre instigated by the PRI at Tlatelolco in Mexico City in 1968. The chapter traces the sharpening social and political crisis that occurred in Oaxaca City in 1977 and its suppression by the military. Attention is then shifted to the rural teachers' protests in Oaxaca in the late 1970s, and the national political 'opening' of the early 1980s, which permitted the election of a 'socialist republic' in the Zapotec municipality of Juchitán (1981–3) in the Isthmus of Tehuantepec (Campbell 1994).

The final section details struggles within the PRI over the 1986 nomination for the Oaxaca governorship. It also examines the municipal elections of the same year, which resulted in 15 out of 570 being taken by the opposition—a clear indication of overall peasant support for, or acquiescence in, the hegemony of the PRI. Although the focus is Oaxaca, changing national styles of leadership and presidential attitudes to democracy and dissent will be alluded to, since they provide a vital context to events at the federal and local level.

Oaxaca is particularly interesting in relation to the nature of, and the challenge to, PRI 'hegemony', since the struggles of the period 1968 to 1986 ran the gamut from peaceful grass-roots opposition via street violence to electoral competition (from the left and right). Indeed, the events in the *municipio* of Juchitán, which encompassed all these aspects, also involved issues of ethnicity and community. Moreover, because the state of Oaxaca has 570 *municipios*, there is the opportunity to enquire into the emergence of a voting opposition on a small scale, since the plethora of small administrative units provides multiple arenas in which opposition to the PRI may be expressed.

It will, however, be clear that neither the extra-electoral opposition of radical elements to the PRI nor the 'socialist republic' in Juchitán were successful;

that they existed is significant, but in each case they were stifled by PRI manip-ulation or contained by its repression. Scrutiny of the electoral results in, and since, 1986 scarcely provides evidence for a terminal weakening of the PRI in Oaxaca. In 1988, when Salinas's share of the national presidential vote was 50.36 per cent, it was 63.81 per cent in Oaxaca, less than two percentage points behind the figure the PRI recorded in the election for state deputies that year. By 1991 the Salinas administration had been sufficiently successful, economi-cally, to lift the PRI vote for deputies, nationally, from 51.11 per cent in 1988 to 61.4 per cent; in Oaxaca the figure was 73.4 per cent. In 1994, however, the PRI vote in Oaxaca for the presidency (when the mandate passed to Zedillo) slumped to less than 50 per cent—but with a massive increase in the turn-out from 46 (in 1988) to 71 per cent.

The burden of this chapter, therefore, is to show that PRI 'hegemony' has not gone uncontested at the state or municipal level. In 1995, the opposition increased its victories from fifteen (in 1986) to forty-six *municipios*. But there is, as yet, no basis for arguing that the 1988 emergence of Cuauhtémoc Cárdenas and the Frente Democrático Nacional, at the national level, has changed Mexican (or Oaxacan) politics for all time. Democratic uncertainty has not broken out nor is the PRI on the verge of losing the electoral and overall polit-ical dominance it has enjoyed for the last sixty-five years.

Oaxaca's Economic Élite and the PRI

Since the Second World War, urban-based *comerciantes*, many of whom are also engaged in small-scale industry and construction, have displaced the *hacendados*, scaled down by the post-revolutionary land reform, as the leading economic element in the state. Although the political élite of Oaxaca is a sepa-rate entity, there is some overlapping membership with the business group. For example, Bravo Ahuja, the governor elected in 1968, came from a power-ful Tuxtepec family, and several of the fifty-seven élite business clans have had members serving in Oaxaca City's municipal government or in different state cabinets (Basáñez 1987; Martínez Vásquez 1990). The political directorate of the PRI in Oaxaca has for decades been drawn, in order of importance, from the Oaxaca Valley, the Isthmus of Tehuantepec, and Tuxtepec—the most dynamic economic regions.

Shared membership of the political and economic élites is especially typical of the Central Valleys, where the *vallistocracia política* is noted for its multiple and diverse contacts with the *vallistocracia económica*. They combine in a cer-tain amount of business; they are brought together through godparenthood, marriage, school attendance, professional services—law, medicine, and accountancy; politicians provide merchants with support and construction work, and the latter reciprocate in a variety of ways. There is also the case of politicians who become businessmen, though this is difficult to detect because

of concealment by the use of third parties in ownership registration (Martínez Vásquez 1990, 107). Even where the membership of these two élite groups does not coincide, both entities are usually mutually supporting; and the PRI is expected not only to maintain the social *status quo*, but to supply the business group with lucrative contracts (Martínez Vásquez 1990, 85–108).

The first major political conflict of the post-revolutionary period in Oaxaca was essentially an inter-regional struggle within the economic élite. It took place between 1950 and 1952, when coffee producers near the Pacific Coast supported one of their colleagues, Mayoral Heredia, for the state governorship. Linked directly to the, then, President of Mexico, Miguel Alemán, through ties of *compadrazgo* (fictive kinship), Mayoral Heredia obtained the PRI's backing at the national level and won the post (Martínez López 1982).

Having assumed the governorship, Mayoral Heredia marginalized the local political class in Oaxaca City, and introduced his own band of bureaucrats with direct links to Mexico City. Almost immediately, he announced plans to modernize Oaxaca's agriculture, especially the export sector. To this end he proposed a new paved road, linking the coffee-growing area around Pinotepa Nacional on the Pacific to Huajuapan de Leon, a staging-post in the Mixteca *en route* for Mexico City and the Gulf Coast. He also introduced tax laws to finance other infrastructural improvements in agriculture, and legislation to provide ten-year subsidies for new industries (Murphy and Stepick 1991*a*).

Oaxaca City's economic élite found themselves not simply outmanœuvred by the nomination and election of Mayoral Heredia, but bypassed in terms of economic strategy; they could foresee little or no benefit to themselves from the stimulation of agricultural exports that would never go near the state capital. Their economic base was local, at that time, and geared to the supply of goods and services to Oaxaca City and its immediate hinterland. Moreover, they believed that the burden of the tax and revenue proposals would fall on them. So, the Oaxaca City merchants, organized through the Cámara de Comercio (CANACO), appealed to the *políticos* who had recently lost their bureaucratic posts on Mayoral Heredia's election and with whom they has personal and professional ties. Many of these bureaucrats were also law professors at the Instituto de Ciencias y Artes; they had taught the economic élite, represented them in law suits, and were tied to them through marriage and *compadrazgo* (Martínez López 1982).

To counter the modernizers and maintain the isolation of the state, the links between the Oaxaca City élite, the university professors, and their students, many of whom were children of the élite, were activated, each group invoking the support of national agencies to which it was affiliated. Events escalated. The state police shot two students. A one-day, national student strike was held. Daily demonstrations in Oaxaca City and a city-wide general strike led to military occupation. The governor lost political legitimacy. He dismissed his cabinet, filled their places with local residents, and appointed a Oaxaca City merchant to be state co-ordinator of agricultural affairs. The latter prevari-

cated; and, after a face-saving period, Mayoral Heredia resigned (Martínez López 1982).

The city's business élite, thereafter, believed they could prevent Oaxaca being drawn into the national economic system. It was their intention to maintain their dominance of local trade, especially in consumption items, with a minimum of competition. Within this overall strategy, their immediate aim was to monopolize the small commercial turnover associated with the low levels of living of the masses, and to increase their profits by catering to the needs of the expanding urban middle class.

These objectives were sustained throughout the 1950s and most of the 1960s, but were destabilized by the activities of the 1968 student movement in Mexico City, especially in the aftermath of the notorious massacre at Tlaltelolco, which took place on the eve of the opening of the Olympic Games. This massacre found immediate resonance among the student body in Oaxaca City, which proceeded to mount a popular movement against the business class and the PRI (González Pacheco 1984), thus ushering in the modern period of political dissent.

Student Radicals: Their Opponents and Allies

Prior to 1968, the PRI adopted a heavy-handed approach to dissent in any form. But after the 1968 student protests in Mexico City, inspired by similar outbursts in Europe, and by the Cuban Revolution of 1959, a different approach was adopted. PRI repression led to a sense of guilt, and to an acknowledgement of the need for greater openness. This policy was initiated under the presidency of Luis Echeverría (1970–6), the minister in charge at the time of the Tlatelolco killings, and partly coincided with the governorships of Bavo Ahuja (1968–70) and his associate, Gómez Sandoval (1970–4), who succeeded him when he resigned to become Minister of Education. Both governors, in turn, reflected national policy, and tolerated opposition to a degree unacceptable to the Oaxaca economic élite.

Tension in Oaxaca, after 1968, hinged on the opposition of radicalized students, peasants, and workers to the economic dominance of the *vallistocracia*, to the undemocratic, permanent government of the PRI, and to its suppression of popular dissent. Land grabs, including one or two urban squats, the creation of independent trade unions—independent of the formal links to the PRI that characterized most syndicates—and strike action at the university were the principal tactics adopted. The élite commercial sector, as the leading element among conservative forces, persistently urged successive governors to repress the militants (González Pacheco 1984; Martínez Vásquez 1990). The response, when it came, under the governorship of Zárate Aquino, involved the dispersal of squatters and strikers and the imprisonment and victimization of the student leadership.

The Oaxaca student movement, which had been spawned by the events of 1968, had strong left-wing, even Marxist, affiliations. It demanded a far greater say, through democratic elections, in university affairs and argued for the autonomy of the Instituto de Ciencias y Artes from the state government. In addition, it seized upon a series of socio-economic disputes that were already occurring in rural and urban Oaxaca, each of which brought it into conflict with either the *vallistocracia política* or the *vallistocracia económica*.

Squatter invasions, the result of cityward migration and the inability of Oaxaca City to employ and house the population in formal circumstances, were a constant challenge to the authorities. So was the outbreak of land disputes between peasants and *caciques* in rural communities. Workers in the swollen urban labour-market, including its informal sector, pressed for unionization, better pay, or reduced outgoings. Peasant vendors in the Saturday market, many of whom were illegal, were subjected to pressure from city-centre merchants who wished to monopolize the retail trade. The student body, which numbered about 300 in the late 1940s, 2,000 in 1968, and 20,000 in 1988 (Martínez Vásquez, 1990), became less élitist in composition and more radical and militant with time. In 1968, students entered the fray against the business class and their political associates in a series of overlapping and intertwining actions.

The Federación Estudiantil Oaxaqueña (FEO), which had been founded to stimulate social activities among the students at the Instituto de Ciencias y Artes, (soon to be converted under dissident pressure in 1971 into the Universidad Autónoma 'Benito Juárez' de Oaxaca or UABJO), rapidly took on a political role. It organized successful resistance to increases in Oaxaca City bus fares in 1969 and 1970—a perennial issue in a state capital with growing peripheral shantytowns. It then proceeded to stimulate vendors' resistance to the merchants' attempts to remove the peasant market from the city centre to the periphery. The Federación de Mercados, representing larger-scale merchants, 'argued that the smaller vendors were unhygienic, the old market was too crowded and too Indian, and that tourists were repelled by all these features' (Murphy and Stepick 1991*a*, 114). But their principal aim was more selfish—to capture a larger share of the retail market from their small-scale competitors by expelling them to the new site on the outskirts, though it took until the repression of 1978 to achieve this.

Confronted by a conservative Directorio Estudiantil, the FEO also found itself locked in a violent struggle over the university buildings that resulted in the army's intervention in 1970, the death of a member of the FEO, and the long-term imprisonment of Castillo Viloria, the FEO leader. This entire episode was essentially a re-run of the events of 1968, which had led to the imprisonment of González Pacheco; it was also a harbinger of the even more turbulent circumstances that were to break out in 1976–7.

The FEO began to equip itself for the struggle ahead. Its new leadership attracted the support of students at the Instituto Tecnológico, the Escuelas

Normales Rurales, Reyes Mantecon and Tamazulapam, as well as a variety of dissident urban and rural groups. A coalition of workers, peasants, and students was formally inaugurated in 1972 with the acronym of COCEO (Coalición de Obreros Campesinos y Estudiantes de Oaxaca) (Yescas Martínez 1982). Key elements in the coalition, in addition to the FEO, were the Partido Comunista Mexicano and the Marxist Bufete Popular Universitario. Based on the Faculty of Law, the Bufete was to provide legal advice to left-wing groups in Oaxaca throughout the decade. Other components of COCEO were the Central Campesina Independiente, and two militant working-class unions, the Sindicato de Trabajadores Electricistas de la República Mexicana and the Movimiento Sindical Ferrocarrilero. An explicit objective of COCEO was to 'achieve the socialist transformation of the country' (Martínez Vásquez 1990, 133 n.11). Later, in 1976, it was to join with other movements to create the Frente Campesino Independiente, which linked peasant movements in Tuxtepec, where it was most active, with those in the Central Valleys and the Isthmus of Tehuantepec (Basáñez 1987; Yescas Martínez 1989).

Government reaction in the early 1970s, though muted compared to its later response, sought to create factionalism among the students, and the FEO was eventually banned. Part of the student movement went underground, notably La Liga Comunista 23 de Septiembre and the Unión del Pueblo, and planted bombs in symbolic locations, including an English-language library (Martínez Vásquez 1990, 136). COCEO, however, continued its activities, helping to organize land invasions by *campesinos* who were trying to recapture property seized by large landowners, notably at Tlalixtac de Cabrera, Zimatlán, Santa Gertrudis (Paz Paredes and Moguel 1979), la Ciénaga, Santa Catarina Quiané, and Xoxocotlán in the Central Valleys. COCEO also supported residents in land disputes in Oaxaca City at San Martín Mexicapan and Santo Tómas Xochimilco (Zafra 1982).

Student radicals also pressed for political prisoners to be released, not only their own leaders, but others, such as Esteban Oviedo Escareño, an Indian from Jamiltepec, who had been jailed for opposing the brutal *cazicazgo* of the Iglesias Meza family. COCEO's anti-establishment activities reached a peak in 1974, when the high rate of inflation triggered widespread strikes in Oaxaca City. It seized the opportunity to organize independent unions of bus drivers, car mechanics, university workers, municipal workers, bakers, social workers at the Instituto Nacional Indigenista, and employees in the city slaughter-house. With recognition of their status came substantial pay rises and fringe benefits that effectively transferred union members into the formal sector of the economy (Murphy and Stepick 1991*a*).

These achievements were terminated in December 1974, with the inauguration of the new governor, Zárate Aquino, backed by the Grupo Oaxaca. COCEO was immediately identified as the enemy: to dismember and annihilate it would be the fundamental objective for property owners and the political regime (Martínez Vásquez 1990, 158). The governor commanded the army

to impose order in those *municipios* where opponents of the PRI had claimed that the recent elections were fraudulent—Zimatlán, Zaachila, Santa Gertrudis, Xoxocotlán in the Central Valleys, and Juchitán and others in the Isthmus of Tehuantepec.

Explosions were attributed to COCEO (though the latter denied involvement), the student underground movement was targeted, the PRI pumped funds and agents into opposing the radical student movement, and the unions of bus drivers and auto mechanics were decertified and disbanded. In 1975, a massive land invasion involving 5,000 people (Martínez Vásquez 1990, 174)—in which COCEO played no part (but for a contrary view see Basáñez 1987, 78)—took place on either side of the Pan-American Highway on the outskirts of Oaxaca City. At the instigation of the governor, the army quickly dispersed the squatters (Murphy and Stepick 1991*a*). Although a small number who were able to pay for basic lots were eventually settled at Santa Rosa, repression of the urban poor began in earnest thereafter, and was completed by 1977.

The main focus of dissident activity in the late 1970s was the Universidad Autónoma 'Benito Juarez' de Oaxaca in Oaxaca City, and within it the recently formed Centro de Sociología. In 1975, the university was paralysed by conflicts over the voting rights of students in elections to the directorships of the various schools. As many part-time professors were also public officials, this issue rapidly spilled over into local politics, and it was resolved only by the intervention of local and federal mediators.

The fragile truce, during which university rectors came and went, was broken by elections to the rectorship in 1976. Two title-holders emerged, one chosen by majority vote (Martínez Soriano of the Frente Democrático Universitario), the other (Tenorio Sandoval, an ex-deputy and president of the Oaxaca Municipality) imposed, so it has been argued, by the state government (Martínez Vásquez 1990). Probably 90 per cent of the students were *democráticos*, but both they and the *restauradores* seized university buildings, and the two groups sniped at, and killed, one another (Lozano 1984). Throughout 1976 the university factions battled both the state and federal governments in actions that embroiled the campus, the city, and the state (Santibáñez Orozco 1982). In Juchitán, in the Isthmus of Tehuantepec, it was alleged that non-PRI candidates had been excluded from municipal office; in Oaxaca City, disputes over bus-fare increases resulted in numerous arrests.

Conservative forces, associated with organized business groups, such as the local Cámara de Comercio (CANACO), the Consejo Coordinador Empresarial (CCE), the Cámara de la Industria de la Transformación (CANACINTRA), and the Centro Patronal (CP), now combined. Merchants, landowners, service clubs, and the PRI formed the Fusión Cívica de Organizaciones Productivas de Oaxaca to oppose subversion and press for peace and stability. As Martínez Vásquez shrewdly observed, FUCOPO 'turned itself into a binding agent and organizer of the actions of the bourgeoisie, the corporate apparatus of the state and the governor' (1990, 188).

Moreover, at the national level, it received the backing of the nationally powerful Grupo Monterrey, while Zárate Aquino himself had the support of the Federal Deputies for Oaxaca, among them Heladio Ramírez López, and the Senator for Oaxaca, General Eliseo Jiménez Ruiz.

At the end of February 1977 FUCOPO announced the closure of all business houses for two days, on the second of which its supporters clashed in the markets with student radicals. Student demonstrators massed at the School of Medicine in the north of the city and marched on the *zócalo*. Just short of the city centre, the state police dispersed them with a display of considerable violence. During the night, federal troops took control of the streets. The next day, 3 March, Governor Zárate Aquino flew to Mexico City and asked President López Portillo for leave of absence. By the evening, a new governor, General Eliseo Jiménez Ruiz, the Senator for Oaxaca, had taken command. General Jiménez Ruiz was known nationally for his anti-communism and his successful military campaign in the state of Guerrero against the guerrilla, Lucio Cabañas. Under his rule, Oaxaca experienced, for two years, a phase of fierce but selective military repression that fragmented COCEO and demobilized the masses politically.

The university problem remained intractable, however. Martínez Soriano and Tenorio Sandoval both stepped down in favour of the new regime's nominee, Fernando Gómez Sandoval, interim Governor of Oaxaca in the early 1970s. But Tenorio refused to hand over the central university building in the core of the city. Gómez Sandoval, who was still unpopular with the *vallistocracia*, withdrew. In mid-March, the federal government imposed a solution over the heads of the Oaxaca élite by giving the army complete control of Oaxaca City and the most important settlements in the state: the central university building was emptied and placed under armed guard (Lozano 1984). The *restauredores* abandoned the UABJO, and founded the Universidad Regional del Sureste.

Oaxaca remained under military control until the next election, which, in 1980, brought Pedro Vásquez Colmenares, the former managing director of one of the two state airlines, to the governorship. As a mark of federal approval and support, the President of the Republic, López Portillo, witnessed his inauguration in Oaxaca City. López Portillo's presence was highly symbolic, since it marked the end of local élite opposition to federal intervention. Events in Oaxaca in the late 1970s had not been entirely to the liking of the commercial élite. They had backed Zárate Aquino until his governorship became untenable, but subsequently found the interim government of General Jiménez Ruiz unsympathetic to themselves, even if he was local. For he had to create sufficient distance from the Grupo Oaxaca of Zárate Aquino to respond to policy emanating from Mexico City, notably from Gobernación (the Interior Ministry) and Defensa Nacional.

The *vallistocracia* feared that the departure of Zárate Aquino had produced a vacuum that was being filled only too rapidly by the federal government

without reference to itself. The military occupation of the university confirmed this. Moreover, Jiménez Ruiz's repression, though frequently resorting to violence, was more specific and less general than they wanted (for its targeted victims on the left it entailed gaol, torture, or death). The commercial élite, inevitably, distrusted the general's Mexico City associates, the Grupo México, whom they called 'los gitanos' (gypsies). A leading figure among the *Oaxaqueños ausentes* was Heladio Ramírez López, a native of the Mixteca. Dubbed by his Oaxaca City opponents as 'tercermundista', he was to play a major part in Oaxaca's politics in the 1980s and 1990s.

Faced with the initiatives of Jiménez Ruiz, the *vallistocracia* split into a hard-line faction bent on the repression of COCEO, headed by Juan José Gutiérrez Ruiz, and a group, led by Carlos Hampshire Franco, which favoured a negoti-ated settlement of what came to be known, nationally, as *el Caso Oaxaca*. The Hampshire Franco element was more closely aligned with the PRI, but in the event lost the support of the Oaxaca Federación de Camaras de Comercio, leav-ing the José Gutiérrez faction in the ascendant. Nevertheless, the latter had eventually to accept the governor's strategy, backed as it was by the López Portillo administration in Mexico City (Basáñez 1987).

Splits among the student body, the real focus of Jiménez Ruíz's attention, were even more dramatic and fatal. Squabbling between different factions of the left reduced COCEO to giving legal advice to peasants and labour organi-zations. Even the guerrilla activities of *el Guero Medrano* in the mountains near Tuxtepec, instead of inciting peasant uprisings, were merely an excuse for blanket military operations in the region.

Intervention by the federal government was civilian as well as military. Federal agencies increased the number of their local offices and staff after 1977, often importing bureaucrats from other states (Basáñez 1987, 142). Oaxaca's infrastructure (roads, telephones, water supply, education, and health) was improved, and the housing agency, ISSSTE (Instituto de Seguridad y Servicios Sociales de los Trabajadores del Estado) undertook the development of a new neighbourhood to the north of the town, specifically to house federal employees.

The Mexican government emerged as an actor at the Oaxaca level with the capacity and intent to nullify the isolationist tendencies of the economic élite, which slipped into a more clientilist role based on government construction contracts. Thus, the 'old commercial elite, without the resources to overcome the external influences, no longer battled external elites directly as they had done in the 1950s and before the Revolution. As the old elite's control slipped away, its members complained that the outsiders were condescending, insensi-tive, and prone to misjudge local needs' (Murphy and Stepick 1991*a*, 120–1).

The final phase of non-electoral dissent in the late 1970s was played out by teachers in Oaxaca (Movimiento Magisterial Democrático) in their con-frontation with *sección XXII* of their union, El Sindicato Nacional de Trabajadores de la Educación. They joined colleagues, notably from Chiapas,

to try to establish, at state level, democratic controls over their union's exercise of power within the educational system, monopolized by a PRI-related clique called the Vanguardia Revolucionaria. They also wished to protest at the low wages handed out to teachers by the government; as the Mexican oil boom of 1978–81 raised inflation to unprecedented levels, teachers found their living standard halved. Street protests, including sit-ins and a silent march in which 12,000 teachers participated, took place in Oaxaca City throughout 1980, backed by COCEO and parents of pupils; news of the 'insurgency' was broadcast through newspapers, radio, and television (Martínez Vásquez 1990, 234).

In early June 1980, protesters from various states, including Oaxaca, camped outside the offices of the Secretaría de Educación Pública in Mexico City, as a result of which they were first threatened and later promised a solution to their grievances. But once they had left the capital, their gains turned out to be far less satisfactory than the teachers had expected (Yescas Martínez and Zafra 1985, 170–1). This was to be only the first stage in a conflict that was to run on, with seemingly endless ramifications, until the end of the 1980s, eluding all attempts by Oaxaca's governors to control it (Sorroza Polo 1992).

Hostility to the dominance of the PRI, reminiscent of that voiced by the Oaxaca teachers, and at an earlier date by COCEO, was echoed by a coalition of social groups in Juchitán. The issues and actors had been present in the Isthmus for some time, and it was the political reform of 1980 that provided the opportunity for dissent to take on the crucial electoral dimension that it did in 1983.

The 1980 Electoral Reform and 'Socialist Republic' of Juchitán

Towards the end of the 1970s an attempt was made at the national level to improve the image of Mexican democracy by allowing more space to opposition political parties, including those of the far left. Cynically, it might be said that the previously 'constrained democracy' presided over by the PRI was now to be slightly relaxed (*reforma política*), but only on (the undeclared) condition that the paramount position of the party was not seriously challenged. This provided an exceptional opportunity for left-wing dissidents in the turbulent *municipio* of Juchitán—with a census population of 45,000 in 1980 (Rubin (1994) and Basáñez (1987) cite 70,000), in the Isthmus of Tehuantepec. Now, according to the constitutional reforms, their movement had the political space to take part in a local election, in alliance with a nationally registered party, to compete with the PRI and to take power (Rubin 1997).

Opposition to the PRI in the Isthmus was spearheaded by COCEI (Coalición Obrero Campesino y Estudiantil del Istmo), an affiliate of COCEO founded in 1974. The success of COCEI as a political force hinged on its appeal to Zapotec and regional identity in contradistinction to the PRI, which was

seen, locally, as an alien force (Campbell 1994). Moreover, it was able to whip up grass-roots support by backing small cultivators and agricultural labourers in their struggles against large landowners and the state (Doniz and Monsivais 1983). According to Rubin, COCEI 'is one of the strongest and most militant grassroots movements in Mexico, in large part because Zapotec Indians in Juchitán transformed their courtyards and fiestas into fora for intense political discussion, gathered in the streets in massive demonstrations, and, in the course of the past two decades, redefined the activities, meanings and alliances of their culture' (1994, 110).

The conflicts in which COCEI intervened so successfully in Juchitán had their roots in nineteenth-century ethnic particularism and regionalism: Juchitán managed to separate itself from the control of Hispanized Tehuantepec, its major rival in 1858 (Campbell 1994). But the immediate origin of the social and political discord lay in the late 1950s, when so-called 'communal lands', which were used for maize and sesame cultivation and cattle rearing, were the subject of dispute between large and small proprietors. To resolve these disagreements and to provide the infrastructure for agricultural development, communal land in adjacent *municipios* was taken into state control in 1964 by the president, López Mateos, and reallocated as *ejidos*, 54,000 hectares of which were irrigated from the newly constructed Benito Juárez dam (Binford 1985). Large landholders persuaded small proprietors to join them in protest: the situation was returned to the *status quo ante*, except that the government exacerbated tensions further by providing credit for irrigated land, the bulk of which went to large landholders, though they, too, still lacked legal title. No credit was received by the majority of small-scale cultivators, who were forced back into their traditional role as agricultural labourers. It was the combination of rural social inequality with differential access to irrigation and credit that provided the students at the *technológico* with the rural support that validated COCEI's reiteration of demands commonplace in Juchitán's political circles since the late 1960s (Reina 1994).

COCEI was formed during President Echeverria's *apertura democrática*; it had his tacit backing and that of several government ministries. The movement won widespread support for marches, strikes, sit-ins in government offices, and Zapotec cultural and artistic activities (Campbell 1994; Rubin 1997). Through these campaigns, improved living and working conditions were achieved for peasants and workers in and around Juchitán. In view of these successes, COCEI was attacked by the right wing of the PRI, by paramilitary groups and the local and state police, and more than twenty deaths were registered between 1974 and 1977 (Rubin 1994, 122).

During the electoral reform of the early 1980s, COCEI formed an alliance with the Partido Socialista Unificado de México (PSUM)—which the constitution now permitted—to secure a place on the ballot. Its poll at the 1980 election was sufficiently close to that of the PRI, for it to decry its defeat as a fraud and elicit mass mobilization in support of its claim to victory. Much of its suc-

cess was, of course, due to the prominent position it gave to the land issue and other local facets of social inequality (Prévot-Shapira and Rivière D'Arc 1983). COCEI was eventually confirmed in government through a further close-run election that it won by the narrowest of margins in early 1981 (Campbell 1994; Rubin 1997).

The success of COCEI's 1980 strategy of mass mobilization, which involved the 'capture' of the *palacio municipal* and extended to occupations in Mexico City and Oaxaca City, was to become the model for opposition groups in other disputed elections in Oaxaca throughout the 1980s. However, a crucial contributory factor in COCEI's victory was a split in the PRI in Juchitán (Martínez López 1985). Juchitán became 'the first and only city in the country with a leftist government' (Rubin 1994, 123), and COCEI-PSUM transformed the face of the town through the implementation of a form of participatory democracy. 'They were collecting money and signing referenda, as well as securing agricultural credit, payment of minimum wages and benefits, and long-absent municipal services. Juchitecos were literally speaking a language (Isthmus Zapotec) that was foreign to their government, a language rich in puns, evocations of local history and fidelity to local experiences and needs' (Rubin 1994, 112).

Juchitán under COCEI was in marked contrast to Juchitán under the PRI, as Rubin records.

Ordinary people in the city's neighbourhoods stated clearly—with new urgency, drawing new connections among their experiences, and with new kinds of actions—that they were poor people (*los pobres*) and that they were exploited in specific ways by local commercial enterprises and government agricultural programmes. They said that they [had been] ruled by a municipal government imposed through fraudulent elections and military force, that they supported COCEI because it fought unequivocally for their well-being, and that they participated in politics—attended meetings and marched in the streets, voted, joined communal work projects, and contributed financially—in order to carry on this struggle. (1994, 121)

Tangible benefits of the COCEI government were a literacy programme, and the setting up of a library and preparatory school (a stepping-stone to university), a teachers' training college, a radio station, health centres, and a book-publishing programme (Campbell *et al.* 1993).

How were the PRI to topple this 'socialist republic', given that COCEI was able to mobilize and deploy so many historical facets of a distinct and self-aware community? (Aubague 1985). The Oaxaca state government under the 'democratic' regime of Vásquez Colmenares, found itself in a cleft stick. On the one hand, it was continuously pressured to oust COCEI by the Juchitán branch of CANACO, whose members carried out a series of strategic strikes; on the other, it felt constrained by the political reforms favouring the opposition that had been enacted by the López Portillo government.

Vacillating though the state government of Oaxaca was, it still had several levers it could operate as and when it chose. These included control of the

municipal budget, manipulation of rumour and violence generated by local PRI militants, and the presence of large state-funded projects that had come on stream during the late 1970s. These included the oil refinery of the Pacific at Salina Cruz and the sugar factory, López Portillo, at Espinal 8 kilometres from Juchitán. Both the oil refinery and the sugar factory had drawn labour from outside the Isthmus—mostly from the oil and sugar areas of Vera Cruz.

These new concentrations of labour were the bastions, impervious or hostile to COCEI, from which the 'reconquest' of Juchitán was to be carried out by the state government during the summer of 1983, backed by army violence (Prévot-Shapira and Rivière d'Arc 1983). By this time, Miguel de la Madrid had replaced López Portillo as President of Mexico, and the oil boom had degenerated into economic crisis. Moreover, the USA, confronted by left-wing revolutionaries in Central America, was pressing Mexico for the removal of the 'socialist republic' of Juchitán from the sensitive region of the Isthmus (Toledo 1995).

Rubin, who arrived in Juchitán in August 1983, witnessed the aftermath of COCEI's repudiation (*desconocimiento*) by fiat of the Oaxaca state government. Twenty-five thousand Juchitecos gathered in the town square to defend the *Ayuntamiento Popular*, the People's Government.

Large Juchiteca women surrounded the City Hall with their fists in the air, dressed in traditional embroidered blouses and gold jewellery, with red confetti streaming over their thickly braided hair. Everything they wore was outlined, ribonned, or bannered in red, the colour of COCEI. In raucous, angry voices, they chanted slogans in defence of COCEI and its mayor, Leopoldo de Gyves, and vilified the official party, the Partido Revolucionario Institucional. (Rubin 1994, 111)

The Mexican government responded to the ousting of COCEI from Juchitán, and the PRI's ensuing electoral victory in November, with a broad-spectrum policy. This involved abuse of human rights in the case of the COCEI leadership (Amnesty International 1986), military support for local PRI moderates, investment in municipal services, electoral competition and comparative freedom of organization for COCEI (Rubin 1994).

By stopping short of outright repression, policymakers in Mexico City hoped to resolve Juchitan's political conflict through what they called economic and political modernization: with massive investment, they would put an end to the pervasive lack of basic services in the city and provide the infrastructure for commercial and urban development; at the same time, national and state leaders would press for the definitive ascendance of well-educated businesspeople and professionals to positions of municipal authority. (Rubin 1994, 123–4)

These machinations by the PRI to retake and hold the ideologically high-profile *municipio* of Juchitán indicate the strict limits that the federal and state governments were to set to the *reforma política*. In insignificant municipalities the PRI was prepared to lose, if the opposition was determined and there were not too many instances of defeat. Even so, electoral fraud and co-optation

might be tried, culminating in manipulation of the electoral roll or of the hours of opening of polling booths; perhaps violence would be used, where the stakes were defined as being sufficiently high—as they were, notoriously, in Juchitán. These conclusions provide a background against which to set the state-wide elections held in Oaxaca in 1986.

The 1986 Oaxaca Elections

The 1986 elections are of importance not only because of the opportunity they provided for 'the extension of the struggle to democratise the *municipio'* (Martínez Vásquez 1990, 245), but because the municipal poll coincided with the hustings for state deputies and the governorship. Moreover, in-fighting within the PRI leadership gave rise to tensions which impacted at the community level. By the second half of 1985 two contenders to the governorship had emerged. Heladio Ramírez López was a former youth leader of the PRI in the Federal District, former federal deputy, former president of the PRI in Oaxaca, and the state's senator, whose local base was in the countryside. His rival was Jésus Martínez Alvarez, a former municipal president of Oaxaca City and member of the state bureaucracy with strong links to the PRI's 'popular' sector.

This, in a nutshell, demonstrates the complex interplay, on a variety of scales, between the PRI, its affiliated organizations, and membership of various government administrations in recruitment to, and selection for, political office. The two competitors, representing distinct power blocks within the Oaxaca PRI, jockeyed for position (Basáñez 1987, 20): Heladio Ramírez (Grupo Heladio) utilized his position nationally, while Jésus Martínez Alvarez (Grupo Oaxaca) relied upon his Oaxacan connections.

In the autumn of 1985, the Governor, Pedro Vásquez Colmenares, was nominated Director de Seguridad Federal de la Secretaría de Gobernación and resigned his state post. With undue haste, the Oaxaca legislature voted Jésus Martínez Alvarez, locally perceived as the stronger of the two candidates, to the interim governorship, thereby making him constitutionally ineligible to compete for that position in 1986 (Yescas Martínez 1991). Outmanœuvred by Ramírez, Martínez, in turn, tried to block his candidature for the governorship.

When, eventually, Heladio Ramírez was nominated, 'the election of municipal presidents became the arena for resolving their political differences' (Díaz Montes 1992*a*, 46). However, Jésus Martínez's brief spell in the state palace gave him only limited scope for interfering in the elections. Moreover, neither politician had a free hand in choosing candidates, since so many other actors—outgoing municipal presidents, local deputies, and various PRI officials with their own axe to grind—were involved.

It is conventional wisdom that the governor intervenes in the selection of PRI candidates in key urban *municipios* (such as Oaxaca City) and sensitive

localities (such as Juchitán). Yet in the vast majority of *municipios* this was unnecessary because in 1986 there was no substantial organized opposition. Opposition parties put up a total of only 150 candidates in 121 out of 570 *municipios*, though that was a substantial increase on the 87 *municipios* contested in 1983 (Martínez Vásquez 1990, 248). As Díaz Montes observed:

There is an important number of rural and Indian *municipios* in which the selection of candidates is made by the community itself through communal assemblies, without much interference from the governor. There are also some *municipios* in which the governor does not intervene, because they are controlled by *caciques*. The relative autonomy of these *municipios* is permitted by the governor and his party, since it represents no danger whatsoever for the system. (1992*a*, 68)

The adoption of communal assemblies long before the formal enactment of 'usos y costumbres' has been confirmed in detail by the situation reported for the Chatino community of Yaitepec. The PRI and PARM competed in Yaitepec for votes in state and federal elections, but local office-holders in Yaitepec were selected through public debate and consensus (Greenberg 1981, 70–1). This traditional system of male, public assembly operated in 490 *municipios* in 1986, in accordance with the 'laws and customs of the communities' (Hernández Díaz 1992*a*).

Sometimes PRI officials imposed candidates on *municipios*, at the behest of *caciques*, notably in Chahuites, Etla, San Juan Mazatlán, and Santa Catarina Juquila (Martínez Vásquez 1990, 249). But in 521 instances, locally chosen candidates (presumably the 490 above and some others) were simply validated by the PRI as their own. In twenty-seven cases there were primary elections for *priístas* (often giving rise to factionalism and later to opposition to official candidates), and in fourteen urban localities the PRI held elections among its affiliated sectors (*obrero*, *agrario*, and *popular*).

Among parties opposed to the PRI in 1986, the only one with a long-run presence in the state was the Partido de Acción Nacional (PAN), characterized, nationally, by its conservative platform and its orientation to business needs. Its influence had been greatest in the Mixteca, where, in 1980, it had won the major *municipio* of Huajuapan de Leon. The Partido Socialista Unificado de México (PSUM), Partido Revolucionario de los Trabajadores (PRT), and the Partido Mexicano de los Trabajadores (PMT), all of which had just been legalized, combined with COCEI to form the Coalición Democrática (CD). Additional oppositional elements included the Partido Auténtico de la Revolución Mexicana (PARM), the Partido Popular Socialista (PPS), and the Partido Socialista de los Trabajadores (PST). Whereas the PRI contested all 570 *municipios*, the CD competed in 32, the PAN in 39, the PARM and the PPS in 35, and the PST in 14.

In both 1983, when the vote was just over 500,000, and 1986 when it rose to 625,000, the PRI received 90 per cent of the vote cast. However in 1986, the level of abstentions was very high (47.4 per cent), especially where there were no

opposition candidates, though lower than it had been in 1983 (51.5 per cent) or 1980 (49.7 per cent). Urban areas were notorious for their abstentionism, the rate rising to 70 or 80 per cent in and around Oaxaca City, where the urban masses were disaffected from all political parties (Martínez Vásquez 1990, 255).

Votes cast in *municipios* where the election was not annulled were: PRI 89 per cent, PAN 3.6 per cent, PPS 2.4 per cent, and CD 1.9 per cent. Such was the dispute over the results that, during the month while the Comisión Estatal Electoral was reviewing the figures, the opposition parties joined forces to create the Frente Cívico para la Defensa del Voto Ciudadano. To keep up the pressure on the PRI, it organized various meetings and hunger strikes on the *plaza* in Oaxaca City (Díaz Montes 1992*a*).

On 14 September, the electoral commission pronounced its verdict: the PRI had taken 537 *municipios* against 5 for the Coalición, 3 for the PAN, and 1 for the PST. In 13 *municipios* the election was declared null and void, and in 11 more no decision was reached. Opposition parties decided to occupy certain municipal palaces to prevent the new regimes from taking possession. On 15 September, 36 buildings were invaded, and the municipal presidents took office in private houses (Díaz Montes 1992*a*, 56). Pressure on the PRI was growing, since in 1983 opposition parties had invaded only 24 municipal buildings.

Some fifty *municipios* remained in dispute after 15 September, when the electoral commission was wound up. At this point the incoming administration of Governor Heladio Ramírez, who had won 91 per cent of the vote cast for the governorship, became dominant. Special bodies were set up, involving one representative of the executive, one of the legislature, and one of the PRI—panels heavily weighted in favour of the dominant party. Although these commissions met with the groups in conflict on various occasions, they managed to resolve only a handful of cases, either because the solutions were unacceptable, or initial agreements were subsequently rejected (Díaz Montes 1992*a*, 57). After Heladio Ramírez was installed as Governor on 1 December 1986, opposition pressure continued and resulted in three plebiscites and six new municipal councils being established to resolve the disputes.

All together, according to Díaz Montes, 73 *municipios* recorded conflicts over the electoral results, leaving 497 (490 recorded PRI victories) undisputed. Out of these 73 contested results, 2 were settled by new elections, 10 by plebiscites, 29 by municipal councils, and 32 by incorporating opposition *regidores* (appointed municipal councillors) in the local government on the basis the votes cast for them. Disputed elections were widely scattered across Oaxaca, though plebiscites and councils tended to concentrate in the Central Valleys around Oaxaca City, in the Mixteca Alta, around Tuxtepec, and in the Isthmus of Tehuantepec, all localities in which anti-PRI activities had occurred in the 1970s and 1980s (Fig. 8.1).

In the case of the extraordinary elections, both were PRI victories. Out of the 10 plebiscites, 7 were won by the PRI or PRI dissidents, 1 by the PAN, and

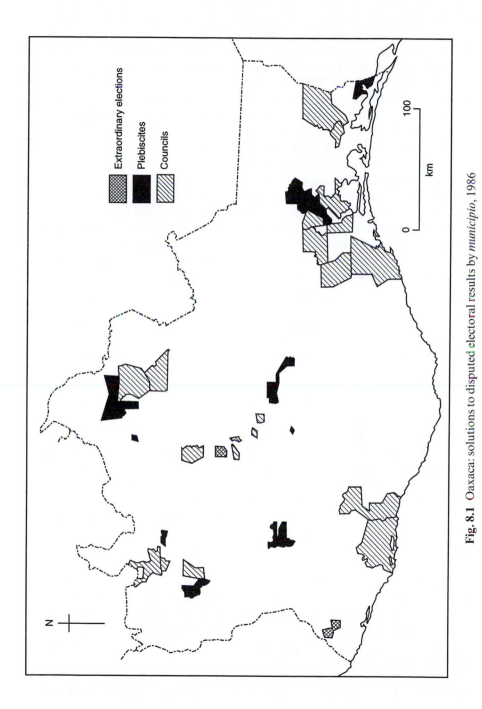

Fig. 8.1 Oaxaca: solutions to disputed electoral results by *municipio*, 1986

2 by the CD. Deliberations in the 29 municipal councils resulted in control of 9 being given to PRI dissidents (therefore not shown on Fig. 8.1), with 2 going to the PAN and 1 to the PPS. All the remainder resulted in PRI dominance, as did 30 out of the 32 cases of incorporation. However, in 8 *municipios* the PRI was forced into acknowledged coalitions with the PPS (5 cases), the PAN, the PARM, and the PST (Díaz Montes 1992*a*, 64, table 3.5).

The final result, which was arrived at only in January 1987, was that the PRI won 555 out of 570 *municipios*, the PAN 6, the PPS 1, the PST 1, the PARM 0, and the CD 7. Out of the 15 opposition victories, only 7 were achieved in the election, the remainder coming from plebiscites and post-electoral pressure—the PRI acknowledged opposition victories unless they were in significant places. A similar pattern of results had obtained in 1983, when the PRI gained 559 *municipios*, and 1980 and 1977 when its tally had been 552 and 561, respectively (Díaz Montes 1992*a*).

The 'reforma politica' of 1980 seemed more apparent than real, the major upturn in opposition fortunes in the *municipios* coinciding with the six-yearly elections to the state governorship. Examination of the spatial pattern of the fifteen *municipios* won by opposition parties in 1986 suggests no simple interpretation, though they formed three concentrations, resembling those of 1980 and 1983 (Martínez Vásquez and Arellanes Meixueiro 1985), in the Mixteca, Central Valleys, and the Isthmus of Tehuantepec (Fig. 8.2). Given that they comprised fewer than 3 per cent of all Oaxaca's *municipios* and victories were split between four political parties or groupings, difficulty in providing a clear-cut interpretation of their distribution is hardly surprising.

Díaz Montes has produced a valuable statistical analysis of Oaxaca's *municipios*. He showed that a large concentration of population (urbanization), high literacy, and a low proportion of the population actively involved in agriculture could be taken together to distinguish between conflictive and non-conflictive cases, based on whether elections were disputed (Fig. 8.1) or not. Generally speaking, rural *municipios* with small peasant populations voted PRI or accepted the PRI label.

Moreover, ability to speak an Indian language was shown not to be significant in a model framework that emphasized the crucial role of modernization in electoral competition and conflict in Oaxaca (Díaz Montes 1992*a*, 81–94). It must be borne in mind, however, that there was a significant difference between disputed elections in urban places (Fig. 8.1), and opposition victories which were, with the exception of Tlacolula in the Central Valleys (Díaz Montes 1992*a*, 113–44), rural and located in *municipios* of little consequence (Fig. 8.2). Furthermore, there were a number of ethnic-ecological disputes going on in the early 1980s in the Sierra Juárez, north of Oaxaca City, and in the Mixteca Alta, which, while important, fell outside the electoral sphere (Basáñez 1987).

Juchitán, then, was clearly distinctive within Oaxaca, in that it was an urban *municipio* with a Zapotec-speaking population in which dissidence had taken

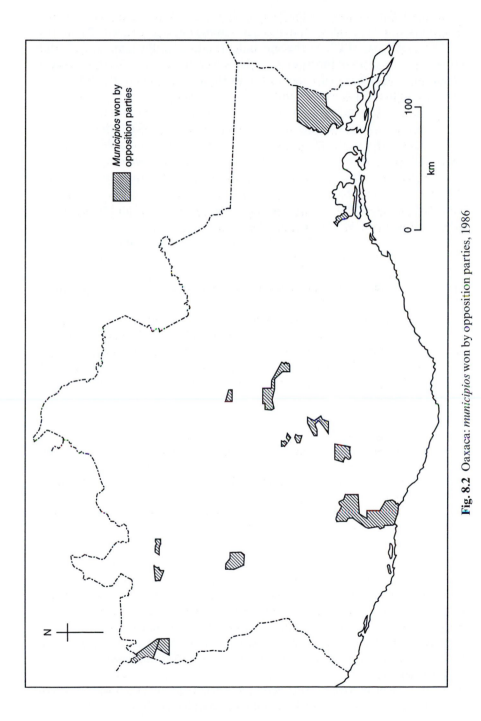

Fig. 8.2 Oaxaca: *municipios* won by opposition parties, 1986

on an electoral dimension. Drawing upon this ethnic identifier, COCEI, against the odds, was able to mobilize thousands of supporters throughout the 1980s. Taking advantage of PRI factionalism, it emerged from a period of repression in and after 1983 to continue mobilizing support on agricultural and urban–workplace issues. In 1986 it joined a coalition municipal government in Juchitán headed by a *priísta*, in an arrangement presided over by the new governor, Heladio Ramírez.

This link between urbanization, ethnicity, and electoral participation was to give a special flavour and durability to COCEI. According to Rubin, 'it demonstrates, contrary to most analyses of Mexico, the continuous importance of electoral competition in post-revolutionary Mexican politics' (1994, 124). But is this judgement correct, when one considers the specificity of Juchitán? One elected, left-wing *municipio*, however significant symbolically, scarcely proves that Mexico is either democratic or socialist.

Hegemony Contested

Rubin has recently proposed a framework for understanding Mexican politics, which abandons the idea of PRI hegemony in favour of an approach that emphasizes competitive variations over time and space. He points to the decline of post-revolutionary regional *cacicazgos*—as in the case of that of Charis in Tehuantepec—during the 1950s and 1960s as a crucial starting-point. He argues that:

National and regional patterns of economic change transformed many of the economic arrangements upon which these regional power structures had been based, and elite and popular mobilizations directly challenged prevailing political procedures. In this context, as the bosses aged and died, conflicts ensued in the 1960s over how politics would be conducted. In many places, the PRI and its affiliated mass organizations barely existed or had only begun to forge procedures for political mediation. Movements for electoral competition, clean government, local cultural identity, and progressive social change met with some successes, but considerable hostility and repression. (1994, 135)

One cannot but be struck by the fact that, in Rubin's words, 'power in Mexico is much more diffuse and hegemony more contested than conventional accounts acknowledge'. He continues, 'the regime's longevity results not from centralization and corporatism, but from the way in which such diffusion and contestation reproduce broad patterns of power' (Rubin 1994, 135).

However, Rubin overstates the case for competition. Concentrating as he does on Juchitán, it is easy to do so (Rubin 1997). Yet the advantage of looking at the whole state of Oaxaca is that it puts Juchitán into its unique context, where urbanization, social inequality, and ethnic identity have meshed in ways unparalleled in other areas. Elsewhere in Oaxaca, the contestation between the

PRI and opposition political parties is much weaker and more sporadic than it has been in Juchitán, and PRI dominance, despite post-electoral disputes, is generally secure, though weakening.

Juchitán excepted, Oaxaca's peasantries and ethnic groups have rarely, if ever, been the basis for mass mobilizations aimed at the PRI as a party. Urban areas have developed into seedbeds of dissent, as evidence from Oaxaca City shows, but the radical link between students, workers, and peasants, in that arena, has born little electoral fruit in the long term, compared to Juchitán. Moreover, non-electoral competition from COCEO and COCEI, while at times virulent, has inevitably and universally led to PRI manipulation, co-optation, and outright repression, including torture and assassination.

There have been no democratic elections in which the PRI was in danger of defeat on a sufficiently large scale to cause the loss of the governorship of Oaxaca or the defection of the majority of *municipios* in Oaxaca. Indeed, the PRI has always tried to win back lost *municipios*: in 1983 it recaptured fifteen out of the eighteen it lost in 1980, and in 1986, it retook eight of the eleven it forfeited in 1983 (Martínez Vásquez 1990, 251). An interesting feature of the finances of *municipios* controlled by opposition parties was that they have been better treated than their PRI-controlled counterparts—as a prelude to their recovery at the polls (Bailón 1995).

The elections for the governorship of Oaxaca in 1992 served not only to re-emphasize the strength of the PRI, but the continuing tussle between the established power groups within it. For example, the two PRI candidates, Luis Martínez Fernández del Campo and Diódoro Carrasco Altamirano, the state senator, were backed, respectively, by ex-Governor Martínez Alvarez and Governor Heladio Ramírez, rivals for the post in 1986 (Díaz Montes and Yescas Martínez 1992).

Diódoro Carrasco, a former state official with privileged connections to President Salinas's Programa Nacional de Solidaridad (PRONASOL), was eventually selected as the official candidate and won with 77 per cent of the vote. The Partido Revolucionario Democratico (PRD), whose candidate had only recently resigned from the PRI, took ten per cent, and the PAN 5 per cent (Díaz Montes 1992*b*). It is a measure of the co-optive power of the PRI and of the frustrations of those opposed to it, that many of the officials in Diódoro Carrasco's 1992 administration had been left-wing university activists in Oaxaca in the 1970s.

Between the Oaxaca gubernatorial elections of 1986 and 1992, however, the PRI vote dropped by 14 per cent, the Coalición Democratica–PRD poll increased by 8 per cent, and that of the PAN by 1 per cent. Even more disturbing for the PRI was the increase in the level of abstentions from 40 to 60 per cent. An additional problem for the PRI was its comparatively poor showing in the urban centres, notably Oaxaca City, where the PAN has a significant power base among professionals (Martínez Vásquez 1992*b*), Huajuapan, and the Isthmus of Tehuantepec (Díaz Montes 1992*b*).

So far as the municipal results are concerned, the PRI took 542, the PRD 14, the PAN 4, and the PARM and the Partido del Frente Cardenista de Reconstrucción Nacional (PFCRN) 2 each. Leaving aside the 438 that used the community vote, the PRI won the adult suffrage in 104 *municipios*, followed by the other parties as listed above. Most of the major urban centres still voted PRI, except Juchitán (PRD) and Salina Cruz (PFCRN) (Martínez Vásquez 1995).

The subsequent municipal elections of 1995 are of special note, since they were the first in which 412 of the *municipios* declared, formally, that their voting would be by the system of 'usos y costumbres'—permitted by the pluriethnic constitution, with all-male public meetings, open debate, and election by consensus. The political parties contested only 158 *municipios*, clustered along the main roads leading through the Central Valleys and in *tierra caliente* on the fringes of the state (Fig. 8.3). The PRI won 110 (with 44.9 per cent of the votes), the PRD 35 (with 27.4 per cent), and the PAN 11 (with 16.7 per cent). The turnout was 54.9 per cent. The Oaxaca Valley, Isthmus of Tehuantepec, Tuxtepec, and Mixteca Baja were the foci of competition between the three parties, and all recorded victories in these regions. In the Mixteca de la Costa, however, the PRD was the PRI's main rival, and here it took 10 *municipios*.

As in the case of the gubernatorial election, there is evidence for increased inter-party competition, with the PRD doing well throughout the state, especially in the urbanized centres of the various districts, where it took Pochutla, Juquila, Sola de Vega, Pinotepa Nacional, Putla, Zaachila, Zimatlán, Nochixtlan, and the much-prized Juchitán. The PAN was successful in the even larger towns, Huajuapan, Tuxtepec, Matias Romero (all, except the latter, district headquarters), and—unthinkable previously—Oaxaca de Juárez, the state capital, where the middle class is well developed and known to be exasperated with the PRI. Nevertheless, the PRI still captured 12 out of the 24 district headquarters where balloted elections for party candidates were held.

An important feature of the development of democracy in Oaxaca has been the increased ability and willingness of the opposition parties to put up more candidates to contest elections. The PRI, in 1995, fielded candidates in 156 out of the 158 *municipios* for which there were competitive elections between the registered parties. But the number contested by the PRD was 120 and for the PAN 53—the figures for the two latter being much higher than for the CD and PAN ten years previously. Against that, however, must be set the weak competitive tendency in the 1995 elections to the Oaxaca state legislature. While the PRI took all 25 seats contested on a 'first-past-the-post' basis, the 17 seats using proportional representation among the other parties were split 5 to PAN, 9 to the PRD, and 3 to others.

The PRI may not be hegemonic, and grass-roots movements may have considerable scope at the local level. Nevertheless, the governing party has a capacity for contesting (or appearing to contest) virtually every political turf in a way that no other Mexican political party can at a municipal, state, and

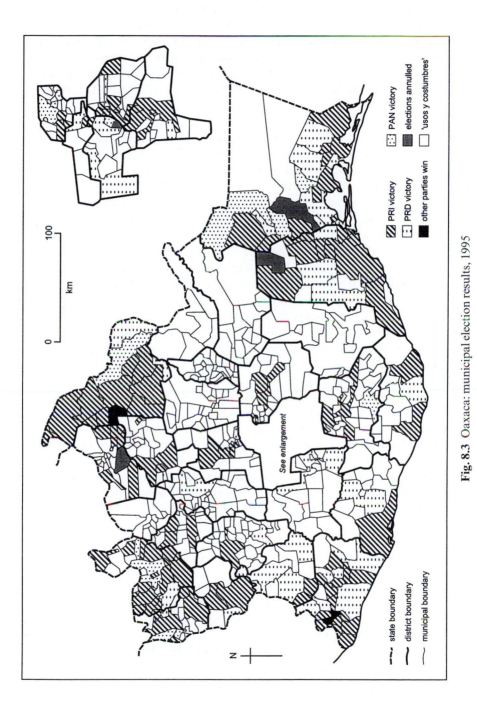

Fig. 8.3 Oaxaca: municipal election results, 1995

federal level. Moreover, it has sufficient *de facto* leverage over the electoral process, despite substantial modification of the law in 1990 (Ward 1994), to hold on to most *municipios* (and virtually all states, as well as national power).

In this way the PRI has retained control of Oaxaca at the state and municipal levels. However, as Chapter 7 showed and this one has confirmed, it has done so largely by letting many *municipios* run their own elections, the results of which, until 1995, were merely validated and claimed by the PRI. It is possible that *municipio* politics, under the system of 'usos y costumbres' adopted in the 1995 elections, will prove just as vulnerable to co-optation by the PRI as before. Indeed, there is evidence to show that the PRI has deliberately used the reform of Article 27 and the land titling of PROCEDE to bureaucratize the countryside and reclaim lost political territory (Pisa 1994).

Conclusion

Coalitions of students, workers, and peasants were important in challenging the axis between the PRI and the Oaxaca economic élite in the context of the constrained democracy of the 1960s and 1970s. Moreover, successful opposition to the PRI was mounted in Juchitán in the early 1980s, based on radical electoral politics and ethnicity. Since the early 1990s, electoral competition at national and state level has provided the main arena for challenging the PRI. In Oaxaca, the PRD has overtaken the more conservative PAN as the major element in electoral opposition, but has not yet been able to vie for the governorship or state power. However, the PAN has wrested the local government of Oaxaca City from PRI control. This pattern of PRI domination of the governorship, PAN control of Oaxaca City, and the consolidation of the PRD as the leading party of opposition was confirmed during the 1998 Oaxaca elections

It is the larger, more urbanized *municipios* that have been successful in installing PRD and PAN governments; Oaxaca's peasantries, whether Indian or *mestizo*, are not contesting, politically, the dominant position of the PRI, though they are active, and often successful, in local-level issues. Oaxaca's peasantries are no more radical now than they were prior to the Mexican Revolution, which helped to create or underpin them (Waterbury 1975).

Part IV

Conclusion

Part IV

Conclusion

9

Conclusion
Oaxaca's Peasantries in Their Theoretical and National Contexts

The previous chapters show that there have been two major historical path-ways into peasantry in Oaxaca. Some peasantries, especially at high altitude, have roots stretching back beyond early colonial times, because they retained (and have had confirmed) traditional lands throughout the intervening centuries. Others, in the tropical lowlands and in the Central Valleys, have received *ejidal* grants since the end of the Mexican Revolution in the early twentieth century. Leaving aside the wilderness areas, which account for two-thirds of the state, the occupied area is now predominantly under *comunidades agrarias*, with the remainder split almost equally between *ejidal* and private land. It is within the privately owned sector that the landed estates are still to be found.

Private lands concentrate in the tropical lowlands of the Isthmus, the north-ern plains around Tuxtepec, the Cañada, and in Pochutla; they also occur at higher altitude in Tlaxiaco, Miahuatlán, and the Central Valleys (Fig. 9.1). Peasantries are associated with *ejidos* in the Mixteca Baja and Mixteca de la Costa, in the Isthmus and the tropical lowlands adjoining Vera Cruz, espe-cially in Tuxtepec, Chaopan, and the Central Valleys. So the *tierra caliente* and the *tierra templada* are contested zones, with histories of land conflict between estates and small farmers. Communal land is literally above these conflicts, occurring in the *tierra fría* in the Mixteca Alta, the Sierra Juárez and Sierra Mixe, Tehuantepec, Yautepec, and the Sierra Madre del Sur.

These regional differences in landholding systems are not the only source of diversity among Oaxaca's peasants. Peasant differentiation is also a product of the variable levels of living and degrees of commercialization which reflect the resource environment at different altitudinal zones, coupled to the availability and quality of communications. Each rural *municipio* is virtually a world unto itself; and many peasants retain linguistic and ethnic identities that distinguish them from one another and from monolingual Spanish speakers. For these reasons, the small farmers of Oaxaca are best described as peasantries.

This conclusion has three aims: to open up a debate about theories relating to peasantry, class, ethnicity, community, and migration; to situate the Oaxaca evidence with reference to those theories, and to compare circumstances in

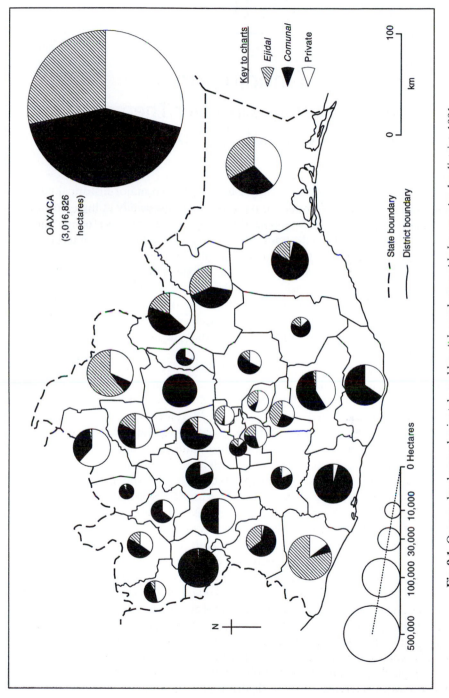

Fig. 9.1 Oaxaca: land owned privately and by *ejidos* and *comunidades agrarias*, by district, 1991

Oaxaca with those existing in other parts of Mexico. My object is less to confirm or refute social theory than to explain the deviation of the 'real world' from the theoretically predicted one. Time and again, however, it will be found that the 'real world' situation in Oaxaca has been substantially 'determined' by the state, and above all by the dominant PRI.

The chapter therefore concludes by drawing out more specifically the role of the Mexican state in the formation of Oaxaca's social structure. It also evaluates the capacity of actors representing peasantry, class, ethnicity, and community to contest the 'hegemony' of the PRI, given the national demand for democracy and transparency, and the deregulatory, free-trade orientation of the Salinas and Zedillo administrations. The uniqueness of Oaxaca is evaluated through a brief comparison with its neighbour, Chiapas, which seized world headlines in 1994, when Zapatista guerrillas, with an ethnic, ecological, and democratic agenda, captured a number of urban centres and subsequently established a bridgehead from which to confront the government. The Zapatista stand-off with the army has persisted since then. Why has Oaxaca, in comparison, been so comparatively trouble free?

Peasantry

Peasants are characterized in social theory as living by family labour applied to the land they farm—usually depicted as their own. They produce what they need to consume—that is, food and drink, clothing, household utensils, and agricultural tools. Their manual labour is often supplemented by animal power, which is used to draw ploughs or pull carts. Typically, the family produces more than it consumes, since peasants have obligations to meet in the shape of tithes, rents, and taxes, which confirm their position as a social stratum subordinate to the occupants of urban administrative and commercial centres (Shanin 1979).

Peasant cash requirements are supplied by market interchange of surplus crops and goods; and the market has the additional function of smoothing gluts and shortages. Another attraction of the market is that it does provide for a modest degree of specialization: individuals may concentrate on certain crops and/or crafts; eventually, entire villages may devote themselves to unique products based on local comparative advantage made possible by the environment (Clarke and Langton 1990). All these features of the market are reflected in Oaxaca, and place-specific specializations are marked both in the Central Valleys and the adjacent and distant mountains.

This self-equilibrating model of peasantry is, of course, an ideal. With capital penetration of a region—such as Oaxaca—from the national economic core, it might be anticipated that some peasants would strive to accumulate cash, acquire more land, dispossess some of their neighbours, and employ them as labour. Output for market sale would increase to meet the purchasing

requirements of the landless, some of whom would enter local craft activities or migrate, as the Oaxaca evidence confirms.

Thus miniature class hierarchies would emerge within the peasantry; and the commercial farming category would be poised for exit from the peasantry into the non-peasant class, where waged work would replace unremunerated family labour and the cash nexus would be dominant. Evidence from Oaxaca suggests that peasants are not evolving *en masse* in this way, though remittances are starting to have this effect in some areas, such as the Oaxaca Valley, the Sierra Zapoteca, and the Mixteca Alta. A paradox is encountered in the Mixteca Alta: one of the poorest and most ecologically devastated areas, it now has satellite aerials bristling from almost every roof paid for by remittances from migrants to the USA.

Access of specialized agricultural and craft products to national and international markets might be expected to produce huge mark-ups in prices as commodity flows extend away from the producer and the producer's local niche. Class differentiation would start to become pronounced, especially where it is possible to retain some of the value-added generated by the production process. These circumstances are precisely reproduced in Oaxaca, by coffee, *mezcal*, weaving, and embroidery products.

Processes of specialized commodity production turn out to be more spotty than agricultural change based on local food staples would normally involve, and give rise to acute differentiation within the peasantry, both within and between communities. Under conditions of rapid but small-scale accumulation, the distinction between capitalism and peasantry dissolves (for example in the *mezcal*, weaving, and embroidery cases discussed in Chapter 4). However, it may be retained for a time in differences of scale and in the role (probably non-remunerated) of the household (Cook and Binford 1990).

A peasant system of organization relies on the household being the unit of production and consumption. Its principal objective is to provide for its own subsistence, with surpluses being disposed of on the open market whenever they occur. Typically, this is achieved by cultivating crops or rearing stock on small units of land, though many rural (and urban) dwellers engage in non-agricultural activities—the norm, according to Cook and Binford (1990), in the Central Valleys, which have been termed petty-commodity production. They produce commodities using the labour power of the household, without the payment of wages. Petty-commodity production is not inevitably a transitional feature within capitalism; its operatives are not necessarily exploited by capital; nor is it to be equated to subsistence activities, though it is often coupled to peasant cultivation.

Two unusual features of the Oaxacan—and, more generally, the Mexican—peasantry require emphasis: firstly, the fact that it has been reinforced by land reform since the 1920s; and secondly that it is not rapidly disappearing in the face of capitalism, though capitalism dominates Mexico at the national scale. The peasantry, established in its modern form through land-reform enact-

ments of the 1920s and succeeding decades, has grown through the accretion of new land distributions, and by population growth. At the same time, industry, commerce, and services have expanded in the urban areas, with the federal government providing the facilitating infrastructure, and the peasantry acting as a reservoir of cheap and rapidly reproduced labour.

However, while Mexico has been modernized, there is no doubt that its economy has remained highly dependent on that of the USA. Mexican capitalism, bolstered by US capitalism, has created enormous spatial disparities. Hence urban core areas of capital accumulation such as Mexico City, Monterrey, Guadalajara, and Puebla, now often outstripped by industrial growth in the Mexico–US border towns, have emerged as part-modernized—if not part-Americanized. Yet peripheral regions such as the South, in general, and Oaxaca, in particular, have remained in the peasant periphery. That is not to say that Oaxaca's peasantry is engaged in a pre-capitalist mode of production (it is penny capitalistic); nor that Oaxaca is without its own state-capitalist nodes in Oaxaca City, the tourist areas on the Pacific, the electricity generating projects near Tuxtepec, and the Tehuantepec oil refinery.

Nevertheless, the weak integration of core and periphery on the Mexican national scale has left Oaxaca in an incipient stage of capitalism. Oaxaca's peasants are unable to accumulate so long as they remain *in situ* in the rural areas. So they migrate, circulate, and emigrate—anything to escape from their marginalized position, especially if they are at the bottom of the peasant class. Hence the 'hidden hand' of population shifts is one of the principal non-state bases for socio-economic change (Kearney 1996).

Migration and Emigration

Zelinsky (1971) has argued that the national demographic transition over time from high fertility and high mortality to low fertility and low mortality is accompanied by a mobility transition comprising five phases. Mexico is currently near the mid-point of the demographic transition, with low and declining mortality and high but slowly reducing fertility. So, in terms of mobility, Mexico ought to be between what Zelinsky calls the early transitional society (phase 2) and late transitional society (phase 3). The former is typified by massive population movements from countryside to city, major outflows to foreign destinations, and significant growth in various forms of circulation. The latter phase experiences substantial but reducing movements from countryside to city, a decline in foreign emigration, and further increases in circulation associated with the growth in social and technological complexity.

Although the pace of Mexico City's growth slackened during the 1980s and 1990s, secondary cities, such as Oaxaca City have kept on absorbing migrants from rural areas, in line with phase 2 of the mobility transition model. Underpinning this process is the urban-orientated nature of the Mexican

capitalist development, the lack of a completed demographic transition, and the overpopulation and economic decay of the peasantry. There has been some change to urban–urban, intra-urban, and urban–rural migration, but the spectacular alteration has been the expansion of circulation, very much as Zelinsky predicted for phase 3. The Oaxacan case is interesting (but not unique), however, because circulation has taken on a long-distance dimension. It reaches the US border zone and includes an international dimension that mobility theory in stage 3 of the transition would deny. This is because of Mexico's recurrent economic crises and the impossibility of policing the Rio Grande border, given the high-wage economy of the USA and its need for plentiful cheap labour.

International circular migration has helped to reduce the rate of population growth in the largest Mexican cities, and through remittances and changed values has underpinned urban–rural convergence in some parts of Oaxaca, particularly the Central Valleys. This is less marked in the Mixteca Alta, and it is not simply because of the impoverishment and environmental degradation. Mixtecs are drawn to poorly paid agricultural work, whereas the Zapotecs of the *sierras* and Central Valleys are concentrated in urban areas, especially Los Angeles. Here they congregate in the service sector and in rented accommodation, both of which are viable long-term attractions to the migrants and their dependants (Klaver 1997).

Generalizing from her study of San Marcos Tlapazola, near Tlacolula in the Central Valleys, and Jaltianguis, near Ixtlán in the Sierra Juárez, Klaver (1997) shows that the pattern of migration is one in which older men have led off, only to be followed later by young adults. Mothers, children, and the elderly are left behind. The Oaxacan sending communities have therefore become heavily dependent on remittances, and migration has emerged as a lifestyle to be emulated. Klaver argues that the system has become so developed that migration has ceased to be a household survival strategy, as it once was; in many instances there is no household left to sustain. Under these circumstances, social rather than economic motivations dominate the decision to migrate among the young; and individual reasons to move have supplanted collective, household ones. Cityward migration to Los Angeles has increasingly involved permanent moves (Klaver 1997).

Nevertheless, intense interactions link sending and receiving communities. The two Zapotec villages studied by Klaver have been developed by gifts from migrants to rural relatives as well as by ideas about modernization transmitted by migrants. This has led to a process of cumulative causation, since life in Los Angeles is seen as an improvement on an agricultural existence among the Oaxaca peasantry. A migration culture has developed that leads to stasis in the sending communities, though this is partially mitigated by migrants' support for their families and the local programme of public works.

Receiving communities in Los Angeles are described as modelled on the home village, with Catholic *fiesta* commitments and communal labour on

neighbourhood infrastructure retained. But replication of home values and environments does not guarantee that home ties will bind forever. Klaver (1997) questions whether the most onerous obligations—to serve in the local government and *fiesta* systems of the Oaxacan community—will be complied with in future generations. Oaxaca's transnational communities, by their very nature, may prove ephemeral, especially if the emigrants experience class mobility and become embedded in the USA.

Class

Most social scientists who deal with class regard it as related in some way to the workings of the economy. Marxists identify two classes in capitalist economies, each with a distinct role: the bourgeoisie, or middle class, who control capital, and the proletariat, or working class, who lack capital and must sell their labour to acquire wages on which to survive. Marxists envisage capitalism as destructive—in two senses. Firstly, the capitalist mode of production destroys peasantry by introducing a market–cash nexus, alienating peasants from their land, concentrating land in the hands of richer peasants, and producing a rural class structure that becomes the precursor of urban-industrial (or, later, financial) capitalism (Harvey 1973). Clearly, capitalism has barely got beyond the cash nexus stage in Oaxaca. That stage was entered during the 1940s and 1950s, and coincided with the construction of the Pan-American Highway.

Secondly, capitalism is based on accumulation: individual capitalists accumulate or are accumulated. The logic of this proposition is that the bourgeoisie must inevitably press the proletarians down to subsistence level, thereby capturing as large a portion as possible of the surplus value produced by the productive process. Conflict will be endemic between the classes over the appropriation of surplus value (the social relations of production); aided by the periodic down-turn in the trade cycle, the inflated population of unemployed will initiate a class revolution and impose the dictatorship of the proletariat (Marx and Engels 1972). This was the line of reasoning of many university students in Oaxaca during the conflicts of the 1970s.

The logic of Marxist thought, then, is that capitalism destroys peasantry (or feudalism) and then itself. The latter proposition does not seem to typify the advanced capitalist countries that are the obvious candidates for revolution. And the first proposition seems not to apply in the Third World, where dependent, or late, capitalism is so derivative and lacking in dynamism that it is incapable of annihilating peasantry, and prefers to capitalize on its persistence—hence Oaxacan peasants' role as a source of cheap food and labour.

What additionally characterizes the Third World is the suffusion of peasantry by capitalism, rather than the articulation of two separate modes of production. An arrested evolution towards capitalism is a quintessential facet of

peasantry under dependent development, notably in rural Oaxaca. The incomplete installation of capitalism also extends to the urban labour force, where, as in Oaxaca City, the majority of employees are engaged in peasant-like, proletarian activities (Murphy and Stepick 1991*a*).

Among non-Marxist theorists of class, Weber is particularly helpful, though he focuses primarily on industrial societies (Parkin 1982). Weber, writing fifty years after 1848 had failed to produce socialist transformations in Western Europe, envisaged classes as having different interests that they negotiated. Whereas Marx had been preoccupied with production, Weber was concerned with consumption; indeed, it was around consumption issues, he argued, that inter-class negotiations would take place. Weber's consumption classes were more heterogeneous than Marx's production classes; the middle class, for example, contained members of the state bureaucracy as well as capitalists. Moreover, the bureaucracy would not only provide a degree of social ballast within the middle class, but, being a product of the state, could be thought of as semi-independent of the mode of production.

So Marx's notion of class relations being the social relations of production, and involving inevitable conflict over surplus value, which, in turn, would lead to a socialist revolution, was rewritten by Weber. Classes, under state tutelage, would negotiate over consumption issues; capitalists would not remain, as Marx alleged, in control of the state; nor would proletarians remain unorganized and potentially available only for revolutionary activity. Weber thought of capitalism as comparatively stable within the mediating framework of the state, and envisaged that class structures would change over time through economic evolution and government intervention.

Although the Mexican Revolution (1910–17) occurred at approximately the same time as the Russian Revolution, it was not socialist. Rather it was characterized by factions orientated to agrarian social justice, on the one hand, and (urban) industrialization and modernization, on the other. So a land reform was initiated to (re-)establish peasantry in the rural areas, and a 'peripheral' type of capitalism was encouraged, especially in the major urban centres.

The state, under the guidance of the Partido Revolucionario Institucional and its forerunners, was of paramount importance in the formation of the twentieth-century Mexican peasantry, not least of all in Oaxaca. It also set about the creation of the urban middle class; the direction and profitability of the capitalist economy; and the provision of the infrastructure that the Oaxacan regional, and Mexican national, economy required. Moreover, the state acted in close association with the capitalist class, which everywhere became essentially urban and, in Oaxaca, was based on commerce rather than industry. But, as the role of the state increased, so the PRI became more exposed to criticism whenever balance between its client sectors (whether peasant, proletarian, or bourgeois) was lost. The latter situation has characterized the period since 1980, although it was prefigured in Oaxaca during the political conflicts of the decade 1968–78.

Ethnicity

Weber saw class as based on three elements, wealth (money), status (esteem), and power (capacity to command), and refused to reduce it to the dichotomy of capital and labour. He also permitted non-class phenomena to play a major social role (unlike Marx), and to that end made a clear distinction between class and ethnicity—a variant of status. Weber construed ethnicity as involving primordial sentiments of group affiliation on the basis of a shared culture and sense of belonging (Parkin 1982). In many instances, members of an ethnic group would have a shared history; furthermore, they might well be distinguished from adjacent populations by physical, or race, differences. So, culture, history, and race distinctiveness frequently combine to define an ethnic group. However, race is not ethnicity, nor is ethnicity race; and cultural distinctions of a greater or lesser kind may or may not equate to ethnicity (a sense of belonging together associated with a shared history).

The essence of race and ethnicity is that they are relative and relational; they require the presence of the 'other'. Hence they are always socially constructed, and it is impossible, as Weber recognized, to theorize which elements will or will not be significant in any particular context. Group hostility may be just as intense in situations where the aggregate physical characteristics of the population are shared, and race difference is not invoked, as where race differences are pronounced. Marked differences in cultural traditions may, prima facie, suggest that segmentation of society will occur; yet very small differences may be elevated into crucially significant markers of social difference (as in Northern Ireland).

Two topics are of fundamental importance at this point. The first is that ethnicity and race have nothing inherently to do with class, though in any social context they are likely to intersect with it. The second is that, although Weber thought it was impossible to theorize about ethnicity, M. G. Smith (1984) has provided a useful framework for doing so through his ideas about cultural, social, and structural pluralism. While Weber thought of ethnicity as leading to segmentation of the class structure, Smith has suggested that class may, in certain circumstances, and, typically, under imperialism, be subordinate to more dominant structures that are culturally (and racially) determined by the colonial state—in this instance New Spain (later Mexico).

Smith's writings on pluralism began with culture, and reflected his anthropological training. Originally, he argued that plurality inhered within the institutional complex of a population—in family and kinship, religion, education, property and economic organization (hunter-gatherer or sedentary activities), and recreation. Systematic divergence in some or all of these institutions would produce 'incompatibility' and give rise to plural cultures (1965). More recently he recognized that social 'incompatibility' may rest on slight institutional divergence in one institution only; and that language should be included

among the features of pluralism, despite the problems of language shift and bilingualism. According to these criteria, most countries are culturally plural (1974).

Smith recognized, in the second phase of his work, that where institutional practices remain in the private domain, they may be of little social structural significance, though their identification is important to an understanding of cultural diversity. However, where institutional differences involve differential treatment of their practitioners, and thus intrude into the public domain, they are structurally crucial. In the former case, the population practising the culture in question is uniformly incorporated into society. In the latter, differential incorporation will probably involve discriminatory treatment (either *de facto* or *de jure*) in terms of civil rights, notably with reference to suffrage and the law (and this may involve land rights, marriage customs, education, and language, to name but a few examples).

Differential incorporation, or structural pluralism, therefore manipulates cultural pluralism to produce social pluralism—the projection of cultural pluralism into the public domain. But structural pluralism may be based, originally, on non-cultural differentiators, most commonly race. Under these circumstances, racism (the belief that one race is superior and another inferior) will become institutionalized. In practice, because ordinary people are not social scientists, they mix up the terms race and ethnicity; so cultural differences are often treated as inherent racial traits.

The relevance of this for Oaxaca is that more than 500 years after the 'encounter' with Europeans, about 40 per cent of the population speak a variety of pre-Columbian languages, which are the principal marker of being Indian: culture has displaced genotype. Indians, as a group, have been treated differentially by the government in terms of their corporate holding of land, and the educational-language and developmental policy that has been directed at them since the Revolution (*indigenismo*). They are differentially incorporated, overtly to their advantage, *de jure*, but covertly to their disadvantage, *de facto*. As peasants, they are located within the lower stratum of the Mexican rural class structure, but with some upward mobility into the rural middle class.

In Southern Mexico, notably in Chiapas, the neighbouring state lying immediately to the east of Oaxaca, the subordinate position of rural Indians has been likened to colonialism and the term 'internal colonialism' has been coined and attached to their status (González Casanova 1969; Stavenhagen 1970). The Indian 'underclass' or corporate category has been construed as rural, and the Mexican or *mestizo* population thought of as typically urban. Surplus value, it is hypothesized, is extracted from rural Indian peasants who are not only exploited in market and class terms, but are culturally dominated, even racially disparaged.

This model of internal colonialism is attractive because it brings peasantry, class, culture, and race into a clear set of interrelationships that are character-

ized as spatial (urban–rural) dichotomies and are reminiscent of core and periphery, developed and underdeveloped. Unfortunately, this is too simple and deterministic a set of linkages: while powerfully suggestive, it is unlikely, on the basis of the above argumentation, that the complex social variables being investigated will in all places fall out in this way. A more confused scenario is probable.

Let us recapitulate. The empirical evidence in Chapters 1–8 has been discussed with reference to three models of class and ethnic relations. The first is class stratification, in which Indians comprise a cultural enclave within the lower, peasant stratum. The second is internal colonialism, according to which the Indian peasant population is dominated culturally as well as exploited economically—modally by *mestizos* operating from urban centres. The third is pluralism, which not only draws attention to the multitude of Oaxaca's ethnic categories, but emphasizes their parallel status *vis-à-vis* one another and their common subordination to *mestizos*.

All three models in combination, it is argued, are useful to an understanding of Oaxacan society and of the linkage between it and the encompassing national stratification. The class model fits Mexico as a whole, and reminds us that, while there is a problem of Indian subordination in Oaxaca, it is not on the scale of Chiapas or Guatemala, though in Oaxaca the Indian category is substantial. Pluralism helps us to separate the cultural from the class dimension, and points to the importance of organization and struggle in the elimination of discrimination through the self-transformation of corporate categories into corporate groups, a process which is currently taking place among Oaxaca's ethnies. Internal colonialism reminds us of the historical and geographical underpinning for ethno-linguistic inequality.

Community

Peasantry, class, and ethnicity are global phenomena that have evolved distinctively in Oaxaca and have been quite specifically constructed by the Mexican Revolution. The same is true of the smaller-scale social feature, community—in Oaxaca enshrined within the political framework of the *municipio*. This is the only unit of local government, a condition that is enjoined by the post-revolutionary federal constitution. In social geography the term community implies a social collectivity below the level of the state—hence urban community, Indian community, rural community.

Two distinct types of rural community have been recognized by Wolf for Latin America: closed and open communities (1955). Closed communities exist at high altitude and often involve traditional, Indian, corporate, landholding groups that were disrupted, but not dislodged, by Spanish colonialism. These are peasant communities, but their closure is now more social than economic, since most are involved in market networks. Open communities are

typical of the tropical lowlands, where peasantries exist in close proximity to plantations, and social as well as economic relations are functionally and spatially less circumscribed than in the closed-corporate units. These community models are, of course, normative; reality is more complex, and there is everywhere a trend towards openness brought about by improved communications, greater reliance on market exchange, and the development of out- and in-migration.

A major feature of the closed corporate community in Oaxaca (and Mexico more generally) has been the existence of *cargos* or obligations which adult men (not women) are expected to take up within the framework of the civil–religious hierarchy. Entering in late youth via the least significant of tasks, men undertake increasingly responsible and expensive offices involving governmental (*municipio*) and religious (Catholic cult and *fiesta*) obligations. In this way the two uprights, civic and religious, are bound together into a ladder up which an individual will climb with age, moving upwards from one side to the other.

The civil–religious hierarchy has been interpreted as a levelling mechanism, stripping potential surplus value from proto-capitalists and redistributing it in the form of community expenditures. The corporate community derives its solidarity from this system, in which, theoretically, social esteem is continually exchanged for capital. Corporateness enjoins peasant rejection of capitalist accumulation, while emphasizing and celebrating masculinity.

In open communities, on the other hand, where corporateness and levelling have been dissolved, if they ever existed, access to capitalist enterprise via petty commodity production or sale of coffee may give rise to small-scale rural class structures. In short, closed-corporate and open peasantries represent either end of a spectrum; under capitalism, it might be anticipated that all closed communities would be moving towards the open and stratified end, involving commercial farming, off-farm work, and landlessness.

In Oaxaca, there is much evidence to suggest that open, class-stratified communities (that are part of the rural national class structure) characterize the low-altitude areas and temperate zones influenced by modernization. However, it is not possible to argue that the closed corporate community, based upon the levelling mechanism of the civil–religious hierarchy, is the norm elsewhere. *Municipios*—even those at high altitude—are ever more open. The forces of socio-economic differentiation are overriding levelling—where it persists. Proportionately fewer people have to serve in the *cargo* system because of population increase. Religious offices are abolished, allocated via queuing, taken over by sodalities, or replaced by individual sponsorships attached to life-cycle events. Civil and religious hierarchies, which became entwined as recently as the nineteenth century, are once again separating under the secularizing influence of the state.

But that does not mean that community is losing its relevance. The fact that over 400 of Oaxaca's 570 *municipios* have opted to run their elections accord-

ing to 'usos y costumbres' is further evidence for the embracing of community difference, and for the association of that difference with a non-Hispanic ethnic identity. However, this does not involve an essentialist harking back to the past, since elections by public assembly are seen as a means of thwarting present-day outside interference, whether from local *caciques* or the PRI—though they are criticized for disenfranchising women. Even where out-migration to the USA is endemic, migrants frequently pay substitutes to fulfil their *tequio* obligation in their home community, and many may return to take up the civil *cargos* allocated to them.

The Role of the State

Oaxaca's social structure, in relationship to the social theory discussed above, has been, in great measure, moulded by policies pursued by the state since the Mexican Revolution. The apparently contradictory post-revolutionary strategies aimed at supporting urban capitalism while reconstructing peasantry, lie at the root of Oaxaca's socio-economic evolution since 1920. However, it must also be recognized that previous state regimes, both colonial and independent, played roles facilitating the persistence of peasantry in Oaxaca, often in contradistinction to what was happening elsewhere in Mexico.

A major reason for the uniqueness of Oaxaca's rural experience over the centuries has been its impenetrable, hostile, and, in places, sterile environment. Peasantries could hold on where their land was too poor to be coveted by *hacendados*; conversely, but with the same result, land could be allocated to the landless where its inferior quality made it expendable to landowners. Oaxaca's impoverished physical conditions are easily understood. More difficult to grasp has been the precise role of the Mexican state.

Different and conflicting theoretical conceptions of the state stress its subordination to the interests of the capitalist class, or its role as adjudicator or umpire in the context of potential class conflict. Other interpretations argue for the state's domination of society, which it fashions to its own ends, usually within the framework of authoritarianism and/or socialism (Badcock 1984). The Mexican state has not fitted permanently into any of these categories; rather it has shifted between categories over time, moving from an authoritarian position in the period 1920 to 1970 to a more flexible stance since then.

After more than sixty-five years in power, it is difficult to disentangle the PRI from the state. A fair approximation to reality is the view that the PRI, over the decades, has not only held the ring between urban capitalism and the rural peasantry, but has also played a leading role in the formation and development of each. However, it has tended to privilege capitalism over peasantry, in part because of the greater driving power of capitalism towards the materialistic goals of the PRI leadership. Moreover, presidential regimes since 1982 have taken an increasingly explicit pro-capitalist stance.

Mexican governments, since the Second World War, have adopted an urban bias in their development projects. This has precluded investment on a sufficiently large scale to turn the land reform into a genuine agrarian reform by funding a green revolution. *Ejidal* agriculture in Oaxaca is notoriously undercapitalized, and lacks machinery, modern seed, fertilizer, and adequate returns; it exists to provide minimum security for peasantries whose basic roles are to reproduce themselves and other sectors of society as cheaply as possible. Its key contributions are cheap labour and inexpensive food.

Two consequences stem from this. There is little dynamic tendency towards commercial agriculture among small farmers, unless they are located in a particularly favourable ecological niche, such as the Etla arm of the Oaxaca Valley. Peasants, otherwise, must diversify their household economies by *artesanias* or out-migration. In the context of rapid population growth, and given the comparatively poor returns for anything but the most sought-after pottery or woven goods, it is hardly surprising that migration, involving oscillatory movements to the US border area or beyond to the USA itself, has emerged as a major strategy.

Migration, of course, involves individual or household choice. But migration can only be understood in the light of government policy towards Oaxaca's peasantries and to population control (or the lack of it until recently). Michael Kearney has very effectively captured this situation, in which migration and transnationalism are omnipresent. 'Whereas the peasant was essentialized as having primordial connection with the land, a condition that made the agrarian issue the fundamental peasant concern, postpeasant rural politics is increasingly elaborated in terms of human rights, ethnopolitics and ethnicity' (Kearney 1996, 8).

As the Mexican state moves into a deregulatory, *laissez-faire* phase, the most significant aspect of which for Oaxaca is the legal change permitting private alienation and sale of land-reform parcels, the recently created, but apparently time-honoured, peasantries may be swept away. There are, however, a number of pointers from Oaxaca's recent experience to suggest that peasantries will not be quickly dislodged. The rural way of life is one into which young people are still being socialized. The physical environment of Oaxaca is inimical to capital penetration, largely because of inaccessibility and poor resources—to which must be added its increasingly eroded or degraded nature. Peasants, especially at high altitude, who are additionally protected from the current reform of the land reform by the communal nature of their land grants, are prepared to fight their corner against outside interference of any kind. Class coalitions at the community level, based on ethnicity, have shown that they have sufficient clout to take on even the PRI—notably in the *municipio* of Juchitán.

The state has played an important role in the definition of community and ethnicity as well as peasantry, but even in these cases there are signs that social agents are mobilizing and gradually moving beyond PRI control. Decentralization is putting more funds into the hands of the *municipios*, and *presi-*

dentes municipales have suggested that, if the PRI wishes to democratize the federal state, it has only to look to the municipal level to see how democracy works. As Chapter 7 showed, it is at the level of the *municipio* that electoral opposition to the PRI has been most fully developed, especially in the Oaxaca Valley, the Isthmus of Tehuantepec, and the Mixteca Alta.

Similar changes are occurring among the ethnic/language groups of Oaxaca. The Zapotecs and Chatinos, the Mixes, the only language group to be encompassed within a single *distrito*, and the Mixtecs, among others, are asking for devolved economic powers so that they can take command of regional change, using their ethnicity as the basis for planning and development. There are, however, considerable difficulties to be overcome, since the unit of local government is the *municipio*. The language groups have no recent history of co-ordinated effort at an ethnic-regional scale, and are only now setting up their own organizations. Nevertheless, the Oaxaca state government has taken the issue sufficiently seriously to have a member of the state cabinet responsible for ethnic affairs.

Although there is ample evidence to suggest that community and ethnicity are becoming more salient, peasantry as a self-sufficient entity is being eroded. Migration and urbanization continue apace, and education is transferring the children of peasants and petty-commodity producers, whether urban or rural, into the semi-proletariat and quasi-middle class. Hence, the Mexican government is faced with a scenario reminiscent of 'the twilight of the gods'. Democracy may not result in electoral defeat for the 'hegemonic' PRI in the short run, but social sectors, once previously controlled, may get out of hand. Moreover, the North American Free Trade Area, so enthusiastically ushered in by the Salinas administration in January 1994, may unleash social forces that can no longer be mediated by the PRI or any Mexican government formed without taking them into account (Gray 1998).

That grass-roots movements have already taken up the challenge to dismantle the PRI-dominated state has been made clear by the rebellion of the Ejército Zapatista de Liberación Nacional in Chiapas in January 1994—which continues to this day, and by subsequent small-scale guerrilla attacks in Guerrero and Oaxaca in 1996. However, the activists involved in 1996 seem not to have been from Oaxaca, where, as I have shown, the *mestizo*–Indian boundary is more malleable, and the land reform has been less blocked, than in Chiapas. In Chiapas, communal lands have rarely been conferred on indigenous communities (Stephen 1998*a*). The Zapatistas (most of them Indian-language speakers) therefore highlight the continuing failure of the government to redistribute sufficient *ejidos* to the land-hungry peasantry (Nash 1995). Indian opposition to present-day PRI agrarian policy, in turn, may be gauged from the fact that no more than 11 per cent of the 2,100 *ejidos* in Chiapas have entered PROCEDE (Stephen 1998*a*).

However, the main influence of the Zapatistas, so far as Oaxaca is concerned, has been refracted from the national level. Mexico's entry into the

North American Free Trade Area and the validity of the presidential election of 1994 were the focus of Zapatista criticism, which they relayed world wide using the internet. Future developments in Chiapas and Mexico will depend on the well-tried manipulative skills of the PRI, and the degree to which it really is embedded in Mexican society. As in the past, however, 'traditional' Oaxaca may prove *not* to be a good guide to the potentialities for radical change at the national scale. There is evidence that, in rural Oaxaca, the image of the revolutionary hero, Zapata, stands both for land reform (1917) and for opposition to its ending (1994), thus challenging the PRI's reversal of its long-run agrarian policy in the early 1990s (Stephen 1997). However, Oaxaca's stability is now based less on subsistence from the land than in the past. Rather, it inheres in the multifaceted activities of its highly differentiated, increasingly mobile, transnational peasantries.

BIBLIOGRAPHY AND REFERENCES

The works in this bibliography have been consulted in writing this book; those marked
* have been cited in the text.

Acevedo Conde, María Luisa (1982), *Desempleo y Subempleo Rural en los Valles Centrales de Oaxaca* (Mexico City: SEP INAH).

—— and Iván Restrepo (1991), *Los Valles Centrales de Oaxaca* (Oaxaca: Centro de Ecodesarrollo).

—— *et al.* (1993), *Etnografía y Educación en el Estado de Oaxaca* (Mexico City: INAH).

*Aceves de la Mora, José Luis (1976), *Climatología del Estado de Oaxaca* (Oaxaca: Ediciones Indeco, 1).

Aguilar Medina, Jose Iñigo (1974), 'Diferencía Etnica y Migración en la Mixteca Baja' (Mexico City: Departemento de Etnología y Antropología Social, INAH, Estudios, 5).

*—— (1979), 'La Mixteca Oaxaqueña: Una Zona de Emigración', in M. Nolasco *et al.* (eds.), *Aspectos Sociales de Migración en México* (Mexico City: Instituto Nacional de Antropología e Historia).

*—— (1980), *El Hombre y el Urbe: la Ciudad de Oaxaca* (Mexico City: SEP INAH).

*Aguirre Beltrán, Gonzalo (1970), 'Los Símbolos Etnicos de la Identidad Nacional', *Anuario Indigenista*, 30, 101–40.

*—— (1973), *Regiones de Refugio: El Desarrollo de la Comunidad y el Processo Dominical en Mestizo América* (Mexico City: Sepini, 17).

—— (1981 originally 1953), *Formas de Gobierno Indigena* (Mexico City: Instituto Nacional Indigenista).

*—— (1984 originally 1972), *La Población Negra de México* (Mexico City: Fondo de Cultura Económica).

*Alcalá, Elio, and Teófilo Reyes Couturier (1994), *Migrantes Mixtecos: El Proceso Migratorio de la Mixteca Baja* (Mexico City: INAH, Colección Científica).

Alexander, Ruth María (1980), *Gramatica Mixteca de Atatlahuca* (Mexico City: Instituto Lingüístico de Verano).

*Alvarez, Luis Rodrigo (1983), *Geografía General del Estado de Oaxaca* (Oaxaca: Edición del Gobierno del Estado).

*Amnesty International (1986), *Mexico: Human Rights in Rural Areas* (London: Amnesty International Publications).

Anguiano Téllez, María Eugenia (1986), 'Los Mixtecos en Baja California', *México Indígena*, 13, 2, 49–52.

*—— (1992), 'Migrantes Agricolas en la Frontera Norte: El Caso de Los Mixtecos', in Jack Corbett *et al.* (1992) (eds.), 105–15.

*Aragon, Aguilar Jacobo (1980), 'El Grave Problema de la Erosión y Agua en Oaxaca' (mecanografía).

Aranda B., Josefina (1990), 'Género, Familia y División de Trabajo en Santo Tomás Jalieza' *Estudios Sociológicos*, 8, 22, 3–22.

Arellanes Meixueiro, Anselmo (1990), *Los Trabajos y los Guías: Mutualismo y Sindicalismo en Oaxaca, 1870–1930* (Oaxaca: Instituto Tecnológico de Oaxaca).

*Aubague, Laurent (1985), *Discurso Político, Utopía y Memoria Popular en Juchitán* (Oaxaca: Instituto de Investigaciones Sociológicas, UABJO).

Autor Anónimo (1981), *Gramática de la Lengua Zapoteca* (Mexico City: Editorial Innovación).

*Badcock, Blair (1984), *Unfairly Structured Cities* (Oxford: Basil Blackwell).

*Bailón Corres, Moisés Jaime (1979), 'Articulación de Modos de Producción: Producción Mercantil Simple y Sistema Comercial en los Valles Centrales de Oaxaca' (Oaxaca: Universidad Autónoma Benito Juárez de Oaxaca, Tesis de Licenciatura en Sociología).

——(1990), 'Los Problemas de Morro Mazatlán: La Lucha por el Control de una Agencia Municipal en el Estado de Oaxaca', *Estudios Sociológicos*, 8, 22, 67–86.

*——(1995), 'Municipios, Opposition Mayorships, and Public Expenditure in Oaxaca', in Victoria E. Rodríguez and Peter M. Ward (eds.), *Opposition Government in Mexico* (Albuquerque: University of New Mexico Press), 205–19.

*Ballesteros, Juan, Matthew Edel, and Michael Nelson (1970), *La Colonización del Papaloapan* (Mexico City: Centro de Investigaciones Agrarias).

Ballesteros, Leopoldo R., and Mauro Rodríguez (1974), *La Cultura Mixe* (Mexico City: Editorial Jus).

*Barabas, Alicia Mabel (1977), 'Chinantec Messianism: The Mediator of the Divine', in Elias Sevilla-Casas (ed.), *Western Expansionism and Indigenous Peoples* (The Hague: Mouton), 221–54.

——(1978), 'Trabajo Propio y Trabajo de la Gente: Articulación Económica y Etnicidad entre los Chatinos de Oaxaca' (Oaxaca: Centro Regional de INAH, Estudios de Antropología e Historía, 13).

——(1986), 'Organización Económica de los Chatinos de Oaxaca', *México Indígena*, 11, 16–22.

*——and Miguel Bartolomé (1973), 'Hydraulic Development and Ethnocide: The Mazatec and Chinantec People of Oaxaca' (Copenhagen: International Work Group for Indigenous Affairs).

——and —— (1984), *El Rey Cong-Hoy: Tradición Mesiánica y Privación Social entre los Mixes de Oaxaca* (Oaxaca: Instituto Nacional de Antropología e Historia).

*——and —— (1986) (eds.), *Etnicidad y Pluralismo Cultural: La Dinámica Etnica en Oaxaca* (Mexico City: Instituto Nacional de Antropología e Historia).

Barbash, Shepard (1993), *Oaxacan Woodcarving: The Magic in the Trees* (San Francisco: Chronicle Books).

Barbosa Ramirez, A. René (1976), *Empleo, Desempleo y Subempleo en el Sector Agropecuario* (Mexico City: Centro de Invesigaciones Agrarias).

*Bartolomé, Miguel Alberto (1979), *Narrativa y Etnicidad entre los Chatinos de Oaxaca* (Oaxaca: Cuadernos de los Centros Regionales).

——(1984), *Sol y Luna: Ciclo Mitico de los Hermanos Gemelos en las Tradiciones de las Culturas Oaxaqueños* (Oaxaca: Cecoax).

——(1986), 'Parentesco y Organización Política Chinanteca' *México Indígena*, 11, 13–15.

*——and Alicia M. Barabas (1982), *Tierra de la Palabra: Historia y Etnografía de los Chatinos de Oaxaca* (Mexico City: Instituto Nacional de Antropología e Historia, Centro Regional de Oaxaca, Colección Científica, 108).

——and —— (1986), 'Los Migrantes Étnicos de Oaxaca', *México Indígena*, 13, 2, 23–5.

*——and —— (1990), *La Presa Cerro de Oro y el Ingeniero el Gran Dios: Relocación y Etnocidio Chinanteco en México*, i and ii (Mexico City: Instituto Nacional Indigenista).

*——and —— (1996), *La Pluralidad en Peligro: Procesos de Transfiguración y Extinción Cultural en Oaxaca* (Mexico City: Instituto Nacional de Antropología e Historia y Instituto Nacional Indigenista).

*——and —— (1997), 'Relocalización y Etnocidio: La Presa de Oro 20 Años Después', *Cuadernos del Sur*, 11, 79–101.

*Basáñez, E., Miguel (1987) (ed.), *La Composición del Poder: Oaxaca 1968–1984* (Mexico City: Instituto Nacional de Administración Pública).

Basilio Rojas (1958, 1962, and 1964), *Miahuatlan: Un Pueblo de México*, i, ii, and iii (Mexico City: Editorial Luz).

——(no date), *Miahuatlan: Un Pueblo de México, Historia General* (Mexico City).

*Baskes, Jeremy (1996), 'Coerced or Voluntary? The *Repartimiento* and Market Participation of Peasants in Late Colonial Oaxaca', *Journal of Latin American Studies*, 28, 1, 1–28.

*Beals, Ralph (1945), *Ethnology of the Western Mixe* (Berkeley: University of California Press, Publications in American Archaeology and Ethnology, 42).

——(1967a), 'The Structure of the Oaxaca Market System', *Revista Mexicana de Estudios Antropológicas*, 21, 333–42.

——(1967b), 'Un Sistema Tradicional de Mercados', *America Indígena*, 27, 3, 566–80

——(1970), 'Gifting, Reciprocity, Savings, and Credit in Peasant Oaxaca', *Southwestern Journal of Anthropology*, 26, 3, 231–41.

——(1971), 'Estudio de Poblados en la Sierra Zapoteca de Oaxaca, México', *América Indígena*, 31, 3, 671–91.

*——(1975), *The Peasant Marketing System of Oaxaca, Mexico* (Berkeley and Los Angeles: University of California Press).

——(1976), 'The Oaxaca Market Study Project', in Scott Cook and Martin Diskin (eds.), *Markets in Oaxaca* (Austin, Tex.: University of Texas Press), 27–43.

——(1979), 'Economic Adaptations at Mitla', in Barbro Dalhgren (ed.), *Mesoamerica: Homenaje al Dr Paul Kirchhoff* (Mexico City: SEP INAH).

Beams, Daniel E. (1989), 'Cattle Economy in Oaxaca, Mexico: Production, Exchange and Consumption' (Waco, Tex.: Baylor University, M.Sc. thesis).

Beltrán Morales, Filemón (1986), 'Migración e Identidad Étnica Zapoteca', *México Indígena*, 13, 2, 41–3.

*Benítez Zenteno, Raúl (1982) (compiler), *Sociedad y Política en Oaxaca 1980* (Oaxaca: Instituto de Investigaciones Sociológicas, Universidad Autónoma 'Benito Juárez' de Oaxaca).

*Berg Jr., Richard Lewis (1974), *El Impacto de la Economía Moderna: Sobre la Economía Tradicional de Zoogocho, Oaxaca y su Área Circundante* (Mexico City: Instituto Nacional Indigenista).

Berlin, Heinrich (1988), *Las Antiguas Creencias en San Miguel Sola, Oaxaca, Mexico* (Mexico City: Ediciones Toledo).

Bernal, Ignacio, and Lorenzo Gamio (1974), *Yagul: Palacio de los Siete Patios* (Mexico City: Instituto de Investigaciones Antropológicas, UNAM).

Bernal Alcantara, Juan Areli (1991), *El Camino de Añukojm—Totontepec y los Salesianos* (Mexico City).

Berry, Charles (1969), 'La Ciudad de Oaxaca en Vísperas de la Reforma', *Historia Mexicana*, 19, 1, 23–61.

*——— (1981), *The Reform in Oaxaca, 1856–76: A Microhistory of the Liberal Revolution* (Lincoln, Neb., and London: Nebraska University Press).

Bevan, Bernard (1938), *The Chinantec: Report on the Central and South-Eastern Chinantec Region* (Instituto Panamericano de Geografia e Historia, 24).

*Binford, Leigh (1985), 'Political Conflict and Land Tenure in the Mexican Isthmus of Tehuantepec', *Journal of Latin American Studies*, 17, 1, 179–200.

——— (1990), 'The Political Economy of the Velas in the Isthmus of Tehuantepec', in Lynn Stephen and James Dow (eds.), *Class, Politics and Popular Religion in Mexico and Central America* (Washington: American Anthropological Association), 77–92.

*——— (1992), 'Peasants and Petty Capitalists in Southern Oaxacan Sugar Cane Production and Processing, 1930–1980', *Journal of Latin American Studies*, 24, 1, 33–55.

*Blanton, Richard E. (1978), *Monte Alban: Settlement Patterns at the Ancient Zapotec Capital* (New York and London: Academic Press).

*———Stephen Kowaleswski, Gary Feinman, and Jill Appel (1981), *Ancient Mesoamerica: A Comparison of Change in Three Regions* (Cambridge: Cambridge University Press).

*Blauert, Jutta (1988), 'Autochthonous Development and Environmental Knowledge in Oaxaca, Mexico', in P. Blaikie and T. Unwin (eds.), *Environmental Crises in Developing Countries* (London: Developing Areas Research Group, Institute of British Geographers).

*——— (1990), 'Autochthonous Approaches to Rural Environmental Problems: The Mixteca Alta, Oaxaca, Mexico' (London: Wye College, University of London, Ph.D. thesis).

*——— and Marta Guidi (1992*a*), 'Strategies for Autochthonous Development: Two Initiatives in Rural Oaxaca, Mexico', in D. Ghai and Marta Guidi (eds.), *Grassroots Environmental Action* (London: Routledge), 188–220.

*——— and ——— (1992*b*), 'Local Initiatives in Southern Mexico', *The Ecologist*, 22, 6, 284–8.

Boege, Eckart (1979) (ed.), *Desarrollo del Capitalismo y Transformación de la Estructura de Poder en la Region de Tuxtepec, Oaxaca* (Mexico City: Escuela Nacional de Antropología e Historia).

*——— (1988), *Los Mazatecos ante la Nación: Contradicciones de la Identidad Étnica en el México Actual* (Coyoacan: Siglo Veintiuno Editores).

*Brading, David (1988), 'Manuel Gamio and Official Indigenismo in Mexico', *Bulletin of Latin American Research*, 7, 1, 75–89.

*Bradomin, José María (1980), *Toponimia de Oaxaca* (Mexico City).

——— (1984), *Monografia del Estado de Oaxaca* (Mexico City).

Brasseur, Charles (1992), *Viaje por el Istmo de Tehuantepec 1859–1860* (Mexico City: Fondo de Cultura Económica).

*Bravo, Helia (1960), 'Algunos Datos acerca de la Vegetación del Estado de Oaxaca', *Revista Mexicana de Estudios Antropológicos*, 16, 31–47.

*Bray, David Barton (1991), 'The Struggle for the Forest: Conservation and Development in the Sierra Juárez', *Grassroots Development*, 15, 3, 13–25.

*Brito de Martí, Esperanza (1982) (ed.), *Almanaque de Oaxaca 1982* (Oaxaca: Gobierno del Estado).

*Brockington, Lolita Gutiérrez (1989), *The Leverage of Labour: Managing the Cortés Haciendas in Tehuantepec, 1588–1688* (Durham, NC, and London: Duke University Press).

*Brown, Betty Ann (1977), 'Fiestas de Oaxaca' (Oaxaca: Centro del INAH, Estudios de Antropología e Historia, 2).

*Browner, C. H. (1985*a*), 'Criteria for Selecting Herbal Remedies', *Ethnology*, 24, 1, 13–32.

*——(1985*b*), 'Plants used for Reproductive Health in Oaxaca, Mexico', *Economic Botany*, 39, 4, 482–504.

*——(1986*a*), 'Gender Roles and Social Change: A Mexican Case Study', *Ethnology*, 25, 2, 89–106.

*——(1986*b*), 'The Politics of Reproduction in a Mexican Village', *Journal of Women in Culture and Society*, 11, 4, 710–24.

——and Sandra T. Perdue (1988), 'Women's Secrets: Basis for Reproductive and Social Autonomy in a Mexican Community', *American Ethnologist*, 15, 1, 84–97.

Brueske, Judith Morisette (1976), 'The Petapa Zapotecs of the Inland Ithmus of Tehuantepec, Oaxaca' (Riverside, Calif.: University of California Ph.D thesis in Anthropology).

*Bustamante V., René *et al.* (1984 2nd edn.), *Oaxaca: una Lucha Reciente: 1960–83* (Mexico City: Ediciones Nueva Sociología).

Butler H., and Inez M. (1980), *Gramatica Zapoteca* (Mexico City: Instituto Lingüístico de Verano).

*Butterworth, Douglas (1973), 'Squatters or Suburbanites? The Growth of Shanty Towns in Oaxaca, Mexico', in R. E. Scott (ed.), *Latin American Modernization Problems: Case Studies in a Crisis of Change* (Bloomington, Ind.: University of Illinois Press), 208–32.

*——(1975), *Tilantongo: Communidad Mixteca en Transición* (Mexico City: Instituto Nacional Indigenista).

——(1977), 'Selectivity of Outmigration from a Mixtec Community', *Urban Anthropology*, 6, 2, 129–39.

Camacho, Juan Pablo (1986), 'Los Mercados de Oaxaca', *México Indígena*, 12, 66–9.

Cámara Barbachano, Fernando (1961), 'Mixtecos y Zapotecos: Antiguos y Modernos', in Santiago Genoves (ed.), *Homenaje a Pablo Martínez del Rio* (Mexico City: Publicación de la UNAM, el INAH, Mexico City College y la Sociedad Mexicana de Antropología), 373–85.

*——(1966), 'Tianguis y Mercados en Oaxaca', in *Homenaje a Roberto Weitlaner* (Mexico City: INAH), 273–9.

Campbell, Howard (1993), 'Tradition and the New Social Movements: The Politics of Isthmus Zapotec Culture', *Latin American Perspectives*, 20, 3, 82–96.

*——(1994), *Zapotec Renaissance: Ethnic Politics and Cultural Revivalism in Southern Mexico* (Albuquerque: University of New Mexico Press).

*——Leigh Binford, Miguel Bartolomé, and Alicia Barabas (1993) (eds.), *Zapotec Struggles: Histories, Politics and Representations from Juchitán* (Washington and London: Smithsonian Institution Press).

*Cancian, Frank (1965), *Economics and Prestige in a Maya Community: The Religious Cargo System of Zinacantan* (Stanford, Calif.: Stanford University Press).

*Carmagnani, Marcello (1988), *El Regreso a los Dioses: El Proceso de Reconstitución de la Identidad Étnica en Oaxaca, Siglos XVII y XVIII* (Mexico City: Fondo de Cultura Económica).

*Carrasco, Pedro (1963), 'The Civil-Religious Hierarchy in Mesoamerica: Pre-Spanish Background and Colonial Development', *American Anthropologist*, 63, 483–97.

*——(1966), 'Cermonias Publicas Paganas entre los Mixes de Tamazulapan', *Homenaje a Roberto Weitlaner* (Mexico City: INAH).

Casillas, Marissa (1986), 'Migración Mixteca', *México Indígena*, 13, 2, 79.

*Cassidy, Thomas (1981), 'Haciendas and Pueblos in Nineteenth Century Oaxaca' (Cambridge: Cambridge University, Ph.D. thesis in History).

Castellanos Martínez, Javier (1989), 'Lo Indio en la Literatura Indigína y en la Narrativa Zapoteca de la Sierra', *El Medio Milenio*, 5, 7–17.

Censo Agrícola, Ganadero y Ejidal 1940: Oaxaca (1948), (Mexico City: Dirección General de Estadística).

**Censo Agrícola, Ganadero y Ejidal 1950: Oaxaca* (1956), (Mexico City: Dirección General de Estadística).

Censo Agrícola, Ganadero y Ejidal 1960: Oaxaca (1965), (Mexico City: Dirección General de Estadística).

**Censo Agrícola, Ganadero y Ejidal 1970: Oaxaca* (1975), (Mexico City: Direccíon General de Estadística).

Censo Agrícola-Ganadero 1990: Oaxaca (1994), (Aguas Calientes: INEGI). This is available in various volumes and on disc and compact disc.

Censo General 1900: Oaxaca (1907), (Mexico City: Dirección General de Estadística).

Censo General 1921: Oaxaca (no date) (Mexico City).

**Censo General de Población 1930: Oaxaca* (no date) (Mexico City).

Censo General de Población 1940: Oaxaca (1943) (Mexico City: Dirección General de Estadística).

**Censo General de Población 1950: Oaxaca* (1952) (Mexico City).

Censo General de Poblacion 1960: Oaxaca (1963)(Mexico City: Dirección General de Estadística).

**Censo General de Población 1970: Oaxaca* (1971, 2 vols.) (Mexico City: Dirección General de Estadística).

**Censo General de Población y Vivienda 1980* (1984, 2 vols.) (Mexico City: INEGI).

Censo General de Población y Vivienda 1990 (1991) (Aguas Calientes: INEGI). This is available in various volumes and on disc and compact disc.

*Cervantes Cortés, Isauro (1992), *Hacia la Reglamentación del Municipal Rural* (Oaxaca).

*Chance, John K. (1973), 'Parentesco y Residencia Urbana: Grupo Familiar y su Organización en un Suburbio de Oaxaca, México', *América Indígena*, 33, 1, 186–212.

——(1976), 'The Urban Indian in Colonial Oaxaca', *American Ethnologist*, 3, 4, 603–32.

*——(1978), *Race and Class in Colonial Oaxaca* (Stanford, Calif.: Stanford University Press).

——(1979), 'On the Mexican Mestizo', *Latin American Research Review*, 14, 3, 153–68.

*——(1981), 'The Ecology of Race and Class in Late Colonial Oaxaca', in David J. Robinson (ed.), *Studies in Spanish American Population History* (Boulder, Colo.: Westview Press) 93–117.

*——(1986a), 'Colonial Ethnohistory in Oaxaca', in Ronal Spores (ed.), *Supplement to*

the Handbook of Middle American Indians: Ethnohistory (Austin, Tex.: University of Texas Press), 165–89.

*——(1986*b*), 'Social Stratification and the Civil Cargo System among Rincón Zapotecs of Oaxaca: The Late Colonial Period', in Richard L. Garner and William B. Taylor (eds.), *Iberian Colonies: New World Societies (Essays in Memory of Charles Gibson)* (private printing).

*——(1989), *Conquest of the Sierra: Spaniards and Indians in Colonial Oaxaca* (Norman, Okla., and London: University of Oklahoma Press).

*——(1990*a*), 'Changes in Twentieth-Century Mesoamerican *Cargo* Systems', in Lynn Stephen and James Dow (eds.), *Class, Politics, and Popular Religion in Mexico and Central America* (Washington: American Anthropological Association), 27–42.

*——(1990*b*), 'Capitalismo y Desigualdad entre los Zapotecos de Oaxaca: Una Comparación entre el Valle y los Pueblos del Rincón', in María de los Ángeles Romero Frizzi (1990*b*) (compiler), 195–204.

*——and William B. Taylor (1985), 'Cofradías and Cargos: An Historical Perspective on the Mesoamerican Civil-Religious Hierarchy', *American Ethnologist*, 12, 1, 1–26.

*Chant, Sylvia (1991), *Women and Survival in Mexican Cities: Perspectives on Gender, Labour Markets and Low-Income Households* (Manchester: Manchester University Press).

Chassen, Francie R. (1985), *Los Precursores de la Revolución en Oaxaca: La Revolución en Oaxaca 1900–30* (Oaxaca: Instituto de Administración Publica de Oaxaca).

*——(1986), 'Oaxaca: del Porfiriato a la Revolución, 1902–1911' (Mexico City: UNAM, Facultad de Filosofía y Letras, Estudios de Postgrado, Tesis de Doctorado en Estudios Latinoamericanos).

*——(1990*a*), *Regiones y Ferrocariles en la Oaxaca Porfirista* (Oaxaca: Cartiles Editores, Colección Obra Negra).

*——(1990*b*), 'El Boom, el Auge Economico y la Crisis', in Margarita Dalton (compiler), *Oaxaca: Textos de su Historia* (Mexico City: Instituto de Investigaciones Dr José María Luis Mora), iv. 70–157.

——and Héctor Gerardo Martínez Medina (1985), *El Primer Gobierno Revolucionario de Oaxaca: La Revolución en Oaxaca 1900–1930* (Oaxaca: Instituto de Administración Pública de Oaxaca).

*——and Héctor G. Martínez (1990), 'El Desarrollo Económico de Oaxaca a Finales del Porfiriato' in María de los Ángeles Romero Frizzi (1990*d*) (compiler), 47–72.

——Leticia Reina, and Guadelope Zarate (1991), 'La Oposición a Porfirio Díaz', *Cuadernos de Investigación*, 13 (Oaxaca: Instituto de Investigaciones Sociológicas, UABJO).

Chayanov, A. V. (1966), *The Theory of Peasant Economy* (Madison: University of Wisconsin Press).

Cheney, Charles Clark (1976), *The Mareños: Tradition and Transition in a Huave Community Organization* (Nashville: Vanderbilt University Publications in Anthropology, 15).

Chiñas, Beverly L. (1973), *The Ithmus Zapotecs: Women's Roles in Cultural Context* (New York and London: Holt, Rinehart and Winston).

——(1976), 'Zapotec *Viajeras*', in Scott Cook and Martin Diskin (1976) (eds.), 169–88.

*Clarke, Colin (1986), *Livelihood Systems, Settlements and Levels of Living in 'Los Valles Centrales de Oaxaca, México'* (Oxford: School of Geography, University of Oxford, Research Paper, 37).

Clarke, Colin (1992), 'Components of Socio-Economic Change in Post-Revolutionary Oaxaca, Mexico', in Miguel Panadero Moya, Francisco Cebrian Abellan, Carmen García Martínez (compilers), *America Latina: la Cuestion Regional* (Universidad de Castilla-La Mancha: Colección Estudios), 147–70.

——(1996), 'Opposition to PRI "Hegemony" in Oaxaca', in Rob Aitken, Nikki Craske, Gareth A. Jones, and David E. Stansfield (eds.), *Dismantling the Mexican State?* (London: Macmillan).

*—— and John Langton (1990) (eds.), *Peasantry and Progress: Rural Culture and the Modern World* (Oxford: School of Geography, University of Oxford, Research Paper, 45).

*Clavero, Bartolomé (1994), *Derecho Indígena y Cultura Constitucional en América* (Mexico City: Siglo Veintiuno Editores).

Clements, Helen Peeler (1980), 'Our Work: Weaving at Santo Tomas Jalieza, Oaxaca' (Texas Technical University, MA thesis).

——(1986), 'Our Work: Weaving at Santo Tomas Jalieza' (Texas Technical University, Ph.D. thesis).

——(1990), 'La Historia de Una Comunidad Artesana: Santo Tomás Jalieza: 1857–1940', in María de los Ángeles Romero Frizzi (1990*d*) (compiler), 353–84.

Cline, Howard F. (1949), 'Civil Congregations of the Indians in New Spain 1598–1606', *Hispanic-American Historical Review*, 29, 351–3.

——(1956), 'The Chinantla of Northeastern Oaxaca, Mexico: Bio-Bibliographical Notes on Modern Investigations', *Estudios Antropologicos Publicados en Homenaje al Dr Manuel Gamio* (Mexico City: Universidad Nacional Autónoma de México y Sociedad Mexicana de Sociología).

*Colby, Benjamin N., and Pierre van den Berghe (1961), 'Ethnic Relations in Southeastern Mexico', *American Anthropologist*, 63, 4, 772–92.

Collingridge, Vanessa (1990), 'Fertility Regulation in Oaxaca, Mexico' (Oxford: Oxford University, BA thesis in Geography).

Comisión Nacional de Derechos Humanos (1991), *Memoria de la Zona Mixe en el Estado de Oaxaca* (Mexico City).

Conejo van Luit, C. (1994), 'Unfree Labour in Oaxaca during the Porfiriato' (Oxford: Oxford University M.Phil. thesis in Latin American Studies).

*Cook, Scott (1969), 'Teitipac and its *Metateros*: An Economic Anthropological Study of Production and Exchange in a Peasant-Artisan Economy in the Valley of Oaxaca, Mexico' (Pittsburg: University of Pittsburg, Ph.D. thesis in Anthropology).

——(1970), 'Price and Output Variability in a Peasant-Artisan Stoneworking Industry in Oaxaca, Mexico: An Analytical Essay in Economic Anthropology', *American Anthropologist*, 72, 776–801.

——(1981), 'Crafts, Capitalist Development and Cultural Property in Oaxaca, Mexico', *Inter-American Economic Affairs*, 35, 3, 53–68.

*——(1982*a*), *Zapotec Stoneworkers: The Dynamics of Rural Simple Commodity Production in Modern Mexican Capitalism* (Lanham, Md., New York, London: University Press of America).

——(1982*b*), 'Craft Production in Oaxaca', *Cultural Survival Quarterly*, 6, 4, 18–20.

——(1984*a*), Peasant Capitalist Industry: Piecework and Enterprise in Southern Mexican Brickyards (Lanham, Md., New York, London: University Press of America).

——(1984*b*), 'Peasant Economy, Rural Industry, and Capitalist Development in the Oaxaca Valley, Mexico', *Journal of Peasant Studies*, 12, 1, 3–40.

——(1985), 'Craft Businesses, Piece Work and Value Distribution in the Oaxaca Valley, Mexico', in Stuart Palmer (ed.), *Markets and Marketing* (Lanham, Md., and London: Monographs in Economic Anthropology, 4), 235–58.

*——and Leigh Binford (1990), *Obliging Need: Rural Petty Industry in Mexican Capitalism* (Austin, Tex.: University of Texas Press).

*——and Martin Diskin (1976) (eds.), *Markets in Oaxaca* (Austin, Tex., and London: University of Texas Press).

*——and Jong-Taick Joo (1995), 'Ethnicity and Economy in Rural Mexico: A Critique of the Indigenista Approach', *Latin American Research Review*, 30, 2, 33–59.

*Cook, Sherburne F. (1949), *Soil Erosion and Population in Central Mexico* (Berkeley and Los Angeles: University of California Press, Ibero-Americana, 34).

*——and Woodrow Borah (1968), *The Population of the Mixteca Alta, 1526–1960* (Berkeley and Los Angeles: University of California Press, Ibero-Americana, 50).

Coplamar (1978), *Programa Integrado, Zona Mixteca, Oaxaca* (Mexico City: Co-ordinación General del Plan Nacional de Zonas Deprimidas y Grupos Maginados, 22).

*Corbett, Jack (1976), 'Aspects of Recruitment to Civil Office in a Mexican Community', *Anthropological Quarterly*, 49, 3, 160–73.

*——and Scott Whiteford (1983), 'State Penetration and Development in Mesoamerica, 1950–1980', in Carl Kendall *et al.* (eds.), *Heritage of Conquest Thirty Years Later* (Albuquerque: University of New Mexico Press).

*——Murad A. Musalem Merhy, Othón Ríos Vázquez, and Héctor A. Vázquez Hernández (1992) (eds.), *Migración y Etnicidad en Oaxaca* (Nashville: Vanderbilt University Publications in Anthropology, 43).

Cordero Avendaño de Durand, Carmen (1982), *Supervivencia de un Derecho Consuetudinario en el Valle de Tlacolula* (Oaxaca: Fondo Nacional Para Actividades Sociales).

——(1986), *El Santo Padre Sol: Contribución al Conocimiento Socio-Religioso del Grupo Etnico Chatino* (Oaxaca: Gobierno del Estado).

——(1992), *El Combate de las Luces: Los Tacuates* (Oaxaca: Museo de Arte PreHispanico de México 'Rufino Tamayo').

*Corona, Rodolfo (1979), *Cuantificacion del Nivel de la Mortalidad en Oaxaca, 1970* (Oaxaca: Centro de Sociología, Universidad Autónoma 'Benito Juárez' de Oaxaca).

Covarrubias, Miguel (1980 originally 1946), *El Sur de México* (Mexico City: Instituto Nacional Indigenista).

*Crumpton, Nicola (1991), 'Cyclical Markets in a Peasant Economy: A study of the Market Systems of Oaxaca, Mexico' (Oxford: Oxford University, BA thesis in Geography).

Cruz Lorenzo, Tomás (1987), 'De Porque las Flores no se Doblegan con el Aguacero', *El Medio Milenio*, 1, 28–54.

*Dahlgren, Barbro (1990), *La Grana Cochinilla* (Mexico City: Universidad Nacional Autónoma de México).

——(1990 originally 1954), *La Mixteca: Su Cultura e Historia Prehispánicas* (Mexico City: Instituto de Investigaciones Antropológicas, UNAM).

Dalton, Margarita (1990*a*), *Oaxaca: Una Historia Compartida* (Mexico City: Instituto de Investigaciones Dr José María Luis Mora).

Dalton, Margarita (1990*b*), *Oaxaca: Textos de su Historia* (Mexico City: Instituto de Investigaciones Dr José María Mora i–iv).

——(1990*c*), 'La Organización Política, las Mujeres y el Estado: El Caso de Oaxaca', *Estudios Sociológicos*, 8, 22, 39–65.

——(1991) (compiler), *La Mujer Oaxaqueña: Un Analisis de su Contexto* (Oaxaca: Consejo Estatal de Población and Coordinadora Interinstitutional de Programas Para La Mujer).

——and Guadelupe Musalem Merhy (1992), *Mitos y Realidades de las Mujeres Huaves* (Oaxaca: Instituto de Investigaciones Sociológicas, UABJO).

Darbellay, Alina Maria Anna (1995), 'Rural-Urban Interactions in North Chuquisaca, Bolivia: Flows of Goods, Relational Exchange and Power Relations' (Oxford: Oxford University, D.Phil. thesis in Geography).

De Cordova, Fr. Juan (1987 originally 1886), *Arte del Idioma Zapateco* (Mexico City: Ediciones Toledo).

——(1987 originally 1578), *Vocabulario en Lengva Çapoteca* (Mexico City: Ediciones Toledo).

De Jong, Lotte (1990), 'Community Discourse: A Family Conflict in Eighteenth-Century Coyotepec, Oaxaca', in Arij Ouweneel and Simon Miller (eds.), *The Indian Community of Colonial Mexico* (Amsterdam: CEDLA), 250–69.

De la Barreda, Nicolás (1960 originally 1730), *Doctrina Christiana en Lengua Chinanteca: Papeles de la Chinantla* (Mexico City: Serie Científica, Museo Nacional de Antropología, II).

*De la Cruz, Victor (1984), *La Flor de la Palabra* (Mexico City: SEP).

De la Fuente, Julio (1947), 'Los Zapotecos de Choapan, Oaxaca', *Anales del Instituto Nacional de Antropología e Historia, 2*, 143–205.

*——(1965), *Relaciones Interétnicas* (Mexico City: Instituto Nacional Indigenista).

*——(1977*a* originally 1949), *Yalálag: Una Villa Zapoteca Serrana* (Mexico City: Instituto Nacional Indigenista).

——(1977*b* originally 1964), *Educación, Antropología y Desarrollo de la Comunidad* (Mexico City: Instituto Nacional Indigenista).

De la Luz Topete, María (1980), *Bibliografia Antropológica de Oaxaca, 1977–79* (Oaxaca: Centro Regional, Instituto Nacional de Anthropología e Historia, Estudios de Antropología e Historia, 22).

Del Paso y Troncoso, Francisco (1981 originally 1890), *Relaciones Geográficas de Oaxaca* (Mexico City: Editorial Innovación).

Del Pilar Sánchez, María (1986), 'Testimonios de Pinotepa de Don Luis', *México Indígena*, 11, 41–7.

*Dennis, Philip A. (1973), 'The Oaxacan Village President as Middleman', *Ethnology*, 12, 419–27.

——(1976*a*), 'The Uses of Inter-Village Feuding', *Anthroplogical Quarterly*, 49, 3, 174–83.

*——(1976*b*), *Conflictos por Tierras en el Valle de Oaxaca* (Mexico City: Instituto Nacional Indigenista).

*——(1987), *Intervillage Conflict in Oaxaca* (New Brunswick, NJ, and London: Rutgers University Press).

De Rouffinac, Ann Lucas (1985), *The Contemporary Peasantry in Mexico: A Class Analysis* (New York: Praeger).

*De Walt, Billie (1975), 'Changes in the Cargo Systems of Mesoamerica', *Anthropological Quarterly*, 43, 87–105.

——and Martha Rees (1994), *The End of Agrarian Reform in Mexico: Past Lessons, Future Prospects* (La Jolla, Calif.: Ejido Reform Research Project, University of California, San Diego, Center for US–Mexican Studies).

*Díaz Montes, Fausto (1982), 'La Producción de Mezcal en Oaxaca', in Raúl Benítez Zenteno (compiler), *Sociedad y Política en Oaxaca 1980* (Barcelona: ICARIA Editorial).

——(1987), 'Los Conflictos Municipales', in *Problemática Municipal de Oaxaca* (Oaxaca: Instituto de Investigaciones Sociológicas, UABJO).

——(1991), 'Union Hidalgo: Recuerdo de una Lucha Municipal' (Oaxaca: Instituto de Investigaciones Sociológicas, UABJO, *Cuadernos de Investigación*, 14).

*——(1992*a*), *Los Municipios: La Disputa por el Poder Local en Oaxaca* (Oaxaca: Instituto de Investigaciones Sociológicas, Universidad Autónoma 'Benito Juárez' de Oaxaca).

*——(1992*b*), 'Elección del Gobernador en Oaxaca', *Cuadernos del Sur* 2, 113–28.

——(1994), 'Elecciones Municipales en Oaxaca: 1980–1992' *Cuadernos del Sur*, 6–7, 93–110.

*——and Isidoro Yescas Martínez (1992), 'Elecciones Federales y Sucesión Gubernamental en Oaxaca' *Cuadernos del Sur*, 1, 5–24.

*Díaz-Polanco, Héctor (1996), *El Fuego de la Inobediencia: Autonomía y Rebelión India en el Obispado de Oaxaca* (Mexico City: Centro de Investigaciones y Estudios Superiores en Antropología Social).

Diskin Martin (1967), 'Economics and Society in Tlacolula, Oaxaca, Mexico' (Los Angeles: University of California, Ph.D. thesis in Anthropology).

*Doniz, Rafael, and Carlos Monsivais (1983), *H. Ayuntamiento Popular de Juchitán* (Oaxaca: H. Ayuntamiento de Juchitán).

Dorsett, James Robert (1975), 'Variations in Isthmus Zapotec Kinship and Ecology at Juchitán and Tehuantepec, Oaxaca' (New Orleans: Tulane University, Ph.D. thesis).

Downing, Theodore E. (1973), 'Zapotec Inheritance' (Stanford, Calif.: University of Stanford Ph.D. thesis in Anthropology).

*——(1974), 'Irrigation and Moisture-Sensitive Periods: A Zapotec Case Study', in Theodore E. Downing and McGuire Gibson (eds.), *Irrigation's Impact on Society* (Tucson, Ariz.: University of Arizona Press, Anthropological Papers of the University of Arizona, 25).

*——(1977), 'Partible Inheritance and Land Fragmentation in a Oaxaca Village', *Human Organization*, 36, 3, 235–43.

*——(1979), 'Explaining Migration in Mexico and Elsewhere', in Fernando Cámara and Richard Van Kemper (eds.), *Migration across Frontiers: Mexico and the United States* (Albany, NY: Institute of Mesoamerican Studies), 159–67.

*Drucker, Susana (1963), *Cambio de Indumentaria: la Estructura Social y el Abandono de la Vestimenta Indígena en la Villa de Santiago Jamiltepec* (Mexico City: Instituto Nacional Indigenista).

Durand, Jorge, and Douglas S. Massey (1992), 'Mexican Migration to the United States: A Critical Review', *Latin American Research Review*, 27, 2, 3–42.

*Eder, Herbert M. (1976), 'Markets as Mirrors: Reflectors of the Economic Activity and the Regional Culture of Coastal Oaxaca', in Scott Cook and Martin Diskin (eds.), *Markets in Oaxaca* (Austin, Tex.: University of Texas Press).

El Guindi, Fadwa (1972), 'The Nature of Belief Systems: A Structural Analysis of Zapotec Ritual' (Austin, Tex.: University of Texas Ph.D. thesis in Anthropology).

*El Guindi, Fadwa (1986) (with the collaboration of Abel Hernández Jiménez), *The Myth of Ritual: A Native's Ethnography of Zapotec Life-Crisis Rituals* (Tucson, Ariz.: University of Arizona Press).

*Enciclopedia de los Municipios de Mexico (1987), *Los Municipios de Oaxaca* (Oaxaca: Gobierno del Estado).

*Encuesta Nacional Agropecuaria Ejidal (1988), *Atlas Ejidal del Estado de Oaxaca* (Mexico City: INEGI).

*Erdinger, Steven (1985), 'Mixtepec: Un Pueblo en la Sierra' (Berkeley: University of California, graduate thesis).

*Escalante Lazúrtegui, Claudia (1973), 'La Depresión Llamada Valles de Oaxaca', *Anuario de Geografía*, Año XIII, Universidad Nacional Autónoma de México, 100–7.

Esparza, Manuel (1974), *Jenifer Holderman: Estudio de Caso* (Oaxaca: Centro Regional de Oaxaca y Sepinah).

——(1980), *Seminario sobre Medicina Tradicional* (Oaxaca: Estudios de Antropología e Historia, 24).

——(1981), *Padron de Casas de la Ciudad de Oaxaca 1824* (Oaxaca: Instituto Nacional de Antropología e Historia).

——(1983), *Padron de Capitación de la Ciudad de Oaxaca, 1875* (Oaxaca: Archivo General del Estado).

——(1985), *Gillow Durante el Porfiriato y la Revolución en Oaxaca (1887–1922)* (Tlaxcala: Talleres Graficos).

*——(1988), 'Los Proyectos de los Liberales en Oaxaca', in Leticia Reina (compiler), *Historia de la Cuestión Agraria Mexicana: Estado de Oaxaca Prehispanico—1924* Mexico City: Juan Pablos Editor), i. 269–330.

*——(1990), 'Las Tierras de los Hijos de los Pueblos. El Distrito de Juchitán en el Siglo XIX', in María de los Ángeles Romero Frizzi (1990*c*) (compiler), 387–434.

——(1991), *Conflictos por Limites de Tierras: Oaxaca, Siglo XIX* (Oaxaca: Archivo General del Estado de Oaxaca, Guías y Catálogos 7).

——(1992), 'Penetración Capitalista en Oaxacxa, 1890–1920', *Cuadernos del Sur*, 1, 51–60.

Estrada, Alvaro (1977), *Vida de Maria Sabina, La Sabia de los Hongos* (Mexico City: Siglo Veintiuno Editores).

Fábregas Puig, Andrés (1986), 'La Transformación de las Formas de Poder entre los Zoques: Una Hipótesis', *México Indígena*, 10, 9–13.

*Feinman, Gary, Richard Blanton, and Stephen Kowalewski (1984), 'Market System Development in the Pre-Hispanic Valley of Oaxaca, Mexico', in Kenneth G. Hirth (ed.), *Trade and Exchange in early Mesoamerica* (Albuquerque: University of New Mexico Press), 157–78.

*Flanet, Veronique (1977), *Viviré si Dios Quiere* (Mexico City: Instituto Nacional Indigenista).

Flannery, Kent V. (1976) (ed.), *The Early Mesoamerican Village* (New York, San Francisco, London: Academic Press).

——(1986) (ed.), *Guilá Naquitz: Archaic Foraging and Early Agriculture in Oaxaca* (New York, London, Toronto: Academic Press).

*——Anne V. T. Kirkby, Michael J. Kirkby, and Aubrey Williams Jr. (1967), 'Farming Systems and Political Growth in Ancient Oaxaca', *Science*, 158, 445–53.

*——and Joyce Marcus (1983) (eds.), *The Cloud People: Divergent Evolution of the Zapotec and Mixtec Civilizations* (New York and London: Academic Press).

*Fox, Jonathan, and Josefina Aranda (1996), *Decentralization and Rural Development in Mexico: Community Participation in Oaxaca's Municipal Funds Program* (San Diego: Center for US–Mexican Studies, 1996, Monograph Series, 42).

Fry, Douglas P. (1992), 'Respect for the Rights of Others is Peace: Learning Aggression versus Nonaggression among the Zapotec', *American Anthropologist*, 94, 3, 621–39.

*García Alcaraz, Augustín (1973), *Tinujei: Los Triques de Copala* (Mexico City: Secretária de Recursos Hidrolicos).

*García Canclini, Néstor (1993), *Transforming Modernity: Popular Culture in Mexico* (Austin, Tex.: University of Texas Press).

García Hernández, Tomás (1989), *Tuxtepec ante la Historia* (Tuxtepec: Culturas Populares).

*——(1994), *La Tragedia de Tuxtepec* (Tuxtepec: Dirección Municipal de Educación, Cultura y Recreación).

——and Roger Merlin Arango (1993), *Muerte Que Vuelves* (Tuxtepec: Culturas Populares).

*García Martínez, Bernardo (1969), *El Marquesado del Valle: Tres Siglos de Régimen Señorial en Nueva España* (Mexico City: El Colegio de México, Centro de Estudios Históricos, Nueva Serie, 5).

*Garner, Paul (1985), 'Federalism and Caudillismo in the Mexican Revolution: The Genesis of the Oaxaca Sovereignty Movement (1915–20)', *Journal of Latin American Studies*, 17, 1, 111–33.

*——(1988), *La Revolución en la Provincia: Soberanía Estatal y Caudillismo en la Montañas de Oaxaca (1910–20)* (Mexico City: Fondo de Cultura Económica).

*——(1995), *Regional Development in Oaxaca During the Porfiriato (1876–1911)* (Liverpool: Institute of Latin American Studies, University of Liverpool, Research Paper, 17).

Garza Cuarón, Beatriz (1987), *El Español Hablado en la Ciudad de Oaxaca, México* (Mexico City: El Colegio de México).

Gay, José Antonio (1982 originally 1881), *Historia de Oaxaca* (Mexico City: Editorial de Porrúa).

*Gerhard, Peter (1972), *A Guide to the Historical Geography of New Spain* (Cambridge: Cambridge University Press).

*Gijsbers, Wim (1996), *Usos y Costumbres, Caciquismo e Intolerancia Religiosa* (Oaxaca: Centro de Apoyo al Movimiento Popular Oaxacaqueño).

Gilbert, Alan, and Peter M. Ward (1985) (eds.), *Housing, The State and the Poor: Policy and Practice in Three Latin American Cities* (Cambridge: Cambridge University Press).

González, Alvaro, and Marco Antonio Vásquez (1992) *Etnias, Desarrollo, Recursos y Tecnologías en Oaxaca* (Oaxaca: Gobierno del Estado y CIESAS).

González Casanova, Pablo (1969), 'Internal Colonialism and National Development', in Irving L Horowitz, J. de Castro, and John Gerassi (eds.), *Latin American Radicalism* (London: Jonathan Cape), 118–39.

*González Circedo, Alicia (no date), 'Relaciones Comerciales entre Grupos Etnicos de la Mixteca de la Costa' (Mexico City: Instituto Nacional Indigenista).

*González Navarro, Moisés (1990a originally 1958), 'Situación Política', in Margarita Dalton (compiler), *Oaxaca: Textos de su Historia*, iv. 12–27.

*González Navarro, Moisés (1990*b* originally 1958), 'Indio y Propiedad en Oaxaca', in María de los Ángeles Romero Frizzi (1990*d*) (compiler), 31–46.

*González Pacheco, Cuauhtemoc (1984), 'La Lucha de Clases en Oaxaca 1960–1970', in René Bustamante V. *et al.*, *Oaxaca una Lucha Reciente: 1960–83* (Mexico City: Ediciones Nueva Sociología), 31–73.

González Santiago, Moisés (1984), *Tlacolula: Presencia Zapoteca* (Mexico City).

González Villanueva, Pedro (1989), *El Sacrificio Mixe* (Mexico City: CEPAMIX).

*Good, Claude (1979) (compiler), *Diccionario Triqui de Chicahuaxtla* (Mexico City: Instituto Lingüístico de Verano).

*Graedon, Teresa Lynn Frost (1976), 'Health and Nutritional Status in an Urban Community of Southern Mexico' (Ann Arbor: University of Michigan, Ph.D. thesis in Anthropology).

Granskog, Jane Ellen (1974), 'Efficiency in a Zapotec Indian Agricultural Village' (Austin, Tex.: University of Texas Ph.D. thesis).

*Gray, John (1998), *False Dawn: The Delusions of Global Capitalism* (London: Granta Books).

*Greenberg, James (1972), 'Closed Corporate Communities—De Facto Reservations: A Study of Internal Colonialism in Highland Chiapas, Mexico' (Ann Arbor: University of Michigan, doctoral candidacy paper).

*——(1981), *Santiago's Sword: Chatino Peasant Religion and Economics* (Berkeley, Los Angeles, and London: University of California Press).

——(1988), 'Money and Violence in Chatino Communities of Oaxaca, Mexico', *Urban Anthropology*, 17, 1, 7–26.

*——(1989), *Blood Ties: Life and Violence in Rural Mexico* (Tucson, Ariz.: University of Arizona Press).

——(1990), 'Sanctity and Resistance in Closed Corporate Indigenous Communities: Coffee, Money, Violence, and Ritual Organization in Chatino Communities in Oaxaca', in Lynn Stephen and James Dow (eds.), *Class, Politics and Popular Religion in Mexico and Central America* (Washington: American Anthropological Association), 95–114.

*Gregory, Lisa (1986), 'Rural Out-Migration in Oaxaca, Mexico: An Historical Perspective' (Athens, Ga.: University of Georgia, MA thesis).

*_Guardian_ (1983, 28 Dec.), 'Juchitan will need more than a quick paint job'.

Gwaltney, John L. (1970), *The Thrice Shy: Cultural Accomodation to Blindness and Other Disasters in a Mexican Community* (New York: Columbia University Press).

Hablantes de Lengua Indígena: Oaxaca (1995) (Aguas Calientes: INEGI).

H. Ayuntamiento Constitucional de Sant Ana del Valle (no date), *Museo Shan-Dany* (Oaxaca: Instituto Nacional de Antropología e Historia).

*Halhead, Vanessa (1984), 'The Forests of Mexico: The Resource and Politics of Utilization' (Edinburgh: University of Edinburgh M.Phil. thesis).

*Hamnett, Brian R. (1971*a*), *Politics and Trade in Southern Mexico, 1750–1821* (Cambridge: Cambridge University Press).

*——(1971*b*), 'Dye Production, Food Supply, and the Labouring Population of Oaxaca, 1750–1820', *Hispanic American Historial Review*, 51, 1, 51–78.

——(1990), 'Oaxaca: Las Principales Familias y el Federalismo de 1823', in María de los Ángeles Romero Frizzi (1990*c*) (compiler), 51–69.

——(1994), *Juárez* (Harlow: Longman).

Harvey, David (1973), *Social Justice and the City* (London: Edward Arnold).

Harvey, Neil (1993), *Mexico: Dilemmas of Transition* (London and New York: Institute of Latin American Studies, University of London, and British Academic Press).

Hasler, Juan A. (1959), 'Organización Social de los Mazatecos de Ichcatlán, Oaxaca', *Revista Mexicana de Sociología*, 21, 1, 173–82.

*Hayner, Norman S. (1966), 'Oaxaca, Town of Old Mexico', in Norman Hayner, *New Patterns in Old Mexico* (New Haven: College and University Press, 39–50).

Heijmerink, J. J. M. (1966), 'La Colonización de un Grupo de Indígenas en la Mixteca Baja, Estado de Oaxaca, México', *América Indígena*, 26, 2, 153–72.

—— (1973), 'La Tenencia de la Tierra en las Comunidades Indígenas en el Estado de Oaxaca, el Caso de Santo Tomás Ocotepec en le Región de la Mixteca Alta', *Revista Mexicana de Sociología*, 35, 2, 289–99.

*Hendricks, Janet, and Arthur D. Murphy (1981), 'From Poverty to Poverty: The Adaptation of Young Migrant Households in Oaxaca, Mexico', *Urban Anthropology*, 10, 1, 53–70.

Hendry, Jean Clare (1957), 'Atzompa: A Pottery Producing Village of Southern Mexico' (Cornell, NY: Cornell University Ph.D. thesis).

*Hensel, Silke (1997), *Die Entstehung des Föderalismus in Mexiko* (Stuttgart: Franz Steiner Verlag).

Hernández Antonio, Juana (1987), 'San Miguel Suchextepec: Costumbres y Creencias en un Pueblo Zapoteco del Sur', *El Medio Milenio*, 1, 50–4.

*Hernández Díaz, Jorge (1986), 'Relaciones Interétnicas Contemporáneas en Oaxaca', in Alicia M. Barabas and Miguel Bartolomé (1986) (compilers).

*—— (1987), *El Café Amargo: Diferenciación y Cambio Social entre los Chatinos* (Oaxaca: Instituto de Investigaciones Sociológicas, Universidad Autónoma 'Benito Juárez' de Oaxaca).

—— (1988), 'Ensayos sobre la Cuestión Étnica en Oaxaca' (Oaxaca: Instituto de Investigaciones Sociológicas, UABJO).

*—— (1992*a*), *Los Chatinos: Etnicidad y Organización Social* (Oaxaca: Instituto de Investigaciones Sociológicas de la UABJO).

—— (1992*b*), 'El Movimiento Indígena y la Construcción de la Etnicidad en Oaxaca', *Cuadernos del Sur*, 2, 47–66.

*—— (1993), 'Etnicidad y Nacionalismo en México: Una Interpretación', in Jorge Hernández Díaz *et al.* (1993), 7–64.

*—— León Javier Parra Mora, and Manuel Matus Manzo (1993), *Etnicidad, Nacionalism y Poder: Tres Ensayos* (Oaxaca: Universidad Autónoma 'Benito Juárez' de Oaxaca).

—— and Jesús Lizama Quijano (no date), *Cultura e Identidad Étnica en la Región Huave* (Oaxaca: Universidad Autónoma 'Benito Juárez' de Oaxaca).

*Hernández Reyes, Raúl (1994), *Educación y Bienestar Social en el Estado de Oaxaca, 1980–1990* (Oaxaca: Instituto Estatal de Educación Pública de Oaxaca).

Hewitt de Alcántara, Cynthia (1984), *Anthropological Perspectives on Rural Mexico* (London: Routledge and Kegan Paul).

Higgins, Michael James (1974), *Somos Gente Humilde: Etnografía de una Colonia Urbana Pobre de Oaxaca* (Mexico City: Sepini, 35).

—— (1983), *Somos Tocayos: Anthropology of Urbanism and Poverty* (Lanham, Md.: University Press of America).

—— (1990), 'Martyrs and Virgins: Popular Religion in Mexico and Nicaragua', in

Lynn Stephen and James Dow (eds.), *Class, Politics, and Popular Religion in Mexico and Central America* (Washington: American Anthropological Association), 187–204.

*Holloway, Annabel (1998), 'An Investigation into the Nature of *Micronegocios* in Oaxaca City, Mexico, with Particular Reference to Urban Workshops' (Oxford: Oxford University, M.Phil. thesis in Latin American Studies).

Hoogshagen, Searle (1960), 'Elección, Instalación y Aseguamiento de los Funcionarios en Coatlan, *Revista Mexicana de Estudios Antropológicas*, 16, 247–56.

——(1966), 'A Sketch of the Earth's Supernatural Functions in Coatlan Mixe', in *Homenaje a Roberto Weitlaner* (Mexico City: INAH), 313–16.

Howard, David (1997), 'Colouring the Nation: Race and Ethnicity in the Dominican Republic' (Oxford: Oxford University, D.Phil. thesis in Geography).

Howard, Sarah May (1993), 'Ethnicity, Autonomy, Land and Development: The Miskitu of Nicaragua's Northern Atlantic Coast' (Oxford: Oxford University, D.Phil. thesis in Geography).

Huerta Rios, César (1981), *Organización Socio-Politica de una Minoria Nacional: Los Triquis de Oaxaca* (Mexico City: Instituto Nacional Indigenista, Colección, 62).

*Hulshof, M. (1991), *Zapotec Moves: Networks and Remittances of US-bound Migrants from Oaxaca, Mexico* (Amsterdam: Netherlands Geographical Studies, 128).

Incháustegui, Carlos (1966), 'Cinco Años de un Programa: El Centro Coordinador Indigenista de la Sierra Mazateca', *América Indígena*, 26, 1, 11–26.

——(1986), 'La Producción de Objectos de Palma', *Mexico Indígena*, 12, 22–6.

——(1994), *La Mesa de Plata: Cosmogonía y Curanderismo entre los Mazatecos de Oaxaca* (Oaxaca: Instituto Oaxaqueño de Culturas).

*INEGI (1997), *División Territorial del Estado de Oaxaca de 1810 a 1995* (Aguascalientes, Instituto Nacional de Estadística, Geografía e Informática), vols. i and ii.

*Infante Cañibano, Lola (1998), 'State and Society in the Mixteca (Oaxaca): *Indigenismo* in the Mexican Regions, 1948–1975' (Oxford: Oxford University, M.Phil. thesis in Development Studies).

*Innis, Donald (1997), *Intercropping and the Scientific Basis of Traditional Agriculture* (London: Intermediate Technology Publications).

*Instituto de Artes Gráficas de Oaxaca (1997), *Memorial de Linderos: Gráfica Agraria de Oaxaca* (Oaxaca: Documentos del Archivo Histórico de la Secretaría de la Reforma Agraria).

*Iszaevich, Abraham (1973), *Modernización en una Comunidad Oaxaqueña del Valle* (Mexico City: SepSetentas, 109).

Iturribarria, Jorge Fernando (1982 originally 1935–56), *Historia de Oaxaca*, i–iv (Oaxaca: Comite Organizador del CDL Aniversario de la Ciudad de Oaxaca de Juárez).

IWGIA (1971), *Declaration of Barbados* (International Work Group for Indigenous Affairs).

Jeffery, Susan E. (1980), 'Invisible Women: How Women Disappear in a Chinantec Community', in 'Processes of Modernization in Mexico', in Colin G. Clarke (issue ed.), *Bulletin of the Society for Latin American Studies*, 32, 90–122.

Jopling, Carol F. (1973), 'Women Weavers of Yalálag: Their Art and its Process' (Boston: University of Massachusetts, Ph.D. thesis).

——(1974), 'Women's Work: A Mexican Case Study of Low Status as a Tactical Advantage', *Ethnology*, 13, 2, 187–95.

*Josserand, J. Kathryn, Marcus Winter, and Nicholas Hopkins (1984), *Essays in Otomanguean Culture History* (Nashville: Vanderbilt University Publications in Anthropology, 31).

Joyce, Arthur A. (1993), 'Interregional Interaction and Social Development on the Oaxaca Coast', *Ancient Mesoamerica*, 4, 67–84.

*Kearney, Michael (1972), *The Winds of Ixtepeji* (New York and London: Holt, Rinehart and Winston).

——(1995), 'The Effects of Transnational Culture, Economy, and Migration on Mixtec Identity in Oaxacalifornia', in Michael Peter Smith and Joe R. Feagin (eds.), *The Bubbling Cauldron: Race, Ethnicity and Urban Crisis* (Minneapolis and London: University of Minnesota Press).

*——(1996), *Reconceptualizing the Peasantry: Anthropology in Global Perspective* (Boulder, Colo. and Oxford: Westview Press).

Kendall, Carl, John Hawkins, and Laurel Bossen (1983), *Heritage of Conquest: Thirty Years Later* (Albuquerque: University of New Mexico Press).

*Kirkby, Anne V. (1973), *The Use of Land and Water Resources in the Past and Present Valley of Oaxaca, Mexico* (Ann Arbor: Memoirs of the Museum of Anthropology, University of Michigan, 5).

*——(1974), 'Individual and Community Responses to Rainfall Variability in Oaxaca, Mexico', in Gilbert White (ed.) *Natural Hazards: Local, National, Global* (New York: Oxford University Press), 119–28.

*Kirkby, Michael (1972), *The Physical Environment of the Nochixtlan Valley, Oaxaca* (Nashville: Vanderbilt University Publications in Anthropology, 2).

*Klaver, Jeanine (1997), *From the Land of the Sun to the City of the Angels: The Migration Process of Zapotec Indians from Oaxaca, Mexico to Los Angeles, California* (Amsterdam: Netherlands Geographical Studies, 228).

*Knight, Alan (1990), 'Racism, Revolution, and Indigenismo: Mexico, 1910–40', in Richard Graham (ed.), *The Idea of Race in Latin America, 1870–1940* (Austin, Tex.: University of Texas Press), 71–113.

——(1994), '*Cardenismo*: Juggernaut or Jalopy?', *Journal of Latin American Studies*, 26, 73–107.

*Kowalewski, Stephen A., and Jacqueline J. Saindon (1992), 'The Spread of Literacy in a Latin American Peasant Society: Oaxaca, Mexico, 1890 to 1980', *Comparative Studies in Society and History*, 34, 1, 110–40.

Krejci, John (1974), 'Leadership and Change in Two Mexican Villages' (Bloomington, Ind.: University of Notre Dame, Ph.D. thesis).

*——(1976), 'Leadership and Change in Two Mexican Villages', *Anthropological Quarterly*, 49, 3, 185–96.

*Kuroda, Etzuko (1993), *Bajo el Zempoaltepetl* (Oaxaca: Instituto Oaxaqueño de Cultura, CIESAS).

La Junta Colombina (1893), *Vocabulario Castellano-Zapoteco* (Mexico City: Secretaría de Fomento).

*Laviada, Iñigo (1978), *Los Caciques de la Sierra* (Mexico City: Editorial Jus).

*Lavrin, Asunción (1990), 'Rural Confraternities in the Local Economies of New Spain. The Bishopric of Oaxaca in the Context of Colonial Mexico', in Arij Ouweneel and Simon Miller (eds.), *The Indian Community of Colonial Mexico* (Amsterdam: CEDLA), 224–49.

*Lees, Susan H. (1973), *Sociopolitical Aspects of Canal Irrigation in the Valley of*

Oaxaca (Ann Arbor: Memoirs of the Museum of Anthropology, University of Michigan, 5).

—— (1976), 'Hydraulic Development and Political Response in the Valley of Oaxaca, Mexico', *Anthropolgical Quarterly*, 49, 3, 197–210.

*Lemoine Villicaña, Ernesto (1954), 'Ensayo de División Municipal del Estado de Oaxaca en 1950', *Yan*, 2, 1, 69–74.

*Leslie, Charles (1960), *Now We are Civilized: A Study of the World View of the Zapotec Indians of Mitla, Oaxaca* (Detroit: Wayne State University Press).

*Lewin, Pedro (1986), 'Conflicto Sociocultural y Conciencia Lingüística en Oaxaca', in Alicia M. Barabas and Miguel A. Bartolomé (eds.), *Etnicidad y Pluralismo Cultural: la Dinámica Etnica en Oaxaca* (Mexico City: Instituto Nacional de Antropología e Historia), 332–69.

*Lewis, Oscar (1952), 'Urbanization without Breakdown: A Case Study', *Scientific Monthly*, 75, 31–41.

*Leyes y Codigos de Mexico (1966), *Codigo Agrario y Leyes Complementarias* (Mexico City: Editorial Porrua).

*Lind, Michael (1979), *Postclassic and Early Colonial Mixtec Houses in the Nochixtlan Valley, Oaxaca* (Nashville: Vanderbilt University Publications in Anthropology, 23).

*Lipp, Frank J. (1971), 'Ethnobotany of the Chinantec Indians, Oaxaca, Mexico', *Economic Botany*, 25, 3, 234–44.

*—— (1991), *The Mixe of Oaxaca: Religion, Ritual and Healing* (Austin, Tex.: University of Texas Press).

Littlefield Alice (1978), 'Exploitation and the Expansion of Capitalism: The Case of the Hammock Industry of Yucatan', *American Ethnologist*, 5, 3, 495–508.

*Lorenzo, José L. (1960), 'Aspectos Físicos del Valle de Oaxaca' *Revista Mexicana de Estudios Antropológicos* 16, 49–63.

Lovell, William George (1975), 'Culture and Landscape in the Mixteca Alta, Mexico (1500–1600)' (Edmonton: University of Alberta, MA thesis).

*Lozano, Miguel (1984), 'Oaxaca: Una Experiencia de Lucha', in René Bustamante V. *et al.*, *Oaxaca una Lucha Reciente: 1960–83* (Mexico City: Ediciones Nueva Sociología), 75–219.

*Luebke, Benjamin Harrison (1959), 'Delineation of Rural Communities in the State of Oaxaca, Mexico' (Gainsville, Fla.: University of Florida, Ph.D. thesis).

*Luque González, Rodolfo, and Reina Corona Juapio (1992), 'La Migración y la Dinamica Demografica en Oaxaca', in Jack Corbett *et al.* (1992) (eds.), 13–18.

MacLaury, Robert Ethan (1970), 'Ayoquesco Zapotec: Ethnography, Phonology and Lexicon' (Mexico City: University of the Americas, MA thesis).

*McMahon, David (1973), *Antropología de una Presa: Los Mazatecos y el Proyecto del Papaloapan* (Mexico City: Instituto Nacional Indigenista).

*Maldonado Alvarado, Benjamín (1996), 'El Estado y la Autonomía desde Oaxaca, Algunas Tendencias Gubernamentales y Ciudadanas' (Oaxaca: Centro de Apoyo al Movimiento Popular Oaxaqueño).

*Malinowski, Bronislaw, and Julio de la Fuente (1982) (trans. and ed. by Susan Drucker-Brown), *The Economics of a Mexican Market System* (London: Routledge and Kegan Paul). See Bronislaw Malinowski and Julio de la Fuente (originally 1957), 'La Economia de un Sistema de Mercados en Mexico', *Acta Antropológica*, Época 2, 1, 2 (Instituto Nacional de Antropología e Historia), 1–186.

*Mangin, William (1967), 'Latin American Squatter Settlements: A Problem and a Solution', *Latin American Research Review*, 2, 419–41.

*Marcus, Joyce (1983), 'The Genetic Model and the Linguistic Divergence of the Otomangeans', in Kent V. Flannery and Joyce Marcus (eds.), *The Cloud People: Divergent Evolution of the Zapotec and Mixtec Civilizations* (New York and London: Academic Press), 4–9.

*—— and Kent V. Flannery (1996), *Zapotec Civilization: How Urban Society Evolved in Mexico's Oaxaca Valley* (London: Thames and Hudson).

*Marroquín, Alejandro (1978), *La Ciudad Mercado* (Mexico City: Instituto Nacional Indigenista, Colección 4).

Marroquín Zaleta, Enrique (1987), 'Aproximaciones a la Religión Indígena de Oaxaca: La Cruz Mesianica y el Culto de los Santos' (Oaxaca: Instituto de Investigaciones Sociológicas, UABJO).

—— (1988), *Reconstrucción de Mitos del Sincretismo Religioso de Oaxaca* (Oaxaca: Instituto de Investigaciones Sociológicas, Universidad Autónoma 'Benito Juárez' de Oaxaca).

*—— (1989), *La Cruz Mesianica* (Oaxaca: Universidad Autónoma 'Benito Juárez' de Oaxaca).

*—— (1992), *La Dinámica Religiosa en Oaxaca* (Oaxaca: Instituto de Investigaciones Sociológicas, UABJO).

—— (1995), *Persecución Religiosa en Oaxaca?* (Oaxaca: Instituto Oaxaqueño de las Culturas).

—— (1997), 'La Religión en Oaxaca: Analisis Sociométrico de una Encuesta' (Oaxaca: Instituto de Investigaciones Sociológicas, UABJO).

Martell Ramirez, Ricardo (1967), *Los Indios Triques de Oaxaca* (Mexico City).

Martínez Gracida, Manuel (1883), *Colleción de Cuadros Sinópticos de los Pueblos, Haciendas y Ranchos del Estado de Oaxaca* (Oaxaca: Imprenta del Estado).

*Martínez López, Felipe (1982), 'El Movimiento Oaxaqueno de 1952', in Raúl Benítez Zenteno (1982) (compiler), *Sociedad y Política en Oaxaca 1980* (Oaxaca: Instituto de Investigaciones Sociológicas, Universidad Autónoma 'Benito Juárez' de Oaxaca), 271–87.

*—— (1985), *El Crepusculo del Poder: Juchitán, Oaxaca 1980–1982* (Oaxaca: Instituto de Investigaciones Sociológicas, Universidad Autónoma 'Benito Juárez' de Oaxaca).

Martínez Medina, Héctor G. (1985), *Los Movimientos Revolucionarios Mederistas en Oaxaca: La Revolución en Oaxaca 1900–1930* (Oaxaca: Instituto de Administración Pública de Oaxaca).

Martínez Vásquez, Víctor Raúl (1985a) (ed.), *La Revolución en Oaxaca 1900–1930* (Oaxaca: Instituto de Administración Pública de Oaxaca).

—— (1985b), *La Educación en Oaxaca: La Revolución en Oaxaca* (Oaxaca: Instituto de Administración Pública de Oaxaca).

*—— (1990), *Movimiento Popular y Política en Oaxaca: 1968–1986* (Mexico City: Consejo Nacional para la Cultura y las Artes).

—— (1992a), *El Movimiento Universitario en Oaxaca (1968–88)* (Oaxaca: Instituto de Investigaciones Sociológicas, UABJO y la Dirección de Comunicación Social del Gobierno del Estado de Oaxaca).

*—— (1992b), 'Información y Comportamiento Electoral en la Ciudad de Oaxaca', *Cuadernos del Sur*, 1, 117–26.

Martínez Vásquez, Víctor Raúl (1993) (ed.), *La Revolución en Oaxaca (1900–1930)* (Mexico City: Consejo Nacional Para la Cultura y las Artes).

*——(1995), 'Elecciones Municipales en Oaxaca (1992)' *Cuadernos del Sur*, 8–9, 145–67.

*—— and Anselmo Arellanes Meixueiro (1985), 'Negociación y Conflicto en Oaxaca', in Carlos Martínez Assad (ed.), *Municipios en Conflicto* (Mexico City: Instituto de Investigaciones Sociales, UNAM).

*Marx, Karl, and Friedrich Engels (1972), *Selected Works* (London: Lawrence and Wishart).

Massey, Douglas S., Luin Goldring, and Jorge Durand (1994), 'Continuities in Transnational Migration: An Analysis of Nineteen Mexican Communities', *American Journal of Sociology*, 99, 6, 1492–533.

*Mathews, Holly F. (1985), ' "We are Mayordomo": A Reinterpretation of Women's Roles in the Mexican Cargo System', *American Ethnologist*, 12, 2, 285–301.

Matus Manzo, Manuel (1993), 'Los Zapotecos del Istmo en el Fin de Siglo', in Jorge Hernández Díaz *et al.* (1993), 111–74.

Méndez Aquino, Alejandro (1985), *Historia de Tlaxiaco* (Mexico City: Compañia Editorial).

Mendieta y Núñez, Lucio (1957), *Etnografía de México* (Mexico City: Universidad Nacional Autónoma de México).

Mendoza Guerrero, Telésforo (1981), *Monografía del Distrito de Huajuapan, Oaxaca* (Oaxaca).

——(1984), *Ciudad de Huajuapan de León: Primer Centenario* (Oaxaca).

Merrifield, William R. (1959), 'Chinantec Kinship in Palantla, Oaxaca, Mexico', *American Anthropologist*, 5, 875–81.

*Messer, Ellen (1978), *Zapotec Plant Knowledge: Classification, Uses and Communication about Plants in Mitla* (Ann Arbor: Memoirs of Museum of Anthropology, University of Michigan, 10, 2).

*Miranda, José (1968), 'Evolución Cuantitativa y Desplazamientos de la Población Indígena de Oaxaca en la Época Colonial', *Estudios de Historia Novohispana*, 2, 129–47.

*——(1990 originally 1959), 'Orígenes de la Ganadería Indígena en la Mixteca', in María de los Ángeles Romero Frizzi (1990*b*) (compiler), 231–9.

*Moguel, Reyna (1979), *Regionalizaciones para el Estado de Oaxaca: Análisis Comparativo* (Oaxaca: Centro de Sociología, Universidad Autónoma 'Benito Juárez' de Oaxaca).

Monahan, John (1990), 'La Desamortización de la Propiedad Comunal en la Mixteca: Resistencia Popular y Raíces de la Conciencia Nacional', in María de los Ángeles Romero Frizzi (1990*c*) (compiler), 343–85.

Montes García, Olga (1992), 'La Migración en la Sierra Norte: Sus Cambios Culturales', in Jack Corbett *et al.* (1992) (eds.), 87–94.

Montiel, Gustavo (1987), *Ejutla de Mis Recuerdos* (Oaxaca).

*Morris, Earl W. (1991), 'Household, Kin and Nonkin Sources of Assistance in Homebuilding: The Case of the City of Oaxaca', *Urban Anthropology*, 20, 1, 49–66.

Mullen, Robert J. (1975), *Dominican Architecture in Sixteenth-Century Oaxaca* (Phoenix, Ariz.: Arizona State University).

*Münch, Guido (1978), 'La Población del Obispado de Oaxaca en 1570', *Anales de Antropología*, 15, 67–81.

——*et al.* (1980), *El Sur de México: Datos Sobre la Problemática Indígena* (Mexico City: Universidad Nacional Autónoma de México).

Münch Galindo, Guido (1996), *Historia y Cultura de los Mixes* (Mexico City: Universidad Nacional Autónoma).

*Los Municipios de Oaxaca (1987), (Mexico City: Enciclopedia de los Municipios en México).

Muñoz Cruz, Hector, and Rossana Podesta Siri (1993) (eds.), *Contextos Étnicos del Lenguaje: Aportes de Educación y Etnodiversidad* (Oaxaca: Universidad Autónoma 'Benito Juárez' de Oaxaca).

*Murphy, Arthur D. (1979), 'Urbanization, Development and Household Adaptive Strategies in Oaxaca, a Secondary City of Mexico' (Philadelphia: Temple University, Ph.D. thesis in Anthropology).

——(1987), 'Studying Housing Areas in a Developing Nation: Lessons from Oaxaca City, Mexico', *Housing and Society*, 14, 2, 143–160.

*—— Martha W. Rees, Karen French, Earl W. Morris, and Mary Winter (1990), 'Crisis and Sector in Oaxaca, Mexico: A Comparison of Households 1977–1987', in Estellie Smith (ed.), *Making Out and Making Do: The Informal Economy in Cross Cultural Perspective* (Lanham, Md.: University Press of America), 8.

*——and Martha W. Rees (1991) (eds.), 'City and Crisis: The Case of Oaxaca, Mexico', Special Issue, *Urban Anthropology*, 20, 1, 1–107.

——and Henry A. Selby (1981), 'A Comparison of Household Resource Utilization in Four Mexican Cities', *Urban Anthropology*, 10, 3, 247–67.

——and ——(1985), 'Poverty and the Domestic Cycle in Oaxaca', *Urban Anthropology*, 14, 4, 347–65.

*——and Alex Stepick (1991*a*), *Social Inequality in Oaxaca: A History of Resistance and Change* (Philadelphia: Temple University Press).

——and——(1991*b*), 'Oaxaca's Cycles of Conquest', *Urban Anthropology*, 20, 1, 99–107.

Mutersbaugh, Tad (1998), 'Women's Work, Men's Work: Gender, Labour Organization, and Technology Acquisition in a Oaxacan Village', *Environment and Planning D: Society and Space*, 16, 439–58.

Nader, Laura (1964), *Talea and Juquila: A Comparison of Zapotec Social Organization* (Berkeley: University of California Publications in American Archaeology and Ethnology, 48).

*——(1990), *Harmony Ideology: Justice and Control in a Zapotec Mountain Village* (Stanford, Calif.: University of Stanford Press).

——and Duane Metzger (1963), 'Conflict Resolution in Two Mexican Communities', *American Anthropologist*, 65, 3, 584–92.

Nagengast, Carole, and Michael Kearney (1990), 'Mixtec Ethnicity: Social Identity, Political Consciousness and Political Activism', *Latin American Research Review*, 25, 2, 61–91.

*Nahmad Sittón, Salomón (1965), *Los Mixes: Etudio Social y Cultural de la Región del Zempoaltepetl y del Istmo de Tehuantepec* (Mexico City: Instituto Nactional Indigenista, 11).

——(1990), 'Reflexiones sobre la Identidad Étnica de los Mixes: Un Proyecto de Investigación por los Propios Sujetos', *Estudios Sociológicos*, 8, 22, 23–38.

——(1994) (compiler), *Fuentes Etnológicas para el Estudio de los Pueblos Ayuuk (Mixes) del Estado de Oaxaca* (Oaxaca: Centro de Investigaciones y Estudios Superiores en Antropología Social).

*Nahmad Sittón, Salomón, Alvaro González, and Martha Rees (1988), *Technologías Indigenas y Medio Ambiente* (Oaxaca: Centro de Ecodesarrollo), 153–97 and 254–6.

———— and Marco A. Vásquez (1994), *Medio Ambiente y Tecnologías Indígenas en el Sur de Oaxaca* (Oaxaca: Centro de Ecología y Desarrollo).

Nash, Manning (1967) (ed.), *Handbook of Middle American Indians*, iv. *Social Anthropology* (Austin, Tex.: University of Texas Press).

*Nash, June (1995), 'The Reassertion of Indigenous Identity: Mayan Responses to State Intervention in Chiapas' *Latin American Research Review,* 30, 3, 7–41.

*Necoechea Gracia, Gerardo (1996), 'Custom and History: Teaching Oral History in the Community Museums Project of Oaxaca, Mexico', *Radical History Review*, 65, 119–30.

Nellis, N. and J. (1983), *Diccionario Zapoteco de Juárez* (Instituto Lingüístico de Verano).

Newbold de Chiña, Beverly (1975), *Mujeres de San Juan: La Mujer Zapoteca del Istmo en la Economía* (Mexico City: SEPSETENTAS).

*Nieto Angel, Raúl (1984), *Tulancingo, Oaxaca* (Universidad Autónomo Chapingo).

Nolasco Armas, Margarita (1972), *Oaxaca Indígena* (Mexico City: Secretaría de Educación Pública).

*——(1981), *Cuatro Ciudades: El Proceso de Urbanización Dependiente* (Mexico City: Instituto Nacional de Antropología e Historia).

——(1986), 'La Migración y los Indios en los Censos de 1980', *México Indígena*, 13, 2, 3–10.

*Norget, Kristin (1997*a*), 'The Politics of Liberation: The Popular Church, Indigenous Theology, and Grassroots Mobilization in Oaxaca, Mexico', *Latin American Perspectives,* 24, 5, 96–127.

*——(1997*b*), 'Progressive Theology and Popular Religiosity in Oaxaca, Mexico', *Ethnology*, 36, 1, 67–83.

O'Brien, Michael J., and Dennis E. Lewarch (1992), 'Regional Analysis of the Zapotec Empire, Valley of Oaxaca, Mexico', *World Archaeology*, 23, 3, 264–81.

Olivera, Mercedes (1962), 'Notas Sobre las Actividades Religiosas en Tlaxiaco', *Anales del Instituto Nacional de Antropología e Historia*, 15, 129–51.

*—— and María de los Ángeles Romero (1973), 'La Estructura Política de Oaxaca en el Siglo XVI', *Revista Mexicana de Sociología*, 35, 2, 227–87.

O'Nell, Carl W. (1969), 'Human Development in a Zapotec Community with Emphasis on Aggression Control and its Study in Dreams' (Chicago: University of Chicago. Ph.D. thesis in Social Sciences).

*Ornelas López, José L. (1980), 'La Migración en Santo Domingo del Valle, Tlacolula', in Raúl Benítez Zenteno (ed.), *Sociedad y Política en Oaxaca,1980* (Oaxaca: Instituto de Investigaciones Sociológicas, Universidad Autónoma 'Benito Juárez' de Oaxaca), 143–65.

*——(1987*a*), *Movimiento Campesino y Desarrollo Regional en Tuxtepec: Tres Invasiones de Tierra en El Mirador, Loma Bonita* (Oaxaca: Instituto de Investigaciones Sociológicas, Universidad Autónoma 'Benito Juárez' de Oaxaca).

*——(1987*b*), 'Los Municipios Indígenas', in *Problemática Municipal de Oaxaca* (Instituto de Investigaciones Sociológicas, UABJO).

*——(1988), 'El Periodo Cardenista (1934–1940)', in Leticia Reina (1988) (compiler), 129–88.

Orozco, Porfirio Santibáñez (1986), 'El Municipio de Oaxaca y sus Problemas' *México Indigena*, 11, 56–9.

*Ortiz de Montellano, Bernard R., and C. H. Browner (1985), 'Chemical Bases for Medicinal Plant Use in Oaxaca, Mexico', *Journal of Ethnopharmacology*, 13, 57–88.

*Ortiz Gabriel, Mario (1982), 'Economía y Migración en una Comunidad Mixteca: el Caso de San Juan Mixtepec', in Raúl Benítez Zenteno (1982) (compiler), 111–42.

*—— (1992), 'El Trabajo Migratorio, una Opcíon para la Supervivencia de las Familias Campesinas de Oaxaca', in Jack Corbett, Murad A. Musalem Merhy, Othón Ríos Vázquez, and Héctor A. Vázquez Hernández (eds.), *Migración y Etnicidad en Oaxaca* (Nashville: Vanderbilt University Publications in Anthropology, 43, 19–24).

*Pacheco Vásquez, Pedro D., Earl W. Morris, Mary Winter, and Arthur D. Murphy (1991), 'Neighborhood Type, Housing and Housing Characteristics in Oaxaca', *Urban Anthropology*, 20, 1, 31–47.

*Paddock, John (1970) (ed.), *Ancient Oaxaca: Discoveries in Mexican Archaeology and History* (Stanford, Calif.: Stanford University Press).

*—— (1983), *Lord 5 Flower's Family: Rulers of Zaachila and Cuilapan* (Nashville: Vanderbilt University Publications in Anthropology, 29).

Parkin, Frank (1982), *Max Weber* (London and New York: Tavistock Publications).

Parmenter, Ross (1964), *Week in Yanhuitlán* (Albuquerque: University of New Mexico Press).

*—— (1982), *Four Lienzos of the Coixtlahuaca Valley* (Dumbarton Oaks, Trustees for Harvard University, Washington: Studies in Pre-Columbian Art and Archaeology, 26).

—— (1984), *Lawrence in Oaxaca: A Quest for the Novelist in Mexico* (Salt Lake City: Peregrine Smith Books).

*Parnell, Philip P. (1988), *Escalating Disputes: Social Participation and Change in the Oaxacan Highlands* (Tucson, Ariz.: University of Arizona Press).

Parra Mora, León Javier (1993), 'Indios y Mestizos: Un Esquema Explicativo, in Jorge Hernández Díaz *et al.* (1993), 67–109.

*—— and Jorge Hernández Díaz (1994), *Violencia y Cambio Social en la Región Triqui* (Oaxaca: Consejo Estatal de Población de Oaxaca).

*Parsons, Elsie Clews (1936), *Mitla Town of the Souls and other Zapoteco-Speaking Pueblos of Oaxaca, Mexico* (Chicago and London: University of Chicago Press).

*Partridge, William L., Antoinette B. Brown, and Jeffrey B. Nugent (1982), 'The Papaloapan Dam and Resettlement Project: Human Ecology and Health Impacts', in Art Hansen and Anthony Oliver-Smith (eds.), *Involuntary Migration and Settlement: The Problems and Responses of Dislocated People* (Boulder, Colo.: Westview Press).

*Pastor, Rodolfo (1987), *Campesinos y Reformas: La Mixteca, 1700–1856* (Mexico City: Centro de Estudios Históricos, El Colegio de Mexico).

—— *et al.* (1979), *Fluctuaciones Económicas en Oaxaca Durante el Siglo XVIII* (Mexico City: El Colegio de México).

Paz Paredes, Lorena y Julio Moguel (1979), *Santa Gertrudis: Testimonios de una Lucha Campesina* (Mexico City: Ediciones Era).

Perelló, Sergio (1989), *Reparto Agrario en Oaxaca 1915–1987* (Oaxaca: Instituto de Investigaciones Sociológicas, UABJO).

Pérez Garcia, Rosendo (1956), *La Sierra Juárez* (Mexico City: Libro Secundo).

*Perez Jiménez, Gustavo (1975), *La Institución del Municipio Libre en Mexico* (Mexico City: Prontuario de Legislación y Administración Municipal).

Peterson Royce, Anya (1975), *Prestigio y Afiliación en una Comunidad Urbana: Juchitán, Oaxaca* (Mexico City: Sepini 37).

Piñón Jiménez, Gonzalo (1987), 'Diferenciación Social de los Campesinos de Boca del Rio, Salina Cruz, Oaxaca' (Oaxaca: Instituto de Investigaciones Sociológicas, Universidad Autónoma 'Benito Juárez' de Oaxaca).

*——(1988), 'Crisis agraria y movimiento campesino (1956–1986)', in Leticia Reina (ed.), *Historia de la Cuestion Agraria Mexicana: Estado de Oaxaca, 1925–1986* (Mexico City: Juan Pablos Editor), ii. 293–373.

Pires-Ferreira, Jane W. (1975), *Formative Meso-American Exchange Networks, With Special Reference to the Valley of Oaxaca* (Ann Arbor: Memoirs of the Museum of Anthropology, University of Michigan, 7).

*Pisa, Rosaria Angela (1994), 'Popular Response to the Reform of Article 27: State Intervention and Community Resistance in Oaxaca', *Urban Anthropology*, 23, 2–3, 267–306.

*Poleman, Thomas T. (1964), *The Papaloapan Project: Agricultural Development in the Mexican Tropics* (Stanford, Calif.: Stanford University Press).

Pozas, Ricardo (1986), 'El sistema de estructuras indígenas actuales', *México Indígena*, 11, 3–5.

*—— and Isabel H. Pozas (1978), *Los Indios en las Clases Sociales de México* (Mexico City: Siglo Veintiuno).

*Prévot-Shapira, Marie-France, and Hélène Rivière D'Arc (1983), 'Les Zapotèques, le PRI et la COCEI. Affrontements autour des Interventions de l'Etat dans l'Isthme de Tehuantepec', *Amerique Latine*, 15, 64–71.

Pride, Kitty (1965), *Chatino Syntax* (Norman Okla.: Summer Institute of Linguistics of the University of Oklahoma).

*Prince, Zack, and Arthur D. Murphy (no date), 'Haciendo Colonia: The Making of a Community near Oaxaca, Mexico', typescript.

Ramos P., Donato (1992), 'La Migración por Micro-Regiones en la Sierra Norte de Oaxaca', in Jack Corbett *et al.* (1992) (eds.), 35–40.

*Ravicz, Robert S. (1965), *Organización Social de los Mixtecos* (Mexico City: Instituto Nacional Indigenista).

Rees, Martha W. and Arthur D. Murphy (1990) (eds.), 'A Student's Guide to Field Work in Oaxaca, Mexico' (Baylor, Tex.: University of Waco).

*—— —— Earl W. Morris, and Mary Winter (1991), 'Migrants to and in Oaxaca City', *Urban Anthropology*, 20, 1, 15–29.

——and ——(1995) (eds.), *Bibliography of Oaxaca* (Oaxaca: Welte Institue of Oaxacan Studies, Welte's Ready Reference, 6).

*Reina, Leticia (1988*a*) (ed.), *Historia de la Cuestion Agraria Mexicana: Estado de Oaxaca. Prehispanico—1924* (Mexico City: Juan Pablos Editor SA), vol. i.

*——(1988*b*), *Historia de la Cuestion Agraria Mexicana: Estado de Oaxaca. 1925–1986* (Mexico City: Juan Pablos Editor SA), vol. ii.

*——(1988*c*), 'De las Reformas Borbonicas a las Leyes de Reforma', in Leticia Reina (1988*a*), 181–268.

——(1988*d*), 'Juchitan 1880–1885: La Defensa de los Recursos Naturales y las Pugnas Electorales' *Guchachi' reza*, 27, 3–7.

*—— (1994) (ed.), *Economía Contra Sociedad: El Istmo de Tehuantepec, 1907–1986* (Mexico City: Nueva Imagen, Editorial Patria).

*Rendón, Juan José (1995), *Diversificacón de las Lenguas Zapotecas* (Oaxaca: Instituto Oaxaqueño de las Culturas).

Rensch, Calvin R. (1977), 'Situación Actual de los Estudios Linguisticos de las Lenguas de Oaxaca', *Estudios de Antropología e Historia*, 17

Riding, Alan (1984), *Distant Neighbours: A Portrait of the Mexicans* (New York: Alfred Knopf).

Rios Hernández, Onésimo (1979), *La Sierra de Juárez* (Mexico City).

Rios Morales, Manuel (1994) (compiler), *Los Zapotecos de la Sierra Norte de Oaxaca: Antología Etnográfica* (Oaxaca: Instituto Oaxaqueño de las Culturas, CIESAS).

*Rios Vázquez, Othón (1992), 'Estudios de la Migración de los Trabajadores Oaxaqueños a los E.U.A.', in Jack Corbett, Murad A. Musalem Merhy, Othón Ríos Vázquez, and Héctor A. Vázquez Hernández (eds.), *Migración y Etnicidad en Oaxaca* (Nashville: Vanderbilt University Publications in Anthropology, 43, 25–34).

*Rivière D'Arc, Hélène, and Marie-France Prévot-Schapira (1984), 'Las Inversiones Publicas y la Región: el Istmo de Oaxaca', in *El Puerto Industrial de Salina Cruz, Oaxaca* (Mexico City: Instituto de Geografía, Universidad Nacional Autónoma de México), 137–70.

*Roberts, Kenneth D. (1982), 'Agrarian Structure and Labour Mobility in Rural Mexico', *Population and Development Review*, 8, 2, 299–322.

*Rodríguez Canto, Adolfo (1996), *Historia Agrícola y Agraria de la Costa Oaxaqueña* (Pinotepa Nacional: Universidad Autónoma Chapingo).

*—— et al. (1989), *Caracterización de la Producción Agrícola de la Región Costa de Oaxaca* (Pinotepa Nacional: Universidad Autónoma Chapingo).

*Rodríguez, Francisco (1984), 'Pemex en Salina Cruz: Especifidades de la Inmigación y el Empleo', in *El Puerto Industrial de Salina Cruz, Oaxaca*, 94–120.

Rodríguez, Roberto, and Imelda García (1985), *Los Pescadores de Oaxaca y Guerrero* (Mexico City: Centro de Investigaciones y Estudios Superiores en Antropología Social, Cuadernos de la Casa Chata, 118).

*Rodríguez, Victoria (1997), *Decentralization in Mexico* (Boulder, Colo.: Westview Press).

*Rollwagon, Jack R. (1973), 'Tuxtepec, Oaxaca: An Example of Rapid Urban Growth in Mexico', *Urban Anthropology*, 2, 80–91.

*Romero Frizzi, Maria de los Ángeles (1975), 'Conflictos por la Tierra en San Martín Huamalulpan, Mixteca Alta, Oaxaca' (Oaxaca: Centro Regional, Instituto Nacional de Antropología e Historia).

*—— (1990a), *Economía y Vida de los Españoles en la Mixteca Alta: 1519–1740* (Mexico City: Instituto Nacional de Antropología e Historia y Gobierno del Estado de Oaxaca).

—— (1990b) (compiler), *Lecturas Históricas de Oaxaca*, ii. *Epoca Colonial* (Mexico City: INAH y Gobierno del Estado de Oaxaca).

—— (1990c) (compiler), *Lecturas Históricas del Estado de Oaxaca*, iii. *Siglo XIX* (Mexico City: INAH y Gobierno del Estado de Oaxaca).

—— (1990d) (compiler), *Lecturas Históricas del Estado de Oaxaca*, iv. *1877–1930* (Mexico City: INAH y Gobierno del Estado de Oaxaca).

*—— (1996), *El Sol y la Cruz: Los Pueblos Indios de Oaxaca Colonial* (Mexico City: Instituto Nacional Indigena y CIESAS).

*Romney, Kimball and Romaine Romney (1973), *The Mixtecans of Juxtlahuaca, Mexico* (New York: Robert E. Krieger).

Ross, Gary N. (1986), 'Night of the Radishes', *Natural History*, 12, 59–64.

*Rubel, Arthur J. and Jean Gettelfinger-Krejci (1976), 'The Use of Hallucogenic Mushrooms for Diagnostic Purposes among some Highland Chinantecs', *Economic Botany*, 30, 235–48.

*——Carl W. O'Nell, and Rolando Collado-Ardón (1984), *Susto: A Folk Illness* (Berkeley and Los Angeles: University of California Press).

*Rubin, Jeffrey W. (1994), 'COCEI in Juchitán: Grassroots Radicalism and Regional History', *Journal of Latin American Studies* 26, 1, 109–36.

*——(1997), *Decentring the Regime: Ethnicity, Radicalism and Democracy in Juchitán* (Durham, NC and London: Duke University Press).

Ruiz Cervantes, Francisco José (1985), *Los Arreglos Finales: La Revolución en Oaxaca 1900–30* (Oaxaca: Instituto de Administración Pública de Oaxaca).

——(1985), *Dos Gobiernos en Oaxaca: De la Soberanía a la Administración Preconstitucional: la Revolucion en Oaxaca 1900–30* (Oaxaca: Instituto de Administración Pública de Oaxaca).

*——(1986), *La Revolución en Oaxaca: El Movimiento de la Soberania* (Mexico City: Fondo de Cultura Económica).

——(1988*a*), 'De Espias, Agentes y Correos durante la Revolución en Oaxaca', *Guchache' reza*, 27, 10–16.

*——(1988*b*), 'De la Bola a los Primeros Repartos', in Leticia Reina (1988*a*) (compiler), 331–423.

Ruiz López, Arturo (1993), *Educación Indígena: Del Discurso al la Práctica Docente* (Oaxaca: Universidad Autónoma 'Benito Juárez' de Oaxaca).

Saldaña, Ángel, *et al*. (1987), *De Sectas a Sectas* (Oaxaca: Instituto de Investigaciones Sociológicas de la Universidad Autónoma 'Benito Juárez' de Oaxaca).

*Sánchez López, Alberto (1989), *Oaxaca, Tierra de Maguey y Mezcal* (Oaxaca: Instituto Tecnológico de Oaxaca).

Sánchez Silva, Carlos (1985), *Impresarios y Comerciantes en Oaxaca: La Revolución en Oaxaca* (Oaxaca: Instituto de Administración Pública de Oaxaca).

——(1990), 'Estructura de las Propiedades Agrarias de Oaxaca a Fines del Porfiriato', in María de los Ángeles Romero Frizzi (1990*d*) (compiler), 107–34.

——(1992), *En la Vispera del Medio Milenio: Condena o Festejo?* (Mexico City).

*Santibáñez Orozco, Porfirio (1982), 'Oaxaca: la Crisis de 1977', in Raúl Benítez Zenteno (compiler), *Sociedad y Política en Oaxaca 1980* (Oaxaca: Instituto de Investigaciones Sociológicas, Universidad Autónoma 'Benito Juárez' de Oaxaca), 309–29.

*Sarmiento Sánchez, Ignacio (1992), 'Migración Étnica Oaxaqueña hacia los E.U.A.', in Jack Corbett *et al*. (1992) (eds.), 99–104.

Sault, Nicole Landry (1985), 'Zapotec Godmothers: The Centrality of Women for "Campadrazgo" Groups in a Village of Oaxaca, Mexico' (Berkeley: University of California, Ph.D. thesis in Anthropology).

*Schejtman, A. (1983), quoted in Ríos Vázquez (1992), 'Oaxaca y Sinaloa: Campesinos y Empresarios en Dos Polos Contrastantes de Estructura Agraria', in *Economía Mexicana*, CIDE, 159–90.

*Schmieder, Oscar (1930), *The Settlements of the Tzapotec and Mije Indians: State of Oaxaca, Mexico* (Berkeley: University of California, Publications in Geography, 4).

Schoenhals, Alvin and Louise C. (1965) (compilers), *Vocabulario Mixe de Totontepec* (Mexico City: Instituto Lingüístico de Verano).

*Segura, Jaime (1988), 'Los Indigenas y los Programas de Desarrollo Agrario (1940–1964)', in Leticia Reina (1988*b*) (ed.), 191–290.

Selby, Henry A. (1966), 'Social Structure and Deviant Behaviour in Santo Tomas Mazaltepec' (Stanford, Calif.: University of Stanford, Ph.D. thesis in Anthropology).

*——(1974), *Zapotec Deviance: The Convergence of Folk and Modern Sociology* (Austin, Tex.: University of Texas Press).

——(1991), 'The Oaxacan Urban Household and the Crisis', *Urban Anthropology*, 20, 1, 87–98.

——Arthur D. Murphy, Ignacio Cabrera Fernández, and Aida Castañeda (1987), 'Battling Urban Poverty from Below', *American Anthropologist*, 89, 2, 419–24.

Seler, Eduard (1986 originally 1905), *Plano Jeroglífico de Santiago Guevea* (Juchitán: Ediciones Guchachi' reza).

*Seminario Franco-Mexicano (1984), *El Puerto de Salina Cruz, Oaxaca* (Mexico City: Instituto de Geografía, UNAM).

Sesia, Paola (1993) (ed.), *Medicina Tradicional, Herbolaria y Salud Comunitaria en Oaxaca* (Oaxaca: Gobierno del Estado de Oaxaca y CIESAS).

*Shanin, Teodor (1979), *Peasants and Peasant Societies* (Harmondsworth: Penguin Books).

Signorini, Italo (1979), *Los Huaves de San Mateo del Mar* (Mexico City: Instituto Nacional Indigenista).

Silva Rivera, Artemio (1995), *Monografía de Santa Cruz, Tacachi de Mina, Oaxaca* (Oaxaca: Instituto Estatal de Educación Pública).

Silva Ruiz, Gilberto (1979), *Examen de una Economía en Oaxaca: Estudio de un Caso de Teotitlan del Valle* (Oaxaca: Estudios de Antropología e Historia, 21).

Sleight, Eleanor Friend (1988), *The Many Faces of Cuilapan* (Orlando, Fla.: Pueblo Press).

*Smith Jr., C. Earle (1976), *The Vegetation History of the Oaxaca Valley* (Ann Arbor: Memoirs of the Museum of Anthropology, University of Michigan, 10, 1)

——(1978), *Modern Vegetation and Ancient Plant Remains of the Nochixtlán Valley, Oaxaca* (Nashville: Vanderbilt University Publications in Anthropology, 16).

*Smith, M. G. (1965), *The Plural Society in the British West Indies* (Berkeley and Los Angeles: University of California Press).

*——(1974), *Corporations and Society* (London: Duckworth).

*——(1984), *Culture, Class and Race in the Caribbean* (Kingston: Department of Extra-Mural Studies, University of the West Indies).

Sorroza Polo, Carlos (no date), *La Crisis Agroalimentaria en Oaxaca, 1940–1985* (Oaxaca: Instituto de Investigaciones Sociológicas, UABJO, Cuadernos de Investigación, 12).

——(1990), 'Cambios Agroproductivos y Crisis Alimentaria en Oaxaca', *Estudios Sociológicos*, 8, 22, 87–116.

*——(1992), 'Sociedad y Política en Oaxaca, 1970–1990' *Cuadernos del Sur*, 1, 99–116.

*Spores, Ronald (1967), *The Mixtec Kings and their People* (Norman, Okla.: University of Oklahoma Press).

*——(1969), 'Settlement, Farming Technology, and Environment in the Nochixtlán Valley', *Science*, 166, 3905, 557–69.

*Spores, Ronald (1984*a*), *The Mixtecs in Ancient and Colonial Times* (Norman, Okla.: University of Oklahoma Press).

*——— (1984*b*), 'Multi-level Government in Nineteenth-Century Oaxaca', in Ronald Spores and Ross Hassig (eds.), *Five Centuries of Law and Politics in Central Mexico* (Nashville: Vanderbilt University Publications in Anthropology, 30).

*——— (1986) (ed.), *Supplement to the Handbook of Middle American Indians: Ethnohistory* (Austin, Tex.: University of Texas Press), includes John K. Chance, 'Colonial Ethnohistory of Oaxaca', 165–89.

——— (1990), 'La Situación Económica de la Mixteca en la Primera Década de la Independencia', in María de los Ángeles Romero Frizzi (1990*c*) (compiler), 129–85.

*Starr, Frederick (1900), 'Notes upon the Ethnography of Southern Mexico', *Proceedings of the Davenport Academy of Natural Science*, 8, 9.

Starr, Jean (1987), 'Zapotec Religious Practices', *Canadian Journal of Native Studies*, 7, 2, 367–84.

*Stavenhagen, Rodolfo (1970), 'Classes, Colonialism and Acculturation: A System of Inter-Ethnic Relations in Mesoamerica', in Irving Horowitz (ed.), *Masses in Latin America* (London: Oxford University Press), 235–88.

——— (1980), *Problemas Etnicos y Campesinos* (Mexico City: Instituto Nacional Indigenista).

Stebbins, Kenyon Rainier (1984), 'Second-Class Mexicans: State Penetration and its Impact on Health Status and Health Services in a Highland Chinantec Municipio in Oaxaca' (East Lansing, Mich.: Michigan State University, Ph.D. thesis in Anthropology).

Stephen, Lynn (1987), 'Weaving Changes: Economic Development and Gender Roles in Zapotec Ritual and Production' (Waltham, Mass.: Brandeis University Ph.D. thesis in Anthropology).

*——— (1991), *Zapotec Women* (Austin, Tex.: University of Texas Press).

*——— (1994), 'Accommodation and Resistance: Ejidatario, Ejidataria, and Official Views of Ejido Reform', *Urban Anthropology*, 23, 2–3, 233–65.

——— (1996), 'The Creation and Re-creation of Ethnicity: Lessons from the Zapotec and Mixtec of Oaxaca', *Latin American Perspectives*, 23, 2, 17–37.

*——— (1997), 'Pro-Zapatista and Pro-PRI: Resolving the Contradictions of Zapatismo in Rural Oaxaca', *Latin American Research Review*, 32, 2, 41–70.

*——— (1998*a*), 'The Cultural and Political Dynamics of Agrarian Reform in Oaxaca and Chiapas', in Richard Snyder and Gabriel Torres (eds.), *The Future Role of the Ejido in Rural Mexico* (La Jolla, Calif.: Center for US–Mexican Studies, University of California, San Diego), 7–30.

——— (1998*b*), 'Between NAFTA and Zapata: Responses to Restructuring the Commons in Chiapas and Oaxaca, Mexico', in Michael Goldman (ed.), *Privatizing Nature: Political Struggles for the Global Commons* (New Brunswick, NJ: Rutgers University Press), 76–101.

*——— and James Dow (1990) (eds.), *Class, Politics, and Popular Religion in Mexico and Central America* (Washington: American Anthropological Association).

Stepick III, Alex (1974), 'The Rationality of the Urban Poor: Ethnography and Methodology for a Oaxacan Value System' (Irvine, Calif.: University of California, Ph.D. thesis).

——— and Arthur D. Murphy (1980), 'Comparing Squatter Settlements and Gov-

ernment Self-help Projects as Housing Solutions in Oaxaca, Mexico', *Human Organization*, 39, 4, 339–343.

Stork, Karl-Ludwig (1984), *Die Zentralen Orte in Becken von Oaxaca (Mexico) während die Kolonialzeit* (Munich: Wilhelm Fink Verlag).

Stuart, James, and Michael Kearney (1981), 'Causes and Effects of Agricultural Labor Migration from the Mixteca of Oaxaca to California' (La Jolla, Calif.: University of California, San Diego, Programme of United States–Mexican Studies, Working Paper, 28).

*Suárez, Jorge A. (1983), *The Mesoamerican Indian Languages* (Cambridge: Cambridge University Press).

Sutro, Livingston D. (1983), 'Changing Use of Zapotec Domestic Space' (Phoenix, Ariz.: University of Arizona, Ph.D. thesis in Anthropology).

Swadesh, Evangelina Arana de (1973), 'Formas de Aprendizaje entre los Indígenas del Estado de Oaxaca', *América Indígena*, 33, 4, 991–1002.

*Swadesh, M. (1967), 'Lexicostatistical Classification', in R. Wauchope and N. A. McQuown (eds.), *Handbook of Middle American Indians*, v. *Linguistics* (The Hague: Mouton), 79–115.

*Tamayo, Jorge L. (1950), *Geografía de Oaxaca* (Mexico City: Talleres Gráficos de la Nación).

Takahashi, Hitoshi (1990 originally 1981), 'De la Huerta a la Hacienda: El Origen de la Producción Agropecuaria en la Mixteca Costera', in María de los Ángeles Romero Frizzi (1990*b*) (compiler), 319–43.

Taylor, Robert B. (1960), 'Teotitlan del Valle: A Typical Mesoamerican Community' (University of Oregon, Ph.D. thesis in Anthropology).

——(1966), 'Conservative Factors in the Changing Culture of a Zapotec Town', *Human Organization*, 25, 116–21.

Taylor, William B. (1970), 'Cacicazgos Coloniales en el Valle de Oaxaca', *Historia Mexicana* 20, 1, 1–41.

*——(1972), *Landlord and Peasant in Colonial Oaxaca* (Stanford, Calif.: University of Stanford Press).

——(1973), 'Haciendas Coloniales en el Valle de Oaxaca' *Historia Mexicana*, 23, 2, 284–329.

——(1974), 'Landed Society in New Spain: A View from the South', *Hispanic American Historical Review*, 54, 3, 387–413.

——(1976), 'Town and Country in the Valley of Oaxaca, 1750–1812', in Ida Altman and James Lockhart (eds.), *Provinces of Early Mexico: Variants of Spanish American Regional Evolution* (Los Angeles: UCLA Latin American Centre Publication, 36), 63–95.

*——(1979), *Drinking, Homicide and Rebellion in Colonial Mexican Villages* (Stanford, Calif.: Stanford University Press).

Tax, Sol, *et al.* (1968 originally 1952), *Heritage of Conquest: The Ethnology of Middle America* (New York: Cooper Square Publishers).

*Tibón, Gutierre (1981 originally 1961), *Pinotepa Nacional: Mixtecos, Negros y Triques* (Mexico City: Editorial Posada, 4th edn.).

Toledo, Alejandro (1994), *Riqueza y Pobreza en la Costa de Chiapas y Oaxaca* (Mexico City: Centro de Ecología y Desarrollo).

*——(1995), *Geopolítica y Desarrollo en el Istmo de Tehuantepec* (Mexico City: Centro de Ecología y Desarrollo).

*Turkenik, Carole Judith (1975), 'Agricultural Production Strategies in a Mexican Peasant Community' (Los Angeles: University of California, Ph.D. thesis in Anthropology).

*Turner, John Kenneth (1969 originally 1911), *Barbarous Mexico* (Austin, Tex., and London: University of Texas Press).

*Turner, Paul R. (1973), *Los Chontales de los Altos* (Mexico City: SepSetentas).

——and Shirley Turner (1971), *Chontal Dictionary* (Phoenix, Ariz.: University of Arizona Press).

*UNDPFAO (1972), *México: Estudios de los Recursos del Estado de Oaxaca, Diagnóstico Socio-Económico del Estado de Oaxaca* (Rome: United Nations).

*Uzzell, Douglas (1977), 'The Myth of Bipolar Migration', *Ekistics*, 44, 263, 216–19.

Van den Berghe, Pierre L. (1967), *Race and Racism: A Comparative Perspective* (New York and London: John Wiley).

Van de Velde, Paul, and Henriette Romeike (1939), *The Black Pottery of Coyotepec, Oaxaca, Mexico* (Los Angeles: Southwest Museum Papers, 13).

Varese, Stefano (1978), 'Defender lo Multiple: Nota al Indigenísmo' (Oaxaca: Centro Regional de INAH, Estudios de Antropología e Historia, 16).

——(1986), 'Multiethnicidad y Construcción Hegemónica: Ensayo de un Inicio', *México Indígena*, 10, 5–8.

Vargas-Barón, Emily (1968), 'Development and Change of Rural Artisanry: Weaving Industries of the Oaxaca Valley, Mexico' (Stanford, Calif.: Stanford University, Ph.D. thesis in Anthropology).

Vásquez Dávila, Marco A. (1995), *La Tecnología Agrícola Tradicional* (Oaxaca: Instituto Tecnológico Agropecuario de Oaxaca).

*Vázquez Hernández, Héctor A. (1982), 'Migración Zapoteca: Algunos Aspectos Económicos, Demográficos y Culturales', in Raúl Benítez Zenteno (1982) (compiler), 67–83.

——(1987), *Division del Trabajo y Grupos Domesticos Campesinos en el Istmo Oaxaqueño* (Oaxaca: Instituto de Investigaciones Sociológicas, UABJO).

Velasco Ortiz, Laura (1992), 'Notas para Estudiar los Cambios en el Comportamiento Migratorio de Mixtecos en el Noroeste de México', in Jack Corbett *et al.* (1992) (eds.), 79–86.

Velasco Pérez, Carlos (1982), *La Conquista Armada y Espiritual de la Nueva Antequera* (Mexico City).

——(1989), *Oaxaca: Patrimonio Cultural de la Humanidad* (Oaxaca: Secretaría de Desarrollo Económico y Social, Gobierno del Estado).

*Velasco Rodríguez, Griselle (1994), *La Artesanía de la Palma en la Mixteca Oaxaqueña* (Oaxaca: Centro Interdisciplinario de Investigación para el Desarrollo Integral Regional).

Villa Rojas, Alfonso (1955), *Los Mazatecos y el Problema Indígena de la Cuenca de Papaloapan* (Mexico City: Memorias del Instituto Nacional Indigenista, 7).

Vogt, Evon Z. (1969) (ed.), *Handbook of Middle American Indians*, vii. *Ethnology* (Austin, Texas: University of Austin, Texas).

*Wall, Miriam Philomena (1982), 'Integrated Regional Development in Mexico: A Case Study of the Mixteca Alta' (Edinburgh: University of Edinburgh Department of Urban Design and Regional Planning, M.Phil. thesis).

*Ward, Evelyn Svec, and William E. (1987), *Folk Art of Oaxaca: The Ward Collection* (Cleveland Oh.: Cleveland Institute of Art).

*Ward, Peter M. (1994), 'Mexico's Electoral Aftermath and Political Future', in Peter M. Ward (ed.), *Mexico's Electoral Afermath and Political Future* (Austin, Tex.: The Mexican Centre, ILAS, University of Texas), 1–4.

*Warner, John C. (1976), 'Survey of the Market System in the Nochixtlán Valley and the Mixteca Alta', in Scott Cook and Martin Diskin (1976) (eds.), 107–31.

*Waterbury, Ronald (1968), 'The Traditional Market in a Provincial Setting: Oaxaca, Mexico' (Los Angeles: University of California, Ph.D. thesis in Anthropology).

——(1970), 'Urbanization and the Traditional Market System', in Walter Goldschmidt and Harry Hoyer (eds.), *The Social Anthropology of Latin America* (Los Angeles: Latin American Centre, University of California), 126–56.

*——(1975), 'Non-Revolutionary Peasants: Oaxaca compared to Morelos in the Mexican Revolution', *Comparative Studies in Society and History*, 17, 4, 410–42.

*——(1989), 'Embroidery for Tourists: A Contemporary Putting-Out System in Oaxaca, Mexico', in Annette Weiner and Jane Schneider (eds.), *Cloth and Human Experience* (Washington: Smithsonian Institution Press), 243–71.

*——(1999), '*Lo Que Dice el Mercado*: Development without Developers in a Oaxacan Peasant Community', in William M. Luker (ed.), *Globalization and the Rural Poor in Latin America* (New York: Lynne Rienner Publishers), 61–91.

*——and Carole Turkenik (1976), 'The Marketplace Traders of San Antonino: a Quantitative Analysis', in Scott Cook and Martin Diskin (1976) (eds.), 209–29.

*Watters, R. F. (1971), *Shifting Cultivation in Latin America* (Rome: Food and Agricultural Organization of the United Nations).

*Weaver, Thomas, and Theodore Downing (1976), *Mexican Migration* (Tucson, Ariz.: University of Arizona, Bureau of Ethnic Research).

*Webster, Steven S. (1968), 'The Religious Cargo System and Socioeconomic Differentiation in Santa María Guelacé' (Stanford, Calif.: Stanford University Summer School).

Weitlaner, Robert J. (1951), 'Notes on the Social Organization of Ojitlan, Oaxaca', in *Homenaje al Doctor Alfonso Caso* (Mexico City), 441–55.

——and S. Hoogshagen (1960), 'Grados de Edad en Oaxaca', *Revista Mexicana de Estudios Antropológicos*, 16, 183–209.

——(1961), *Datos Diagnósticos para la Etnohistoria del Norte de Oaxaca* (Mexico City: Instituto Nacional de Antropología e Historia).

——and Carlo Antonio Castro (1954), *Papeles de la Chinantla*, i. *Mayultianguis y Tlacoatzintepec* (Mexico City: Serie Científica, Museo Nacional de Antropología, III).

——and Mercedes Olivera de Vázquez (1969), *Los Grupos Indigenas del Norte de Oaxaca* (Mexico City: Instituto Nacional de Antropología e Historia).

——and Carlo Antonio Castro (1973), *Papeles de la Chinantla*, ii. *Usila (Morada de Colibries* (Mexico City: Serie Científica, Museo Nacional de Antropología, VII).

——(1977) (compiler), *Relatos, Mitos y Leyendas de la Chinantla* (Mexico City: Instituto Nacional Indigenista).

*Welte, Cecil (1978), 'Population Changes in the Valley of Oaxaca, 1826–1970' (Oaxaca: Welte's Ready Reference Release, 4, 7–9).

*Whitecotton, Joseph W. (1977), *Zapotecs: Princes, Priests and Peasants* (Norman, Okla.: University of Oklahoma Press).

Williams, Aubrey (1979) (ed.), *Social, Political and Economic Life in Contemporary Oaxaca* (Nashville: Vanderbilt University Publications in Anthropology, 24).

Williams, Barbara J. (1972), 'Tepetate in the Valley of Mexico', *Annals of the Association of American Geographers*, 62, 618–26.

Willis, Katie D. (1991), 'Women's Work and the Use of Social Networks in a Low-Income Settlement in Oaxaca City, Oaxaca' (Oxford: Oxford University, M.Phil. thesis in Latin American Studies).

*—— (1993) 'Women's Work and Social Network Use in Oaxaca City, Mexico', *Bulletin of Latin American Research*, 12, 1, 65–82.

*—— (1994), 'Women's Work and Social Network Use in Oaxaca City, Mexico: An Analysis of Class Differences' (Oxford: Oxford University, D.Phil. thesis in Geography).

*Winder, David (1992), 'From Timber Concessions to Community Forestry: Political, Economic, and Social Change in the Sierra de Juárez, Oaxaca, Mexico'. Unpublished typescript.

Winter, Marcus Cole (1972), 'Tierras Largas: A Formative Community in the Valley of Oaxaca, Mexico' (Phoenix Ariz.: University of Arizona Ph.D. thesis in Anthropology).

—— (1990) (compiler), *Lecturas Históricas del Estado de Oaxaca*, i. *Epoca Prehispánica* (Mexico City: INAH y Gobierno del Estado de Oaxaca).

*Winter, Mary (1991), 'Interhousehold Exchange of Goods and Services in the City of Oaxaca', *Urban Anthropology*, 20, 1, 67–85.

*Wolf, Eric (1955), 'Types of Latin American Peasantry: A Preliminary Discussion', *American Anthropologist*, 57, 452–71.

—— (1959), *Sons of the Shaking Earth: The People of Mexico and Guatemala—Their Land, History and Culture* (Chicago: University of Chicago Press).

—— (1966), *Peasants* (Englewood Cliffs, NJ: Prentice Hall).

—— (1986), 'The Vicissitudes of the Closed Corporate Peasant Community', *American Ethnologist*, 13, 2, 325–9.

*Yescas Martínez, Isidro (1982), 'La Coalición Obrero Campesino Estudiantil de Oaxaca: 1972–74', in Raúl Benítez Zenteno (1982) (compiler), 289–308.

—— (1989), *Los Desengañados de la Tierra (Una Experiencia de Lucha Campesina en Tuxtepec, Oaxaca)* (Oaxaca: Instituto de Investigaciones Sociológicas, Universidad Autónoma 'Benito Juárez' de Oaxaca).

*—— (1991), *Política y Poder en Oaxaca* (Oaxaca: Gobierno del Estado).

*—— and Gloria Zafra (1985), *La Insurgencia Magisterial en Oaxaca, 1980* (Oaxaca: Instituto de Investigaciones Sociológicas, Universidad Autónoma 'Benito Juárez' de Oaxaca).

*Yescas Peralta, Pedro (1958), 'Estructura Social de Oaxaca', *Revista Mexicana de la Sociología*, 20, 3, 767–80.

*Young, C. M. (1976), 'The Social Setting of Migration: Factors Affecting Migration from a Sierra Zapotec Village in Oaxaca, Mexico (London: London University, Ph.D. thesis in Social Anthropology).

*Young, Kate (1980), 'The Creation of a Relative Surplus Population: A Case Study from Southern Mexico', in Colin G. Clarke (issue editor), *Bulletin of the Society for Latin American Studies*, 32, 61–89.

Ysunza Ogazón, Alberto (1996), *No Que No?* (Mexico City: Instituto Nacional de la Nutrición Salvador Zubirán).

*Zafra, Gloria (1982), 'Problemática Agraria en Oaxaca: 1971–75', in Raúl Benítez Zenteno (1982) (compiler), 331–49.

*Zeitlin, Judith (1984), 'Colonialism and the Political Transformation of Isthmus

Zapotec Society', in Ronald Spores and Ross Hassig (eds.), *Five Centuries of Law and Politics in Central America* (Nashville: Vanderbilt University Publications in Anthropology, 31).

*Zelinsky, Wilbur (1971), 'The Hypothesis of the Mobility Transition', *Geographical Review*, 61, 2, 219–49.

Zepeda, Eraclio (1985), *Magia del Juego Eterno* (Photografias de Flor Garduño) (Juchitán: Publicación Guchachi' reza).

Zúñiga, Rosa María (1982), *Toponomias Zapotecas* (Mexico City: Instituto Nacional de Antropología e Historia, Colección Científica, 117).

INDEX